D1237218

# AFTER THE REBELLION

## The Later Years of William Lyon Mackenzie

Lillian F. Gates

# AFTER THE REBELLION

## The Later Years of William Lyon Mackenzie

*Lillian F. Gates*

Toronto & Oxford
Dundurn Press
1988
Published with the assistance of the
Ontario Heritage Foundation,
Ontario Ministry of Culture and Communications

Design and Production:Andy Tong
Printing and Binding:Gagne Printing Ltd., Louiseville, Quebec, Canada

The writing of this manuscript and the publication of this book were made possible by support from several sources. The publisher wishes to acknowledge the generous assistance and ongoing support of **The Canada Council, The Book Publishing Industry Development Programme** of the Department of Communications, **The Ontario Arts Council,** and the **Ontario Heritage Foundation.**

Care has been taken to trace the ownership of copyright material used in the text (including the illustrations). The author and publisher welcome any information enabling them to rectify any reference or credit in subsequent editions.

*J. Kirk Howard, Publisher*

**Dundurn Press Limited**
1558 Queen Street East
Toronto, Canada
M4L 1E8

**Dundurn Distribution**
Athol Brose, School Hill,
Wargrave, Berkshire
England RG10 8DY

**Canadian Cataloguing in Publication Data**

Gates, Lillian F., 1901-
        After the rebellion : the later years of
William Lyon Mackenzie

Bibliography: P.
includes index.
ISBN 1-55002-025-0

1. Mackenzie, William Lyon, 1795-1861. 2. Politi-
cians - Canada - Biography. 3. United States -
Politics and government - 19th century. 4. Canada
- Politics and government - 1841-1867. I. Title.

FC451.M3G38 1988    971.03'8'0924    C87-094973-X
F1032.M3G38 1988

_to_
_Paul Wallace Gates_

# CONTENTS

Illustrations are between page 192 and 193

# PREFACE

This study of Mackenzie's post-rebellion years has never been intended to be a full-scale biography of Mackenzie. At the time it was begun, it was expected that Dr. Catherine McLean's account of Mackenzie's life up to and including the rebellion would soon go to press and therefore I confined myself to the post-rebellion years, with which she did not plan to deal. (Dr. McLean was the author chosen and subsidized by Mackenzie's grandson, W.L. Mackenzie King.) McLean's study was still incomplete and unpublished at the time of her death. Although I have become aware of this fact, I have kept my own account of the period up to December 1837 as concise as possible for two reasons: this period had been dealt with in detail by Lindsey, Dent and Kilbourn, and since I started writing several other accounts have appeared; and I needed to save my space for the later period, about which what I call only the surface facts have been given.

In the post-rebellion years politics and journalism filled Mackenzie's life and that is what I have emphasized, plus the influence upon him of American ideas and his actual experiences in the United States. My object has been to present Mackenzie as a determined radical reformer for whom "responsible government" was not enough. He fought a losing battle at tremendous personal cost for an ideal not yet achieved in Canada. Although he failed, he was not a useless and obstructionist member of the legislature. This could not be shown by mere assertion. It has required detailed analysis of his role as Member for Haldimand.

I have included such details of his personal and family life as rest on documentary evidence and seemed relevant to this study of the post-rebellion years. Stories that rest on family reminiscences or traditions, endearing or pathetic as the case may be, had already been fully set forth by Lindsey and others. With my space at a premium, I saw no need to repeat them.

My concluding chapter is an overall estimate of Mackenzie which brings out some of the reasons both for his failures and for the warm spot he kept in many hearts. I have tried not to exaggerate Mackenzie's importance, but I hope I have raised more than "a perfunctory little tombstone" to his memory.

In doing the research for this book I have been assisted by two grants from the American Philosophical Society, and in the publication by the Ontario Heritage Foundation. I have also had most appreciated help from my editor, Professor Roger Hall. My acknowledgements are due to Cornell University, which has once again generously allowed me the use of its libraries and research facilities. The staffs of the Public Archives of Canada, the National Library of Canada, the Archives of Ontario, the Metropolitan Toronto Library, the Library of the University of North Carolina and the New York Historical Society have also given me much appreciated assistance. Parts of Chapters II and V appeared in the *Canadian Historical Review* and part of Chapter VI in *Ontario History*. I thank them both for permission to include that material here.

The frontispiece is from a photograph of a pen and ink sketch of Mackenzie in his old age, speaking to the Assembly (courtesy of the Public Archives of Canada).

Dr. Blake McKelvey of the Rochester Historical Society, Mr. Richard D. Hupman, formerly librarian for the United States Senate, Prof. Maurice Neufeld of Cornell and Mr. R.E. Doane have promptly responded to my requests for help and information. Mr. John B. Johnson, editor of the Watertown *Daily Times*, kindly gave me access to his file of the *Watertown Jeffersonian*. My special thanks are due to Prof. Joel Silbey of Cornell for his advice and encouragement and his kindness in reading what I call the American half of this study. I am deeply indebted also to the late Col. C.B. Lindsey who permitted the use of his great-grandfather's papers, which he had deposited in the Archives of Ontario. I enjoyed many pleasant and enlightening conversations with him while this work was in progress.

I acknowledge with love and gratitude the many hours of labour that my daughter Annette spent in checking the text and in making the bibliography and index. Finally I must thank my husband who shared my time with "Old Mac" with some reluctance but who nevertheless has supported my research, and the production of this book, with great generosity. It is with pleasure that I dedicate it to him.

Ithaca, New York                                           Lillian F. Gates
November 1986

Rebellion! foul dishonoring word,
Whose wrongful blight so oft has stained
The holiest cause that tongue or sword
Of mortal ever lost or gained.
How many a spirit born to bless
Hath sunk beneath that withering name,
Whom but a day's, an hour's success
Had wafted to eternal fame!

Pen and ink sketch of William Lyon Mackenzie in a typical pose.

# Chapter I

# NAVY ISLAND AND HICKORY ISLAND

On December 11, 1837, William Lyon Mackenzie, fleeing from Upper Canada after an abortive attempt at rebellion against the British authories there, crossed the Niagara River to take refuge in the United States. The life of Mackenzie prior to his arrival in Buffalo has been told in detail by his son-in-law, Charles Lindsey, and the events of the rebellion have been discussed by many able writers. Consequently, a summary of these topics is all that is necessary as a preface to this study of Mackenzie's post-rebellion career.[1]

Mackenzie was born in Springfield, a suburb of Dundee, Scotland, on March 12, 1795. His father died when he was an infant and subsequently his 45-year-old mother had a hard struggle to maintain herself and her child. The boy was sent to the parish school and here he proved to be a bright scholar, quick with figures. As a youth he was indentured as a clerk to a Dundee merchant in whose service he learned accounting. Dundee had a good subscription library. Mackenzie became a member and for a time acted as secretary of the organization. In its reading room he absorbed the poetry and the history of Scotland. Here too he read works on political economy and political theory, the accounts of travellers in the United States and Canada, histories of the American Revolution and the autobiography of Benjamin Franklin.

When Mackenzie was about nineteen he went into business for himself by opening a small general store in a nearby village. By 1817 his venture had failed. His creditors did not have him imprisoned for debt (as they might have done) but left him free to pay them when he could. This experience seems to have made a lasting impression upon him. As a legislator in Canada, he tried to have imprisonment for debt abolished and to obtain for honest debtors the right to retain a minimum of household goods essential for their families and tools to start over again in their trade or occupation. Mackenzie's difficulties seem to have been caused by the unstable level of prices in the immediate post-Napoleonic years.[2] Throughout his life no topic interested him more than methods of maintaining a stable currency and easing the plight of poor but honest debtors.

Dundee was a turbulent city: here the influence of the French Revolution was marked; here a liberty pole had been erected; here the street urchins shouted for Liberty and Equality and their elders demanded a more liberal franchise and parliamentary reform. Some of the agitators were sentenced to transportation. The young Mackenzie, intelligent, inquisitive, alert, emotional, was caught up in this political ferment, so much so that in 1819 he paid a visit to France, the country from which these exciting ideas about liberty, equality and the rights of man had come.[3]

After about two years of intermittent employment in England, Mackenzie emigrated to Upper Canada in April 1820, perhaps at the suggestion of Mr. Edward Lesslie of Dundee.[4] At York he managed a book and drug store for John Lesslie; later he operated a general store at Dundas, at first in partnership with Lesslie, afterwards alone. In 1824, by which time he had removed to Queenston, he made what he came to regard as a fateful decision: to abandon a mercantile career for journalism and to engage in politics.

Mackenzie came to Canada deeply influenced by both the British radicals and the American Revolution. He hoped that this new world would become a democratic society in which every man would have an equal opportunity to develop his abilities unhampered by legal restraints and by privileges to a favoured few. On May 18, 1824, he began to publish the *Colonial Advocate*, first at Queenston, later at York. In his first number he set forth the list of moderate reforms he hoped for in Canada: equality of all religious sects before the law, abolition of the law of primogeniture, independent judges not removable at pleasure and an independent Legislative Council instead of one chiefly composed of placemen. From time to time he advocated additional reforms relating to the bench, the bar, the banks, the educational system, the land policies of the province and the control and management of its public revenues.

Mackenzie came to be an admirer of Andrew Jackson but he was at first critical of him and, as J.E. Rea has pointed out, he did not openly rejoice when Jackson won the election of 1828. He may have been unable to follow the complicated electoral campaign of that year during which very different Jacksons were presented by the two parties in the American press and inconsistent policies were promised on his behalf by the supporters of the future president. As a result of his visit to Washington and to the White House in 1829, Mackenzie concluded that Jackson was "the fittest choice a nation of freemen could have made." He praised Jackson's course during his first term as "wise and prudent" and he rejoiced in his re-election.[5] His newspapers show that prior to the rebellion he was greatly influenced by the ideology of the Jacksonians and, later, by their most radical wing, the Equal Rights Party of New York State.

In 1828 the County of York elected Mackenzie to the legislature. During the session of 1831 hostile members of the Assembly brought about his expulsion from that body on a charge of libel. "Our representative body," he had written, "has degenerated into a sycophantic office for registering the decrees of the... Executive...."[6] Mackenzie was re-elected and again expelled. In April 1832, after another triumphant re-election, he went to England to protest his expulsions and to inform the Colonial Office of the grievances of Upper Canada as expressed in the petitions he carried with him, bearing some 24,000 names.

These grievances in part related to the land regulations. They bore hard on poor men wanting land and required scattered reserves amounting to one-seventh of the lots in every township to be set aside for the benefit of "a Protestant clergy." The interpretation of this phrase to mean only the Anglican clergy was resented by other Protestant denominations. Additional grievances were the inability of the Assembly to control the disposition of all the public revenue, the inequalities of the system of representation and the want of a system of local government. Above all, the Reformers wanted the Lieutenant-Governor's Executive Council to be composed of only those who "possess the confidence of the people...."

The Colonial Secretary questioned the legality of the Assembly's expulsions of Mackenzie and warned the Crown officers not to be party to such acts again. The triumph of the Reformers in the general election of October 1834 finally enabled Mackenzie to take his seat when the new legislature met in July 1835.

Meanwhile the Town of York, having become the incorporated City of Toronto, had elected its aldermen in March 1834. Mackenzie, one of their number, was elected by his colleagues to be the new city's first mayor and he had served Toronto in this capacity for a year.[7] In November 1834 he had given up publishing his newspaper, explaining that the reform movement was now well under way and could be carried on by others. His paper was consolidated with W.J. O'Grady's *Correspondent* as the *Correspondent and Advocate*. But Mackenzie was still to carry on the work of reform by other means. On December 9, 1834, the Reformers of Toronto organized the Canadian Alliance Society. Mackenzie submitted to the members a series of resolutions which they accepted and on which they based their reform program. It included many of the objectives for which he was to work consistently throughout his political career both before and after the rebellion. The Alliance made Mackenzie their corresponding secretary.[8]

During the session of 1835 Mackenzie was made chairman of the Assembly's Committee on Grievances. He compiled its famous report which again emphasized the need for a responsible government as well as a long list of other desired reforms. The Colonial Secretary's response to this document raised the expectations of Reformers, but their hopes were soon dashed by the conduct of a new lieutenant-governor, Sir Francis Bond Head. In 1836 Head called an election in which he used his influence against the Reformers, who found themselves in a minority at the next meeting of the legislature. Mackenzie himself was defeated. He attributed Reform losses to the personal interference of the Lieutenant-Governor and to his corrupt use of the Land Department to create voters qualified with the necessary 40/- freehold.[9] Hope of securing reform by constitutional methods seemed to be at an end. Mackenzie now became a journalist again. The first issue of his new paper, significantly named the *Constitution*, appeared on July 4, 1836, its last on November 29, 1837.

In October the Toronto Reformers reorganized as the Toronto Political Union with W.W. Baldwin as president.[10] Mackenzie became seriously ill after his defeat in July. He had no office in the Toronto Political Union which, under the leadership of the Bidwells and the Baldwins, did not exert itself to rally support for the calling of a convention of Reformers. By July 1837, however,

Mackenzie was again active in Reform politics; Bidwell and Baldwin had withdrawn.

Mackenzie and other Toronto Reformers now drew up a Declaration of Grievances, many of them similar to those in the American Declaration of Independence. The Toronto document, formally adopted on July 31, 1837, expressed sympathy with the grievances of the people of Lower Canada, and declared it to be the duty of Upper Canada Reformers to make common cause with them. A Vigilance Committee was created which appointed Mackenzie its agent to establish political unions outside Toronto and to secure their approval of the declaration. Mackenzie drew up a draft constitution for a State of Upper Canada for submission to a proposed convention after a provisional government should have been established. Some of the political unions in Upper Canada drilled their members with arms. In the first week in November Mackenzie, who was now ready to use force if organized demonstrations of discontent proved futile, sent Jesse Lloyd to inform the Lower Canadians about his plans and to learn theirs. Thomas Storrow Brown, one of Papineau's supporters, claims that at this moment Papineau and other Lower Canadian malcontents had no policy except what was publicly expressed at meetings, had acquired no arms or ammunition, and that Mackenzie's intentions were "unexpected."[11] Years later Mackenzie admitted to his son that he had urged the Lower Canadians to "make their movement." He called them "nerveless and dilatory" and criticized Papineau, Speaker of the Legislative Assembly of Lower Canada, as not equal to the risks of a revolutionary leader.[12]

After violence had broken out in Lower Canada, first at Montreal on November 6, and some arrests had been made on the 11th, Papineau sent Théophile Dufort to Mackenzie on November 13 asking the support of the Toronto Reformers.[13] At a meeting hastily called on receipt of Papineau's message, Mackenzie argued that as the troops had *all* been sent away to strengthen Sir George Colborne, the Commander of the Forces in Lower Canada, it would be possible for a few determined men to seize the unprotected Lieutenant-Governor of Upper Canada, seize the vital supply of arms in the City Hall, take possession of Toronto, alert their friends in the countryside and proclaim a provisional government forthwith. The meeting could not be persuaded by the impetuous Mackenzie to put this plan for a *coup d'état* into immediate operation, while its prospects for success were at their best. Mackenzie claims that a similar plan was later agreed to at a meeting of 12 leading Reformers with this difference, that supporters from the countryside were to be assembled at John Montgomery's Tavern, four and a half miles north of Toronto, up Yonge Street, for a march on the city to take it by surprise. It was expected that a majority of the inhabitants would then rally to their support. Whether there ever was such a gathering, and whether this plan was fully agreed to in advance by Mackenzie's associates in Toronto, whether Dr. John Rolph, a leading Reformer and M.P.P. for the County of Norfolk, had consented to be the rebels' executive, are points in dispute.[14]

During the first week of December Mackenzie distributed a handbill entitled "Independence in the rural townships of the Home District." It called

15

upon Canadians to "get ready" their rifles, promised them rewards in land at the expense of the Clergy Reserves and the Canada Company, assured them that "one short hour" would give them success and threatened vengeance upon those who opposed them. The uprising was set for December 7 but, without Mackenzie's knowledge, the date was advanced to December 4 by Rolph when he feared that Mackenzie was about to be arrested. The result was the arrival at Montgomery's of a much smaller force than expected, inadequate preparation of supplies, discouragement, confusion, divided counsels and delays that favoured the government. On the 5th Head sent a Flag of Truce to the rebels with an offer of amnesty if they would disperse at once. Their reply was to ask that the offer be put in writing. The Lieutenant-Governor refused, withdrew his offer of an amnesty and sent the flag back with this message. On December 7 the rebel force at Montgomery's was routed and fled. Mackenzie succeeded in evading capture. By December 11 he had reached the farm of Samuel McAfee on the banks of the Niagara in the township of Bertie, minutes ahead of a troop of dragoons searching residences for him. Mackenzie and a companion, Samuel Chandler, were rowed to safety across the Niagara by their intrepid host. The two exhausted refugees found shelter in the home of Dr. Chapin in Buffalo. Such are the essential points in the history of the Upper Canada rebellion and the life of Mackenzie until the day he sought refuge in the United States. Years later he was enabled to return to Canada by the passage of an amnesty act in 1849.

* * *

What activities filled Mackenzie's American years? What light do they throw on him as a Reformer and how did they affect his post-rebellion career in Canada? The attitude of American state and federal authorities to the rebellion, Mackenzie's share in the events of the Patriot war and his subsequent trial and imprisonment have received more attention from historians but even on these topics some things remain to be said. And what were Mackenzie's relations with two other prominent Reformers who took refuge in the United States, Dr. John Rolph and Marshall Spring Bidwell? Finally we may ask, is Mackenzie to be regarded as one who made a trade of agitation, a mere "pot-house brawler," a dishonourable, scrounging journalist who neglected his family and left a trail of debts behind him wherever he went, a bitter, vengeful, spiteful man, an erratic person of no consistent principles or constructive ideas and a ranting useless member of Parliament after his return? Or should he be regarded as a devoted, incorruptible, radical Reformer not to be contented with the achievement of responsible government, but determined that the economic policies adopted for the development of the province should not enrich a few and lay a heavy burden on the back of the common man? Was he "the people's friend," consistently waging war against corruption in high places and fighting for the democratization of the political and social structure of Canada? And what did he accomplish?

* * *

On the 14th of December, three days after Mackenzie's arrival in the United States, 24 sympathizers with the Canadian rebellion, under the leadership of Rensselaer Van Rensselaer and accompanied by Mackenzie, took possession of a small bit of Canadian territory, Navy Island, in the Niagara River. Here the provisional government of the State of Upper Canada was proclaimed. From time to time this group of Patriots, as they called themselves, was joined by Canadian refugees and American sympathizers until it amounted to at least 450 men.[15] The Patriots successfully resisted the efforts of the British forces in Canada to dislodge them until January 14, 1838, when they withdrew to the American mainland.

Mackenzie disclaimed responsibility for the Navy Island affair. His account of its origin is substantiated to a considerable degree by Van Rensselaer, by Thomas Jefferson Sutherland, the latter's second-in-command, and by contemporary newspapers. Days before Mackenzie arrived in Buffalo men who were expecting rebellion in Canada were planning to raise a force of volunteers to assist the rebels if a rising should occur. They had held three meetings for this purpose, a private one in late November, after news had arrived of the first outbreak of violence in Lower Canada,[16] and two public meetings, one on November 28 and another on December 5.[17] Popular interest having been aroused by these meetings, their organizers twice invited Mackenzie to come to Buffalo to speak, and on December 5, before they knew that rebellion had actually occurred in Upper Canada, they sent him "an unsolicited offer of aid towards rendering revolt in Canada successful."[18] Thomas Jefferson Sutherland, who attended the meeting on December 5th, left Buffalo for Toronto after this meeting. It was probably he who carried the offer of aid to Mackenzie. James Latimer, a journeyman who had been employed by Mackenzie, testified that on the 6th Mackenzie had read to the men at Montgomery's a letter from "Mr. Cotton" of Buffalo, stating that 200 men were coming to their assistance.[19]

> While prospects of success remained unclouded [Mackenzie later wrote] I never dreamed of asking aid from New York or Buffalo. On Wednesday morning, December 6, those of you who were with me judged such a course necessary....

On that day he wrote to the *Buffalo Whig and Journal* asking "all the assistance which the free citizens of your Republic may choose to afford."[20]

On December 11 another Canada meeting was held in Buffalo. Mackenzie's arrival in an exhausted condition was made known by Dr. Chapin,[21] who promised that he would speak on the following evening. On the 12th the Eagle Theatre was filled to overflowing. Rolph was in the city and Marshall Spring Bidwell[22] at Lewiston, but neither of these prominent Reformers attended.[23] Mackenzie, when introduced, acknowledged the cheers of the audience with several low bows, spoke of himself as "not the principal man," and went on to talk for over an hour about the grievances of the Canadians and their efforts to obtain redress.[24] The Buffalo *Commercial Advertiser* reported him as saying that only 200 of the "3500" who came to Montgomery's were armed and that as a body they lacked arms, powder, ordnance and blankets. The *Advertiser* interpreted Mackenzie's words as a direct appeal for assistance. The mayor of the city, Dr. Trowbridge, put the same interpretation upon them in a letter to President Van Buren.[25]

Thomas Jefferson Sutherland[26] claimed that he, a number of the inhabitants of Upper Canada and "others" had been preparing to bring about a political revolution in Upper Canada and that Mackenzie had no knowledge of it. When asked not to interfere, Mackenzie agreed, but insisted that he must speak at the meeting as Chapin had promised he would. Sutherland states that on this occasion it was he, not Mackenzie, who asked for volunteers.[27]

Van Rensselaer substantiates Sutherland's statement that an American expeditionary force of assistance was being planned before Mackenzie's arrival in Buffalo.[28] His account of his own activities raises questions about the degree to which American assistance had been planned for in advance by conspirators in Upper Canada, questions which cannot be answered conclusively from the surviving evidence. As Van Rensselaer travelled westwards from Albany in late November 1837, ostensibly to get news and new subscribers for his Albany *Daily Advertiser*, a paper which as early as 1831 had predicted a revolt in Upper Canada if grievances were not redressed,[29] he heard rumours of the probability of an uprising. At Lewiston he learned that the rebels in Upper Canada had been defeated on the 7th and was *"grievously mortified, irritated and disappointed"* at the news.[30] Surely there is more than the disappointment of a sympathetic bystander in these words? From Lewiston someone, most probably Van Rensselaer, wrote to the Rochester *Republican*, "We do not find the cause of the patriots as far advanced *as we anticipated* when we left home."[31]

Lindsey claims that Van Rensselaer was induced to involve himself in the affairs of Canada by John W. Taylor and Dr. Rolph.[32] Taylor represented Saratoga City in Congress and had been Speaker of the House 1825-27. When, and if, arrangements were made by Rolph for American help is uncertain. Before leaving Lewiston, however, Van Rensselaer wrote that Mackenzie was no military man — he should have marched on the city as soon as the rebels' designs became suspected — but that a proper military leader "will be found."[33] All this sounds like the result of a conversation with Rolph, who had arrived there on the 8th and who always maintained that Mackenzie should have marched on the city without delay.

When Van Rensselaer reached Buffalo on the 11th, Sutherland called on him, presenting a letter of introduction from Taylor,[34] who had been acquainted with him for some years.[35] Sutherland told Van Rensselaer that he had already enrolled 400 volunteers and had collected arms.[36] All this supposedly had been accomplished by the afternoon of the 11th — before Mackenzie made his speech on the 12th.[37] But Sutherland was a person of no standing and this was not the only occasion in his life on which he tried to thrust himself forward.[38] He had found that he needed a name to give his project "the proper tone," and Van Rensselaer, the son of a distinguished American hero of the War of 1812, was just the person to do that and he just happened to be right on the spot.[39] Sutherland urged him to take over the command, assuring him that he would have ample support and no interference. Rolph, who had been at Lewiston, where it is almost certain that he had talked with Van Rensselaer, had now come to Buffalo. It is probable that he, together with other prominent persons in the city, decided that Van Rensselaer would be a more suitable person to take the lead than Sutherland. At any rate, on the 12th, Rolph, Sutherland and Mackenzie went together to receive Van Rensselaer's promised decision. He consented to take command of the Patriot force once the men were on Canadian soil.[40]

The Toronto *Patriot* believed that after the British captured Sutherland on the lake ice while en route from Detroit to Sandusky on March 4, 1838, he made some disclosures which revealed that the plans of the rebels had rested wholly on American aid. "Nor were the military services of Van Rensselaer and Sutherland thrown into the scale accidentally from a sudden burst of sympathy. No. No. These men were ready at a call and had received considerable sums of money in advance from Toronto." Disclosures were made but they were not made by Sutherland. Captain Spencer, his aide, was captured with him and it was this man, a son of Chief Justice Spencer of New York, who gave Head information on the understanding he would be pardoned. Sir George Arthur kept the promise made by Head. When Sutherland returned to the United States he was indicted for violating the Neutrality Act, but he was never brought to trial. Mackenzie commented that the U.S. District Attorney dropped his case "like a hot potato" when he threatened to "tell all."[41]

Van Rensselaer claims to have derived his authority from Dr. John Rolph, "president of the Executive Council organized before the rising in Toronto, and William Lyon Mackenzie member of the same." But Rolph dominated the arrangements. He promised Van Rensselaer that no one would interfere with him in the exercise of his military powers, and he "went so far as to propose and insist that I should have the power to arrest any member of the Executive Council, providing it became necessary to do so, in order to prevent his interference in my department." "THIS PLEDGE of *non-interference* was both unasked and unexpected on my part, but it was the suggestion of Dr. Rolph... himself, and *exacted* by him from Mackenzie who at first evinced somewhat of a non-concurring disposition."[42]

At the Eagle Theatre on the 11th, a Committee of Thirteen had been chosen by sympathizers with the Patriot cause. Ebenezer Johnson, the former mayor of Buffalo, was named chairman.[43] On the 13th, this committee posted a handbill asking for donations of supplies for the cause. Another notice directed Patriot volunteers to assemble in front of the Eagle Theatre at 9:00 p.m., prepared to take up the line of march. No name was signed to this order. About 100 volunteers —an idle ragamuffin band of men and boys according to one witness—turned up and were marched off by Sutherland to Van Rensselaer's lodgings. Here Sutherland tried to present Van Rensselaer to the men as their general and to get him to accept a flag. He refused to take a public stand on United States soil.[44] After robbing the courthouse of 22 stand of arms, Sutherland and his men went to Black Rock, N.Y. The next morning Mackenzie went there, uninvited, and unwisely got into a dispute with the sheriff, who recovered some of the arms.[45] This circumstance was to tell against him at his trial.[46] Later the Patriots acquired ordnance and ammunition by stealing from the state arsenals.[47] From Black Rock Sutherland took his men to Whitehaven on Grand Island, sent Van Rensselaer word that he was about to leave for Navy Island from that point, and asked him to join the expedition there.[48]

Sutherland states that it was he and some others who conceived the Navy Island scheme without consulting Mackenzie. The latter had wanted the friends of Canada to go over to Fort Erie on the Canadian side and there organize a force that should join Dr. Charles Duncombe, the leader of rebels in the London District. Sutherland claims that there was no leading of a military expedition from Black Rock to Navy Island by Mackenzie nor was there any arrangement that Mackenzie should join him there. He was sent there by Sutherland's other collaborators against Sutherland's wishes. In his petition to President Van Buren in 1840, asking for Mackenzie's release from prison, Sutherland stressed that he was seeking no favour for a friend or for one he admired. He was asking for the release of one who was not guilty of organizing a military expedition against a country with which the United States was at peace and he added that if Mackenzie became associated with the enterprise, it was not as its leader.[49] Of this there can be no doubt.

Van Rensselaer substantiates this account of the circumstances under which MacKenzie went to Navy Island. The Committee of Thirteen had become disgusted with Sutherland's lawless course — open recruiting and theft of state arms — and were about to dissolve as a committee. But when they heard from Van Rensselaer of the Navy Island plan, they were "elated[50]... resolved to hold on and forward... an abundance of supplies... and they were particularly anxious that I would move off without delay, and take Mackenzie with me because Governor Head had made a requisition upon Governor Marcy for his person....."[51] Head had not yet done so, and did not until December 22, but it is quite obvious that the Committee of Thirteen had become a little uneasy and one way of mending matters was to shift the base of operations to Canadian soil — Navy Island. When asked, Marcy refused to surrender Mackenzie on the grounds that his offence was primarily a political one, and, in any event, he was now on Canadian soil.[52]

Only 24 persons accompanied Van Rensselaer and Mackenzie to the island early on the morning of the 15th. This — this miserable handful of supporters — was all that the excited meetings and Sutherland's boasted success in recruiting had produced in the end. No wonder Mackenzie seemed "inert and spirit-broken" on the passage to Navy Island.[53]

Solomon Van Rensselaer reproached his son with having violated American neutrality, but was mollified when he subsequently learned that the Patriot army was not being organized on American soil.[54] The Neutrality Act of 1818 was evidently well understood by father and son. As soon as he had learned about Mackenzie's speech, the Secretary of State had instructed the U.S. District Attorney, N.S. Benton, to go to Buffalo and to arrest violators of the Neutrality Act.[55] At Benton's request its pertinent sections had been printed on December 13, 1837, in the Albany *Argus*, the official organ of the Van Buren Democrats in New York State. Nevertheless, the editor of the paper, Edwin Croswell, who was reported to have Papineau as his guest,[56] made it clear to Benton that vigorous enforcement of the law was not desired. He wrote:

> You will perceive by the *Argus* of this morning that we have published your communication with considerable omissions. The truth is... that the popular feeling — the democratic feeling particularly — is all with the suffering patriots. For one I believe their quarrel just and I am unwilling to afford or to appear to afford unnecessary facilities for the prosecution of supposed offenders. On the contrary I shall not regret to see them afforded all *legal* aid. We have thought it best, upon consultation with Mr. Flagg & other friends here, to publish only so much as will advise our citizens of their duties & their legal liabilities & shall serve to show the British government the prompt action of our own government .... Beyond this, in my judgment, it is powerless, for I do not believe unless the infraction of the law were open and palpable, no [*sic*] jury in this country would be found that would convict. [57]

On the Niagara frontier the initial enthusiasm for the Canadian rebels seems to have waned quite promptly owing to the lawlessness of Sutherland's men and the failure of Rolph and Bidwell to associate themselves with Mackenzie. "I begin to doubt as to future dependence upon the professed liberals of Canada. At any rate it is not for us to drive on a revolution for them," a correspondent of the Buffalo *Commercial Advertiser* commented.[58] This paper, while not unfriendly to Canadian independence, had from the outset taken a realistic and cautious stand. Later the paper warned that there could be no question but that America's policy would be one of neutrality and it pointed out that the people of Upper Canada as a whole had rallied to the defence of the government.[59]

On December 19, Governor Marcy, who had been stirred up to action by the Secretary of State, issued a proclamation calling upon the people of New York State not to allow their sympathies to lead them into violations of the law.[60] Public criticism of the Patriots now began to be expressed.[61] From the Canada side criticism of Mackenzie for having set back the cause of freedom by rebellion drifted across the lakes.[62] On the American side Rolph and Bidwell denounced him, asserting that he was "not a proper person for a leader" and had not the confidence of the most influential radicals, who wanted only the correction of certain abuses and an elective Legislative Council. Their criticism of the rising is significant: it had been "entirely *premature*."[63]

Prior to leaving for the island on the 15th, Mackenzie had spent December 13 and 14 preparing a proclamation announcing the formation of a provisional government for the State of Upper Canada, with himself as chairman *pro tem*, and an executive committee composed of 11 persons who were named and "two distinguished gentlemen" who were not named. Presumably Rolph and Bidwell were meant.[64] The document had been sent to the printers dated Navy Island, December 13th. Its confident tone reflected the excitement of that day and its wording must have given the impression to Canadians, to whom it was addressed, that the entire Navy Island enterprise was under Mackenzie's control. The proclamation called upon them to rise, promised "any volunteer" 300 acres of land, and gave the basic principles of a constitution for the new state, which an elected convention would be asked to adopt. These were: abolition of hereditary honours and the laws of entail and primogeniture, civil and religious equality, declaring the St. Lawrence open to the trade of the world, and the wild lands of the country available to "the industry, capital, skill and enterprise of the worthy men of all nations," freedom of the press, trial by jury, vote by ballot, an elected senate and assembly, and election of all officials, militia officers, justices of the peace, the governor and other members of the executive. Years later Nelson Gorham claimed that in framing this Navy Island proclamation Mackenzie "discarded the ceremony of consulting with anyone." It came "fully fledged from the incubator of his own brain."[65] A few days after landing on the island, Mackenzie ventured to the Canadian side of the river by night in a yawl to distribute the document, probably with Samuel Chandler as his companion.[66] Although the proclamation was addressed only to Canadians, the references to land were clearly intended to attract American volunteers. Despite the offer of 300 acres of land, the forces on Navy Island augmented slowly. A second proclamation, this one not addressed only to Canadians, was issued on December 19, promising volunteers $100 in silver as well, "on or before the 1st of May next." A third proclamation appeared on December 21.[67]

By letters to the Buffalo and Rochester papers and to the New York *Commercial Advertiser*, Bidwell made it clear that he was not associated with the provisional government on Navy Island.[68] Mackenzie had had an interview with him at Lewiston, perhaps on the 13th when he was supposed to have gone to Youngstown to recruit men.[69] It was the last time they talked together.[70] One can imagine Bidwell's icy reception of Mackenzie, who probably had come to get Bidwell's consent to the use of his name, and who no doubt became enraged at the refusal of this prominent Reformer to help the cause.

Rolph's course was more devious. He permitted Mackenzie to add to the tail of the proclamation, "I am personally authorized to make known to you that... Dr. John Rolph now decidedly approves of the stand we are taking...." Rolph could hardly do less. After all, he had participated in the negotiations with Van Rensselaer, had promised him to get in touch with Dr. Duncombe and had defended the rebel cause in conversation at Lewiston.[71] But meanwhile he had privately disparaged Mackenzie and told a delegation from Canada that his actions there had been "without consent."[72] The Rochester *Democrat* of December 10 published a letter stating "apparently on the authority of Dr. Rolph himself, that he took no part in the insurrection any more than Mr. Bidwell." The New York *Commercial Advertiser* of December 19 commented: "Thus we find the whole outbreak the work of Mackenzie and was neither advised nor countenanced by any of the respectable gentlemen whose names were so freely used by him." Rolph did not visit Navy Island until December 26, when he came with a committee from Rochester to confer with Van Rensselaer. This was probably the committee that noted "a lack of discipline, especially in the commissary department" and "a great want of energy in the commanding officer."[73] Rolph shared in their conclusion and perhaps helped them to it. Bidwell informed a friend: "You are wrong in your conclusions about Rolph. He has been opposed to the proceedings on Navy Island. He exerted himself to break up that establishment.[74] On December 28, when the provisional government proposed to appoint Rolph to receive cash contributions to the Patriot cause, he declined to act in that capacity.[75] From this point on Rolph turned his back on the Navy Islanders and busied himself trying to get re-established in his profession. John A. Dix, Marcy's secretary, wrote to the U.S. Attorney-General, Benjamin F. Butler, on Rolph's behalf, suggesting a patronage appointment in a public institution for him, pleading that he had "conscientiously abstained from violating our laws." "His only crime was discussion."[76]

Van Rensselaer and Mackenzie had hoped that Charles Duncombe and the rebels in the London District would make it possible for them to land in Canada. After learning that Duncombe's followers had been dispersed, Van Rensselaer sent Sutherland to Detroit to organize a force there that would make a diversion in his favour at Malden. Some days later he sent Bill Johnston to French Creek to do the same on the St. Lawrence.[77] On the 28th a steamboat chartered by the Patriots, the *Caroline*, went down from Buffalo to Schlosser to carry supplies to Navy Island and to be ready to take Van Rensselaer's forces to the mainland whenever he should be informed that his diversionary tactics were succeeding. The destruction of this vessel on the 29th by a cutting-out party sent from Canada, who seized her while tied up at Schlosser, is an incident too well known to need recounting here at length. It spoiled Van Rensselaer's plan for landing on the Canadian mainland.

The seizure of the *Caroline* in American waters and the killing of one American in the process immediately rekindled enthusiasm for the Patriot cause in lake-shore towns and upstate communities. "Not one man in forty but espouses Mackenzie's cause," the Secretary of the Treasury was informed.[78] Papineau went to Albany and there "warmed up" the Chancellor, the judges and other prominent men of New York State in favor of the Patriots. Thurlow Weed commented, "I new [sic] the whole thing was wrong but I always left Papineau full of sympathy and solicitude for the Patriots. I mean I knew it was wrong for us to interfere."[79] On January 4, "the largest meeting ever held in the city of Albany" assembled to sympathize with the Canadians and to adopt measures for their relief.[80] Arms, ammunition, provisions and recruits poured into Navy Island.

Meanwhile the British were daily expected to attack the island, if not Buffalo itself.[81] The city was aroused to a frenzy of excitement. Allan MacNab had collected boats at Black Creek and canoes at Chippewa to attack the island, but he seems to have been in no hurry to start. Sir Francis Bond Head and J.B. Robinson also were averse to attempting an attack; it might mean that the British boats would be caught in the current and swept over the falls, two miles downstream. Besides, there was always the danger of defeat, a risk they did not want to run, since a defeat would give an impetus to the Patriot cause and bestow upon it "the character of regular warfare."[82] "On the other hand," argued the Lieutenant-Governor, "if we allow them to undertake the dangerous business of attacking *us*, we have science on our side instead of on theirs." The *Caroline* incident, the subsequent increase in the number of men on Navy Island, the growing excitement on the American shore and his fear that it would be "impossible to prevail upon the militia to remain... much longer," caused Head to change his mind.[83] On January 5 he informed Sir John Colborne that MacNab was preparing to attack. People in Buffalo believed that on January 6 the Canadian militia had refused to go into the small boats when ordered. Dr. Bryant Burwell, a resident of Buffalo, recorded that:

> About 450 volunteered. The rest were driven to their boats and when ordered to start not an oar was lifted.... The attack was abandoned for the present. [84]

MacNab then attempted to rout the Navy Islanders by continuing the cannonading he had begun on December 27. On January 11, when Head again reported that MacNab was "on the point of attacking," he was superseded in command by Colonel Hughes.[85]

One wonders who was reluctant to attack Navy Island. Was it the militia from cowardice or from secret sympathy with Mackenzie and the rebels; or was it MacNab who did not dare to take the risk? Lieutenant-Colonel Charles Grey, who visited Navy Island a few months later, informed his father that there was "an excellent landing place at the upper end of the Island" where there was "not the slightest risk from the current" and that 4,000 or 5,000 men had been assembled and kept

> watching without daring to attack for six weeks an accessible island garrisoned *at most* by 500 Ragamuffins. It is an eternal disgrace to Colonel MacNab and Sir F Head and such is the opinion of every Volunteer I have spoken to, officers and men in the neighborhood. [86]

Matters were gradually approaching a crisis for both sides. After the *Caroline* was destroyed negotiations for another steamboat had to be made if supplies, particularly munitions and ordnance, were to reach Van Rensselaer and his men. By January 8 Johnson's committee had made arrangements for the use of the *Barcelona*.

In the meantime the attitude of the government of the United States had become clearer. Up to this point President Van Buren and Governor Marcy had not condemned the Patriots outright: they had merely drawn attention to the Neutrality Act. The complaints of the government of Upper Canada about the assistance being given to the Patriots, complaints strongly reinforced by the British Minister at Washington, H.S. Fox, at length led President Van Buren, on January 5, to issue his first proclamation warning American citizens that they would receive no aid or comfort from their government if they got themselves into difficulties through violating that act. Those who had believed that the

President would sooner or later show sympathy with the Canadian rebels ought to have become convinced that his policy had been — and would continue to be — peace.[87] Joel R. Poinsett, the Secretary at War, now ordered General Winfield Scott to the frontier and Scott persuaded Governor Marcy to accompany him.[88]

By January 10 the public's attitude also had changed. Mackenzie, as will appear shortly, had angered some of Buffalo's citizens. Besides, everyone was getting tired of Navy Island; those upon it and those supplying it. After all it had served its purpose: a place, not on American soil, where a military expedition against Canada could be organized. But nothing had been accomplished.

The U.S. Marshal now stationed himself at Schlosser to prevent arms and supplies from being smuggled across to the island in small boats.[89] On January 10 the British authorities were informed that the citizens of Buffalo had begun to assist him. No provisions had reached the island for several days and the Patriots' funds were said to be exhausted.[90]

Scott and Marcy arrived on the frontier by January 10. Poinsett proposed that they should have a conference with Head at which they should suggest that the excitement could be pacified if the Canadian authorities would disavow any participation in the *Caroline* affair, offer redress and permit the Navy Islanders to lay down their arms and go home! Scott reported that this unofficial suggestion arrived after Governor Marcy had left and after Head's recall by his government had become known. Moreover, "a most exasperating bloody spirit" prevailed in Upper Canada where "a barbarous bill of pains and forfeitures" was about to pass the legislature at Toronto. On the day that Scott wrote, three such bills passed.[91]

Before the arrival of Marcy and Scott, Van Rensselaer had made plans for leaving the island as a letter to his father shows.[92] His intentions were to land his men at Chippewa. The "golden opportunity" for landing at Chippewa was lost, however, because the promised steamboat, the *Barcelona*, did not arrive:

> The men would not hazard the passage of the Niagara without the tow of the Steamboat... although [on the11th] we stood under arms from sunset to midnight waiting for One... it did not appear.[93]

Van Rensselaer then became willing to leave the island. After conferences with the Committee of Thirteen and with Marcy and Scott, who both strongly urged this course upon him, he agreed to withdraw and to disarm his men.[94] Some field pieces and about 200 men were landed at Schlosser. The main body, 400 to 600, went to Grand Island during the night of January 14 to hide their small arms and some of their artillery. They then marched across the island to Whitehaven where the *Barcelona* picked them up and landed them on the American shore, an unarmed body of men. It was expected that the Navy Islanders would disperse themselves throughout New York State, but what most of them did was to rendezvous west of Buffalo at Silver Creek, waiting for a steamer to take them to Canada.

At heart General Scott sympathized with the Patriots and hoped their cause would be successful.[95]Van Rensselaer more than hints that he had expected co-operation from Scott. After the withdrawal, however, he complained to his father of the faithlessness of Marcy and Scott and accused them of failing to live up to their "implied understanding." Nelson Gorham also complained of the treachery of Scott. On the day he agreed to leave the island, Van Rensselaer had been "buoyed up... by fresh promises of boats provided I would take my men up to Buffalo and embark there."[96] Mackenzie states that the plan had been to land the Navy Islanders at Long Point. It may be that Scott's treachery consisted in coaxing Van Rensselaer off Navy Island and then chartering all available steamboats to prevent him moving his men and supplies.[97] Van Rensselaer was then obliged to tell the men to "foot it" up to Detroit.[98] They were surprised by Colonel Worth on January 22 and reportedly deprived of "all the arms and ammunition that had been saved from Navy Island" before they could leave Silver Creek.[99]

The contrast between the official policy of the United States and the conduct of the authorities of New York State was noted by contemporaries. The Buffalo *Commercial Advertiser* commented:

> During his stay here [Governor Marcy] displayed more of the qualities of a popularity seeking demagogue than of a chief magistrate sworn to execute the laws.... His most intimate and confidential advisers while in this city were those who have most actively engaged in the recent movements on the frontier.... [100]

Chance enabled Sir George Arthur, when passing through Albany, to observe Bidwell's intimacy with Marcy and to note the latter's embarrassment on Arthur's discovering it.[101] Thomas C. Love, a former Whig congressmen from Buffalo, complained that despite the presence of the governor, three brigadier-generals and the New York State militia, the Navy Islanders "with their arms" had been permitted to travel over 60 miles of territory to a point west of Buffalo from which they expected to pass into Canada. Love added:

> I have been impressed from the beginning with the belief that the *Regency* at *Albany* with a view of presenting a new issue for popular attention, have fomented this excitement to the extent of their power. If I had entertained doubts on that subject before Governor Marcy's visit to this place they would now be dissipated. [102]

Papineau requested E.B. O'Callaghan to:

> Learn from my good friend the Chancellor and Judge Cowan all you can of the views which led Mr. Van Buren to be so excessively timid as he has been towards England. Without naming names, you know how many of his numerous friends... in New York State have been more hardy than he.... [103]

Governor Marcy's taste for Patriot intrigues, lukewarm at best, soon diminished. "The Canada business threatens to become more embarrassing than was anticipated," he informed his friend, General P.M. Wetmore.[104] The Governor seems to have become anxious to wash his hands of the whole affair which, owing to the *Caroline* incident, the failure of the Patriots to accomplish anything, divided opinion in upstate New York and the attitude of the President, had indeed become embarrassing to him. In a separate interview with Van Rensselaer Marcy obtained from him a promise "to move his men out of New York State as speedily as possible."[105] At the same time he did not want to create political enemies among those who had espoused the Patriot cause. Subsequently he became politically obnoxious to them for his vigorous enforcement of the neutrality laws, and during the elections of 1838 he was charged with having given information to the Canadian authorities.[106]

While on Navy Island Mackenzie conducted the correspondence for the Patriot forces. How long he stayed there is uncertain. Van Rensselaer's statement implies that he left some days prior to the withdrawal, "safely ensconced" himself in the home of a friend in Buffalo and remained there. We know that on January 4 Mackenzie left the Island, temporarily perhaps, to take his wife, who had arrived there on December 25, to Captain Appleby's home in Buffalo.[107] En route he was arrested by the Marshal on a charge of violating the Neutrality Act. This event can only have been a terrible shock to Mackenzie who, after the *Caroline* affair, had been confidently expecting continued American aid and sympathy. Van Rensselaer charges that, when arrested, he became "extremely abusive towards everything American... and... disgusted all his benefactors in that quarter by the violence of his language."[108] His wild outburst was described as a "vulgar two hour tirade... against this country and its officers," although a more friendly account was published in some papers.[109] Three Buffalo men went his bail for $5,000 and he was released.[110] Mackenzie seems to have permanently damaged his prospects in Buffalo, for he subsequently complained of the very limited support his newspapers received there and of the failure of the Buffalonians to relieve his personal misfortunes.[111]

\* \* \*

The decision to withdraw from Navy Island was made not by Mackenzie but by the Buffalo Committee of Thirteen and the officers of the Patriot forces. As Donald M'Leod put it, "The island could not land on the Canadian shore, nor could the loyalists make any impression on the island."[112] While the committee was debating what to do, Mackenzie had written to them urging the evacuation "so that we get at once into Canada." This was what he had contended for all along, and with reason. He believed that the full strength of the rebels had not been mustered on December 4 and that many men on their way to Montgomery's on the 7th had turned themselves into loyal subjects coming to the support of the government when they heard that Mackenzie's supporters had been routed. It was reasonable to think that the prompt arrival of men, and particularly of arms, from the American side might yet call forth support for the rebel cause. Sir George Arthur and his Executive Council became convinced that the disaffected feeling in Upper Canada was "far wider and deeper" than Head had supposed. Bishop Alexander Macdonnell was of the same opinion. A year after the rebellion even J.B. Robinson confessed that "if a lodgement could be made on our frontier — a rebel camp formed — I am not sure that even thousands would not flock to it."[113]

Although from the outset Mackenzie had not been in favour of occupying Navy Island, in his opinion it had not been a completely futile affair, since it had decreased the revenue of Upper Canada by hindering trade across the lakes, increased doubt in Great Britain about the value of colonies, and had aroused American hostility towards her. Nevertheless a month had been wasted on the island while the Tories had entrenched themselves and filled the jails with Reformers. There was no more time to lose. Mackenzie therefore strenuously opposed Van Rensselaer's plan for sending the Navy Islanders to Detroit. He wanted them to return to Buffalo, seize boats by force and embark for Canada.[114] A violent quarrel, by no means the first, broke out between the two men. One can imagine that the impetuous and energetic Mackenzie had not been deterred from speaking his mind by the powers which had been conferred on Van Rensselaer by Dr. Rolph and that subordination to this commander-in-chief, who had "spent the principal part of his time lying on a buffalo skin"[115] had infuriated him.

In the end it was decided that an attack on Fort Henry, the key to the naval base at Kingston, should be made about February 22.[116] Van Rensselaer was to use the westward retreat of the Navy Island forces under Donald M'Leod as a feint, and to go east himself to prepare for the attack with the help of Bill Johnston while both the British in Canada and the government of the United States would be watching the Detroit frontier. Van Rensselaer was selected to head this new expedition apparently by the Buffalo group supporting the Patriots. He states that Mackenzie was irritated at being passed over by them and by "the contempt for him which my inattention indicated," but he was again made to promise not to interfere, and "we parted as friends."[117]

Mackenzie's account of this affair is very different. Mackenzie, like Donald M'Leod a few months later, resented the attempt of Americans to take control out of Canadian hands. Here was the nub of the difficulty. Was the Patriot war to be managed by Canadians (i.e. Mackenzie) with the assistance of personally disinterested Americans, or was it to be taken over and run by Americans, some of whom regarded it as a chance to get in on the ground floor in Upper Canada in the event of success? Mackenzie suggested to Van Rensselaer that if he still wanted to help, he should remain with the volunteers who were on their way to Detroit, and that he should accompany them into Canada when opportunity offered.

When Mackenzie parted from Van Rensselaer at Buffalo it was his understanding that the latter "would not desert his men."[118] Bill Johnston claimed for himself the credit of suggesting the attack on Fort Henry and the manner in which it should be carried out.[119] When Van Rensselaer attempted to take the control, Mackenzie continued to work for the success of the plan, relying on

Reformers in Lennox and Addington counties to turn out to support the invaders. He did so, according to Johnston, not because he had confidence in Van Rensselaer, but because he hoped for success by sychronizing the attack with the movements of the Patriots in Lower Canada.[120]

After the stormy meeting at Buffalo Mackenzie, accompanied by his wife, David Gibson, and Daniel Heustis, left for Watertown.[121] By January 21 he was at Rochester, where George Dawson, editor of the Rochester *Democrat*, had offered him hospitality.[122] In Rochester Mackenzie tried to raise money for the Patriot cause but met with a discouraging response owing to the recent failure at Navy Island.[123] Van Rensselaer subsequently accused him of trying to obtain money for himself to start a newspaper. He states that the Rochester committee gave Mackenzie $100 to get rid of him. However, it is clear from the letters of a member of this committee that they knew what Mackenzie was about and regarded *him* as the leader of the enterprise.[124] He had already learned from a former Belleville resident, C.H. McCollum, that 482 Patriots in Hastings County had been prepared to march on Kingston if the movement behind Toronto had succeeded. McCollum believed they could still be aroused and that support would come from Americans in Jefferson County.[125] Mackenzie kept in touch with the Patriots across the lake and also with the leaders of the French Canadian rebels who hoped that an attack on Fort Henry would cause Colborne to divert troops to its assistance and thus their planned invasion of Lower Canada from Vermont would be facilitated.[126] Before making final arrangements Mackenzie planned to see Papineau who, he remarked, "sits at the helm, quiet and still and moves all."[127] But Papineau is reported to have been nervous for his personal safety on account of the reward that had been offered for him and to have been considering withdrawing to Europe. By January 1 he had broken with Dr. Robert Nelson and Dr. Cyril Côté (two influential Lower Canadian rebels) because he disapproved of the frontier adventures being planned by them. He had discovered that Van Buren was "determined on enforcement of the neutrality laws to prevent misunderstanding with Great Britain."[128]

Van Rensselaer certainly regarded the Fort Henry plan as his own and he protested both for Bill Johnston and himself when he learned that Mackenzie was already active in the neighbourhood of French Creek (Clayton). Fearing that if his presence and Mackenzie's at French Creek became known Kingston would be put on its guard, Van Rensselaer proposed that he himself should go openly to Buffalo and Mackenzie to Albany to throw people off the scent.

Van Rensselaer claimed that Mackenzie agreed to his proposals except that he preferred to go to Lower Canada instead of to Albany. Mackenzie, on the contrary, states that he refused to accept Van Rensselaer's stipulations and again urged him to join the force in the west so as to draw the attention of the British to the Detroit frontier. Van Rensselaer did not go. It is clear that the two leaders did not come to an understanding and that each of them stubbornly decided to go ahead with his own plans.[129]

On February 9, Colonel Worth having mistakenly reported that Van Rensselaer was on his way west to join the Navy Islanders, General Scott hurried off to Detroit.[130] The whole of the American frontier from Buffalo to Plattsburgh was now clear. There were no garrisons of importance on the Canadian side; the greatest number of men in Fort Henry and Kingston was thought to be only 300 militia, many of them friends of the Patriot cause prepared to spike the guns and open the gates. A crossing on the ice could be made to within half a mile of the fort without observation and so could the rest of the distance, according to Van Rensselaer, "had the preparations been conducted as secrecy and promptitude intended."[131] "Their plan of attack is admirable," wrote R.H. Bonnycastle, three days before it was scheduled to take place, adding, "The only folly they have shown is in confiding it to too many."[132]

Mackenzie, meanwhile, succeeded in keeping out of sight at Watertown until he left for Ogdensburgh on February 5.[133] From Ogdensburgh he went to Plattsburgh, accompanied by David Gibson, to consult with the leaders of the French Canadians. After his return a convention of Patriot sympathizers is thought to have been held in St. Lawrence or Jefferson County and a plan of campaign agreed on.[134]

One of Mackenzie's supporters in Rochester, C.H. Graham, now informed him that Van Rensselaer had left the Niagara frontier with the avowed intention of supplanting him. He suggested that Mackenzie should use the executive authority with which the refugees and the Patriots resident in Canada had entrusted him to depose Van Rensselaer from the command. "[He] has disgusted all the friends of the revolution who have come in contact with him."[135]

It is not worthwhile to go into all the charges and counter-charges exchanged between the two men. Suffice it to say that when Van Rensselaer returned to French Creek on February 17, some of the Patriots insisted that he should have the command while others sided with Mackenzie. So acrimonious did the quarrel become that Van Rensselaer threatened "to shoot Mackenzie or give him over to the authorities in Canada as being an injury to the cause."[136]

Mackenzie differed from Van Rensselaer not only about the command of the expedition but about the policy to be followed. He did not want the men to leave French Creek as a body, but to cross as individuals and to be organized in Canada. In that way he thought the provisions of the Act of 1818 would be evaded. Nor did he want "large bodies of Americans invading Canada."[137] One hundred and fifty men from the American side, he was convinced, would be adequate with the forces he expected to join him in Canada. He informed his Rochester friends that provisions, clothing, money, munitions of "peace," all had been abundantly contributed, that the arsenal at Watertown had been robbed, and that he had reason to expect "a simultaneous movement at Montreal." This account of the extensive preparations made by the Patriots both on the American side and in the "Bidwell country" (the town of Belleville and the county of Lennox and Addington in Upper Canada) is well confirmed.[138]

Early on the morning of the 22nd, hearing that Colonel J.E. Wool was approaching, Van Rensselaer and an advance guard crossed to Hickory Island, four miles from Gananoque, with the arms, to prevent them being seized under the provisions of the Neutrality Act of 1838.[139] Wool, however, remained at Plattsburgh to watch the movements of the French Canadian leaders, Nelson and Côté, convinced that their scheme was to entice him away to French

Creek.[140] On the 21st he sent General Skinner of the militia to Watertown without a force, merely to investigate and report, but with the power to call for a battalion of militia should he find as many as 200 or 300 men "actually embodied for Canada."[141]

Despite the abundance of supplies, less than 100 men followed first Van Rensselaer and second Daniel Heustis over the ice to Hickory Island on the evening of the 22nd. A force of at least 1,000 had been expected to follow. Some of them never left French Creek and most of those who did visit the island did not stay. Only 51 men answered the third muster and then Van Rensselaer, deciding it was folly to invade the Canadian mainland with so small a force, withdrew to the American side and gave up his commission.[142]

Privately, Mackenzie attributed the failure to attack Fort Henry to Van Rensselaer's drunken incompetence; publicly he merely said, "Aside from deficient skill his worst failing must have been too apparent to everyone who knew him to require any comment from me."[143] Others commented on the "pot-valiant" Van Rensselaer, and Bill Johnston, in a letter to C.A. Hagerman wrote, "If Mackenzie or any other decent man had been at the head... they would have taken... Kingston."[144]

Van Rensselaer excused his failure to act by the small size of the force that had actually followed him to Hickory Island and blamed that on Mackenzie's interference. On the very day the expedition was to leave, the Watertown *Jeffersonian* published a letter from Mackenzie stating that he had

> neither seen nor corresponded with Mr. Van Rensselaer in his recent movements on this frontier but have earnestly and invariably urged my friends to withdraw all confidence from him in matters connected with Canada.[145]

Because neither Mackenzie nor David Gibson took part, the men from Jefferson County likewise abstained, and there were 20 or 30 sleigh loads of them, well supplied with arms.[146] Mackenzie's own explanation of his last-minute withdrawal is simply that he did not wish to take upon himself "the disgrace of a failure."[147] That it would have been a failure, whether there had been harmony between the two leaders or not, Bonnycastle and General Wool leave no doubt, and Mackenzie seems to have realized it. A full month before the attempt on Kingston Sir John Colborne was made aware of the preparations being made at French Creek and at Plattsburgh and had protested to Governor Marcy and General Wool.[148] Moreover the robbery of the Watertown arsenal on the 18th had alerted both the District Attorney and Wool.

After returning from Hickory Island Van Rensselaer was arrested at Syracuse and, unable to find bail, was jailed at Albany to await trial.[149] He promised the Syracuse Onondaga Standard to prove that the abandonment of the Fort Henry expedition was chargeable to Mackenzie, "a cruel, reckless, selfish madman,... the greatest curse of the cause he pretends to espouse...." His parting advice to the Patriots was, "Turn the meddling craven out of your ranks."[150]

The promised exposé, under the heading "A Voice from Albany Jail,'", appeared in the Albany *Advertiser* of March 29, 1838, and in the Toronto *Patriot* of April 10, 1838. Van Rensselaer claimed that Mackenzie had tried to take over the direction of the Fort Henry expedition, which Van Rensselaer had originated, and had disclosed the secret to every committee in the region in his efforts to raise money and supplies and had thus destroyed the necessary secrecy of the enterprise. When he found out at Plattsburgh that the affairs of the Lower Canada Patriotes were not in as flourishing condition as he had led the Upper Canadians to believe,

> he suddenly turned about... concocted the magnanimous desire of overthrowing the expedition so that the censure should be taken from his shoulders and placed on mine.

> [Van Rensselaer blamed also Dr. A.K. Mackenzie of Lockport, later said to be a spy for the British,[151] who was supposed to come with teams and reinforcements and who did not turn up until the withdrawal had begun.]

> To this scoundrel in conjunction with his ingrate namesake [W.L. Mackenzie] I am indebted for the bitter tone of public sentiment after the failure.... [152]

There is no doubt that Mackenzie and Gibson did not obtain cheering news from the Lower Canadians. They were somewhat discouraged by the failure of Papineau to exert himself. A rift had developed between Papineau and the more radical Lower Canadian leaders. Robert Nelson observed that:

> Papineau has abandoned us for selfish and family motives regarding the seigneuries and his inveterate love of the old French laws. We can do better without him. He is a man fit only for words and not for action.... [153]

Papineau's attitude greatly disturbed Gibson, who regarded Papineau as "the author of the whole revolution... Upper Canada would never have attempted revolt alone.[154] In late January Robert Nelson instructed one of his subordinates to try to engage Colonels Worth, Wool, or Scott of the U.S. Army for the Canadian cause by promising them 10,000-20,000 acres of land partly improved, with several sawmills and grist mills on it.[155] The location of this prize and the name of its then owner were not stated. This and other desperate expedients achieved little. On February 12, Papineau himself wrote to Mackenzie informing him that he was opposed to the plans of the group at Plattsburgh.[156]

After Mackenzie and Gibson had left Plattsburgh, General Wool arrived there and made it plain to Robert Nelson what the attitude of the United States — and his own attitude — towards any movement of the Patriots would be. Wool said:

> We do not see the slightest shadow of hope for you *at present*...
> as an attempt, followed by failure would surely... expose the
> resident people of Canada to harsher treatment than they
> might otherwise experience, we are out of humanity, deter-
> mined to suppress any movement on your part.... you cannot
> get... money or... arms; so you must give up... for the present.
> If you are about any preparation for invasion, pray... abandon
> your project. [157]

On February 21 Nelson wrote to Mackenzie that owing to the lateness of the season (the ice was expected to break) and the vigorous opposition of the United States, they had decided to abandon their projected invasion of Lower Canada for that year.[158]

From a letter written to the Rochester committee on the 22nd, it appears that Mackenzie was still hoping that all would "go well," and that Bill Johnston, Colonel Woodruff and others would make up for Van Rensselaer's lack of energy.[159] Mackenzie made no mention in this letter of the notice he was that very day to publish in the *Jeffersonian*. He did, however, state that General Wool was expected to arrive on the scene.[160] As has been seen, it was not Wool but Skinner who left Plattsburgh on the 21st for Watertown. It is probable that Mackenzie's interview with Skinner, the arrival of Nelson's letter of the 21st and perhaps additional information that Kingston was well prepared were what led him, at the last moment, to deter his friends from taking part in what would have been a disastrous attempt to take Fort Henry. For this he cannot be blamed, but he certainly did not do the fair thing in placing all the blame for the failure of the elaborately planned project upon Van Rensselaer. The Navy Island enterprise was not of Mackenzie's designing; nor can he be blamed for its futility. For the Hickory Island affair he must bear a full share of responsibility.

Nelson and Côté, however, persisted in their plans.[161] Nelson's letter of the 21st had only been a blind. On the 25th the Lower Canadian Patriots succeeded in robbing the state arsenal at Elizabethtown, evaded Wool, and crossed into Lower Canada on the 28th. But it was Wool's opinion that their leaders had no serious expectations of success. He believed they hoped to provoke the British into following them across the border and into committing acts of aggression against the frontier inhabitants, thereby bringing about war between Great Britain and the United States.[162] Wool informed Nelson that if he did not surrender before he was attacked by the British and if he should be driven back, Wool would "repel his return to the states by force."[163] Nelson and Côté advanced only one mile north of the frontier. Overnight their force of 700 men dwindled to 160. E.B. O'Callaghan was unable to explain this sudden diminution to Erastus Corning, who had offered to supply the Lower Canada Patriotes with lead.[164] On March 1 Wool achieved the ignominious withdrawal and surrender of the Lower Canada Patriotes with all their arms and equipment.[165] Nelson and Côté were turned over to the civil authorities of Vermont and jailed for a time.[166]

The withdrawal from Lower Canada, the failure to attack Fort Henry, and the quarrels of Van Rensselaer and Mackenzie had an unfortunate effect upon public opinion in upstate New York. Both men came in for a share of the blame. Within 48 hours, Van Rensselaer was being denounced as a drunken coward by the very people who had been ready to empty their purses for him.[167] Mackenzie, observed the Ogdensburgh *Republican*,

> has shown himself equally selfish, heartless, unprincipled and cowardly; and so great is the revulsion of feeling here, that I verily believe, if he should return here again, he would be handed over to the Canadians. [168]

The ignominious failure left a bad impression on the Canadian side too. "Being shamefully imposed on by that affair, leaving half the county to suffer imprisonment — we cannot now get action from them," one of Mackenzie's supporters wrote at a later date.[169] S.C. Frey observed:

> People cannot understand why you should be the life and soul in getting up that expedition and then on the very day of its embarkation come out with a card and disavow any connection with it. Your intimate friends understand it but in the meantime, time only and prudent movements can turn the current of public opinion. [170]

## Chapter II

# MACKENZIE'S GAZETTE AND THE PATRIOT WAR

After the failure at Hickory Island Mackenzie left the frontier lest he should be arrested again for violating the Neutrality Act. He travelled west as far as Milan, Ohio, in company with Calvin Willcox, seeking support for the Patriot cause. Meanwhile, the Navy Islanders had reached the Detroit area in a wretched state for want of food and clothing.[1] Dr. Duncombe had been trying to organize a Patriot force at Detroit to co-operate with the disaffected in the London District of Upper Canada and recruiting for the Patriot service had been continuing in Michigan, Ohio, Kentucky, and Illinois.[2] These western forces were defeated at Malden on December 9, at Fighting Island and Comstock Flats on February 25, and at Pelee Island on March 3.[3] Willcox and Mackenzie then concluded that, for the time being, any further efforts on their part to obtain support for the Patriots would only expose them to ridicule.[4] Bill Johnston proposed raiding Canada to obtain hostages high in rank and holding them until the Patriot prisoners taken by the British were released.[5] Mackenzie either disapproved of or ignored this suggestion. By March 4 he had returned to Albany, where friends tried to convince him that the Canadians' cause was hopeless. By March 10 Mackenzie and his wife were in New York City at the home of an old friend, James Smith, printer to the Methodist Book House.[6]

Mackenzie planned to go on to Washington for a month.[7] S.C. Frey suggested that while there he should make the acquaintance of Senator Silas Wright of New York, and others of his friends thought northern politicians could be interested in adding free territory to the Union.[8] The isolated adventures of the Patriots had accomplished nothing, but if war between Great Britain and the United States should come about as a result of the *Caroline* affair, there was still hope of freeing Canada. If Mackenzie went to Washington, he did not stay long. By March 17 he was in Philadelphia and by the end of the month back in New York, busy establishing his newspaper, *Mackenzie's Weekly Gazette*.

It is surprising that Mackenzie did not choose to publish his newspaper at Buffalo, from which point it surely would have been easier to get copies into Canada and to keep in touch with Canadian news. He had proposed it — to the Buffalo Committee of Thirteen, on the very day the withdrawal from Navy

Island was decided upon. His proposal received a lukewarm response: the Committee would consider it when they had leisure.[9] After all, Buffalo already had several struggling papers, some of which had given generous support to the Patriot cause. Moreover, Mackenzie had lost prestige in that city. When, at a later date, he decided to take his newspaper closer to the frontier, it was to Rochester, not to Buffalo, that he went.

The prospectus for *Mackenzie's Gazette* appeared in the *National Gazette* of Philadelphia on March 15, 1838, and in the *United States Gazette* on March 17. Its editor disclaimed any intention of adopting any course contrary to the policy of neutrality which the United States wished to maintain. He did propose to discuss subjects in dispute between Great Britain and the United States: the boundary of Maine, the *Caroline* affair, Texas, the navigation of the St. John and St. Lawrence Rivers. Apart from these topics he would discuss the politics of the United States only incidentally.[10]

Henry O'Rielly, editor of the Rochester *Daily Advertiser*, and a former employer of Mackenzie's son James, was in New York at this time. He sympathized with the Patriot cause and helped Mackenzie to get his paper started,[11] on credit, not an easy matter since Mackenzie had left Toronto still in debt to the Bruce Brothers, a New York firm of type founders. George Bruce had him arrested for debt as a non-resident alien. He was released, with O'Rielly's help.[12]

For a few weeks Mackenzie was able to keep the dark devil of despair from overtaking him. He cheered himself and his family by reflecting upon the career of William Cobbett who, after eight years as a refugee in America, had returned to England to become a successful journalist and "comfortable in his worldly circumstances."[13] But in April Mackenzie was plunged into gloom by the news that his close associates, Samuel Lount and Peter Mathews, had been hanged. They had been captured while trying to escape after the defeat at Montgomery's. "The news came upon me like an electric shock. I was utterly unprepared for such an event," he confessed.[14] By July he was in a more cheerful mood. His family, then consisting of five daughters and his mother, had arrived from Toronto. On May 12 the first issue of his paper appeared, with a boasted circulation of 4,000. Although Mackenzie had been indicted at Albany on June 10 for violating the Neutrality Act, his trial had been postponed and he had not been held in jail.[15] Moreover, his hopes for Canada were still high since he knew in a general way, if not in detail, that an organization of Canadian refugees and American sympathizers, headed by "General" Henry S. Handy of Illinois, was planning a widespread rising all along the frontier for July 4.[16]

For a brief time *Mackenzie's Gazette* continued to be what it had promised to be: a paper primarily concerned with defending the Patriot cause and providing news from Canada and the United Kingdom. By harping on such topics as the grievances of the Canadians, the similarities with the causes of the American Revolution, the burning of the *Caroline*, the arming of blacks in Upper Canada, the treatment of Americans in that province, the question of double allegiance, the Maine boundary and the "right" to navigate the St. Lawrence, the *Gazette* did its best to make American public opinion actively hostile to Great Britain. War between the two powers would afford the Patriots an opportunity to call forth what they believed to be their latent support in Upper Canada and for a time the *Gazette* tried hard to provoke war. "One short war well managed," its editor wrote, "might give this continent perpetual peace. Until Canada is freed the revolution in America will not be complete."[17]

Mackenzie also used his *Gazette* — too much of it — to defend himself and to criticize Dr. John Rolph and Marshall Spring Bidwell, who had disassociated themselves from the Canadian cause — and from Mackenzie — and now seemed to be interested only in looking out for themselves.

Bidwell had been born in the United States. His father, at one time a member of Congress and subsequently Attorney-General of Massachusetts, had fled to Canada in 1810 to escape trial on a charge of corruption levied by his political enemies. In early manhood the younger Bidwell acknowledged that he was a "True Blue Yankee."[18] After he entered politics he became one of the leaders of the Reform Party in Upper Canada and was twice elected. Nevertheless Lieutenant-Governor Head and Richard Henry Bonnycastle regarded him as a leader of the group that favoured breaking the imperial tie and the one who directed "the secret workings of the anarchists."[19] The imprecise account that Bidwell gave to the New York *Commercial Advertiser* of the circumstances under which he had been obliged to leave Canada intimated that before the rebellion good relations had been restored between him and the Lieutenant-Governor. It concluded in a manner that threw the blame for his predicament upon Mackenzie.[20]

Mackenzie acknowledged that he did not expect evidence connecting Bidwell with the revolt to be in Head's hands. "Bidwell," he wrote, "was as well aware as myself of the approach of the revolt, although he took no public part in it."[21] This statement does not clear Bidwell of sympathizing with and planning for *a* break with the mother country. The strongest evidence against him of attempting to hasten that day, apart from his political course in Canada, is his intimacy with Governor Marcy, which shocked Sir George Arthur,[22] the statements of John W. Birge[23] and the prompt favours he received in New York State. On January 2, 1838, Bidwell was admitted to practise as attorney and counsellor in the Supreme Court and as solicitor and councillor in the Court of Chancery of the State of New York, *ex speciale gratia*, and thus got his feet firmly placed on the ladder of professional success in the Republic.[24] He established himself in New York City with the firm of Strong and Griffin and thereafter "laid down republicanism with all his soul."[25]

Mackenzie had been accused of trying to injure Bidwell's prospects in the United States in some manner not specified but, if true, he only injured himself. Henry O'Rielly had tried to interest Senator Silas Wright in Mackenzie but he could not persuade Wright to exert himself for Mackenzie, because Mackenzie had "sought to bar against another unfortunate the gate of sympathy within whose walls he is himself seeking refuge."[26] Whatever may have been Mackenzie's conduct in this respect, it did not differ in principle from Bidwell's. Bidwell had disassociated himself from the refugees and had disparaged Mackenzie both publicly and privately. Moreover, when an Upper Canada Patriot was on his way to Pittsburgh to buy arms, Bidwell had taken it upon himself to inform the Secretary at War.[27]

Both Mackenzie and his son came to the conclusion that Bidwell's "attachment to liberty" had been governed by selfishness. James, who for a time had reported the debates in the Assembly, wrote:

> I never knew him ever openly to give his support and influence to a question which was not certainly popular — or even to speak when the tide of feeling was evidently against the motion. [28]

Even the editor of the *Christian Guardian* criticized Bidwell for "double dealing" and supported his accusation in some detail.[29] According to James, Bidwell and Rolph were jealous of Mackenzie's influence with the people and of the attention his Report on Grievances had received. Moreover, the report had "recommended changes they did not want." Mackenzie aimed at economic and social reforms more fundamental than merely getting rid of the Clergy Reserves and establishing a "responsible government," and he never budged from this position either before the rebellion or after his return from exile.[30] James went so far as to say that Bidwell, irritated by Head's failure to consult his Executive Council, of which Rolph was a member, "suggested revolution to father which a year before it occurred he had not contemplated. This I know as far as I can know anything." This strong accusation is weakened by the fact that James had earlier stated that Mackenzie was the first to propose rebellion and had told his son it had a startling effect. The two statements are reconcilable only if Bidwell and Rolph were maturing longer range plans when Mackenzie came forth in early November 1837 with his proposal for an *immediate* attack upon Toronto.[31]

In the first issue of his *Gazette* Mackenzie began the republication of his "Narrative of the Rebellion." It had originally appeared on February 1 in the Watertown *Jeffersonian* at Mackenzie's request to "correct" the account of that even which the Jeffersonian had taken from the *Upper Canada Herald*. At the Eagle Theatre on December 12 Mackenzie had covered up the reasons for the disastrous change of date from the 7th to the 4th in a manner not precisely accurate, yet one which did not openly blame Dr. John Rolph. In the Watertown version he referred to a meeting of 12 leading Reformers in November 1837 at which rebellion had been decided upon and at which an "Executive in the city" (Toronto) was named. He disclosed that it was the "Executive" who had changed the date of the uprising to the 4th. Mackenzie now prefaced the republication of his narrative with additional material and named the "Executive" — Dr. John Rolph. Rolph denied this honour. There had been no such gathering at which he had been appointed executive. This is one of the most disputed points in the history of the rebellion.[32] Certainly Van Rensselaer believed Rolph had been the chosen executive.

Mackenzie also republished an article from the *United States Magazine and Democratic Review* entitled "History of the Recent Insurrection in the Canadas" which, referring to the change of plans from the 7th to the 4th, said that:

The movement [of organizing for revolt], however, went on with the expected success until it was precipitated either by the treachery or the criminal indiscretion of one of their leaders....[33]

By republishing this statement without comment, it appeared to Henry O'Rielly and other reproachful Rochester friends that Mackenzie had sanctioned a charge against Rolph far stronger than he himself had originally made. In response Mackenzie pointed out that in the same June 9 issue in which the critical article had been published he had taken care to say that

if Dr. Rolph's act was indiscreet, as it certainly was, it was done with the purest and most honourable motives, and might have given us the means of success if Dr. Rolph had followed it up as he ought to have done. When I say this I say enough... I have neither questioned his patriotism or integrity publicly or privately. But I have stated facts and I have added that the Dr's courage did not sustain him when the trial came. Further I have not gone. [34]

Mackenzie certainly believed O'Rielly to be his friend, yet Rolph was able to persuade him to send a protest to the *Democratic Review* accompanied by an article very critical of Mackenzie which Rolph had written. The article was not a straightforward factual account of the events of December 4-7, adequately supported by evidence from others, but a turgid argumentative account full of implications and Rolph's own interpretations of events. The *Review* rejected the article "because its readers would need an acquaintance with localities which the general reader does not have." Also, although Mackenzie had shown "incapacity" in conducting the rebellion, his conduct was, in the editor's opinion, "hardly worthy of the unqualified censure and imputation of bad motives interspersed throughout your article."[35] J.C. Dent, who found the rough draft of the article among Rolph's papers, but who apparently did not discover why it had not appeared in print in 1838, published it as an appendix to the second volume of his *Upper Canada Rebellion*.

John Louis O'Sullivan who, with S.D. Langtree, published the *United States Magazine and Democratic Review*, was an ardent Jeffersonian. In Mackenzie he saw "a bold earnestness and sincerity of character, coupled with untiring devotion to the people's cause."[36] O'Sullivan came to believe that it was the "manifest destiny" of the United States to embrace the entire North American continent.[37] In 1837, however, O'Sullivan was not as ardent an expansionist as he later became. He did praise the Canadians — and Mackenzie — for their efforts to remodel their institutions along more democratic lines and to loosen the colonial tie, but he thought the proper policy for the United States was neutrality and peace with Great Britain.

If the Canadian people wish to be free from their dependence on
a foreign country, they have but to rise in their strength... and
say so; — they need no assistance of money or volunteers from
us. If it is not the will of the people — or if that will is not
sufficiently strong to carry them through the ordeal of revolution — we ought not to desire it. [38]

At this moment, the great question of the day for O'Sullivan was not the
Canadian rebellion but the banks. Like Mackenzie, O'Sullivan was a hard-
money man, ever ready to denounce the paper money and credit system as a
"stupendous modern fraud upon the industry of the mass of society." For him
the arch villain in the banking world was the Bank of England whose policies
had stimulated inflation in the United States and had precipitated the panic of
1837. This was an explanation of the crisis of 1837 also advanced by Jackson and
the New York *Evening Post*.[39] O'Sullivan predicted:

The present generation will not pass away without witness-
ing... the radical reform of the Bank of England, and its whole
paper money system. [40]

Here was grist for Mackenzie's mill! Here were two themes he could treat as one:
the abolition of the paper money system and the abolition of British power and
influence in the New World.

Throughout the summer, however, Mackenzie continued to give the major
part of his space to Canadian topics: in the issue of July 7 he criticized the land
policies of Upper Canada, not in his own words, but by reprinting a long extract
from an article in the *British and Colonial Review*.[41] The author regarded the land
system of the United States, with its cash sale and uniform price policy, as the
model to be followed. He denounced the sale of more than two million acres to
the Canada Land Company, and criticized Wakefield's proposal for an Imperial
Land and Emigration Commission. To interfere for the benefit of the mother
country was in effect to tax the colony:

Leave the colony to manage its own affairs and it will take from
us all [the emigrants] that it is desirable for itself to receive; to
force upon it that of which we might be glad to get rid is simple
tyranny.

Opinions such as these Mackenzie was happy to reprint, stamped with his
approval.

In the next two issues of the *Gazette*, the rebels' Draft Constitution for Upper
Canada was reprinted. "It contained," Mackenzie observed, "my long cherished opinions, especially the fifth section."[42] This section, printed in italics,
provided for equality before the law and subjected corporations to the same
legal liabilities as individual partnerships. Other sections emphasized by italics

proposed to create an endowment of one million acres of the best public land in the province for *common* schools and to place the Crown and Clergy Reserves, the endowent of King's College and the unsold land of the Canada Company at the disposal of the legislature, forbade the imposition of religious tests, defined legal tender as gold or silver and declared that the River St. Lawrence ought to be a free and common highway to all nations.

But if, during July, *Mackenzie's Gazette* was still discussing Canadian questions, by September the thoughts of its editor had turned to other topics. Discouraged, perhaps, about the prospects of a successful rebellion in Upper Canada, Mackenzie made up his mind to abandon his neutralist attitude in American politics[43] and to become a citizen of the United States.[44] The Short Hills Affair in June had failed. The St. Clair raids had accomplished nothing of importance, and the widespread uprising long planned for July 4 and dependent for success upon arms to be obtained by robbing the Detroit arsenal had been foiled by the vigilance of the American authorities.[45] As James Mackenzie put it, it seemed to be "all over in Canada."[46] Moreover, the leading Lower Canadian rebels, Papineau, Nelson and Côté, were no longer able to work together. Mackenzie had contrived to bring about an interview between Nelson, Papineau and O'Callaghan in the hopes of reconciling them, but without success.[47]

Personal considerations, too, added their depressing weight to the burden of these failures. Before *Mackenzie's Gazette* was two months old its editor was in straitened circumstances and facing the stark truth that on the whole the New York press was hostile to him and his *Gazette* and that its influence was minimal. Free circulation of his paper in Canada was forbidden and anyone caught reading it was subject to a fine of $20.00.[48] The circulation of 4,000, of which his first issue had boasted, had not been a paid circulation. Some subscribers had paid for only four months, some had not paid anything, and some, it soon became obvious, would never pay anything. No wonder that the once ebullient Mackenzie, who had often delighted his friends by singing with impish glee, "I care for nobody, no, not I," now seemed to one of them a "blunted & broken down" man, despairing of the cause he once had led.[49]

Although Mackenzie had decided to become an American citizen, he was still determined to give the Patriot cause all the help he could through his *Gazette*. He would, however, no longer refrain from discussing the political and economic problems of the country to which he was shortly to belong. After all, could a newspaper devoted chiefly to Canadian and British news, yet forbidden to circulate in Canada, flourish on the support of the impoverished Canadians in exile and their American sympathizers? Was not its base too narrow? If his paper were to survive and to do any good for Canada, was it not necessary to broaden its appeal? Considerations such as these may well have influenced him.

In Canada Mackenzie had fought on a wide front for the establishment of social democracy; in the United States he continued to fight for this same ideal.

> Most of the political economists [he wrote] have ingeniously
> organized mankind into machines for the production of the

greatest quantity of riches and seem little concerned with the distribution of it. [50]

In issue after issue of the *Colonial Advocate* he had attacked the Family Compact and the Bank of Upper Canada. Translated into American terms, these same villains became the Whigs and the "monied interest" and Mackenzie continued the battle against them. Just as in Upper Canada he had attacked those churchmen who supported the provincial administration and benefited from the Clergy Reserves, so in the United States he criticized those clergy who preached submission to the established order of things. Mackenzie preached the social gospel and again, as in 1837, he borrowed the language of Orestes Brownson to do it.[51]

In the Boston *Quarterly Review* Brownson had quoted at length from the writings of the Abbé de Lamennais, a liberal Catholic, and had applied the Frenchman's ideas to American society. Mackenzie reprinted the entire article in the *Gazette* of October 6, stating that it well expressed his own ideas. The Abbé believed that the people of Europe were struggling to reconstruct the social order on the basis of equality, and he called upon the clergy to league themselves with the people rather than with the aristocratic governments of Europe. Brownson accused the clergy of the New World of being no better democrats than those of the old. The purpose of Christ's mission, he reminded them, had been to found a new order of society in which there would be peace between men and nations, and every man would sit under his *own* vine and fig tree with none to molest him and none to make him afraid. His own vine and fig tree with none to molest him and none to make him afraid! Here is a description, in scriptural words,[52] of Mackenzie's ideal society and one he had used more than once in the columns of the *Colonial Advocate*. Beneath all the inconsistencies — and shortcomings — of Mackenzie's conduct, this was his guiding ideal, the "true" republic he struggled to create on both sides of the border.

The great questions of the day in American politics concerned the banks. What should be their relation to the national government and to the treasury and what restrictions should be placed on their power to issue paper money?[53] These had been important questions for Mackenzie in Canada,[54] and they were still fundamental questions for him. He could not keep silent on them. Moreover, there was now no need to. The *Democratic Review*, hostile to the Bank of the United States and to the Bank of England which, the *Review* was convinced, controlled it, had already shown him how to relate these issues to the cause of Canada.

Mackenzie made his plunge into the roiled waters of American politics at a moment when even President Martin Van Buren was finding it difficult to steer his course through its cross currents. The coalition which had elected Andrew Jackson, confident that he stood for states' rights and limited government, had been shaken partly by his conduct during the nullification crisis, partly by his anti-bank and hard money policies. Van Buren had succeeded by conciliatory tactics in holding together enough of this coalition to win the election of 1836 but he had not been able to weld it into the united party based on Jeffersonian principles that he had hoped to create. His attempt to solve the financial problems arising from the Panic of 1837 added to the strains among his supporters. Jackson had removed the government's deposits from the Bank of the United States to various state banks (the Pet Banks), and to check speculation and inflation he had issued his Specie Circular, which required gold or silver in payment for public lands. Most of the banks, including the Pets, had suspended specie payment during the Panic of 1837. Temporary arrangements for the care of the government's revenues by the Post Office Department and Treasury agents had then been made. As a permanent solution Van Buren was now advocating the establishment of an Independent Treasury which would accept the paper only of specie paying banks and, by its demands for specie, would have a regulating and restraining effect on their note-issues. This proposal was widely regarded as an attack upon state banking institutions. The alternatives to Van Buren's Independent Treasury were the national bank wanted by the Whigs or continued dangerous reliance on the still inadequately regulated state banks.

In addition to disputes among Democrats on the national and state levels, there were many sharp conflicts among politicians in New York City where Tammany was being opposed by the Equal Rights Party, which had come to be called the Loco-Focos. These radical Jacksonians were anti-monopoly, anti-bank, hard-money men, who supported the proposed Independent Treasury, but would have it accept only specie. They had fought for various democratic reforms, advocated direct election of the president, and short terms for office holders. Their decision to run their own nominees in several New York City contests, including that for mayor, had deprived Tammany of victories it otherwise might have had.[55] With the political and economic program of the Loco-Focos Mackenzie heartily agreed.

In Canada Mackenzie had been the determined enemy of the Bank of Upper Canada, which enjoyed a monopoly of the government's deposits and exercised too much political influence to suit Reformers.[56] He had also opposed granting charters for additional banks unless their note-issuing powers would be adequately safeguarded and restricted. He was now observing the increasing discord among Van Buren's followers with dismay. To O'Rielly he wrote, "This great struggle on the public monies I see is exhausting their energies but it is, I must admit, all important, perhaps more so than that of Canada."[57] It was therefore perfectly consistent for Mackenzie to support Van Buren's financial policies and it was important to him to do his bit to prevent a Whig victory in the forthcoming elections of 1838.

Mackenzie's decision to support the President meant that he had to accept his policy of peace with Great Britain. Up to this point Mackenzie had been doing his best to inflame American public opinion against her in the hope that the outbreak of war would give the Patriots their chance. Now it was necessary for him to do an about-face — and to account for it to his readers. He began by explaining to Bill Johnston, in the *Gazette* of July 21, that Canada could be freed by peaceful means. Continued agitation would hinder immigration, hurt trade, diminish the revenue, increase the expense of holding the Canadas and consequently oblige the British government to set those provinces free. (This was not an unrealistic argument: it was exactly what was worrrying officials in Upper Canada.)[58] If the Americans helped by an economic boycott, added Mackenzie, no war would be necessary. Two weeks later he came out for Van Buren and urged the Friends of Freedom in Upper Canada, as well as those in exile, to "do nothing that may in any way involve the American government or amount to a breach of that neutrality it is desirous to observe." Van Buren, explained Mackenzie, was striving to carry out the principles of Jacksonian democracy and to defend the labourer and farmer against the speculating, cheating monopolists who would reduce them to the level of the tenants and labourers of the Old World. Therefore it was with the Jacksonians that the true friends of Canada should identify themselves. The Whigs might appear to favour the emancipation of Canada more actively than Van Buren, but it was only in order to exploit the resources of the continent more effectively. Canada would gain little from exchanging the Colonial Office for Webster and the Whigs. "One swarm of locusts would leave us, it is true, but another more keen in the bite would alight in their place."[59]

Mackenzie's departure from neutrality in American politics cost him dear. In upstate New York, Whigs who had exerted themselves "to save his carcase from famine and his neck from the halter" denounced it as an act of treachery and ingratitude.[60] Bill Johnston sent him a bitter letter protesting his

> taking up politics at the very moment when we wanted your services the most in the cause of Canada.... [The second Lower Canada rebellion and the attack on Prescott were not two months away.] From the Democrats I have met with nothing but cruelty. For God's sake don't take Van Buren's part. [61]

From agents for the *Gazette* in Jefferson, Monroe, St. Lawrence and Fuller counties cancellations came in. By September some 200 subscribers had been lost, and by the end of October the *Gazette's* circulation had fallen below 3,000.[62]

Not all of Mackenzie's mail consisted of criticisms and cancellations. Ardent Patriots like S.C Frey rejoiced at his stand:

> I am a thorough going Loco-Foco and so are you [Frey wrote]. I always agreed with you while some of our milk and water reformers in Canada used to think you was too hot and too rank.... God knows if Canada never got freedom till she got it by the exertions of such men she would be in Tartarian bondage for ever. [63]

E.B. O'Callaghan believed that if Van Buren's political strength were increased he might adopt a tone towards Great Britain more favourable to the interests of the Patriots. "Such a result would be cheaply purchased even by the ruin of the *Gazette*," were his closing words of comfort to its struggling editor.[64]

James Mackenzie disapproved of his father's policy. He brushed aside the latter's elaborate argument that the triumph of Van Buren was vital to the cause of true liberty on the continent.

> My object is Canada, not the United States [wrote James]. The cause of Canada... is now... dragged down by the expression of your personal opinions to a question of party....

James regarded the choice between Whigs and Democrats as simply a choice of evils. Both had "an Augean stable of aristocratic tendencies which will require a new party to change." It was futile and dangerous for Mackenzie to embroil himself in disputes over a paper currency and chartered monopolies. The trend of the times was against him. Banks had become too deeply rooted, so much part of the business of the country. Moreover, James added:

> The hate which monied men now feel for the cause of liberty — Canadian liberty — before a shadowy prejudice — now assumes a tangible shape — your opposition to their interests.[65]

James reminded his father that even in Canada his friends had "looked aghast at the monstrous absurdity" of his attacking the bank interests and had been jealous of his success. Some of them had been as eager as the Tories for liberal charters for banks of issue and they had let Mackenzie know that they disapproved of his officious interference in this matter at the Colonial Office in 1832.[66]
Mackenzie vigorously defended his right to speak his mind on American politics, even though he was not yet a citizen:

> We ought to feel that the struggle now going on in this republic between the sons of commerce, organized monopoly and foreign aristocracy on the one hand and the American government and the plain and honest farmers... on the other is the battle for freedom for the American continent as much for Canada as for the 26 states.... I have therefore... begun here as I left off at Toronto... I will not prove traitor on this side of the St. Lawrence to the democratic principles we fondly cherished on the other side. [67]

Canadian Patriots, however, were less interested in these long run calculations than in the immediate struggle with Great Britain. Mackenzie tried to convince them that British investors in American bank stock and western lands had laid the United States under tribute. "There are other ways besides fighting to reduce a government under foreign sway," he observed, in words that for Canadians have a very modern sound. It was this foreign control of the American economy, and consequently of the country's political and social character, that he believed Van Buren intended to break by his banking legislation. Therefore, by supporting Van Buren, Canadian Patriots would be helping to weaken their own enemy, Great Britain.[68] "If your country will seriously adopt the hard-money system," he informed Senator James Richardson, "all border warfare is useless. That would give liberty to Canada."[69] This cryptic summing up of Mackenzie's line of reasoning must have been a puzzle to the Chairman of the Senate's Committee on Foreign Relations.

Mackenzie clung to the hope that a strengthened Van Buren administration would use economic sanctions against Great Britain and thus induce her to loose her hold on the Canadas. He could plainly see, however, that the United States would not involve itself in war over Canada before Canadians had demonstrated a determination to achieve their independence. In the meantime he disapproved of further military operations on the frontier. "If there cannot be a formidable force raised," he warned, "it would be cruelty to entice the farmers to join."[70] In this realistic appraisal of American sentiment and in this cautious advice from their once impetuous leader, there was little comfort for Patriots. Meanwhile his *Gazette* was filled with discussions of the Loco-Foco program and the danger of a monied aristocracy triumphing in America and preventing her from becoming a "true" republic.[71]

In the New York State elections of 1838 Mackenzie supported Marcy for governor "as the best means of strengthening Van Buren."[72] He was ready to believe that experience had opened Marcy's eyes to the defects of the banking system and to the weakness of the New York Safety Fund. The Loco-Focos, however, did not find Marcy an acceptable candidate because he had not broken with the conservatives in the party who were opposed to Van Buren's proposed Independent Treasury. Discussion of the results of the election of 1838 in the *Gazette* was limited to a brief announcement of the failure of the Democrats to carry New York City.[73] The exciting news from Canada left no room for more extended comments.

# Chapter III

# THE BATTLE OF THE WINDMILL

A general assault on the Canadian frontier had been planned for November 1838 by the Hunters organization, a secret society of Patriots and their American sympathizers similar to fraternal organizations to which members are admitted by degrees and on oath. It had its origin in Vermont during the summer of 1838,[1] spread rapidly throughout the frontier communities of New York, westward to Michigan, to Ohio and to Kentucky. The members were pledged to work for the Patriot cause and to contribute to the funds of the organization. Mackenzie's son James became a member; he published the Hunters' newspaper, *The Freeman's Advocate*, at Lockport.[2] Hunters' Lodges also existed in Upper and Lower Canada.

On November 3, 1838, Robert Nelson aroused the Lower Canada Patriotes to a second rebellion which was not terminated until November 10. On November 11 the western Patriots, who had failed to synchronize their movement with Nelson's, launched an attack upon Prescott and on December 4 on Windsor. Van Buren, the Loco-Focos, and the Independent Treasury were now relegated to second place in *Mackenzie's Gazette* and space given first to hopeful accounts of these struggles at their commencement, later to grim accounts of their failure in both provinces, to lists of those imprisoned, killed, or wounded, and to bitter denunciations of Sir John Colborne.

Mackenzie took no part in organizing these Patriot adventures,[3] although he knew they were imminent,[4] but since they greatly affected his attitude towards Van Buren and his own future political course in the United States some account of them cannot be omitted.

At a convention held in Cleveland in September, the western Hunters chose civil and military officers for the Republic of Upper Canada that they expected to establish. American military men regarded these people as "of little consequence."[5] The convention also authorized a republican bank for Upper Canada. When $70,000, less than one per cent of the authorized capital, had been paid in, the bank was to issue notes secured on the revenues of the new republic and its public domain. The officers of the bank were three Oswego men.[6] Meanwhile $10,000 was to be borrowed for the Patriot cause on the strength of the bank, and those who had been made its directors were said to be busy raising this fund. The Montreal *Transcript* reported a rumour that a loan fund to help the cause of revolution in Canada had been opened in New York.[7] "If we succeed," predicted S.C. Frey, "we will make short work of the U.C. Land Co., rectories and Clergy Reserves."[8]

Donald M'Leod was not so sanguine as Frey. He states that out of the $10,000 the Cleveland committee planned to raise in a fortnight, they actually obtained $300. This amount was probably the cash received, not the amount subscribed. M'Leod characterized the organization at Cleveland as a group of American speculators, men of poor fortune, whose integrity was open to question, who had got the management into their own hands, left the minor posts to the Canadian Patriots, talked big and were likely to accomplish nothing.[9]

Four days before the attempt on Prescott, James Reid wrote from Rochester that the time was "almost up," and that 500 Polish refugees with more or less military experience were then on their way from Schenectady to Salinas and would soon be "at their work."[10] Much of this information about the activities of the Patriots, the part being played by Charles Duncombe at Detroit, the movement of military supplies across the frontier into certain townships, even the name of Von Schoultz, upon whom the command devolved in the Battle of the Windmill, did in fact reach Sir George Arthur. He was made anxious by his realization that "the ardor and loyalty of the people had certainly abated" and that the militia was not to be relied on.[11] Arthur sent the information his spies had gathered to Washington and to Governor Mason of Michigan. The latter would not take it seriously, and, although Van Buren appeared to, the Commander of the United States' northern forces, General McComb, thought it politically inexpedient to exert himself until after the elections.

Lucious V. Bierce, the Commander of the Western Patriot Army, planned to invade Upper Canada at Malden. He had been in correspondence with Niels Von Schoultz, a Polish army officer who had recently emigrated to the United States and who offered his services to the Patriot cause.[12] Von Schoultz gave the impression that he had "300 veteran Poles under his command" but he is reported to have succeeded in obtaining only a few Polish emigrants when he opened a recruiting office in New York City.[13] Von Schoultz proposed a detailed plan for Bierce's Canadian campaign, as part of which he would precede him into Canada from Detroit. Whether Bierce accepted this plan is not known, but he did order Von Schoultz to the Detroit frontier.[14] In New York State John Ward Birge was in command of another Patriot force at Buffalo, and these men were directed by Bierce to be ready to cross to Fort Erie as soon as they should learn that he had taken Malden.[15] Bierce had been led to expect thousands of men, and when he found only hundreds awaiting him at the rendezvous he tried to persuade the men to abandon the hopeless project of invading Canada. Stung by the charge of cowardice, in the end he led them across to attack Windsor — and to defeat.[16]

When Bierce did not move promptly, Birge, without the knowledge or consent of his superior, took the initiative, countermanded Bierce's orders to Von Schoultz according to one account,[17] and directed him and his men to Oswego, from which point Patriots were to leave to attack Fort Wellington at Prescott. Birge had reconnoitred this invasion point in advance and perhaps chose it because it was not strongly defended.[18]

The story of the Patriots' attempt to land at Prescott and their subsequent defeat at the Battle of the Windmill are well-known events of the Patriot war, but the political aspects of the story are not so well known. The background of the affair is still shrouded in mystery and the conduct of the leading actors confusingly and contradictorily reported in the sources.

The Patriot expedition started from Oswego on November 11, 1838, on board the S.S. *United States* bound for Ogdensburgh. Three of the vessel's owners travelled with her: Theophilus S. Morgan, Lucius B. Crocker of Oswego and Hiram Denio, a judge of the Fifth Circuit Court of New York. Her passengers included Niels Von Schoultz, Martin Woodruff, Bill Johnston, E. Wingate Davis and Christopher Buckley. In October Davis had visited various places in Upper Canada to learn the state of Canadian feeling and had been told by members of Hunters' Lodges on that side of the border that Canada was ripe for rebellion.[19] Von Schoultz, Wingate, Buckley and Davis had left Salina early in November, the two latter accompanied by 125 men they had recruited from the "salt boilers" at Salina and from neighbouring communities. Feeling against the British was especially strong in Salina, where it had been learned that four American prisoners taken at Short Hills had been sentenced to be hanged. (These sentences were later commuted to transportation.)

The Salina party found that the *United States* was not ready to leave port on the 8th as expected. By November 10 two schooners, the *Charlotte of Oswego* and the *Charlotte of Toronto*, had arrived to take on freight and had departed. Subsequently these vessels were found to have on board men and supplies for the Patriot expedition.

The *United States* left on the 11th. At several points en route (Sackett's Harbor, Cape Vincent, French Creek) she picked up young men waiting for the tardy steamer, their numbers now depleted by departures. At Millan's Bay the steamer found the two schooners waiting. Captain James Van Cleve complied with the request of one of his passengers to tow them down the river to Ogdensburgh. After the schooners had been lashed to the steamer, some of their Patriot passengers clambered aboard her. The unhappy Van Cleve then proposed to the owners that he run the ship aground in Alexandria Bay, but they would not consent. It was then decided that the *United States* should put in at Morristown, 10 miles above Ogdensburgh. She remained there three hours, during which time her owners sent an express to alert the U.S. Marshal at Ogdensburgh that a Patriot expedition was en route to that port.

Before the *United States* entered the harbour of Morristown some of the Patriots and their officers returned to the schooners. Bill Johnston took command of the *Charlotte of Oswego*, Von Schoultz of the *Charlotte of Toronto*. The two schooners, now separated from the steamer and lashed together, dropped down with the current to Prescott. They arrived there before dawn on the 12th, but the vital surprise landing was bungled in some manner. Contemporaries have explained it in three different ways. The result was that the unwieldy vessels, still lashed together, were swept by the current over to the American side. The larger of the two, the *Charlotte of Oswego*, grounded on the bar at the mouth of

49

Oswegatchie Creek; the *Charlotte of Toronto* was then cut loose and continued on to the harbour of Ogdensburgh.[20]

According to Captain Van Cleve's account,[21] John W. Birge, who had been in Ogdensburgh for some days, now took command of the expedition. It was decided that as the surprise landing at Prescott had failed Von Schoultz should take the *Charlotte of Toronto* down to Windmill Point, a short distance below Prescott, and make a landing there. It was expected that Canadian Patriots would come to join him.

When the *United States* docked at Ogdensburgh, Bill Johnston and members of the Hunters' Lodge in that locality seized her and took her down to Windmill Point with men and supplies. On the return trip Johnston attempted to get the *Charlotte of Oswego* off the bar, without success. The *Charlotte of Toronto* then came up to take the men off but could not reach her. In this attempt the smaller schooner was sheltered by the steamer from the fire of a small British vessel, the *Experiment*. The *United States* then went down again to the Windmill, with Captain O.B. Pierce now in command. On the way back the steamer was fired upon by the *Experiment*, which was unable to do her much damage, but the pilot had part of his head blown off. Pierce then called on Captain Malcolm, who had been forced on board, to pilot her back, and he deliberately ran her aground in Oswegatchie Creek. Some of the vessel's machinery was then removed and she was made useless to the Patriots.[22]

Hiram Denio went on board at this point and found "General" Birge lying on a settee in the cabin. He had gone out on the steamer but soon became so ill he could not keep the deck. "It is known on all hands that his illness is a subterfuge," wrote Denio, but others acknowledge that it was the horrible fate of the helmsman that had unnerved him.[23]

The Patriots at the Windmill elected Von Schoultz as their commander. It is doubtful whether the Polish veterans he was supposed to bring with him ever arrived, at least in the expected numbers. Martin Woodruff admitted there were "only 5 - 160 men altogether."[24] Only three Polish names besides that of Von Schoultz are on the list of prisoners taken at the Windmill.[25] One of the Poles escaped. How many of them remained safe with Birge in Ogdensburgh and how many were among the dead cannot be stated.

The British at Kingston, who had been informed by a spy at Sackett's Harbor that a Patriot expedition was under way, alerted Colonel Worth. He left that port with two companies of United States troops on board the *Telegraph*.[26] Worth arrived at Ogdensburgh on the night of the 12th. He seized the *United States* and the schooners, thus effectively isolating the Patriots at the Windmill from reinforcements from Ogdensburgh and rendering their position hopeless. They defended themselves valiantly against the British regulars and the Canadian militia sent against them, but after armed British vessels came from Prescott with heavier guns to batter the stone Windmill, in which they were holding out, the end came for the Patriots.

The account of the relations between Bierce, Birge and Von Schoultz in M'Leod's *Brief Review of the Settlement of Upper Canada and... the Commotion of 1837*, a book published in 1841 by one who had been closely in touch with the

Hunters' organization in the west, is supported by statements later made by Bierce in his *Reminiscences*. M'Leod states that Birge "announced himself" as the commander of the eastern division of the Patriot forces and prevailed upon Von Schoultz to join him. Bierce, he claims, had for weeks been waiting for Von Schoultz, went to Buffalo, could hear nothing of him, returned "very disappointed" and knew nothing of the Prescott expedition until he heard of its failure.[27]

Birge sent Mackenzie a different account of the Prescott expedition which only adds to the mystery surrounding its origin. Birge states that he had been in Ogdensburgh for four days prior to the arrival of the expedition. Here he had met "many" from the Canadian side who had told him that if Prescott were to be taken by surprise "they would rally to our side"; otherwise they would be obliged to defend the town at the call of Colonel Young. That surprise, he emphasized, had not been achieved because the expedition had been spotted as it passed Brockville (by Lieutenant Fowler in the *Experiment*) and because the bungled landing at Prescott had alerted the sentry. Birge wrote:

> I rest myself on this single point: that unless Prescott could be taken by surprise no one would be justified in landing unless in secret. Here was sealed the fate of the expedition. No courage from any source could have averted its fate. [28]

Birge stated that he was "willing to lay aside many important considerations that destroyed us." He claims that both Bill Johnston and Von Schultz were not aware of the causes of the expedition but does not state what they were. Such details as he did give Mackenzie about the progress of the expedition once it was under way, and about his own much criticized conduct in failing to join the Patriots at the Windmill, although the expedition's commander, are not supported by other sources. Birge promised to send Mackenzie a pamphlet history of the affair which his friends were to publish "next week."[29] Two years later he was still promising it. So far it has not been found, but there is a brief letter in the Albany *Argus* of December 24, 1838, in which Birge blamed Von Schoultz for disobeying his orders and asserted that he himself had not set the expedition on foot. Again he did not explain who had. In November 1840 the United States District Attorney informed Birge that he was not ready to try his case and that he need not appear in court to renew his bail. Evidently the case was dropped. Birge was tried, however, at a convention of the Hunters' organization which met in Auburn in January 1839. The charge was deserting his men after getting them into difficulties. Whether he was present or tried *in absentia* is not known. James Mackenzie claims that his father was one of the "triers." Birge was acquitted on the grounds that Von Schoultz had disobeyed his orders.[30]

Prisoners taken at the Windmill named prominent men in Oswego, Watertown, Ogdensburgh, Auburn, Salina and Sackett's Harbor as having had a hand in organizing the affair. They claimed they had been deluded by these persons into believing that the Canadians were "oppressed" and would welcome their help in "freeing Canada, but they found that none came to assist them. Many of the men named did attempt to have the Patriots at the Windmill rescued before it was too late and begged Colonel Worth to allow them to surrender to him. Worth had an interview with the British commander, Colonel Plomner Young, who responded that he had no authority to allow them to withdraw but expressed the hope that they might escape.

> We parted perfectly understanding each other... every avenue was left unguarded... but through cowardice and treachery but a feeble effort was made....[31] I have not a doubt [Worth added] there are those who desired a scene of slaughter in order to exhibit a striking case of martyrdom by which to appeal to, and arouse the sympathies of the people.[32]

Subsequently citizens of Ogdensburgh and its vicinity tried to induce the court-martial at Kingston and Sir George Arthur to show clemency to the prisoners.[33] The youths among them were released after a short imprisonment, but the older men were transported to Van Diemen's Land and their leaders paid with their lives.[34]

The Prescott expedition had important political repercussions in the United States. Whig and Democratic newspapers hurled charges and counter-charges back and forth respecting the responsibility of the two parties for the unhappy affair. The following letter from Thomas V. Russell to a relative in Canton, New York, illustrates the belief of some Democrats:

> Facts in relation to the invasion are beginning to develop which are utterly astounding to all of us, from which it appears that many very prominent men in these frontier counties have been actively engaged in the matter for several months past becoming members of the secret societies of the patriots.... These men it is supposed did not intend that they [sic] expedition should proceed farther than Ogdensburgh, expecting that it would there be arrested by our authorities, and the odium of its failure cast upon the government. In this they were... disappointed — they had raised a mightier devil than they had power to lay. The invaders went whither they were sent, and it is to be hoped that the sacrifice of so many brave men will work a salutory reformation in the popular party on this subject....[35]

Support seems to be given to the foregoing charge against the Whigs by the attempt made at Morristown to alert the U.S. Marshal at Ogdensburgh that a Patriot expedition was en route to that port. As it happened he had already left for Sackett's Harbor. Morgan and Crocker and Van Cleve all averred that they had been taken by surprise, but the latter was not believed and lost his post.[36] As for Denio, Davis's account refers obliquely to a U.S. judge who had a hand in the affair. The misuse of Patriot meetings for political purposes was made known to Mackenzie two months before Prescott,[37] but there is not enough evidence to enable one to decide the truth of this charge against the Whigs.[38] All one can do is to say, with Thomas Russell, that Patriotism had become a new method of political warfare.

During the Navy Island campaign, the Whigs had accused Van Buren, and particularly Marcy, of being too tender towards the Patriots. Subsequently it was their ploy to blame the administration for being too vigorous in enforcing the neutrality laws. The Patriot cause had proved to be popular all along the northern frontier and therefore both political parties tried to profit by posing as sincere friends of the refugees. The Democrats, who happened to be the party in power, and therefore obliged to prosecute those who violated the country's neutrality laws, were hampered in this contest. In every northern state except Ohio the Whigs triumphed in the election of 1838. The Patriot cause was, however, only one reason for the defeat of the administration and less important than Van Buren's economic policies.

In upstate New York, particularly in Oswego County, the Patriot cause also contributed to divisions within the Democratic Party. The Prescott fiasco was blamed not so much on the Whigs for mounting an offensive which they had no intention of carrying on seriously, but on Van Buren's neutrality policy. The Patriots, it was argued, were really defeated by the authorities of the United States in the persons of Marshal Garrow and Colonel Worth, who seized their vessels. Administration men who supported Van Buren's policy of neutrality accused those Democrats who had been Patriot sympathizers of deceiving young men into entering a service which never had any prospect of success. They demanded that all such Democrats who were state or federal officials should be dismissed. But severity towards Patriot sympathizers had its dangers. Van Buren was informed through Judge Turrill of Oswego that Benton was arresting many of them and that his activities were likely to have unfortunate political results.[39] "The year 1839 — and for nearly a decade — the political life reflected in Oswego County the effects of the prejudices and predilections of the patriot war."[40]

After printing completely inaccurate accounts of rebel movements and "victories," Mackenzie had been obliged to admit that the Lower Canada rebels had been defeated, their leaders had retired to the United States, and Patriots were in misery and want. His Extra of November 14 began an account of the Battle of the Windmill and his regular issue of November 25 acknowledged the failure of the Patriot movements in both provinces.

Mackenzie and others then began to hold sympathy meetings for the relief of the Patriots, particularly those in Lower Canada. The first of these meetings was held in New York City on November 14. Alex Ming Jr., a radical Jacksonian who was an official of the New York Customs House, presided. One of the speakers was E.A. Theller, who subsequently published *Canada in 1837-8... with the personal adventures of the author*. After being captured at Malden, Theller had been imprisoned in the citadel at Quebec, from which he escaped. Before leaving with Mackenzie on a speaking tour, he supplied the *Gazette* with an account of his experiences.[41] On November 17 Mackenzie and Theller addressed a well-attended meeting in Philadelphia, where the *Ledger* was actively supporting the

53

Patriot cause.[42] On November 19 they reached Washington. Here Mackenzie tried to induce George Washington Custis to take the chair at their meeting. Although Custis expressed sympathy, he refused. So also did the mayor of the city. Mackenzie now found that the Van Buren administration was trying to obstruct the meeting. Several of the newspapers would not advertise it. With difficulty he got handbills printed instead. The Secretary of State warned the clerks in his department not to attend. Nevertheless, Mackenzie and Theller claimed that about 1500 people turned up and gave them an excellent hearing, but the New York *Sun* contemptuously described the gathering as "two hundred miserable loafers."[43]

After a meeting held in Baltimore on November 22, Theller and Mackenzie separated, the former going home to Detroit, Mackenzie to Albany. Here he failed to draw a crowd and lost money on the hall. His "organ of self-esteem," reported O'Callaghan to Louis Perrault in a letter commenting on "Mac's touchy disposition," was wounded by this failure,[44] and his growing bitterness towards Van Buren, to whose influence he attributed his cool reception, was increased.

On November 21, the day after Mackenzie's Washington meeting, President Van Buren issued a proclamation calling upon citizens of the United States to give no aid to those of their fellow countrymen who had assisted the Canadian Patriots and who, by disregarding the obligations of neutrality, had thereby forfeited all claim to the protection of the republic. His message to Congress of December 4, 1838, declared that those acts of American citizens that had troubled the peace of the Canadian frontier were as much deserving of punishment as breaches of the peace within the United States itself.[45]

What angered Canadian Patriots and their American supporters was that in the proclamation and the message Van Buren had not confined himself to reaffirming neutrality but had gone on to comment on the merits of the struggle and to proclaim the weakness of the insurgents. The Patriots' projects were said to be "impracticable of execution" and their activities were branded as "criminal enterprises." In the opinion of Patriots, the government had not been neutral itself. By seizing their vessels it had assisted, if not ensured, the victory of the British in the Battle of the Windmill. The *Gazette* laboured this theme at length.

What angered Mackenzie was that Van Buren knew in October, from reports of customs officials, that a Patriot expedition was being prepared. Supplies of arms were permitted to be assembled and kept, cannon were openly moved over the roads of New York State, some government officials had assisted in the preparations, but the President had not interfered. His proclamation, which might have served as a warning to his countrymen, was not issued until after the Prescott expedition had failed — and after the Congressional elections.

> He allowed them to rush upon destruction with the predetermination to disown them if they failed [wrote Mackenzie]. "When they stood in need of his protection it was denied them." "Verily he will have his rewards. Our eyes are opened.

We mistook a dexterous politician for an upright American statesman.... Never will we fall into that error again.[46]

The British Minister at Washington, H.S. Fox, was equally critical of Van Buren's conduct and for the same reason.[47]

What angered Americans other than friends of the Patriot cause was Van Buren's statement that American citizens who had been taken at Prescott (and were in danger of execution) had forfeited their claim to the protection of the republic. This was inviting the British authorities to proceed to extremes. A.C. Flagg, State Comptroller of New York, had tried to warn Van Buren:

> It is extremely important that nothing should be said in the message which could be tortured into censure of the cause for which the Canadians have been contending, and which they, and thousands of our own people, consider identical with the cause of liberty for which our fathers contended. An expression which could be construed as harsh towards the Canadian cause might encourage the British to harshness. Also, an expression of indifference to the cause of freedom would rivet itself on the minds and prejudices of thousands on our frontier.

Van Buren replied that the "least temporizing" would lead to greater evils and that there was nothing he could do but rigidly perform his duty, however painful.[48] Judge Joel Turrill of Oswego informed Van Buren of the damage the proclamation had done to the party. The people were much excited. What they objected to was those parts of the proclamation that related to American citizens. "Were an election to take place now this would injure us very materially in this section of the state."[49]

Van Buren's proclamation drew criticism also from Sir George Arthur because it contained the words, "disturbances having broken out both in Upper and Lower Canada...." This was not true of Upper Canada prior to the attack on Prescott, nor subsequently, as Upper Canada did not support the invaders. Arthur, however, admitted to Colborne that a widespread organization of Patriot Lodges had been created in the province and "had matters taken a different turn in Lower Canada we should have been in a blaze long before this." The British Minister obtained from the Secretary at War a promise that the offensive words would be corrected and in the President's message, issued a few days later, a phrase condemning the efforts of American citizens "to disturb the peace where order prevails" was substituted for them.[50]

After the failure of the Patriot movements, Mackenzie had to reconsider his position. The election was over, he had backed the wrong horse, the Whigs had carried New York, Van Buren had openly denounced Patriot activity, and Mackenzie had become his bitter opponent. And yet the avowed principles and program of the Democratic Party were what he approved. What was he to do? Moreover, sympathy for Canadian rebels was declining. Not $250 had been collected from New York and Philadelphia for the relief of the refugees, and $100 of that had come from a single donor, Frances Wright D'Arusmont.[51] The execution or transportation of Americans taken at Prescott and the refusal of their government *publicly* to intercede for them had sharply checked American interest in frontier adventures. Moreover, the failure of the Canadians to support Von Schoultz had led Americans to question whether the Canadians really wanted independence and to charge them with being too cowardly to fight for it.

Why had the widespread organization which the Hunters were thought to have created throughout Canada failed to bring forth the expected results? Between December 27 and January 10 Mackenzie visited the frontier to find out for himself what had happened and what was now the state of public sentiment.[52] In this interval he also attended the convention of delegates from Hunters' Lodges at Auburn, New York, previously referred to. He reported to his readers that, far from being cowardly, the people were ready to rise whenever there was a reasonable chance of success, but that without arms they could neither rise against a government backed by regular troops nor give effective aid to movements initiated from the United States. The failure had been due to dissension among the leaders, lack of the element of surprise, the presence of spies in the Hunters' Lodges, and the interference of the authorities of the United States at Ogdensburgh and Detroit. In fact, neither of the recent ventures had had a chance from the start against the fully prepared and forewarned Sir George Arthur. Mackenzie, if he was realist enough to see this fact, naturally did not put the matter in these terms to his readers. He covered up the failures as best he could but acknowledged that he "had grown weary of prophesying good and chronicling bad news from Canada."[53]

Mackenzie was far from content with the manner in which American Hunters were dominating Canadian Patriot activities and exploiting sympathy for the Canadian cause. He knew that the directors of the proposed Republican Bank of Upper Canada had intended to lose no time in disposing of valuable lands in the province. Like Frey, M'Leod and Theller, he came to the conclusion that the Patriot expeditions had been promoted by Americans motivated not by a desire to establish a "true republic" in Upper Canada but by a spirit of speculation.[54] The historian of St. Lawrence and Franklin Counties, New York, Franklin B. Hough, shared this judgement.[55]

Mackenzie abhorred land speculators. When the Auburn Convention created an executive committee of five, to which he was not named,[56] he decided that the entire Patriot organization would have to be rebuilt and remodelled on entirely different lines if it were to accomplish the kind of revolution in Upper Canada for which he stood. The delegates agreed that a separate Canadian Association should be organized under his leadership.[57]

Mackenzie decided that he could guide the work of a separate Canadian Association more effectively from Rochester than from New York. Later he was to claim that when he left New York City his paper had a large circulation and was paying well, and that it cost him $500 to remove to Rochester to be near his revolutionary friends.[58] There can be little doubt, however, that one of Mackenzie's reasons for leaving New York was the unsatisfactory condition of his *Gazette*. He needed at least 3,000 punctually paying subscribers to maintain his paper and he did not have them. Mackenzie's influence in New York, as perhaps he now realized, had from the outset been negligible. He had lost influence on the frontier too. It had become essential for him to re-establish his paper elsewhere and to rebuild his influence in upstate areas.

The last number of *Mackenzie's Gazette* published from New York was dated January 26, 1839. The family had planned to leave the city on the 17th and had everything, including the types, packed for the journey when, on the 16th, Mrs. Mackenzie gave birth to her 11th child, a son.[59] In consequence the journey was postponed.

The first number of the *Gazette* issued from Rochester did not appear until February 23. The first step towards organizing the Canadian refugees was taken when a confidential circular, dated March 12 and signed by Mackenzie and John Montgomery, was sent to persons favourable to Canadian independence inviting them to meet at Mackenzie's home on March 21. Those who responded then drew up a constitution for the new Canadian Association, elected Montgomery president, Mackenzie secretary, and Samuel Moulson treasurer. Membership was limited to those who had left Canada within the last two years, or were refugees or emigrants for political reasons, or were British born and favourable to the cause of Canadian independence.[60] The avowed purpose of the Association was to obtain relief and employment for Canadian refugees, to work for Canadian independence, but to discountenance "hasty and ill-planned expeditions" whether organized on American soil or elsewhere, and all attempts to take revenge against the persons or property of political enemies.

> I know thousands of you wish for a successful revolt because it would greatly enhance the price of land [Mackenzie wrote]. With such men I have no feeling in common.... It would be a poor recommendation to the laboring people that a successful revolt would raise the price of land on them and their children, and drive them back further into the wilderness. [61]

To James he confessed:

> Had we gained the day in Canada... only to get a monopoly fastened on us in the shape of a parliament upheld by speculators and adopting popular forms the better to deceive, I would have felt worse than I do, and surely I feel bad enough. [62]

Mackenzie did not intend his new society to waste its strength on abortive frontier raids. His object was to keep the Patriot organization alive until a favourable moment arrived. Should war come, or a rising take place in Canada, Patriot sympathizers could then seize the moment to establish an independent Canada. In preparation for these possibilities, the Canadian Association sent out another circular inquiring what support in men and materials could be expected from the recipients' locality and what supplies of arms Patriots might have concealed there.[63]

Mackenzie was not the first to establish an organization for the relief of Canadian refugees. A similar association had been formed earlier at Lockport, in March 1838. Dr. A.K. Mackenzie had been chosen as its president.[64] Mackenzie was put on the Executive Committee although he was then in New York getting his *Gazette* under way. He was informed about what had been done by A.K. Mackenzie,[65] who did not tell W.L. Mackenzie that on the very day this organization was formed he had written to Sir George Arthur

> to express his desire that the Lieutenant Governor would meet with a delegation of the refugees, or at least to enter into a correspondence with them in the hope of reaching a reconciliation with them. [66]

There is some evidence that Mackenzie's Canadian Association attracted those among the refugees who, while willing to accept American aid to free Canada, did not want to see her swallowed up in the process by the United States. By circularizing the Hunters' Lodges, Mackenzie made an effort to draw Canadians out of those organizations into his and to discredit the Cleveland committee of Hunters by charges of peculation and mismanagement. Reports of the strength of the Hunters were denounced as "Mother Goose fables" in his *Gazette*.[67] Canadian exiles in Youngstown and Lockport met, and sent delegates to the Association at Rochester.[68] The new Association, however, never acquired strength in men, money or arms and it naturally aroused hostility. Such replies to its circular as are extant show little enthusiasm for it. Among Canadians in exile hope was "next to gone".[69]

The initial convention, the circular and one or two meetings in Rochester and nearby communities were not followed up by more definite plans. By May 13 James Mackenzie was inquiring of his father whether the Association had been abandoned,[70] and by June 19 his father was in jail.

Meanwhile "General" Lucius V. Bierce had resigned his command of the Western Patriot Army and Henry S. Handy had replaced him. The Hunters' organization had by this time given up hope of winning a victory on Canadian soil. The line of policy still open to them was to create a standby organization that would be ready in the event of war. During 1839 Sir George Arthur began to receive alarming reports of the success of Handy's subordinate, "Major-General" Donald M'Leod, was having in organizing a network of supporters in Canada.[71] James Mackenzie states that Handy's organization was distinct from the Hunters and that for a time he belonged to both of them. In later years he dismissed Handy's and M'Leod's reports of their widespread success as "paper marvels."[72] However numerous its Canadian supporters may have been, Handy's organization did not succeed in supplying them with arms. There were rumours that an invasion of Upper Canada was being planned for July 1839, later for October, but all the talk came to nothing.

By May 1839 Mackenzie was admitting that there was nothing his Canadian Association could do at the moment. One of his warm admirers in Washington was Thomas Fitnam, a Democratic Irish ward-heeler from Philadelphia who had been appointed to a minor post in the State Department. Throughout his correspondence with Mackenzie, Fitnam pretended to more influence and knowledge than he had and he fed Mackenzie expectations of war which the latter believed for a time. Certainly the tense situation on the Maine-New Brunswick boundary and the passage of an act giving the President of the United States power to raise a force of 50,000 volunteers and appropriating the funds to equip them justifies these expectations.[73] But Caleb Cushing was of the opinion that Van Buren would take no decisive action and that the summer would pass in negotiations.[74] In the end Mackenzie put more faith in the judgement of this important member of the Committee on Foreign Affairs than in the opinions of the ever-hopeful Irishman. Consequently, when indignant friends wrote him about the sale at auction of seized Patriot arms for a song, he advised them publicly through the *Gazette* to recognize the hard realities of their situation. There would not be war. All the help that Canadians could expect from the United States was "an asylum for exiles."[75] A handful of penniless exiles could not bring about a successful rebellion by themselves. Mackenzie's best advice to the exiles was to make their peace with the British authorities in Canada if they could, try to get permission to return to Canada to sell their property, and then emigrate west. He added, however, "Truth compels me to acknowledge my fears that they will not find all the advantages they anticipate in a removal hither."[76]

Nevertheless Mackenzie urged the Canadian Association not to dissolve. There were a thousand ways, he told them, in which the members could assist the Patriot cause, but he specified only one: by contributing to the cost of publishing the documentary account of the rebellion which the Association had authorized, "for I confess that to that publication I attach a great deal of importance." It is easy to be cynical about this advice and to regard it as a selfish request backed by vanity and a desire to publish a *pièce justificative*, but it should be remembered that Mackenzie was a printer with confidence in the power of the press. He was always more interested in a wide circulation of his publications than in profit from them and he distributed them in large numbers freely. He had seen the influence of the Seventh Report on Grievances and was noting the influence of the Durham Report. Would not a post-rebellion report that contained, in addition to the old grievances, an account of the peaceful steps taken to secure redress, the events of the rebellion, the treatment of prisoners, the conduct of the government of Upper Canada, and the similarity of the fundamental issues involved to current political troubles in Great Britain and on the Continent have its influence too? Unhappily for historians, the "great report" of the Canadian Association which the *Gazette* of June 8 referred to as "about to be submitted" never appeared.

Mackenzie's attempt to raise funds to publish 5,000 copies of this report enabled his critics to charge him with using money collected for distressed Canadians for his own benefit, an accusation he repeatedly and indignantly denied.[77] By June 1839 the funds of the Association amounted to only $126.00, the greater part of which was subsequently spent on the expenses of Mackenzie's trial and the printing of an account of it.[78]

Mackenzie had hoped that the move to Rochester would put new life into his *Gazette* but it did not flourish any better than the new Canadian Association. "It is difficult to make people understand how they are to help the cause of Canada by taking... the *Gazette*," wrote S.C. Frey.[79] It was more difficult still to get them to view the cause of Canada in the enlarged light that Mackenzie did, as part of the great struggle for human liberty throughout the world. From February 23, 1839, when the *Gazette* was first published in Rochester, to June 11, when its editor went on trial, many columns were devoted to the Chartist agitation in England. Mackenzie believed Canada had much to hope for from the expected triumph of the Chartists. "Regenerated England will never give a dollar to keep in subjection, at the point of a bayonet, a colony which wishes to be free," declared the *Gazette*,[80] anticipating the course of imperial history by roughly a century.

Mackenzie did not neglect American politics in his *Gazette*, despite the advice he received from one of his well-wishers to be a looker-on in Venice and to attend less to politics and more to the needs of his large family.[81] On Washington's Birthday a young lawyer of Buffalo, James R. Doolittle, made an address in which he enquired:

> What have we to gain by shaking off the oppression of the
> privileged classes of Great Britain if we are to grant the same
> power in ten fold magnitude to a thousand incorporated ty-
> rants which... never die.

Here was the great enemy — the privileged corporations with their special charters. Mackenzie had fought them in Canada, was then fighting them in the United States, and was prepared to fight them in the future. He predicted that:

> It is after Canada becomes politically independent that the
> fearful struggle will commence between the antagonistic prin-
> ciples of monied aristocracy and bible democracy. [82]

It was all no use. From neither Canadian exiles, American Hunters, friendly Whigs, Chartist sympathizers, ardent Loco-Focos or Irish Americans, whose accounts of Ireland's sufferings were given great play, did enough paid subscriptions come in. By May 11 he was down to an edition of 1,300.

On June 1 Mackenzie made another effort to expand his subscription list by reducing the price of his paper and by a candid statement of his editorial policies. He would follow no party line further than he thought the party supported political reform, and the object of his paper would be to keep alive the spirit of liberty and to show up the evils of colonial and monarchical misrule. His advice to the refugees had been and would continue to be to wait until the people of Canada themselves would act. On this basis he pled earnestly, almost desperately, for support.[83] Before the end of June he was editing his paper from jail.

# Chapter IV

# THE MONTHS OF IMPRISONMENT

Mackenzie's trial for breach of the Neutrality Act of 1818, which had been postponed twice, finally took place at Canandaigua on June 19, 1839, before Judge Alfred Conklin, of the Circuit Court of the Northern Division of New York, and Judge Smith Thomson, of the U.S. Supreme Court.[1] From the outset Mackenzie had decided to conduct his own defence. At Canandaigua he had 14 witnesses present, thanks to the financial help of the Canadian Association,[2] but several key witnesses, upon whose evidence he later stated he had been depending for acquittal,[3] failed to turn up. John Montgomery was there, but Dr. Rolph conveniently missed the stage. James Doyle, one of those Mackenzie had sent to Buffalo after receiving an offer of aid from that city; Philip Dorsheimer, at whose hotel the Buffalo committee had met prior to the outbreak in Upper Canada; and Elisha Huntley, the proprietor of the Eagle Tavern, all were absent. Sutherland was still in jail in Quebec, but after his release he did his best to establish Mackenzie's innocence while at the same time belittling his importance.[4]

Subsequent to his conviction, in memorials for his release, Mackenzie argued that the Neutrality Act had been a dead letter for nearly half a century and had not been acted upon during the South American, Greek, Mexican, or Texan revolts, in which American citizens had taken part; and that if he had offended it, it had been done within 48 hours of his arrival in the United States and before the government had called attention to this "long forgotten law".[5] This plea was not accurate. Mackenzie may have been ignorant of the law, but it had not been long forgotten. Van Rensselaer and his father were well aware of it,[6] and its essential provisions had been printed in the Albany *Argus* of December 13, 1837. Also, in 1835 the act had been discussed by the judges on a complaint by the Mexican consul at New York about public recruiting to aid the Texans against Mexico. It was considered again when Robert Nelson and Dr. Côté were tried at Windsor, Vermont, in the summer of 1838.

So far as the statute had been interpreted in these cases, it had been related only to military expeditions carried on from United States territory, not to acts of individuals, or even to acts of individuals acting in concert unless they had been bound by oaths of obedience. Indeed, at Mackenzie's trial the court pointed out to the jury that if a civil war existed in Canada, any individual was free to shoulder a musket and to take part on either side without violating any statute.[7]

N.S. Benton, the District Attorney for the Northern District of New York, attempted to prove that the substance of Mackenzie's speech at the Eagle Theatre had been an appeal for men and arms and for the kind of assistance France had given the United States during the American Revolution. He accused Mackenzie of having been part of a military procession which had formed at the close of the meeting, had marched from the Eagle Theatre to Black Rock, to which place the arms stolen from the city hall were taken, and had there set up a military array with sentinels. He contended also that Mackenzie had tried to prevent the sheriff from recovering the arms, and had been present when the Patriots' colours were presented to Van Rensselaer. Most important, it was Mackenzie who had drawn up and circulated the Navy Island Proclamation. By doing so he had associated himself with Sutherland and Van Rensselaer, and these acts constituted a violation of the Neutrality Act.

In cross-examining Benton's witnesses Mackenzie was able to throw doubt on the accuracy of their testimony and to make them admit that they were not certain he was part of the military parade formed after the meeting on the 12th, nor were they sure where it went. (It went to Dr. Chapin's house, where it disbanded.[8] It was Sutherland's recruits who went to Black Rock on the 13th.)

Mackenzie admitted showing a "natural anxiety" that the Patriots should retain the arms taken to Black Rock, but he obtained an admission that his resistance to their removal had been purely verbal and consisted in his urging that there was a committee in Buffalo ready to pay for the arms or give security for them.[9] He acknowledged the Navy Island Proclamation but argued it had been addressed to Canadians and distributed only in Canada. He had not authorized the printers to circulate it in the United States or to publish it in the *Buffalo Journal*.

In opening his defence Mackenzie first tried to counteract the prejudices which Benton had attempted to create in the minds of the jury by telling them that it was Mackenzie who had caused all the frontier difficulties and had cost the United States $1,000,000. To this end, he reviewed the entire history of the rebellion. The cause of Canada, Mackenzie insisted, was similar to that of the American colonies, which, he reminded the jury, had been aided in their struggle for independence by citizens of other countries. By referring to the unfortunate prisoners taken at Prescott, he attempted in his turn to arouse anti-administration prejudices in this upstate jury.

Mackenzie then dealt with that part of the indictment which charged him with making war upon the dominions of the Queen, with whom the United States was at peace. He had prepared an elaborate and ingenious argument, more useful as propaganda for the Patriot cause than relevant as defence. He challenged the Queen's right to rule, argued that conquest and robbery gave her no title to Canada, and that, in any case, maladministration of the province had released her people from their allegiance. He contended that since the "murder" of Durfee, when the *Caroline* had been cut out and burned, the United States and Great Britain had *not* been at peace.[10] Judge Thomson made short work of these arguments. The executive part of the government had already recognized the

Queen's title to Canada and it was for Congress, not the court, to say whether the United States was at war or not.

Mackenzie seized upon the court's admission that individuals were free to take part in civil wars and tried to show that prior to the rebellion there was no government in Canada, but anarchy, as Lord Durham's *Report*, which he offered in evidence, would show. This move was also blocked by the court, which ruled that since Canada was not recognized as an independent country the court could not permit the introduction of evidence concerning its internal affairs. Thus Mackenzie was defeated in his efforts to get Lord Durham's *Report* before the jury. When the trial was resumed on the second day, Mackenzie made another effort to establish that civil war existed in Canada before the Navy Island episode, and called Dr. James Hunter to testify on this point, but again the court refused to allow the testimony on the ground that it was for Congress to determine whether a state of war existed between the mother country and her colonies, and Congress had not so considered it.

Blocked on the general lines of his defence, Mackenzie then turned to the Navy Island episode itself. He attempted to prove that the citizens of Buffalo had offered their help before the outbreak in Upper Canada was known, that the whole Navy Island episode was of their devising, not his, and that he had not organized a military expedition from the United States and did not possess the means to do so. Here he was hampered by the absence of Rolph, Dorsheimer and Doyle. Montgomery testified that he had seen a letter which the Buffalo committee had written to Mackenzie asking in what way they could help, but the court refused to let him testify about a letter which Mackenzie claimed Sutherland had sent.[11] It might have revealed a Texas-like readiness on the part of some Americans to intervene. Neither was he permitted to testify as to the nature of Mackenzie's reply. At this point, completely frustrated, Mackenzie refused to call any more witnesses and rested his case.

Mackenzie' eloquent defence was weighted with historical allusions to the American Revolution, the Monroe Doctrine, the South American, Greek, and Mexican revolutions, and to the history of Upper and Lower Canada. One of his friends termed it "masterly and comprehensive" but "over the heads of the jury".[12] Long before he concluded the jury must have lost the thread of his argument, overwhelmed by the mass of names, dates, facts and historical allusions which Mackenzie had always at his command. No doubt they heard with relief Judge Thomson's statement that the greater part of it was irrelevant to the points before the court.

The judge's charge was distinctly adverse to Mackenzie. It stressed that after the meeting at the Eagle Theatre Sutherland had asked for volunteers "in the presence and nearby the defendant who urged them to turn out immediately." By so doing, Mackenzie had associated himself with the expedition. If he participated in getting it up in any way, not necessarily as its leader, he was guilty; and it made no difference to *his* guilt whether the entire city of Buffalo participated with him. It was "surely proven" by the proclamation, said Thomson, "that Mackenzie had associated himself with Sutherland and Van Rensselaer."[13]

The proclamation was the key point of the whole case. Mackenzie subsequently admitted that it showed co-operation with Sutherland and Van Rensselaer but "after I returned to Canada, not before." This was a worthless rejoinder based on the fact that the printed proclamation was sent to him on Navy Island "five days after we crossed the Niagara."[14] It was the proclamation that convicted him. Mackenzie never realistically faced this fact. He seemed to think that the main point against him was that at Black Rock, in a "few casual remarks," he had opposed the recovery of the stolen arms.[15] The trial illustrates some of Mackenzie's most unfortunate failings: his verbosity, his inconsistencies, his over-confidence in his own abilities, his tendency to incriminate others and to find excuses for his own failings. He was sentenced to 18 months imprisonment in the county jail and a fine of $10.00. He chose to be imprisoned at Rochester instead of Canadaigua to be near his family and place of business. This was a decision he was subsequently to regret. On the advice of "able lawyers" (whom he did not name) he decided not to appeal.[16]

The effect of Mackenzie's trial and sentence was to bring in gifts and new subscriptions to the *Gazette* from liberal editors and sympathizing Americans, among then Solomon Southwick, onetime editor of the *Albany Register* and candidate for Governor of New York; W.J. Duane, formerly secretary the Treasury under Jackson; Senator Samuel Hazard of Delaware; Hobart Berriam, editor of the Washington Metropolis; James Ronaldson, author of *Banks and Paper Currency: Their Effects Upon Society*; Mathew Carey, author of *The Olive Branch*; the widow of Wolfe Tone; H.R. McNally, an ardent Irish Anglophobe who promised Mackenzie $50.00 a quarter while he remained in jail, earned it and sent it; David Bruce of Bruce Bros., a New York firm of type founders; and Adam Ramage of Philadelphia.[17]

Mackenzie's imprisonment lasted from June 21, 1839, to May 10, 1840, when he was pardoned. It is unnecessary to tell again the story of his miseries while in jail, or to recite his complaints against his jailer, subjects which have been treated at length elsewhere. Mackenzie insisted that his status should be that of a political prisoner and for that reason refused "felon's fare" and had his meals brought to him by his family.[18] To occupy his time the prisoner read the files of the *Workingman's Advocate* with which its editor, George Henry Evans, supplied him. He compiled and saw through the press his *Caroline Almanac*. He busied himself devising a constitution and a code of laws for a "true" republic[19] and he continued to publish his *Gazette*. Without his press Mackenzie felt himself to be nothing. He *had* to publish his paper, no matter at what cost to himself or his family. Several of his friends urged him on, arguing that the real object of the prosecution had been to silence him to please Great Britain.[20] Mackenzie also wrote innumerable letters of complaint to friends, politicians and fellow editors, asking for his release.

Although friends and editors of Rochester papers rallied round, Mackenzie's son, it is sad to find, did not. James was working in Lockport and, when asked by his father to come to Rochester to help edit the *Gazette*, felt it wiser to say no. He feared that his irascible temper would be aroused by some trifle and cause him to "talk foolishly and give offence" as had happened in the past.

James's boyhood in Canada had evidently been far from a happy one. This eldest son wrote:

> Consider in your lonely hours my situation. Consider how seldom I saw you but to receive punishment and how little of love such a course could call forth.... Remember that the delight — the softening influences of home were never mine — that save my grandmother no one looked upon me but as being both silly and bad.

But the passionate anger of an adolescent son was now giving way in James, if not to filial piety, to filial pity.

> We have been in life so much divided. One thing I most sincerely hope is that the kindly feeling you manifest towards me and the true return I feel in my own heart growing daily stronger will not while we live be ever again by any folly broken. [21]

In place of James, Mackenzie procured the services of William Kennedy. This man had been one of his employees in Toronto. After the rebellion Kennedy petitioned Head for permission to leave the province. He had been imprisoned for three weeks, subjected to "daily insults," and had, he pointed out, little prospect of employment.[22] Two other employees of Mackenzie, who had already sought refuge in the United States, had been taken on by the *Watertown Jeffersonian*.[23]

With its editor in jail, able to see people only at the whim of the jailer and able to gather information only by letter, there was little fresh news in the *Gazette*. For three months its columns were devoted chiefly to a detailed account of Mackenzie's trial, petitions for his release, and the miseries of his situation. But the paper could not be kept alive on sympathy and on an endless recital of its editor's grievances. Before long Mackenzie turned to topics of more general interest. For Canadians these were Lord Durham's *Report* and the Act of Union; for Americans in general, slavery, the Independent Treasury and the presidential election of 1840; for the people of upstate New York in particular, bank charters, canals and the pending state election of 1839.

What stand would Mackenzie now take in American politics, or would he take a stand at all? In 1838 he had supported the Van Buren administration and Governor Marcy, but both before and after the elections he had criticized Van Buren for "truckling" to Great Britain and strengthening the neutrality laws of the United States. The result was, as one of Mackenzie's friends put it, "no one could be sure where to find you in politics."[24] For a time Mackenzie was not sure himself. He began to realize that American politics were more complicated than they had once appeared to be. The politics of New York State were closely allied to national politics and far from being a simple juxtaposition of Jacksonian Democrats and Hamiltonian Whigs. The Albany Regency, a group of Democratic politicians who could not be regarded as speaking for the common man or as eager to restrain banks of issue, had been Van Buren's supporters. The question now was, had Van Buren been washed of his past sins, and the taint of his relationship with this clique, in the waters of the Potomac? He was advocating an Independent Treasury and seemed to have become a hard-money man. In consequence, Democrats in New York State and elsewhere had become divided.

Before his trial Mackenzie had begun to modify the harsh criticism of the President which he had indulged in after Prescott.[25] By August 1839 he was hoping that in the end Van Buren's policy would prove to be less subservient to Great Britain than it appeared to be and he had begun to praise his state papers for setting forth principles of political economy that were "pure and faultless, generally speaking."[26] Yet he still had lingering doubts about Van Buren, caused in part by the various compromise proposals he had reluctantly accepted in attempting to win over opponents of his Treasury bill in his own divided party.[27] By September 1839 the United States had experienced another period of financial stringency and bank suspensions. By September, too, Mackenzie had convinced himself that Van Buren now would really insist on an Independent Treasury and restrictions on the use of paper money.[28] Even though Van Buren had called Americans who took part in the Prescott affair "lawless criminals" and had signed the act of 1838 under which Patriots' arms had been seized, it seemed to Mackenzie he was the only person the Equal Rights Party could trust to fight for a sound and stable currency and to oppose the creation of corporations and monopolies, including a national bank. "On Mr. Van Buren's honesty and faithfulness, then, it appears to me that much depends for the happiness of the continent."[29] He was therefore ready "to give a thousand votes for him if he had them."[30]

W.J. Duane in vain tried to make Mackenzie take a more realistic view of American politics. Duane had grasped the change that had come over them in New York State since 1820 at the hands of Van Buren and Thurlow Weed.[31]

> Party or faction is everything [wrote Duane]. The people at elections move as armies do under command. The country is in the hands of an oligarchy of leaders.

What the leaders were concerned with was not carrying out the wishes of the people but perpetuating themselves in power.

> You have not yet formed a true estimate of men and proceedings in this republic [he warned]. Neither Congress nor the Executive is likely to act under the influence of exalted and generous considerations. [32]

To his well-wishers who counselled him to keep silent on politics, Mackenzie explained once again that he could not, without stultifying himself. His course in the United States would be what it had been in Canada. There his aim had always been "the establishment of republican institutions of the purest kind."[33] He had upheld the principles of Jacksonian democracy in Canada and in the United States in 1838. He would uphold them still, no matter at what cost to the *Gazette*.

> What would Canada gain [he demanded] if she exchanged the English yoke for a band of smooth tongued quacks and supple sharpers with their schemes and nostrums? If they stand their ground here, would any form of government prevent their migration beyond the St. Lawrence? [34]

To various suggestions that his imprisonment might be made to bear on party politics to his advantage and to Van Buren's disadvantage, Mackenzie returned a decided negative, and he persisted in his support of Van Buren even when it became apparent that his punishment was to be no brief and easy imprisonment, and that the efforts his friends were making for his release would not soon succeed. "We must not injure a good government because it won't do what we want in a minor matter," he wrote.[35] He assumed, indeed, a *very* noble stance. His language in his letter to O'Rielly was not that of a prisoner under sentence but of one who fancied himself to be a person of great political influence free to negotiate with the administration.

> If he [Van Buren] is not to do it [pardon Mackenzie] we should be told so at once so that we may manage not to hurt the elections in Michigan and in this State.... Hasten on those papers and tell them [!] at Washington to decide at once if they can and if it is unfavorable, much as I would dislike it, I would cheerfully put up with it for the good of the country in its negotiations. [36]

For some months Mackenzie continued to maintain this lofty tone, insisting he would sooner remain in jail than be the means of losing one vote for the Independent Treasury, and consoling himself with the thought that his imprisonment might speed the release of more of the Americans taken prisoner at Prescott. In this mood of self-abnegation he went so far as to ask his friends to stop all agitation and all further efforts to obtain signatures to memorials for his release lest they injure Van Buren. When, in September, the President visited Oswego and made a conciliatory speech in which he acknowledged that the *sympathy* shown the Canadians was understandable, Mackenzie gave it a friendly summing up.[37] This was too much for some of the Patriots.

> You have in your last paper [wrote one of them] turned traitor to the cause of the Patriots.... as the apologist and admirer of Martin Van Buren's Tory speeches... I pity and despise you. [38]

By October Mackenzie had changed his mind and was no longer content to "sit quiet" under his imprisonment. He was suffering from ague, had become worried about his health and was being hampered in the conduct of his paper by the hostility of the jailer. Neither Mackenzie's family, nor his friends, nor his employee William Kennedy, could visit him except at this man's whim. Winter was approaching. His family was ill-provided for and some of its members had become seriously ill. This was almost more than he could bear. "It really unmans me," he wrote, adding that he had been "maddened" by the treatment he had received.[39]

> The whole hubbub here and in Buffalo [declared the disillusioned prisoner] was caused by the prospect of easy acquisition of the country over the lake. Sympathy had little to do with it.[40]

> I wrote eighteen letters to the men in Buffalo who really got up the movement for which I am unjustly punished and not one of them returned me an answer. [41]

Then on October 22 a shot was fired through the window of Mackenzie's cell. It may have been a stray bullet, but the prisoner did not think so. From then until his release in May 1840 his complaints were unending. When the memorials of his friends elicited no response from Van Buren, Mackenzie petitioned the President himself, offering to remove to Texas or to any other state Van Buren would name and to give up his newspaper and all connection with the press for the next 14 months, the balance of the term imposed on him.[42]

There can be no question that Mackenzie fully expected Van Buren to respond favourably to the numerous petitions for his release and to acknowledge in this way the support *Mackenzie's Gazette* had given the Independent Treasury. These hopes were dashed by a letter from S.D. Langtree, who had interviewed the Secretary of State on his behalf. "The President would be in difficulties were he to pardon you, especially if any fresh disturbances should break out. It would be interpreted as approval of your course," Langtree explained,[43] probably reiterating the reasons advanced by Secretary Forsyth. Mackenzie's own petitions were ignored. From this time on he grew increasingly hostile to Van Buren and was evidently planning to take his revenge some day. For the time being his personal grievances had to give way to questions of public policy. He made up his mind to make no "fuss" until after the state elections of 1839. "After that," he warned O'Rielly, "I'll grumble louder."[44]

> Throughout the fall of 1839 *Mackenzie's Gazette* urged the voters to strengthen Van Buren at the polls. The President, it was true, had declared he would not pardon Mackenzie "were he sure his refusal would cost him the entire election of New York."

> What if he has [demanded the victim].... Is he not opposed to filling state treasuries from the sale of public lands? To a

National Bank? To the creation of soulless corporations by the federal power? To receiving uncurrent paper for the lawful taxes? To receiving and retaining bank notes in the Treasury? To confining the franchise to the landowners? To imprisonment for debt? Did he not steadily oppose federal appropriations from the national revenue to be used log-rolling fashion... where will the real friends of liberty and justice find a man who never held a share in a monopoly bank with so many good qualities, with so few... pernicious opinions...? If Mr. Van Buren gain New York in the fall election I shall consider it a triumph for the Canadian cause.... If I had 100,000 votes the man who now hold the reins should have them. FOR WHERE WOULD WE FIND A BETTER ALTERNATIVE? [45]

Despite this public endorsement, suspicion of Van Buren lingered in Mackenzie's mind. The very issue which praised Van Buren as a national statesman denounced the Albany Regency crowd through which he had risen to power.[46] "With such democrats... we hold no commerce. While they pretended to war on the great monster at Philadelphia, they nursed a brood of little ones."[47] A constant struggle, a constant re-evaluation seems to have been going on in Mackenzie's mind. He distrusted Van Buren for his past history, approved of his current domestic policies, and hated him for personal reasons and for his current attitude towards the Patriots. The result was carping criticism in his *Gazette*.

By November 1839 Mackenzie's *Gazette* was in a bad way. Its subscription list had dropped to about 1,000 and it was not paying its editor the wages of a journeyman printer to keep his family upon. Only the donations of friends enabled him to keep his paper going, and he was also dependent upon contributions to finance the printing of his *Caroline Almanac*, then in preparation. Mackenzie had got himself into a difficult position as an editor. He had given the Van Burenites his support, and he and his pitiful little paper had been ignored. And no wonder. The *Gazette* had criticized the leaders of both political parties and had sneered at the very principle on which Van Buren insisted, party discipline: "as if," it said, "confidence in office seekers and office holders was the test of democracy."[48] Apparently Mackenzie had not yet arrived at that more realistic assessment of American politics which Duane had advised. It was hardly worth Van Buren's while to complicate his relations with Great Britain for so undisciplined and uncertain a supporter as Mackenzie.

When the President's message of January 1840 came, denouncing the "chain of dependence" by which the banks of the United States were tied to "the money power of England,"[49] favouring the specie clause as completely as the message of 1837, and proposing to substitute for the Pet banks sub-treasuries which could not lend the public funds, Mackenzie acknowledged that "it did his heart good" to read it. "It is like the grand idea of American honor and greatness I loved to cherish beyond the St. Lawrence...."[50] Yet in subsequent issues, although he denounced the Whig candidate for the presidency, William Henry

Harrison, as a high tariff, national bank and monopoly man, he criticized Van Buren also for his foreign policy and continued to subject all his moves to suspicious scrutiny. Like a squirrel in a cage, Mackenzie went back and forth, and finally confessed that he was at a loss to understand the little Magician's moves on the political chessboard.[51]

Friends in Rochester, Philadelphia and Washington who were still working hard to secure Mackenzie's release, or at least amelioration of the conditions of his imprisonment, were dismayed by his continuing criticism of Van Buren. The President's justification for his refusal to release him was that in the present state of negotiations with Great Britain it would not be expedient for him to interfere with the sentence of the court, but that he was willing that everything that could be done to ease the conditions of Mackenzie's imprisonment should be done.[52] G.M. Keim, a member of Congress from Pennsylvania who had an interview with the President, thought that if Mackenzie should authorize his friends to appeal to the Governor-General of Canada he would be released at his request and thus the question would be relieved "of the embarrassment in which it seems involved."[53] Mackenzie spurned this proposal:

> I presume the suggestion came from yourself, [he wrote to Van Buren] and whether it did or not, I beg to state it is humiliation enough to ask you for relief from an unjust and very harsh sentence .... To go to the men who have bathed themselves in the blood of the best in Canada and humble myself before them I never will. [54]

When Mackenzie sought the help of the Governor of New York State, William Seward, Van Buren took a legalistic position: he was willing that Mackenzie should have the benefit of whatever leniency the State of New York showed offenders against *its* laws in analogous cases.[55] But what *state* offence was analogous to Mackenzie's?

Mackenzie's friends tried to console him by assuring him that Van Buren would release him before long — perhaps by summer — because to keep him in jail until the expiration of his sentence in December would hurt the President's chances for re-election. "No. Matt knows better than that," wrote one of them. If Matt didn't, the Democratic Central Committee of Ohio enlightened him.[56] Thomas Storrow Brown, safe in Florida, enquired whether Mackenzie would not "rather suffer the tortures of the inquisition than aid those who were trying to revive the Hamilton system and principles of 1798." Brown urged him to believe, at least until after the elections, that Van Buren had been governed by high and patriotic principles.[57] Meanwhile, the fretting prisoner, whose access to books and papers was limited, watched his newspaper shrinking into insignificance. The *Gazette*, which had started out in New York as an eight-page paper with a boasted circulation of 4,000, had come down to six pages by May 1839, to four by March 1840, had occasionally skipped publication, and its paid circulation had shrunk to 1,000.[58] Neither was this Mackenzie's only grief. His family had been suffering severe privations, one of the children

70

had become seriously ill and his 90-year-old mother had died in September.[59]

Henry O'Rielly, a staunch Democrat, attempted to convince Mackenzie that in the end he would have to admit that his criticisms of Van Buren were unjustified.[60] He could not overcome Mackenzie's bitterness.

> To be made a tool of, a mere catspaw by those I cherished and confided in, [he raged] ...to be insulted and abandoned and every humble memorial... met by contemptuous silence... it is not in human nature not to feel this. [61]

This is an amazing letter. Were those Tories of Upper Canada who insisted that Mackenzie had been made a tool of by more astute scoundrels behind the scenes right after all? And whom did Mackenzie mean by those he had confided in: certain supporters on the American side? Van Buren, in a message to Congress, stated that few Americans were concerned in the efforts to free Canada and these were "inexperienced persons." "I could show the incorrectness of that statement by such evidence as Mr. Van Buren would not like, but it is better not," Mackenzie commented.[62]

Having failed in a personal appeal to the President,[63] Mackenzie's next move was to put political pressure on him through numerously signed petitions to Congress. In December 1839 Caleb Cushing assured Mackenzie that an effort would be made in Congress in his behalf, but month after month passed and nothing more was heard from Cushing.[64] A committee of Rochester citizens was formed which circulated a memorial and obtained, Mackenzie claimed, 3,000 signatures to it.[65] In Albany E.B. O'Callaghan circulated another petition and in upstate New York, Michigan and Ohio communities similar petitions were circulated.

Mackenzie supplemented these efforts by printing a *Gazette* which contained a five-page appeal of his own to the Senate and the House. This was a most tortured account of the rebellion in which it was argued that the uprising had been provoked not only by Lieutenant-Governor Head but in accordance with the deliberate policy of the British Government, whose purpose had been to give occasion for dissension with the United States and to put that country in the wrong. This production can only have been a desperate effort by one whose nerves and reason had been frayed by privation, ill health and grief.[66]

On March 27 a petition was presented to the Senate asking for Mackenzie's release and, on the motion of Henry Clay, it was sent to the President. In April more petitions were presented to Congress, including ones from Michigan, Illinois, Ohio and Maine, asking either for Mackenzie's release or mitigation of his punishment.[67] On April 29 and 30 Cushing brought his case up in the House by objecting to the appropriation for his safe-keeping.[68] At the same time he exhibited a long petition for his release. Cushing was "stopped by captious questions of order raised by Van Buren men." The Speaker's decisions in Cushing's favour were overruled.[69] On April 30 Senator John Norvell of Michigan, formerly postmaster at Detroit, introduced a resolution requesting the President to pardon Mackenzie.[70] On May 5, before the resolution came up for debate, Van Buren, motivated perhaps by what had become politically expedient, remitted the balance of Mackenzie's sentence and at 7 p.m. on May 10 he was set free.[71]

## Chapter V

# THE FAILURE OF THE *GAZETTE*

During his imprisonment Mackenzie became aware that the situation in Canada was changing in ways that left little hope of arousing Reformers to another effort at rebellion. Lord Durham, the British High Commissioner sent out to investigate the causes of the rebellion, had made his report; and Canadians, believing he advocated the granting of responsible government, were expecting the imperial government to implement his recommendations.

Before his trial Mackenzie had received copies of Durham's *Report*, Head's *Narrative*, and printed correspondence between Fox, Arthur, Colborne, Durham and the Colonial Office.[1] He had used this correspondence in his *Gazette* to deepen hostility on both sides of the border to British rule. All the contemptuous remarks about Americans made by Fox and Arthur were publicized. Likewise Arthur's disparaging comments on the militia of Upper Canada and his distrust of their loyalty were quoted. They made the militia appear so unreliable that Patriot expeditions from the American shore could no longer be regarded as utterly hopeless adventures that had never had a chance of success.[2]

Mackenzie had followed Durham's course in Canada with close attention and from the outset he had been critical and distrustful of him. Shortly after his arrival in Canada Durham had sent a confidential agent to interview Mackenzie, who was then in New York City. Despite his intimacy with O'Callaghan and his correspondence with prominent French Canadians, Mackenzie had professed to know nothing of Lower Canada. Stewart Derbyshire reported that:

> From him I could extract no reference to any specific grievance beyond the composition of the Legislative Council and the vague statement that they wanted "to lift the hand of tyranny from the soil."[3]

When Mackenzie learned in July 1838 that Dr. Wolfred Nelson and seven other Lower Canada prisoners had been banished to Bermuda, he promptly accused Durham of having broken faith with them. He pointed out that the prisoners had not admitted being guilty of high treason. They had simply — and carefully — acknowledged that they had taken a part that had "eventuated in a charge of high treason." Yet they had been banished without trial by an ordinance of June 23, 1838. Lord Brougham, as is well known, brought about the disallowance of this ordinance and thereby Durham's resignation.[4]

For months following the departure of the exiles for Bermuda *Mackenzie's Gazette* was filled with anti-Durham comments quoted from English sources[5] and from Lower Canada correspondents eager to offset pro-Durham propaganda in government-controlled Lower Canada newspapers.[6] Mackenzie made public also Durham's treatment of Louis Michel Viger, a member of the Legislative Assembly of Lower Canada who was kept in jail for months while repeatedly and unsuccessfully demanding a trial.[7] Mackenzie's comments on the commission appointed by Durham to inquire into the municipal institutions of Lower Canada were inaccurate and slanted to support his statement that he "had known all along that Buller, Durham and Co. were all humbug."[8] Adam Thom, one of the commissioners, had not called for wholesale butchery of the prisoners because "it would be absurd to fatten felons all winter for the gallows";[9] he had simply demanded that they be tried speedily; and Thom and his fellow commissioners were not averse to the introduction of local government in Lower Canada, but favoured it.[10]

Before Lord Durham's *Report* was completed, his despatches revealed that he interpreted the long struggle in Lower Canada as fundamentally one between two races, and from the proclamation which he issued shortly before leaving Canada it became known that his policy was "to elevate the province of Lower Canada to a thoroughly British character" and "to raise its defective institutions... to the level of British civilization and freedom."[11] The radical newspaper the *London True Sun* subjected his pronouncements to a scathing criticism which Mackenzie republished under the heading "Falsehoods Refuted".[12]

Mackenzie's copy of Lord Durham's *Report* may have been sent to him by Joseph Hume, but perhaps he had only extracts translated by E. Parent for *Le Canadien*. One can imagine the eagerness with which he perused the report and the glee with which he extracted quotable quotes to bolster his contention that Upper Canada had been provoked into rebellion and that the grievances complained of did in fact exist.[13] In Great Britain the report was praised by the *London Spectator* and by the London *Weekly Despatch*.[14] Mackenzie passed on their favourable comments to his readers but he provided them at the same time with his own succinct list of the report's shortcomings. Durham proposed a new form of government for a united Canada under which her public lands would be managed by Great Britain, the existing land monopolies would be continued, her governor and judges would come from Great Britain, her permanent civil list would be prescribed by the home government, her commerce would be regulated by the imperial parliament, an appointed Legislative Council would be an effective check on the elected assembly, and self-government would be limited to matters of no imperial concern.

> We scout this report, the great produce of Ellice and his titled friend, [wrote Mackenzie] and say give us the means of permanent happiness to Canada only through the strait path of independence.[15]

Durham's recommendations respecting the institution of a system of local government and the choice by future governors of executive councillors who could command the confidence of the Assembly did not receive the extended, reasoned and sympathetic treatment in the *Gazette* that one might have expected. Mackenzie had no faith in the proposed reform. "It is impossible to believe that British noblemen will consent to part with substantial despotism in Canada until they give up the country with it," he observed. Neither Mackenzie nor his son believed that Upper Canada's power to manage her own affairs would be effectively increased. Durham's proposal was not worth "a farthing." Besides, as the *Gazette* reminded its readers, Durham had given "the lie" to his own report and had declared responsible government to be a term he had "never made use of." This was unfair. Although Durham admitted that he did not advocate the *immediate* institution of a responsible government, he had in that same speech warned ministers that unless responsible government were conceded "there would be no satisfaction in the colony."[16] Arthur's reference to responsible government as "the darling object... advocated by Mackenzie" did not go unnoticed in the *Gazette*, but Mackenzie did not enlarge on the topic.

Years before the rebellion Mackenzie had made it clear that he did not regard responsible government as an adequate remedy for Upper Canada's grievances, nor by itself likely to create the kind of society he wished her to become.[17] After 1837 he turned a deaf ear to Joseph Hume's repeated suggestions that he should write an account of the rebellion making it clear that all the rebels had ever wanted was a responsible government. Mackenzie called it "a humbug,"[18] and after his return to Canada, when he was once again a member of the legislature, he called it a mockery. He wanted more extensive reforms and economic and social legislation that would abolish privileges, prevent the development of a monied aristocracy in Canada, and leave every man to find his own level according to his merits in the public esteem. When chronicling Durham's death, Mackenzie acknowledged that he had "exposed the wretchedness of the Canadian colonial system" but he added that Durham had "proposed no useful changes."[19] No further comments on Durham's *Report* appeared in the *Gazette* after April 1839; its space was devoted instead to accounts of its editor's trial and imprisonment.

In the spring of 1839, shortly after he went to jail, Mackenzie seems to have received from England information that gave him hope that the Whig government would be able to carry a measure with which the majority of Reformers would be "content." He advised them to wait with patience to see what it would be, and meanwhile to annoy the government as little as possible.[20] The measure, however, proved to be a bill for uniting the two provinces of Canada on the basis of equal representation in the legislature. When this project had been under consideration in 1828 Mackenzie had condemned it. He considered that a union of all five British North American provinces under a government empowered to deal with lands, roads, trade, canals and the post office might prove useful, but he thought a local union of the two Canadas would only prove to be "a source of vexation and discord."[21] He was still of that opinion. Since he did not expect Russell's bill to pass, he refused to waste time on its details. Some of the provisions of the bill, it is true, were more liberal than those of the Union bill finally passed, but Mackenzie's solution for Upper Canada's troubles was independence.[22]

The Upper Canada Tories objected to this Union bill, particularly to the provision giving the two provinces equal representation in the new legislature.[23] Charles Poulett Thomson, later Lord Sydenham, was sent to the Canadas as Governor-General to obtain their consent to the Union on the basis of equality. By February 1840 their concurrence had been obtained through his shrewd political management. Moreover, the governor-general, with the help of James Stewart, Chief Justice of Lower Canada, drew up and sent home a different — and decidedly more conservative — Union bill which, in somewhat altered form, was enacted by the imperial parliament in April 1840 in place of Russell's bill.[24]

Neither radical Reformers in Upper Canada nor Patriotes in Lower Canada found the provisions of this Act of Union satisfactory. In the imperial parliament radicals criticized its inadequacies and treated with skepticism Russell's statement that Canadians favoured union. Hume could not see that one Canadian grievance would be remedied. The Canadians, said Hume, wanted to control their civil list — instead, one was to be imposed on the revenues of the united provinces by imperial fiat; they wanted a system of local self-government in place of rule by appointed justices of the peace — instead, the local government clauses originally in the bill had been dropped at the instance of Edward Ellice; Upper Canada had asked for changes in the Legislative Council to make its membership more acceptable to the people and Lower Canada had gone further by demanding a wholly elective council — instead, all members of the Legislative Council of the united province were to be appointed, and for life. Above all the Canadas wanted a responsible government, yet there was nothing in the bill to ensure responsibility and to give satisfaction to the popular branch of the legislature.[25] All that the imperial government would openly do was give the vague promise that the government of the united province would be administered in accordance with the well understood wishes and interests of the people, and instruct the governor-general "to maintain harmony between the Executive and the Legislature." To this end colonial officials were informed that they could be called upon to resign whenever the governor considered that public policy made it expedient to require them to do so.[26]

While Canada was thus moving rapidly towards union and a new constitution, Mackenzie was mewed up in jail and Canadian affairs were being settled without him, and along lines that would not permit the growth of the kind of political democracy he had come to favour or create the egalitarian social order in which he believed. One can imagine the sense of frustration that consumed him. What use now all his anxious considerations of an ideal constitution for an independent republic of Upper Canada, unless he could halt the untoward march of events? Was there any hope of arousing Canadians to fight for freedom as he understood it? It is clear that Mackenzie's fevered thoughts began to turn in this direction while the union was under discussion, while confinement was daily growing more irksome to him and his health was declining.

Prior to his imprisonment Mackenzie had organized his Canadian Association on a standby basis and James had persuaded Patriots in the Lockport area to keep the peace lest activity on their part should hurt Mackenzie's chances of a pardon. Mackenzie himself had restrained Ben Lett from guerrilla warfare against the British in Upper Canada and had urged him to go to Texas and not to "hover around the mouth of the pitt until he fell in." But by December Mackenzie had changed his mind. There seemed to be no prospect of his being released and no prospect either of a settlement in Canada satisfactory to radical Reformers. He therefore began to sound out the exiled Canadians about resuming border activities. To James he wrote, "Advise Ben Lett not to go to Texas on any account.... If I determine to do what I spoke to you about I will need both you and Lett."[27]

The responses Mackenzie received to his queries varied. From E.A. Theller in Detroit he received encouragement. Donald M'Leod in Cleveland also urged him on, arguing that "Something effectual must be attempted now or the business must be given up."[28] Bolder spirits among the Hunters had all along been impatient with the policy of watchful waiting. If their organization did not attempt something worthwhile soon, its supporters would drift away. One shrewd observer predicted that the new governor-general would put back the cause of reform by his "soft sawder" system of granting a little here, flattering a little there. The same man warned Mackenzie that, as a result of the Hickory Island fiasco, it would be impossible to get Canadians to turn out as they had on that occasion. On the other hand, C.H. McCollum, a merchant of Oswego, N.Y., formerly of Hastings County, shared Mackenzie's hope for war, proposed organizing a secret committee in every township to support the Canadian Association of Rochester, and offered to work the district east of Toronto himself.[29] Dr. James Hunter, of Hartlands, N.Y., formerly of Whitby, Upper Canada, was firmly opposed to a renewal of border hostilities since he believed independence for Canada would never be achieved by such means. In his opinion an independent Upper Canada was physically impossible owing to her landlocked situation and total dependence on the United States and Lower Canada.

> Far better it would be to let the contemplated settlement of the British monarchy go into effect and let the poison in its veins produce its own dissolution... [advised that foresighted man, adding] But if you can suggest a plan that can reach that cold blooded murderer Prince? [30]

And ended his letter with that query.

Late in December "General" Handy came to Rochester. By this time the prospects of war with Great Britain over Maine were fading. Negotiations over the boundary had begun, but it was still possible that a campaign of guerrilla warfare — a series of hit-and-run attacks on the Canadian shore, with destruction of property, if not of life — would bring about war. It cannot be stated that

Handy had a chance to discuss such a line of policy with Mackenzie but it is certain that Handy saw John Montgomery.[31] A short time later, Lieutenant-Governor Arthur discovered that two men were distributing commissions in the Patriot Army signed by Handy and Montgomery and he had them arrested.[32]

The first issue of *Mackenzie's Gazette* to appear after its editor regained his freedom announced, in general terms, his intention of continuing to work for the Canadian cause.[33] The second issue carried John Montgomery's "Letter to the Friends of Liberty on the Northern Frontier." This long production, full of historical allusions, probably chiefly Mackenzie's work, was an open invitation to Canadians to commence guerrilla warfare and incendiarism against their government and its officials, and all but an open invitation to Canadians in exile to resume border raids and to American sympathizers to join them.

At this time Mackenzie was resolved to wage war on British commerce, "the weak point" in British power, by burning steamships, warehouses, and barracks, and he told M'Leod that he was willing to go the full extent and "three steps beyond" what M'Leod had urged him to consent to in 1839.[34] He commended the burning of the *Sir Robert Peel*, the blowing up of Brock's monument and the Kingston Fire of April 1840.[35] French Canadians were urged not to "stand on trifles with their tyrants" but to use every means in their power to dislodge them, even by fire, and all Canadians were reminded that they could carry on guerrilla warfare as successfully in their country as the determined Seminoles had in Florida. The advice of an American editor, disgusted by Prince's shooting of Patriot prisoners at Windsor, was quoted:

> Give all foreign British army and navy officers, judges, governors and magistrates one month to leave Canada or to denounce British rule. After that, shoot them where found.

This, said the author, would be the way to force the tyrants to emigrate rather than the residents. These grim proposals, these methods of protesting against the establishment of that day and the inadequate reforms of the Act of Union, may have originated with Montgomery — possibly with Handy — but they were put to the public in Mackenzie's language and in *Mackenzie's Gazette*, scarcely three weeks after he had regained his liberty.

Mackenzie's son, evidently consulted by his father as to his opinion of "Montgomery's" letter, replied that he had no objection to its proposals provided they would lead to the desired end — war between Great Britain and the United States — and lead Canadians to wish for a change for the sake of security. "Official station," observed James, "will not be so much wanted if it makes a man a target for a rifle."[36]

After the publication of Montgomery's letter, the *Gazette* was suspended until September 17. In the meantime Mackenzie travelled, he tells us, 2,000 miles, "weighing matters" and talking with people. In Washington and Philadelphia he met with little encouragement.[37]

There is no shadow of hope for us save in our own exertions [he informed M'Leod] ...and they are amply sufficient if we go to work in earnest the right way as I am determined we will....[38]

Support for the policy of renewed raids on the Canadian frontier was not forthcoming from some influential Canadian Patriots either. E.B. O'Callaghan, when informed by Mackenzie from prison that he was "reluctant to give up the ship," had told him bluntly that it was "waterlogged" and advised him to "relax, read less, and not fatigue [his] brain."[39] T.S. Brown, while boasting that he was "as much a soldier of democracy as ever," now announced his unwillingness to be "food for gallows," and Charles Durand confessed he saw no hope in a Patriot war.[40] From the Vermont frontier came an intimation that Mackenzie was not wanted there, although Ben Lett would be welcome at the office of the *North American*.[41]

On second thoughts, even James changed his mind. "In choosing our means," he wrote, "we cannot choose those we have condemned in others: hanging of persons, indirect assassination, confiscation of property for opinion's sake... I would rather see you look back with honorable regret on the past than align yourself with this scheme which cannot succeed and with which justice can have no sympathy."[42] Years later, James informed Charles Lindsey that he had belonged to Handy's organization but that after learning his plans "did not divulge them but refused to act with him or those connected with him." James did not mention Mackenzie's own proposals for guerrilla warfare.[43]

Whether Mackenzie was moved more by his son's arguments or by the discouragement he met with in Washington and when he went to the Niagara frontier in August, it is impossible to say. At all events, he informed James that his plans, "whatever they were could not be carried out and were consequently deferred or abandoned."[44] It may be that rest and improved health had brought Mackenzie to a calmer and more realistic frame of mind. By the end of August he was planning to publish the *Gazette* again and trying to get his son to come to his assistance. James, who had refused once before lest his temper should lead to unfilial scenes, reluctantly consented to come for three months if no better person could be found.[45]

When the *Gazette* reappeared on September 17, 1840, it made no mention of Montgomery's letter, denounced the Hunters and those who had begged money for the Canadian cause and lived off it, and came out unreservedly for Van Buren. Meanwhile M'Leod was waiting in vain for him to come to Cleveland. Mackenzie now informed him of the complete reversal of his policies. "That is our abiding interest, to secure Van Buren's election." He added that men of honour could not be found to engage in guerrilla warfare.[46] The feelings of the old professional soldier were outraged. He protested indignantly that he had never advocated guerrilla warfare. What M'Leod wanted was to continue the careful organization of Hunters' Lodges on both sides of the frontier in preparation for any move. This had been his occupation and, presumably, his living. In his bitterness and disappointment he overwhelmed Mackenzie with reproaches and accused him of having received "a new light" in Washington. Had Van Buren shown him "the shining bottom of the Sub Treasury well," he inquired. In a subsequent letter he softened this accusation a little, but warned Mackenzie that rumours he had been bribed to support Van Buren were being circulated.[47] Bill Johnston did not mince words. His letter to William "Lying" Mackenzie accused him of having seen "Matty Kendall and Blair" while in Washington and of agreeing "for a paltry sum" to quit the cause.[48] Subsequent to the election, Mackenzie's agent at Cape Vincent reported that the town, heretofore Democratic, had given a majority of 150 for the Whigs, and that Mackenzie was being accused by some of his former Patriot friends of having accepted a bribe of $1,000 and liberation from prison on condition of coming out for Van Buren.[49] The *National Gazette* of Philadelphia, a paper friendly to the Patriot cause, made a similar accusation.[50] All these charges Mackenzie vigorously denied. It was always his boast that his was an independent and unbought newspaper.

It is unlikely that Mackenzie bargained or could have bargained with Van Buren for his release from prison or that he received a bribe to support him in 1840. The *Gazette* simply was not influential enough for that, and one can well imagine that Van Buren would have preferred to do without its editor's imprimatur. Mackenzie was and remained personally hostile to and distrustful of Van Buren, but he did want the program of the radical wing of the Democratic Party to succeed and Van Buren was its candidate. "With unspeakable pleasure" Mackenzie saw the sub-treasury bill pass, with, however, a modified specie clause that would not be fully operative until 1841.[51] It was signed on July 4 while his paper was suspended. His doubts and hesitations were now resolved. He could give the administration unstinted support, and as one who had long argued that public money should not be utilized by private banks felt it his "duty" to do so. He later informed Caleb Cushing that:

> I supported Van Buren at the sacrifice of personal feeling and frontier support because I thought his course of upholding states' rights and an independent treasury was the true means of preventing conflicts that might split the union.[52]

It would have been more realistic if he had admitted also that, having failed to drum up support for the Patriot cause in the United States, he had decided to turn his *Gazette* "into a regular thorough going Democratic weekly," that being the only party he could with any degree of consistency support.[53]

Point by point *Mackenzie's Gazette* contrasted the record of the two parties from the point of view of an anti-bank, anti-monopoly Democrat. The Jacksonians had got rid of a national bank and a national debt and had refused to assume the state debts; the party of Harrison, Clay, and Webster would recreate both these evils. The Van Buren administration had introduced a pre-emption bill in May 1839; Harrison and Clay had attempted to kill it and to "deprive the pioneers of their log cabins." Large sums had been expended in removing the Indians and in buying their land; what had the nation got in exchange? Worthless paper money! By issuing the specie circular the party of Jackson and

Van Buren had halted this robbery of the public by land speculators. Between 1813 and 1837 the United States treasury had suffered a loss of $34,974,722[54] from the deposit banks and bank notes. The administration's Sub-Treasury Act now required collectors to demand treasury notes or specie. Finally the Whig candidates were denounced for the support they enjoyed in the Tory papers of Canada and Great Britain. In summary, Mackenzie characterized the forthcoming election as a "trial of strength between English influences and democratic institutions." "Disregard any petty complaints of mine," he urged his readers. "Vote for Van Buren."[55] Five issues of the *Gazette* appeared at irregular intervals between September 17 and November 7, when Mackenzie had the unhappy duty of announcing:

> Messrs. Van Buren and Kendall are rejected... because they fought boldly against the English money power and American gambling, we shall ever rejoice to do them honor.

The *Gazette* was now on its last legs. Its circulation had declined to no more than 1,360 and its editor, despite the liberal bribe he was supposed to have received, was in debt for presswork done for him by the Rochester Daily Advertiser. From week to week the *Gazette* struggled to survive. Only a contribution from Henry O'Rielly and friends "in token of gratification at his devotion to the [Democratic] cause" kept it going.[56] The November 17 issue announced what was apparently Mackenzie's last desperate attempt to maintain his paper — a plan to publish a one-cent daily entitled the *Rochester Sun* in connection with his weekly *Gazette*. It never appeared. December 23, 1840 saw the last issue of *Mackenzie's Weekly Gazette*.

Before the final number came out Mackenzie's entire printing establishment, which had cost him $925.00, was being offered for sale for $350.00.[57] It was purchased by the publisher of an anti-slavery paper, the *American Citizen*, which was already being printed in Rochester using Mackenzie's equipment.[58] It is probable that Mackenzie's creditors had threatened to seize his equipment and that the demise of the *Gazette* was not voluntarily permitted by its editor.

"A Letter to the People of Upper Canada," the major item in the final issue, documents Mackenzie's despair at this moment. Three years' residence in the United States, he confessed, had lessened his regret for the failure of the rebellion. He now foresaw, as a result of the election, the triumph of an aristocracy of monied monopolists in the republic he had once admired. Mackenzie's faith in political democracy had been shaken and his hope of seeing social democracy in the New World was fading. Worse still, he had come to doubt his own fitness for the role of a public journalist and in this black moment acknowledged it. As for a federal union of the British provinces of North America, he did not expect it to come about. Reformers and Patriots with whom he had talked simply did not understand federalism; they thought of it only as involving a sacrifice of petty local interests and power. The chances for a larger federal union with the United States were "marred by the slavery issue." Besides, there was no unanimity of feeling either north or south of the border.

"It was a wonderful dream," concluded Mackenzie sadly, "the whole continent working together harmoniously."[59]

It is easy to see why *Mackenzie's Gazette* failed to maintain itself. It had appealed for support primarily to Canadian Reformers and their American supporters and this foundation proved to be too narrow. Although circulation of the *Gazette* in Canada could not be entirely prevented, it was severely restricted because it was unlawful and dangerous to possess a copy. Moreover, Mackenzie's was not the only paper published for the refugee market. Others had got into the act.[60] Mackenzie's quarrel with Van Rensselaer and the subsequent divergence between his policies and those of the Hunters cost him the support of some sympathizers with the Canadian cause. His bitter comments on American sordidness and selfishness, his criticisms of both Whigs and Democrats, and his stand on slavery all cost him other subscribers he might have had.

Soon after Mackenzie started publishing his *Gazette* in New York City he had been sounded out about his stand on slavery. Friends urged him not to involve himself in the abolitionist controversy.[61] For a time he took this advice, but unfortunately he later saw an opportunity to use a southern grievance, as he had used the Maine boundary dispute, to arouse hostility towards Great Britain. What started him off was the speech of Francis W. Pickens of South Carolina on the *Enterprise* case.[62] This vessel, with American-owned slaves aboard, had been driven by stress of weather into a port in Bermuda, where the British authorities had liberated the slaves.

In discussing this dispute Mackenzie accused Great Britain of attempting to induce American slaves to desert and to rise in arms against their owners. Although she had given "pretended" freedom to her West Indian slaves, she was not a true emancipator. Her Emancipation Proclamation had been intended to create unrest among American negroes, to harass the United States and break the union.[63] Mackenzie was not alone in his suspicions of Great Britain's motives.

> There are many intelligent men in the south [wrote Duff Green] who believe that the true secret of the abolition of West India slavery was jealousy of our manufacture and of our commerce. [64]

The foregoing is apt to strike one as an example of the kind of exaggerated argument that Mackenzie sometimes made use of. It diverts attention from his thoughtful and rational discussion of the slavery question and his basic attitude towards the South's peculiar institution. When in Canada he had expressed himself in favour of freedom, education, and equality of treatment for all men regardless of their colour. As mayor of Toronto he had presided at a meeting of one of Upper Canada's anti-slavery societies held in the city hall in 1837, and in the proposed constitution for the State of Upper Canada, published in the *Constitution* of November 15, 1837, he had included a clause providing that "there shall be neither slavery nor involuntary servitude in this State...."[65]

> I am opposed to slavery of whatever races it may be the curse.
> The breaking up of slave families grieves me to the heart... but
> the mode of cure must be mild and gentle, temperate and
> Christianlike.

Forcible interference with the institutions of a sovereign state did not seem to him the sensible way.

> If this community of nations shall trample on the sovereign
> power retained by each of them for self government on the
> pretence of removing negro slavery, the result must be a violent
> separation which would in all probability end, not in removing
> bondage from the blacks, but in burying both blacks and whites
> under the iron yoke of monarchical power and strong govern-
> ment.... For the sake of the best interests of mankind this
> Union, this last and best refuge of the oppressed of the earth
> must never, never, be dissolved. [66]

Mackenzie proposed that the federal government abolish slavery by purchasing all the slaves at a fair valuation and paying for them in federal bonds:

> Any attempt to remove slavery exclusively at the expense of
> the slave owner will be likely to create difficulties more formi-
> dable than slavery itself. [67]

Mackenzie believed that the day would come when the South would be glad to be freed of its burden of slavery but that, in the words of the *Boston Quarterly Review*:

> The day of emancipation is not yet. It were useless to emanci-
> pate the slave to-day because we should be merely changing
> the form not the substance, of his slavery. [68]

Like Orestes Brownson, whose final article in the review he quoted, Mackenzie believed that:

> Slavery is doomed.... There are causes at work which will free
> the slave, and free him too with the consent and the joy of his
> master. [69]

The willingness to wait for economic forces to make emancipation acceptable to the South, this policy of gradualism, and the *Gazette's* support of Van Buren, who was regarded as an apologist for slavery, earned for Mackenzie the hostility of the abolitionists, many of whom had refused to sign petitions for his liberation.[70] Vigorous criticisms of his stand came from his own son:

Union with the United States.... No. No. Union would couple us with that detestable slave system... if its effects are not to make labour disgraceful and idleness honourable I much mistake it.... I by no means approve of your views on the subject.....

I am an abolitionist and will never (as you have done) pretend to justify for a crime by apologizing with the assertion that England is the greater criminal. [71]

Subsequently Mackenzie stated vigorously his hatred of slavery, but he did not accept the abolitionists' position.[72]

With considerable justification the peace-minded regarded Mackenzie as a war-mongerer; the Whigs resented his ingratitude to Whigs who had supported the Patriot cause; and the Van Burenites did not find in him a consistent, loyal and uncritical party supporter. The *Gazette* was no party-line paper. It advocated today and deprecated tomorrow, lashing out at friend or foe as its independent-minded editor saw fit, and this in a country where, as James observed, "it is so unfashionable."[73] In addition to the foregoing faults of the *Gazette*, there was Montgomery's letter inviting Canadian exiles and their supporters to renew the frontier outrages that had so recently been quieted, and finally there was the paper's support of Van Buren in 1840. However consistent and logical this decision was in one who held the views Mackenzie did on banking and currency questions, it could not win him subscribers in upstate New York, Ohio and Michigan, all predominantly Whig and strongly abolitionist, and it must have been regarded by some as a desperate crawling bid for financial support from the party whose "heartless" leader had humiliated and broken him.

## Chapter VI

# THE UNION AND THE
# *VOLUNTEER*

$S$hortly after the election, which resulted in an overwhelming victory for the Whigs, Mackenzie began looking about for some way of earning a living, realizing that his *Gazette*, the final issue of which was to appear on December 23, was doomed. The financial situation of the Mackenzie family was now extremely precarious and a twelfth child — another son — was to be born in February.[1] Mackenzie first attempted to get admitted to practice law in the courts of Monroe County. To his bitter disappointment his application was rejected "in open court by four Democratic judges." There was no instance on record, he was told, of a foreigner being admitted to the bar of the Supreme Court who was not a counsellor before he arrived.[2]

There was one gleam of sunshine at this dark moment but Mackenzie turned his back on it. Friends in Cincinnati urged him to come there to establish a truly Democratic newspaper and offered to provide a printing establishment for him. Mackenzie refused to go, telling them "for if I have a heart it is in Canada with those who suffered for their... principles, and there only will I be at home."[3]

During the spring of 1841 the elections to the first parliament of United Canada were being held. Mackenzie could not bear to stand idly by, watching the consummation of the Union and the acceptance by Reformers of a constitutional settlement so far from his ideals. He got in touch with Reformers in the Niagara District, evidently proposing that he should visit the area to persuade farmers to vote against candidates who were expected to become the Governor-General's tools.[4] This offer was declined.[5] "There are not now above one in ten of those who formerly professed to be your friends that still remain so sincerely..." wrote one of them.[6] "I cannot see that you can do any good by coming on the farms and it might do harm if it were found out," warned another. "Go to Cincinnati for the sake of your family."[7] But Mackenzie was not yet willing to give up.

In the Niagara District a little group of radical Reformers was doing its best to defeat David Thorburn and to elect Gilbert McMicking. Thorburn's influence, Mackenzie's friends admitted, was greater than that of any of the Reformers in the Niagara District, but he had become unacceptable to the more radical because he had "joined Merritt"[8] on the civil list question.

Thorburn was one of those who, when the terms of the proposed union were under debate, had voted for a sufficient civil list to secure the independence of the judges, and to give the executive "that freedom of action necessary for the public good."[9] Sydenham interpreted this vote to mean that the Assembly had left it to him to decide the amount of the civil list and the manner in which it would be apportioned. His recommendations were made part of the Act of Union. Reformers like Francis Hincks were astounded by these clauses.

> I would have no objection that high offices should have salaries attached *provided always*, as I have said before, we had an annual civil list as would make the Executive completely dependent on us to go on. This last is with me a sine qua non. It is our security for Responsible Government. With a control over supplie [sic] we can secure anything; without it we are powerless. [10]

Opposing Thorburn proved to be uphill work. The radicals had no press of their own, could not get printing done for them at Toronto, or even at Niagara unless they were "very moderate." Since Sydenham had the press pretty well under his control, they were unable to reply effectively to Thorburn and Merritt's argument that the Governor-General "only wanted the civil list placed in his hands to show that they had confidence in him," and that afterwards "he will give it back again."[11] This of course was nonsense. The civil list provisions were part of the Act of Union and could be altered only with the consent of the imperial parliament. During the campaign one of Mackenzie's letters came to Thorburn's knowledge and was used by him on the hustings to show that McMicking's opposition to him was really being directed by Mackenzie, and this did the unfortunate McMicking no good.[12]

Mackenzie also took keen interest in the contest for the fourth riding of York, which his wife's brother-in-law, John Mackintosh, had represented in the 12th and 13th parliaments of Upper Canada.[13] He was enraged when he learned that Mackintosh, who had voted against the union, had been reluctantly persuaded by the Reformers to withdraw in favour of Robert Baldwin. "Can it be possible," he inquired of George Lount, "that 221 inhabitants of the county of York have declared themselves ready to support Robert Baldwin against John Mackintosh...?" He characterized Dr. W.W. Baldwin's "pretended leadership" of the Reform party as

> the vilest mockery I ever witnessed. While Mackintosh sat for years as Chairman of the Committee of the Home District Reformers, endeavoring to get responsible government conceded from England, where were the Baldwins? Who heard of them? Nobody! [14]

All this was far from accurate, although it is true that after being defeated at the polls in 1830 the Baldwins took no active part in politics for a time. Dr. Baldwin gave as his excuse "the fickleness of the public" which seemed "indifferent into whose hands they commit the preservation of their rights." He refused to be a delegate to the Metropolitan District Nominating Convention which elected John Mackintosh president and which required its candidates to pledge their support to demands for responsible government and an elective Legislative Council.[15] Nor did he become a member of the Canadian Alliance Society formed in December 1834 to create province-wide support for these changes and for many other reforms including vote by ballot. However in 1836 W.W. Baldwin became president of the more moderate Constitutional Reform Association created in that year. Robert Baldwin became a member of Head's Executive Council, only to resign when he discovered that Head did not intend to govern with the advice of his Council.[16] Robert Baldwin then went to England to persuade the imperial government to bring about this change in the relations of the Lieutenant-Governor and his Executive Council. But the "great change" Mackenzie wanted for the province could not have been comprised within the narrow limits of responsible government. With reform as Mackenzie understood it, Baldwin had as yet shown no sympathy.

Between the fiery and impetuous Mackenzie and the cold and cautious Baldwin there had never been a bond of sympathy. Furthermore, Mackenzie was now aware that Baldwin had done very little to defend Lount and Mathews and other Reformers who had been arrested subsequent to the rebellion. At a later date he was publicly to accuse Baldwin of not doing that little for free, as Baldwin could well have afforded to do. Mackenzie's accusation is well supported by a scathing letter to Baldwin from John Carey.[17]

In addition, Baldwin had raised grave doubts in Mackenzie's mind as to his sincerity by accepting the post of Solicitor-General for Upper Canada from Lord Sydenham and by entering the first ministry put together after the union as solicitor-general for what had now become, officially, Canada West. In both instances, however, Baldwin had made it plain that he accepted office in the expectation that the government would be carried on in accordance with the principles of responsible government and that, if it were not, he would resign.

Francis Hincks, who was trying to get the Reformers of both sections of the united provinces to work together and to form a party that would have a majority in the new legislature, was able to convince the French Canadians and the Reformers of Upper Canada that Baldwin could be trusted and that he would resign should Sydenham fail to remodel his ministry after the election had given the Reformers the majority they expected. As for Mackintosh's seat, Hincks argued that the fourth riding of York was a safe constituency in which Baldwin was sure to be elected, that he was needed in Parliament and would be more use than Mackintosh. Under this pressure Mackintosh withdrew and Baldwin was elected. Hincks, who had master-minded the Reformers' campaign, felt that his political judgement had been vindicated,[18] but Mackenzie was not to be reconciled to the loss of Mackintosh from the legislature. In his opinion Hincks was not to be trusted. "When did he become a Reformer," he asked. "When it became gainful."[19]

Of the 44 Tories who had sat in Upper Canada's last parliament, Mackenzie rejoiced to find that only seven had been re-elected. "Never did a set of men stink so in the public nostrils as the wretched squad just cashiered."[20] The rest of Upper Canada's representatives were either ministerialists, or Reformers, not all of whom were prepared to stand up and be counted in opposition to the Governor-General. Yet Mackenzie did not give up hope of creating a "true" republic north of the border. Five of the Upper Canada Reformers could still be classed as radicals and there was a sizeable bloc of 23 representatives from Lower Canada hostile to the union. Perhaps it would be possible to influence the malcontents in both sections of United Canada, even to win some old Reformers back to the cause of independence, and so to guide their obstructive tactics as to make efficient government impossible under the union. Thus it would become apparent that independence was the only answer for Canada. In addition there was still opportunity to make relations between the United States and Great Britain worse by harping on their unsettled disputes: the boundary of Maine, the *Caroline* affair, and the "guilt" of Alexander McLeod, who was accused of being one of the party that had seized that vessel. If war could be brought about, Mackenzie believed it would result in the independence of Canada. It was with these twin lines of policy in mind that he made another venture into the field of journalism shortly after the results of the Canadian election became known.

The Rochester *Volunteer* appeared on April 17, 1841. It was a small sheet, scornfully described by the Toronto *Patriot* as a "napkin."[21] Mackenzie began in a moderate way. Among the members for Upper Canada, he professed to see "a clear majority of men who might be expected to support responsible government," concealing for the time being, except from E.B. O'Callaghan, his dissatisfaction with the composition of the legislature and his fears that many of the Reform members would not prove true to the cause.[22]

The first issue of the *Volunteer* restated the principal grievances complained of by the Assembly of Upper Canada in 1835 and pointed out that only one of those who had voted against the adoption of its Seventh Report on Grievances had been elected. This was an indirect reminder to the Upper Canada members that the Act of Union had not given the province what the Reformers had struggled for and what Mackenzie believed their constituents still wanted: responsible government, an elective Legislative Council, impartial judges and juries, control of all the provincial revenues and resources, and the appropriation of the Clergy Reserves for education.[23] Mackenzie did not intend Upper Canada to forget these grievances nor would he allow the bitterness of the rebellion years to die down if through the *Volunteer* he could prevent it. He held the re-elected Tory members up to scorn for the role they had played as members of militia courts martial, or as legislators who had voted for harsh treatment of suspected persons, and for the confiscation of the property of rebels. Milk and water Reformers who had not ventured to oppose these measures were criticized.[24]

To French Canadians the Act of Union was abhorrent. Mackenzie rubbed salt into their wounds by pointing out, with the help of O'Callaghan who seems to have supplied the statistics, exactly how the electoral districts in Montreal and Quebec had been altered to the disadvantage of French Canadian voters.[25] He had great hopes that the French members would make the union unworkable.

> They are a glorious sedition spreading club, [he wrote] and we
> must do our best to get a head over them that will use them in
> that way. [26]

Mackenzie's hope of influencing the course of the Reformers during the first session of the first parliament of united Canada rested on arrangements he had made with a part-time journalist, Dr. John Smyles,[27] who had been hired by James Gordon Bennett of the New York *Herald* to send him weekly letters from Kingston, where the first parliament of united Canada was to be held. The *Herald*'s reporter was an ardent Loco-Foco (a radical Democrat) who shared Mackenzie's views on banking and currency questions, "soulless corporations," and "the breed of lawyers." Smyles was also an ardent sympathizer with the Patriot cause who hoped to see the Canadas part of the United States. He was an astute observer but his reports to his newspaper were not objective and Bennett subsequently complained of their violence.[28]

Smyles had introduced himself to Mackenzie by letter while the latter was still publishing from New York, had been present at the first meeting of the Canadian Association, had visited him in jail, and had contributed several articles to the *Gazette*.[29] He now agreed to supply the *Volunteer* with news from Kingston, but this arrangement could not be publicized because it would have restricted his ability to get information and might have subjected his letters to Mackenzie to interference. Smyles's letters were not always printed verbatim in the *Volunteer*, Mackenzie having been told he might edit them and add such comments as he pleased. Sometimes Smyles's realistic and discouraging predictions as to Sydenham's ability to manage the legislature were, understandably, omitted. In addition to supplying news, Smyles undertook to give the members letters from Mackenzie and to see to it that the *Volunteer*, which could not go through the mails, was distributed in Kingston. He was the "careful and sure conveyance" by which Mackenzie proposed to send every member of the legislature a free copy of the *Volunteer* for six months, if only someone would provide his out-of-pocket expenses — $10.00 for paper and press work. A contribution from the Canadian Association in Cincinnati soon made this possible.[30] Another outlet for the *Volunteer* was the office of the Toronto *Mirror*. This was a Roman Catholic Reform paper edited by Charles Donlevy and "devoted to the attainment of an independent local government."[31]

In Kingston Smyles ran into difficulties. When he presented Mackenzie's letter of introduction to Hincks, he received "a very cool reception." This is not surprising. Hincks was coaching Reform strategy in Kingston and he was not disposed to have Mackenzie interfering from across the border as he had attempted to do during the elections. Hincks had accepted the union and wanted it to work — on the basis of responsible government — and he looked forward to making a united Canada attractive to British capital. Mackenzie was bent on destroying the union and was hostile to the kind of economic changes Hincks wished to encourage. Moreover, in the *Volunteer* Mackenzie had cast doubt on Hincks' integrity by *hoping* that his conversion from conservatism to liberalism would continue "whatever sacrifices of worldly advancement this may entail."[32]

Smyles's efforts with other Reformers were not any more successful. He informed Mackenzie that:

> I have not presented many of your letters as they were received, I thought, rather cooly [*sic*]. You need look for no aid of any kind from folks in correspondence with you and losing cast or influence therefrom. [33]

Mackenzie and Smyles were striving to sharpen differences and to keep bitterness alive, whereas it was Sydenham's policy to get the moderate Tories and the moderate Reformers to work together. Many of the latter were "anxious for moderation" and were willing to work with the Governor-General. Others, "neither honest nor independent" were being won over by one inducement or another.[34] Thomas Parke, the Reform member for Middlesex, whom Mackenzie at first characterized as "a thoro' republican," a Methodist who had voted for the grievance report, and "an excellent legislator" was made surveyor-general, "hooked with a golden bait," as Smyles put it.[35] Even Reformers would not take the *Volunteer* from Smyles openly. He had to address those Mackenzie sent and leave them on the table in the legislative hall. He reported that:

> All are afraid of being asked or taunted with being in correspondence with you. There is nothing for it but to keep up domestic squabbles and thereby keep alive the belief that the government will not do anything for the permanent benefit of the country and by and by bring about the conviction in the minds of men that they *cannot* and that there is nothing for it but separation. [36]

The accounts of the session which appeared in the *Volunteer* were on the whole accurate but coloured by Mackenzie's — and Smyles's — desire to show that the new constitution was nothing but "a costly mockery" and the Parliament of Canada a mere instrument for Sydenham to manipulate at will. The members of the Legislative Council were still appointees. In the Assembly of 84 members, only 20 were necessary for a quorum. Consequently the vote of 11 persons could, on occasion, decide matters. To Mackenzie this meant that "placemen" could weary out honest members who had to earn their bread. As for the famous debate on responsible government with which the session opened, Smyles interpreted W.H. Draper's tergiversations to mean that responsible government, as Hincks and Baldwin understood it, had not been obtained, and Mackenzie added that the country need not look for "a manly critical opposition" or "a full declaration of principles by thorough going Reformers." Responsible government, as Sydenham and Draper explained it, was "one grand humbug."[37]

Smyles recorded the failure of three attempts made by Neilson, Hincks and Baldwin successively to include in the answer to the Speech from the Throne an amendment critical of the Act of Union, each one milder than the preceding one.[38] Then W.H. Merritt proposed a still milder amendment, reserving to the House the modification of the union if found expedient. It carried by a majority of 16, but subsequently, reported Smyles wrathfully,

> the near slavish bankrupt pretended reformers reversed their stand of yesterday. They struck out "hereafter may think expedient" and put in "subject to modification as *experience* may dictate." Hincks pointed out that this was tantamount to an acknowledgement that they accepted the Act of Union as it was. Of the reformers, only Baldwin, Price, Smith and Cooke supported him. [39]

The government, Smyles guessed, had put pressure on the others to reverse themselves, as indeed it had. Sydenham wrote:

> They introduced some rather ambiguous words about the Union. I sent for the members who I knew had voted from ignorance... and away they went directly and voted the words out again... by a very large majority. [40]

Merritt himself seconded the change in his original amendment, whose words, the Governor and his supporters affected to fear, might become "a trap" for the unwary.[41] What Sydenham wanted was an unequivocal acceptance of the union and a pledge to give it a fair trial.

As the session wore on, the Reformers of Upper Canada one by one came under Smyles's suspicion. Thorburn, Parke, even Boswell, who had pressed Draper hardest for a clear statement on responsible government, were denounced along with "the other rats" who were "throwing off the cloak of the hypocrite and coming out regular tories."[42] Among the French Canadians, Cuvillier, Parent, Caron, Debartsch and (possibly) Morin were classified as supporters of Sydenham.[43] Viger was referred to as a "venerable patriot" and "the most logical" of the representatives from Lower Canada. Smyles regretted that not one of his speeches was reported, the reporters being "all Tories" and "gorged with prejudice.[44] The only Upper Canadian Reformers who remained true to the cause were Hincks, Baldwin, Price, Durand and Smith (presumably Smith of Wentworth). Praise these men in the *Volunteer*, urged Smyles, and "give it to the others,"repeating old stories against them as if they had just been reported from Kingston.[45]

While these discouraging developments were occurring in Kingston, Mackenzie in Rochester was having difficulty in financing the *Volunteer*. It was not paying its way and publication had become irregular.[46] Mackenzie's last resources, from the sale of cherished possessions, were almost exhausted and he realized that he would be unable to carry on much longer.[47]

Mackenzie had been desperately trying to get the Upper Canada Reformers to unite on some course in opposition to Sydenham. Smyles's letters of July 15 must have ended his hopes of upsetting the smooth implementation of the union and of creating a demand for independence. The *Volunteer* had not been welcomed, and Smyles reported that there was little he could do to help its circulation. People were either loyal or afraid, and no one had any principles about the kind of "organic change" the *Volunteer* advocated. For example, before the opening of the session, a meeting in the London District, with Elias Moore, a former MPP and a Reformer, in the chair,[48] had resolved to advise Reform members to test the stability of the ministry upon some question involving the economic welfare of the province rather than upon the abstract principles of responsible government.[49] Here was a clear indication that the proposed British loan was having the effect Sydenham and Lord John Russell expected. Smyles predicted that after the British corn and timber duties should have been repealed, as they would have to be, time would show that it would be better for Canada to be a part of the United States. But this was a process that would take half a century. The only events that would accelerate annexation were war between Great Britain and the United States — or a revolution in England against a Tory government.[50]

Some opposition to Sydenham's policies did develop during the latter part of the session but it was not of a nature to give either Smyles or Mackenzie much comfort. Yet "the Lords of Thomson's creation" proved not to be completely pliable. Respecting the District Council's Bill for Upper Canada Smyles learned that there was "some chance of its being so altered and amended as to defeat the ministry on one of its own measures."[51] That was in effect what happened. An important provision of the bill was rewritten to make the bill less obnoxious to the Legislative Council: the tax these elective local government bodies could impose on wild land was reduced.[52] The bill was not acceptable to staunch Reformers either. Baldwin fought every clause that gave the Governor power to name the officers of the councils, but he could not obtain the united backing of Reformers. Even Hincks went over to the government's side. Only six Upper Canada Reformers marked their dissatisfaction with the District Council's Bill by negative votes.[53]

Four weeks later Smyles had become completely disgusted and had given up hope of seeing effective opposition to Sydenham. His Naturalization Bill, Board of Works bill, Court of Requests bill, District Councils bill — all had been accepted. The Governor-General, in effect, not the House, disposed of the provincial revenue, since no appropriation bill could be introduced without his approval;[54] he controlled the press and could silence criticism. The "Parlement" simply registered his "edicts." All that remained was the Bank Bill. Sydenham's plan for a government bank which alone should have the power to issue bank notes was expected to win the support of liberal French and English members and to be opposed by Tories, speculators, and the Montreal merchants and bankers.[55] Smyles would have approved of the creation of such a bank but not if that meant another feather in Sydenham's cap. He predicted that the bill would pass and that Francis Hincks would be appointed inspector of the new institution. Smyles informed Mackenzie that:

> 3 weeks more and the Governor will have reserved all the power and patronage of the colony to himself.... Your labor of years, your loss of life so to speak, will be in vain unless McLeod is *hanged*, of which there is no probability. [56]

But the bill did not pass. Opposition came from frightened debtors as well as from the bankers.[57] Smyles explained:

> He cannot carry it. The country is so much indebted to the banks that in the event of its being brought into operation they will call in all their debts and produce ruin and confusion. [58]

The bill was debated at length in committee and then negatived, on Baldwin's motion, as inexpedient. "Mr. Hincks, of the Toronto *Examiner*, lost thereby £1,500 per annum — the price at which Lord Sydenham bought him up," reported Smyles with grim satisfaction.[59]

Smyles's letters to Mackenzie and to the New York *Herald* completely ignored the constructive aspects of Sydenham's work in Canada, and therefore when Hincks went over to the Governor's side Smyles could only regard him as a "bare faced scoundrel" who ought to be "*hanged*." Smyles did not see, as Hincks did, that Sydenham was forcing through changes in parliamentary procedures that were necessary to the development of ministerial responsibility, and departmental reforms essential to sound financial practices. Hincks had realized also that responsible government would make unified, disciplined political parties essential, but his earlier efforts to mold Reformers into such a body were now made a reproach to him.

> His violence against the government was one of the main causes driving Thorburn, Boswell and others from supporting Baldwin [wrote Smyles]. In a caucus the night before Parliament met he drove Thorburn off in a rage because he wanted him to oppose Sydenham *nolens volens*, right or wrong. [60]

Hincks had not actually been appointed to any office before the Governor-General died, but an appointment was generally expected, and therefore Smyles, who was burning to injure Hincks, urged Mackenzie to put his "whole strength into a circular addressed to the electors of Oxford" — where Hincks would have to stand for re-election once he accepted office. Smyles wanted a circular "full of scorching fire" and supported with documents that would show Hincks up as "a public liar." "As you keep everything," he wrote, "maybe you will be able to aid us...."[61] But Mackenzie, although he may have replied to this request, had already turned his attention to influencing the politics of Canada by other means than the printed word.

Smyles remained in Kingston until after Sydenham's death, noting the increased restlessness of the Legislative Council after the defeat of Sydenham's Whig supporters in England, the failure of the government's bank scheme, Neilson's unsuccessful attempt to get a resolution recommending an all-inclusive amnesty, and the resolution of the House that it was expedient to tax all American produce entering the province.

> This [Smyles predicted correctly] will not go through. It would hurt the carrying trade and benefit Upper Canada farmers at the expense of Lower Canada farmers who grow no wheat. [62]

The scramble for a share of the British loan, district against district, section against section, inland communities against those on the waterways, moved Smyles to sarcasm. He likened their representatives to a crowd of ragged urchins scrambling for the handful of coppers thrown into the air by a gentleman who wanted to amuse himself watching them fight for his largesse.[63] Detailed accounts of the closing days of the session were, however, no longer sent to Mackenzie. His *Volunteer* had been suspended after the issue of July 24.

Mackenzie had come to realize that it now seemed hopeless to expect the old Reformers of Upper Canada to create the kind of democratic society he dreamed of, and even more hopeless to think they might achieve the independence of the colony. The one hope remaining lay in war between the United States and Great Britain, and to this topic the *Volunteer* was devoted for the rest of its short life. Peace or war rested on the outcome of the trial of Alexander McLeod. Several persons reported to have participated in the burning of the *Caroline* had been arrested when they ventured to cross the lakes. One by one they were released for lack of evidence but when McLeod, Deputy Sheriff of the Niagara District, was arrested — for the third time — at Lewiston in November 1840, he was held for trial without bail, charged with the murder of Amos Durfee, the one person known to have been killed in the *Caroline* affair. Great Britain demanded the release of McLeod on the ground that, even if he had helped burn the *Caroline*, which was not admitted (although Lord Sydenham intimated that McLeod had gone around boasting of his participation[64]), the United States had no right under international law to try on a criminal charge one who had acted under military orders. Secretary of State Forsyth would not acknowledge this principle of international law. His successor, Daniel Webster, did. Webster tried to get New York State not to try McLeod, but Governor Seward insisted on the state's right to do so. The interference of the federal government and its efforts to secure McLeod's release were in Thurlow Weed's opinion a mistake, likely to hurt the Whig party in New York. "All our border folks want war," he wrote. Weed was convinced that the court would not convict McLeod and that if his case "had been left to New York's grooming, all would have been quietly over in three weeks." In fact, Governor Seward assured the President that McLeod had a sound alibi and that if he should be convicted, he would be pardoned.[65]

Mackenzie had been following the McLeod case with intense interest. He tried to change Cushing's attitude on the case by sending him long articles on the subject which he had written for the Rochester *Daily Advertiser* under the pseudonym Donald McDonald,[66] but Cushing continued to support Webster's policy. It was one thing for Cushing, as a member of the Whig opposition, to embarrass the Van Buren administration by furthering petitions for Mackenzie's release, advocating independence for the Canadas in close association with the United States, and calling down the vengeance of Heaven on the British authorities in Canada in an impassioned Fourth of July address: "God of Justice, where sleeps thy thunder?" It was quite another matter for him to do so now as a member of the party in power on whom the responsibility would fall for leading the country to the brink of war, and perhaps over it.[67]

Cushing's attitude was a great disappointment to Mackenzie. "I continue to write you, although you take no notice of my letters," he explained,

> because looking to your whole course of years, so far as I have known it, you appear to me earnestly to seek the removal of British power from this continent. [68]

> Much might and would be done if those who worked knew it was of any use. Is there any way we could properly know that? [69]

Cushing maintained his discreet silence about Whig policy, nor did he respond to Mackenzie's hint that he had in progress a 48-page almanac "on the regular war principle" which could be printed in New York, with engravings — if only he could get credit.

After Webster became Secretary of State in March 1841 Mackenzie and other ardent Patriots watched with mounting anger his efforts on McLeod's behalf. When his trial, scheduled to take place at Lockport in March, was postponed until June, E.B. O'Callaghan and Donald M'Leod became convinced that, from the Patriot point of view, it would end in "nothingness." "Dan is cock of the walk," wrote M'Leod. "Harrison is just in the White House."[70] Articles attacking Webster and recalling American grievances against Great Britain began with the first issue of the *Volunteer* and continued to appear. Finally, in the last issue of the paper before its suspension on July 24, by which time it had become crystal clear that neither Whigs nor Democrats when in power would take an unyielding stand towards Great Britain, Mackenzie hinted that some Patriots were advocating the renewal of border warfare, although he himself was still counselling patience.[71]

No further issue of the *Volunteer* appeared until September 25, just two days before McLeod's trial was scheduled to take place at Utica, to which city a change of venue had been granted the accused. Nelson Gorham asked Mackenzie to "contrive" by some means to procure evidence against McLeod. "Right or wrong he should be hung," if not for the *Caroline* affair, then "for murdering those poor negroes at Niagara."[72] As the New York *Herald* suspected, Mackenzie was also asked by the district attorney, L.S. Woods, to suggest witnesses for the prosecution. He did his best to oblige and in the *Volunteer* of September 25 he disparaged the character of the women who were to provide McLeod's alibi.[73]

Mackenzie did not feel vindictive towards McLeod as an individual. He was much more anxious for a public trial that would spread the "horrid details" of the affair throughout the United States and thus increase hostility towards England than he was for the punishment of McLeod himself. Yet he seems to have been aware that only if McLeod were hanged would the hoped-for war come to pass. Mackenzie went to Utica to cover the trial. Precisely what he thought of it cannot be learned from his *Volunteer*, since the issue of November 17, in which presumably it was discussed, is missing, but his letters show that he thought the trial had been a "sham battle" and that the "murderer" had been acquitted by "intrigue," an opinion not without justification.[74]

While the trial was pending, the authorities of both the United States and Canada had begun to fear there would be a revival of Patriot activities if McLeod were acquitted. Indeed, some Patriot sympathizers did not wait for the verdict, or even for the trial, which at one point seemed unlikely to take place at all. Sometime in March 1841 Benjamin Lett attempted to burn the S.S. *Minos* but failed.[75] He then planned to destroy a lock on the Welland Canal with the assistance of E.A. Theller and Samuel McAfee. Lett was captured at Buffalo on September 6, before the plan of the conspirators could be carried out. Theller then did the job, McAfee being "timid about it," although he took Theller and the powder as far as Port Robinson.[76] There was another attempt to destroy British vessels, which did not succeed, and another attempt to blow up a lock on the Welland, which did minor damage.[77] Sometime in September a cache of powder believed to belong to the Patriots was destroyed at Syracuse with the loss of several lives. On September 24, 65 kegs of powder were stolen at Lockport to replace it.[78] It was doubtless this series of events that led President Tyler to issue his proclamation of September 25 denouncing the Hunters' organization and warning its members that if they fell into the hands of the British the government would not interfere on their behalf.[79]

One of Mackenzie's ardent old coadjutors, S.C. Frey, was not in favour of a renewal of border activities. He had lost all confidence in the Hunters, approved of Mackenzie's plan for forming associations of "true" Patriots for "true" purposes, but otherwise favoured letting the Canadian reformers "sweat it out" under Tory management until they were ready to act with unanimity.[80] Donald M'Leod, also, had no further use for the Hunters and, months before the trial, had given up hope of anything being accomplished by the Canadians themselves. "It's all over at last," he wrote, as soon as the results of the Canadian election became known.[81]

Since the rebellion Louis J. Papineau had not favoured "partial and weak insurrections & invasions when the result would only be but disastrous to all concerned." But it now seemed to him that the tense diplomatic situation favoured the Patriots. Papineau was eager for Alexander McLeod's conviction and sure that it would mean war. If McLeod should be acquitted, then he hoped that war could be provoked by other means. He enquired of Mackenzie,

> Are you not inclined to think that with a demonstration next
> winter on the part of Fairfield [the Governor of Maine] and his

people, a few bold and disastrous invasions of Upper Canada from this side would soon arouse the ire of the Tory government... as things are now, would not a few attacks on Canada bring on a quarrel and Canada's emancipation? Are the reports to be credited that the Hunters are organized and doing? Are those reports true?

Papineau urged Mackenzie to write to Governor Fairfield, and to "Blow the Fire."[82] But the poor *Volunteer* had no strength left. The missing issue already referred to was the last blast from its feeble bellows for many months.

The trial of McLeod proved to be a damp squib. It did not arouse the expected public interest at Utica, where spectators never filled the courtroom,[83] nor did the verdict produce the disturbances on the frontier that the New York *Herald* had expected.[84] Apathy prevailed among Americans and discouragement among the Canadians. "What a sad turn the trial of McLeod has taken," Papineau observed. "Where are now the prospects of war?"[85] James Mackenzie wrote:

> There seems to be a general conviction that McLeod was let go. But there seems to be the utmost apathy.... Nothing but war between the two nations will awake matters again. [86]

Shortly after the trial, James went to Ohio and began to teach school, an occupation he intended to be only a stepping stone to the bar.[87] Mackenzie did not neglect to act on Papineau's hint that he should get in touch with people in Maine, but from this potential trouble spot also discouraging responses came: Maine would await the negotiations to be undertaken by the federal government.[88]

Mackenzie now gave up hope. Further attempts on Canada "in defiance of both governments" would, it was plain, be useless. Moreover, he had not the means to continue his propaganda warfare any longer. On October 20 he noted that the family had not a grain of flour, nor meal, nor money when, fortunately, a $3.00 subscription arrived.[89] About the end of January he published not a full issue of the *Volunteer* but a small extra — not much more than a handbill — in which he told his subscribers in effect that he was turning his back on Canadian problems. He announced:

> Believing that my further interference in Canadian politics would be unavailing, and having more than fulfilled my solemn pledge to the gentlemen of Lower Canada where the revolt began... I intend to devote myself to the study and practice of law.... [90]

Mackenzie seems to have wavered from this decision when Dr. A.K. Mackenzie of Lockport, a double dealer who posed as an ardent Patriot while acting as an informer to the government of Upper Canada,[91] tried to get him to create another McLeod affair. This man proposed that Mackenzie should bring about the arrest of J.S. Hogan[92] when the latter should visit Rochester. There was no doubt Hogan had been one of the *Caroline* party and he was expected to raise precisely the issue the Patriots wanted by admitting it with pride and looking to his country to defend him. Dr. A.K. Mackenzie, who had known Hogan since childhood, did not want the young man harmed, but he seemed to think he could use Hogan to keep up Patriot agitation on the frontier, from which it is likely the doctor profited, without putting his life in danger. He tried to persuade Hogan that by consenting to this scheme he would "immortalize himself" and he acknowledged to him that the Patriots were anxious to prevent the *Caroline* case being settled by the commissioners who were negotiating the Webster-Ashburton Treaty.[93]

Hogan agreed to co-operate with A.K. Mackenzie, but W.L. Mackenzie at first refused to have anything to do with the plot, since he could not answer for the results to the young man.[94] Hogan was arrested at Lockport, released because the warrant was improperly made out, and advised by W.L. Mackenzie to leave Lockport without delay. Subsequently Mackenzie changed his mind about Hogan and decided to have him arrested if he should cross the lakes again. Meanwhile Hogan had become a little uneasy and sought an assurance from Sir Charles Bagot that the British government would protect him if he went to the United States. He received a somewhat noncommittal reply and was advised that any British subject "who may be obnoxious to the Americans would not act wisely in putting himself into their power."[95] Hogan did not take this advice. On March 31, 1842, when he arrived at Rochester, Mackenzie was informed and got Dr. Theller to have him arrested.[96] At the hearing before a police justice Dr. A.K. Mackenzie testified that several times, both in Canada and in the United States, Hogan had boasted of being one of the *Caroline* party and of having suggested the plan to MacNab, who took the credit. The Rochester *Evening Post* reported:

> Hogan behaved with spirit. He placed his trust and confidence
> in the power of his country — in the wooden walls of old
> England.

The court, however, decided that it could not enquire into a case of murder in the county of Niagara on a Monroe county warrant which, moreover, had not set forth the facts sufficiently and had been issued by one magistrate and made returnable before another.[97] Hogan was placed under police protection until he could return to Canada. A correspondent of the New York *Herald* reported that the captain of the *Gore* had refused to take him, saying he "would not have such a puppy on board unless he were put in a box and regularly labelled." Hogan's confessions were dismissed as "braggadocio" and the results of the hearing termed "gratifying," since no further agitation over the *Caroline* was desired. "The Patriots," added this writer, "are awfully chagrined."[98] In the end the whole affair, which Mackenzie had expected to cause "some noise in the world"[99] fizzled out. Public interest in the Patriot cause was gone.

A few months later Congress passed an act to prevent any new McLeod or

Hogan incident from disturbing the peace between Great Britain and the United States. Federal judges were to take cognizance of cases in which any subject of a foreign state claimed that his act had been done under the authority of a foreign government. The constitutionality and expediency of this measure was contended for on the grounds that "the peace of the Union ought not to be jeoparded by a fragmentary part." Its constitutionality has never since been questioned.[100]

It will be recalled that the judges of Monroe County had already rejected Mackenzie's application for admission to the bar. Nevertheless, after he gave up the *Volunteer* he opened an office for the practice of law, in the hope that he would be admitted when he should have become a citizen. Meanwhile he intended to study law and to earn a living by collecting debts, auditing accounts and performing minor legal services at the courts such as filing papers. During the three months following the cessation of the *Volunteer* he found the pickings from these sources so slim that he began to solicit his friends in Albany and Philadelphia for a patronage appointment and raged with bitterness against some of his former associates in Buffalo, such as the then attorney-general of New York, George P. Barker, when he did not succeed.[101] "Your luck in these regions, I suspect, is problematical. You are too much of a Leggett," explained O'Callaghan in answer to one of these diatribes.[102] Leggett was the radical editor of the *Plain Dealer*.

Mackenzie then revived the *Volunteer*, announcing euphemistically that he found editing a weekly paper would not interfere with his other engagements. This time the *Volunteer* was not to be a Patriot paper but simply a liberal political journal, not opposed to banks of discount but still opposed to banks of issue; anti-tariff, but rejoicing in the new trade regulations established between the United States and Great Britain; still hostile to the latter country but not advocating or expecting war. As James Mackenzie had predicted,[103] the new venture was not a success. It lasted for two issues, April 25 and May 10, 1843. Mackenzie then abandoned the *Volunteer* — and left Rochester for New York City, literally "starved out",[104] and helped on his way once again by the ever-generous Henry O'Rielly and by John Allan, mayor of Rochester and owner of a line of barges and boats on the Erie Canal.[105]

## Chapter VII

# THE RETURN TO THE METROPOLIS

$M$ackenzie arrived in New York for the second time on June 12, 1842. First he had to face his creditors in that city, and second he had to find some way of earning a living. He was still in debt about $3,000 to George Bruce & Co.,[1] the type founders who had supplied him in Canada, and he was also in debt some $330.00 to Harper Bros. for books sold him in 1837. He could have taken advantage of New York's Bankruptcy Act, but he scorned to do so. Instead, he gave Harpers his note and they acceded to his request for four more years' credit, but they did not enable him to start the bookshop he had thought of establishing.[2] The Bruce firm likewise agreed not to bother him but to "leave him to his best discretion" to liquidate his debt to them.[3]

While his American friends were negotiating for a patronage appointment for him — which was not forthcoming at this time — Mackenzie was not idle. He kept body and soul together by collecting some of his old debts due for his *Gazette*, and he compiled an Irish Repeal Almanack which he expected to publish, but which seems not to have appeared.[4] He also began to write for the *Plebian Weekly* and was soon offered a sub-editorship on that and other papers. Because these subordinate posts would have limited his cherished independence Mackenzie refused them.[5] The *Plebian* published James Gemmell's detailed account of the sufferings of the Canadian and American prisoners in Van Diemen's Land, from which Gemmell had recently escaped, and it deplored the failure of the American government to interest itself in the fate of the exiles. It is probable that Gemmell, who visited Mackenzie in New York, had his editorial assistance in preparing this vivid account, in which Gemmell said of Mackenzie:

> I saw that he faithfully performed his duty behind Toronto and
> if some who do not know him have blamed him in the United
> States, I am sure that those who were his companions cannot
> have done so.[6]

On August 2, 1842, Mackenzie was elected actuary and librarian of the

Mechanic's Institute of New York City. He did not obtain the post without some opposition on account of his political course in the United States but, thanks to the support of Thomas Ewbank, the President, and of the Bruce brothers, who were members, only eight votes were cast against him.[7] Mackenzie at first professed to "delight" in the duties of his position at the Institute, which had a good library and an extensive collection of foreign and domestic newspapers and magazines. After a few months he wrote to O'Rielly that he was doing well. This turned out to mean that he was getting by without adding to his debts.[8]

Mackenzie worked incessantly. He solicited friends for aid in securing memoirs or brief biographies of eminent Irish-Americans, and he planned to follow this compilation with a similar work about "illustrious" Scotsmen in America who had supported the American Revolution.[9] He began to put together also "a true sketch of the political career... of Martin Van Buren."[10] Before long he found it necessary to lay aside the books he had projected. His life, he complained, had become one of "continuous and wearisome drudgery," the duties of the Institute detaining him every night until ten.[11] His fatigue is perhaps to be attributed to the presence of another baby,[12] to the serious illness of his wife and of one of his daughters, and to his poverty.

The post of actuary did not prove to be as profitable as expected. The Institute had 1,400 members who should have paid a fee of $2.00 each. Mackenzie was supposed to collect the fees and was entitled to keep 60% for himself, but less than a fifth of the members paid. "I never could have made $500 out of it unless I had pressured many to pay who could ill afford it," he explained. Since he could barely keep his family on the fees, he resigned at the close of the year for which he had been engaged. On October 14, 1843, his official connection with the Institute ended.[13] But this was not the whole story. Mackenzie admitted that he had spoken his mind "so very plain" that he had lost many friends in the Institute, a majority of whose members were Whigs, and one suspects that he was eased out of his position.[14]

For some months prior to his resignation from the Institute Mackenzie had been dreaming of publishing a newspaper once more.[15] He had said he was through with politics, both American and Canadian, but cut off from politics Mackenzie was, as Adam Ramage observed, "like a fish out of water."[16] There was as yet no hope of returning to Canada, and besides, since April 11 he had been an American citizen. Another presidential election was in the offing and another Democratic candidate had to be chosen. Mackenzie could not keep silent. Martin Van Buren, who had failed of re-election in 1840, was hoping to be the candidate of the Democratic Party in 1844. Mackenzie, who had supported him in 1840, specifically on the Independent Treasury issue, decided this time to do him all the damage he could and to prevent his nomination. Van Buren had hurt the Patriot cause! He had treated the help given him in previous campaigns by *Mackenzie's Gazette* as if it had been utterly worthless, when in fact it had been given at the sacrifice of personal feeling and out of sincere regard for the public welfare! He had kept Mackenzie in prison, thereby inflicting intense mental suffering and physical privations on him and his helpless family! Mackenzie would now take his revenge; and he could do it without harping on his own grievances. He would destroy Van Buren's credibility as a public figure. The thought was sweet to him. It was for this purpose, not to discuss Canadian grievances or to advocate more border warfare,[17] that he established his New York *Examiner*, an eight-page paper that appeared for the first time on September 30, 1844, was soon reduced to four pages, and lasted for only five issues.

While still at the Institute Mackenzie had begun to write a sketch of Van Buren's political career based on "many documents" he had "accepted."[18] Among these were the "16,000 American newspapers, some 400 a year for the last 40 years" which the Institute possessed.

> Every moment of my time is spent at the quill [he wrote]. I must get ahead and I prepare quietly in these rooms to the best of my power. [19]

With concentrated energy and feverish haste he attacked that mountain of source material, reading, clipping and scribbling away, night after night, compiling his indictment of Van Buren and his Regency supporters. No wonder his eyesight became impaired![20]

In the first issue of the *Examiner* Mackenzie admitted that his earlier ideas on public men and public questions had undergone some revision. He now proclaimed himself a party man and a Democrat, but he asserted that in Van Buren he had been "cruelly deceived." Van Buren had undermined the safeguards of democracy by an organized spoils system and had pretended to be opposed to paper money although in the past he had actually favoured chartered banks of issue.

During Van Buren's eight years in the Senate of New York, 1812-1820, a large proportion of the banking capital of the state had been incorporated. Van Buren claimed that most of the applications for charters that were rejected were so disposed of on his motion, every application but one having his vote recorded against it.[21] Mackenzie rightly branded this statement as untrue: Van Buren had voted for some charters, withdrawn his opposition to others, and permitted his "tail" to vote for others while he himself abstained. He and his infamous Regency had actually caused "an immense number of banks with anti-republican charters to be made," that is, with charters that did not contain the restrictions and safeguards Mackenzie thought desirable for banks of issue. Van Buren had also pretended hostility to the Bank of the United States, a feeling really rooted in the failure of his petition for a branch of that bank at Albany.[22] To top all, as Governor he had been the "author" of the "Safety Fund plunder scheme" which required banks to contribute in advance to a general fund to be used in case of bank failures.

There can be no question that Van Buren, like other New York State politicians, had turned the legislative power to grant or withhold bank charters and to distribute the stock of the new institutions to the advantage of himself and his party, and that the administration of some of these banks had been scandalous. But the *Examiner* related their unsavoury histories as if all their misdoings had been Van Buren's personal sins. Mackenzie damned the Albany Regency right and left, ignoring the fact that the restraining law requiring banks of issue to have a state charter, undemocratic as it was in the eyes of the Loco-Focos, had at least limited the number of the "rag-paper shops" he was fond of denouncing. He ignored also the fact that the charters issued in the late 1820s and 1830s contained more stringent requirements than the earlier ones — even if they were not enforced.

Prior to Van Buren's short term as Governor of New York State there had been numerous serious bank failures. In the sessions of 1826 and 1827 not one bank charter could be obtained or renewed. New York's General Bank Act of 1827 imposed such severe personal liability clauses on directors and stockholders of banks that no new banks were chartered in 1828. When the unpopular sections of that act were repealed, so far as they related to the personal liability of stockholders, Van Buren introduced his Safety Fund Device to give the public some degree of protection and one that bankers would accept.[23] Subsequently in that session the legislature granted or renewed some 30 bank charters.

Experience revealed the weaknesses of the Safety Fund Act, and at the time Mackenzie was writing they were being laid bare in legislative documents.[24] Mackenzie gives the impression that Van Buren, as Governor, had deliberately lent his support in 1829 to the creation of a device for plunder. The truth is that in this period New York State, like other political communities, was gradually feeling its way towards the enactment of — and public acceptance of — sound legislation respecting banks and paper money.

Mackenzie also unjustly accused Van Buren of being "the author" of the "pet bank" scheme under which, after the removal of the federal government's deposits from the Second Bank of the United States, certain "pet" state banks had received them. Not until Van Buren "thought he saw a chance of keeping the presidency by turning to honesty for a time" did he denounce the chartered banks and advocate an Independent Treasury.[25]

Mackenzie seems to have been close to the truth, although he did not put his conclusion fairly. An Independent Treasury had been under discussion for some time. One important New York State Democrat pointed out that it might serve to restore the Jeffersonian image of the Democratic Party in the minds of the "thousands" of honest men who had left it, disgusted by the "memorable Bank and speculating era from '33 to '37."[26] It was important to Van Buren to keep his Jacksonian image as an advocate of sound money. He had expected that the deposit banks, the Pets, which were subject to Treasury regulations regarding their specie reserves, would be a means of checking over-issues of paper by the banks with which they dealt. After May 1837 most of the government's deposit banks were involved in the general suspension of specie payments. Van Buren had then been obliged to come up with some other proposal for keeping the public revenues, an Independent Treasury.

How had Van Buren betrayed democracy? In 1821 he had opposed the establishment of universal manhood suffrage in New York State. (It had since been achieved, except for Negroes, and by 1843 Van Buren had come around to praising the amendment.) He had also opposed direct popular election of justices of the peace because he thought elected justices would find it difficult to be impartial in those days of open balloting. He wanted them to be named by the Governor from lists presented by the (elected) supervisors and the judges of the Court of Common Pleas.[27] No class of officials had been more bitterly criticized in Upper Canada by Mackenzie than the appointed Tory justices of the peace. He could see in Van Buren's argument nothing but a desire to retain an extensive and disciplined body of patronage appointees throughout the state, ready to support him and his Albany Regency friends. Van Buren's centralizing system, he declared, was a threat to democracy in America.[28] Throughout his political life Mackenzie balked at party discipline, but in his more judicial moments he acknowledged that political warfare, to be effective, had to be something more than guerrilla warfare. In his less temperate moments he was ready to beat an opponent, in this instance Van Buren, with any stick that came to hand.

Criticisms of Van Buren, vindictive certainly on Mackenzie's part, were also being made by some within Van Buren's own party. The years 1820-1840 comprised a period in which disciplined political parties were being organized from the state to the township level. There were those within New York State clearly unhappy with this development. It had been an experience that independent-minded men resented. Lorenzo Sherwood, of Hamilton, New York, subsequently informed O'Rielly that:

> For two months preceding the convention [of 1844] scarcely a voice was to be heard in our party in this section of the State that did not express regret at the prospective nomination of Van Buren.... I have never known him guilty of being a pioneer in reform of governmental abuses... he has stood aloof from the bold heart & staunch hands through whom... the popular security was to be effected. [29]

Mackenzie's criticism of Van Buren was no harsher than this. Henry O'Rielly reported the general astonishment at Mackenzie's intimate knowledge of the political history of New York State, which it has been possible only to hint at here. He was somewhat distressed at Mackenzie's attacks on some prominent Democrats, although he was perturbed by the degree of corruption in the state and admitted that Van Buren had "a rotten conservative bodyguard." O'Rielly, once a staunch supporter of Van Buren, had come to doubt whether the state could be carried for the Democrats if Van Buren were nominated.[30] "I can scarcely tax my memory with a single remark in favor of renominating Mr. Van Buren," he acknowledged.[31]

James Mackenzie had long been trying to convince his father that Van Buren was nothing but a selfish schemer, a "cold calculating character." "Nothing but party machinery can keep him afloat," he wrote. "He has no abiding place in the hearts of his countrymen."[32] Some of Mackenzie's correspondents were troubled by the inconsistency of his position. Not so James. "I agree with you," he wrote, "that though you once supported Mr. Van Buren, you are consistent in opposing him upon the data you have furnished in your *Examiner*.[33]

After three issues had been published it was plain to Mackenzie that he would have to stop the *Examiner*, his third unsuccessful venture into journalism in the United States. He had hoped to continue his paper until the fall of 1844 and had "laid in a mine of facts" to use against Van Buren, but "for want, not of gun powder but of match paper" his mine failed.[34] O'Callaghan and a group of his Whig friends tried to make it possible for Mackenzie to use the rest of his "gunpowder." They raised $120.00 for him, which he received through Dr. A.S. Doane, who had been Health Officer for the Port of New York while the Whigs were in power. This sum enabled Mackenzie to bring out two more issues of his *Examiner*. Beyond that, all Doane could suggest was sending a subscription list around among the Whigs of New York. Mackenzie decided he would sooner let his paper fail than have it said he had become a mere puppet of the Whig party.[35] He preferred to cherish his independence even in defeat.

Mackenzie was now faced with the prospect of unemployment once more. He had begun the *Examiner* with about $200.00 which he had managed to scrape together, no doubt by pinching economy, and the venture was on the point of failing. At this moment, when he was perhaps unnerved by the prospect of scattering his family or putting them through another winter of destitution such as they had known in Rochester, temptation was put in his way by Thomas Fitnam, an Irish friend in Philadelphia who held a minor appointment in the State Department.

President John Tyler was hoping that the Democratic Party would select him as its candidate in 1844. Originally a Democrat, Tyler had broken with the Jacksonians and had been elected Vice-President on the Whig ticket in 1840. He had succeeded President William Henry Harrison when the latter had died a month after his inauguration. The Whigs, however, wanted to re-establish a national bank, and on this issue Tyler broke with them, became again a Democrat, and strove to build a party following of his own.[36] It seemed to Fitnam that conflict between the supporters of J.C. Calhoun and those of Van Buren would result in Tyler's being nominated at the Democratic Convention in May 1844. He therefore suggested that Mackenzie speak of Tyler occasionally "in terms of kindness..." in his *Examiner*. Fitnam, who was on friendly terms with the President's son Robert, proposed to try to secure a patronage appointment for Mackenzie, and to do so in such a way that it would not be supposed that Mackenzie "desired anything of the kind." "There are times," he wrote, "when a little prevarication for expediency's sake is absolutely necessary."[37]

Mackenzie promptly fell in with Fitnam's plan. He wrote that he would "rejoice" to accept a humble appointment, deplored bitterly his inability to continue publishing, and praised Tyler's stand while still a Democratic member of Congress.

> Perhaps even you are not aware that President Tyler was the first to propose a divorce of bank and state [he informed

Fitnam]. He did so in Congress in 1819. His speech against Banks and paper I find in the *National Intelligencer* of that year....
[38]

Fitnam had intended to show Mackenzie's letter at the White House, but its tone was too humble. He decided it would be better for him "to keep up an appearance of respectability and independence." Fitnam arranged an interview in New York for Mackenzie with the President's son, who handled patronage matters for his father in New York and Philadelphia,[39] and he carefully coached him to avoid expressing a doubt about his ability to continue his paper, or at least to put this on the ground of his duty to his family, not want of means. The interview with Robert Tyler took place, Mackenzie managed it well, and on November 7 Fitnam was able to inform him that Robert Tyler had promised that he should have an inspectorship in the New York Customs House.[40]

In the interval Mackenzie had maintained his "appearance of... respectability and independence" by producing a fourth issue of the *Examiner*, and its tone and contents evidently were approved. This fourth issue is missing. Its major feature praised Tyler's Exchequer plan, if we may judge it by this complaint from a subscriber:

> His odious Exchequer, which... would be nothing else than a huge paper money machine... a national bank in disguise... shows him anything but an orthodox member of the republican school.... You have given him too much credit. [41]

President Tyler believed that "the naked Sub-Treasury" had been condemned at the polls, and early in his administration he had signed a bill repealing Van Buren's act. Nothing had been done by that act to restrict the issue of paper money and to establish a stable currency. Tyler wanted a Treasury arrangement that would answer both these purposes. What he proposed was the establishment of agencies in important cities to receive the dues of the United States in gold or silver or in the notes of specie paying banks. Under the supervision of a Board of Control, those agencies were to pay out U.S. Treasury notes redeemable in gold or silver on demand and were to maintain a metallic reserve of one-third against such notes. By issuing and recalling these notes, the Board would be able to control the volume of paper in circulation.[42]

All the provisions of Tyler's Exchequer plan cannot have pleased Mackenzie, but there were features of it which he must certainly have approved. In his Canada days, recognizing that paper money had come to stay, he had advocated a government bank of issue, and he still preferred one big bank to a thousand lesser "monsters." But he regarded "all this babble about banks" as useless. The important thing was "stability of the currency."[43] Tyler's Exchequer plan was not designed to abolish private banks of issue but it would have prevented the public revenue from being used for private profit and it placed the power to control the currency in the hands not of private banks but in those of a Board of Control appointed by an elected president and confirmed by an elected Senate.

In thus acknowledging the right of the people to control the banking system through their elected representatives, Tyler did not go as far as Charles Duncombe had in his little book *Free Banking*, a copy of which Duncombe sent to Caleb Cushing who was in charge of drafting a bill based on Tyler's proposals.[44] Tyler's Exchequer plan, a compromise between Van Buren's Sub-Treasury scheme and the national bank desired by the Whigs, pleased practically no one. Cushing's bill received an unfavourable report from the Committee on Ways and Means.

In his fifth and final issue, of November 1, 1843, Mackenzie reported the rumour that the President would propose the annexation of Texas. "Others may make a bugbear out of Texas but he, Tyler, hopes to see the republic extend over the whole continent."[45] How could Mackenzie bring himself to support a candidate who advocated the immediate annexation of Texas? Tyler insisted that he had national interests, not those of the slave states, in mind. Yet it was obvious that the slavery interests would be strengthened by the addition to the union of the Republic of Texas, where the peculiar institution already existed.

In his *Gazette* Mackenzie had taken a vigorous anti-slavery though not abolitionist stand.[46] In coming out for Tyler he was guilty of a glaring and discreditable inconsistency. Moreover, in committing the *Examiner* to his support, Mackenzie tarnished his hitherto shining independence as an editor. He had never been a party man. He had campaigned for Van Buren in the past without fear — and certainly without favour! He had refused to enlist under the banner of the New York Whigs. But when Fitnam intimated that a patronage appointment might be forthcoming from Tyler Mackenzie leaped at the bait. An appointment would mean that he could maintain his family and his *Examiner*. To take his revenge on Van Buren had become an obsession with him.

Mackenzie's elation on learning that Robert Tyler had promised him an inspectorship was shortlived. Fitnam had led him to think that the support of his *Examiner* was desired and that the inspectorship would enable him to continue it.[47] James also thought that what Tyler was interested in was the support of his father's "powerful pen."[48] Expecting to need more room to get out his paper, Mackenzie moved his family to a large house at 220 Williams St., New York.[49] But Edward Curtis, the Whig Collector of the Port of New York, had first to implement Robert Tyler's promise by recommending the appointment to J.C. Spencer, the Secretary of the Treasury, who had power to confirm or reject it. When confirmation did not come, Mackenzie asked W.J. Duane, a former secretary of the treasury, to write to Spencer on his behalf. Duane doubted whether the appointment had been made in consideration of Mackenzie's "past merits and sacrifices" as the latter evidently wished it to seem, but rather because he had assailed Van Buren "whom many men in power hate." He declined to write to Spencer, for whom he had no respect. The anxious Mackenzie then wrote twice to Spencer himself.[50] Spencer objected to the appointment on the ground that Mackenzie was an outlaw of the British government "for crimes not merely political."[51] Moreover he had violated the neutrality law of the United States, and he was the outspoken enemy of Van Buren whom, of course, no office-seeker like Spencer could yet afford to offend. His letters were ignored.[52]

Robert Tyler and Fitnam kept assuring Mackenzie that although the inspectorship could not be obtained some other appointment would be given him.[53] Eight months of misery, poverty, humiliation and despair followed. Mackenzie had at this time no regular source of income. His eyes troubled him, he suffered from rheumatism, his children had whooping cough and measles. Sometimes he had not a shilling in his pocket or a meal for his family. Every little item that could be spared went to the pawnshop to keep them in food. Mackenzie's later grim comment suffices: "Last winter tamed me and mine."[54] Meanwhile the promised appointment dangled before his eyes, just out of reach.

For some time Mackenzie had been at work upon a life of Van Buren, and in the November 11 issue of his *Examiner* he had announced his intention of publishing such a work. By April it had become his one financial asset. If the biography was to prevent Van Buren's nomination by the Democrats, all along Mackenzie's objective, it had to be published before their convention in May.

President Tyler was trying to build a personal party that would back his Texas policy and either make him the Democratic nominee for President in 1884 or enable him to throw the nomination to the candidate of his choice. In the spring of 1843 he had begun to purge the Post Office and Treasury Departments of Whig appointees, but he did not tackle patronage problems in New York State until the spring of 1844.[55]

In April, Dr. A.N. Miller, Tyler's brother-in-law, came to New York on a "political pilgrimage," and an interview with him was arranged for Mackenzie. Fitnam, who had begun to doubt whether Tyler could get the Democratic nomination after all, advised Mackenzie to get the Van Buren biography out before the convention and to make the best bargain he could with Miller.[56] The interview took place and once again Mackenzie was promised an appointment as soon as Curtis could be removed from the Customs House. But while Congress was in session he could not be removed, not only because Congress would not confirm a Tyler appointee as his successor, but also because Tyler feared to lose votes for his Texas treaty by removing him.[57] "This is where the difficulty lies," Fitnam explained.[58]

Meanwhile O'Callaghan was trying to convince Mackenzie that Tyler's supporters were not to be trusted and that the Whigs would buy the biography if Van Buren were nominated. O'Callaghan arranged an interview for Mackenzie with Thurlow Weed and urged the latter to lend him a press and types so that he could publish his anti-Van Buren *Examiner* throughout the campaign.[59] No definite arrangement had been concluded by Mackenzie with either side when, on May 29, the Democratic Convention at Baltimore nominated — James K. Polk! Neither Whigs nor Tylerites now had any need of the biography on which Mackenzie had lavished so much labour.

Mackenzie regarded Polk's nomination — and possible election — with disfavour. "Is slavery forever to dictate the chiefs of this great empire?" he enquired,[60] overlooking the fact that out of hatred for Van Buren (who, he felt, had "got his deservings") he himself had supported the pro-Texas Tyler.

After Congress adjourned, President Tyler gave Cornelius Van Ness an interim appointment as Collector.[61] He took office in mid-July and immediately began "cutting away the Clay and Webster vines that clung to the walls of the federal agencies." Sixty men were summarily dismissed from the Customs House and hundreds of temporary $3.00-a-day appointments were created which brought forth applicants "so numerous that they actually blocked up the street leading to the Customs House."[62] It was with this hungry mob that Mackenzie was competing for a place, still clinging to the shreds of his dignity as an independent editor and publisher, and acutely uncomfortable in the knowledge that some other poor devil would be dismissed to make room for him.[63] "You will be lucky if you go in with the first batch of appointments," Fitnam informed him.[64]

Certain that Mackenzie was at last to get a worthwhile appointment, O'Callaghan, O'Rielly and Fitnam loaded him with good advice, cautioning him to be prudent in what he said in the Customs House, "that den of sharks," advising him to keep quiet and remember his responsibility to his starving family.[65] Mackenzie's nomination as an inspector at $1,100 a year was made on July 25, but no sooner did the fact become public than Van Ness was criticized for making the appointment by two Whig newspapers, the New York *Express* and the *Commercial Advertiser*.[66] When the Secretary of the Treasury required the nomination to be withdrawn, Van Ness conferred on Mackenzie a temporary, much less valuable appointment. On July 27 Mackenzie began work in the archives office of the Customs House as a clerk at $600 a year.[67] Van Ness evidently regarded these minor clerkships as bits of patronage under his own control and throughout his tenure of office disregarded the peremptory orders he received to report the clerks' names and the authority for their employment.[68]

Mackenzie was not left to enjoy even this minor appointment in peace. M.M. Noah, editor of the *New York Messenger*, led off the attack with a "savage article" entitled "Corruption in the Customs House." It called Mackenzie an "incendiary foreigner," charged him with cowardice and treachery, and accused him of fostering frontier disturbances that had cost Americans their lives and liberty. When he was attacked by other New York and Philadelphia papers as well, Mackenzie sent the New York *Herald* a long and spirited defence.[69] He stated that the inspectorship had first been offered to him without any previous application on his part either directly or indirectly, without any political views on the part of those offering it and, as he sincerely believed, solely out of good feelings for an exile who had struggled for liberty.[70] Surely an honest pen would have scratched in protest at being required to indite these lines.

Replying to the charge of the *Commercial* that native sons had been passed over for foreigners, Mackenzie took a firm stand: at naturalization aliens become entitled to all the rights of natural-born citizens. He recounted the history of the alien question in Canada, relating that "orders came" to naturalize Americans by a new law after they had renounced their American citizenship but would have denied them the right to vote or to hold office or be elected to the Assembly. A committee of which he had been the confidential secretary had sent Robert Randal to England to protest against confirmation of this act [of 1827]. The result had been that the Colonial Office gave in:

Americans were confirmed in all their rights "without an oath of abjuration" and the benefits of the act were extended to aliens "who had been an hour in the province."

This was a decidedly inaccurate summary of the history of the Naturalization Act of 1828. It did not make clear the concessions that had been sought and exaggerated those that had been obtained.[71]

Mackenzie asserted, with considerable exaggeration:

The first political essay I ever penned was in defence of American in Canada.... I stood well with the government and its officers; they had never refused me a favor. I quarrelled with them on account of the Americans.

This surely was a fanciful rethinking of his relationship with the government of Upper Canada.

I was no printer when I began on the eve of a Canadian general election to sound the republican tocsin.... From that day to the hour I crossed the Niagara... in 1837, I pursued at all risks an undeviating republican course.

Here is an acknowledgement that Sir John Colborne might have been glad to make use of in 1835. Mackenzie's defence was an able one, temperately expressed, tailored to appeal to American readers, but it was factually inaccurate. Mackenzie was vigorously defended by the *Working Man's Advocate*, which explained to its readers "the secret" of Noah's hostility and that of other Whig papers.[72] The Whig attack upon Mackenzie was occasioned by the appearance of a circular addressed to the candidates for President and Vice-President, enquiring what their policies would be on the naturalization laws and whether they repudiated the support of the Nativist Party or not.

The rise of the Nativist movement in New York in the 1840s had been occasioned by a heavy influx of immigrants who did not share the Protestant and largely Anglo-Saxon traditions of the older inhabitants. In New York City, where Whigs and Democrats were fairly evenly divided, the votes of naturalized citizens had become important. Competition for employment, the bestowal of minor patronage appointments on newcomers, disorders at the elections which were attributed to them, added to social and religious prejudices, caused disgruntled native Americans to organize a new party, the Nativist Party. Its object was to exclude all but the native-born from certain offices and to extend the period of residence required before naturalization from five years to 21.[73] With Whig and Nativist hostility to new immigrants Mackenzie, now one of them, naturally had no sympathy.

Mackenzie believed that he would not be suspected as the author of the circular, but Noah, whom the document called the father of the Native American party and "a political Jew," immediately accused him of being its author and of obtaining signatures to it.[74] He demanded to know, "What right had this foreigner to address a circular to the American candidates for the Presidency?"

O'Callaghan advised Mackenzie:

> If you could keep quiet I think it would be better for you. Anyone acquainted with your style would know you. Your scissors, not your pen, betray you.[75]

The circular, like Mackenzie's defence at his trial, had roamed over ancient history, quoting the words of early presidents and recounting the aid of the foreign-born in the revolution,[76] Mackenzie denied, in a letter to the New York Democrat, that he had "addressed" the circular to the candidates for the presidency or had asked people to sign it.[77] Whatever restricted meaning he gave to the word "addressed," he certainly composed it, and acknowledged the fact to his son[78] and to Thurlow Weed.[79]

During the difficult spring and summer of 1844 Mackenzie had been practically penniless, dependent upon an occasional $5.00 from an old friend or a bit of hack work such as the compiling of almanacs.[80] In this period of anxious waiting he published part of his "Lives of 1000 Remarkable Irishmen," a compilation which he had begun shortly after his return to New York. The entire work was intended to appear in 10 parts, each containing 100 biographies. Number one appeared on February 21, 1844, under the title *Sons of the Emerald Isle*. It was a 64-page pamphlet advertised at 1/- York (12 1/2 ¢). The publishers, Burgess Stringer and Co., drove a hard bargain. Mackenzie feared he would make nothing out of it, and he didn't.[81]

Mackenzie's pamphlet was something more than a collection of sycophantic biographies. It was a tract against nativism. Mackenzie reminded his readers that the first settlers in America were "all aliens" and he denounced the Nativist associations whose members looked upon newer settlers as if they came of inferior stocks. "It is to make the youth of America ashamed of such associations and such principles that this volume is published." Mackenzie attacked the then current concept of the Irish as an ignorant and benighted people, and emphasized the part that men of Irish birth or ancestry had taken in the struggle for American independence. Once or twice he pointed out similarities to the course of events in Canada during the thirties, and he quoted Grattan's words:

> Let no people ever consent to be a Province who have strength enough to be an independent nation.

While waiting for a federal appointment to be made, Mackenzie developed a new interest into which he poured his restless energy and which, no doubt, helped him to endure the endless weeks of uncertainty. This was the National Reform Association of which George Henry Evans was the guiding spirit. Evans had edited and published a daily paper, *Man*, and a weekly, the *Workingman's*

*Advocate*, until ill-health and financial difficulties forced him to retire to a small farm in New Jersey in 1836. Mackenzie, while editor of the *Colonial Advocate*, had exchanged papers with Evans, had found him a kindred spirit and had received from him, while in prison, a file of the *Workingman's Advocate*. In June 1841 Evans began publishing a continuation of the *Workingman's Advocate* under the title *The Radical*. This was a monthly paper which appeared irregularly until April 1843. In its columns he worked out more fully the ideas on land reform which he had expressed in his earlier publication. Man had a natural right to life and to a living, therefore he had a right to land enough for subsistence. Monopolies were the great evil, and land monopoly, which kept surplus labourers confined to great cities, where their numbers depressed the rate of wages, was the greatest evil of all. The principles of the Declaration of Independence called for republican equality. Therefore the public domain must be kept open to the poor and out of the hands of land speculators if a landed aristocracy was to be prevented and unemployment and urban misery relieved. Rightly administered the public domain could become "a great outlet of relief for surplus labor and could free the workmen from absolute dependence upon the employer class." Translated into practical terms, Evans' theories required free public land for actual settlers, limitations upon the quantity of land an individual could own and exemption of settlers' homesteads from seizure and sale for debt.

In February 1844 a group of friends, among them Mackenzie, met "in a room behind John Windt's little New York printing shop," to discuss with Evans his plans for reform of American society through reform of the nation's land policies. Out of this meeting came the National Reform Association, organized on a formal basis in June. The aims and ideals of the Association were set forth in a tri-weekly paper, *The People's Rights*, which Evans and Windt formed a partnership to publish. This paper soon gave way to a new series of the revived *Workingman's Advocate* and in 1845 to a paper called *Young America*.[82] The National Reform Association held public meetings indoors and out, gradually won adherents, including Horace Greeley and Gerritt Smith, obtained the support of other reform organizations and of many newspapers, created an organization on a national scale, and became an effective voice in national politics. The Association was to gain a partial victory with the enactment of the homestead law of 1862, which offered free land to the landless, but the important principles of preserving the public domain for actual settlers, limiting land ownership and making the free homestead inalienable, were not written into the act.

From the outset Mackenzie took a keen interest in the work of the National Reform Association. Until July 24 his name appears as one of the central committee and some of its sessions were held at his home. He was frequently a speaker at the Association's public meetings. The *Workingman's Advocate* wrote that he was

a terrible fellow for long speeches, but somehow or other the audience always thinks them too short and an ordinary speaker may as well hang up his fiddle when the great Canadian orator comes into the room. [83]

Evans' plan for townships six miles square within which free farm lots would be granted to actual settlers only and sites in a centrally located village made available to craftsmen, and in which the mineral lands, timber resources and water power of the township would be retained in public ownership and managed by the township's local governing body — all this must have seemed to Mackenzie a blueprint for the agrarian democracy he longed for:

> So help me God [said he], I see no plan so likely to perpetuate liberty as this plan of allowing every man who chooses to become a landholder; and if Congress would make the experiment on one hundred miles square of territory, I would be among the first settlers. [84]

Mackenzie denounced the existing land sales system which, from the other side of the border, had looked so desirable to him and his fellow Reformers. He now realized that it permitted speculators to buy up soldiers' bounty land warrants at a discount and to enter large tracts of land with them at the government sales without limitation. The squatters, or pre-emptors, whose quarter sections were to be offered at the government auction had to find $200 in cash before that day arrived or risk losing their land. In many instances they were obliged to sign a note for $400 at 12% to secure a loan of $200. Often the desired land was entered for them by speculators with land warrants for which they had paid much less than $1.25 an acre.[85]

The meetings and publications of the National Reform Association gave Mackenzie a chance to express his opinions again on old grievances and to link them up with the cause of land reform. The paper money system, he told an audience, was a great evil which had to be destroyed, but land monopoly was the greatest evil. America still cherished "the British system of land monopoly." With that statement as a point of departure, he was off on a denunciation of "the voluminous mass of British common law" with its tangle of technicalities and precedents, which ought to be swept away. The monopoly of law business by lawyers, which he had unsuccessfully challenged in Rochester, he denounced once more. "If you do not rise up in your might and abolish these law and land monopolies, the history of the past will be the history of the future," he warned. To the *Workingman's Advocate* he contributed two articles on judicial reform, signed "Franklin," in which he advocated that the laws of New York be revised, the code of procedure be simplified and practice in the courts be opened to all citizens of the United States.[86] It was folly, he remarked, for Americans to object to naturalized foreigners while permitting themselves to be governed by the unjust laws and technicalities inherited from England's legal system, and he concluded:

The principles of the Revolution and of the constitution are yet to be extended to the public courts and the public lands of the United States. [87]

After Mackenzie entered the Customs House, his name ceased to appear as one of the central committee of the National Reform Association and he wrote nothing more touching on politics until his resignation in June 1845.

## Chapter VIII

# THE LIVES OF BUTLER AND HOYT, AND THE LIFE OF VAN BUREN

W̲hen Mackenzie actually started working in the Customs House on July 27, 1844, the members of his long-suffering family no doubt experienced a tremendous feeling of relief that at last the long agony was over. Perhaps they even believed that its unpredictable head had finally settled down to his fundamental duty of providing for them. It is apparent from Mackenzie's letters that he undertook the task in no spirit of calm resignation. His vendetta against Van Buren had proved to be a useless waste of his time and resources. Out of it he had obtained his patronage appointment but at the sacrifice of his independence and his honesty. After a long, humiliating public struggle he had finally obtained a petty clerkship, only to discover in a few weeks' time that he would never receive the worthwhile inspectorship which he had expected,[1] and he was tortured by the knowledge that, should the Van Buren Democrats show strength in the November elections, he would lose the petty appointment and salary he had just secured. As Polk's inauguration day approached his nervousness increased, stimulated by a warning from Fitnam.[2]

Mackenzie's letters to O'Callaghan at this time were querulous, suspicious and tinged with self-pity. He jealously contrasted his own hard lot with Papineau's good fortune in becoming free to return to Canada, regain his property and see his relatives placed in well-paid government posts.

> When yourself and friends sent to Toronto in Nov., 1837 to urge us to rise [he wrote] ...it certainly would not have come into my thought that the men who did that would in the event of failure make a treaty with England for the patronage of Canada to themselves and our Tory enemies and forget that I have an existence. [3]

O'Callaghan did his best to quiet Mackenzie's suspicions. The political situation in Lower Canada, he reminded him, was "in a state of chaos;" no town or county organization existed, the schools were in ruins, there was no jury law, and sheriffs only for districts almost half the size of the State of New York. D.B. Viger and D.B. Papineau (French Canadian members of the Draper-Viger ministry) might well have decided to support Governor Metcalfe for patriotic reasons, believing that the administration of the country would be better in their own hands then if their posts were held by Tories. "We may believe they will be disappointed but we should not asperse their motives," he observed.[4] Mackenzie was not ready to be consoled. He was galled by his humble position, could see no prospect of advancement, his family had whooping cough and scarlet fever, and he himself was suffering from rheumatism and a "tic doloreaux" [sic] in his face.[5]

Mackenzie was a man of restless energy and an inveterate scribbler. He no longer had a press and without it he felt himself to be nothing. He was frustrated, muzzled. He told O'Callaghan:

> I have clung to the hope of office from these folks for no other
> object on earth than that I might get enough to keep the family
> under one roof and enable me to save enough to... purchase a
> small [printing] establishment. [6]

But if he had had a press, what would he have done with it? He still clung to remnants of the Loco-Foco program: restrictions on the issue of paper money, opposition to the piling up of state debts and to the creation of monopolies and limited liability corporation. These had been his opinions in Canada and during his early years in exile. They were still his opinions and should have made him support the Barnburner wing of the Democratic Party and its leaders, Silas Wright and Martin Van Buren, whom he mistrusted and hated. Would he have used a press to agitate for the annexation of Canada to the United States? Only recently he had written to O'Rielly:

> I feel sorry, very sorry sometimes, that I had not the advantage
> of a seven years' residence in these states before I engaged in the
> Canada revolt. With my present experience there would have
> been no outbreak — for I would have stopped short of that and
> made others do so also. [7]

It is clear that by 1844 Mackenzie did not know what course he should advocate for Canada nor where he stood in American politics either. Nativism had cured him of any desire for annexation.

Lacking a press of his own and wisely, for once, refraining from taking part in the political controversies of the moment, Mackenzie spent his spare hours working on the second portion of his *Sons of the Emerald Isle*. The publishers of the first portion, however, were reluctant to take the second.[8] Fully 30 of the 50 persons selected for inclusion, while "illustrious" in their homeland, had never set foot in the United States. Not until October 1845, when Mackenzie, as we shall see, was once again very much in the public eye as an author, was he able

116

to get the pamphlet published. The *Tribune* alone gave it a few kind words; other papers ignored it.[9]

To O'Callaghan Mackenzie proposed that together they should get out a new edition of Theller's *Canada in 1837-8,* with critical notes. Theller had praised the conduct of Wolfred Nelson and others but had referred to Papineau's "unaccountable desertion" and flight from the battleground of St. Charles.

> Papineau, in whose person the love, admiration, and confidence of a whole people was concentrated... [promised] to guide them in... the sacred cause of freedom... instead of the brave, devoted, leader, the Canadians found in him the pusillanimous coward. In him they had raised a colossus;— he crushed them in his fall. [10]

O'Callaghan, the friend of Papineau, declined Mackenzie's proposition..[11] Before long Mackenzie had much more fascinating work to occupy his time than editing a new edition of Theller's book.

In 1845 the Democratic Party in New York State was badly split between the Van Burenites and the more conservative Democrats who had never favoured his Independent Treasury scheme and who, Van Buren believed, were responsible for his losing the nomination for the presidency to Polk.[12] Both factions of the New York Democrats were trying to secure patronage appointments from Polk so as to strengthen themselves within the state and with an eye to the next presidential election. The adherents of ex-President Tyler were also badgering Polk, who was trying to conciliate the various factions in his party and at the same time to be master of his own administration.[13]

While this struggle within the Democratic Party was in progress, Mackenzie made a discovery that played into the hands of Van Buren's enemies. In the New York Customs House there were several locked boxes of papers which the assistant collector, C.J. Bogardus, ordered the clerks to break open and sort. When one of these, labelled "J & L Hoyt's Law Papers," was opened, it was found to contain miscellaneous correspondence of Jesse Hoyt, a previous collector, with various members of the Albany Regency that revealed their private negotiations with one another respecting bank charters, loans, election bets and appointments to office.[14] Mackenzie copied some of the letters and, by the middle of May, had got in touch with Duff Green, one of Polk's advisers, making known to him his wish to expose the doings of the Albany Regency to the President and to the public.[15] Green, no friend of Van Buren, regarded the discovery of the letters as "providential,"showed some of them to Polk, and informed Mackenzie that his information was "duly appreciated in the right quarter."[16] To Calhoun, who led the segment of the Democratic Party most feared by the Van Buren men, Green wrote:

> As if to put an end to Van Buren's influence, letters going as far back as 1824 between the leading partners of the old Albany Regency ... showing their operations and their combinations

and intrigues for office and the manner of obtaining the control of Jackson and managing the elections and the establishment of presses has been discovered in the Customs House of New York and the originals secured, and copies multiplied so as to prevent any arrangement for the suppression of the originals. Some of the copies have been exhibited to the President and he now understands that he has nothing to hope by identifying himself with that clique. [17]

One of the difficult decisions Polk had to make was whether to retain Tyler's appointee, C.P. Van Ness, as Collector of the Port of New York. Tyler had been anxious to leave behind in office some of his friends in the hope of retaining political influence in his party, perhaps even of being nominated in 1848, and the collectorship carried with it extensive patronage in an important state. Polk, who did not plan to run again himself, had no sympathy with the discredited Tyler. By the end of May the reluctant and hesitating Van Ness had been induced to resign. Polk then offered the collectorship, not to John Coddington, the nominee of the Van Buren men, but to a conservative Democrat of his own choosing, C.W. Lawrence, who accepted.[18]

Van Ness's resignation as collector was to take effect on June 30. Mackenzie sent in his own resignation to take effect on the same date. He explained to his son, and to the surprised O'Rielly, that the reason for his resignation, "or at least one immediate reason" for it, was that he did not want to serve under Van Ness's successor, the conservative banker C.W. Lawrence, whom he had criticized in the first number of his *Examiner*.[19] As will be seen, this was not the whole story.

After leaving the Customs House Mackenzie began to prepare for the press his *Lives and Opinions of Benjamin Franklin Butler and Jesse Hoyt*, based in part on the letters he had obtained there. He would have liked to publish the Butler and Hoyt material in a newspaper if only he could have got hold of "an independent press."[20] But a press was not to be had. Dr. A.S. Doane, who had earlier supplied some money from Whig sources to support his *Examiner*, assisted him in getting the Butler-Hoyt book published. Mackenzie stipulated that the publisher should put out a large and cheap edition and take no more than the usual trade profit. "I will take no profit, no copyright, no advantage whatever beyond my bare labour... and would not take that if poverty did not press me to the ground." He asked only $100.00 for his "two months hard labour" and his expenses to and from Boston, where the book was to be printed. These sums were advanced by Doane.[21]

Mackenzie's book, strictly speaking only a pamphlet, was hardly a biography of Hoyt and Butler. It consisted of some of their correspondence found in the Customs House and numerous extracts from newspapers, all strung together by Mackenzie's comments, supported by numerous footnotes. The work revealed, according to its author, how Democratic politicians had intrigued for office and how they had used office "for the basest and most wicked personal and party purposes" and not for the public welfare. The *New York Tribune* described the book as:

> [a] lucid and startling exposition of the enormous frauds and
> villainy which have for years... misled the people of New York
> under the abused name of Democracy.... [22]

The modern reader finds the work no longer lucid, so full is it of obscure contemporary references. Neither is it well organized. It seems to have been very hastily compiled from the letters and from Mackenzie's extensive file of clippings. But it was a "startling" exposé. The charters of banks had been obtained by political jobbery; their stock and their directorships had been distributed to political friends who had in many instances paid their subscriptions in promissory notes and speculated in the stock of their own institutions. The directors had borrowed from their own banks for investment in lands, issued floods of paper, subsequently bought up the notes when they had depreciated and paid off their debts to their banks in this nearly worthless paper. Several of the institutions so fathered and so managed were obliged to close their doors, in some instances within a year of being chartered.[23]

Readers of Mackenzie's book were shown how little merit and integrity had entered into the appointments even to judicial offices made by the Regency and how much party loyalty and political jockeying had to do with them. The *New York Tribune* remarked that it had long believed Van Buren to be a corrupt and heathen gambler in politics, a fake pretender to democracy and that "now we have the incontrovertible evidence."[24] This was rather more than Mackenzie supplied. His readers learned of the unsavory background of many persons who had been supported by leading Democratic politicians for office despite their connection with broken banks and fraudulent insurance companies, but corruption on the part of Van Buren himself was only intimated, not proved. He was discredited by his associates.

Van Buren had conferred an important office of trust, the Collectorship of the Port of New York, upon Jesse Hoyt, a man who, as his correspondence now revealed, had been Van Buren's personal and political lackey — and his son's. Hoyt was known to be "overwhelmed with debt and bankrupt in credit."[25] He provided only "straw sureties,"[26] failed to pay over his collections promptly to the Treasury, left them in his private account and ended a defaulter for some $200,000.00. Governor Silas Wright bemoaned the fact that he had not resisted Butler's wish to have Hoyt appointed. "I trembled at the thought and felt chills."[27]

The Poindexter Inquiry into the New York Customs House had provided ample proof of Hoyt's misconduct and of the dishonesty of many other officials appointed for their services to Van Buren's party. The Whigs charged that a large proportion of the money withheld by Hoyt had not gone into his own pocket but had been expended corruptly in the elections "for Mr. Van Buren's benefit and we believe with his knowledge."[28] Hoyt had received a warning from Van Buren at the end of January 1841 *after* the President had failed of re-election, but he was not removed until February 27.[29] Van Buren states in his autobiography that, after removing Hoyt, he appointed John J. Morgan for a few "years," when actually Morgan held the office for less than one month.[30]

The reaction of the press to Mackenzie's book varied with the political stand of the paper. Not all Whig papers approved of it. For four columns the *Tribune* quoted from the work and editorialized on its contents, enlarging upon "the enormous frauds and villany" which had "duped and misled the people of New York under the absurd name of Democracy" with the watchwords of "Harmony of the Party," "Regular Nomination," "usages of the Party." In subsequent days the *Tribune* gave additional extracts and underlined the lessons Mackenzie wished the forthcoming convention to draw from his pages. The real value of the letters was that they pointed up the necessity of a change in the method of filling important offices. They must be made elective, declared the *Tribune*, and the people must be induced to use their power "discriminatingly without slavish subservience to party."[31] It suggested the use of split ballots and the writing in of names.

The *National Intelligencer* did not give unreserved approval to Mackenzie's conduct in publishing private correspondence and, like the *Courier and Inquirer* and the *Commercial Advertiser*, refrained from printing extracts. It observed that Mackenzie had drawn needed attention to the Poindexter Report on the New York Customs House. This document had not previously received enough publicity or been made available to the public, owing to the small number of copies printed. "The large volume of the report deterred public journalists from the attempt to publish them [*sic*]; and the labour of analysis was almost as appalling."[32] These difficulties had not deterred Mackenzie! No one was better able than he to understand the intricacies of the Poindexter Report and to bring to light the political connections and past history of the culprits named in it, equipped as he was with training as an accountant, with inside knowledge of the Customs House and with information derived from researches into 40 years of New York newspapers. The New York *Express* thought the book would become a classic like Machiavelli's *Prince*. Mackenzie's labour, it noted, must have been "prodigious."[33] Mike Walsh's *Subterranean*, whose motto was "Independent in Everything — Neutral in Nothing," remarked:

> There is more manhood and principle in one hair of [Mackenzie's] head than there is in the united composition of the whole brood of [domestic politicians].[34]

The *Courier and Inquirer*,[35] the politically neutral *Journal of Commerce*,[36] and the Whig *Commercial Advertiser*,[37] all commented upon the damage Mackenzie's book had done to the political and personal reputation of Van Buren and his friends.

Hostile Democratic papers, instead of meeting the charges in Mackenzie's book squarely and defending those members of the party it had attacked, railed against the person who had exposed them. Mackenzie had made public private correspondence without the consent of writers or recipient! And for mercenary motives! Mackenzie had stolen correspondence! Mackenzie had forced open locked boxes in the Customs House, boxes marked private, to obtain it! He had been guilty of "a despicable piece of knavery." There was astonishment that Mackenzie, a recent immigrant, should know so much about the past political and business history of New York. He must have had accomplices. The Washington *Union* suggested that Mackenzie had been "guided to the papers by some more cunning rascal" and had used Customs House time in copying them.[38] All those accused by different papers were exonerated by Mackenzie.[39] The most restrained and judicious comment came from the New York *Commercial*:

> It is evident that Mackenzie has worked himself into the belief that he is performing a duty to the country.... Samson-like he appears reckless of consequences to himself, provided he can show certain public men to the world in their proper colours. That he has accomplished his object no one can doubt. [40]

In his preface Mackenzie took pains to justify at length his publication of Hoyt's private correspondence:

> Has not treason been committed against the state? The safety of the state, which is superior to every other consideration, makes it necessary to use all possible means to unmask the machinations of treason.... [41]

But this argument of *salus populi, suprema lex*, repeated to friends like W.J. Duane,[42] O'Callaghan[43] and O'Rielly,[44] satisfied none of them.

James Mackenzie, who was editing the Kalida (Ohio) *Venture*, upon consideration accepted his father's justification of his conduct but, a more realistic man than his father, he was not disposed to view the conduct of those Mackenzie exposed in the same harsh light.

> Bargain, compromise and concession is so essential to our Republican system [he wrote] that it requires a strong mind to tell where it merges into corruption.

James was troubled, also, by the fact that the book aided the Whigs and injured the Democratic Party, "the party of progress".[45]

In long, defiant and bold letters to the *Tribune*, Mackenzie defended himself. His motives had not been mercenary but "to uncloak and rid the public offices of dishonest officials" like Hoyt, whose misdeeds and whose trial had been ignored by the Democratic press.

> Party bound by manly principle has done much good and may do more; but when party editors shield dishonest public servants by libelling those who have the courage to accuse them... their object must be a wicked one — they love "the spoils" more than their country.... I here publicly repeat that I feel I deserve well of the republic.

A letter to the *Tribune* signed Anti-Humbug pointed out that Benjamin Franklin had obtained Governor Hutchinson's private letters and had made use of them without his consent and had justified himself with the same argument that Mackenzie used, *salus populi*. This letter may have been written by Mackenzie himself. Throughout his life he was greatly influenced by the career of Franklin.[46]

Neither in his letters to the *Tribune* nor in his later publication, *The Life and Times of Martin Van Buren*, did Mackenzie make it entirely clear how he came to make copies of the letters or to publish them. He claimed that his immediate superiors all were aware that he was making copies of Hoyt's correspondence. This statement was publicly denied by the Keeper of the Archives, but publicly supported by Ingraham Coryell, another Customs House employee, who accused his superiors of bearing false witness against Mackenzie.[47] In the book itself Mackenzie refers to the papers as "parts of a correspondence which was, it is presumed, intentionally placed before him."[48] Van Ness acknowledged that he had been informed of the discovery of the Hoyt papers, but he did not admit that he knew of or had authorized the copying. He was displeased when he learned from Duff Green what Mackenzie had been doing.[49]

Henry O'Rielly, who was much upset by Mackenzie's conduct and wanted to know exactly how the papers had come to his attention, asked him for "the facts" and enquired, "I think you told me you copied those letters — not taking the originals — is it so?"[50] O'Rielly may have learned the facts when he visited Mackenzie in New York shortly thereafter, but he has left no record of this visit.[51] However, it is clear that Mackenzie had possession of the originals;[52] 142 of them are now in the Archives of Ontario, 11 in the Public Archives of Canada — but whether Mackenzie stole them or was permitted to take them, and if so by whom, cannot be stated. To his son Mackenzie gave no information beyond remarking, "As yet, I dare not explain all."[53]

The exact relations between Mackenzie, Duff Green and the Polk administration cannot be determined. In a letter of May 30, before he knew of Mackenzie's resignation, Duff Green offered to give him "any aid in my power." Mackenzie seems to have interpreted this indefinite statement to mean that he would be assisted to commence a weekly paper.[54] Whatever help Green had in mind when he offered to aid Mackenzie, it did not extend so far as to put a press at his disposal. Green feared that the connection which Polk and most of the members of his cabinet had had with the parties implicated by Mackenzie's disclosures would weaken the administration.[55]

If Mackenzie had entertained any hopes of benefit from the Polk administration, by mid-July they were gone.[56] It is clear that persons close to Polk knew in advance that Mackenzie intended to publish the Butler-Hoyt letters. When they turned down his request for help he made his arrangements with Doane instead. Bitterly disappointed at his treatment by Duff Green and Polk, he wrote to O'Rielly:

> I have neither press nor types, money, friends or influence —
> and what is worse than all I have seen enough to take away the

soul stirring enthusiasm that warmed me in Canada. I hate your country, deceitful, two faced plausible race of politicians from my soul.... [57]

From a publisher's point of view the *Lives of Butler and Hoyt* was a success. The first edition of 5,000 was sold out within 24 hours of its appearance on September 22. The work was then stereotyped and published by several houses.[58] Before sale of the book was halted on October 1 by an injunction, thousands more were sold. The *New York Herald* reported on September 27 that 50,000 copies had been disposed of at 37 1/2 cents each, or $18,750, of which it is estimated $12,000 was profit. Not a cent of this went to Mackenzie. O'Rielly wrote:

What a rush there is for that publication. In steamboats and railroads you see it with travellers. At Philadelphia it is placarded and talked about as much as in New York, among active men, and here in Pittsburgh, even, the demand for it & for the New York papers respecting it exhausts quickly the supplies.... I never recollect such a rush for any book.... [59]

In New York the streets were placarded with announcements about it, and after the injunction was issued boys were selling copies of it for one dollar. In Rochester the book was not to be had.[60]

It is impossible to estimate the effects of the book upon national politics. Duff Green thought the work would be "a death blow to caucus dictation... the public are capable of choosing their own public servants without the aid of a corrupt caucus machinery."[61] Whig journalists, led by the *Tribune*, insisted that the exposé had destroyed the image of the Van Burenites as true Jacksonians, true democrats and friends of the common man.[62] Secretary Walker's *Daily Globe* saw it as justifying Loco-Foco criticisms of the Regency.[63] Fitzwilliam Byrdsall, a leading Loco-Foco politician whom Lawrence removed from the Customs House as one of his first acts, predicted that the Democratic Party in New York State would have to be reorganized under a new leader. He explained to Polk:

The fact is, the old Regency has had its day and must now be as one of the things that were. There have been coolness and divisions among those men that composed it formerly and its fall is accelerated by the letters published. [64]

Jesse Hoyt was accused of having deliberately left his private papers in the Customs House and of conniving at their publication. The *New York Herald* remarked that Hoyt owed it to himself to prosecute Mackenzie, and he did.[65] Hoyt obtained from the Vice-Chancellor an injunction which forbade the further publishing or dissemination of Mackenzie's pamphlet or the sale of the plates. All proceeds from the work were to be held subject to the orders of the court.[66] When the case was heard, the court refused to dissolve the injunction.[67]

123

Mackenzie's *Lives of Butler and Hoyt* was criticized by the Washington *Union* as "a shameless and inferior production and its author was called "a thief."[68] This newspaper, edited by Thomas Ritchie, was the official paper of the Polk administration. A remark of this kind, coming from administration sources, when friends of Polk had been informed in advance about the letters, had made use of them, and could have stopped the copying, angered Mackenzie. He promptly announced that he was bringing out another book that would prove "more unpalatable" to them than the earlier one.[69] Uneasy about what further revelations Mackenzie might be in a position to make that might damage the Polk administration, Duff Green enquired of him whether he had anything that placed the President in the same boat as Benjamin F. Butler.[70] No answer to this query appears to be extant. Green then went to New York to see Mackenzie. He found that

> he was very sensitive on the subject of the book... said he would not subject himself to the charge of being an informer for *pay* & that therefore before he published he stipulated that he was to have no pecuniary interest whatever in the book. It is not surprising therefore that Mr. Ritchie's comment in the *Union* has given him great offence and hence his determination to write another book in which to assail the President and Mr. Ritchie.

Finding that Mackenzie's "ruling passion" was hatred of Van Buren, Duff Green attempted to convince him that he would injure Van Buren more effectively if he concentrated his fire on him than by assailing Polk, Ritchie and a dozen other persons at the same time. "But he left me declaring... that he would retaliate on Mr. Polk and Mr. Ritchie for the manner in which Ritchie had assailed him."[71]

Mackenzie's second book based on the Customs House material did not appear until the end of April 1846.[72] It was entitled the *Life and Times of Martin Van Buren: The Correspondence of His Friends, Family, and Pupils*. There was a long subtitle, listing 51 politicians, editors and office-holders, including Polk. Green's remonstrances had gone for naught. Polk was criticized for his inconsistency, his appointments, his attitude towards slavery and his support of the Pet banks.

Mackenzie had intended his *Life of Van Buren* to follow his earlier book promptly but, as he planned to use in it both the letters originally published as well as additional ones, he felt that the Vice-Chancellor's injunction of October 15 hindered him from going ahead with the work. He wished to appeal, but was "so wretchedly poor" that he could not employ the necessary legal talent. Also, in appealing, he was very anxious not to have to answer the question where the letters then were. They were not at his home. He had placed them "beyond the reach of a replevin writ," and was disposed to imitate Franklin who had demurred to the question where he got the Hutchinson letters and to whom he had sent them[73] In this dilemma Mackenzie appealed to Thurlow Weed and laid his problem before him. Mackenzie was sufficiently encouraged to go ahead with his plans for publication although he was without resources of his own. Doane helped him to make arrangements with William Taylor by which Taylor was to pay him $1,000 for the copyright of his *Life of Van Buren*, $400 of which was to be paid in advance and the balance when the work should be completed, approximately January 15.[74]

Mackenzie's *Life of Van Buren* was dedicated, like his earlier book, to the members of the New York State Constitutional Convention. The *Life* was not, of course, a biography of the President tracing his career in chronological detail. It consisted of a 150-page commentary on American politics in which a justification by the author of his use of the Butler-Hoyt correspondence and an account of his relations with the officials of the New York Customs House was included.

All 176 letters which had appeared in the earlier work were now reprinted along with 137 new ones. These, said Mackenzie, were all the Hoyt letters "that ever will or ought to be published."[75] Commentary and letters were reinforced by extensive footnotes. Mackenzie burdened his argument with a undue weight of illustrative material, quotations and references to recent political events, in many cases cryptically expressed. He inserted names and incidents by the hundreds and skipped back and forth between elections with a bewildering disregard for chronology. Nevertheless, he piled up a telling indictment not only against Van Buren but also against other factions of the Democratic Party as well. In addition, Mackenzie added a detailed account of the maneuvres among the factions of the Democratic Party before and during the Baltimore convention of 1844, and a special section on Van Buren's stand on slavery in which he argued that Van Buren had been the "tool" of the southern interests and had not really been opposed to the annexation of Texas. A few years later when Van Buren became identified with the Free Soil Party in a last effort at a political comeback, Mackenzie denounced his stand as hypocritical, "a humbug and a mockery".[76]

The most effective part of his book was that which recounted the relations of Van Buren and his supporters with the banks, but much of this material had already appeared in his *Examiner* and his *Lives of Butler and Hoyt*. The account he now gave of the safety fund was intended to deprive Van Buren of all merit for attempting a worthwhile reform: "It was because not one charter could be got... that the sleek party leader opened his budget in 1829 with the panacea of a safety fund."[77] The weaknesses of the safety-fund law were fully set forth in the Safety Fund Commissioner's Report of January 30, 1843. Mackenzie quoted its general remarks at some length and gave the history of the failure of various safety fund banks, taking care to name the prominent Democrats who had been connected with them.[78]

Mackenzie's statements about Van Buren are fully supported by the Assembly's *Journals*; his interpretation of Van Buren's career is another matter. There were many inconsistencies in his own conduct. "They call me changeable," he confessed to James. "And so I am, I yield to new facts if important and well proved...."[79] To Van Buren, however, he was not willing to allow the benefit of changed circumstances, wider experience or alterations in the political position of men and groups with whom he had to work. Nor did he regard him as a statesman trying to make his party "an effective coalition of state interests bound together by agreement on the need to limit federal authority and allow local diversity,"[80] thus assuring the preservation of the union. He saw in Van Buren's career only the tortuous course of a self-seeking intriguer devoid of principle.

The Life of Van Buren created less excitement than the Lives of Butler and Hoyt. It could not have the same impact. The revelations in the additional letters were not as fresh or as embarrassing and it seemed like a warmed-over sort of production, although there were more documented criticisms of Polk. On the part of the Democratic journals there was a systematic effort simply to disparage the work as of little consequence and to deny it the publicity of denunciation, which had stimulated the sale of the earlier pamphlet.[81] The New York Tribune of course paid Mackenzie's new production glowing tributes.[82] Not all Whig journals were so unstinted in their praise of his conduct. To print letters written in privacy and confidence was characterized by the American Review as the act of an unprincipled man. Revenge for real or fancied injuries had been Mackenzie's motive. "If [the correspondence] is of any service it will chiefly be in showing the democracy ... what shameful dupes they have been for so many years."[83]

In his autobiography Van Buren pictures himself as having taken the publication of Mackenzie's book with indifference.

> The general sentiment elicited by this publication, on the part of both my political opponents and friends, was that I could well have afforded to defray the expense of bringing out in such a form, my portion of the correspondence. [84]

This can be admitted — and Mackenzie did admit it. What was important was the commentary. "Separated from their context, they [the letters] must be regarded as the sweepings, dross and rubbish of literature, utterly worthless."[85] One of Van Buren's biographers states that:

> all relations were broken between Polk and Van Buren when it was publicly revealed... that the President was responsible for the savage attack on him [that appeared in Mackenzie's books]. Polk of course, could not afford to place himself before the nation as endorsing the unjust attacks on Van Buren which Mackenzie worked into his pamphlet; so Mackenzie was removed from his customs house berth.... [86]

These statements are completely wrong. Mackenzie resigned before his first pamphlet was written and it was published with the help not of Polk but of the Whigs.

Van Buren suspected that his political enemies had drawn Mackenzie's attention to the trunkful of Hoyt s letters and had employed Mackenzie to cause him annoyance. He believed that Daniel Webster had been aware that Mackenzie's pamphlet was to be published from Boston and was ready to be put into circulation at the time of Van Buren's visit there. Van Buren thought that Webster's failure to meet him on this occasion was to be explained by Webster's fear that

> the attentions he had designed to show me, if coincident with a publication of confidential letters of a political and personal bearing... expected seriously to annoy and injure me, would be both awkward and impolite. [87]

However, Mackenzie's *Life of Van Buren* did not appear until after the ex-President had left Boston. Publication was deliberately delayed for a few days for "a cause" which Mackenzie did not specify,[88] but whether at Webster's suggestion or not cannot be stated.

When the *Life of Van Buren* appeared, Jess Hoyt's lawyers promptly made a motion in Chancery to have the property of William Taylor, the publisher, attached for violating the injunction already obtained, claiming that the material in the new book was also covered by the injunction. This motion was denied. But Mackenzie was not yet free of his legal troubles. His appeal from the Vice-Chancellor's decision to the Chancellor was pending. Thurlow Weed attempted to get legal help for him from Webster, who acknowledged that Mackenzie "had done the state some service in exposing the hypocrisy of the pretended patriots." Webster regretted that he had not the leisure to act himself and suggested someone else who he thought might serve for a moderate fee.[89]

The Chancellor, Reuben Walworth, heard Mackenzie's appeal in December 1845, but held back his decision for two and one-half years, until June 22, 1848, eight days before his office became extinct. He then reversed the Vice-chancellor on the ground that Hoyt's letters were not literary property, as Hoyt had contended. Walworth's decision, however, had a sting in it. "No one," said the Chancellor, "whose moral sense is not depraved," would justify the purchase and publishing of private letters for the purpose of wounding the feelings of individuals or of gratifying a perverted public taste,

> and he expressed his disbelief that the letters had been honestly obtained. His court, however, a court of equity, could not restrain or punish crime or enforce the performance of a moral duty since no right of property was involved. [90]

The Chancellor ordered a full restitution to Mackenzie of the book and the proceeds. The *Tribune* commented:

> This is slow justice. In the meantime the interest of the work has in good part subsided... the proceeds of copies sold have been dissipated through the bankruptcy of a publisher and the costs

of litigation; and now Mr. Mackenzie's property is thrown back to him after it has ceased to be of any practical value. He gave up a competence to be in a position to publish the book. Law has destroyed his property. [91]

The polemic disregarded the fact that Mackenzie had asserted he had no financial interest in the *Lives of Butler and Hoyt* and that he had sold his copyright of the *Life of Van Buren*. If anyone suffered financial loss from this injunction, it was the publishers. Mackenzie suffered lasting damage to his reputation from his use of the Hoyt papers. It was always something that his enemies in the United States, and later in Canada, could throw in his teeth.

# Chapter IX

# THE CONSTITUTION OF NEW YORK STATE

By 1846 Mackenzie was ready to return to Canada if he could.[1] In Canada there was still a chance that he could redeem his career and labour usefully for the reforms he had at heart. In the United States his prospects were reduced to the bare hope of making a living. Almost four years were to elapse before the exile could safely cross the St. Lawrence. Meanwhile, as the ever-pressing problem of providing for his family had to be solved promptly, he became the *New York Tribune's* reporter at the New York State Constitutional Convention, and on May 1 moved to Albany. This new, and to Mackenzie exciting, opportunity reconciled him to a further stay in the United States. He regarded his position as "one of some importance." (He had to think of it in these terms. It mattered to him, particularly after his humble clerkship.) "I am a connecting link in the chain of communication between my fellow citizens and the Delegates through a leading newspaper of immense circulation."[2]

The original constitution of New York State had been made a more liberal document partly by legislative action, partly by the constitutional convention of 1821. Property qualifications for voting and for holding office had been swept away, for whites, and the small Council of Appointment which had named all officials, state and local, had been abolished. Nevertheless an immense amount of patronage was still at the disposal of the Governor and of the legislature. By 1846 there was a widespread demand from radical elements in both political parties for reforms in order to destroy the highly centralized power structure at Albany and to allow the voters a greater voice in their government.

In New York State the Democratic Party had become split into two factions, Barnburners and Hunkers as they came to be called. The Barnburners included the adherents of the old Equal Rights party (the Loco-Focos), which had joined with the Van Buren Democrats in support of the Independent Treasury. During the years 1838-1842 an increasing strain had developed within the party as conservative Democrats (the Hunkers) and Whigs voted together to increase the state's debt so as to assist railroads and expand the canal system. They had not, however, provided for tax revenues to service the debt. The result was that the state's credit had become impaired. In 1842 the Barnburners, who had regained control of the Assembly, passed their "stop and tax" law. The severity of their policy of retrenchment, which caused work on the canals to be suspended, finally split the Democratic Party into two factions that could no longer work together.

In 1844 Silas Wright, Van Buren's most trusted lieutenant, reluctantly accepted the Democratic nomination for Governor in the hope of pulling the party together. He won the election but the schism in the party was not healed. The Hunkers wished to modify the stop and tax law so as to permit the completion of some of the unfinished canals.[3] The Barnburners were determined to erect a permanent defence for the principle of this law by amending the state's constitution so as to prohibit the legislature from running the state into debt without the direct consent of the people obtained by a referendum. They also wished to deprive the legislature of the power to lend the state's credit to private enterprises, and they wanted a general incorporation law which would make stockholders of a corporation fully liable in their individual capacities for its debts.

Mackenzie was delighted at the prospect of a constitutional convention in New York State. "What more did we wish — what more did we struggle for in Canada," he reminded his son.[4] In Mackenzie's opinion many reforms were needed in New York. Some of those he now advocated acquired added urgency in his mind from his own grievances. Some had been part of his planned reforms in Canada. This was particularly true of those relating to the law and the judiciary, the election of officials, the banking system, public debts and education.

The constitutional convention sat from June 1 until October 12, 1846. Mackenzie sent the *Tribune* daily accounts of its proceedings by the evening boat from Albany until the telegraph went into operation. Greeley's only instruction to him was to be impartial in his comments.[5] A Williamsburg paper, the *Democratic Advocate*, also received some reports from Mackenzie over the signature "Adverb."[6] As a rule his reports were not as detailed as those of the three Albany papers, which had two reporters apiece. Sometimes he referred his readers to them for the exact wording of a committee report or for a complete account of an important speech, and thus saved space in his own account, which rarely exceeded two columns, to editorialize on the conduct of the convention and to press for reforms which he regarded as most important.

The convention was slow in getting down to business. Mackenzie feared that these delays would prevent the convention from coming to grips with vitally needed reforms until the closing days, when lack of time might prevent changes from being given adequate consideration. Matters turned out as he expected. Eleven reports were crowded into the final week of the convention, as Mackenzie had predicted,[7] and these included such important topics as the franchise, education, municipal affairs, banking and currency, and revision of the tax laws to provide for equalization of assessments throughout the state. Mackenzie strongly advocated "direct taxation, equally applied," in the belief that it would lead to the breakup of large properties and the creation of "more freeholders." Nothing was done on this last subject.[8]

Reporting Bascom's motion on the judiciary gave Mackenzie a chance to express his own views on reform of the law, the courts and the election of judges. He allotted more space to this topic than to any other. Mackenzie hoped the convention would recommend the compilation of "an American code of laws instead of keeping the judiciary dependent on British precedents."[9]

New York's constitution provided for seven levels of courts. The numerous appeals possible under the existing system, and the burdensome costs, had produced a general demand for reform. Some delegates were primarily concerned with reducing the accumulation of cases in the higher courts; others urged that it was equally important to reform the inferior courts which were closer to the people and where a substantial amount of the judicial business of the country was carried on.[10]

Mackenzie favoured the courts of the elected justices of the peace. Election of the justices had been one of the provisions in his Draft Constitution for Upper Canada. The labouring classes did not need the other courts where costs were so much higher. What they needed was cheap and speedy justice close at hand from men who had been entrusted with judicial power by their neighbours. But Mackenzie did not favour a multiplicity of appeals. On this point he approved of the ideas of Enoch Strong, a Whig delegate from Monroe County, who proposed that the justices of the peace should have exclusive jurisdiction in matters involving up to $100, and that only one appeal should be allowed.

> It was a court near their own homes, which they could attend
> with little expense and loss of time, and where witnesses and
> jurors could be got near their own doors that the people asked
> for.... [11]

In Canada the comparable courts dealing with small sums were the Courts of Requests, after 1841 the Division Courts. Mackenzie repeatedly urged the extension of their very limited jurisdiction when he returned to Canada.

In New York State the justices' courts themselves were in need of reform. Some delegates contended that only one justice was needed in most of the townships. He should be salaried and his court should have juries.[12] Prior to the rebellion, Mackenzie had repeatedly argued that these small claims courts, whose commissioners were government appointees, ought to have juries.[13] In the end, the convention left the courts of the justices as they were, except that the extent of their jurisdiction was to be established by the legislature.

The most lively debates turned on the question of whether the judges should be appointed or directly elected by the people. What did the old phrase "independence of the judges" mean in a republic? Should they not be required to obtain public approval of their conduct from time to time? Surely the people were able to make a fit choice? The troublesome question was, would judges in county courts, who were bound to know who had supported them and who had been against them, be able to hold themselves above local politics. Noting that Van Buren's opposition in 1821 to the institution of elected justices of the peace was being used again as an argument,[14] Mackenzie counter-attacked with a quotation from Jefferson, who had favoured popular election of the judges over either nomination by the executive or election by the legislature. Even if the people did not select men learned in the law, they would, Mackenzie believed, elect men of good common sense.

> One thing I am sure of. We would not have those Judges of loose life and conversation who have found their way to the Bench under the system of appointment by the Albany Regency or any other.

His final criticism of Van Buren quoted the latter's admission, in 1821, that to elect justices of the peace "would break down the party to which he belonged."[15]

If the judges were to be elected, on what basis should this be done? On a general ticket or individually? Mackenzie, of course, strongly advocated direct election of the judges individually. In that way the electors would know the candidates and it would not be possible for bad men to be "smuggled in" on a general ticket along with the good ones.[16] In the end it was decided that the judges of the Supreme Court should be elected by judicial districts and that half the judges of the Appeals Court should be taken from among the judges of the Supreme Court, half should be elected on a general ticket.[17] "It will be eight years a party bench," Mackenzie observed with disgust. "Tammany will control the nominations."[18] When he returned to Canada he did not suggest that the judges should be elected except at the county level, and he did not press the question.[19]

The constitution of 1821 had authorized a revision of the statutes of New York State. The revision, carried out chiefly by Benjamin F. Butler,[20] had not gone so far as to

> codify the whole law... in the sense of substituting positive written... enactments for the law as existing in the common law and equity systems and as interpreted and applied by the courts....[21]

*That* was what was being demanded in 1846 and by no one more vociferously than Mackenzie. Simplification and codification of the law had been a favourite topic with him from his Canada days on, and the subject of various letters to American newspapers.

When the Committee on the Rights of Citizens made its report, it submitted an article providing that:

> such parts of the common law as were in force in New York on April 19, 1775, should continue to be the law of the state, subject to such alterations as the legislature had or should make.[22]

Mackenzie at once took alarm, pointing out that all the costly uncertainties of the unwritten law and of the thousands of precedents derived from it would remain to plague the ordinary man and to profit the lawyers.[23] "I am for Nativism in the law," he proclaimed. "English Chancery and common law are unfit for Republican America."[24]

At first the Committee could only agree to have the rules of procedure simplified and codified.[25] Some members, however, were determined not to give up the fight for codification of the substantive law — "one of the greatest reforms called for by the people" — and Mackenzie supported this fight by one vigorous article after another in the *Tribune*. Three days before it closed the convention decided that the legislature should appoint commissioners to reduce to a written code the whole body of the law of the state as far as practicable and then report to the legislature. Mackenzie reported triumphantly, "They have voted for the codification of the law. A great reform."[26] He rejoiced too soon. Commissioners were appointed in 1847 who reported a code of substantive law, but "so great was the hostility it encountered from the bar that it was never enacted."[27]

Mackenzie denounced the Court of Chancery as vigorously as he did New York's retention of the common law. It was an "English importation," "a fearful scourge;" it had "meddled with everything;" it had decided "one way today, another way tomorrow;" it was "the terror of the free press;" its procedure was slow and costly; and there had been interminable delays in handing down its decisions.[28] The reader will recognize here Mackenzie's personal grievances against this court. Everywhere Courts of Chancery had become detested. In England Jeremy Bentham had denounced this court. In United Canada abolition of the court was under discussion in the Assembly.[29] In New York State Julian Verplanck, a former Democratic congressman turned Whig, had acknowledged that:

> Equity as a separate system can hardly be said to have worked well anywhere. Its uncertainty, its immense power and still more its delays and expenses have always been a subject of public complaint.[30]

In 21 of the 29 other states no separate court of chancery existed.[31] At the previous constitutional convention Erastus Root had tried to have New York's court abolished but, Mackenzie reminded his readers, "Van Buren and his tail" had been too much for him.[32]

From the outset there was not much doubt that the convention would decide to abolish the Court of Chancery. Its jurisdiction passed to the 32 judges of the new Supreme Court. The new constitution also provided that testimony in equity cases should be taken as in courts of law. The question that gave rise to extended debate was whether the undefined powers of the court, described in the detested phrase, "co-extensive with the powers of the Court of Chancery in England," should be transferred to the new court or should be specifically defined.[33] Mackenzie, and others, could not see that merely transferring jurisdiction in equity from one court to another would be much of a reform. Instead of eight chancery courts there would be 32. Nothing would be accomplished unless provision were made for blending the jurisdictions and simplifying the forms and proceedings in both equity and law. In the end, a safeguarding clause was adopted merely giving the legislature the power it already had under the old constitution to alter and regulate jurisdiction and proceedings in law and equity. As Mackenzie noted with regret, the clause could mean anything or nothing.[34]

Another proposal whose progress through the convention Mackenzie watched with interest related to what was called "the lawyer-licensing system," the power of judges to control admissions to the bar. Mackenzie was opposed to monopolies of every description, whether composed of capitalists, professional men or mechanics. When publisher of the *Colonial Advocate* in Toronto he had denounced craft unions because he feared they would "split up the community into so many selfish and mischievous monopolies like the guilds."[35] In his reports to the *Tribune* he repeatedly urged that the "democratic principles of the revolution" should be extended to the courts.[36] He believed that no such exclusive provision was to be found in the present or any previous constitution of New York State. In this he was wrong; the judges had exercised this power against him in 1838;[37] but he was right in claiming that several states permitted all citizens to practise — Missouri, Maine and New Hampshire.[38]

Mackenzie's views were shared by many who, unlike him, had no personal grievance to motivate them. In the convention of 1821 there had been almost twice as many farmers as lawyers. In the convention of 1846, there were 42 farmers, 46 lawyers. De Toqueville's aristocracy of lawyers was coming into existence and was disliked; they were thought to charge excessive fees and to increase court costs unnecessarily.[39] It was Strong, a farmer delegate from Monroe, who vigorously opposed any rule for "the establishment of any superior or privileged order of human beings," claiming "it ought not to be engrafted on the constitution of a free people."[40] Strong's effort to prohibit the judges from preventing any citizen from practising "except for want of good moral character" met with some vigorous support, but not enough. In the end a clause which entitled any citizen of good moral character who possessed "the requisite qualifications of learning and ability" to be admitted to practice was adopted.[41] A contemporary historian claimed that the convention established "a liberal rule" for the admission of attorneys and counsellors.[42] Mackenzie did not think so. He pointed out that this wording, unwarily accepted by the liberals in the convention, continued the existing power of the judges to exclude; and now, being "riveted" in the constitution, would be more difficult for the legislature to change.[43] Mackenzie observed:

> What I have witnessed in this chamber fully satisfies me that "the privileged order" combined in action as they are with the very wealthy part of this community, are the real sovereigns of this state in a greater degree than 99/100 of the community are aware of.... [44]

Another reform which Mackenzie hoped to see adopted provided for the institution of courts of conciliation so as to reduce the amount of litigation and bring about the settlement of disputes at minimal cost.[45] This proposal was not welcomed by the committee on the judiciary, one of whose members sarcastically compared such courts to old women talking over a tea table. Other members found it more sensible, and on September 3 the committee reported a provision for creating courts of conciliation. An emasculated version was adopted which permitted, but did not require, the legislature to establish them, and which stated that their judgements were not to be binding unless the parties agreed in advance to accept them.[46]

In no article of the new constitution did Mackenzie take keener interest than in that relating to the judiciary. After his return to Canada he was to propose the abolition of the Court of Chancery and the lawyer licensing system, and he attempted to obtain conciliation courts, elected justices of the peace, elected sheriffs and a judicial system that a poor man could afford to utilize.

Another change for which there was widespread demand in New York State was that assemblymen be elected by single electoral districts. This was a reform that Horace Greeley had long kept before the public,[47] and the arguments in support of it were the same as those advanced for single judicial districts. This "great and most desirable reform" was accepted by the convention.[48]

The new constitution abolished many minor offices and provided that most state and local offices should be filled by election, but it did not go far enough in reducing the Governor's patronage to suit Mackenzie. The Governor had had the power to make 2,238 appointments with the consent of the Senate and 289 alone.[49] Mackenzie listed 953 appointments that were still to be filled by him with the concurrence of the Senate.[50] On the last day of the convention John A. Kennedy, a Democrat from New York County, proposed that all appointments made by any legislative body or official board should be made by open voting. This check on log-rolling was defeated. "If the ballot is a protection to the voter, it ought not to be a screen to conceal the acts of their official agents from the voters," Mackenzie observed.[51] The use of the patronage to undermine the independence of the legislature was, however, restricted in the new constitution by a provision that senators and assemblymen accepting a civil appointment from either the state or federal government should lose their seats. Here was "a real check upon intrigue,"[52] a reform that Mackenzie hoped to secure in Canada after his return.

The institution of single electoral districts for Senate and Assembly, the reduction of patronage, and the election of judges and state and local officials, all were intended and expected to return power to "the people." For Mackenzie all this was not enough. "Unless the power of nominating is in the people," he wrote, "they do not actually have the power of election."[53]

Among the delegates to the constitutional convention were 13 who were classified as "Anti-Renters." These men represented half-a-dozen Hudson Valley counties where great estates were being cultivated by tenants holding their farms on long or perpetual leases. Since the fall of 1839 disputes over payments in kind had been raging between the landlords and their tenants.

Arrears of rent had accumulated from farms now no longer able to raise wheat profitably, and the landlords were refusing to commute the leases into outright freeholds on what the tenants regarded as reasonable terms. Payments called quarter-sales, due when tenants sold their holdings to someone other than the landlord, and reservations by the landlords of mill sites, water rights and timber rights were additional grievances. The efforts of the landlords to collect their back rents through the sheriff, who seized and sold the tenants' cattle, and their attempts to evict stubborn tenants, led to organized resistance to the law, and to the death of a deputy sheriff. By the fall of 1845 some 60 Anti-Renters were in prison.[54]

The convention appointed a committee (later referred to as the "anti-rent committee") to inquire whether the character and permanency of American republican institutions would not be "increased" by multiplying the number of freeholders, reducing the landed monopolies and forbidding the acquisition of more than 320 acres by any man.[55] The first section of its report proposed to declare all feudal tenures, with their incidents, abolished. This provision was accepted with the addition of a proviso saving "all rents and services certain already lawfully created or reserved." The second section limited leases of agricultural land to 12 years. The third section made all restraints on alienation invalid *for the future*.[56] The committee made no recommendation respecting methods of breaking up the large estates, nor did it take any action on a memorial from the National Reform Association which had been referred to it. This memorial proposed that the public lands of the state be granted, as inalienable homesteads, to actual settlers having no other land, and it asked that the Anti-Renters "now in prison for opposing land monopoly" be liberated.[57]

Mackenzie was eager to see every remnant of feudalism rooted out of the institutions of New York State. In Canada he had advocated liberal land regulations and had criticized the policies of the Canada Company. In New York City he had been an active member of the National Reform Association, denouncing land monopoly and aristocracy in ringing phrases and with a wealth of historical allusions. He now sent the *Tribune* a letter signed with one of his favorite pseudonyms, "Roger Sherman,"[58] advocating the liberation of the imprisoned Anti-Renters, praising the idea of exempting homesteads from seizure for debt and the proposal for land limitation. The plight of the English and Irish masses in the Old World where land monopoly existed was graphically described.[59] But Mackenzie did not write the *series* of trenchant articles or pour forth the "perfect Niagara of facts" in support of anti-rentism that he produced in favour of judicial reform.[60] Yet here was an issue that one would expect to have called forth his most passionate efforts.

Perhaps it was not necessary for Mackenzie to wage a campaign in behalf of anti-rentism. After all, on June 25 Horace Greeley had placed the *Tribune* squarely behind the cause of land reform and of free homesteads, and had shown his sympathy with the Anti-Renters. Could the reporter add weight to the editor's words? But the remedies Greeley suggested were legal and for the future; he did not advocate interfering with existing property rights.[61]

Mackenzie was of the opinion that "anti-rent lawyers" in the convention had not done the tenants any good. Although they had prevented future leases being made on the old terms, they had not touched existing leases or the question of land limitation.[62] Greeley politely yet firmly and publicly disagreed with his reporter. What the convention had accomplished was "of decided worth" if only as indicating public disapproval of land monopoly and tenancy and sympathy with the unfortunate prisoners who had resisted landlordism in the Hudson Valley.[63]

There was nothing Mackenzie was more anxious to see the convention do than require the legislature to establish a system of free public schools, supported by taxation instead of by the inadequate state and local grants supplemented by school rates paid by the parents.[64] Not until October 3, just a week before its scheduled closing, did the convention get around to debating the important subject of education. Michael Hoffman, a prominent Barnburner, tried to cut off discussion by remarking that:

> any attempt to discuss the subject of education would bring the Convention to its certain death; for although the Convention might not adjourn, its members would.

Then a proposition to submit to the people separately a section requiring the legislature to provide for free common school education was defeated. Mackenzie's comment was:

> The Democratic equality-loving Convention have refused to allow the people to say what they prefer.... This is left to the Legislature.[65]

Three other subjects gave rise to extended debate: the public debt of New York State, banks and corporations.

One of the standing committees created by the convention was instructed to report of "Lands, internal improvements, public revenues and property and public debt." This committee proposed borrowing money to complete the unfinished canals and using the surplus canal revenues for the creation of a sinking fund to reduce the state's debt. Mackenzie approved some parts of the committee's report. "Money borrowed for internal improvements," he remarked, "would fill the state with wealth," but from debts contracted for wars, "the people suffer."[66]

A second report of this committee recommended that the legislature be forbidden to lend the credit of the state to any individual or corporation. The committee also proposed that the state's borrowing powers be limited to $1,000,000, except in case of invasion or insurrection. With these exceptions, all laws contracting debts on behalf of the state should provide for a direct annual tax sufficient to redeem the debt in 18 years and should be submitted to a referendum for approval by the people. These two restrictions on the legislature — the heart of the Barnburners' program — proved acceptable to the convention.[67] Mackenzie had included similar restrictions in his Draft

Constitution for Upper Canada, by requiring the legislature to provide by taxation for the liquidation of loans.

The convention's standing committee on currency and banking had as chairman C.C. Cambreling, one of the leading Barnburners. Several of the reports of his committee were readily accepted by the convention. The legislature was denied the power to grant special charters for banks but might incorporate them under a general law. It was also restricted from sanctioning the suspension of specie payment. In future banks were to be required to give security for the redemption of their notes in specie. In addition, Cambreling proposed first, to limit the total quantity of bank notes that might be issued by the banks of New York State and second, to make stockholders individually responsible without limit for their banks' liabilities, both notes and deposits.[68] Here was the big issue on which Mackenzie had agitated in Canada: control of the currency, regulation of the banks and liability of their stockholders. Here were the reforms he had provided for in sections 5, 18 and 56 of his Draft Constitution for Upper Canada.[69] Here was the radical program he had supported in his *Gazette*. But both these propositions were being vigorously opposed by the Whigs and by his employer, Horace Greeley, who called imposing on stockholders unlimited liability for the debts of banks "an act of pure hostility" to banking, especially as the state had already taken security for their notes.[70] Mackenzie perforce limited himself to factual reporting of the debates, but he took care to include in one of his letters to the *Tribune* statistics from Comptroller Flagg's report showing up the unsatisfactory character of both the safety-fund and the free-banking systems.[71] The safety fund had proved to be inadequate to the demands upon it, and the securities deposited by the free banks, when sold to redeem their notes, had likewise proved to be inadequate.

Cambreling found himself obliged to yield on his two proposals. The first one was defeated, 44 to 58.[72] Ultimately he modified the second to secure passage of a liability clause as strong as he could get it.[73] In the form finally submitted by his committee, it passed 49 to 35. It made a bank's stockholders responsible for all its debts and liabilities of every kind merely to the amount of their shares of stock. Thus the convention never got a chance to vote on the question of unlimited liability.

Radical delegates were uneasy about the proliferation of non-banking corporations. In many instances they had been promoted by men who, standing on a flimsy financial basis of their own, had succeeded in wangling charters from the legislature with limited liability privileges. This topic gave rise to extended and confused debate.

The Committee on Corporations recommended that they be created by a general law. It also accepted the principle of unlimited liability, though with stockholders' shares of that liability made proportionate to the amount of stock they held.[74] The first recommendation proved acceptable to the convention. The second was replaced by an ambiguous substitute which merely provided that "dues from corporations shall be secured by such individual liability of the corporators and other means as may be prescribed by law."[75] An attempt to

138

impose liability equal to double the amount of stock held was defeated in the convention.

Mackenzie's account of the debates on this topic was factual and limited. His Whig editor approved of creating corporations under a general law but was opposed to the principle of unlimited liability for stockholders or even proportionate liability, and had promptly said so. Mackenzie did venture to say that he wished the corporation article could be submitted to the people and he asked why responsibility for debt "should be one way for partnerships and another way for corporations."[76] That, evidently, was as far as he dared go on a topic on which he had formerly expended reams of argument and which had found a place in both his Draft Constitution for Upper Canada and his Navy Island proclamation. It was granting limited liability to corporate stockholders that Mackenzie opposed. He favoured general incorporation laws of which all could take advantage without having to purchase the favour of politicians.

In the early forties the same distrust of trading and manufacturing corporations existed in Canada, and not only among radical Reformers. Moderates like Robert Baldwin and J.H. Price opposed granting corporations limited liability privileges. By the time Mackenzie returned to Canada, however, attitudes had changed, and it was too late for him to renew his old fight on this subject even if he had still been inclined to do so. In the session of 1850, in response to repeated petitions, a general incorporation act had been passed granting limited liability privileges simpler than the complex privileges of an earlier measure.[77]

In Mackenzie's opinion, while the New York State convention had done some useful things, it had failed to provide for a truly democratic society. It had done nothing to break the control of professional politicians over the nomination of candidates for public office. To remedy this situation he suggested that the law should provide for the election of one delegate from each assembly district to the various party nominating conventions, whose members should, by open votes, select their candidates for all state offices. "That would be real democracy."[78] The system Mackenzie advocated, at the instigation of O'Rielly,[79] was later to be instituted in New York State, but unhappily it was not to eliminate the "traders in politics" nor the "dealers in votes" whom he castigated. Nor had the convention concerned itself with the wretchedness and misery which existed in the cities of New York and Brooklyn.

> I am well acquainted with it. What madmen those politicians are who think that a State or Nation that does not make unceasing efforts to remedy such a condition of things can ever be truly good or happy. In this Convention very few seem to think of the accumulating masses of wretched beings rendered dangerous because they are injured. [80]

Privately, Mackenzie gave James a more generous estimate of the work of the convention:

> With all its faults it goes further than any constitution I know
> in the way of placing in the people's hands the judicial,
> legislative and executive power of government. Much that was
> valuable failed, but on the other hand, much that was bad was
> changed for the better.... [81]

Mackenzie was strongly in favour of submitting the constitution to the people for adoption, article by article, but such a proposal was defeated in the convention, 70 to 40. However, he planned to vote for the new constitution for the good that was in it, disregarding the convention's sins of omission and the rather shabby way in which it had left too many ticklish questions to be solved by the new legislature.

Horace Greeley, who had loyally defended his reporter against attacks made on him by several delegates and by other newspapers,[82] was not as critical as Mackenzie of the work of the convention. He thought the land tenure provisions were "of practical as well as theoretical value," and commended the single member assembly and senate districts, and the new restrictions designed to prevent the polls being swamped by batches of newly naturalized voters or by voters imported from other districts. The requirement that all laws be passed by a majority of those elected and the "ayes" and "noes" on the final vote be recorded would enable the public in future to determine exactly where "responsibility" lay.[83]

What estimate can we make of Mackenzie's reports on the work of the convention? On the whole he was impartial. It is true he went out of his way to blame the Van Burenites for the accumulated errors of the past and he took care to commend radical Whigs who took the initiative in proposing reforms and condemned Democrats who opposed them. But Whig, Barnburner and Hunker delegates alike were criticized or praised by him as he saw fit. He rode his hobbies, fought hard for economic and social reforms as well as political ones that especially interested him, and enriched his letters to the *Tribune* with statistical material from special reports to the convention that did not become part of the printed official debates published by the *Atlas* and the *Argus* newspapers.

Mackenzie was always grateful to Greeley for employment and for favours in the way of advances and loans. While at Albany he received $12.00 a week. In addition he obtained an intensive political education. The rapid economic and social changes which had occurred in New York State in a quarter of a century were described as he listened. Some of the ablest men in the state — and its shrewdest politicians — discussed the practical problems and the demand for changes which had arisen and worked out their compromise solutions, yielding a key word or phrase as he watched. Radical reformers had it demonstrated to them that politics is the art of the possible. Thoughtful men, troubled by the direction of social change and concerned with the preservation — or the creation — of a "good" society, a "true Republic," in America, debated their various ideals of it with eloquence. Mackenzie was soon to return to a Canada in which the transition from a predominantly rural and agrarian economy to a partly urbanized society and more mature and diversified economy was already under way. It has been said that it was to a different Canada, no longer interested in the old issues that had given rise to the rebellion, that Mackenzie returned. It was a different Mackenzie that returned — but there was still much of the old leaven in him.

# Chapter X

# GREELEY, O'RIELLY AND THE PAPERS OF PRESIDENT MONROE

With the end of his employment as the Tribune's reporter in sight, Mackenzie began to plan for the future. Early in November George Bruce purchased the steam press and printing office of Perry and Reed at a sheriff's sale for $10,000. He proposed that Mackenzie continue the business with one of the partners, who could not get along with one another, and even offered him the chance to buy the business on the installment plan.[1] To his son Mackenzie admitted he might have accepted the offer if he could have had his help. He had not the courage to face a heavy burden of debt at his time of life alone.[2] Moreover, he would have had to take a partner. This was something he would not do, perhaps aware of the limitations of his own irascible temperament.

By mid-November Mackenzie was once again pinched for funds. He asked Thomas Ewbank to help him buy a stove on credit. Ewbank, in refusing to aid him on this occasion, replied with more justice than kindness:

> Those who insist on bending the world to their view instead of conforming themselves — at least reasonably — cannot expect to sail through life with the wind always on their poop.... What might your surprising energy & untiring industry have accomplished were they invested in anything else but politics. The worst business for you here — whatever it may have been in Canada. But why repeat what I have often told you.[3]

Mackenzie tried to persuade Greeley to employ him to report the doings of the New York State legislature, but the Tribune's editor thought they would be "of subordinate consequence and interest" to most of his readers.[4] Mackenzie's reluctance to leave Albany was based on the hope that he would get an appointment from the legislature as Assistant Clerk to the Assembly. Greeley did his best to obtain from the Whigs this bit of patronage for Mackenzie, but he failed.[5] It is hardly to be wondered at. Mackenzie's course in politics since his arrival in the United States had certainly been zig-zag. He had latterly done the Whigs some service but he had also criticized conservative Whigs in the convention and had deplored the election of lawyers to the legislature. There were 28 of them in the new assembly. None of these influential men could be expected to enable a polemicist like Mackenzie to keep a gimlet-eyed watch on their conduct in the legislature and expose them in Greeley's radical Whig newspaper.

Mackenzie remained in Albany until May 1847. He was asked to edit an issue of the Albany *Patriot* (an anti-slavery paper) in the absence of the editor, and this gave him a chance to plug several of his favourite topics: codification of the law, reduction of federal patronage, a free public school system and the cost of the iniquitous Mexican War. Before long he was writing for the *Tribune* again under various pseudonyms. There was a letter on anti-rent, one on land limitation and free homesteads, one on prison reform, two on the necessity of more generous support for education and in support of the local option provisions of the excise law.[6]

Mackenzie used his spare time putting together a history of the rebellion and he seems to have got in touch with George Bruce about obtaining the use of a press and types.[7] O'Callaghan, who was once again writing to him although not as frequently or on the old relaxed and intimate basis, questioned the prudence of this project. He advised Mackenzie:

> Reflect on the consequences of your acts beforehand. It matters little who goes to a Governor's levee but it matters much whether anything should be done which can weaken the influence of the Liberal Party in Canada or give their enemies an advantage against them.

He evidently feared that Mackenzie, embittered by the failure of the Liberals to include him in an amnesty, might make indiscreet revelations. "Are personal grievances to weigh in times like these..." he enquired, adding, "I will do nothing to embarrass the movements of those with whom I have acted in Canada." He signed his letter "Yours, as long as you merit it."[8]

Mackenzie's history may have got beyond the stage of a collection of notes, for he informed his son that he was "writing out my book upon Canada."[9] He also told O'Rielly that he had been working hard on the book, and that, aided by his latest remittance, he would get "through" the book during the next fortnight, and that it would be an octavo pamphlet, minim, of some 100 or 144 pages.[10] Subsequently he informed Wolfred Nelson that he *had* written the book but had decided to postpone publication.[11] Mackenzie did publish in the *Tribune* a four-column account of his escape from Canada 10 years earlier,[12] but his history of the rebellion never appeared. After his death his son-in-law stated that it was not to be found among his papers.[13] Various memoranda survive, and what was probably the title page for the intended manuscript.[14]

In April 1847 Mackenzie decided to give up the struggle to remain in Albany. He had been having a thin time of it — to Henry O'Rielly's generosity his family owed its Thanksgiving dinner — and by spring he could no longer pay his rent.[15] Thomas Ewbank induced the publishers of the *New York Tribune* to find work for him again, although they complained that Mackenzie had been "too fond of finding fault" in his letters.[16] By May 12 the family was settled in the house Horace Greeley had occupied on 50th St. near 3rd Avenue.[17] Mackenzie remained with the *Tribune* only until August, when Henry O'Rielly found other employment for him.[18]

While at Albany Mackenzie had appended to one of his daily reports a request for employment after the convention in some literary capacity such as arranging and editing historical documents.[19] It produced no offers at the time, but in June 1847 O'Rielly informed him that President James Monroe's papers had been placed at his disposal for extending a memoir of the life of the fifth President and that if Mackenzie cared to undertake the task he might draw on O'Rielly for money.[20]

> The only limitation is [wrote O'Rielly] that Mr. G[ouverneur] shall ultimately have a voice in case anything should be embodied of no public use and of private annoyance.

Henry O'Rielly had gone through various vicissitudes.[21] He had been editor of the Rochester *Daily Advertiser*, postmaster of that city, a promoter of the convention for the reform of the constitution of New York State, secretary of the association formed for this purpose and recording secretary of the state's Agricultural Society. In 1845 he had become interested in the electric telegraph and was at this time organizing telegraph companies and constructing lines in the Ohio Valley.[22] He asked Mackenzie to write and get published in the *Tribune* and other newspapers articles supporting him in his disputes with the patentees of the Morse telegraph. O'Rielly had no leisure for literary work at this moment, therefore sought Mackenzie's help with the Monroe manuscripts also. From time to time he sent him remittances for his services on both accounts.[23]

President Monroe had left a one-third interest in any profits that might arise from the use or publication of his papers to his son-in-law, Samuel L. Gouverneur, and one-third to each of his two daughters, Mrs. Gouverneur and Mrs. E.K. Hay. Gouverneur was also too busy to extend and document the memoir of Monroe's life which the ex-President had begun.[24] He entrusted the memoir and some of the Monroe papers, perhaps a good half of those in his possession at the time, to O'Rielly.[25] The financial arrangement worked out between them provided that O'Rielly should publish the life, manuscripts and papers of Monroe at his own expense and receive three-eighths of the profits from publication.[26] Gouverneur reserved the right to suppress or exclude such portions of the material "as a due regard for Mr. Monroe's memory or respect for the feelings of others or their descendants may render proper."

In August Mackenzie obtained the trunk of Monroe papers and began to read and arrange them. The collection remained in his care from August 1847 to January 1849. Its whereabouts in this interval have not hitherto been known. Mackenzie was greatly excited by the Monroe papers:

> The topics of the day (our day) are discussed at great length by the great men of the republic [he named some thirty-five of

them]... with unquestionable candour.... Such a collection of important ms. correspondence it was never before my fate or fortune even to glance at. [27]

O'Rielly also sent Mackenzie the "145 closely written manuscript pages... contain[ing] a sketch of the public life of Mr. Monroe up to 1806...."[28] Mackenzie soon began to realize that there were important gaps in the correspondence and he suggested that Gouverneur might be able to supply the missing letters. He surmised that the sketch of Monroe's life had been written by a southern man, an intimate of Monroe's home, perhaps by Gouverneur. He did not realize that, although in the third person, it had been written by Monroe himself, but he guessed correctly that some of the references in it were to Monroe's own writings.[29] He was aware, too, that some of the letters and parts, at least, of the sketch had been published before and, like a careful editor, he tried to obtain definite information on this point.[30]

Mackenzie proposed that he should prepare a fully annotated edition of the Monroe papers and that the correspondence should be put into print direct from the precious originals, without the necessity of recopying them, and under his own careful supervision. He thought that the notes and letters, together with the sketch of Monroe's life to 1806 as it then stood, would run into several volumes which could be issued seriatim as they received Gouverneur's approval.[31] But O'Rielly was so absorbed in his telegraph business that he could not attend to this proposal promptly and left Mackenzie to his own devices. The latter therefore went on chronologically arranging the letters, summarizing and indexing them.[32]

At the end of November 1847 Mackenzie began working for the *Tribune* again, seven days a week for $15.00, funds from the hard-pressed O'Rielly no longer being an adequate source of income.[33] Mackenzie was reluctant to return to the *Tribune*, where George M. Snow, one of the assistant editors and a staunch Nativist, was unfriendly to him.[34] He also found the late hours very hard on him. "I would leave this concern if I could do better," he admitted.[35] In April 1848 he did resign, one of the partners being dissatisfied with his work.[36] Perhaps it was not up to par. In the spring of 1848 Mackenzie was much depressed and wrote of his "inability to be of material use to any one as now situated."[37] He was restless and unsettled, awaiting news of the amnesty, and he was very unhappy. He nearly lost his two sons by drowning; one daughter, Janet, was absent in Toronto; eight-year-old Margaret was seriously ill and Mackenzie had been told nothing more could be done for her — she died in June — and the eldest daughter, Barbara, was also stricken and had to be hospitalized for a time.[38]

Then, also, journalistic styles were changing and with them the duties of reporters. News was coming to be written briefly, impersonally, without editorial comment and long excursions into past history.[39] The new way was not Mackenzie's way. Special articles were his strong point. As a free-lance writer and irregularly paid publicity man for O'Rielly, Mackenzie could not afford the house on 50th St. and moved to cheaper quarters.[40] Greeley found work for him compiling almanacs. He did the Whig almanacs for 1848 and 1849 and the *Business Men's Almanack* for 1848.[41]

Mackenzie continued to press O'Rielly to come to some decision on the Monroe papers, at least to arrange for the publication of a select number of them, not only because he hoped soon to be in Canada where his time would be otherwise occupied, but also because he thought some of the correspondence had a bearing on current political questions.[42] O'Rielly put the matter up to Gouverneur, whose response was unfavourable.[43] At this time Gouverneur thought it possible that Congress would make a grant in aid of publishing the Monroe papers, as it had the Hamilton papers. Publication of a selection of Monroe's papers, which it would be assumed comprised the cream of the collection, would only depreciate the value of the rest.

O'Rielly did ask Mackenzie to find Monroe's manuscript notes on what he would have done if the Missouri Compromise bill had failed and also any other notes of Monroe's "about those slave matters." The material was to be sent to Senator James Westcott (Florida) "leaving your note anonymous as if I write it."44 The search was unsuccessful, but Gouverneur found the wanted document among those he had retained. Westcott received also some 24 other extracts from the Monroe papers, several of them supplied by Mackenzie. He used them in his speech on the Oregon Territorial Bill to fortify his view of the proper interpretation of the Missouri Compromise.45 He wished to show that Monroe had been prepared to veto it and signed it only after he had been assured by all the members of the cabinet, except John Quincy Adams, that although by its terms Congress did, and constitutionally could, restrict slavery in the territories, the Compromise placed no restriction on the territories when they should become states. O'Rielly also asked Mackenzie to extend the memoir of Monroe's life by inserting the most important documents that supported it into the text, and to point out those years for which letters seemed to be missing so that the Monroe heirs might search for them.[46]

Despite Mackenzie's urging, O'Rielly never succeeded in arranging for the publication of any portion of the Monroe papers. By October 1848 it had become clear to O'Rielly that he was not going to profit from the papers as readily as he had imagined he would. Senator Westcott now informed him that Gouverneur had suggested to him that he (Westcott) should extend the memoir of Monroe's life. Westcott proposed that O'Rielly should bring the papers to Washington where the three of them could consult on the subject. "Great prudence must be observed in reference to political subjects and to them who were his [Monroe's] contemporaries...." Westcott did not doubt the Congress could be got to patronize the work but he warned, "How & by whom it is edited will be with some an influential consideration."[47]

O'Rielly next discovered that Gouverneur had consulted Eliab Kingman, who had been a clerk of the House of Representatives from 1840-43, about the possibility of his completing the memoir. It is clear that O'Rielly was not keen on Kingman's becoming the editor and having the advantage of all the work that had already been done.

> Will you not be named as Editor [he enquired of Gouverneur]. You
> know how sensitive many public men will be about the contents

of Mr. Monroe's papers. And it is well that it should be decided whose name shall appear as Editor, bearing the responsibility. [48]

Meanwhile poor Mackenzie went toiling on, ignorant of these developments and of how soon his hopes of being the ghost editor of the papers were to be crushed. In all the negotiations O'Rielly did not reveal — and dared not reveal — that he had entrusted the Monroe papers to the man who had published the Butler-Hoyt correspondence and that he planned to use that man's services in editing them.

Gouverneur now began to press O'Rielly to bring the papers to Washington where they could be inspected if required. [49] On December 23 a contract was signed between Gouverneur and O'Rielly reciting the terms of the existing agreement between them, which was to stand unless the papers should be purchased by the government for not less than $20,000. In that event Gouverneur was to get 70%; O'Rielly was to get 30%, 10% of which was to go to Kingman for helping to negotiate the sale. [50]

Towards the end of January 1849 Mackenzie, as requested, sent the papers, together with a chronological index which he was not given time to complete, to O'Rielly who was now impatiently waiting to submit them to the inspection of a committee of the Senate. [51] Congress purchased those of the Monroe papers that were not of a private character for $20,000. [52] Subsequently Gouverneur paid off Kingman "and others" and O'Rielly, and received a clearance from the latter. [53]

Mackenzie was evidently deeply disappointed by the sale of the papers to the government. He wrote somewhat reproachfully,

I had supposed that I would superintend the printing and had therefore prepared many notes not now desirable under the new arrangement.

He reminded O'Rielly that he had first been requested to arrange the unorganized papers, to extend the memoir and to prepare the most suitable letters for publication. He had done so, attaching relevant newspaper clippings to them, marking passages in the letters fit to be omitted, and had summarized the contents of many letters for headings. But he had used slips of paper that he had previously used in noting debates in Albany "never dreaming the papers would come before a committee of the Senate." When requested to send them for the committee to see, he left in the clippings he had added but felt it necessary to remove most of the notes and memoranda he had attached to the letters. [54] They might have given his identity away. All his work in preparing the Monroe papers for publication was thus made useless.

There were two documents that Mackenzie did not return, whether by accident or design cannot be stated. They both relate to Canada. The first is a draft letter of Sept. 23, 1813, written by President Madison to General Mason about the treatment which British prisoners in American hands were to receive in retaliation for the way in which American prisoners in British hands were being treated. A couple of lines written by Monroe and his signature were added to this draft letter. Mackenzie published the document in his *Message* of June 18, 1858, with the statement that the original draft letter was then before him. The second document, a letter of Nov. 28, 1818, was written by ex-President Madison to President Monroe. It stated Madison's belief that Canada "whenever rich enough to be profitable [to Great Britain] will be strong enough to be independent." Mackenzie published it in his *Message* of December 31, 1859, and in his *Almanac for Independence and Freedom*. This letter is now in the Ontario Archives.

Mackenzie's services to O'Rielly as a promoter of telegraph companies came to an end about this time also. For 18 months he had been writing articles at O'Rielly's request, defending him in his disputes with Samuel Morse and the other patentees of the Morse telegraph, and he had constantly badgered the *Tribune* and other newspapers to insert them. A brief account of O'Rielly's telegraph business now follows.

In June 1845 the patentees of the Morse telegraph had signed a contract with O'Rielly for the construction of a line which should connect a point on their seaboard line (Philadelphia as it turned out) with Harrisburg, Wheeling, Cincinnati and other towns as far west as St. Louis and also with the principal towns on the lakes. The contract gave O'Rielly the right to construct lines linking the western cities with one another but reserved to the Morse patentees, although not in clearly exclusive language, the right to connect these western points directly to New Orleans. O'Rielly had many difficulties to contend with, some of them occasioned by helping the Morse interests in the construction of their own seaboard line. When he did not complete the Harrisburg-Philadelphia portion of his line within the time set by his imprecisely worded contract, F.O.J. Smith, an ex-congressman from Maine who held one-fourth of the patent, insisted on the contract being declared void. Smith had begun to see that the telegraph companies O'Rielly was organizing so vigorously in the Ohio Valley would become a very profitable telegraph "empire." He regretted that he had let it slip from his control.

Embittered by the treatment he received, O'Rielly disregarded the declaration that his contract had become void, went on organizing companies and building lines north of the Ohio, other lines south to New Orleans, and finally a line from Boston to New York. In all he constructed over 4,000 miles of telegraph lines. O'Rielly used the Morse instruments north of the Ohio, as his contract permitted him to do. When his enemies tried to secure an injunction to stop him, they failed. His contract was upheld and his cause was popular. He appeared as the champion of freedom, fighting those who were trying to profit from other men's exertions and attempting to make of the telegraph industry one huge monopoly. For his other lines O'Rielly used the Columbian telegraph and the chemical telegraph of Alexander Bain. (These inventions were to be declared violations of the Morse patent.[55]) Meanwhile O'Rielly had gone on building lines, hampered by lack of capital, ruinous rate wars, the patent dispute and by the refusal of the Morse lines to transmit messages which had originated on non-Morse lines. In 1849 the irrepressible promoter tried to interest Congress in a telegraph line to the Pacific coast. In 1851 he became bankrupt.[56]

Mackenzie entered into O'Rielly's struggle with the Morse patentees with all his heart and soul. He was much more than a paid publicity man. O'Rielly was his old friend and moreover he was fighting Mackenzie's old enemies: the forces of corporate monopoly and privilege. Mackenzie condensed the lengthy circulars O'Rielly sent him into briefer articles and saw to it that from time to time reports of the progress of the O'Rielly lines appeared in the Tribune.[57] When, on September 4, 1847, the Morse patentees adopted their non-intercourse ruling, refusing to accept messages that had to be forwarded from or to O'Rielly lines, Mackenzie was able to have a vigorous letter published under the pseudonym "Mercator" which denounced the non-intercourse ruling and claimed that in making it the Morse patentees violated one condition of their patent, which was that they would act as common carriers for the benefit of the country.[58] His letter gained the more force in that it was prefaced by an editorial that accused the Morse patentees of "High-handed... usurpation of public and private right." "Mr. Greeley endorses your strictures most nobly. Heaven bless him," wrote the delighted O'Rielly.[59]

In a memorial to the legislature of New York O'Rielly asked for enactment of a general telegraph law giving equal protection and equal rights of way to all who wished to erect lines "so that there may be fair competition in this as in all other things."[60] Mackenzie drew attention to O'Rielly's memorial in a letter to the *Tribune* signed "Stephen Girard." He argued that enlistment of lightning in the service of man had originated with Franklin and asked,

> Shall the agency of this almost universal messenger be monopolized to the injury of millions and the gain of a few, or will the Legislature hasten to set bounds to human avarice... by... a Telegraph Law in accordance with the free spirit of American institutions.... [61]

From material supplied by O'Rielly Mackenzie prepared a lengthy review of the controversy over the O'Rielly contract. Copies were sent to other newspapers, to the influential Thurlow Weed and to the Speaker of the New York Assembly.[62] The latter agreed to introduce a bill such as O'Rielly wanted and suggested Mackenzie should supply one. Mackenzie took it upon himself to draft a bill, modelling it on the telegraph company law of Ohio.[63] It was introduced but not proceeded in.[64] At the next session, at the instigation of Representative Brooks, one of the proprietors of the New York Express, a bill was passed providing that any association of capitalists might be incorporated as a telegraph company and have rights of way upon public highways. They were to be required to accept despatches from or to other lines and to serve the public on a first-come, first-served basis.[65]

Then, for a few months, Mackenzie seems to have turned his attention to matters other than O'Rielly's telegraph lines. As has been noted, he had serious domestic troubles, he still had the Monroe papers to work on at this time, and the inevitable hack-work, almanacs. He was also trying to finish his book on Canada. "The object in getting it out now," he informed O'Rielly, "is to set myself right with all parties and to help the cause of freedom." He was expecting the amnesty at any moment.[66] But when Bain and O'Rielly tied to obtain a patent for the Bain chemical telegraph, Mackenzie came to their assistance again with two articles signed "Morion."

Mackenzie's services to O'Rielly as a promoter of telegraph companies were now about to come to an end. Greeley offered to send him to Washington as a correspondent for the *Tribune* at $20.00 a week. Mackenzie accepted, although it meant leaving his family behind, because it would enable him to complete his editing of the Monroe manuscripts and his "political education."[67] He was to leave New York on November 30th, but at the last minute he rejected this employment because, as he told O'Rielly, he thought it "right" to do so. His decision is curious and was not fully explained even to his son.[68] Greeley had been elected to Congress in November 1848 to fill out an unexpired term, and he served until the end of the lame duck session. One would have expected Mackenzie to jump at the chance of being there at the same time. But he was a touchy person, proud and sensitive, and he knew that other members of the *Tribune's* staff did not regard him with approval.

> Had I gone to Washington [he explained] I would have been blamed for many things, and Robinson[69] would have reviewed and permitted or rejected what I might have written. I am afraid I would not have pleased him so easily as Mr. Greeley.[70]

About this time Greeley felt obliged to intimate that he was reluctant to endorse any more of Henry O'Rielly's notes. The latter, always short of ready money, had been paying Mackenzie in this way and Greeley had been endorsing the notes so that Mackenzie could get them discounted.[71] When O'Rielly wanted the *Tribune* to give publicity to his memorial against a proposal to "reform" the patent laws, claiming that his enemies were trying to "smuggle through" a "villainous bill" to make patents proof conclusive in a court of justice,[72] Mackenzie had to confess that he no longer had influence in the *Tribune* office and that Greeley was disinclined to court further newspaper controversy.[73] About this time, when Mackenzie's prospects of earning a living in the United States except by hack-work seemed to be vanishing, the long awaited amnesty was finally granted him.

# Chapter XI

# THE AMNESTY AND
# THE ANNEXATION CRISIS

$M$ackenzie was the last of the exiles to be enabled to return to Canada. His failure to receive this boon earlier embittered him towards some of his former associates in both sections of that province, and led him to accuse them of indifference towards him.[1] The question of an amnesty that would include Mackenzie had, however, been under discussion in Canada since 1841 and he had repeatedly had his hopes raised only to have them dashed when nothing was done for him. In the first parliament of united Canada, Colonel John Prince, who was thought to be trying to regain popular favour after executing Patriot prisoners at Windsor, brought up the subject of an amnesty for "worthy men entrapped... [by] artful and cowardly leaders." So did John Neilson who, however, asked for a general amnesty.[2] After a six-hour debate on whether an amnesty should be made general or not, during which both Baldwin and Hincks said they would vote for a general amnesty, an address carried, but in an amended form. It now asked only that pardons be granted to all those whose return would be compatible with the safety of the Crown and the province. Obviously these words were meant to exclude Mackenzie.[3] The Governor-General, Lord Sydenham, consented to forward the address,[4] but failed to do so. His promise was made the very day he received the injury that was to prove fatal.[5] His successor, Sir Charles Bagot, did forward the address and recommended an amnesty for those against whom no legal proceedings had been taken. For those who had been convicted or attainted he was ready to recommend pardons provided their presence would be no danger to the province. Wolfred Nelson, John Montgomery, John Rolph, David Gibson, Nelson Gorham and Charles Duncombe were pardoned in 1843. All but Duncombe returned to Canada.[6] The efforts made by the Mackintosh family on Mackenzie's behalf did not succeed.[7]

After the first Baldwin-Lafontaine government took office in September 1842 the question of an amnesty for political offences was again raised in the Assembly. On this occasion William Dunlop, representative for Huron, remarked that he was surprised Mackenzie had not been pardoned since worse men than he had been allowed to return; Mackenzie had this redeeming quality:

He had the courage to face the danger he had brought upon himself unlike Rolph and some others who had been pardoned, who kept back and pushed better men than themselves forward to bear the brunt of the contest.

During the debate Baldwin remarked that he had not changed his mind about the desirability of a general amnesty but that it did not depend upon him and his colleagues.[8]

Mackenzie confidently expected that with a Reform government in power an amnesty would be obtained. The failure of the Baldwin-Lafontaine government to make the return of the Van Diemen's Land prisoners a cabinet question and to ask for a general amnesty before they went out of office in November 1843 filled him with bitterness. Francis Hincks informed Rolph that he had received a letter from Mackenzie threatening, if Hincks did not write to him immediately,

> to publish another *Welland Canal* showing up Baldwin, Dunn, Price and myself... Mackenzie pretends to believe that we are opposed to an amnesty. Some of his friends in Toronto, one would think, might set him right on this point, but as I feel assured that money is what he wants I think it would not be worthwhile taking any notice of him whatsoever. [9]

Hincks did not quote Mackenzie's letter (written, it should be noted, about the time his *Examiner* was failing and when he and his family were in great need of the money an amnesty might have enabled him to collect), but put his own interpretation upon it. This seems to be the basis of the charge of attempted blackmail that has been levelled against Mackenzie by some of his critics.

Sir Charles Metcalfe's appointment to succeed Bagot did not disturb Mackenzie. Joseph Hume informed him that Metcalfe was an able and upright man from whose rule in Canada he hoped much. Mackenzie's estimate of Metcalfe was prophetic: "I should think he would conciliate as far as he can without giving up any real power to any party."[10] In December 1844, on the motion of Lafontaine and James Leslie, the member for Verchères, an address to the Crown for a general amnesty was passed unanimously. Metcalfe consented to forward the address and supported the Assembly's request. The response of the Colonial Secretary, Lord Stanley, was not a promise of a general amnesty: it referred only to the release of natives of Canada under sentence of transportation.[11] In January 1845 38 Canadians arrived in New York City from Van Diemen's Land.[12]

Stanley did give Metcalfe permission to proclaim a general amnesty if he found it politically essential to do so, but he hedged his reluctant permission with exceptions that made Metcalfe decide not to use it. Metcalfe was persuaded to use his discretionary powers in favour of most of those still in exile. He permitted a *nolle prosequi* (an order not to proceed in the case) to be entered for

E.B. O'Callaghan, Thomas Storrow Brown and, finally, at Lafontaine's urging, for Papineau.[13] Brown returned in 1844, Papineau waited until 1845, and O'Callaghan never returned.[14] Lafontaine advised Wolfred Nelson that the time was not propitious for either his brother Robert or for Mackenzie, and especially the latter.[15] Francis Hincks, in conversation with Mackenzie at the New York Customs House in June 1845, did not raise his hopes either.[16]

In November 1845 Isaac Buchanan, a wealthy businessman and moderate Reformer, sent Mackenzie a more encouraging estimate of popular sentiment and an offer of financial assistance to enable him to establish himself in business in Canada when he should return.[17] The exile would have welcomed an amnesty but was not yet ready to return or to confess guilt.[18] He did want to collect some of the money still owing to him in Canada, which he put at $9,000, and to be able to prosecute the claim of the heirs of Robert Randall to property in Bytown. (He had been bequeathed an interest in Randall's estate.[19]) While the outlawry hung over him none of these things could be accomplished.

By 1846 Mackenzie was ready to return. Nativism and Duff Green's failure to enable him to start a newspaper had soured him on the United States. William J. Duane undertook to write to Papineau, whom he had befriended in exile, requesting him to see what he could do for Mackenzie with his friends in the legislature.[20] John Ryan of Montreal advised him not to wait for the indictment against him to be quashed but to apply for a pardon.[21]

After his employment at the New York State constitutional convention ended, Mackenzie began to act on this advice in a roundabout way. He admitted to James Lesslie that:

> I now see, as I could not see ten years ago, how frivolous many measures were which I then thought of primary importance, and that a union of the states with Canada would be far from promoting happiness.... The slave power governs here.... [22]

To his son he acknowledged that had he known how things were managed in the United States he would never have dreamed of becoming an American citizen "if outlawed by England until doomsday."[23] Even that much desired reform, elective judges, had disappointed him; it had been made to subserve the ends of party. As for American foreign policy, it presented the sad spectacle of "an elective republic grasping at more territory and more slavery while England is expending her treasure to set the slaves free."[24] In November 1846, in an open letter to Earl Grey, and in a somewhat different private one protesting the continuance of his outlawry, Mackenzie expressed regret that the Reformers had not limited themselves to constitutional opposition, as Joseph Hume had advised, but he reminded the imperial government that they had repeatedly tried to obtain reforms in a system which even Sydenham had denounced as "abominable," and he accused the government of Upper Canada of having excited the revolt and of having gloried in it.[25] When Lord Elgin succeeded Metcalfe as Governor-General in January 1847 Mackenzie confidently expected that a general amnesty would be granted. However, another two years were to pass before it was obtained. Meanwhile the exile became more and more eager to return, his impatience whetted no doubt by the knowledge that George Bruce was ready to help him re-establish himself in business in Canada if he should decide to go.[26]

Lord Elgin inherited an unstable political situation from his predecessor. The existing Draper-D.B. Papineau ministry had no enthusiastic support, and when it was reorganized in May 1847 with Henry Sherwood in Draper's place its strength was not increased. Mackenzie described the new administration as "a poor helpless collection of odds and ends."[27] Reformers in both parts of the province were looking forward to winning the elections of 1847-8 and to getting the principle of responsible government fully recognized at last. Mackenzie was unwilling to mar their chances of success by having the question of a general amnesty raised at this juncture.[28] At this time Janet Mackenzie was visiting her aunt and uncle in Toronto. She attended Lord Elgin's levee and, to her father's "utter astonishment," presented Lady Elgin with a petition for his pardon that had been drawn up by James Lesslie.[29] Mackenzie's Toronto friends also began to circulate a petition; one of them expected it would receive over 20,000 signatures.[30] When the Tories made a fuss about the petition and when the liberal papers began to fear it would damage the Reform cause at the elections, Mackenzie's friends decided to stop circulating it for the time being.[31]

Although Mackenzie would have preferred the amnesty to come without solicitation on his part,[32] a letter from Joseph Hume moved him to take a hand in the matter himself and not to wait upon the "tender mercies" of a Reform government. Hume reminded Mackenzie that he had always condemned the attempt at revolution but he acknowledged that no one had tried more persistently than Mackenzie to get the abuses of Canada removed by constitutional means. Hume informed him that he had six times applied for an amnesty for him on the ground that the rebellion had been caused by misrule, and that therefore "there should be oblivion." When Baldwin and Lafontaine were in office Hume had sent them copies of his correspondence with the British government concerning a general amnesty and had suggested that they apply to the Colonial Office for one. "They said the day was not yet come and they never did it." On January 15, 1848, Hume had again applied to Earl Grey for a general amnesty. Grey refused to originate any steps for Mackenzie's pardon as the charges against him were serious, but he undertook to "receive favourably" any representation from the government of Canada in his favour. Now that the elections were expected to return the Reformers to power, Hume promised to write at once to Baldwin asking him to take steps to procure the amnesty.[33]

After the receipt of Hume's letter Mackenzie wrote to Lord Elgin's Civil Secretary a letter which both justified the revolt and regretted it. Mackenzie claimed that it was only when attempts to secure reform from the imperial government seemed to have failed that he turned to the idea of independence and a closer relation with the United States. He admitted that, although not opposed to elective governments, he was no longer enamoured of the "beauties of Democracy" as exemplified in the United States — the spoils system, slavery and the waste of the public revenues in an imperialistic war against a weak neighbour, Mexico.

Had I seen things in '37 as I do in '48 I would have shuddered at the very idea of revolt no matter what our wrongs might have been... I ought... to have stood by the Government... to the last, exerted every energy I possessed to make it better, more just, more perfect.... Surely, Surely, there was cause for complaint — but, we took the wrong course to get redress.

Referring to his history of the rebellion, Mackenzie said:

I would do it [publish] now, but the dissention [sic] which the facts I have carefully treasured up and arranged would produce in Canada would come amiss just now. It would be impossible not to arouse feelings and passions which had better slumber.

He did, however, assert that Rolph had been appointed executive and he denied that he had had anything to do with the death of Colonel Moodie,[34] an accusation that was holding up the amnesty.

Mackenzie also wrote to Robert Baldwin demanding to know "How long am I to be proscribed and outlawed by a responsible government?"[35] Hume's letter had caused him to believe that Baldwin and LaFontaine, when in power in 1843, had declined to ask for a general amnesty. He told O'Rielly:

It is not Earl Grey nor the Whigs in power in England that have kept me here so long. It is the pretended Canada friends who were with me when the wind was in my sails.... [36]

This was not quite fair. Even if Sir Charles Bagot or Sir Charles Metcalfe had been persuaded to recommend a *general* amnesty without exceptions, Sir Robert Peel would have opposed it.[37] Hincks assured Mackenzie that Hume had misinformed him; a general amnesty had been one of their first considerations but the Colonial Office would not agree to it.[38]

The second Baldwin-Lafontaine ministry took office on March 11, 1848. Before the end of the month the legislature was prorogued to give the new ministry time to mature its measures. In this short space of time neither the government's leaders, nor Wolfred Nelson, nor Papineau, both of whom had been elected to the legislature after their return from exile, said a word about an amnesty. Papineau indeed made a long and violent speech, but his list of matters that ought to be inquired into did not include an amnesty.[39] Dr. J.E. Barker, editor of the Kingston *British Whig*, who had been publishing letters from Mackenzie under a pseudonym, thought he might safely return without a pardon. "As for expecting the Reform party would enable you to return legally — that's hopeless. They know you too well," he wrote.[40] Probably Barker meant by this that the leading Reformers were well aware Mackenzie would not rest content with the achievement of responsible government; he would agitate for additional political and economic reforms that they were not ready to incorporate into their program. However, other friends in Upper Canada assured Mackenzie that an amnesty would be proposed at the next session of the legislature, which was called for January 1849.[41] Meanwhile Mackenzie wrote to Lord Elgin himself, a rather pointless letter, half sycophantic, half critical of his government, particularly of the appointments to the bench.[42] By mid-October Mackenzie had become convinced that the Baldwin-Lafontaine ministry would do nothing. To Wolfred Nelson he characterized them as "shabby, crouching, and mean in grain."[43] Nelson tried hard to convince him that his friends had not been idle, but that one difficulty was Papineau's conduct since his return:

> He is moving heaven and earth to bring himself to the top again.... He maintained utter silence while his brother was battening on the government and until he had received his $20,000 and then having nothing more to expect, he has all at once come out with his old violence and rancour, not a spark of gratitude... I was wrong and my brother was right in his estimate of this man's character. All is self with him. His present course, if there were not other influences at work, would prevent an amnesty. [44]

To Lafontaine it was politically important to obtain credit for securing an amnesty. In fact, Lord Elgin feared he would resign if one were not granted. Papineau and Lafontaine had become rivals for political leadership in Lower Canada, the former anxious to destroy the union, the latter to utilize it in the interests of French Canada. In both sections of the province there were those who had returned quietly without benefit of either a pardon or a *nolle prosequi* and there were others who had received a conditional pardon which did not restore all their civil rights or property. The position of such persons would be regularized and their civil and political rights restored if a general amnesty were obtained.[45] Lord Elgin thought that in Upper Canada the "best part" of the Reform party did not favour an individual pardon for Mackenzie but was willing he should benefit from a general measure.[46]

When Parliament assembled the Governor-General did not wait for a general amnesty to be requested. He announced that the Queen intended to pardon all persons still liable to penal consequences from political offences arising out of the events of 1837-8. The Toronto *Examiner* did not find this enough. It remarked:

> The amnesty to be acceptable must be thorough and complete. The disabilities which attach to those who temporarily left... and have since returned must be removed. These disabilities render them ineligible to... serve as representatives of the people till after a residence of seven years after their return. This must be removed. The amnesty will not be... what it ought to be if it does not meet cases of this description. [47]

Papineau was elected to the Assembly about two years after his return. The restriction referred to rested on an Upper Canada act (4 Geo.IV, cap.4) still unrepealed. Moreover, Mackenzie had become an American citizen and, under the act of 1845, could not be naturalized for five years.[48] At this session the period was to be reduced to three years. These acts were not to be enforced against him. Presumably the legal position still was that a man could not divest himself of his status as a British subject and an amnesty restored all civil rights.

A general amnesty bill, phrased in the broadest terms, was introduced into the Legislative Council on January 30, passed by that body after one reading and by the Assembly on the same day.[49] It forgave all manner of treasons, all felonies, all misdemeanours arising out of the rebellion or the subsequent disorders. All attainders were reversed, all forfeited land or property was to be restored unless it had actually been seized for the Crown and sold. Elgin's purpose in not waiting for a request was to give the Crown, not the Baldwin-Lafontaine ministry, credit for initiating the amnesty. Thus the Queen's confidence in the future loyalty of Canadians would be demonstrated at a time when there were revolutionary movements in Europe, considerable unrest in Ireland and fear of raids on the Canadian frontier by Irish sympathizers in the United States. The Governor-General was anxious that the correspondence between himself and the home government about the amnesty should not be made public and he succeeded in having a motion for papers, made by Sir Allan MacNab, defeated.[50]

Information that the amnesty bill had been signed reached Mackenzie by February. He wrote to Hincks that it seemed to be "a most satisfactory document." Later he was to criticize the amnesty as having done him more harm than good.[51] In now accepting it, Mackenzie laid his cards upon the table, warning the minister what his course would be on his return to Canada. He would demand to know why an amnesty or a *nolle prosequi* had not been obtained for him by a Reform government earlier. He would ask for the settlement of his claims against the government, particularly for his services investigating the accounts of the Welland Canal, since the amnesty restored him in his legal claims but also made him liable for old debts. He would press for reforms as he had in pre-rebellion days, but he would advocate peaceful reform without thought of annexation to the United States.[52]

On February 20 Mackenzie left for Montreal accompanied by his son William. He felt uncertain of his reception but planned, if all went well, to remove his family to Canada in the spring.[53] His visit did not pass off peaceably. He reached Montreal by February 25 and remained there until March 6, observing the discussion of the Rebellion Losses Bill in the legislature. One day, after being assured by the librarian that as an ex-member he needed no card of introduction to enable him to use the legislative library, he ventured into its reading room. The librarian was not present but Colonel John Prince, Member for Essex, entered, demanded to see Mackenzie's card of introduction, and declared he would kick him downstairs if he did not leave. Mackenzie went out into the lobby, where Prince reiterated his threats. A messenger of the House, "emboldened by Prince's language," came forward to the door of the assembly chamber and tried to excite those present to do Mackenzie violence, calling him

157

a rebel and a murderer and accusing him of having his son's blood and that of Colonel Fitzgibbon's son on his hands.[54] The dispute ended when John Sandfield Macdonald, Member for Glengarry, offered to introduce Mackenzie in the library. A.N. Morin, Speaker of the Assembly, let the messenger off with a reprimand, at Mackenzie's request. Prince subsequently expressed regret for his impulsive action, apparently when he learned from Mackenzie's friends of his changed opinions.[55]

Before leaving Montreal Mackenzie wrote to the Montreal *Herald* denying once again that he had murdered Colonel Moodie and pointing out that he had been one of a party of four who had already left the rebels' headquarters for Toronto at the time Moodie was challenged and shot by the rebel guard at Montgomery's. He quoted the account of one of Moodie's companions, Captain Stewart, R.N., to the effect that Moodie had fired first when the guard halted him and that the guard had fired back. Subsequently four other persons exonerated Mackenzie and substantiated his account of the death of Colonel Moodie.[56] The charge of murder had first been publicized in the 1841 edition of Bonnycastle's work on Canada. It was repeated in the editions of 1846 and 1849 but was not included in that of 1852.[57] When the accusation first came to Mackenzie's attention, he had written to the then Colonial Secretary, W.E. Gladstone, asserting his innocence and his readiness to be tried on the charge before any court, judge or jury in Canada. He had received no reply.[58]

The unpleasant incident in the legislative library at Montreal was only the first of several. Mackenzie received threatening letters; at Kingston he was burned in effigy; at Belleville there was a riot; and at Toronto there were several days of great violence. Mackenzie was burned in effigy in front of John Mackintosh's house, where he was staying. A mob gathered in front of the house

> threw vollies of stones at every part of the building.... Sashes,
> glass and all went to shivers — the panel of the front door was
> broken and the police did nothing. [59]

When Mackintosh asked the city council for protection for his home, one of its Tory members advised him to turn Mackenzie out of doors and another boasted that if it were not for the law he "would not hesitate an instant" to take Mackenzie's life. The city council passed a resolution declaring that the people of Toronto were peaceable and incapable of such an act as the late riot unless their feelings had been "deeply insulted." Two weeks after the incident none of the rioters had been arrested.[60]

Despite the threats and the violence, Mackenzie remained in Toronto nine days. Subsequently he visited Dundas, Oakville, Hamilton, Bertie, Wellington Square, Smithville, Queenston and Dunnville, and by April 4 was back in New York.[61] The whole experience must have been a bitter one for Mackenzie. Had he, one wonders, dreamed in his days of exile and poverty that one day he would return to be welcomed by Reformers as one who had fought the good fight for the benefit of the common man, perhaps even of being carried in triumph down Yonge Street, as he once had been, surrounded by enthusiastic supporters? If so, that fantasy was now shattered. Yet the visit, though ill-timed and far from pleasant, was not without its usefulness. Mackenzie had not been closely in touch with developments in Canada for several years; nor had he kept abreast of the complicated political maneuvers that had taken place. The increase in population and the economic progress the country had made since 1837 exceeded his most sanguine expectations. "No idea that I had of men and things would have told the truth," he confessed.[62]

After Mackenzie's departure, his friends explained to him why his visit had been somewhat inopportune. He had arrived just when the Rebellion Losses Bill had reopened old wounds that had almost healed.[63] This bill provided for the payment of property losses caused by the suppression of the rebellion in Lower Canada. Property owners in Upper Canada had already been compensated for their losses by an act of 1841. To ultra-loyalists the bill for Lower Canada was not a belated measure of equal justice but an iniquitous measure that would permit men who had aided or sympathized with the rebels but who had not been convicted to be compensated for their losses. The government's supporters argued that to attempt to distinguish between the loyal and the actively disloyal, except those regularly convicted, would be both unwise and hopeless and would undo the effects of the amnesty.[64] James Lesslie wrote:

> I think that had it not been for this circumstance [the Rebellion Losses Bill] you would have met with little molestation. The Tories seized upon the measure as a means of alarming Lord Elgin — peradventure he might be led to dissolve Parliament and give their expiring cause one more chance to be resuscitated and your arrival was a kind of god-send to them.[65]

"What I have seen compels me to give up all idea of an immediate return to Canada," Mackenzie informed his son. "Ministry and opposition are opposed to my return and unfriendly. The public mind must be prepared."[66] He prepared it by publishing a narrative of his visit. It appeared in installments in the *New York Tribune* under the heading of "A Winter's Journey through the Canadas," and was republished in the Toronto *Examiner*.[67] These articles commented on the marked economic progress that had occurred in Canada since the Union, gave the history of and justified the government's Rebellion Losses Bill, denounced the Tories as now the disloyal party advocating annexation, criticized the selfish conduct of Papineau both before and since his return from exile, and praised the reform program of the ministry so far as it went. Reforms still badly needed were pointed out: a more equitable assessment law, abolition of imprisonment for debt, an increase in the membership of the Assembly, single member districts, greater economy in government and provincial control of the post office in Canada. As for himself, Mackenzie wrote, "I deeply regret our eventual resort to force; but who is there that believes that but for our resort to physical resistance... a Durham, an Elgin or a Sydenham... would ever have been sent to redress grievances in Canada...?" He summarized the causes of discontent that had led to the rebellion by quoting Sydenham's words:

When I look to the state of government, and to the departmental administration of the province, instead of being surprised at the condition in which I find it, I am only astonished it has been endured so long. I know that much as I dislike Yankee institutions and rule, I would not have fought against them, which thousands of these poor fellows, whom the Compact calls rebels, did, if it were only to keep up such a government as they got.... [68]

Mackenzie still felt that, however unwise their course, he and his supporters had been justified in what they had done, and he did not pretend to think otherwise, but he announced, "It is not my intention ever again to meddle with political revolutions."

Lord Elgin is said to have remarked that he hoped Mackenzie on his return to Canada would not take Papineau's course. Mackenzie wrote to reassure the Governor-General on this point. While he would still agitate for reforms, *he* did not intend to advocate annexation and he should not be held responsible for everything that might appear in the columns of the *New York Tribune*,[69] a journal which did.

Elgin had some reason to feel uneasy. After collecting from the government the $20,000 he claimed as his unpaid salary as a former speaker of the Legislative Assembly of Lower Canada, Papineau had been elected in opposition to the government of the day. At the opening session he made an attack upon the union and the ministry which ran on for three days. He advocated extension of the suffrage, vote by ballot and the institution of elective practices at all levels of government until Canadians should have nothing to envy Americans. In Elgin's opinion, he had made "a pretty frank declaration of republicanism."[70] This was the moment when annexationist sentiment was rising in Canada, not only among Papineau's followers but also among English Canadians alarmed by the recent changes in Great Britain's commercial policies. Papineau's correspondence with Erastus Corning (mayor of Albany, who had given him financial help in 1838) shows that long after the annexationist crisis of 1849 had passed Papineau still believed annexation would be achieved and hoped to live to see it.[71] When Mackenzie was in Montreal Papineau called upon him, but Mackenzie did not return the visit, well aware of the disfavour with which Papineau was regarded by moderate Reformers, and not himself in sympathy with Papineau's desire for annexation.

Upon his return to New York Mackenzie was hard up for cash and once again faced with the problem of earning a living. "He is back here, poor, dispirited and helpless. What shall be done," Horace Greeley enquired of Thurlow Weed.

I offer him work and will pay for it all he will take [added that kindly man], but he persists in believing that I do so only out of charity and that he cannot support his squad of girls on what he ought to take from me... but [thinks that] from the Whig party he has the right to something on the score of justice. [72]

Greeley proposed that Weed should secure for Mackenzie one of the secret inspectorships in the New York Customs House and he arranged an interview for him with Weed.[73] Mackenzie applied, humbly, merely for a petty clerkship, remarking that he probably would not want it for more than six months.[74] He did not get an appointment, and it is not to be wondered at. Mackenzie had made up his mind to return to Canada, as his letter of application to Thurlow Weed shows. Why waste patronage upon him?

In May Mackenzie received a tempting offer to become the principal editor of the New York *Sun* at a liberal salary. This paper, which had a circulation of 40,000 and was produced on a steam press, had recently been inherited by two young men, the Beach brothers, who needed an editor of experience, energy and judgement. Mackenzie knew he possessed the first two qualities but the years had battered his self-confidence. He had come to mistrust his judgement about Americans and their politics. He therefore refused to undertake the "trust" for the young men lest the paper, under his management, should lose circulation.[75] The New York *Sun* was not the type of paper Mackenzie would have enjoyed editing. It appealed to the emotions, and supplied its working class readers with human interest stories, sensational accounts of crimes and accidents, romantic fiction and moral advice.[76] Moreover, the paper was to be neutral in politics. "You conduct a neutral paper! As well engage you to turn monk! You could not if you would...." commented Thomas Ewbank, in whose opinion Mackenzie had done right in refusing the tempting offer.[77]

After failing to get the Customs House berth Mackenzie earned a living by compiling the *Business Men's Almanack* and the the Whig *Almanac* for 1850, and by assisting in the editorial room of the *Tribune*.[78] He wrote the *Tribune's* obituary editorial on the life of Albert Gallatin, taking the opportunity to denounce the Nativists, whose principles would have excluded Gallatin from office,[79] and he contributed occasional unsigned articles on Canadian affairs based on Lesslie's letters to him.

In addition Mackenzie was contributing almost weekly letters to the Toronto *Examiner*. This paper, founded by Francis Hincks in 1838, had originally been a vigorous Reform journal, critical of Lord Sydenham and his supporters — until Hincks became one of them. Subsequently it had taken a more moderate position. On its sale to James Lesslie in 1844 the paper passed into less able hands and was soon down to 600 or 700 subscribers.[80] The thing above all others that Lesslie was interested in was secularization of the Clergy Reserves and establishment of the voluntary system in church affairs. In 1845 a group of Upper Canada Reformers had established a new journal, the *Globe*, with George Brown as editor. When the Baldwin-Lafontaine government came into power in 1848 it was the *Globe* that received the government's patronage, and the *Globe*, although also an upholder of voluntaryism, defended the ministry's cautious approach to the Clergy Reserves question. Within the old Reform Party, in Upper Canada, there was still a radical element, soon to be known as the Clear

Grits, who were impatient with the Baldwin-Lafontaine ministry. Until the foundation of the North American in 1850, the Toronto *Examiner* was the mouthpiece of this section of the party. "I am determined," wrote its editor, "to drive the ministers into doing their duty — or out of power so far as the *Examiner* can do it."[81] Mackenzie's letters were designed to point out that duty to them — and to Canada.

It has been said that when Mackenzie returned to Canada he was a "spent force."[82] On the contrary, his pungent articles found a welcome and evoked a warm response from the *Examiner's* readers. His vigour blew the fire of reform into a brighter blaze even before his return. Mackenzie had condemned the Act of Union on many counts and he had never regarded achieving responsible government as an adequate goal for Reformers. But unlike Papineau, Mackenzie was ready to acknowledge that Canada had made great progress, both political and economic, since the rebellion. His point was that a great deal remained to be done and Reformers should bestir themselves to do it before all hope of creating a democratic society based on a wide distribution of wealth vanished.

The Baldwin-Lafontaine ministers had been in office since March of 1848. The session of 1849 had now closed and several important reforms, some of which they had criticized their predecessors for not making, had not been initiated. For example, they had not yet enacted a new assessment law. All grist mills, all merchants' shops, were assessed alike, without reference to their situation or size; all frame houses of the same number of storeys were assessed alike regardless of their size or character. All cultivated land was assessed at 20/ -, all unoccupied land at 4/-, regardless of quality or location. "The present law is a premium in favor of land sharks," remarked Mackenzie, adding that for a Reform ministry to "play the game of land speculator and keep the burden on the poor man's back was scarce to be looked for." As long ago as 1834 he had pointed out the injustice of the assessment law, and Baldwin himself had acknowledged it in an election manifesto. Yet nothing had been done.[83] Other long overdue measures which the ministry had not yet introduced were: bills for the simplification and codification of the laws, for honest juries, for a free public school system supported by a general tax; bills for abolishing the property qualification for members of the Assembly, the laws of entail and primogeniture, the right of a creditor to imprison his debtor; bills to reduce the profligate civil list, to extend the franchise, and bills that, by increasing the membership of the Assembly and placing restrictions on the members' freedom to accept appointments to office, would at least limit the executive's ability to corrupt them. This was the hard work of reform, the "up-rooting of pine stumps and clearing of heavy timbered land" which the Baldwin-Lafontaine ministry was not prepared to undertake nor its Upper Canada organ, the *Globe*, prepared to press for. That job would be done by the *Examiner*.[84]

A measure for which the ministry had found time was the Judicature Act of 1849. This act reorganized the Court of Chancery and had created a new Court of Common Pleas for Upper Canada, an "unnecessary duplication" in Mackenzie's opinion, since its jurisdiction was to be the same as that of the Court of Queen's Bench. These changes had made possible three new judicial appointments and it was rumoured that two of the new appointees were to be Robert Baldwin Sullivan and Henry J. Boulton and that the clerk of the new court was to be Sheriff Jarvis. Jarvis, who had sold up Mackenzie's personal property and had not yet accounted fully for the proceeds! Sullivan, whom even Hincks had accused of having no principles and of acting purely from expediency,[85] and who had been president of the Council that had advised Arthur not to stay the execution of Lount and Mathews! Boulton who had cheated Mackenzie's friend Robert Randall and had kept him seven years in prison for debt! Boulton who had voted for the expulsion of Mackenzie from the Assembly! Boulton who had been dismissed as Attorney-General! Boulton who had subsequently been made Chief Justice of Newfoundland and again dismissed! Boulton who had only then turned Reformer! Boulton, "one of the meanest, perhaps the most unprincipled of the Family Compact whose wicked conduct is known to every old settler!" Week after week Mackenzie wrathfully denounced the expected appointments and the "shameless reform ministry" that had recommended them while overlooking the claims of able and staunch Reformers like John Rolph.[86] If this was responsible government, could Papineau be blamed for calling it "a trap"?[87] In the end, Sullivan's appointment went through but Boulton did not obtain the coveted judgeship. He was a first-rate lawyer but the ministry could not outrage public feeling by raising him to the bench.[88] Even the semi-official *Globe* admitted there were "strong objections to the appointment... heard from almost every quarter."[89] Instead, Alexander McLean was translated from the Court of Queen's Bench to the new Court of Common Pleas and R.E. Burns, of whom Mackenzie did not approve either,[90] but whom Lesslie described as "the best of a bad lot" and had suggested in place of Boulton,[91] was selected to replace McLean.

Impatient though radicals like Lesslie and Mackenzie were for more reforms, the ministry — and the province — had more pressing problems at the moment: the commercial depression, the demand for a reciprocal trade agreement with the United States and, when that apparently could not be obtained, the growth of annexation sentiment. It is not necessary here to do more than refer to the general causes of this development. They were: the loss of preferential duties for Canadian wheat and the reduction in the preferential duties on timber in the British market; changes in imperial policy that had brought about a commercial depression in which the merchants were the most vocal sufferers; the enactment of the Rebellion Losses Bill to compensate those whom the Tories classed indiscriminately as rebels; and the refusal of the British government to heed Tory petitions for the restoration of the preferential duties.[92] In October 1849 a group of Montreal merchants issued a manifesto calling for peaceful separation from Great Britain and annexation to the United States as the most effective and permanent remedy for the economic ills of Canada.[93]

Outright annexation sentiment was limited in Upper Canada. Nevertheless the movement made some progress until Lord Grey's despatch of January 9, 1850, made it absolutely clear that the British government was not prepared to acquiesce in the separation of Canada from the Empire and its annexation to the United States. Shortly thereafter the annexationists in Upper Canada, one of whose strong arguments had been the alleged weary indifference of Great Britain towards her colonies, acknowledged their defeat.[94]

The Toronto *Examiner*, never an outright annexationist paper, criticized the British government for having failed to demand free access for Canadian products to American markets when it opened Great Britain's own markets and ports to American products and American shipping.[95] In addition, its editor used the annexation movement as a stick with which to beat the slow-moving Baldwin-Lafontaine government. The *Examiner* warned that unless the Clear Grit demand for secularization of the Clergy Reserves was satisfied *soon*, that section of the Reform Party would advocate annexation. Said the *Examiner*:

> If fear of Imperial influence restrains them [the ministry] from doing their duty to the Canadian people, the sooner the illusion about responsible government is dispelled the better. [96]

Mackenzie must have been dismayed by the flare-up of annexationist sentiment in Canada at a time when he was eagerly looking forward to re-establishing himself there and had burned his bridges behind him with both political parties in the United States. James Lesslie was quite willing, even insistent, that the pros and cons of annexation should be fully discussed.[97] Mackenzie, therefore, was quite free to do what he could to counteract annexationist propaganda through the *Examiner* and other papers. He conceded that independence would probably come about some day, but the country was not yet ready for it and, in any case, independence was a very different thing from annexation. American markets would certainly be open to Canada's natural products with annexation, but it would be at a high cost. Canada would lose control of her customs revenue and of her public lands,[98] and she would have to bear a share of Washington's large military expenditures. The costs of her own defence, a burden being borne by the British taxpayer, would fall on her shoulders, partly under annexation, fully with independence. As for the naive notion of some Montreal annexationists that the only change in their constitution would be that Canadians would elect their own governors, Mackenzie, who had been behind the scenes and had learned how nominations and elections were managed, could tell them that "the people of the states have very little to do with electing their governors."[99] The cure for Canada's economic ills was not the restoration of duties on "the bread of the British poor," but for Great Britain to repeal the Navigation Laws and negotiate for the province a reciprocal trade agreement with the United States.[100] He advocated also the opening up of the Hudson's Bay Company's territories to Canadian enterprise and settlement.

In discussing annexation Mackenzie did not spare the Tories. A pampered faction that had once wanted to get rid of all Yankee schoolmasters and that would have hanged the Reformers in 1837 is about to rebel, he jeered.[101] As merchants, their loyalty had proved to be but pocket deep and as large

164

landowners they expected annexation to increase the value of their properties. Annexation, Mackenzie warned, would not lessen their hold upon the industrious farmers of the country. He quoted effectively Patrick Shireff's prediction that Canadians would find it difficult to get rid of the power of these Tory land speculators and mortgage holders.

> Separation from the mother country in all probability would lessen their chances. Upper Canada is likely to separate from Britain in seeking to retain monopolies.[102]

Mackenzie was well aware that annexationist sentiment was growing among old Reformers, disillusioned at the slow progress of reform under a responsible government.[103] The radical Peter Perry's triumphant election for the third riding of York, where the government did not venture to oppose him even though he would not commit himself on the question of annexation except to say that the time had not come, was clear proof of the prevalence of such sentiments.[104] Dr. J.E. Barker, editor of the Kingston *British Whig*, saw a chance to capitalize on this development, and suggested that Mackenzie should join him in issuing an annexationist paper from Toronto. His offer was rejected.[105] In Mackenzie's opinion the annexationist movement was diverting attention from needed reforms. "Let the Tories be annexationist and the Reformers stick to their old principles," he advised. There was a great deal that needed to be done and could be done without any modification of the Act of Union or appeals to Great Britain. The Baldwin-Lafontaine government should use its powers under the existing constitution for the general good. If the *Examiner* would boldly take this course, it would "steer clear of the annexationist reef."[106] In an open letter to that paper Mackenzie stated that if he had been able to settle in Canada,

> every effort that man could make would have been made by me not only to keep Canada separated from that country but also to preserve the British connection and make it worth preserving.[107]

Annexation would link Canada with the slave-holders of the South and would reduce Canadians to the level of second class citizens in the union, scorned by the Nativists and excluded from office.

> If annexation takes place, not one spot on this continent will remain on which a native of the United Kingdom can rest the sole of his foot, and say he is the equal of any man.[108]

Nativism, slavery, and the shortcomings of American democracy; these offset all the commercial advantages of annexation for Mackenzie, the more so as he hoped some of the latter could be achieved without resort to so extreme a measure.

In late November Mackenzie paid another visit to Canada which lasted about four weeks.[109] Not much is known about it except that he visited Lloydtown, townships north of Toronto and the Niagara Peninsula.[110] The way was prepared for this visit, which gave rise to no unpleasant incidents, by Mackenzie's articles in the *Examiner* and by his signed address to the Resident Landowners of the County of York. In this detailed article he reminded the province of his past services in fighting for numerous reforms, some of which had since been obtained and the necessity of others generally recognized. As for the great reform, responsible government, he too had sought to remedy Canada's grievances by this means rather than through rebellion. In 1835 he had moved for the creation of an administration possessing public confidence[111] and the grievance report he had compiled had demanded "thorough responsibility to public opinion." If in the end he had erred, it had only been "through excessive zeal" for the public interest. He acknowledged that the people were better off than they were but he did not consider that they had yet obtained a really responsible government. An executive council "appointed by the governor during pleasure," with no responsibility but losing their places, not subject to impeachment, wielding an immense patronage with which they could influence a small Assembly of 84 members, half of whom were office holders and many of whom were chosen by small constituencies — this surely could not be called responsible government.[112]

Mackenzie returned to the United States on December 24, 1849. Although his visit had passed off quietly he did not think it quite time to settle in Canada.[113] He had found that his stand on annexation had cost him the sympathy of some radical Reformers.[114] On the other hand it had won him the support of others who argued that if he was not "right at heart" he would have supported the movement.[115] Mackenzie decided to wait for the political atmosphere to clear a little. In January 1850 he was persuaded to go to Washington as the *Tribune's* correspondent. He does not seem to have been sure of himself in this post or to have enjoyed the experience,[116] and he did not complete the session. While there he contributed a few news items to the *Examiner* under a Washington dateline, but its proprietor wanted more from Mackenzie than letters from Washington. His paper, once the vigorous voice of the Reformers in Upper Canada, had been losing ground to George Brown's *Globe*. Lesslie, who was now about to lose the assistance of Charles Lindsey (subsequently Mackenzie's son-in-law and his biographer) found that he could not give adequate attention to his newspaper because he also had on his hands the needs of his bookstore and his printing shop. He wanted Mackenzie to assist him with editorials as well as correspondence from Washington, and he proposed that Mackenzie should take charge of the *Examiner* entirely if he should return to Canada. Lesslie wanted his paper "creditably maintained" and knew of no one who could do it for him better than Mackenzie. On most of the great questions of the day — the university, the Clergy Reserves, law reform, education, elective offices, primogeniture laws, retrenchment — the two men were at one. They did not see eye to eye on annexation. Mackenzie opposed it; Lesslie felt that "rule by a bureau in London is absurd. There must be an end to that" — but he did not go beyond this point and he was willing to let Mackenzie express his own views on the question.[117] Lesslie made it clear, too, that he hoped to see Mackenzie in the Assembly again before too long and that his help was needed to strengthen the Reform Party and prevent the formation of a coalition government that would never push through the reforms desired by the radicals.

Grateful though he was for Lesslie's offer, Mackenzie declined it.

> I have no sympathy with [annexation] and foresee very clearly that... I would either have to make converts of many of your friends or lose their support and get their ill-will.

His visits had shown him that he would also have to face "a hostile collection of factions" — the bench, the bar, the sheriffs, the Orangemen and his old adversaries. Much as he wished to sit in the Assembly again and edit a newspaper, he was not disposed to truckle to any of these interests to ease his way in Canada and might, after all, decide to end his days in the United States.[118] Moreover, he was unwilling to conduct a paper that he did not wholly own and control. "I will not be trammelled in any way in the expression of my sentiments," he declared.[119]

Lesslie, though disappointed, did not give up. He and his brother Joseph continued to pique Mackenzie's interest in Canadian politics by accounts of the increasing unpopularity of the Baldwin-Lafontaine ministry. "There will be a glorious field for the application of your talents before long," Mackenzie was assured.[120] Mackintosh wrote of his fear that the growing division in Reform ranks would result in the formation of a coalition ministry.[121] Whether it was the political news from Canada or dissatisfaction with (perhaps even the loss of?) his situation in Washington cannot be stated, but during the first week of April Mackenzie finally made up his mind that the time had come to return to Canada. "Gladly would the *Tribune* keep me here and I may come back but not if I can help it. I've seen enough," he told James.[122] By May 1 he and his family had arrived at Toronto.[123]

# Chapter XII

# THE RETURN HOME

Upon his return to Canada Mackenzie established his family in a house on Yonge Street. Writing to his daughter Barbara, who was staying with her Baxter cousins in Buffalo, he said:

> Our house is about two-thirds as large as the old one — better
> furnished — comfortable — but the gardens and outhouses of
> 1837 are not to be had now. [1]

No. It was a different Toronto, a city lit by gas to some extent, provided with a water system, although an inadequate one, sewers, and some macadamized streets. Daily steamboats connected Toronto with other lake ports and omnibuses left the marketplace at frequent intervals for neighbouring rural communities. The population of about 30,000 was three times what it had been at the time of the rebellion, the number of common schools had increased from one to 15 and the number of newspapers to 10. [2]

Mackenzie did not at first attempt to establish a newspaper of his own, although he had originally planned to do so with the promised financial help of George Bruce. He had also hoped to persuade James to return to Canada and join him in this enterprise. This paper was to have been published in Montreal, a city where there was a large English-speaking population and the one Mackenzie then regarded as most suitable for the capital of Canada. The disturbances that had occurred during his first visit, both in Montreal and Toronto, had made him hesitate to introduce a large borrowed capital into Canada [3] and may well have made Bruce hesitate also.

Some of Mackenzie's friends thought he should now be content to accept some sinecure, if one could be found for him, and to stay out of political life. To settle down quietly to the task of providing for his family was what Mackenzie could not discipline himself to do, either in the United States or Canada. [4] He contributed frequent articles to the *Examiner* and the *Niagara Mail* but his weekly letters to the *New York Tribune* were his only other source of income for some time.

*Mackenzie's Weekly Message*, his last journalistic venture, was not to be established until December 1852. Its editor claimed it never really paid. How

Mackenzie contrived to live after his return to Canada cannot be adequately explained. His present-day descendants are unable to throw any light on the question. His wages as a member of the Assembly and the irregularly paid rent from his property in Dundas can hardly have been sufficient for him and his family.

It has been said that Mackenzie was out of touch with politics in Canada when he returned, and he himself felt this to be so at the time of his trial visit, but Lesslie's letters and his own articles written for the *Examiner* during his final months in the United States show that he was rapidly catching up. After he was settled in Toronto again he set about making himself thoroughly familiar with all that had gone on during his absence, when he was dependent upon friends for bits of political gossip and for an occasional Canadian newspaper. He obtained a file of the *Examiner* for the years during which Hincks had edited it, a file of the *Mirror* for 1840-43, and a complete set of the Journals of the Legislature, the latter supplied by John Sandfield Macdonald.[5] One can readily believe that the man who had been able to master the facts of New York's political history with a speed and thoroughness that astonished natives of that state would have no difficulty in becoming *au courant* with developments in Canada.

Despite his disclaimers, Mackenzie seems to have made up his mind to re-enter public life as soon as he could. He must confidently have expected to play an important role again. Had he not this time been urged to return and to take a hand in the good work of reform? Could he not now count on a welcome from Reformers and hearty support from the real radicals in the party? Promptly, through the *Examiner*, he made his stand on public affairs known.

> I am for railways, reciprocity and retrenchment — not for rebellion [he wrote]. I am opposed to separation and annexation.[6]

Mackenzie's task in re-establishing himself in Canadian political life was to be difficult—more difficult than he realized. Not only was it a different Toronto but a different Canada that he had come back to. He had left a province that was in the depths of a depression; he returned to one about to enjoy several years of great prosperity. In such a period a critic of the government of the day would not find it as easy to attract a personal following as in a period of depression. The country was filling up. The rural communities were no longer isolated pockets of settlement; through the elected district councils they had effective means of helping themselves. The area under cultivation in Upper Canada, 1,440,505 acres in 1837, had become 3,705,523 acres by 1851, and during the next decade it was to increase to 6,051,619 acres. The exports of the province in grain and lumber were already recovering from the loss of the imperial preferences and were finding expanding markets in Great Britain and the United States. Canada's small water-powered grist and saw mills had begun to be replaced by large steam-driven flour and lumber mills; her economic life had become more diversified and urbanized. For her growing industrial enterprises and maturing agriculture she now needed capital and additional financial services — more banks, insurance companies and savings and loan associations. Prior to the rebellion Upper Canada's problem had been to devise and enforce a land policy that would put settlers on her agricultural lands and to provide improved means of water transport to get her staples to market. By the fifties little good agricultural land remained. What had become important was finding the funds for railways, not only to prevent the export-import trade of the province from being diverted more and more into American channels, but also to stimulate the internal trade and economy of the province itself. Soon it was also to become apparent that if the province was to dissuade her energetic farmers' sons from slipping away to the American prairies, she must secure for them the Canadian prairies. Mackenzie has been accused of being out of step with his time. It needs to be emphasized that he appreciated these economic problems as well as the next man, as his public statements show. Where he differed from many of his contemporaries was about the methods by which these desirable ends were to be obtained and about the economic and social side-effects they were willing to risk to achieve them. His experiences in New York State, particularly at the constitutional convention of 1846, had taught him that these costs might be heavy.

In Canada the battle for responsible government had been won. The Governor-General would now accept a ministry supported by a majority in the Assembly and would take its advice, even on questions of patronage, although he would still try to use his personal influence to affect its policies. Several of Upper Canada's old pre-rebellion problems remained — effective parliamentary control of the revenue, reform of the representation, education, the Clergy Reserves, in fact the whole question of state-church relationships. The solution of these problems would be no easier now that Upper Canada and more conservative and clerically-dominated Lower Canada were tied together in the union. Then there were the new demands for a wider franchise, an elective upper house and elective officials. These came from old Reformers and from young ones in both parts of the province — who had been influenced by the English Chartists, or the European revolutions of 1848, or by the example of nearby American states. These problems were not susceptible of simple solutions and there were more political cross-currents in both parts of the province than there had once been. In upper Canada new men had come to the fore in the Reform Party and on some points Mackenzie did not yet agree with them. It would not be easy for him to step back into his old niche.

Before Mackenzie could consider devoting himself to public affairs, the family's ever-pressing need for money had to be addressed. There were several sums owing to him that he was anxious to collect. First, there was his claim for $1,200 from the county of York — three years' wages owing to him as its representative in the Assembly of Upper Canada, even though repeated expulsions had prevented him from serving his constituents during that time. Then there was the £250 to which he believed himself entitled for his services during 1835 as one of the commissioners appointed by the Assembly to investigate the affairs of the Welland Canal. The commissioners had not been paid because no supply bill had been passed in 1836. Eager to lay the results of his investigation before the province, Mackenzie had published three issues of a newssheet entitled The *Welland Canal* at his own expense. This he did before the Assembly of Upper Canada had accepted the report or consented to its publication and after Mackenzie had failed to persuade Papineau and O'Callaghan to get it published for him in Lower Canada. Mackenzie now claimed to be not only unpaid for his services as commissioner but $300 out of pocket as well.[7] In addition Mackenzie wanted an accounting from William Jarvis, Sheriff of the County of York, who, on the complaint of some of Mackenzie's creditors that he was an absconding debtor, had seized and sold the contents of his newspaper establishment and bookstore. Finally, there was the Randall estate which included a claim to a valuable property in Bytown and to -£500 from the old province of Upper Canada. Mackenzie was one of the executors of this estate and had been left a share in it.

Mackenzie collected his wages from the county of York more promptly than his claims on the legislature. He reminded the county of the various good measures he had advocated as their representative, particularly when he had presented a petition from the township of Vaughan in 1832.[8] He stated that he would not take his case to court but would accept the decision of the Council as final and as a mark of approbation or disapproval of his conduct on that occasion. This was shrewd. The Vaughan petition had asked for the abolition of the Crown and Clergy Reserves, regulation of the public lands by law, provincial control of all provincial revenue, the creation of township and county councils with power to impose assessments, a more equal system of representation and an executive council possessing public confidence.[9] These were hardly sentiments that the County Council could afford to seem to be repudiating in 1850. A special committee of the Council, chosen by ballot, recommended that Mackenzie be paid £293, the amount of his claim plus interest. This recommendation was accepted.[10]

After the amnesty and during his visit to Montreal in 1849 Mackenzie had raised the question of the sums he claimed from the Province of Upper Canada and was told to wait, since a discussion of his claims might add to the prevailing excitement.[11] A year later he was still waiting. In June 1850 Mackenzie and I.J. Culp, who had been appointed an executor of Robert Randall's estate while Mackenzie was in exile, submitted a petition to the legislature on a claim of Randall's for £500 that had been approved by the Assembly of Upper Canada but blocked by the Legislative Council. Hincks explained that the government of the day *must* oppose a claim unless it was prepared to recommend a money vote to sanction it, and that the Randall claim was in the same class as other claims against the old Province of Upper Canada upon which no decision had yet been made.[12] This explanation did not deter Mackenzie from pestering other members of the government.[13] In 1851, without further appeals on his part, payment of the claim was provided for in the supply bill of that year.[14]

In May 1850 Mackenzie applied for payment of his Welland Canal claim and pestered Hincks to present his petition. Hincks did as requested but made no motion to refer the petition to a committee.[15] Mackenzie also tried to secure the help of William Hamilton Merritt, President of the Council and former president of the Welland Canal Company. He warned Merritt that unless his claim received prompt attention he would resort to "agitation" through the press. Irregularities revealed by Mackenzie's investigation of the company's affairs 15 years previously were recalled to public memory and spread on the pages of the *Examiner* in considerable detail.[16] Mackenzie also wrote to Etienne Taché, the Receiver-General, whose clerk, Dufort, had been sent to Toronto in 1837 to seek the help of Upper Canada. Taché's reply, although not unfriendly, complained about the "irrelevant matter" Mackenzie had included in his letter.[17] In a similar vein Mackenzie wrote to Lafontaine. In a second letter Mackenzie included an article prepared for publication and a request for an interview and for an explanation of the government's treatment of him.[18] Lafontaine took this to mean he was being threatened with the same sort of exposé inflicted on Merritt. His reply to Mackenzie amounted to saying, "Publish and be damned to you."[19]

After the supply bill of 1850 passed without any provision for paying him, Mackenzie wrote to Robert Baldwin, evidently accusing him of neglect and indifference. The minister replied, rather coldly, that it was not for him to become his private counsel in the matter and intimated that his claim would receive attention when other claims against the Province of Upper Canada were disposed of.[20] In February Mackenzie appealed to Hincks again. Hincks, less abrupt and perhaps politically more cautious in dealing with Mackenzie than other members of the cabinet, assured him a decision would be made soon and on March 6, 1851, he was informed that his claim for £250 had been approved.[21] Thus, after a tedious two-year struggle, Mackenzie's claim based on services rendered 16 years before was finally paid, without interest.

In 1837 Mackenzie had possessed a substantial personal estate in Toronto — the contents of his home, his printing establishment, bookstore and bindery. After his flight Eastwood and Goodell, the papermakers to whom he was in debt, obtained a writ of attachment against his property; but before the Sheriff could seize his goods and chattels the mob pillaged his bookstore and printing establishment. He was informed:

> There has been a most shameful destruction of property. Many valuable books stolen — the types in pye — the presses asunder....[22]

Subsequently the goods were sold by the Sheriff, William Botsford Jarvis. Mackenzie did not know for years how much his possessions had sold for or what had happened to the proceeds. He was under the impression that a substantial sum must still be in the Sheriff's hands. When he returned to Canada in 1850 he tried to obtain an accounting and wanted Robert Baldwin to force the Sheriff to give one. Baldwin declined to intervene in the matter.[23] In 1852 Mackenzie's request was acceded to by the Hincks-Morin administration. The Sheriff's account showed that the sale of Mackenzie's possessions, valued by him at various times at $9,000 to $12,000, had brought £520/3/3. After payments to creditors, about £70 remained, which he was now entitled to claim.[24] In late October 1853 Mackenzie was still petitioning the government to oblige Jarvis to pay up.[25]

In pushing for a speedy settlement of all these claims Mackenzie got off on the wrong foot. He was too impatient to go through proper channels, perhaps too needy, and perhaps too convinced that a Reform government ought to exert itself on *his* behalf more promptly. When writing to the members of the government from Lower Canada he traded, one has to say, on his knowledge of their connection with the events of 1837 to pressure them into a quick decision on his claims. He annoyed old friends in Upper Canada who had assisted him, made enemies of the Baldwin-Lafontaine administration already irritated by his public criticism of their conduct, and gave those who still regarded him as a traitor and murderer a chance to vilify him. The methods to which he resorted — only, it should be remembered, after his importunities had failed to bring a prompt decision — must have caused some members of the administration to conclude that he had returned to Canada a bitter and vengeful man, determined to do everything the hard way and to make himself as unco-operative and obnoxious as possible. From his point of view, they were an ungrateful lot who owed their present power as members of a responsible government to the sacrifices he had made. He could not help contrasting the treatment Papineau had received with the grudging treatment meted out to him — and he was not without public sympathy in Upper Canada.[26]

It will be recalled that after Mackenzie sold his *Colonial Advocate* he started to publish another paper, the *Constitution*. Since this paper received no government patronage Mackenzie had been obliged to borrow from the Bank of the People to sustain it. One of his notes for $100 was endorsed by John Doel and John Montgomery and another by J.H. Price. After Mackenzie fled to the United States, Doel and Price had to pay those notes. In 1837 Mackenzie had owned a 200-acre lot in East Garrafraxa township and two town lots in Dundas, on one of which he had built a small two-storey frame house. With his treason this property became forfeit to the Crown. Mackenzie's creditors, however, were permitted to present their claims against his estate, and the property was sold for their benefit.[27] Doel bought it for £81, reimbursed Price in part, paid some other small sums owed by Mackenzie and the taxes on the real estate. He was out of pocket more than £200 by 1850, but he offered Mackenzie all his land back for this sum (the house had burned) and accepted £50 in cash and the balance as a note, not a mortgage. Thus Mackenzie was helped to qualify as a freeholder when he became a candidate for the Assembly in 1851.[28]

Mackenzie acknowledged that Doel had treated him with kindness. Relations between the two families evidently remained cordial. The reminiscences of Doel's son, W.H. Doel, about the events of 1837, not written until 1880, may give a contrary impression, but in 1855 we find the young man writing to Mackenzie:

> One person cannot honor & esteem another for the principles
> he not only professes but unflinchingly carries out more than

I do you. I consider that you have done more for this my native country than any other one man and any one taking the stand you have taken of right against might will be annoyed and persecuted by such men as are at present in power. [29]

In October 1850 Mackenzie began preparing the way for his return to political life as an independent member by publishing an Address to the Electors of the County of York asking whether one of the ridings was disposed to elect him to the legislature again.[30] (He had represented the undivided county from 1828 to 1834, and the Second Riding from 1835 to 1836.) There was no seat vacant at the moment but a vacancy was expected to occur before long.[31] Mackenzie reminded the county that in 1849 he had taken a strong anti-annexationist stand and had opposed independence for Canada "situated as we now are." He could see no disloyalty, however, in acknowledging that a permanent or everlasting colony is an impossibility.

> The independence of this province may be half a century distant... but it is nevertheless inevitable.

He repeatedly expressed his regrets for his share in the rebellion while reminding his readers, in a way that must have made some of them secretly uncomfortable, that it was absurd

> to lay on my shoulders a movement which, had it been successful, would have been owned in its incipient stage by thousands. [32]

He now appealed to the gratitude of his old constituents, recalling his political services to the province in the pre-rebellion years. The great boon of responsible government had been demanded by him and conceded, he believed, largely as a result of his efforts. Now that it had been won he urged old Reformers to regard it as a beginning, not an end. They had obtained a tool which they should use to reshape the social and political structure of Canada nearer to their heart's desire.

In his letters to the *Examiner* in 1849 Mackenzie had vigorously attacked the "slow-coach" Baldwin-Lafontaine ministry. He now conceded that during the past two sessions it had enacted many useful reforms. The jury law, the assessment laws, the law of libel had all been improved; provision for township polling places and for the election of country and township officers had been made. But the ministry had only begun "to walk in a good road when we had made it for them." There was still a long way to go. Mackenzie's proposals for economic reform called for economy and retrenchment on the part of the government, a reciprocal trade treaty with the United States, reduction of Canada's tariff, a stable currency, abolition of seigneurial tenures, opening the navigation of the St. Lawrence and its canals to the ships of all nations and further improvement of that waterway. The social reforms advocated were:

prompt secularization of the Clergy Reserves, not by means of procedure by address but by a bill which the imperial parliament should be asked to accept; abolition of the rectories; establishment of a system of completely free public schools supported by the proceeds of the Clergy Reserves and of the Jesuit estates and by the land revenue; a sharp reduction in college and university fees so that "the plain farmer may have a chance to give his sons the highest course of instruction;" abolition of the laws of primogeniture; and the enactment of temperance legislation. His political program demanded an increase in the membership of the Assembly, single member districts of equal size "without consideration of the dividing line between the provinces," the abolition of plural voting and of the high property qualification for members of the Assembly. Mackenzie also proposed that the Assembly should be elected for three years instead of four. "Four is too long — it is allowing three years to sin and one to repent." But the important reform needed other than secularization of the Clergy Reserves was the creation of a legal system that a poor man could afford to utilize. This meant abolition of the Court of Chancery, reduction of lawyers' fees, simplification of legal procedures and establishment of courts of conciliation.[33]

Many of the changes Mackenzie wanted were advocated also by the Clear Grits and the Lower Canada radicals, les Rouges. The Grits, however, also wished to institute certain American practices that Mackenzie was not at this time as ready to accept as he once had been. These were an elected governor, an elective legislative council, fixed biennial parliaments, extension of the franchise and vote by ballot.[34] The radicals got no support from the *Globe*, which accused them of republicanism and upheld the administration, although not uncritically. The *Examiner* was sympathetic to their point of view but the younger radicals did not find this "erratic and discursive" paper, many of whose columns were written by Mackenzie, a satisfactory mouthpiece for their ideas.[35] Consequently in May 1850 the Clear Grits had founded their own newspaper, the *North American*, under the editorship of William McDougall. Mackenzie did not identify himself with the Clear Grit section of the Reform Party.

> As for this new attempt to divide those who desire good
> government into ministerialists and clear grits [he wrote], I am
> an enemy to it; united we stand — divided we fall... division,
> through a demand for things impracticable without revolution
> would deeply injure the reform party.

Things which he thought the mother country was unlikely to concede, and therefore "impracticable," were an elected legislative council and an elected governor-general. "The Clear Grit platform... is annexation under a new cloak," he declared.[36] Later he was to come closer to their position.

In February 1851 David Thompson, the Member for Haldimand, died. This event gave Mackenzie an opportunity to get into Parliament before the general election was held. Early in March he announced his candidacy for the vacant seat. The *Examiner* referred to him as "the old staunch friend of people's rights" who had performed herculean labours on their behalf and shown "unceasing vigilance and unswerving fidelity" to the cause and who now "with enlarged knowledge and wider experience" again presented himself to the public.[37] Neither Clear Grits, Reformers nor Tories welcomed Mackenzie's return to political life. They all looked upon him with suspicion because, as the Hamilton *Spectator* explained, he stood aloof from all parties. The editor had no desire to see Mackenzie in Parliament and thought he might do "a great deal of mischief if he got there."[38]

William McDougall made similar criticisms in stronger terms: Mackenzie denounced all political parties, attacked Papineau "the eloquent, the learned, the consistent republican, whose opinions are the convictions of a philosophical mind, not the whims of the moment." Mackenzie, on the other hand, laid down no intelligible principle for a party of his own. "Even if his principles harmonized with ours," wrote McDougall, "we should not support him as a public man." He was rash, headstrong, opinionated. He regarded no man's advice. "Under a representative system of government, which implied government by and through a party — there is no place for such a politician." McDougall could not see that Mackenzie could do any good by trying his hand at politics again. "The government of Canada unless we are to revert to the old system must be carried on by a party."[39] The Clear Grits' criticisms of Mackenzie as a man and as a politician were justified, but his platform was as timely as theirs and it does not substantiate the belief of some writers that on his return to Canada he was out of touch with the questions of the day. He was behind the times only on extension of the franchise to others than freeholders. His previous experience in Canada, reinforced by what he had seen of election practices in the United States, had made him wary on this point.

Among those who wished Mackenzie success in his canvass was Joseph Hume. His letter of April 1, which he gave Mackenzie permission to publish, did not arrive before the election was over but was nevertheless published in the *Examiner*.[40] In the accompanying private letter Hume went on to emphasize once more the inadequate interpretation of the rebellion he preferred to believe: that all that was ever wanted was responsible government which "if granted when you were despatched to England to obtain it, would have prevented the rebellion...."[41]

The country of Haldimand was composed of 10 townships, eight of which were part of the Grand River Tract granted to the Six Nations of Indians. By 1851 most of the land had passed into the hands of whites by gift or sale.[42] Although the original grants or purchases of Indian land had been divided, there were still some large properties in the county. There were 4,848 males of voting age in Haldimand in 1851, 2,038 persons occupying more than 20 acres of land and 1,977 classifying themselves as farmers, but only 786 freeholders voted.[43]

Between 1848 and 1851 the population of Haldimand had increased by one-third[44] and the amount of land under cultivation had more than doubled. Several flourishing villages had grown up on the banks of the Grand River, whose water power maintained sawmills, planing mills, grist mills and woollen mills. There were also steam mills, tanneries, breweries and two foundries. The county that was to accept or reject Mackenzie was, therefore, no raw backwoods area or stagnant community, but a flourishing agricultural and lumbering county to which the terms of Canada's export trade in wheat and forest products were important and in which industries related to these products were established.

Initially numerous candidates came forth for Haldimand but their number was finally reduced to four. Ronald McKinnon, a prosperous merchant and mill owner who had been a contractor for the Grand River Navigation Company was the candidate for the Tory Party.[45] George Brown, editor of the *Globe*, and H.N. Case, owner of the plaster works in Haldimand, both claimed to be the regular candidate of the Reform Party, but neither of them received the accolade of the ministry, which chose not to take a hand in the contest. Brown, though a supporter of the Baldwin-LaFontaine administration up to this point, had become suspicious that the government was marking time on the Clergy Reserve question owing to the influence of Lafontaine and his Roman Catholic supporters in Lower Canada. Brown was a voluntaryist and as strong an opponent of state-churchism, Anglican or Catholic, as any of the Clear Grits. His purpose in seeking a seat in Parliament was to give the ministry a push in the direction of secularization of the reserves.[46] It is therefore not surprising that Baldwin and Hincks should have been reluctant to add the forceful George Brown to the number of Upper Canada members dissatisfied with their handling of that question. When informed of Brown's candidacy, Hincks wrote him a rather neutral letter stating that if he could be brought forward for Haldimand without dividing the party it would be "satisfactory" to the ministry and hinting that Brown should act with "discretion."[47] The ever-suspicious Mackenzie was under the impression that the government had induced Brown to oppose him in Haldimand in order to mark their sense of Mackenzie's "ingratitude." Hincks replied:

> You are wholly mistaken in supposing that Mr. Brown was sent to Haldimand to oppose you.... I feel assured that you will have no cause for complaint on the score of government interference in the election. [48]

He didn't. It was Brown who complained: "Never did candidate in similar circumstances receive less support from his party."[49] No party leader came to his assistance.

Mackenzie and Brown soon became the principal combatants, two non-residents opposing each other and opposed by two local businessmen.[50] Accompanied by his daughter Janet, Mackenzie was driven about the constituency by a shoemaker, Thomas J. Wiggin.[51] In a lengthy address to the electors issued on April 2, Mackenzie announced his platform, elaborating the proposals for further reforms made in his earlier address to the electors of York. He argued that Brown, the recipient of government advertising and printing and the holder of a government appointment as one of the commissioners for the penitentiary, would not be a really independent member no matter what professions he might make during the campaign. He accused him of defending a government that had bestowed undeserved and extravagant pensions, perpetuated the "Chancery job," and been guilty of waste, corruption, and "all sort of rascality." Above all, Brown had up to this point defended the government's dilatory course with respect to the Clergy Reserves.

On the eve of the election George Brown believed that the real contest was between him and Mackenzie and that as "of course" he was "the least objectionable choice" the Tories would throw their votes to him. He was confident he would get 310 votes which, in a four-way contest in which he expected 700 to 750 votes to be cast, would give him the victory.[52] Out of the 786 votes cast, Mackenzie obtained 294, McKinnon 266, Brown 165 and Case 61.[53]

How are we to account for Mackenzie's victory less than a year after his return to Canada and against as redoubtable an opponent as George Brown, who, no less than the Tory candidate McKinnon, took care to remind the voters of the events of 1837?[54] Brown grossly miscalculated the strength and the staying power of his Tory opponent in a county where the Anglicans were the strongest denomination.[55] Fear of Mackenzie's victory did not win them over to Brown. Second, the county contained a sizeable body of Roman Catholics. Their votes were lost to Brown who had roused the active hostility of the Toronto *Mirror*, a Catholic reform journal, by his criticism of the Papacy and of the hierarchy in Canada.[56]

To the *Examiner* and other reform journals in the province Mackenzie's victory in Haldimand had a significance beyond the boundaries of that county. It was not merely George Brown who had been defeated but the Baldwin-Lafontaine government. "The reformers in the county have ceased to be ministerialists and time will show this is true elsewhere," predicted the *Examiner*.[57] The *Bathurst Courier* declared: "Mr. Mackenzie is a stronger man in the country than many supposed." The *Peterborough Weekly Despatch* observed:

> The Haldimand Election has offered a fair trial of strength between the two sections of the reform party, ministerialists and progressives;... in one of the oldest and staunchest reform constituencies in Upper Canada lately represented by a staunch supporter of the ministry. Out of 785 votes only 165 were recorded in favor of the ministerialist candidate. These results ought to convince our present rulers that the country is not satisfied with their rate of progress. [58]

Mackenzie's friends of course interpreted his victory as a criticism of the "shuffling and deceptive" policies of the Baldwin-Lafontaine administration. One wrote:

> The spell of their craft as reformers seems to be broken.... [They] are traitors to the implicit confidence placed in them by the people. [59]

Another asked:

> Where are we? After all our toil and suffering the Great
> Questions have been swolled [sic] up in the struggle for
> Responsible government, we may say almost lost sight of in
> pursuit of this Phantom. To begin the catalogue, where are the
> Clergy reserves, the intestate Bill, the Vote by Ballot
> retrenchment &c., &c. [60]

During the months after the election Mackenzie's correspondence was swollen
by letters of congratulation and advice and information about these and other
grievances that needed to be remedied, among them the tariff, the assessment
laws, the extensive powers of the Superintendent of Education, Egerton
Ryerson, the manner in which timber limits were disposed of, the inadequate
powers of the division courts and the improvident sales of public works to
private capitalists.[61] "Everyman in the province is looking for something great
from you," he was informed. A Wesleyan Methodist wrote:

> I would be glad to hear that faithful voice again demanding in
> our Legislature equal civil and religious privileges for all
> classes of the people. [62]

It was buoyed up by such letters of confidence — and by the news that
McKinnon had decided not to question his legal qualifications for the
Assembly[63] — that the new member for Haldimand took his seat in the fourth
session of the third parliament of united Canada.

# Chapter XIII

# THE MEMBER FOR HALDIMAND

The fourth session of the third parliament of united Canada opened at Toronto on May 20, 1851. Dr. Wolfred Nelson had planned to introduce Mackenzie to the Assembly but his professional duties prevented him from being present. Instead, this office was performed by Jacob DeWitt, Member for Beauharnois and president of La Banque du Peuple. There was much speculation as to the course the new member would take. Nelson had assured the administration that Mackenzie did not intend to be obstructive but would support them whenever he conscientiously could, using "every occasion for the common good irrespective of all private feeling" — latitude unlimited for one of Mackenzie's temperament. While acknowledging that the work of reform had only begun, Nelson warned: "Let us be cautious lest we mar the whole by trying to go too fast."[1] The impetuous new member was not to be restrained. One of his admirers wrote, with some exaggeration of the fact, that it was said he had not been in his seat two minutes before he was up with a motion.[2]

Mackenzie's first move reveals his concern for the kind of society he hoped Canada would become. He tried to repeal a portion of the Upper Canada Trust and Loan Company Act of 1850. This company, which had received a charter in 1843 empowering it to lend money on real estate at the legal rate of 6%, claimed it could not attract capital under that restriction. An act had then been passed allowing it to lend at 8%.[3] Mackenzie objected to the act because it gave the company, controlled by directors in London, a *special* privilege other lenders in Canada did not have. In a lengthy speech, not all of it relevant, he deplored what he believed would be the pernicious result of such legislation: "There was no power in the country so potent for reducing the number of freeholders as the money power." If it was necessary to secure capital to improve farming in Canada, he thought it would be far better for the government to borrow it at 3 or $3\frac{1}{2}$% and lend it to the farmers at 8 or 9%, applying the profit to the uses of the province. Permission to introduce the repeal measure was refused on the ground that action of that kind would weaken the credit of the province.[4]

Mackenzie also objected to the manner in which the bill of 1850 had been passed "at the fag end of the session," when many of the members were absent, "with the rules suspended," and when no one knew what was being done.[5] John A. Macdonald subsequently accused Mackenzie of stating what he knew to be untrue, claiming that the bill was not passed at midnight, the House was full, and 40 subjects were taken up afterwards as the record showed.[6] The wily MacDonald referred to the final passing of the bill along with many other engrossed bills, but Mackenzie was referring to what happened when the bill was reported out of committee and ordered to be engrossed. Mackenzie might well have been even blunter. Newspapers of the day reported that the bill "had been pushed through with railroad speed" at a time when the House was in a disgraceful and uproarious condition. Several of the members were "reeling drunk" and others, far from sober, were throwing ink wells at one another and making paper bullets out of the bills ready for their consideration.[7] Four attempts were made at this session to amend the usury laws so as to raise the legal rate of interest. All were defeated with Mackenzie's help.[8] At the next session Mackenzie moved that the Trust and Loan Co. be required to furnish detailed information about the loans made, rates charged, land held and mortgaged estates acquired. The return was ordered but when presented in summary form it did not show that the farmers of Upper Canada were losing their land to the "foreign" usurers and bloodsuckers he had denounced.[9]

Law reform had been one of the main planks in Mackenzie's platform. Popular distrust of lawyers as a class, resentment at the charges of this monopolistic self-regulating profession and at its stranglehold on the political machinery of the state had been revealed in the speeches of a number of delegates at the New York State constitutional convention. A similar distrust of the profession existed in the Upper Canada of 1850. "Lawyers nowadays are going at ninety percent discount," observed a resident of York West.[10] An innkeeper complained: "We are worse off now than we was under the old tory compact, unless we can get the lawyers thrown out of the house of parliament...."[11] Baldwin's conduct as head of a Reform government had intensified this distrust in the minds of some Reformers. "The whole aim of the Baldwinites seems to be to create a law aristocracy which unless arrested will shortly swallow up the wealth of the Province," a Glengarry physician predicted.[12]

Mackenzie began the session with a determination to do all he could "to relieve the country of the lawyers' monopoly...."[13] On May 27 he made his first effort in this direction by introducing a bill to establish conciliation courts in Upper Canada, remarking that such courts existed in France and Jamaica and were permitted by the constitution of New York State. He proposed that the county judges should hear, without fee, cases of assault and battery, breach of promise, libel, malicious persecution or violence of any kind, should reason with the parties and endeavour to bring them to a settlement. Such a measure, he reminded the legislators, had been passed by the Assembly of Upper Canada in 1831, but had been killed by the Council. (That bill had not provided for county *judges* and had been rejected by the Council on the ground that such conciliation courts would sap the foundations of jurisprudence "and give to a popular meeting the appointment of judges who, though householders, might be foreigners."[14]) Mackenzie's bill of 1851 was derided as a "nonsensical scheme that only jackasses would favor," and in the course of the debate he was subjected to personal abuse which the Speaker did not attempt to halt.[15] Lafontaine remarked that Mackenzie had been denied the respect of all political parties; Henry Sherwood called him a rebel and a robber.[16] His bill was given the six months hoist.[17] At the next session Mackenzie introduced another conciliation courts bill. It was criticized as not being well drafted. Mackenzie claimed, without justification, that it was copied word for word from one drawn by one of the ablest lawyers in New York State "where it had given much satisfaction." Again his bill was ridiculed. "Our Clear Grits were to a man dumb," he complained. "Not a reformer had a word to say for a bill that contemplated lessening lawyers' fees." He concluded that it would be hopeless to introduce the measure again.[18]

On June 23 Mackenzie attacked the lawyers' "monopoly" by introducing a bill to abolish the distinction Queen's Counsel and to authorize any man to plead for himself or another in a court of law. He pointed out that in France any person could practise and that in New York State and in Nova Scotia anyone could sit for the bar no matter where he had studied law. In Upper Canada, however, admission to the bar was controlled by the Law Society. Only after five years' apprenticeship to one of its members, three years in the case of college graduates, was a young man admitted to practice.[19] The country wished to get rid of this principle of monopoly, Mackenzie claimed, because it was "contrary to the spirit of the age." He failed to obtain a second reading for his bill and was again subjected to personal abuse. Henry Smith, of Frontenac, held up a commission in the Patriot forces bearing a representation of the American eagle running away with the British lion. Amid laughter of the House, Mackenzie rose to a point of order, asking "what that had got to do with it." Smith explained that he wanted to make a comparison between the commission in the rebel army and a lawyer's commission.[20] Other attempts which Mackenzie made in subsequent session to ease access to the profession, provided a candidate could prove his qualifications, proved equally futile. Both admission to apprenticeship and to the final qualifying examination (not instituted until 1857) were controlled by the Law Society.[21]

On June 26 Mackenzie made his best-known motion: that the Court of Chancery of Upper Canada be abolished and that equity jurisdiction be conferred upon the courts of common law. A court of equity did not exist in the upper province until 1837.[22] Mackenzie had opposed its establishment, he explained,

> not that I thought the system complete without it, but because I did not believe its institution of secret examinations in lawyers' offices for open ones before the world — its practice, exceedingly arbitrary and artificial... its questionable barriers as to what cases were doubtful, obscure, and therefore fit for equity courts... would be an improvement. [23]

It was Head's Bread and Butter Parliament that established the Upper Canada Court of Chancery. The handful of Reformers who had succeeded in retaining their seats fought the proposal every step of the way and tried in vain to add restrictive riders to the bill.[24]

The Court of Chancery was unpopular from the start for its expense and its delays. In 1845 the House of Assembly had seriously considered abolishing it,[25] but in the end commissioners were appointed to make recommendations for reorganizing this court. In 1849 the Baldwin-Lafontaine government undertook the task. The Vice-Chancellor, R.S. Jameson, was pensioned off early. The Court was then given three judges, a chancellor and two vice-chancellors, who were empowered to make new rules to reduce costs of chancery suits and to expedite the tedious processes of the court. Mackenzie, as has been seen, found fault with this act on account of the new judicial appointments it made necessary. He objected to Jameson's pension, which facilitated them, because it had been made without the consent of the legislature.[26]

In his speech proposing that the Court of Chancery now be abolished, Mackenzie pointed out that France, Lower Canada and 15 of the states had no Court of Chancery, that New York and Ohio had abolished theirs, and that Nova Scotia was considering doing the same. He objected to the enormous costs of the Court and to the fact that evidence was taken in written form instead of verbally in the presence of judges,[27] and he criticized the appointment of W.H. Blake to the chancellorship because, as a member of the Assembly, he had voted to create the office he now held.[28] Mackenzie's motion was defeated 30 to 34,[29] but since 23 Upper Canada members, a majority of her 42, had voted for the abolition of the Court Baldwin resigned from the cabinet. Six of the 23 had previously been supporters of the ministry; three of them had voted for the Act of 1849, and 13 of the 23 were members of the bar.[30] With the exception of John A. Macdonald, all the Upper Canada Tory members supported Mackenzie's proposal, although several of these also had voted for the Act of 1849. Baldwin complained that he had remodelled the court in accordance with the wishes of the bar of Upper Canada, which was dissatisfied with it and with Vice-Chancellor Jameson personally.[31] His predecessor's measure had had 12 years' trial, but he could not get two for his. Under such circumstances, he enquired: "What prospect had he of being able to protect any of the institutions of the country from mere demagogues?"[32] Although Baldwin withdrew from the cabinet he reluctantly remained Attorney-General West, at Lafontaine's request, a course which was not in harmony with his own theories of responsible government as H.J. Boulton pointed out.[33] The Colonial Secretary also found this state of affairs "very objectionable" but was persuaded by Elgin to accept it.[34]

Although Mackenzie's motion failed, it was not without significance. A scene of disorder occurred when another member remarked that purely Upper Canada questions were being decided by Lower Canada votes. This circumstance led the *Examiner* to call the union "a union of force and fetters," "a living lie."[35] It earned Mackenzie praise from staunch Reformers both within and without his constituency. One of them wrote:

> Your famous motion on the Chancery bill... shook the whole faction to its centre. Mackenzie men in Haldimand can about be picked up on every door step. [36]

Another constituent called his Chancery Bill "a laurel on your head" and remarked that he would deserve the thanks of the country even if he had done nothing else during the session.[37]

Abolition of the Court of Chancery was not merely one of Mackenzie's crotchets, part of the ideological baggage he had brought back from the United States. Francis Hincks was of the opinion that those who supported him did so "only as a factious attempt to embarrass the government," and recent historians have agreed with him.[38] In his *Reminiscences* Hincks wrote, "I am not aware that between 1851 and 1884 any similar proposals have been made."[39] Hincks' statement belittles the importance of this controversy and gives an inaccurate impression of its future course. Reformers in the legislature had kept a hostile eye on the Court of Chancery from the start and had repeatedly called for returns respecting its activities and its costs. The changes made in 1849 had not satisfied them.[40] During the session of 1850 six petitions had been presented from various parts of the upper province asking for the court's outright abolition.[41] The support which Mackenzie's motion of 1851 received was, therefore, a response to a long-continued popular protest against it.

Mackenzie made other attempts to have the Court abolished and its jurisdiction transferred to the common law courts, but obtained less support. The explanation probably is that the Court had become acceptable because chancery suits in which the ordinary man was likely to be concerned — partnerships, wills, mortgages — could, after 1853, be heard in the county courts of Upper Canada.[42] Mackenzie predicted that Upper Canada would never get rid of the Court of Chancery until she was no longer hampered by Lower Canada votes. By that time, however, the procedures of the Court had been much improved, its fees lowered and its judges required to go on circuit. The Court was to remain under a different name a permanent part of Ontario's legal system. Fusion of the courts of law and equity and simplification of their procedures, reforms for which Mackenzie contended, were not to be fully achieved until Oliver Mowat's administration passed the Ontario Judicature Act of 1881.[43] During the intervening years it had been J.A. Macdonald's policy to achieve this result by degrees, following the example of England rather than the "hasty & inconsiderate legislation of the United States."[44] Mowat's act likewise followed the British example set by the Imperial Judicature Act of 1873.[45]

With one exception, all the measures that Mackenzie introduced so promptly during the session of 1851 failed. On June 6 he brought in a bill for the election of sheriffs, instancing the conduct of Sheriff Jarvis, who had not yet given him an account of the sale of his property, as an argument in its favour.[46] "Even if it fails," observed a Belleville friend, "it will make them [the sheriffs] less overbearing."[47] The bill was given short shrift.[48] His bill requiring the votes of members on the final passage of bills to be recorded, a provision he had seen made part of the constitution of New York State, was given the six months hoist. Later attempts, in the sessions of 1852 and 1857, were likewise to fail.[49] His acceptance of the office restriction bill was designed to prevent executive councillors and members of the Assembly from obtaining lucrative offices which they had voted to create. This was a point Mackenzie had made much of during his election campaign. His bill was refused a second reading and at the next session was turned down again.[50] The bill had a tactless preamble, certain to ensure its rejection. It was stated to be "contrary to British precedent and practice," "derogatory to the character of the judiciary... that those concerned in creating courts and offices should be appointed to fill them" and was, moreover, likely to bring the representative of the Crown who acquiesced in such proceedings into "disrepute." His bill for the relief of creditors of Indians in Upper Canada, one which would have benefitted his constituents, was denied a second reading. (At the previous session an act had been passed preventing creditors from obtaining a confession of judgment for debt against an Indian unless he was possessed of land in fee simple.[51]) A resolution asking for the improvement of the Grand River, introduced by Mackenzie at the request of his constituents, was negatived.[52] It almost seems as if a majority in the Assembly was determined to show the people of Haldimand that next time they would do better to elect someone else. The only measure Mackenzie succeeded in getting through was a minor local act to permit the closing up of a certain street in the town of Cayuga.[53]

This trifling result is not a measure of Mackenzie's usefulness in the Assembly. During the election campaign, and in his letters to the *Examiner*, he had complained that the province was not being fully and promptly informed about what was being done with its revenues, nor was it obtaining adequate information from various chartered corporations to which special privileges or financial aid had been granted. Consequently he called for and obtained a number of detailed returns which cannot have endeared him to the government departments, to the corporations concerns or to Francis Hincks.

On the occasion of the debate on the postal revenues, as in his speech on conciliation courts, Mackenzie delivered one of his discursive discourses "darting off to the burning sands of India" to drag in a reference to the conduct of Clive, touching for three-quarters of an hour "on all imaginable subjects" before returning to the question at issue.[54] This type of thing tried the patience of testy members and reduced his effectiveness in the legislature. Yet Mackenzie could also speak — and write — vigorously and to the point, bolstering his case with a wealth of often unwelcome facts. His letters to the Freeholders of Haldimand, published week after week by the Toronto E*xaminer* while the session lasted packed a real punch.

Mackenzie, never a party man, gave his support to measures of reform no matter by whom they were introduced. Baldwin's bill for abolishing the laws of primogeniture, bills to reduce law expenses and register's fees, a mechanic's lien bill and a bill to forbid the payment of mechanics in truck all had his support. None of them was enacted except Baldwin's bill.

Mackenzie also spoke in support of H.J. Boulton's bill to prohibit the expenditure of public money for purposes not authorized by law.[55] On this occasion he was attacked by Colonel Bartholemew Gugy, a Lower Canada Tory, who called him a traitor, a liar, a scoundrel, a robber, a murderer, half cat and half monkey, half tiger and half goat. Mackenzie kept his temper, merely protesting that the Speaker should not have allowed such latitude of speech to Gugy. Some of his constituents were disposed to complain to the Assembly about the insults that had been offered to the county of Haldimand in the person of their representative.[56]

The law of Upper Canada provided that no one might be arrested for a debt of less than £10 unless there was reason to expect that he would abscond, and no one might be kept in jail for debt who could prove that he was not worth £5, exclusive of £20 worth of essential household equipment and clothing.[57] During the session of 1841 Colonel Prince had attempted to have imprisonment for debt abolished in Upper Canada and in this session H.J. Boulton tried to secure this reform. Mackenzie supported him and moved for a return of the number of debtors in close confinement for debt or for the payment of law costs. There proved to be only ten such cases, but there were approximately 80 persons who were bailed to the jail limits, that is, to the boundaries of their counties.[58] Throughout his political career Mackenzie continued to interest himself in the plight of debtors and would have imposed imprisonment only on those guilty of fraud. He had in his early days escaped a debtors' prison, thanks to the mercy of his creditors, and he knew what his friend Randall had suffered as a debtor.[59]

It was not until 1858, Mackenzie's last session in Parliament, that John A. Macdonald became convinced that there was "a general desire in the country for abolition of imprisonment for debt" and, stimulated no doubt by the depression of 1857, he decided to "indulge" the people.[60] But Macdonald's legislation did not go that far. The £20 limit was raised to £24/10 for debtors tried in the division courts and to £25 in the superior courts. The efforts of Mackenzie and others to amend the law failed. Some provisions of the law were liberalized in 1859. Imprisonment for non-payment of law costs was abolished and the restrictions on debtors who were bailed were eased,[61] but imprisonment for debt was never *totally* abolished in united Canada. Debtors could still bring this penalty upon themselves by fraudulent conduct, and that fact, if proven, determined the length of their imprisonment.

During the Haldimand campaign Mackenzie's main criticism of George Brown had been that he continued to support the Baldwin-Lafontaine administration despite its failure to declare itself frankly in favour of secularizing the Clergy Reserves and abolishing the rectory endowments, which Reformers held to have been illegally created by Sir John Colborne. The status of these hoary disputes by 1850 was as follows: the imperial "settlement" of the Clergy Reserves question in 1840 had provided for the gradual sale of the remaining reserves and for the distribution of the Clergy Reserves funds in a manner that left Anglicans and Presbyterians dissatisfied with their respective shares, gave the government power to aid other denominations of Christians, and displeased those who believed the ministers of all denominations should be supported entirely by the voluntary contributions of their parishioners. Sales of the reserves to lessees and squatters had given rise to endless disputes since 1840 over the valuation of the lots they claimed and the terms on which they should be allowed to acquire them. Squatters on clergy land in the township of Erin, for example, had complained that they had been on their land 17 or 18 years and were now being required to buy it at valuations which had been delayed and then raised at the request of the Church. It was grievances of this kind which made Reformers determined to secularize the reserves and to use the revenues for general purposes.[62]

Baldwin acknowledged his reluctance to disturb the Clergy Reserves settlement of 1840, but he was regarded as having pledged himself to secularization during the election campaign of 1847.[63] Because his government had taken no steps towards secularization in 1848 and 1849, he had come to be mistrusted by radical Reformers. Section 11 of the Imperial Clergy Reserves Act of 1840 had repealed those sections of the Constitutional Act that related to the reserves and had thereby deprived the province of the power, which that act had given her, to legislate on the subject. Baldwin took the view that before any settlement of the reserves question could be achieved that power had to be regained. In this interpretation of the act of 1840 Elgin and the colonial secretary had concurred.[64]

In 1850, when no mention of the Clergy Reserves was made in the Speech from the Throne, it seemed to voluntaryists just another indication of the ministry's reluctance to secularize. Then on June 18, 1850, J.H. Price, "the firmest voluntaryist in the ministry,"[65]proposed 31 Clergy Reserve resolutions as a basis for an address to the Crown. These resolutions, which were adopted, did not *commit* the ministry to secularize. They merely asked the imperial parliament for an enabling act giving Canada power to dispose of the reserves as she saw fit, on condition that those stipends and allowances being paid out of the Clergy Reserve fund should be continued for the lives of the incumbents. Although both Baldwin and LaFontaine voted for the address, it became clear during the debate that the ministry was divided. Baldwin declared he put justice to the Church first and Lafontaine said he preferred to have the reserves retained for religious purposes.[66] Clear Grits could well doubt whether such a ministry would secularize. This was the status of the Clergy Reserves dispute when Mackenzie took his seat.

Mackenzie could not see any need for waiting for an enabling act. Why could not the imperial parliament legalize a Canadian Clergy Reserves Act as it had a Canadian post office act? From two of the townships in Mackenzie's county a petition had come signed with 400 names asking for secularization of the reserves. Mackenzie was determined that the government should not shirk its duty any longer. Early in the session of 1851 he presented a petition asking that the Clergy Reserves be sold for the benefit of free schools and that the rectories be abolished. Never one noted for brevity, he spoke for two hours on this occasion. The Assembly grew impatient with his long harangue and defeated his motion 9 to 47.[67] Mackenzie was just wasting the Assembly's time; Elgin's ministers, who were determined to wait for an enabling act, had already announced that they would not take up the Clergy Reserves question at that session.[68]

When Baldwin resigned from the cabinet the notion that he had done so because of Upper Canada's votes on Mackenzie's chancery court motion was derided by his critics. A month earlier it had been rumoured that he would not stand for the north riding of York again. A Sharon innkeeper was convinced "he couldn't possibly be elected. He has deceived the people."[69] Another disgusted voluntarist remarked:

> They say Baldwin gives up on account of the Chancery vote, but I believe it is on account of the rectories and reserves which his Puseyite soul cannot disturb after all his bunkum speeches in former days. [70]

The Toronto *Examiner* regarded Baldwin as one of the most conservative members. It declared his popularity had been steadily declining and that the cause of reform would not lose by his resignation.[71]

In Upper Canada it was believed that despite the strong feeling on the rectory question Lord Elgin was creating new rectory endowments and permitting vacancies to be filled.[72] On June 5, 1851, J.C. Morrison introduced a bill to repeal sections 38-40 of the Constitutional Act so as to prevent the creation of rectories in future or the presentation of incumbents to existing rectories when they became vacant. This bill, which did not touch the legality of existing rectory patents, was referred to a committee which added a third clause providing that, in the event of its being judicially determined that the rectories were legal, the Church Society of the diocese should have the right of presenting to the rectories. In this form the bill was unacceptable to both Morrison and Mackenzie and they tried, unsuccessfully, to have it recommitted.[73] The day before the amended bill was reported the Assembly requested the Governor-General to submit the legality of the rectory patents to the Court of Chancery with the right of appeal to the Privy Council and with the expenses of all proceedings for both sides being guaranteed by the Assembly.[74] Mackenzie and Morrison's attempt to give the bill the three months hoist failed, and the bill passed. It was a reserved bill. On the last day of the session Hincks moved an address asking the imperial government to sanction the bill. Mackenzie tried to prevent the passage of the address by talking for 45 minutes before the hour of adjournment. No one aided him to continue this filibuster. The address passed, 28 to 3, to shouts of triumph from the impatient members.[75] The validity of the patents was upheld by the Court of Chancery and by the Court of Error and Appeal.[76] The Conservative government in office at that time did not appeal this decision.

In his pre-rebellion days Mackenzie, like other Reformers, had objected to the charter of the University of King's College, which placed that institution, endowed with Crown land, under the control of those whom he called "our clerical exclusives." The charter was later modified to make it more acceptable to non-Anglicans but it still failed to satisfy them. In 1849 King's College was converted into the University of Toronto, its faculty of divinity abolished and all ecclesiastics excluded from its government. Bishop Strachan would not accept this "godless university" as a replacement for King's College. He therefore went to England to secure a charter and private funds for a new Anglican college, Trinity. A royal charter was not to be granted until 1858, but in the session of 1851

Sir Allan MacNab introduced a bill to incorporate Trinity that set no limits to the amount of land it might hold, and would also have permitted the Church to establish preparatory schools in connection with it.[77]

Mackenzie opposed the bill. Was Bishop Strachan, after all the efforts of the Reformers, to get an exclusively Anglican institution permanently endowed with Upper Canada land? In a long speech Mackenzie pointed out that the bill proposed to set aside the Statute of Mortmain for the benefit of Trinity, a provision to which Mackenzie, always anxious to prevent the growth of tenancy, strongly objected. He tried to have the Assembly resolve that as the Church of England had been arrayed against the people of Upper Canada

> in their long effort to get equal civil and religious rights, abolish rectories and appropriate the reserves to education, it is dangerous and inexpedient to... strengthen the said church... by granting its request for the special incorporation of an exclusive sectarian college for itself.

Only one vote besides his own was cast for this declaration and against the final passage of the Trinity College bill.[78] Mackenzie's opposition to this bill again caused him to be subjected to personal abuse in the Assembly.[79] His opposition was hardly in keeping with his own principle of religious equality. Other sectarian institutions had special charters. There was no reason why the Church of England should not, especially as in its final form the bill incorporating Trinity gave it only a limited privilege of holding land in mortmain — real estate to the value of £5,000 annually — and permitted only one school connected with it.[80]

Another religious controversy of a different sort was aroused by the Wesleyan Methodist Benevolent Societies Incorporation Bill, introduced by Billa Flint, Member for Hastings. This bill, which was strongly desired by Egerton Ryerson, would have created a corporation chosen by the Methodist conference of ministers to hold and control the property of various Methodist benevolent societies, and it would have given the corporation power to name its officers and made it self-perpetuating. Ryerson defended the bill in a pamphlet entitled "Remarks on Religious Corporations" in which, by way of showing "the tolerant and enlightened spirit of our American neighbours" as an example, he included several New York State statutes incorporating religious enterprises with which Marshall Spring Bidwell had supplied him.[81] Even so, Mackenzie's help in defeating the measure was sought by those Wesleyan Methodists who were no admirers of Ryerson and who resented his efforts to force acceptance of this plan upon the denomination. They wanted the laity to have a voice in the affairs of the church and some control over its funds. "The ministers should not take all these matters into their own hands. It has made bad and ambitious men of them," wrote one member of the denomination.[82]

Mackenzie attempted to amend the vague provisions of the bill so as to provide that the corporation should be composed of three elected

189

representatives, lay or clerical, from each circuit, one-third of whom were to retire every two years. The amount of property that the corporation might hold was to be limited to £25,000. This amendment failed. Those who opposed it included some 17 Lower Canada members who resented the criticisms of the Roman Catholic Church and the state of education in Lower Canada that Mackenzie had unnecessarily and unwisely included in his remarks.[83] While grateful to Mackenzie for his efforts, Methodists who disliked the bill begged him instead to support their petition that the bill be dropped even though some changes in its original wording had been made. "The Ryersons will continue in a thousand ways to avoid the new clauses," one of them wrote. They also objected to the bill because it would create another ecclesiastical corporation "subversive of the laws of mortmain and destructive of the voluntary principle."[84] What they had tried to deny to the Church of England, they did not want for themselves. The upshot of the matter was that the bill was not withdrawn, some clauses John Ross found objectionable were omitted, and then the bill passed, 37 to 17, with Mackenzie, of course, in the negative. In its final form the bill limited the amount of real estate the Methodist corporation could hold to £5,000 annual value and obliged the corporation to account to the Governor-General if required.[85]

Although parliamentary reform had been promised by Reform candidates during the election of 1847, and had been before the legislature three times, nothing had yet been accomplished. The Act of Union required a two-thirds majority on both the second and third readings for such bills. That had proved difficult to obtain. Mackenzie had criticized the government for its failure to amend the representation clauses, which now worked to the disadvantage of Upper Canada and over-represented the small towns at the expense of the county constituencies. He believed that an increase in the membership of the Assembly would make it less easy for the administration to secure a majority by bribing the representatives with appointments and he proposed to base the increase on the principle that every man's vote should have equal weight. This meant the creation of single member constituencies, equal in size, a reform which New York had obtained in 1846. Moreover Mackenzie wanted the seats apportioned "without consideration of the dividing line between the provinces." Two years later George Brown was to begin his vigorous campaign to give the more populous upper province a larger share of the representation, calling for "Rep. by Pop.," "without consideration of the dividing line between the provinces."[86]

Lafontaine's representation bill of this session would have increased the membership of the Assembly from 84 to 130 and reapportioned the seats, but it would have maintained equality of representation between the two parts of the province despite the disparity in their populations.[87] In a discursive speech that caused the Speaker finally to call him to order, Mackenzie approved of the proposed increase in the membership of the Assembly and did not on this occasion object to the equal division of the seats with Lower Canada, but he voted against LaFontaine's bill on account of the unequal representation of the constituencies in both sections of the province.[88] The bill passed its second reading one vote short of the required two-thirds majority, which an affirmative vote by Mackenzie would have provided. Mackenzie had placed himself in the position of having prevented a reform for which he himself contended: the creation of a larger, more representative, and hopefully less corruptible Assembly. As it was he had laid himself open to the reproach of having voted with the Tories. "Liberal members ought to have held together upon the principle of enlarged representation for the counties," he was told.[89]

A Territorial Divisions Bill for Upper Canada also passed at this session.[90] Mackenzie voted for it but criticized some of its provisions in the *Examiner*, observing that three small towns represented by Tories — Cornwall, Brockville and Niagara, with a total population of 7,545 — would together have three seats, while the three counties into which the county of Waterloo was to be divided (for judicial purposes only) would have only one representative among them although their total population was 54,612. He reminded the ministers of Lord Durham's words, "It is not in North America that men can be cheated by an unreal semblance of representative government or persuaded that they are outvoted when in fact they are disenfranchised."[91] Mackenzie's long speech on this occasion caused him to be attacked for going into a lot of extraneous and irrelevant matter. However true this may have been in some instances, on this occasion his remarks seem to have been very much to the point.

In conformity with his belief that the people should be left free to manage their own local affairs, Mackenzie supported unsuccessful attempts to allow the people, not the government, to select the new county seats which Hincks's bill for the division of certain counties would make necessary.[92] Similarly, when the Municipal Corporations Act came up for amendment he attempted to provide for lower property qualifications for the councillors and for direct election of the mayors of cities,[93] a privilege, he reminded the members, already enjoyed by the people of Montreal, Philadelphia, New York, Boston, Buffalo, Albany and Detroit.[94]

Mackenzie had frequently criticized the government for extravagance. On various items in the supply bill of 1851 for pensions, salaries, contingencies and grants to sectarian colleges he voted in the negative.[95] But when H.J. Boulton moved that the salary of the Governor-General should be borne by the imperial government he voted with the majority against the motion. To cavil about the Governor-General's salary was, he argued, an indirect way of advocating annexation.[96] At a later date, when he had become a bitter critic of Elgin, he was not so ready to have his salary paid out of Canadian revenues.

Mackenzie was on the alert to prevent valuable privileges from being granted away as private monopolies. A bill to incorporate a company to make a canal at Sault Ste. Marie had reached its third reading and would have passed, Mackenzie informed O'Rielly, "had I not risen and argued against the folly of our making a ship navigation up to Sault Ste. Marie and then giving a company of private persons power to make a gainful monopoly of the last half mile." The government was criticized for letting matters get to that stage without opposition. Hincks then moved that the third reading be postponed.[97]

When Mackenzie began to take an active part in Canadian affairs again he was as well aware of the importance of railways as any other legislator and drew attention to the way in which the economy of the neighbouring republic was being transformed by them.[98] Haldimand's municipal council and many of his constituents had for some years been interested in the projected Niagara and Detroit Railway, a company that had been chartered in 1836.[99] Its proposed route ran close to the shores of Lake Erie and of course through the township of Haldimand. In 10 years time the company had accomplished nothing and its charter had therefore expired. Petitions and bills for the restoration of the charter had been before the legislature repeatedly, but had been successfully opposed by those interested in the Great Western, who feared that if the Niagara and Detroit, which had the best and shortest route across the peninsula, were constructed it might prevent the Great Western from being completed.[100] Mackenzie supported the route from which his constituents would benefit pointing out that, unlike the proposed Niagara and Detroit, the Great Western was to be built upon a longer and circuitous route (Windsor to Hamilton via London and Hamilton to Suspension Bridge) part of which would be "difficult and expensive to work." So it proved.[101] But the Great Western and Sir Allan MacNab had more political influence than Colonel John Prince, president of the Niagara and Detroit, whose backers were for the most part Americans interested in the prosperity of Buffalo. The charter was not renewed.[102] Haldimand then began to rest its hopes on another road, the Brantford and Buffalo.[103]

Mackenzie regarded legislative charters—and all who sought them—with deep suspicion. To him they meant special privileges not available to all, political intrigues, and the corrupt use of power by the people's representatives. This had been his attitude towards the chartered banks before the rebellion, during his Loco-Foco period in the United States, and while he was agitating for a general telegraph law, a general incorporation law and a free banking system in that country. It was a point of view shared in Canada by many old Reformers. To the 20th century, talk of free trade in telegraph lines and railways seems absurd. But it was not so absurd to the men of 1840-60. Mackenzie and men like him believed that if the right to found banks, construct plank roads, telegraph lines or railways were open to all *without special favour or assistance* from government, men would take care to risk their *own* money only in those ventures which were sound.[104]

After the Reformers came to power in Canada in 1848 a general act was passed governing the creation of companies for the construction of gravelled or macadamized roads. At the instance of Malcolm Cameron, representative for Kent and at the moment a Clear Grit, this act was extended to apply to railways and tramways.[105] Under the terms of these two acts the Buffalo and Brantford Railway Company was organized to build a road from Brantford to Fort Erie. It was to cross the Niagara to Buffalo on a steam ferry. Here was a project that would serve Haldimand County as well or even better than the Niagara and Detroit, and Mackenzie was urged to watch over its interests rather than attempt to recharter the defunct Niagara and Detroit.[106]

The Brantford and Buffalo needed safeguarding. In the session of 1851 an

The Parliament Buildings in Toronto where Mackenzie sat as a member of the legislature. These buildings were used in Toronto from 1832 till 1841 as the seat of the Upper Canadian legislature and from 1849 to 1851 and 1855 to 1859 for the legislature buildings of the United Province.

Marshall Spring Bidwell, a moderate Reformer. Bidwell was defeated in the election of 1836. He left Upper Canada at the time of the rebellions and later practiced law in New York State.

Robert Baldwin circa 1845 by Hoppner Francis Meyer. Baldwin was a member of the moderate reform family who inaugerated responsible government in the late 1840's.

Isabel Mackenzie, Mackenzie's wife who supported Mackenzie unflinchingly through his trials and tribulations and outlived him by 12 years. This portrait was painted while her husband was Mayor of Toronto (1832-1834).

Portrait of William Lyon Mackenzie in his later years.

Toronto, Canada West about 1850.

Mackenzie House, 82 Bond Street, Toronto. Mackenzie moved into this house in 1859 and spent the last two years of his life here. It had been purchased for him by a group of friends and admirers numbering over 3000 subscribers led by James Lesslie.

# DISSOLUTION
## OF THE UNION
## With Lower Canada.

# WILLIAM LYON MACKENZIE

### INTENDS TO DELIVER

# A LECTURE

In the several places hereinafter named, at Two o'clock, in the Afternoon of each day, which will be explanatory of the extent, nature, and effects of the Political Union, now subsisting between Upper and Lower Canada, viz:

**IN CAYUGA,** on Wednesday, September 26th, at Two, afternoon.

**CALEDONIA,** on Thursday, Sept. 27th, at same hour.

**DUNNVILLE,** on Friday, Sept. 28th, Two, afternoon.

**RAINHAM CENTRE,** on Saturday, September 29th, same hour.

**BELLAS' SETTLEMENT,** Oneida, Monday, October 1st, same hour.

**CANBORO',** Tuesday, October 2nd, same hour.

**SMITHVILLE,** Wednesday, October 3rd, Two, afternoon.

**FONTHILL, PELHAM,** Thursday, October 4th, same hour.

**DRUMMONDVILLE,** (Niagara Falls,) Friday, October 5th, same hour.

**ST. CATHERINES,** Saturday, October 6th, same hour.

**TORONTO, Sept. 17, 1855.**

J. CLELAND, PRINTER, 62 YONGE STREET, UP TWO STAIRS.

Poster announcing a lecture by Mackenzie on one of the controversial political issues of the day — the dissolution of the union of Canada West and Canada East. Although responsible government had been achieved while he was in exile, Mackenzie remained unhappy with the new political organization .

amalgamation act was brought in by MacNab to consolidate into one act measures previously enacted relating to railways. This act was to apply to all railways to be constructed after its passage, and therefore to the Brantford and Buffalo. The act required a company to show that 10% of the subscribed stock had been paid in before a charter of incorporation could be applied for.[107] In addition it contained many unexceptional provisions relating to railways. Mackenzie was the only one to vote against the bill,[108] but not out of pure cantankerousness. The railway in which his constituents were interested had just been incorporated under the earlier legislation with only 6% of the capital paid in, and its incorporators were afraid that MacNab and Hincks would find some way of preventing their enterprise from going on. On July 23 MacNab brought in a bill to repeal what Mackenzie called "Cameron's free trade in railways bill" of 1850. An attempt to get rid of MacNab's bill was unsuccessful but, before it passed, the friends of the Brantford and Buffalo succeeded in adding an amendment saving the rights of that railway acquired under the repealed legislation.[109]

The subsequent history of the Brantford and Buffalo may conveniently be given at this point. During the next session this railway was reincorporated as the Brantford, Buffalo and Goderich and authorized to extend to the latter city. By 1854 trains were running over the road as far as Paris. Mackenzie boasted that the Brantford, Buffalo and Goderich, unlike other roads, had been constructed without government aid and at the low cost of £5,000 a mile.[110] And so it had, but the road was in a very shaky condition, physically and financially, and its friends were petitioning for government aid to complete it to Goderich. By 1856 this railway, which had never been adequately financed, was bankrupt. It was taken over by a new company incorporated for that purpose, the Buffalo and Huron, which later was to be absorbed by the Grand Trunk.[111]

From the point of view of Francis Hincks the most important bills to come before the Assembly in 1851 were those relating to the Grand Trunk Railway. Since the mid-forties the province of Canada had been striving to construct railways that would serve not only her own needs but also would capture the trade of the American midwest and draw it to the St. Lawrence and Montreal. In 1849 the province had passed the Guarantee Act.[112] It empowered the government to guarantee as a loan 6% interest on the capital required to complete any railroad not less than 75 miles in length, half of which had already been completed by its promoters. In 1851 the imperial government agreed to guarantee the interest on a loan to build an intercolonial railway from Halifax to Quebec once the three provinces had agreed on the route and provided that route was entirely through British territory. In June 1851 the premiers of the two maritime provinces and Canada's Inspector-General, Francis Hincks, held a conference at Toronto and reached an agreement.[113]

Hincks then made public the 18 resolutions on which his railway legislation was to be founded. Two bills came out of them. One of them authorized the government to make arrangements for the construction of its share of the Halifax and Quebec as a provincial work with the aid of the proposed imperial guarantee. Authority was also given to build a railway from Quebec to

Hamilton, or some point on the Great Western, as a provincial work provided the imperial guarantee could be obtained for this part of the railway as well. If it could not be obtained, the money for the Quebec to Hamilton might be raised half on the credit of the province, provided the other half was subscribed for by municipal corporations. The second bill authorized the government to borrow £4,000,000 for the construction of the province's share of the Quebec to Halifax, and the Quebec to Hamilton, on the above conditions.[114] All preliminaries necessary to obtaining the imperial guarantee for the Quebec to Halifax had apparently been completed during this session. The benefits of the Provincial Guarantee Act of 1849 were now restricted to lines already begun under its terms or that should form part of the main trunk line. The guarantee, however, was extended to principal as well as interest on half of the cost of construction and it was also liberalized in other ways.[115]

Mackenzie voted against both railway bills. To his constituents he explained that while he could "comprehend" the idea of a railway from Halifax to Detroit he could not approve of pledging the country to a debt of £4,000,000 "merely for a military road," a railway from Halifax to Quebec.[116] Mackenzie saw no need for this railway. There was no prospect of traffic for the line. There was no justification for it except that Lower Canada wanted it. The St. Lawrence and Atlantic would give Montreal a connection with Portland.[117] Moreover there was no security that after the sum necessary to build Canada's share of the Quebec to Halifax had been provided there would be anything left out of the £4,000,000 to build the Quebec to Hamilton, the part that Canada really needed. That would be left to "chance."[118] That Mackenzie's misgivings about the Quebec to Halifax were shared by other Upper Canada representatives is clear. Eleven of them voted for the bill, eighteen against it, while twenty-seven Lower Canada members voted for it, only two against it. Lower Canada radicals (les Rouges) shared Mackenzie's view that the money would be wasted. It would be better, they argued, to spend the money on model farms for the benefit of the nine-tenths of the population which was engaged in agriculture.[119]

The fourth session of the third parliament closed on August 30th. It had been a busy three months for Mackenzie. It has not seemed necessary to analyze in detail all his negative votes, either at this session or at subsequent ones. They show his persistent opposition to all measures that would increase the patronage at the disposal of the government, increase the public debt, raise the legal rate of interest, abolish the usury laws or grant special privileges by charters of incorporation to the legal and medical professions. His lengthy speech in opposition to a bill to incorporate the medical profession caused Colonel Prince to remark that he was "unfitted for a deliberative Assembly" and had cost the country £1,000 "by his useless and absurd speeches." Nothing daunted, Mackenzie, who had been requested by some of his constituents to oppose the bill, declared he would continue moving adjournments until the bill was abandoned — or the House rose — and he did.[120]

Throughout his parliamentary career Mackenzie was to be criticized as an obstructive, if not a useless member who voted most frequently in the negative.[121] In addition he irritated his colleagues by persistently calling for roll-call votes, sometimes when his was the only negative vote to be recorded. He exasperated them also by terribly long speeches, sometimes on topics the members regarded as irrelevant to the proper business of a Canadian legislature. In one instance a hostile member from Lower Canada remarked that if he had known how much trouble Mackenzie would give the House he would never have voted for the amnesty. If half a million were voted to put him out of the country he thought the province would be the gainer.[122] Worse still, in this his first session Mackenzie dragged in references to the rebellion, not always in the best taste, and then complained of those who threw his past in his teeth.[123]

During his first term a Lower Canada member, Dunbar Ross, tried to get rid of him by introducing a bill to vacate the seats of members who had been guilty of treason or who had taken an oath of allegiance to a foreign power. The bill received the six months hoist on the motion for a second reading by a vote of 39 to 3. Neither Baldwin, Price, nor Lafontaine voted. Hincks voted with the majority, and of the other 38 votes that disposed of Ross's bill 26 came from Lower Canada.[124] The bill would have struck at Papineau and others in Lower Canada and would have deprived some of them of the benefits of the general amnesty.

On the other hand, numerous letters testify to Mackenzie's industry during the session and to the satisfaction of old Reformers with his conduct there. "You are just what your old friends expected... still the faithful opponent of corruption," one of them wrote.[125] From Haldimand he was assured that: "The general opinion of the County is that you are the most useful man in the House." The *Examiner* called him "the sentinel of Freedom."[126] Long before the session closed he was asked to represent Haldimand again. He was advised that at the general election in December he would stand "a fair chance against any man, the Apostle Paul not excepted."[127]

Chapter XIV

# CLEAR GRITS AND MINISTERIALISTS

Before the parliamentary session of 1851 ended Lafontaine announced his intention to retire.[1] Reconstruction of the ministry then became inevitable and it was expected that Francis Hincks would be asked to undertake the task. Political realists among the Upper Canada Reformers were disposed to stand by Hincks, conscious of the difficulties the government had had with its Lower Canada supporters and appreciative of Hincks's past services to the cause of reform. One of them wrote:

> Let old reformers... remember that their old leaders... led them to the brink of the precipice by want of discretion; that the party was scattered to the four winds of heaven. It was Hincks that came out in the *Examiner* with power and strength and gathered together the wretched remnants of the once powerful body.... If the reformers are mad enough to divide themselves & let the Tories in —, then goodbye to further reform for the next 10 years.[2]

During the summer of 1851 Hincks succeeded in bolstering his position and in giving the Reform Party in Upper Canada some semblance of unity for the time being. Overtures were made in July to William McDougall, the Clear Grit editor of the *North American*. McDougall and his political friends consented to make an alliance with Hincks to prevent the Tories getting in, but only on condition that Hincks intended to *advance* the work of reform. McDougall suggested that taking Malcolm Cameron and John Rolph, both ardent advocates of secularization, into the cabinet would be the best guarantee Hincks could give them. On these conditions, and on being assured that the French would allow the Clergy Reserves question in Upper Canada to be settled by a majority of the Upper Canada votes, McDougall agreed to put the support of the *North American* behind Hincks.[3]

There was skepticism among the rank and file of the Reform Party and in the minds of other voluntaryists about these arrangements. George Brown opposed the coalition of Grits and Hincksites. He believed that Hincks had "sold them" (the voluntaryists) and that Rolph and Cameron had undertaken not to oppose sectarian schools, not to question the validity of the rectory patents, and to await the passage of the enabling act before pressing the Clergy Reserves question to a solution.[4] Finally, even the *Examiner* was won over and promised "some of the pap." Shutting his eyes to the fact that the cracks of distrust had merely been papered over, Lesslie announced that the union of the Reform Party had been achieved "without any compromise of principles."[5] A.N. Morin took Lafontaine's place as leader of the French Canadian supporters of the government, Rolph became Commissioner of Crown Lands and Cameron, President of the Council. The new ministry was expected to take prompt steps to secularize the reserves, abolish seigneurial tenures, increase the representation and make the Legislative Council elective.

McDougall believed that although the Clear Grits had agreed to support Hincks and to postpone their demand for wholly elective institutions their "entrance into office would ultimately mean the triumph of their principles." Hincks, on the other hand, expected to absorb the troublesome radicals.[6]

Mackenzie distrusted the arrangement that McDougall had made with Hincks. So did radical Reformers in Oxford, Hincks's own constituency. They were ready to nominate Hincks as their candidate for re-election provided he would accept the platform they had drawn up and sign it. Hincks refused to sign or to have anything to do with getting up a platform or to consider himself the nominee of a convention of delegates in Oxford. He would run as the representative of the ministerial party. "Monarchical and constitutional government cannot be carried on with republican forms," he observed.[7] These Oxford Reformers then turned to Mackenzie for help in choosing a real Reform candidate from among several aspirants and in uniting Reform sentiment behind him. "Hincks must not be tolerated any longer in Oxford," declared one of them.[8]

Mackenzie, who was now very busy composing his Election Circular of October 25 and his Voters Guide, did not go to Oxford to speak as requested, nor did he choose between various would-be candidates. Instead he published in the *Examiner* a long article in which he acknowledged Hincks' abilities but expressed his conviction that Hincks no longer put Reform principles above the desire for office. He then proceeded to list Hincks's sins of omission, or rather those of the ministry in which he had been Inspector-General: its failure to settle the reserves and rectories questions promptly, to lower the tariff on articles of common consumption, to account adequately for the revenue and to bring about economy in government by reducing salaries and pensions. Hincks's negative votes in opposition to reforms advocated by the Clear Grits, such as abolition of the Court of Chancery, equalization of the representation among constituencies, simplification and codification of the law, expansion of the suffrage and establishment of the elective principle for all country offices — all were recounted. Hincks had bidden his constituents to "look to his past" when refusing to sign a platform. Mackenzie did the job for them — thoroughly — referring not only to Hincks's conduct in the last parliament but to his very different protestations when he had been editing the Examiner as the Reform newspaper.[9]

In the end the divided Oxford Reformers could not agree on a candidate to replace Hincks. An attempt was made to nominate John Scatcherd,[10] but when he found that he was not receiving the whole-hearted support of Reformers in all the townships of Oxford he withdrew on nomination day, and his committee agreed to support Hincks after receiving a verbal assurance from him that he would work with Rolph and Cameron for secularization of the reserves. At the last minute Mackenzie also threw his support to Hincks, making this decision known in a handbill issued on November 28, 1851.

> We are all in one ship together; give me Hincks but not before Scatcherd & Co. but far, very far before Vansittart [the Tory candidate]. Hincks may... go for the reforms the county requires. Who expects as much from Vansittart?[11]

Hincks carried the constituency by the narrow margin of 76 votes over his Tory opponent. On the first day of the polling he had been 137 votes behind — an indication, remarked the Examiner "of great differences in reform ranks."[12] Fearing a Tory victory, Reformers rallied to Hincks on the second day, giving him in the end 51% of the total votes cast.

If some Clear Grits distrusted the arrangement made between McDougall and Hincks, some of the ministerialists distrusted it also. They had expected there would be no opposition to the nominations of Hincks as the Reform candidate for Oxford, Baldwin for North York and Price for York South. They were angered at finding that these nominations would not go through smoothly. Moreover, they distrusted John Rolph, who had seemed to be intriguing for a nomination by acclamation for the late Peter Perry's seat in York East and who seemed to be all too eager to speak his mind about the Clergy Reserves in York North, Baldwin's constituency. Baldwin's suspicious son-in-law, John Ross, wrote:

> The very way in which Rolph's name has been put forward by his friends convinced me that no ministry will last six months unless he is the one man power. They will intrigue under his direction to make him premier. [13]

This distrust of Rolph was shared by Price who, in 1849, had informed George Brown:

> Rolph is a blackhearted rascal... he always was a Tyrant and he is bitter, gloomy, unforgiving, vengeful — he wants power and cannot get it — one man power is all over & he now as he always did concocts mischief in the dark and employs Tools who are soft enough to appear in public.... Rolph will... quietly plot the destruction of any ministry that will not make him its pilot in everything. [14]


198

In the end Rolph stood for the County of Norfolk, where he won 70% of its votes.[15]

In York North John Mackintosh contested the Reform nomination against Baldwin and John Hartman. Mackenzie took time to visit the riding to speak in favour of the faithful Mackintosh. The platform adopted enumerated the reforms advocated by the Grits. Baldwin, when asked to sign their "list of principles," refused, and called the practice of giving written pledges "unconstitutional."[16] In the end Mackintosh withdrew in favour of Hartman, a much more progressive Reformer than Baldwin. Hartman carried the riding against Baldwin and the Tory nominee, obtaining 58% of the votes cast while Baldwin received only 12%, although he had obtained 50% in 1847.[17]

Nomination day in Haldimand was December 1 and election day December 10. There had been a little uncertainty among Mackenzie's supporters as to whether he would choose to stand for them or would prefer to be nominated for some other Reform constituency. Mackenzie announced his willingness to represent Haldimand again on November 5, but he did not visit his county until the first week of December.[18] He was re-elected by a vote of 537 to 309 for his Tory opponent, 63% of the vote in this two-way race, as compared with 294, or 38% of the total vote in the four-way race at the by-election in the spring.[19]

Prior to the election the Upper Canada members of Parliament had included 16 Tories or Conservatives. Afterwards, Conservatives held 21 seats. An advanced Reformer had obtained the seat for Cornwall at the expense of a Conservative, but six constituencies previously represented by Reformers had fallen to Conservatives: York South, York West, Peterborough, Lanark, Welland and Middlesex.[20] In three of these constituencies the fact that the Reform vote had been split between two candidates had given the Tories the victory. Hincks blamed the loss of these seats on Lesslie of the *Examiner* and on Mackenzie. He was particularly bitter about the defeat of Baldwin by Hartman, whom he had been unable to persuade to withdraw. After his defeat Baldwin announced his retirement from politics. "Some of the oldest and best Reformers all over the country regret the course you have been taking," Hincks informed Mackenzie. "As to Mr. Baldwin in *my humble opinion* it was *suicidal* for the *party*." Baldwin was one who carried weight with:

> cautious slow judging men.... Be assured Toryism *has gained* by the separation forever of Mr. Baldwin from the party of progress .... All that you and your friends have accomplished has been by the policy of getting a *minority* of the liberals to act against the majority leaving consequences out of the question.... I don't desire to break up the party which is weak enough at best & I shall continue to blame those who do.... My firm belief is [added Hincks, thoroughly irritated by the monkey-wrench Mackenzie had thrown into his political machine] that if every man who voted the *liberal ticket* in U. Canada at last election were polled for *you* or me I would beat you 3 to 1 at least.[21]

A trial of strength between the influence of the two men was to come three years later.

For all his boasting, Hincks's victory in Oxford had been a narrow one. Moreover it was doubtful whether his ministry would last four years, as John Ross realized. He warned Hincks's election agent:

> The southern townships saved the county. You must set to work making votes against another election. They need not be recorded. Get fathers to deed part of their land to their sons.

The same advice was repeated a few months later.

> We are at work here [Belleville] getting our county ready for another contest if it should come. The votes will be good when the four years come round if not required now.[22]

It is not surprising that Hincks did not accord Mackenzie his share of the patronage that usually fell to county members of the party in power. Mackenzie had denounced the patronage system in the United States but he seemed determined to get his share in Canada. To John Rolph he complained that his recommendation for census taker had been disregarded and a person known to be opposed to him had been appointed instead. Neither had he been consulted about the justices of the peace and the militia officers named for his county since the by-election in April. "I am not opposing the government. I know not its measures nor interfered in the movements to form a ministry," Mackenzie protested. All he had done was to help "weed the Assembly of sham Reformers"[23] — an argument not likely to conciliate Hincks.

Radical Reformers in the western counties showed their satisfaction at Mackenzie's re-election for Haldimand by giving him a complimentary dinner at Berlin in April and by inundating him with correspondence about matters they wanted attended to when the session opened. For example, squatters ejected from Indian land during the heavy snows of March and deprived of their improvements besought his help. Those who wanted the navigation of the Grand River improved to Brantford, and perhaps beyond, at government, *not* county, expense, presented their case to him. Country doctors opposed to the Medical Society Incorporation Bill that they regarded as an effort by the Toronto physicians to get control of the profession into their hands urged him to oppose this would-be "monopoly." And of course the old grievances pertaining to the reserves, the assessment acts and the courts were again pressed upon his attention.

The new legislature was not to be called into session until August 19, and in the meantime Mackenzie had to deal with an awkward personal problem. One of the "sham" Reformers Mackenzie had helped to weed out of the Assembly was J.H. Price. Until his resignation in October 1851 Price had been Commissioner of Crown Lands in the Baldwin-Lafontaine government. He had always been regarded as sound on the question of secularizing the reserves and had tried to give Baldwin's "slow-coach" policy a push.[24] Yet he had refused to disassociate himself from Baldwin, had supported Hincks and had helped to negative reforms that Mackenzie and some Reformers wanted. Mackenzie visited the south riding of York, distributed his Voters' Guide and charged Price with having betrayed his constituents. The Reform convention of the county nominated David Gibson as their candidate in place of Price. In the three-way contest the Tory candidate, J.W. Gamble, received 632 votes, Price 321 and Gibson 278.[25]

This incident terminated an old friendship between Price and Mackenzie. Price had been one of the few staunch old Reformers to oppose Sydenham. Even though he had talked of retiring from politics, he had some reason to feel bitter towards those who had engineered his defeat for the Reform nomination when he changed his mind at the urging of Robert Baldwin and Marshall Spring Bidwell.[26] Moreover, Price had in the past befriended Mackenzie. It will be recalled that he was one of those who had paid Mackenzie's notes to the Bank of the People and had been repaid only in part when Mackenzie's real estate was sold.

Prior to Mackenzie's return to Canada, both Price and Doel had assured Lesslie that although they would expect Mackenzie to pay them if he could, they would not "molest" him for the money.[27] Mackenzie states that it was on this understanding that, on October 10, 1850, he gave Price a note at 12 months for the balance he claimed.[28] However, since his return Mackenzie had criticized the Baldwin-Lafontaine administration of which Price was a member, and he seems to have referred publicly to the sale of his real estate and to the demands of his creditors in Canada for the payment of old debts in ways which Price found offensive.[29] As his letters to Baldwin show,[30] Price had certainly been anxious to have Mackenzie's property sold so that he might be paid. Mackenzie took the view that his real estate had been sacrificed and that, if it had not been sold, he would have been regained it after the amnesty like other persons whose forfeited but unsold property was returned to them. Relations between the two men deteriorated rapidly. On November 14, 1851, Price requested Mackenzie to pay his note, warning that if he was not paid "forthwith" he would sue him. Two days after the election he did sue, won his case and was paid. "My offense," observed Mackenzie, "was my Voters' Guide and going to the Riding and confronting him with his betrayed constituents."[31]

Mackenzie betrays here an inability to see anybody's point of view but his own. Prior to the rebellion, he had put all his energy into the struggle for reform and had, as he truly said, risked all — and lost. He thought of the sums his political associates had enabled him to borrow to keep his paper going more as a contribution to the cause than as personal loans, and he regarded their demands for payment as utterly selfish. Price, no longer as radical a Reformer as Mackenzie, or at least no longer as ready to disregard political consequences, looked upon him as a debtor who expected consideration from one he felt free to criticize publicly and to damage if he could. Price was embittered by his defeat after 15 years of faithful service to the cause of reform.

Between the general election and the commencement of the session on

August 19, 1852, Mackenzie seems to have been in a despondent mood. His own victory and his successful exertions for others should have exhilarated him but he seems to have feared that a hard struggle was ahead for Reformers such as he and that his own strength for the fight was waning.[32] The long years of privation and incessant toil had taken their toll. "I'm only 57 but you'd take me for 67," he told James. "I have only four teeth in my whole upper jaw and not many below."[33] In New York he had lost one daughter and now in Toronto the health, mental and physical, of another failed, owing her father believed to the privations the family had endured.[34] A letter to Donald M'Leod was evidently so gloomy that M'Leod commented on "how whining" he had become.[35] But it was poverty as well as age that was bothering Mackenzie. He had little on which to support his family except his wages as a representative, irregular rent from his property in Dundas and occasional newspaper articles for which he might be paid. No wonder he fought so tenaciously and impatiently to collect all that he thought was his due from a slow-moving government, or that he resented the efforts of his old associates in Canada to collect every cent from him — and with interest.

Moreover, he was now about to be faced with the double expense of maintaining his family in Toronto while he spent the legislative session in Quebec. How could he look forward to it with pleasure and confidence, remembering the criticisms and insults to which he had been subjected during the previous session and his failure to accomplish anything worthwhile?

Dr. Rolph was now a member of the government. He had been appointed Commissioner of Crown Lands, a post he held until 1853 when he became President of the Council and Minister of Agriculture instead. Rolph's response to Mackenzie's letters about the Clergy Reserves and to his complaints about patronage were pleasant and friendly,[36] but if Mackenzie expected that he would become a political intimate of Rolph he was to be disappointed. Rolph went off to Quebec without giving him a hint as to the principles on which he had accepted office or what the intentions of the Hincks-Morin government might be.[37]

Rolph was well aware from Mackenzie's own letters of his straitened circumstances. He may well have concluded from Mackenzie's references to his efforts on Rolph's behalf after his return to Canada[38] that, as Commissioner of Crown Lands, it was being hinted to him that an appointment of some kind would be acceptable. At any rate, John Rolph enquired of Mackenzie whether he would care to undertake investigations for him into the disposal of Crown lands in Canada West, assuring Mackenzie that the remuneration would be satisfactory.

> The duties will of course embrace everything I want to do and ought if possible to do myself,... inquiries, the correction of abuses and the saving to the public the no doubt, large sums of money yearly lost.... It will not vacate your seat.[39]

The investigation of abuses! Here was a tempting offer — something right up Mackenzie's alley — and a chance to earn something too.

Mackenzie's reply of June 14 is not to be found in the Rolph papers that have survived, but according to a copy in the Mackenzie papers his letter said:

> No man... with a large family... would be unwilling to labor for their subsistence. Therefore I accept your proposition.... Had it been made six or eight months since I could readily have perceived how it might be useful to me but what work can I perform in Upper Canada on the eve of a session held 500 miles hence is not quite so clear. You, however, wish to serve me and as my seat will not be affected nor my independence in or out of the legislature I stand ready to fulfill your orders when received. [40]

(There had been no mention of Mackenzie's independence in Rolph's letter.)

On June 14 the Committee of Council recommended that the Commissioner of Crown Lands be allowed to employ two confidential agents, one for Canada East, one for Canada West, at £1/-/- a day and 10/- expenses. This recommendation was approved.[41] Subsequently Mackenzie discovered that the offer was not without strings. The intention was to employ him after the session was over. Rolph explained that to employ him beforehand might subject them both to suspicion,

> and impair your usefulness and *apparent* independence of office during legislation. All this must be private and confidential between us. [42]

It was clear to Mackenzie now. The offer was a "job", and he spurned it.

James Lesslie and other friends tried to persuade Mackenzie to accept Rolph's proposition but he would not consent.[43] In a draft reply dated June 28 Mackenzie wrote:

> Had you reflected on the proposition you made to the council I am sure it would not have been made. You yourself would have blushed that I after 30 years of honest advocacy of Canada rights became an agent where no agent is or can be needed or ever has been needed by any commissioner.

Referring to his struggle to get an accounting of the sale of his property, Mackenzie added: "Probably the agency matter was intended in your mind and meant as some compensation for the injustice done me."[44] Mackenzie's actual reply does not remain in the Rolph papers but is briefly summarized in the Mackenzie papers.[45] It was apparently similar to the draft, and it may have cost Mackenzie a struggle since it was not sent until July 17. Rolph denied there was any jobbing intended by his offer and thanked Mackenzie, "especially for the spirit in which you regard the sincerity of my desire to serve you."[46] One wonders whether there was a touch of sarcasm intended in these words. Subsequently, when Mackenzie learned that it was the government's intention to appoint a commission to compile a revised edition of the statutes, he wrote that he supposed the job would be bestowed after the session upon a couple of lawyers who, being secretly informed beforehand, would support the government throughout the session.

> No private whisper from our immaculate rulers will have told
> them that they were hired; it will all be the government's
> motion....[47]

John Rolph's offer of temporary work had made the naturally suspicious Mackenzie very suspicious indeed.

Early in August Mackenzie left Toronto for Quebec, indebted to Lesslie for the money to travel with and accompanied by his son William who was to attend school there.[48] From Quebec he began writing weekly letters for the *Examiner* under the pseudonym Abraham Adams, but the disguise was soon penetrated and was given up.[49] He was appointed to the Committee on Contingencies and to that on printing.[50] This committee accepted several of his suggestions which brought about economies in the printing of the *Journals*.[51] His attempt to have the Office of Queen's Printer abolished and the public printing done by contract, the first of several efforts, did not succeed.[52]

For Francis Hincks the important business of the session was to put through the Grand Trunk Railway Bill and several measures designed to attract additional capital to the underdeveloped province of united Canada. In the spring Hincks had gone to England in the expectation of completing the arrangements for the imperial guaranteed loan for the railway and of being able to return in triumph to face Parliament in August with an announcement that would stimulate the entire economic life of the province, divert attention from the grievances of the voluntaryists and the reforms wanted by the radicals, and strengthen his political position. Lord John Russell's ministry had consented to an imperial guarantee for an intercolonial railway but not to the inclusion of a line linking Halifax and St. John with Portland, Maine, on which Joseph Howe of Nova Scotia was insisting. Neither would the Derby ministry, which had come to power in February 1852, consent to its inclusion in the guarantee.[53] To Hincks's chagrin, the whole scheme fell through. Instead of returning empty-handed, Hincks negotiated a contract with an English firm for the construction of a main line from Montreal to Toronto.

The charter of the Grand Trunk was put through only after some complicated negotiations with holders of previously granted railway charters that threatened to obstruct it. The carrying out of these deals required the passage of the Railway Amalgamation Act and the chartering of the Grand Trunk of Canada East.[54] The result of Hincks's railway legislation of 1852-53 was that the province undertook to assist a railway not limited to the essential 330-mile stretch between Toronto and Montreal, but a system 1,100 miles long which was to extend from Sarnia to Trois Pistoles and which included the St. Lawrence and Atlantic Railway. This line would give Montreal a connection at the international boundary with an American line from Portland. In addition, the

Grand Trunk East was promised that if it extended its main line from Trois Pistoles as far as the eastern boundary of the province, it should have the help, not of the provincial guarantee, but the aid of one million acres of Crown land in the counties of Rimouski and Bonaventure.[55] This portion of the Grand Trunk would be part of the projected Quebec to Halifax.

Mackenzie certainly advocated the prompt construction of railways in Canada but he voted against all these bills. His chief objection to the Quebec and Halifax was that the money would be wasted. On the rest of the project his thinking was clouded by his distrust of the honesty of Hincks and his political associates and he never came up with any practical alternative to Hincks's policy of obtaining the necessary capital by methods that added to the public debt and required raising the tariff to provide revenue for the interest and sinking fund.

Mackenzie criticized the Grand Trunk and its chief promoter, Francis Hincks, in season and out of season. He regarded the entire enterprise as illegal and unauthorized because the railway had turned out to be not the provincial enterprise assisted by a British loan at 3% for which the province had voted, but a private enterprise assisted by the Canadian government with the loan of 6% government debentures to the extent of £3,000 a mile. Moreover no provision was made, originally, for accounts to be submitted to the legislature until 14 years had elapsed, although the company's work was to be inspected as it proceeded.[56] When George Brown, who had successfully contested Kent as an Independent, moved that the government produce the contract with the British firm, his motion was defeated.[57] Not until 1856 were its details made public. Mackenzie complained that the entire contract had been given to one English firm without competitive bidding. They were asking $38,000 a mile although Hincks had assured the Assembly that the road could be built for $20,000. Even after construction had started and inflation had occurred, Mackenzie continued to argue, quite unrealistically, that the railway could be built for half the sum the English contractors were asking.[58] Mackenzie later referred to the bill creating the Grand Trunk as "an iniquitous measure that will prove a greater curse to Canada than the Clergy Reserves."[59]

It was not only for the foregoing reasons that Mackenzie consistently opposed the Grand Trunk; it was because he was convinced it was corrupting the political life of the country. Hincks was provided with additional patronage and it was believed he found opportunities to enrich himself at the public expense.[60] Members of the government and of the Assembly obtained railway contracts or held paid offices with the Grand Trunk or other railways. Independence of judgement and concern for the public interest could not, in Mackenzie's opinion, be expected from members so situated, and from time to time he took care to let the electorate know through his *Message*, a paper he began to publish in December 1852, who they were.

Another government measure intended to attract capital to the province and stimulate railway building was Hincks's Consolidated Municipal Loan Fund Act.[61] It also was to meet with Mackenzie's disapproval. This measure was designed to enable the government to borrow for Upper Canada municipalities on better terms than these small and unknown authorities could obtain for themselves. In future municipal councils wishing to raise money for public works, or to assist railways or other enterprises by which they would be benefitted, could market their debentures through the Receiver-General as part of the Consolidated Municipal Loan Fund. The treasurers of the borrowing municipalities were required to levy annual rates for the repayment of their debts to the loan fund and if they did not do so the Governor was to order the Sheriff to levy them. The government's supervision and what amounted to its guarantee would, it was expected, prevent the financial weakness of one municipality from spoiling the market for Canadian securities.

Mackenzie was the only one to oppose a second reading of this measure and one of the few to vote against it in the end. Since the government's approval of loans was required, the act tended to centralize power in the hands of a ministry he distrusted and to add to its patronage powers. Subsequently he was to complain of the government's readiness to assent to the requests of certain municipalities while rejecting those of other constituencies represented by radical members, "in short to lend the public credit or refuse it where they pleased."[62]

Under existing legislation the consent of the majority of ratepayers had to be secured before a bylaw could pass to borrow money to assist railways or other enterprises, and the bylaw had to provide for the levy of a rate sufficient to repay the loan in 20 years, irrespective of any income that might be expected from tolls or dividends. These requirements had obstructed the financing of some local improvements.[63] Hincks's bill, in its original form, dispensed with the ratepayers' assent; approval by the Governor-in-Council of proposals coming from the municipal councils would have sufficed. When the bill was in committee Mackenzie and others criticized it strongly for this reason.[64] The final version of the act included such a requirement, but restricted it by an alternative provision which really left power to the County Council, not to the ratepayers.

At first Mackenzie had no objection to local aid to railways but before his first session in the legislature was over he had begun to fear that the people were running mad in their desire for railways.[65] He predicted that in their scramble for railway connections the councils would plunge their municipalities too deeply into debt. The Loan Fund Act provided that if municipalities expected or believed there would be an income from the undertaking in which they had invested they might deduct the expected sums from the amount they were otherwise required to raise annually for servicing the loan. This provision proved to be a snare and a delusion. Neither the municipal councils nor the government that supervised them exercised a wise restraint in the matter of loans to railways. Almost $6,000,000, or 85% of their borrowings down to 1858, were for this purpose.[66]

At this session, as at the previous one, several bills to raise the legal rate of interest were offered by those who argued that the existing restrictions were impeding the flow of investment capital into Canada. They were defeated, with Mackenzie's help. The bill introduced by George Brown maintained the legal rate of 6%, except for institutions authorized by law to charge more, but it took the teeth out of the law by repealing the penalties for usury. Where the rate of interest was not specified, 6% was to be understood. Mackenzie regarded Brown's bill as the least objectionable of those offered.[67] Nevertheless he did his best to stave off a measure which he feared "would expose the farmers to extortion." He was vigorously supported by an Upper Canada Conservative, J.W. Gamble, who drew attention to the fact that several American states had reinstituted their old usury laws and a legal interest rate of 6%.[68] All these efforts failed. The bill finally passed 42 to 31, with most of Mackenzie's and Gamble's support coming from Lower Canada.[69] Mackenzie attempted also to block the charter of the Canadian Loan Company, authorized like the Upper Canada Loan and Trust Company to lend at 8%. He could not this time complain that privileges were being granted to foreign capitalists, but he was just as ready to denounce the domestic ones as "a vile nest of usurers."[70]

Clear Grits and Independents had looked forward to this session of the legislature with some misgivings. Would the Clergy Reserves be secularized? Could the Hincks-Morin administration work together harmoniously for long and would it have the strength and the desire to push this measure through? In the legislature Upper Canada's Reformers were about equally divided between progressives and non-progressives — to use the term McDougall had stressed with Hincks. Conservatives held 21 of her 42 seats. Therefore the ministry would have to rely on its Lower Canada supporters, 24 of whom were thought to be "under priestly influences" and unlikely to sanction measures that the radicals expected.[71] John Rolph seems to have realized from the start that he would be in a "very horrid and unenviable situation" and had begged Mackenzie to be reasonable and to aid him.[72]

Prior to the opening of the session Hincks had learned that the new government of Lord Derby would not bring in an enabling act at the current session of the imperial parliament. Derby's excuse was that, a general election having taken place in the province, the imperial government was uncertain what the views of the new assembly would be. The government, the Colonial Secretary explained, could not

> place it in the power of an accidental majority of the colonial legislature, however small, to divert forever from its sacred object the [Clergy Reserve] Fund....

He had intimated, however, that a little tinkering with the distribution clauses of the Act of 1840 might be allowable.[73] Hincks, in response, vigorously defended Canada's right to settle the reserves question herself; but when the Colonial Secretary's despatch was made known as part of the Speech from the Throne, the government's reply was merely a tactful promise to give consideration to its contents and a mild expression of regret that the imperial parliament had not passed the desired enabling act.[74]

This language outraged the two Independent members, George Brown and Mackenzie. Brown demanded that the government state clearly what its position was.[75] In a long speech he accused Hincks of having pledged himself to secularization to the several Reform candidates in Oxford who withdrew in his favour. Hincks denied the truth of these accounts. Mackenzie reviewed the history of the Clergy Reserves dispute at length, pouring scorn on the notion that it would be any "accidental majority" that would pass a secularization bill and urging that the British government was pledged to let Canada settle the question.[76]

In an effort to convince the more radical Upper Canada members that his government did intend to secularize, Hincks introduced several resolutions as the basis of an address to the Crown to make it clear that Canada would regard a refusal to pass an enabling act as a violation of her constitutional rights.[77] In the course of the debate Hincks acknowledged that he believed it would be impossible to arrive at any other solution of the Clergy Reserves question short of secularization. George Brown interpreted this statement as committing the government to secularize. Therefore he voted for Hincks' resolutions, as did Mackenzie. The resolutions, however, were not completely satisfactory to the two Independents because they did not call for the unconditional repeal of the Act of 1840 and did not specifically commit the government to secularize. In fact the Speaker had refused to allow Brown to move a last minute amendment to the resolution to this effect.[78]

Lord Derby remained uninfluenced. Hincks bided his time. At length his patience was rewarded. In December 1852 the Derby government was replaced by the Aberdeen government which did provide the enabling act. Canada learned the news before the end of May;[79] at last she had the power to settle the reserves question herself. The ministry had finally got the reserves "just where we had them in 1837 except," Mackenzie noted, "that the fund has been pillaged for fourteen years."[80] Nothing more was attempted before the session closed, but it was generally expected that when the legislature met again the Hincks-Morin administration would promptly introduce its Clergy Reserves bill.

One important reform promised in the Speech from the Throne was an increase in the membership of the Assembly. Although a "rep. by pop." amendment introduced by George Brown was not accepted, Mackenzie this time voted for the government's bill, which received the required two-thirds majority.[81] Both sections of the province were now to have 65 members instead of 42 and single member constituencies were created except for the cities of Montreal, Quebec and Toronto. Mackenzie was not content with the distribution of Upper Canada's seats: too much weight was still allowed to some small towns and small eastern constituencies like Prescott, Russell and Renfrew.[82] The division between Conservatives and Reformers of all sorts in Upper Canada was now so close that Mackenzie did not this time think it advisable to fail to support a bill that Reformers believed would increase their strength, even though it was in his opinion "as pinched an affair" as it was possible to make it.[83]

Several of the restrictions imposed upon the legislature by the Act of Union had long been resented by radical Reformers. Mackenzie wanted the imperial parliament to give Canada power to make changes in the representation by majority vote. While the two-thirds restriction stood it would be impossible to obtain "rep. by pop." He suggested that a majority of the Assembly be required for a quorum, not a mere handful of 20 members, and he proposed that the Governor-in-Council be deprived of the power to determine the time, place and duration of sessions and the summoning and dissolution of parliaments, and that these matters be established by law. Most important, he wanted the high property qualification for election, £500 worth of real property, to be abolished and the requirement to be set by the legislature. Under the Constitutional Act Upper Canada had had this power and had set the qualification at £80.[84] All these proposals were part of the Clear Grit program, but only two members supported Mackenzie in asking for these changes,[85] one of which was incompatible with English parliamentary government. Later in the session Brown moved for an address asking only for abrogation of the two-thirds requirement. He received more support than Mackenzie but his proposal was defeated also, 22 to 48.[86] The Clear Grits were now safely in the government's camp and it would not offend its French Canadian supporters by any move in the direction of "rep. by pop."

During the session of 1851, J.C. Morrison had introduced a bill, which was not proceeded in, to extend the franchise to tenants of the Canada Company occupying land under a purchase agreement and to those purchasing land from the Crown or holding on location tickets.[87] Mackenzie regarded this bill as "an artful proposition."[88] He had always been opposed to allowing tenants and location ticket holders to vote. Like other Reformers in the pre-rebellion years, he had feared the executive would sway the elections by creating voters by grants of Crown land, and that tenants on Canada Company or clergy land would be subjected to pressure to vote for the government's candidates. His ideal was still a society of independent freeholders ready to stand up and be counted. By 1851, however, the situation in Upper Canada had changed. No longer were the votes of indigent immigrants, discharged soldiers or outright paupers to be feared. The classes presently disenfranchised included the sons of older settlers and recent immigrants from Great Britain purchasing land on credit or renting improved land in the more settled townships. There was also a rapidly increasing class of mechanics and artisans in the towns to be considered. Under the Franchise Act of 1849 this group could vote if they owned a house and lot worth £5 a year or paid £10 in rent. Radical Reformers were convinced that the time had come to widen the franchise and broaden the basis of political society. Some were even ready to advocate manhood suffrage and vote by ballot.[89]

Responding to Clear Grit pressure for progressive reforms, the Hincks-Morin ministry introduced a bill to extend the franchise in Canada West to tenants, occupants and owners of property assessed at £7/10 annual value or upwards in cities or towns, if entitled to representation, and £50 or £5 annual value elsewhere. Voters' registers were to be made up from the assessment rolls. Squatters on Crown land and persons in debt to the Crown for rent, or behind in their installment payments, were to be excluded.[90] Mackenzie objected to these provisions because he foresaw the difficulty of administering them and the possibility of corruption. These restrictions were later to be modified to provide merely that no one was to be deemed an occupant of land unless he held it with the consent of the Crown and with the intent that, on certain conditions, he should become an owner.[91]

Mackenzie was still uneasy about giving the vote to tenants and debtors unless they were to be protected by the ballot from pressure from their creditors or landlords. He moved for a committee to report a bill for voting by ballot at all elections, local or provincial, in both sections of the province. His motion was defeated, 6 to 39. Among those who voted no were leading Reformers like Hincks, who had once favoured the ballot.[92] Mackenzie evidently felt he could not support the franchise bill without the safeguard of the ballot and therefore refrained from voting. At the next session he introduced another ballot bill, bolstering his argument by quoting from Kaye's *Selections from the Papers of Lord Metcalfe* the latter's approval of the ballot.[93] His proposal was defeated, but even the ministry now admitted that it was "thinking" about introducing a ballot bill as a government measure.[94] Ontario was not to obtain the ballot for provincial elections until 1874, the same year the Dominion Ballot Act was passed.[95]

Several reform measures brought in by the government had Mackenzie's support although some of them disappointed him because of their limited nature — the Upper Canada Assessment Act, for example,[96] and the act to extend the jurisdiction of the division courts for the settlement of small debts. Some of his correspondents had been complaining of the cost of the county courts [97] and of the extortions practised by the bailiffs and clerks of the division courts.[98] The government's bill did enlarge the jurisdiction of the division courts but not to the extent that some of Mackenzie's correspondents had proposed. The new act did, however, provide for unification of the rules of practice by a commission of county judges and various clauses attempted to regulate more closely the conduct of clerks and bailiffs.[99]

A measure which Mackenzie introduced for the benefit of poor men was a bill exempting goods and chattels up to a limited value from seizure and sale for debt. In 1851 Mackenzie had introduced a bill exempting goods to the value of £62/10, justifying the bill with a preamble on the principle that "want of sympathy with the people weakens the state in time of danger."[100] His more moderate bill of this session exempted a long list of items to the value of £40. Mackenzie's list of necessities to keep a poor man and his family from utter despair in times of adversity is surely a reflection of his boyhood in Scotland. It was a generous provision compared with the limited exemption allowed by the existing law — wearing apparel, bedding and tools to the value of £5.[101] His bill passed the Assembly, with the exemption reduced to £30, but not the Council.[102] He tried again in 1854. They had legislated enough for the rich, he told the members. Time now to legislate for the poor. The bill again failed to get by the Council.[103]

Mackenzie was not discouraged. "There is great good to come from the agitation of well founded principles even if they are not at once successful," he observed.[104] In 1857 he made his fourth and final attempt to secure this protection for the poor. J.A. Macdonald, then Attorney-General for Upper Canada, promised that the government would move in the matter.[105] The promise was fulfilled — in a niggardly fashion.[106] Unsuccessful in amending Macdonald's clauses, Mackenzie then brought in a more generous bill of his own. It died in committee.[107] In 1859, after Mackenzie was out of Parliament, the Upper Canada Division Court exemption for tools was increased and in 1860 an act was passed giving in all courts of Canada a really generous exemption such as Mackenzie had proposed a decade earlier.[108]

When Mackenzie returned to Canada in 1850 the Crown lands were being managed under the provisions of the Land Act of 1841. A cash sale policy had been established except for school land and Clergy Reserves, which could be purchased on 10 years' credit. In Lower Canada land was priced at 4/- an acre, in Upper Canada at 8/- except lots long on the market which could be had for 4/-.[109] One exception to the cash sale policy was permitted: on certain colonization roads in new areas 50-acre free grants were available to settlers, with the adjoining 50 acres reserved for them to purchase. Mackenzie did not approve of these small and inadequate free grants. He thought the system "more nominal than real" since the liberality of the free grants was neutralized by the cost of the reserve.[110] Land could be obtained for less than the cash price by the use of the scrip that had been issued in satisfaction of U.E. and militia claims to free grants, but this scrip had fallen chiefly into the hands of speculators and suspicion had been aroused about the methods by which they had got hold of it.[111]

By 1852 the colonization road and free grant policy was not being actively pursued. Dissatisfaction with the Land Act of 1841 had led to some reductions in price and to the institution of the credit system. Settlers buying on credit were limited to 200 acres and required to perform settlement duties. This system proved less of a boon to settlers than to speculators, who acquired assignments from them.[112] Some Clear Grits were advocating a return to a policy of strict cash sale at sharply reduced prices. Mackenzie thought it more important to give the settler time "than to offer him a tantalizing bargain which he cannot take the first step to get possession of."[113] Reducing the price of land was only a half-way answer to Canada's land and settlement problems. The result might be that any really desirable land would promptly be snapped up by the Canada Land Company or other speculators.[114] Land policies that favoured speculators and enabled them to keep in a state of wilderness land that other men needed received his unsparing condemnation. What title had any man to land except for the common good and general welfare?

The chief complaint in the 1850s, however, was the shortage of land open to settlement. In the United States railways were beginning to open up the fertile prairies and pressure for a homestead policy was increasing and seemed in a fair way to succeed before long. Mackenzie could not see why Canada should "stand still," keeping her undeveloped territory closed to native sons and immigrants alike and intensifying her squatter problem. He urged that the Ottawa-Huron area be surveyed and thrown open to settlement as soon as possible. He wanted townships to be laid out six miles square, nine to a county, with reserves for county towns, for town plots and for schools. He proposed that alternate quarter sections be granted to landless families, be protected from seizure for debts, and that the intervening quarter sections be offered for sale to actual settlers only under the pre-emption system.[115] His proposals show the influence of the American land system and of the schemes of the National Reform Association. Mackenzie finally put his proposals in the form of an address to the Governor-General. It was ordered, but there seems to have been no response to it.[116]

In the session of 1852 Mackenzie prodded the Hincks-Morin administration to make good on its election promises to liberalize the land system. No radical changes in existing policies were made but authorization was given for the opening up of colonization roads and specific portions of the land revenue were allotted for this purpose. On these roads settlers were to be offered free grants, not exceeding 100 acres, subject to settlement duties. It appeared to Mackenzie that the government was beginning to move in the right direction at last, save that it was concentrating its attention on building a trunk line of railway following the St. Lawrence and the lakes while ignoring the need for interior routes to open up the country,[117] and it was continuing the policy of making free grants that were too small.

Ever since 1824 old Reformers had been protesting the sale of a million acres of Crown land in the Huron Tract and 1,332,000 acres of Crown Reserves to the Canada Company. One would expect this transaction to have come to be regarded as water over the dam by the 1850s, but the Canada Company's policies had kept popular resentment alive, and hope of overthrowing its charter had not yet died. Indeed down to Confederation protests and petitions hostile to the company continued to be received by the legislature. One man even proposed that the government should buy the company out with Canadian debentures and "liberate their slaves,"[118] a method of dealing with "foreign" capitalists nowadays well known.

The evil influence of the Company on public policies was an old and favourite theme with both Mackenzie and the editor of the *Examiner*. In 1842 the Company had instituted a system under which settlers could lease land for 10 years at a rent equal to 6% on the value of the land, and with the option of purchasing at any time during the lease at an advance of 20% upon the price at the time of leasing. For example, one of Mackenzie's constituents was told he might purchase 100 acres in Walpole (a township in Haldimand County) at £5 an acre, or lease them at £30 a year, paying three years' rent in advance, with the option of purchasing the property for £600 at the end of 10 years.[119] This was land that the Company had held for a quarter of a century and had acquired nominally at 3/6 an acre, actually for 2/4.[120] The "calamitous leasing system" was the most hated aspect of the Company's policies and came to be regarded by the settlers as a "trap."[121] After 10 years' labour creating their farms they were obliged by the terms of their lease to give up possession peaceably if they had not purchased or could not meet the new terms the Company might then demand. Mackenzie remarked:

> We dislike absenteeism, leasing, tenancy, middlemen as they
> exist in Ireland on improved land; but to institute the Irish

212

system here and apply it to the unbroken forest is a refinement on European cruelty. [122]

The plight of the Canada Company's lessees in Downie (a Perth County township in the Huron Tract) was drawn to Mackenzie's attention after the session closed. Here there were 90 persons whose leases were due to expire in February 1854 and who feared they would be compelled to leave their farms. [123] The Company's records show that for 60% of them leasing proved not to be a step towards ownership.

It was Mackenzie's policy to call for annual returns from corporations that had received special charters from the legislature. He had no difficulty in getting support for his motion that the Canada Company be requested to furnish answers to his numerous queries, which were in themselves a comprehensive indictment of its policies and an evidence of the deep hostility Reformers had always felt towards it. There was not an aspect of the Company's business into which he did not intend to pry. But the Company had an imperial, not a colonial charter, and Fred Widder, its resident commissioner, refused the information asked for on the grounds that he could not supply it without the permission of the proprietors in England. They would not consent. [124] Mackenzie regarded this refusal as "a standing insult to the people of Canada." [125] A later effort to obtain these returns was equally unsuccessful. [126]

By 1850 the proper management of the timber lands of Canada had become as important — and as controversial — as the policies to be followed for the limited amount of agricultural land remaining. No sooner had Mackenzie been elected to the legislature in 1851 than he began to receive complaints about the monopoly of timber limits. [127] Anyone who knew Mackenzie of old was aware that the word "monopoly" was to him as a red rag to a bull and that he could be counted on to bring their complaints before the legislature.

The problem was threefold. First, there were the complaints of owners of sawmills near the lakes, especially in the Midland and Eastern Districts, that whole townships in their vicinity had been leased to one person, giving him a monopoly and depriving the sawmill owner of his source of raw material unless he paid tribute to the monopolist, who often had no capital of his own invested in sawmills. An additional grievance was that such persons sold their logs, or even their licenses, to Americans who exported the logs out of the country in their rough state. [128] Second, there were those lumbermen, cutters of sawlogs, who did not bother to take out a license but who were ready to pay the Crown dues — if and when caught. The Act of 1849 [129] was intended to put an end to this practice, which had been condoned for years. It provided that a lumberman with a license could claim and seize all the timber cut on his berth, with or without his leave. The grievance was that the licenses were taken out by scheming men who had no intention of working the berth themselves but moved in to take advantage of the labour of unlicensed operators by seizing their sawlogs. This was in effect the squatter problem in the timber industry. Third, there were those engaged in cutting timber on the Ottawa and its tributaries. Extensive limits were held by a few persons or firms such as Allan Gilmour and Company. The latter was believed to hold a stretch of timber land 140 miles in length and five miles deep and to be using a device well known on the American continent, dummy-entrymen

One of Mackenzie's correspondents explained what had happened to the industry. The Crown Timber Regulations required a lumberman to cut a certain quantity of timber annually. Failure to work his timber berth could mean that he would lose it. The larger firms were suppliers to lumbermen and marketed their rafts for them. During 1847 and 1848, when the trade was depressed, owing in part to the overstocking of the market caused by this regulation, they had acquired

> the limits held by their customers... and... all vacant ones so that
> now there is not a vacant mile on the Ottawa and its tributaries. [130]

The ground rents imposed at a progressive rate on unworked limits by the regulations of 1851 had not yet grown heavy enough to oblige the large firms to relinquish berths on which they were not cutting. In consequence the working lumberman was now at the mercy of those monopolists for a chance to use his men and equipment. The holders of the timber limits required the lumberman to pay a lump sum for each gang he put into the woods, supplied him with working capital at the legal rate of interest, with goods at 25% to 40% interest, and sold his raft at the end of the season for a commission of 5%. "They run very little risk," Mackenzie was informed, "as they hold timber, horses and oxen and come in after the men's wages." The system was in effect a subcontracting system with most of the risk borne by the small operator.

Mackenzie was asked to move for a return that would show the extent of timber lands held by each person or firm. "It would exhibit the amount of fraud and corruption and the number of land agents engaged in the business who hold limits," he was told. [131] In the session of 1852 Mackenzie asked for a map that would show the unoccupied limits and for a return showing the timber licenses granted during the years 1848-52 and those transferred. The return supplied gave only the licenses granted in 1852. No information was given on one vital point — transfers. [132] Of the 27,972 square miles of timber limits granted in 1852, 30% had gone to just three persons or firms: the Gillmours, John Egan and G.B. Hall; and 50% of the whole had gone to 10 persons including those mentioned. This was the kind of information Mackenzie took pains to elicit and lay before the public. [133] He charged that timber berths were granted in quantities too large for men of limited means to handle, with the result that they were denied what he regarded, in true Jacksonian fashion, as "their fair and legitimate right of participation." "Is this dealing with public property for the advantage of the people at large," he inquired. [134] That indeed was a moot point, particularly as it applied to an industry that in some areas had peculiar problems very different from those of small-scale agriculture. Mackenzie was always ready — sometimes over ready — to air the complaints of the small man. In this instance

214

that was all he accomplished.

As part of their bargain with Hincks, the leaders of the Clear Grits had agreed to postpone their demand for wholly elective institutions, part of the radical program previously resolved on at Reform meetings in 1849, 1850 and 1851.[135] The coalition with Hincks was an uneasy one which the Tories, now more entitled to be called Conservatives, stood a good chance of breaking apart if they could introduce some measure that would reveal the differences within Reform ranks. On September 13, J.W. Gamble, the Conservative who had defeated Price for York South, introduced two resolutions proposing that certain taxing powers be conferred on the county councils of Upper Canada, and a third resolution, that these elective bodies be given the right to name certain county court officials including the sheriffs.[136] When Hincks opposed Gamble's third resolution, saying that he objected to this transfer of patronage from the government to the county councils, he was twitted by his Conservative opponents who observed that a Reform ministry should not object to *this* proposal.[137] Mackenzie supported Gamble's resolutions, but moved in amendment to the third that these officials, including the sheriffs, should be elected by freeholders of the county. The fat was now in the fire.

Mackenzie had already introduced a bill of his own for the election of sheriffs.[138] The preamble used words similar to those of George Dunning's famous resolution in the imperial parliament of 1780: "The patronage of the Crown is increasing and ought to be diminished."[139] It continued with a long justification of the bill, unlikely to win support for it. At the time Gamble introduced his proposals it had made no progress.

Gamble's third resolution was not acceptable to Mackenzie because he feared that the county councils would become corporations with patronage to bestow; therefore it would be far better to have the sheriffs popularly elected for three years. If they were made ineligible to succeed themselves immediately they would be obliged to account for monies in their hands at the end of the term of office. Some Reform members supported Gamble, some Mackenzie.[140] The ministry opposed both Gamble's and Mackenzie's proposals respecting the office of Sheriff. The Attorney-General admitted that if any change was to be made Mackenzie's proposal was the reasonable one, but knowing the importance of retaining the patronage he opposed any change. Hincks said that the election of sheriffs would lead to republican independence, but W.H. Merritt said that it was not a question of republicanism and monarchy but between centralization and decentralization.[141] This was precisely the issue Mackenzie had raised himself with respect to the Consolidated Municipal Loan Fund, the Medical Incorporation Bill and other issues. It seemed likely that between the Conservatives and radical Reformers the ministry would be left in a minority as far as Upper Canada was concerned, as Baldwin had been on the chancery question.

"Great was the consternation in ministerial ranks," George Brown reported with glee.[142] Hincks rose to the occasion, "pitched into his supporters with a vengeance," demanded that they give his government the support it was entitled to from them, and pointed out that otherwise there would be "a change that they would not like."[143] He accused Mackenzie of adopting a course unfriendly to his administration although he had been warned that the Reformers of Upper Canada were in favour of keeping it in power. Hincks declared that he was not afraid of Mackenzie. He despised him and "all his missiles" — "the broad sheets he sent... all over the country with votes and speeches and all the rest of it."[144] "Dr. Rolph followed in the same vein and laid the lash on Mr. Mackenzie's back without mercy." He called it "political suicide" for Mackenzie to ally himself with the Tories to embarrass the government, and his course dishonourable. As a Clear Grit, supposedly favouring the election of local officials, Rolph got out of the situation for himself quite neatly. He declared he would not vote on the principle involved either way; he would vote to support the government.[145]

A few days later Mackenzie's own bill for election of sheriffs in Upper Canada came up for a second reading and was the occasion of further criticism of him by Rolph and Hincks. They advised the people of Upper Canada to turn him out of Reform ranks, accusing him of cooperating with the Tories, of dishonourable conduct and of introducing a measure he knew would not be passed merely to embarrass the government. Mackenzie defended his political conduct, pointing out that *he* was not pledged to support the government. He had no desire to introduce measures of his own but he had promised his constituents to bring in his bill for the election of sheriffs. He would support the government's measures if he could agree with them "but he would not consent to place his head under the feet of the ministry." He added that he did not wish to overthrow the government and ended by asking leave to withdraw his motion for a second reading of his bill. The Conservatives would not let the Clear Grits — and Hincks — off the hook so easily. Permission to withdraw was refused and then Mackenzie's bill was killed by a vote of 5 to 42.[146] In 1856 he was to make another attempt to procure elective sheriffs.[147] The province of Canada was never to obtain them.

Unhappily a break in Mackenzie's long-standing friendship with James Lesslie was occasioned by this bill. A letter from Mackenzie to the electors of Haldimand, which Lesslie would normally have printed in the *Examiner*, was not inserted. This letter had justified Mackenzie's political course and had given an account of the defeat of his amendment to Gamble's bill. Certain expressions were used in it which Lesslie wanted to change. Mackenzie had on previous occasions permitted changes to be made in his letters, but on this occasion he would not consent. Lesslie therefore would not print the letter because, in his judgement, it would do harm to Mackenzie himself and to the cause of reform.[148] He reminded Mackenzie of the political realities of the situation, which Mackenzie had previously acknowledged:

> We may choose whether we shall retain the present men in power, who are by far the most progressive we can hope to get at the present, or we may get back the Tories to power.... You are in great danger of throwing the country into the arms of the enemy and of blasting your own reputation... [he warned,

adding] Your personal hate to Rolph and the loss of some favorite measure seems to destroy your equanimity & warp your judgment. [149]

On October 5, in the course of the debate on his election of sheriffs bill, Mackenzie referred to Lesslie's refusal to publish his letter. His words were a public criticism of his old friend and an insinuation of corrupt motives that made Lesslie very indignant.[150] After this incident no more of Mackenzie's letters to his constituents appeared in the *Examiner*. Mackenzie had now deprived himself of his only important medium of communication with the province. To maintain his influence in the Reform Party at the level it had been during the elections, there was only one thing Mackenzie could do — establish a press of his own again.

*Mackenzie's Weekly Message*, subsequently the *Toronto Weekly Message*, was not welcomed by the editors of the other reform journals. William McDougall wrote to Rolph:

> Mackenzie is about bringing out a weekly paper to make confusion more confounded in the Reform ranks.... I told him he always was a marplot and seemed determined to remain so.... His paper will be extensively read and will injure my paper and the *Examiner*.... Lesslie is in no very good humour at the prospect. He is not entitled to much sympathy for he has defended him and upheld him in abuse of others and now he will find the viper he has warmed to life ready to sting him. [151]

In an equally gloomy letter to Charles Clarke, McDougall predicted that extremists like Mackenzie and George Brown would break up the Reform Party, alienating hundreds who would otherwise support a rational progressive reform party.

> His [Mackenzie's] efforts will be directed to make mischief in the party — not to advance its interests.... If he is sustained in his crotchets, whimsical, contradictory and anti-reform movements let it be so, but I am determined to put him in his true position towards the Reform Party at the outset. [152]

McDougall feared that Mackenzie's present line of policy would divide and ruin the Reform Party.

> It is evident then that a man who believes all wisdom centers in himself, and cannot, when in opposition, agree to work with others is out of place under a constitutional party system.... The only effect of this wretched self-willed demagogue under our system is to destroy or postpone every good measure which the demagogue may happen to bring up.... [153]

Eighteen months later McDougall was to seek the help of this same self-willed demagogue.

The editor of the *North American* believed that Mackenzie started his *Message*

> more for the purpose of putting "money in his purse" by stirring up this old matter [the Randall claim] than anything else. The paper will give him additional influence and by managing to strike while the iron is hot he hopes to get the Gov't and Parl't to resuscitate Randall's properties. I know his objective and the motives which activate him for he has avowed them and therefore I am determined to bring him out in his true colors at once. [154]

It is true that Mackenzie's petition asking for an investigation into the proposed disposition by the government of the land Randall's estate claimed was presented shortly after Mackenzie broke with Lesslie, but the preliminary steps respecting this petition had been taken much earlier and before Mackenzie could have foreseen that he would lose the help of Lesslie and his *Examiner*. [155]

The early issues of the *Message*, which commenced publication on December 25, 1852, were printed at some job printing office. In February 1853, when the legislature was in recess, Mackenzie made a trip to New York where he arranged with George Bruce to provide him with types and other printing material on credit. Subscriptions to the *Message* came in promptly and before long Mackenzie could boast that he had "more subscribers than he ever had before at any time in 30 years." [156] George Brown, who thought Mackenzie still too tolerant towards French Canada and Roman Catholicism and guilty of misrepresenting Brown's views at times, nevertheless saw fit to praise the paper.

> Mackenzie [wrote his competitor] tells more truth in one number of his *Message* than the [ministerial] organs do in six months and we are glad to hear he has many readers. [157]

Although the Clear Grits stood by Hincks against Mackenzie on the sheriff question, they became disenchanted with Hincks before the session was over. One reason for this was that action on the Clergy Reserves had been put off until the next session. A second reason was the Upper Canada Supplementary School Bill which came up in May. Mackenzie had long been an advocate of free schools. He considered the fact that 100,000 of Upper Canada's 250,000 children aged five to sixteen were not being educated a disgrace to her, but he was also a staunch opponent of sectarian education. He advocated a common and secular school system under which children would not be taught "blindly to follow and revere any one set of men or ideas but to exercise their reasoning powers." [158] In 1851 he had tried to have the separate school provisions of the Common Schools Act of 1850 repealed. [159] The government's school bill of this session exempted from local school assessments those who sent their children to separate schools or supported them, while still allowing separate schools a share in the legislative grant for common schools. Mackenzie supported George Brown's unsuccessful motion to delete from the bill all recognition of any portion of the community in a sectarian capacity.[160] When the bill came up for its third reading, 10 Upper Canada members voted with the ministry, 17 against them, but the bill passed with the aid of its Lower Canada supporters. By the passage of this detested bill what the *Message* called the "real" wishes of Upper Canada had again been defeated by the Lower Canada vote.[161]

A third reason for the Clear Grits' increasing dissatisfaction with the ministry and its Lower Canada supporters was the plethora of bills to incorporate Roman Catholic charitable, educational or ecclesiastical institutions. Mackenzie, who was growing weary under the triple burden of his parliamentary duties, his correspondence and writing articles for his *Message*, complained particularly about these bills.

> Of all annoyances this is to me the most insufferable; for I am pledged, and voluntarily so, against unfairness to any religious sect; and would rather agitate effectively for the repeal of the Union of the Canadas than to see the Upper Province... compelled to build up a state church....[162]

What he objected to about these ecclesiastical incorporation bills was that they gave power to hold land in mortmain, which meant that a class of dependent tenant farmers would come into existence where there might have been independent freeholders.[163] He noted that between 1841 and 1850 24 bills had been passed enabling ecclesiastical corporations to hold real property to an extent that could produce £78,000 a year.

Early in the session the ministry moved to reduce the irritation caused by the numerous ecclesiastical corporations bills by introducing a general measure for this purpose. This bill permitted any five persons, whoever they might be or what their qualifications, to apply for incorporation for charitable, educational or religious purposes and to obtain this status by the simple act of registering a document stating the nature and purpose of their organizations with the Provincial Secretary, who was required to publish the fact in the *Canada Gazette*. Only two restraints were placed upon such bodies: they could acquire real property only up to the value of £2,500 yearly, and an annual report to the government was required.[164]

George Brown was strongly opposed to this loosely drawn bill which, he believed, would stimulate rather than check the proliferation of ecclesiastical corporations and would deprive the legislature of control over them.[165] "Had it passed," he wrote, "Romanism would have obtained a lift it has not had for many a long day."[166] Brown thought he had secured enough votes from Conservatives and Clear Grits to defeat the bill—and perhaps the ministry. One of the planks repeatedly included in Clear Grit platforms had been "No ecclesiastical corporations." Yet when Brown attempted to give the government's bill the three months hoist, to his chagrin his motion was defeated 33 to 39 with the Clear Grits voting against him.[167] "The ministry frightened them by threatening to resign if the bill were thrown out," Brown declared, and J.A. Macdonald asserted that they had been promised that if they would save the government, which really feared defeat, they would never see the bill again.[168] It was not proceeded in.

It was on the occasion of this vote that the weary Mackenzie was caught napping. When aroused he voted aye, in support of a hostile amendment made by Brown, believing that he was supporting the government's bill; but on realizing his mistake he was permitted by the Speaker to change his vote to nay, and therefore in favour of giving the government's bill a second reading.

Mackenzie's vote was not given to keep the government in power and the Tories out. Mackenzie had always favoured general measures of which all could take advantage on the same terms. They saved the time of the legislature and made lobbying for special favours unnecessary. His object in voting for a second reading was to obtain an opportunity to improve the bill by amending it to restrict the amount of land these ecclesiastical corporations could hold in mortmain.[169] Later in the session he tried to obtain a more satisfactory general ecclesiastical corporations bill.[170]

The advantages of a general ecclesiastical corporation act were not provided by law until 1859, a year after Mackenzie had resigned his seat, and then it was done as part of an amendment to the Joint Stock Companies Act of 1850. This amendment then included corporations for the construction of buildings for various educational and religious purposes. Rephrased in the Consolidated Statutes of 1859, Title 5, cap. LXIII, the law empowered five or more persons to form a joint stock company for educational or religious purposes. The amount of land they were empowered to hold was not specifically limited but was vaguely expressed as land necessary to carry on their operations. How strictly this phrase could be or ever was interpreted is not known at this writing.

The long legislative session of 1852-53 ended on June 14. On the final day the contingencies had yet to be voted. The Committee on Contingencies had been importuned throughout the session to recommend increased salaries for officers of the Assembly. Both Brown and Mackenzie were members of this committee. They had tried to persuade the Assembly to establish the salaries of all permanent officials by legislation in order to put an end to this pressure, and had failed.[171] Mackenzie then tried to get the House not to leave the vote on the report of the Committee on Contingencies until the last minute, and failed.[172] On the last day of the session a surprise motion was made to set aside the Committee's report, rearrange the status and salaries of the officers, and "without reference to efficiency or terms of service" give nearly all of them increases. This proposal came after twelve noon, without notice, when two-thirds of the members had already departed and with prorogation set for two o'clock. Brown "resisted the trick, which was to force a vote by a handful of members" and he insisted on speaking in opposition. Mackenzie reported:

I was in the chair. Bedlam broke loose.... I was again and again threatened with personal violence as was Brown but he insisted on being heard. Other members did so also, twelve members talked at once — others stamped, honked, imitated roosters, yelled, and still they failed.

The *Globe's* account of this scene is similar.

> Fortunately Mr. Mackenzie was in the chair and stood firm as a rock amid the din raised by... Lower Canada members.... As two o'clock approached the uproar waxed more furious than ever... threats of personal violence were uttered....

At two o'clock the Speaker resumed the chair. The debate continued with increasing uproar. The chairman was attempting to put the motion to a vote when, as Mackenzie put it, "The governor's arrival [to prorogue] barely saved a dishonest vote.[173]

The session was over. The weary member for Haldimand could now go home. There was not much on which he could congratulate himself. He had done his best for the poor man with his mechanics' exemption bill, his opposition to the repeal of the usury laws, and his attempt to liberalize the land system and to bring the conduct of the Canada Company to public attention. As a radical Reformer he had tried to put the representation of the people on a fairer basis, to secure the safeguard of the ballot and to make the sheriffs elective. As a staunch believer in equality before the law he had tried to give the ministers of all denominations the right to perform marriages on the same basis and he had tried to make the registration of all marriages, births and deaths a civil matter.[174] He had also supported a bill to enable women to retain after marriage all their rights in their real property.[175] As a voluntaryist he had opposed sectarian schools and all sectarian legislation. And he had accomplished practically nothing. Moreover, he had seen enacted three measures that he thoroughly detested: the Upper Canada Supplementary School Bill, the Grand Trunk charter, and the Consolidated Municipal Loan Fund Bill. He had witnessed growing sectional feeling and he had become increasingly doubtful whether much could be accomplished under the union. What was worse, he had lost the help of Lesslie and by his sheriffs bill and by his criticisms of John Rolph he had angered those Clear Grits still willing to work with Hincks for expediency's sake.

Chapter XV

# THE ELECTION OF 1854

Upon his return to Toronto Mackenzie took over the management of the *Message* from his nephew, Peter Baxter, who had been in charge during the legislative session. Mackenzie's paper was now six months old. It was paying its way — or rather it was not yet running its publisher into debt. He was able to meet George Bruce's bills and he still had hopes of having a press of his own again, a steam press no less.[1] He even dreamed of starting a daily.[2] But the *Message* was not putting any money into his pocket, although its circulation had increased and on the face of things it seemed to be flourishing. There were the old difficulties: delinquent and disgruntled subscribers. There were new difficulties too: the competition of more newspapers edited by young and vigorous men, the increased capital costs of the business and the fact that the want of political information was no longer felt as it had been in the days of the old *Colonial Advocate*.[3] Then there was Mackenzie's discursive style of writing[4] and his practice of raking over old coals. These deprived some of his articles of the pithy character they might have had. Mackenzie's paper did not have 3,000 cash subscribers at the end of its first year[5] and no doubt its editor envied the 10,000 subscribers of which the *Globe* could boast. Nevertheless, throughout 1854 the *Message* held on and gradually increased its advertising. Its editor was not so prosperous, however, as to be able to keep both his sons in Upper Canada College. He had them helping him in the office of the *Message* during the summer. William never returned to the school, but George completed four years.[6]

When parliament was prorogued on June 14, 1853, it was expected that it would be called into a second session before the close of the year to use the power it had received to settle the Clergy Reserves question.[7] Instead, repeated prorogations were proclaimed. In December it was officially announced that the government considered that the existing parliament ought not to deal with weighty matters like the Clergy Reserves and the seigneurial tenures; those questions should be put off until a new parliament could be elected under the terms of the new representation and franchise acts.[8] But this latter act[9] was not to go into effect until January 1855, by which time the voters' registration lists, based on the new assessment franchise, would have been compiled. To get earlier action on the reserves by a more representative parliament it was therefore necessary to summon the existing one again to amend the Franchise Act so as to bring it into force in 1854.

Radical Reformers were in no mood to put up with delay. Canada now had the power to determine the disposition of the reserves itself. The moment for action had come. It was feared that, in a country grown more populous and more prosperous, interest was likely to be diverted from this hoary dispute to other political problems of importance — the railways, the tariff and corruption in government. One man, who fully realized that the voluntaryists were contending for a principle, informed Mackenzie that secularization of the reserves did not appear to be as popular as it once had been. "The clergy," he observed, "are generally good men and do not do much harm." Were the reserves to be secularized and sold, he feared "an immense amount of jobbing" would occur and little would be derived for education. Besides, everyone was thinking about railroads, giving "scarce a thought to other questions."[10] Clear Grits suspected that to get the issue settled Hincks would not live up to his understanding with them and would agree to some other solution of the reserves question more acceptable to the Conservatives than secularization. McDougall feared Hincks was getting ready to make a new political combination and "with the shamelessness and indifference to principle which... characterizes him... making ready for the turn of the wheel."[11] The disillusioned editor of the *North American* now offered his newspaper for sale.[12] James Lesslie came to the same conclusion as McDougall: Hincks had deceived the country. He was playing up to the French Canadians and the Tories of Upper Canada, hoping for another four years in office with their support.[13] Lesslie also was growing weary of the struggle. Before Parliament reassembled he, too, offered his newspaper for sale.[14] Its circulation had dropped to between 2,000 and 2,500 subscribers. Both the *North American* and the *Examiner* were to be acquired by the *Globe*, the former in February 1855, the latter in August of the same year.[15]

All sorts of rumours, surmises and accusations were in the air. Why, it was asked, had not the government at least introduced its Clergy Reserves Bill towards the close of the last session, when there was still time? Why had Hincks asserted that the representation bill would not shorten the life of the existing parliament, that it was competent to legislate on any question, and why did he now say that it should not? If Parliament was not competent, why had he not asked for a dissolution and provided for an election promptly?[16] Between the *Message*, the *Globe*, the *Examiner*, and the *North American* on the one hand and the ministerial papers on the other, charges and counter-charges were bandied back and forth. They can all be passed over without detail now except one — that the government's decision to delay action on the Clergy Reserves was due to Lord Elgin.

Hincks was disposed to conceal the influence the Governor-General undoubtedly had exercised.[17] The government's paper, the *Leader*, announced:

> We are authorized to say that the policy of deferring legislation
> on important questions like the Clergy Reserves and the
> Seigneurial Tenures... proceeds from the spontaneous and

> united volition of the cabinet, it.. was deliberately taken
> without any prompting from the Governor-General. [18]

This statement was received with skepticism and rightly so.

Dr. Rolph was in the awkward position of having to justify the government's policy to the Clear Grits, who had regarded his inclusion in the cabinet as a guarantee that secularization would take place promptly. He warned his friends that since Elgin's consent was necessary to the introduction of any measure by his ministers, they would be obliged to resign if he refused it. The consequence would be that a Tory ministry would be installed and it would have all the resources of government at its disposal during the next election.[19]

Malcolm Cameron, the other Clear Grit in the cabinet, admitted in a speech at Perth on February 3 that it was Elgin who would not consent to legislation by the existing parliament.[20] It was the ministry's intention, Cameron said, to summon Parliament, pass a bill to bring the Franchise Act into operation in 1854 instead of in 1855, and merely introduce a measure to place the Clergy Reserves funds in the general revenue of the province. Parliament would then be dissolved and the ministry would go to the country on the merits of its Clergy Reserves Bill.[21]

From Donald M'Leod, at this time employed in the Patent Office under Dr. Rolph, Mackenzie heard much the same story. Dr. Rolph was as true as ever on this question. The delay was due to Lord Elgin, who felt that a House "fresh from the people" should settle the question so that hereafter there could be no doubt what the wishes of the province had been.[22] This argument rested on the dangerous assumption that the election would turn on the single issue of the reserves.

Mackenzie had professed in sentimental and exaggerated language that when Lord Elgin, a distant descendant of Robert Bruce, had been appointed Governor-General of Canada, hopes that had almost died had been revived in him.[23] Disappointed in these high expectations, he gradually began to indulge in criticisms of one who had accepted and supported Francis Hincks as his leading minister. More than once Mackenzie remarked that responsible government was a sham, that all it amounted to was government by means of a purchased majority.[24] Asked why he named Lord Elgin in connection with his criticisms of the ministry, he replied that with a weak ministry the Governor-General could do as he pleased.[25] He summed Elgin up as a moderate, forbearing man, tactful in the management of cabinet and legislature and with the skill to keep in the background.[26] He attributed the changes made in the cabinet during the summer of 1853 to his selection and accused him of having assigned the government to speculators and stock jobbers.[27] Lord Elgin's interference in the matter of the reserves caused him to indulge in even more outspoken criticism.

The short and final session of the fourth parliament had to be postponed until June 13, 1854, longer than anticipated, owing to two fires at Quebec that damaged the buildings in which it was to have been held. In addition, both Elgin and Hincks were out of the country, first in England, then at Washington, where the negotiations for the Reciprocity Treaty were being brought to a successful conclusion. In this interval Hincks and his "Judas Reformers" lost ground.[28] The Reform Association of Whitby, for example, declared that the extensive patronage enjoyed by the administration had made responsible government a "nullity" and its attitude on the Clergy Reserves question had disorganized the Reform Party.[29] When it became known that the Prime Minister had participated in the financial deal known as the £10,000 job,[30] William McDougall, who, with Charles Clarke, had helped to organize the coalition of Clear Grits and moderate Reformers, informed Clarke that he was "prepared to break up the present combination." McDougall claimed he had overlooked many things but that this scandal was too much. "Rolph cannot stay in the government with honor, after these disclosures," he observed.[31] By February 15, Lesslie's *Examiner* was calling Hincks "as corrupt and as unprincipled a statesman as ever carried the province." Efforts seem to have been made at this time to induce Rolph to resign, but he did not formally break with his colleagues until after Parliament met.

Mackenzie participated in the attacks on the ministry and its supporters using every weapon in his armoury, whether fact or rumour, particularly those relating to railway contracts, stock jobbing, land sales and the financial scandals in which Hincks had got himself involved.[32] In anticipation of a general election he busied himself preparing another Voters' Guide and tried, not very successfully, to raise money for an edition of 20,000 copies.[33] Meanwhile in his *Message* he reviewed the voting records of those Upper Canada Reformers who had failed to keep their promises to their constituents. The two Clear Grits in the cabinet came in for special criticism: Cameron for subsequently trying to minimize his embarrassing disclosures about Lord Elgin and for his failure to live up to his election pledges about the ballot, retrenchment, election of country officers and legislative control of appropriations.[34] Rolph was criticized for a long list of votes opposing Mackenzie's pet reforms. Although nominally one of the Clear Grits, he had voted in favour of separate schools, ecclesiastical corporations and grants to sectarian colleges and had given his general support to the government's Clergy Reserves policy. On such questions as the adoption of a temperance law, amnesty for Irish agitators and abolition of the rectories he had "skulked," and he had failed to support vote by ballot and abolition of property qualifications for the Assembly.[35]

When George Brown ran for Kent as an Independent in the general election of 1851 after his break with Hincks, Mackenzie had given his candidacy tacit approval. Hincks had had no more vigorous and outspoken opponent in the fourth parliament than Brown and one might have expected Brown and Mackenzie to co-operate, temporarily at least, against Hincks. At the close of the session they had stood together against a rowdy and hostile Assembly. Yet in the weeks before the election there was constant sparring between the two men. George Brown was a doughty fighter but in the brawl between Scots Mackenzie held his own. One suspects that he was motivated in part by a jealousy that he did not acknowledge even to himself. The *Globe* was flourishing. It had more than twice the circulation of the *Message* and was soon to become a daily, leaving the *Message* far behind in the race for subscribers. Moreover, the session that had just closed had brought the younger and more vigorous Brown to the fore as the government's most influential critic outside the Tory ranks, a role which Mackenzie had expected to fill.

On many questions the two men did not differ, or did not differ much. Both of them favoured a trunk line of railway, but not Hincks's bill, nor the contracts that had been made for construction of the road. Both were uncompromising voluntaryists. On secularization of the reserves, abolition of the rectories and opposition to separate schools they agreed. Both men had voted for the extension of the franchise but when Mackenzie had proposed the use of the ballot if the franchise were granted to others than freeholders Brown had not supported him.[36] Mackenzie favoured making the Legislative Council elective; Brown was strongly opposed to a change which he regarded as one which would not fit British parliamentary institutions.[37] Mackenzie had opposed repeal of the usury laws and the creation of the Upper Canada Consolidated Municipal Loan Fund. The more practical Brown, realizing the stimulus these measures would give to the commercial life of the province and to the construction of local improvements and railways, had supported them.[38]

Although Brown and Mackenzie both advocated representation according to population, they had not yet come to the same point of view on the union. In 1853 Brown was opposed to dissolution, primarily for economic reasons. If the unity of the St. Lawrence were lost, then Upper Canada might be left to face trade barriers on both routes, the St. Lawrence and the Erie Canal. Dissolution of the union would place the West "at the mercy of Brother Jonathan and Jean Baptiste."[39] Mackenzie had never approved of the Union because, among other reasons discussed in his *Gazette* and *Volunteer*, it was unjust to Lower Canada and he did not think it likely to last because it was now unjust to the other part of the province.[40] Upper Canada, which had come to exceed Lower Canada in population, provided for its own local roads and took care of its poor out of local taxes, but Lower Canada, where there was scarcely any local taxation on residents or non-residents, was always dipping into the general revenue for these purposes and, in addition, was constantly petitioning for and receiving grants for her eleemosynary and educational institutions. As Mackenzie put it, Upper Canada provided two-thirds of the revenues and Lower Canada siphoned it off.[41] Nevertheless Mackenzie was willing that the Union should have a further trial with an elective legislative council; but if Lower Canada's representatives in the new assembly should unite with an Upper Canada minority to thwart the wishes of the people of the upper province (on the Clergy Reserves it was implied) he was ready to "go at once for dissolution."[42]

Hostility between Brown and Mackenzie developed out of the debate on the Ecclesiastical Corporations Bill. Mackenzie felt that the *Globe* had unfairly reported his stand and had tried to deceive its readers into believing that he had pledged himself to a bill that would have made the creation of ecclesiastical corporations all too easy.[43]

Mackenzie took his revenge. He twitted Brown, who was touring Upper Canada, attacking the Hincks-Morin administration he had once supported, with his political inconsistencies and his rabid anti-Catholicism. Brown protested indignantly that although he had supported Baldwin, Lafontaine and Hincks, he had never approved of their ecclesiastical legislation and had remonstrated consistently in private. He accused "the restless little creature" Mackenzie of paying "fulsome compliments" to the Roman Catholics. In a letter to the *Haldimand Independent* Mackenzie had pointed out that Catholics, Anglicans and Dissenters alike had been guilty of persecuting other faiths. They all believed in miracles: the Protestants, for example, in such Old Testament wonders as the creation of Eve from Adam's rib, the parting of the Red Sea, the story of Jonah and the whale and the ability of Balaam's ass to talk "excellent sense, good grammar, and the best of Hebrew." "Why then quarrel over creeds? Why deride Catholics for their belief in miracles," Mackenzie had inquired. In response, Brown accused the editor of the *Message* of attempting to bring the Bible into contempt and to deny the truths of revelation.[44]

Nothing daunted, Mackenzie challenged Brown to a debate in St. Lawrence Hall, Toronto, but Brown seems to have been reluctant to meet him on a public platform.[45] At length a confrontation between the two men was brought about at Guelph. The Wellington County Committee for Reform invited Brown to speak at a public gathering of Reformers, followed by a dinner. A group of Reformers hostile to Brown secretly asked Mackenzie to be present and to speak also. "We expect great sport... Brown is not any match for Mack," wrote George Thomson, one of the leading spirits in the affair.[46] The secret became known too late for Brown to back out. What followed was so differently reported by various newspapers that one would not think the accounts relate to the same event. Mackenzie's friends declared he had "totally routed that hypocrite George Brown."[47] On the whole it seems likely that Mackenzie was used by the mischievous George Thomson merely to annoy Brown and that the occasion did nothing to help the unity of the Reform Party.

In the long interval between sessions, while there was a dearth of political news for the *Message*, Mackenzie indulged in much speculation about the probable course of events and filled his columns with accounts of his financial losses and personal grievances. He argued that he should have been paid interest in addition to the principal of his Welland Canal claim and that he should be reimbursed for the expenses of his journey to England in 1833 to present Upper Canada's grievances to the Colonial Office.[48] He complained also of the repeated insults to which he had been subjected in the Assembly. On one occasion they had been of so unrestrained a character that even *Punch* had commented: "On the whole, Mr. Punch is disposed to suggest to his colonial friends that there is a species of self-government to which they seem hardly to have given sufficient attention. It is personal."[49]

It was probably the absence of interesting news for the *Message* that led Mackenzie to fall back upon material relating to the rebellion. His "Western Wanderings, Seventeen Years Ago" appeared in the issues of September 7 and 15, 1854. The Wanderings was a revised edition of the story of his escape to Buffalo that he had published in the *New York Tribune* of 29 September, 1847, only this time he gave the names of those who had assisted him or at whose homes he had called. "Head's Flag of Truce," which appeared as an article in the issue of April 7, 1854, related to a dispute that had occurred in the Assembly about the propriety of Dr. Rolph's conduct when entrusted with the Flag of Truce by Lieutenant-Governor Head. The dispute did not originate with Mackenzie but with W.J. Boulton, who accused Rolph of taking government money to which he was not entitled. This Rolph denied. Boulton had also tried to get some information from Rolph as Commissioner of Crown Lands that Hincks did not want to release.[50] His queries related to money that the government planned to take out of the Crown lands revenues for roads, although under an act of 1849 it was supposed to go for schools.[51] In replying to Boulton Rolph accused him of betraying a confidence. Boulton retorted that Rolph, after agreeing to accompany Head's Flag of Truce, had betrayed the trust he had accepted, had privately advised the insurgents to attack Toronto, "and then skulked from the country leaving his victims [the deluded rebels] to ruin and misery." Rolph denied this accusation of treachery and declared that Robert Baldwin knew that "everything connected with his conduct on that occasion... was proper, honorable and strictly correct." According to Mackenzie, Rolph added that he regretted that the late Samuel Lount had stated "what was false" about the incident.[52]

Lount had testified before the Treason Commission that when the flag had come up the *first* time Rolph had privately advised the rebels not to attend to Head's message but to go on with their proceedings.[53] Rolph, on the contrary, claimed that he had no private conversation with the rebels until the *second* visit of the flag, and after it was formally declared at an end. It was *then* that he had advised the rebels not to delay their march into Toronto. To bolster his account, Rolph published in the Quebec *Gazette* of November 1, 1852, an affidavit procured from the flag-bearer, Hugh Carmichael, that supported his assertion.

When Boulton raised the Flag of Truce issue, Mackenzie had twice objected to the turn Boulton's remarks had taken and had pointed out to the Speaker that if Boulton were permitted to refer to the events of 1837 there was "no knowing to what it might lead."[54] After Carmichael's letter was published, Mackenzie felt it incumbent on him to defend the veracity of his friend Lount, and in the legislature he renewed the discussion about Rolph's conduct. Two of the Clear Grits, David Christie and John White, tried in vain to dissuade him from reopening the discussion and attacking Rolph, a key member of the coalition Hincks had put together, but he would not listen to them.[55] Mackenzie had angered Rolph by supporting Boulton and in retaliation Rolph had denounced Mackenzie's "vituperative speeches" and had characterized him as a useless and troublesome member who seldom carried a measure to redress a wrong or benefitted the country either within the legislature or out of it.[56]

The Flag of Truce controversy did not receive much attention at the time. Mackenzie and Rolph's interchange came about in a closed session. Some information about the verbal battle got out, but the *Examiner*, whose editor had recently quarrelled with Mackenzie, did not publish a statement from him and other papers did not give the dispute much space. Mackenzie, with a newspaper of his own again, now was able to publish evidence supporting his side of the story. Limitations of space have made it necessary to omit a discussion of all the points of the controversy and of the value of the 69-page document compiled in rebuttal by Rolph's friends which he — wisely — did not see fit to publish in Mackenzie's lifetime or his own.[57]

There is one letter which Mackenzie would have been glad to know about and which hitherto has not been related to this controversy. It is a letter from Thomas G. Ridout, cashier of the Bank of Upper Canada, to John J. Morgan, Robert Baldwin's uncle by marriage, written on December 19, that is, about a month before Lount's statement to the Treason Commission:

> Dr. Rolph, before his departure acted a very treacherous part towards Robert Baldwin, on the occasion of being the bearer of the Flag of Truce... for it appears that, after delivering their message and *receiving* a reply, Dr. Rolph lingered a few minutes behind Robert, and took *that opportunity* to advise the rebels not to lose another half hour in making their attack upon the city from which they were only one mile distant. This advice, it seems, they had not the courage to follow; and the doctor, feeling that the rebels had lost their only chance of success, decamped from town that night, and made his escape across the river Niagara.... His papers have since been seized and it is discovered beyond a doubt that he was the prime mover of all our disturbances. [58]

(Baldwin's statement to the Treason Commission acknowledged that Rolph had a private conversation with the rebels after the Flag of Truce had come up a second time, and when it technically had ended. He made no statement about Rolph's conduct during the first visit of the flag, to which Ridout's letter refers, and this is the nub of the dispute.)

When Mackenzie's Flag of Truce article appeared, the Montreal *Gazette* of April 17, 1854, commented that if Mackenzie had falsely accused Rolph of being a double traitor he ought to be punished; if true, Rolph should be ostracized; adding:

> Rolph's public conduct since he became a minister has not been such as to make the world believe that he would not sneak out of a disagreeable responsibility if he had any opportunity whatever....

On the whole, however, the Flag of Truce article did not excite much attention in the press. The government papers wisely ignored it. When the election came Rolph was again returned for Norfolk but with a reduced majority. He received about 55% of the total vote as compared with 70% in the previous election.

The incident in the legislature was 18 months old by the time the Flag of Truce article was published, and by reviving the topic Mackenzie did himself no good and gave ground for the charge that he was animated more by personal hatred for Rolph than by concern for Lount's memory. James Mackenzie stated that "the real cause" of his father's changed attitude towards Rolph was his feeling that as Commissioner of Crown Lands Rolph had not supported him in the matter of the claim of the Randall heirs to valuable property in Bytown.[59] Rolph had declined to make any recommendation on the claim and had left the controversy to be decided by the Executive Council. He had even avoided acknowledging in a forthright manner that he had voted in Randall's favour when his claim was before the Legislature of Upper Canada.[60] In addition to this equivocal behaviour, there were many recent occasions in the legislature when Rolph's conduct would cause a radical Reformer like Mackenzie to become increasingly hostile to a man who had come to be known as "Old Dissolving Views."

A pleasanter occupation for which Mackenzie found time in the extended interval between sessions was paying his long-desired visit to his son James. He left Canada in late April and arrived at Columbus on April 26. James was now a member of the Ohio House of Representatives and Chairman of its Committee on Finance.[61] The Free Democrats, to which section of the party James belonged, were busy organizing their protest against the Kansas-Nebraska Act, and perhaps for this reason Mackenzie did not go to his son's home in Kalida, and his visit was surprisingly brief. By April 28 he was on his way home again.

Mackenzie utilized the information obtained during this visit to point out to Canadians some advantages which the people of Ohio enjoyed. The seat of government was within 300 miles of every man's home, not "on the verge of civilization." The legislature met at a fixed time annually for a brief period and was convened in the forenoon, not late in the day. The Senate was elected; the Assembly represented single-member districts. A majority of the elected members was required for final passage of bills. No handful of members, 10 out of quorum of 19, could legislate at three in the morning after wearying out the others. The distinction between the courts of equity and the courts of common law had been swept away and the old complicated forms of action at common law had been abolished; a simplified uniform code of procedure was now in use. "To this we will yet come in Canada..." Mackenzie prophesied, "the people... in the long run... will turn their backs on those who pillage them."[62]

On June 13 the session opened at Quebec. Everyone had expected a short session, but no one had expected it to terminate as abruptly as it did. A hostile amendment was made to the Speech, criticizing the government for not promising to introduce measures to secularize the Clergy Reserves and to abolish the seigneurial tenures. This wording, for which Mackenzie voted, proved unacceptable to the majority. A subsequent amendment simply criticized the government for not promising to introduce measures to *settle* these questions. Mackenzie felt he could not vote for an amendment so imprecisely worded, one that a Tory minority might take advantage of should the existing government be defeated. Unable to get the floor to explain his position, he left the Assembly before the final vote was taken at 1:40 a.m. This second amendment, which passed, amounted to a vote of no confidence from both sections of the province. The House then adjourned.[63]

It would have been possible for the defeated ministry to ask the co-operation of the opposition to pass the legislation necessary to bring the Franchise Act into operation and to grant supplies before asking for a dissolution, and Sir Allan MacNab was prepared to pledge his party to this. However, when the Assembly met again on the 28th the members found that Parliament was to be prorogued immediately with a view to dissolution and without a chance to enact even one measure, as was constitutionally required for a session. MacNab, angered at being deprived by the government's manoeuvre of a chance to form a new administration, denounced its course as unconstitutional. Mackenzie followed with an impassioned protest against the dismissal of Parliament without the opportunity to pass vital legislation or to inspect the public accounts. His speech was interrupted by the Speaker's reading a notification from Lord Elgin that Parliament was to be prorogued forthwith, and soon after Black Rod knocked. Mackenzie continued to speak, proposing a suspension of the rules so that the bill to bring the new Franchise Act into earlier operation could be put through all its stages at once. The Speaker replied that the rules could not be suspended if any member objected. Mackenzie demanded that his motion be put and walked towards the Speaker's desk with it.[64] The House was now in an "indescribable uproar," several members trying to speak at once and John A. Macdonald at the top of his voice accusing the ministry of asking for a dissolution so as to prevent an inquiry into their corrupt practices. Meanwhile Black Rod had been admitted, but his message summoning the members to the Council's chamber for the prorogation could not be heard. The Speaker, who had been standing for some time, ruled that all further discussion was irregular. The House then rose. The Quebec *Gazette* reported that:

> The storm lasted forty-five minutes. Meanwhile Lord Elgin waited seated on the throne, awaiting in dignified neutrality the disobedient — rightfully disobedient — and insulted Commons.[65]

The abrupt dismissal of Parliament gave Mackenzie a theme which he continued to embroider throughout the elections, denouncing not only the ministry but Lord Elgin for taking the advice of his responsible ministers and granting them a dissolution.[66]

Preparations for the general elections had been warming up all through the long period between sessions and criticism of the Hincks-Morin administration had been rising. To older Reformers it seemed that the province was as far from genuine reform as it had been in the days of the Family Compact.[67] Some Clear Grits were confident that the "Judas Reformers" would be thrown out at the election and that even Rolph would be defeated.[68] But between two of the leading Clear Grits, Charles Clarke and William McDougall, there was a difference of opinion. McDougall's *North American* had come out in opposition to the government:[69] Clarke was still prepared to work with the ministry. He was convinced that the "democratic leaven" would eventually make the present Reform Party a truly progressive party and that editors like Mackenzie and

Lesslie were playing into the hands of the enemies of reform and would destroy the "unity of the party on which our chance of success alone rests."[70]

The Voters' Guide that Mackenzie had hoped to publish before the elections "with all the votes in book form" did not appear. Instead he put out a special issue of the *Message* entitling it "The Voters' Guide".[71] It was largely a reprint of comments he had made earlier on important topics. The *Globe* also came out with a special issue which gave the important decisions. It was more complete than Mackenzie's "Guide." He decided to purchase 5,000 copies of it for distribution to his own subscribers and for general circulation.[72]

Mackenzie, who had been losing ground in Haldimand, was warned that he would have to fight for his re-election.[73] Two of the country's newspapers, the *Cayuga Sentinel* and the *Haldimand Independent*, were against him. The former said that he was "no earthly use" as a representative because he never visited the county except at election times and did not know the wants of the people, unlike his opponent, McKinnon, an early resident who had "grown up" with the county. The *Sachem* charged that Mackenzie was only opposing the ministry on account of the Randall claim, which they would not grant. "If he could once get that into his clutches his mouth would be stopped." As their representative, Mackenzie had "done nothing" for the county and even if he should introduce a useful measure, it would be voted down "so much do the representatives in the Assembly detest him."[74] (There was some sad truth in this.) The *Independent*, once his supporter, thought the voters should choose a resident to represent them instead of a man who used "his position to create distrust in the party he professes to belong to," and who retarded the business he was sent to perform "to gratify his private feelings against individuals."[75] Mackenzie had alienated some Haldimand officials by publishing a complaint that the accounts of the county were in confusion and, relying on information given him, had made some incautious assertions that could not be fully proved.[76] His attitude on separate schools had hurt him with Roman Catholic voters, his attack on Rolph had hurt him with Clear Grits and the tone of his *Message* was hurting him with moderate Reformers who objected to his loading with "obloquy and rank contempt" almost every officer under the government, even those holding the most minor appointments.

Mackenzie's agent in the township of Rainham, William Holmes, had sent him a frank warning.

> Assuredly this [course] can do no good.... We returned our Member at the last election with a sweeping majority and it is humiliating to know that unless some measures be soon adopted to reconcile matters the majority at the next general election will be materially cut off... many of your warmest supporters are decidedly adverse to your course as an Editor and have determined to use their influence against you. [77]

Mackenzie did not take this warning sufficiently to heart. He did not visit his county until nomination day, July 20. Four candidates presented themselves, of whom two dropped out. The show of hands favoured Mackenzie two to one, but to his disappointment the Tory candidate, McKinnon, demanded a poll.[78] This made it necessary for him to make more speeches in Haldimand, whereas he had hoped to be free to work against Hincks and his supporters in other constituencies. Mackenzie took a confident tone throughout. In the middle of the wheat harvest, it was McKinnon who was putting the county to the trouble and expense of a poll for which Mackenzie claimed there was no excuse, since *he* was sure to be re-elected.[79] The result, however, was what William Holmes had predicted: Mackenzie was elected by a greatly reduced majority of only 54 votes. He secured 54% of the total votes cast, whereas at the general election of 1851 he had secured 62% and a majority of 228.[80] In Haldimand county 130 fewer votes were cast than in the preceding election. Mackenzie complained that Hincks had unfairly called the election in the middle of the wheat harvest. One wonders how many of the farmers who stayed at home were men who would not vote for McKinnon but who would not this time exert themselves to vote for Mackenzie either.

Mackenzie attributed his narrow victory to his absence from the county, helping Hincks's opponent in Oxford.[81] He asserted that money had been expended liberally to defeat him, and he even accused Lord Elgin of "compelling" the Indian agent, David Thorburn, to electioneer against him. No doubt both Tories and Hincksites made a determined effort to keep Mackenzie out, but the fact is that he had lost ground in Haldimand and the *Message* was doing him as much harm as good.

Although Mackenzie's critics both within and without the government declared he had no influence with any political party,[82] his help was sought by progressive Reformers in other constituencies as eagerly in 1854 as in 1851. He gave much space in his *Message* to their platforms, and between Reformers of various shades made his preferences clear.[83] In Lambton, George Brown was opposing the ministerial candidate, Malcolm Cameron. Mackenzie had criticized Brown for his rabid anti-Catholicism and for misrepresenting Mackenzie's more moderate stand, but he made it known that he preferred Brown to Cameron, whom he denounced as a corrupt, pretended Reformer.[84]

The candidate Mackenzie was most eager to have defeated was of course Hincks himself. Prominent Clear Grits were confident that this time the corruption issue would defeat Hincks. "We should be able to organize a true blue radical government," McDougall predicted to Charles Clarke, who had by this time also broken with Hincks. A central committee embracing all the liberal press and many old Reformers was formed in Toronto. They were "all of the right stamp except Brown," and he, as an opponent of the government, was taken in "of necessity".[85] McDougall, who had written so disparagingly about Mackenzie when his *Message* first appeared, was now eager for his help not only against Hincks in Oxford and a Conservative candidate in North Wellington, but for himself. McDougall was contesting North Waterloo against the ministerial candidate, M.H. Foley. He sent Mackenzie several appeals for help, the final one saying, "If you come to Berlin Saturday the county will be saved." It wasn't. Foley won the seat by a majority of 90 votes.[86]

Since the last election, in which Hincks had carried Oxford with difficulty, the constituency had been divided. Hincks intended Malcolm Cameron to contest Oxford South for the government. He instructed Thomas S. Shenston, his agent and the Registrar of Brant, to procure a requisition for Cameron.

> Mr. C must be got into Parliament or very bad consequences may come ... my honor is concerned in his being returned for Oxford or for Renfrew and I am now able to say that it will not do to bring him forward for Renfrew. His defeat would be to say the least probable.... That he can easily be returned for Oxford there is no doubt. [87]

Hincks's supporters seem to have been reluctant to accept Cameron. When the election came off it was Hincks himself who ran for Oxford South as well as for Renfrew. He was elected for both constituencies, chose to sit for Renfrew, and intended Cameron to take up the vacancy thus created in Oxford South, but in the end the seat went to Ephraim Cook, with Hincks's support.[88]

In Oxford South Hincks was opposed by a radical Reformer, William Carroll, a friend and a brother-in-law of John Mackintosh,[89] and by D.B. Miller, a Conservative. Mackenzie made several speeches in Oxford, once facing Hincks on the same platform. The Oxford *Sentinel* reported as follows:

> "Glad am I", says Mac. to the great financier, "to meet you on your own ground that I may give you your desserts—an awful thrashing" — and well did he keep his word.

Mackenzie delivered a detailed indictment of Hincks's administration, the high points of which were its management of the revenue, the undue proportion of it given to Lower Canada, the increase of the public debt, the "scandalous" Grand Trunk contract, the government's failure to abolish unsecured bank notes, their proposal to distribute the Clergy Reserves fund to municipal councils instead of using it for education or as part of general revenue, their failure to bring the new Franchise Act into operation, to abolish rectories and to put all religious denominations on a basis of legal equality, their opposition to vote by ballot and to the election of local officials, and the speculation and jobbing by some members of the government. According to the *Sentinel* Hincks appeared very uncomfortable and Mackenzie never to better advantage. At the close of his speech there were "deafening cheers".[90] There may have been cheers, but there weren't votes. Poor Carroll got exactly 23. Hincks got 625, and a majority of 359 over his Conservative opponent.[91]

The *Cayuga Sachem*, a paper decidedly hostile to Mackenzie, gave a different account of his election activities in Oxford. The *Sachem* predicted that Hincks would be elected by a large majority and it reported that Mackenzie had left Oxford "perfectly crestfallen." At Ingersoll he had "amused the people by his jokes and antics" and made them laugh, but did not convince them. At Ottersville and Norwichville he and Carroll had found they would receive little support. Then, according to the *Sachem*, they proposed to the Conservatives that they should work together against Hincks, with either Carroll or Miller agreeing to withdraw in the other's favour.[92] The proposal, if made, obviously was rejected. Carroll had no strength to offer. One wonders how he came to be a candidate in the first place. Did an over-zealous Mackenzie force him upon a reluctant constituency? Mackenzie's correspondence is of no help here since, some years after the election, he returned all Carroll's letters.[93]

A sarcastic correspondent asked Mackenzie to explain why Carroll, a wealthy, respected Reformer who had been a councillor and reeve of Norwich and had the *Globe*, the *Examiner*, the *North American* and the *Message* all supporting him, and Brown and Mackenzie speaking in his favour "against the most vulnerable candidate," had been so crushingly defeated. Mackenzie briefly referred his questioner to Carroll, saying that to him the result was "unaccountable."[94] Elsewhere in the *Message* he intimated that the cause was what it had been in 1851 — the influence of storekeepers and merchants over their debtors.

The explanation is not so simple. Approximately 1,850 fewer votes were cast for all candidates in Oxford South in 1854 than in 1851, an indication that here, as in Haldimand, farmers could not be drawn away from their harvest and/or they were apathetic to Hincks as well as to his opponent, Carroll. But this figure does not tell enough. It is necessary to ask how many more persons were entitled to vote in 1854 than in 1851 and didn't, how many old voters refrained from voting this time, how many of those who did vote were the new voters that Ross had suggested should be "made." Only a comparison of the poll books for the two elections could answer these questions. In any event it is clear that Hincks's victory was by no means a great triumph. He received only 33 more votes than he got in 1851 from the five townships composing the constituency of Oxford South. From three of the townships he received fewer votes than in 1851. His gains came in the township of North Oxford, 47 votes as against 18, and in Norwich, where 45 additional votes were cast, he received 272 votes as against 192 in 1851. The Conservatives, whose candidate had received 195 votes in this township in the previous election, obtained only 79 in 1854.[95] The radical Reformers in Oxford had been much divided in 1851. They did not rally to Carroll in 1854. He received only a smattering of votes in four of the townships and only 16 from his own township, the most populous in the constituency and the one that had formerly elected him reeve and councillor. The *Globe* attributed Hincks's success to the fact that he had not been opposed by an able person. "Properly speaking there was no contest." If the election in Oxford was not a smashing victory for Hincks, it certainly was a smashing defeat for Carroll and for his campaign manager, Mackenzie. Although his own campaign had suffered from his absence and from Hincks's hostility, Mackenzie declared he would have imperilled his own return ten times over rather than omit his efforts to defeat Hincks.[96] Mackenzie had retained his seat, but what he had lost — permanently — in this election was influence in the Reform Party. When Parliament opened, the opposition was prompt to make him feel that he had become insignificant.

# Chapter XVI

# REFORM AND DISILLUSIONMENT

When Parliament met at Quebec on September 5, 78 new members took their seats. The election had strengthened the critics of the Hincks-Morin administration in both parts of the province, and on the right as well as on the left. The question was, could they combine to overthrow the government?

In the Speech from the Throne the great unsettled questions of the day—the Clergy Reserves and the seigneurial tenures — were referred to in the most cautious language. "A final and conclusive adjustment" of the reserves question "in the interest of *religion* and social harmony" was promised, but secularization was not mentioned, although reference was made to the fact that the opinion of the country had been expressed "in no unequivocal terms" at the elections.[1] In his *Reminiscences* Hincks called this phrase "indicating, as plainly as such documents ever do, that a measure for secularizing the Clergy Reserves would be submitted."[2] John Rolph had accepted the wording of the speech, including the use of the word "adjustment." He later explained that he had done so because he believed his colleagues were not only pledged to secularize but willing to.[3] A "determination" on the seigneurial tenures was promised but no reference was made to their abolition and emphasis was placed not on the condition of the censitaires but on the importance of the security of *property* to economic progress.

Before the speech was even debated, the Hincks-Morin administration fell, the Clear Grits and Rouges (the radicals of Lower Canada) having come to the conclusion that Hincks was not to be trusted. When the government tried to prevent the House inquiring into the conduct of a Lower Canada returning officer, six of the Upper Canada ministerialists took this opportunity to vote against it.[4] Among them was Rolph, a member of Hincks's cabinet up to this point. Radical members from Upper Canada charged Hincks with corruption and stated openly that it was on his account alone that they voted against the ministry. Having lost majority support in Upper Canada, Hincks resigned. In announcing his resignation, he stated that he did not propose to evade inquiry into the charges of corruption made against him during the elections; on the contrary he welcomed inquiry. At this point Mackenzie was unwise enough to indulge in an ironical cheer, whereupon Hincks taunted him with his attempts to defeat him in Oxford and with the miserable showing of his candidate Carroll.[5]

With Hincks's blessing, a coalition ministry was then formed by Sir Allan MacNab and A.N. Morin, supported by the Conservatives of Upper and Lower Canada, some of Hincks's followers, and all the Lower Canada supporters of the former administration.[6] It was agreed that the Clergy Reserves Bill that Upper Canada wanted and the Seigneurial Tenures Bill that Lower Canada wanted would be pushed forward together, supported by the government's adherents in both sections of the province. A critic referred to the new ministry as "the maculate conception."[7] Radical Reformers were angered that Lord Elgin sent for MacNab instead of giving some prominent Upper Canada Reformer a chance to form a ministry.[8] It did not seem unreasonable to them to hope that, since the Upper Canada Tories held only 25 seats, the 30 Upper Canada Reformers and the Rouges who had voted against Hincks would be able to attract enough additional support from Hincks's ministerialists in both parts of the province to support a radical government. David Christie reported that the Governor-General was cooly received at the agricultural show in London, and predicted that he would leave Canada "dishonored." He observed:

> We must add another plank to our platform — elected governors. We have had enough of pauper aristocrats from England or High Church Tory governors. [9]

Mackenzie was enraged that any Upper Canada Reformer should support the MacNab-Morin coalition. He accused those who did of "falsifying the pledges of a life time" and declared the composition of the new government almost made him "puke." As for Hincks, he had betrayed the Reformers and by his speculations and corruption had made the name of reform "stink."[10] Rolph, in explaining to the Assembly why he could not support the new coalition, made similar accusations. He was replied to by John Langton, who implied that Rolph had lost the reputation he once had and cast the Flag of Truce incident up to him once more. In rebuttal Rolph rehearsed in detail the events of December 5, 1837, defending himself against the charge of improper conduct while entrusted with the flag.[11] Mackenzie praised Rolph's speech so far as it related to the Clergy Reserves. On the Flag of Truce question he contented himself this time with the observation that he could not have endorsed all the concluding paragraphs of Rolph's statement.[12]

The charges of corruption against Hincks could not be disregarded by the new government. As John A. Macdonald observed, "We were obliged in taking office to wash the dirty linen of our predecessors...."[13] The Committee of Investigation presented a whitewashing report, as Mackenzie had predicted it would.[14] He was called before the Committee, as Hincks had wanted him to be, but he was unable to substantiate from *personal* knowledge any of the charges against Hincks to which he had given publicity in his *Message*.

The MacNab-Morin ministry, which had professed, on taking office, to be ready to carry out the legislative program of its predecessors, allowed six weeks of the session to elapse before it proposed to consider, not the Clergy Reserves and seigneurial tenures, but the seat of government question and the reform of the Legislative Council. The frustrated Clear Grits, including Mackenzie, protested vigorously and successfully at the attempt to put these time-consuming topics first, fearing an adjournment before the two former long-awaited measures could be passed.[15] Even after the bills were introduced, the ministry showed no disposition to dispose of them promptly. What this administration considered of first importance was securing more capital for railways and banks, not the grievances of the voluntaryists or the plight of Lower Canada peasants. Several measures to increase the capital of the chartered banks were brought forward before the Clergy Reserves and Seigneurial Tenures Bills had been disposed of. When Mackenzie attempted to block this move, he was told that the commerce of the country was entitled to "precedence."[16] One member of the Assembly observed, "Surely the Hon. member for Haldimand's interest was not of so prevailing a character generally as to induce gentlemen on the Treasury Bench to postpone any important question on his solicitation?" Here is a clear indication of the damage the election of 1854 had done Mackenzie. He had no parliamentary "tail" to follow him. He had won his own seat by a small margin and the showing of his candidate Carroll seemed to indicate that his influence with the farmers of the western peninsula had become minimal. When Mackenzie persisted in his opposition and raised a point of order, he was overruled by the Speaker who, on appeal, was unanimously supported by the House. When he still persisted in speaking, the impatient members began banging the lids of their desks and MacNab appealed to the Speaker to prevent the Member from Haldimand from impeding the business of the country. Mackenzie tried to shout MacNab down, declared his feelings had been outraged "after suffering so many years of exile" — and broke down in emotion and confusion.[17]

The Clergy Reserve Bill of the MacNab-Morin ministry differed in some respects from that which Francis Hincks had intended to introduce. He had planned a secularization bill to create separate funds for the two parts of the province from sales of their Clergy Reserves. The stipends of those clergy and religious bodies to whom the faith of the Crown was pledged were to be a first charge upon the interest earned by these funds. Any balance was to be divided annually among the municipalities according to population, but if a municipality was in debt to the Consolidated Municipal Loan Fund, its share was to be retained by the Receiver-General.[18] Hincks's scheme, as the *Examiner* pointed out, would not have meant the final secularization of the Clergy Reserves. It meant only the secularization of the funds, and it would not have precluded the reopening of the whole question as long as the reserves were not merged into the mass of Crown lands.[19] The new government's bill provided for the creation of separate Clergy Reserve funds as before. After payment of the stipends to incumbents, who could, however, have them commuted for a capital sum,[20] the balance of the funds, not merely the interest, was to be divided annually among the municipalities as before, or placed to their credit under the Consolidated Municipal Loan Fund. The commutation clause had not been part of Hincks's bill, at least as far as it was made known during the election campaign.

These provisions were no more satisfactory to Clear Grits and voluntaryists than Hincks's intended bill had been. Mackenzie supported George Brown's attempts to require that the existing funds and the unsold lands be transferred to the Crown at a valuation and that, after a sufficient sum had been set aside to provide for the annual stipends to incumbents, the balance of the Clergy Reserve monies should be distributed "forthwith" to the municipalities according to population. This proposal would have destroyed any possibility of tampering with the settlement at a future date. Mackenzie also supported a motion to delete the commutation provisions of the bill. This clause was most distasteful to Clear Grits and voluntaryists since, if the commutation money should come to be controlled by the denominations and invested by them in land, the end result would be that, despite the long struggle of the Reformers, ecclesiastical endowments would be indirectly created out of the reserves.

W.H. Merritt's motion that the municipalities be required to use their money for common schools and for district libraries was defeated. Since Mackenzie had always preferred that the reserves be used for education, it is surprising to find that his vote is not recorded in favour of Merritt's motion. He complained in the *Message* that he *had* voted for it but that Solicitor-General Smith had moved to expunge his vote because he "was for a minute outside the bar." (He had returned from the gallery while the Speaker was putting the question.) Mackenzie "entreated" Smith to allow his vote on this question, which was so dear to him, to stand, especially as it would not affect the result. His pleas were in vain. He was laughed at.[21]

William McDougall advised Reformers to amend the government's bill if they could so as to have the unsold lands converted into school lands and the existing funds appropriated to schools also. Above all they should see to it that the conditions of commutation were clearly established, and that the commutation money could not be invested in land by those whom Lesslie called "our clerical banditti."[22] But MacDougall confidentially advised Mackenzie that the Reformers ought not to oppose the bill even if they could not succeed in amending it. They ought not to let "that rascally coalition" have the credit for passing a secularization measure, something that Reformers had fought for and Tories opposed for years.

> The people [he warned] have been bamboozled so long, and by Reformers too, that they are ready to take anything that can be called secularization and from any party that will give it to them.... The people are wearied out and disgusted with the very name 'Reserves' and will take a sham settlement rather than none.[23]

Despite McDougall's warning, the commutation clause slipped through not adequately safeguarded. Originally the clause had read that commutation would be made at the discretion of the Governor-General and "by agreement with the church bodies." When this wording was changed to satisfy protesting voluntaryists it read, "with the consent of the parties and bodies interested," and it was also provided that the commutation money might not be invested in land. With these changes the bill had passed. Mackenzie is reported to have said he would sustain the government "through thick and thin" until the secularization bill was passed, but if he did say it, he voted against the bill in the end and so did George Brown.[24]

The MacNab-Morin ministry assured voluntaryists that the words "and bodies" were merely intended to cover Roman Catholics and the Wesleyans, to which denominations lump sums, not individual allowances, were being paid. Subsequently the government interpreted the words to mean that the consent of other denominations was necessary to commutation agreements being made with their clergy. This interpretation enabled the Church of England and the Church of Scotland to get their clergy to consent to their commutation money becoming part of a common fund which the denomination would invest and administer. Dozens of printed petitions, which Mackenzie helped to circulate, were presented protesting this interpretation of the commutation clause. The rage of the voluntaryists at the "trickery" of the government, and of the Governor-General as a consenting party to it, was unbounded.[25] Column after column of the *Globe* and the *Examiner* were filled with discussion of the topic.

Abolition of the seigneurial tenures had been one of the points in Robert Nelson's Declaration of the Republic of Lower Canada that had displeased Papineau, owner of the seigneury Petite-Nation.[26] By 1838 censitaires holdings, partitioned and repartitioned among heirs, had become too small, their grain fields worn out and infested with rust and the midge, their harvests progressively poorer while the demands of the seigneurs, often not justified by ancient custom, had become more insupportable. Moreover, they were not willing to grant unoccupied lands in their seigneuries on the old terms. By 1837 abolition of the tenure was being demanded by some who spoke for the cultivators of the soil and by merchants and industrialists who found the restrictions on the sale of property and on the use of water rights an obstacle to their projects. Several laws already existed under which both seigneurs and censitaires could commute their tenures, but it seemed unlikely that these laws and others subsequently enacted would soon bring about the extinction of the system. The habitant was rarely in a position to pay the lump sum required to compensate his seigneur and the validity of the seigneurs' claims was often in dispute.[27]

In 1851 the Assembly had appointed a committee to draft a plan under which the seigneurs' legal rights would be defined and a scheme devised to enable the censitaire to commute his tenure. Mackenzie realized that the seigneurial system had been an important factor in the rebellion and he had recently been informed that it might drive the people into rebellion again, since its burdens were "progressing daily."[28] His acquaintance with the anti-rent disturbances in New York State would cause him to take this grievance seriously. He therefore cheerfully voted for the committee's proposal "to do justice to the deeply wronged cultivators of Lower Canada."[29] The bill reported by the committee did not provide for the abolition of the tenures. Lafontaine objected to the declaratory features of this bill, which merely set the maximum rents seigneurs could demand according to pre-conquest customs. He wanted one that made commutation obligatory and provided for compensation to the seigneurs. Unable to bring the Lower Canada members around to his point of view, he flew into a rage and announced his retirement from politics. The bill was withdrawn.[30]

In 1852 L.T. Drummond, Attorney-General East in the Hincks-Morin administration, introduced a bill the main purpose of which was not to force a commutation of tenures, in which, it was argued, the habitants were not much interested, but to bring about a reduction of those rents which were alleged to be excessive and illegal.[31] In future, seigneurs were to be required to concede land in farms of not less than 40 or more than 120 arpents, and the size of the domain they could keep for themselves was to be limited. Such future concessions were to be made *en franc aleu roturier* and the only charge upon them was to be a fixed annual rent of 2d an arpent. The annual rent to be demanded on land already conceded, whether hitherto expressed in money, kind or services, was not in future to exceed in value 1d an arpent and could be redeemed by the censitaire at his option for this amount capitalized at 6%. The seigneurs were to be compensated by the government for any difference between this sum and the value of existing rents so far as the courts should find them legal.[32]

When it came to voting on the bill as a whole, Mackenzie was in a quandary. He was sympathetic to the peasant population of Lower Canada but he disliked placing an unspecified burden on the Consolidated Revenue Fund as the compensatory provisions of the bill would do. He believed that the change of tenure would benefit them — and the province as a whole — but he was convinced that the seigneurs would receive more than their due from courts composed chiefly of seigneurs.[33] Many seigneuries were no longer held by the original grantees or their heirs. They had been purchased by men who treated their properties like ordinary business investments and sought to maximize the income from them.[34]

Up to the very eve of the third reading Mackenzie could not decide which course to take. In the end his was one of the twenty negative votes cast against Drummond's bill. It passed the Assembly but was promptly rejected by the Council.

The Seigneurial Tenures Bill of the session of 1854-55 was substantially the same bill, a measure to define and limit seigneurial rights, to facilitate but not to require their redemption, and to abolish the *lods et ventes*. To the extent that existing rents were found legal by a special court to be established for this purpose, the seigneurs were to be compensated by the province for the difference between those rents and the maximum to be established for the future, this time 1d an arpent. These annual rents and the seigneurs' right to *lods et ventes* (one-twelfth of the purchase money when the censitaire sold his holding), could be redeemed by the censitaires at their option and at their expense.[36] Certain other casual rights such as the seigneur's right to require the use of his mill and to control the use of water power on his seigneury were to be abolished.[37] Compensation to the seigneur for any reduction in annual rents was to become a charge upon the Consolidated Revenue Fund. If the payments taken from the fund should exceed the amount paid into it from certain Lower Canada sources of revenue named, Upper Canada should be compensated by a sum equal to the excess. The seigneur was to be allowed a domain of a certain size as his private property. The remainder of his unconceded land was to be vested in the Crown. Rights which he had in his unconceded land were to be valued and he was to receive such a proportion of that sum as would compensate him for the loss of his rights in the whole. For any holdings to be conceded in future seigneurs could demand only a fixed rent redeemable by the tenant at his option.

Upper Canada Clear Grits were opposed to burdening the Consolidated Revenue Fund with payments to the seigneurs, especially as it was not proposed to sweep the whole system away. Mackenzie believed they would receive enormous sums to which they were not legally entitled. Since the burden was to be placed upon the Consolidated Revenue Fund, it would be borne chiefly by Upper Canada, which was providing the major portion of that revenue and was seeing it granted away liberally to Lower Canada for local services and for the support of institutions which the upper part of the province provided for itself.[38]

> I will not [Mackenzie wrote] keep the detestable tenure with which the Canada Co. curse their unfortunate tenants without improvement while Upper Canada may have to pay two million of dollars to better the lot easier tenure of Lower Canadians who, or whose ancestors, never paid a shilling for their farms —to pay the vast treasure, too, to "Lords of the Manor", who have been pillaging their peasants ever since... 1760 in spite of previous law and usage.... We had better get rid of Lower Canada altogether. She is a drag on us. [39]

Mackenzie moved two amendments, that the compensation to seigneurs should not be paid by the province but by the parties benefitted, and that it was "improper, unprecedented and dangerous to pledge the Consolidated Fund and thereby increase the provincial debt to an unknown and unlimited amount." These motions were made in the very words John A. Macdonald had used with respect to Drummond's bill of the previous year, as Mackenzie took care to point out, but Macdonald, who was now Attorney-General for Upper Canada in the coalition government, had reversed his stand.[40] Both amendments were rejected.[41]

When the bill came up for a third reading Mackenzie moved the six months hoist and that a committee be appointed to take steps towards the dissolution of the union for various reasons given, one of which was that "this far away French government" was "drowning" Upper Canada in debt. There is no record of this motion in the Journals. The *Message* tells us that he was interrupted "by loud and derisive cries." The Speaker was asked not to allow such a motion to be put. Mackenzie withdrew it. "I will bring it up again," he promised the readers of the *Message,* and he advised them in the meantime to get up township, county and ward societies for the repeal of the union.[42]

This tenure bill passed the Assembly by a vote of 71 to 32, all the Clear Grits and some of the Rouges voting against it.[43] It came back from the upper house with its provisions radically altered — one might almost say reversed. The changes were accepted by the Assembly.[44] Seigneurial tenures were abolished outright, and commutation was no longer to be voluntary. In future seigneurs and censitaires were to hold *en franc aleu roturier*. No maximum legal rent of a penny or two an arpent was set by this law. *Rentes constituées* were to be established for the annual *cens et rentes* and also for the casual seigneurial rights to which the censitaires' holdings had been subject. No assistance was to be provided by the province to redeem the annual rents except to the extent that they exceeded 1d an arpent, and then only if the indemnity fund should prove sufficient after certain other charges upon it had been met. The provincial appropriation, in addition to the Lower Canada sources of revenue specified for this purpose, was to be limited to £150,000. These funds together were to prove insufficient even for the complete redemption of the *rentes* substituted for the seigneurs' casual rights. They remained an obligation of the censitaires until additional appropriations were made out of the Lower Canada Clergy Reserve Fund and the Consolidate Revenue Fund to relieve them of these burdens.[45]

The effect of the tenures act, as amended by the Council, was to get rid of those seigneurial rights which were a hindrance to the development of industry and to the transfer of real property. No reductions were effected for the benefit of the censitaires, and most of them were to be unable to redeem the *rentes constituées* that replaced the old payments.[46] Even as late as 1940 not all these ancient rentes constituées had been redeemed. The wild lands of the seigneurs became their unrestricted property which they could hold, sell or rent as they pleased. In Mackenzie's opinion the cultivators of the soil were placed "more and more at the mercy of their landlords."[47]

When the Council's amendments came up for a second reading, 30 Lower Canada members, including all the Rouges, voted no, as against 21 Lower Canada members who voted yes. The government's majority was provided by its Upper Canada supporters.[48] It has been said that Mackenzie never really understood French Canada. In this instance, at any rate, he fully understood that the so-called reform which was being given her was not what the majority of the cultivators of the soil wanted at that time, whatever other benefits it might produce, an opinion shared by a substantial block of Lower Canada representatives.

George Brown attributed the drastic changes in the bill to Lord Elgin and Francis Hincks.[49] Mackenzie also accepted the idea that the revised bill had been forced upon the ministry by Elgin, who was reported to have said that he would never sanction the Assembly's version. Drummond's similar bill of 1852 had alarmed the seigneurs. They protested that they would not be adequately compensated for the loss of their rights. One of the most influential of them, Edward Ellice, seigneur of Beauharnois, used a familiar device: he attempted to convince the Colonial Secretary, the Duke of Newcastle, that the question of the tenures had been raised only by "agitators." Newcastle wrote to Elgin pointing out how undesirable it would be for the Canadian legislature to give the impression that it did not have

> rigid respect for the rights of property.... I will not hamper your discretion, [he added] but I am confident you will prevent such a discredit to the Colony as any violation of private rights by an Act of the Legislature.

Elgin did not accept Ellice's limited view of the tenures controversy and intimated that some of the disputed points about the tenures would be decided adversely to the seigneurs in any settlement that could be made.[50] To Francis Hincks, the maintenance of Canada's credit, and therefore the market for her railroad and municipal securities, was a matter of prime concern. He produced a pamphlet advocating the changes in the Assembly's bill and in the application of the government's indemnity already noted. Hincks's *Reminiscences*, in which part of the pamphlet is quoted, substantiates Brown and Mackenzie's charges that Elgin had wanted the Assembly's bill to be modified.[51] The comments of Elgin's guest, the Hon. Amelia Murray, who discussed the pending legislation with L.J. Papineau, show that both he and Elgin were opposed to the Assembly's bill,[52] although for different reasons.

In addition to the bill to give effect to the Reciprocity Treaty, which of course Mackenzie favoured, the other major topics to come up before the Christmas recess were the bank acts, which will be discussed later, and the farewell address to Lord Elgin.

On December 16, when many members had already left, Sir Allan MacNab moved the address. The opponents of the government, led by A.T. Galt, were not prepared to accept an address which referred to the happiness and prosperity of the province under the existing administration or that of Francis Hincks. They proposed to amend the address so as to make it complimentary only to Lord Elgin personally. It passed as originally worded. Only one of the Rouges present voted for it; of the members of the opposition from Upper Canada who were present, only two. One of these was George Brown, either willing to join in doing the formal, polite thing to a departing Governor or, as the *Colonist* put it, cajoled into it by the wily Governor-General himself.[53] Not so Mackenzie! He delivered a slashing attack on Lord Elgin to an increasingly restive and perhaps embarrassed Assembly, since he read newspaper accounts of the insults MacNab had levelled at the Governor-General in 1849. Mackenzie accused Elgin of caring little for the fortunes of Canada, of having encouraged a profligate government, and of being "a willing traveller through all the mazes of corruption" through which his ministers had led him. On this occasion Mackenzie discussed responsible government in terms which have enabled his detractors to say he never really understood it. But, as W.M. Whitelaw has pointed out,[54] at this time the Governor-General was not without influence and power, and Mackenzie seems to have been well aware of that. "His Excellency came here to carry out responsible government which surely means that when he sees one set of councillors pursue a corrupt or unjust course he should change them or check their measures and stop the wrong...."[55] This was what Elgin had failed to do. But there were other occasions, particularly prior to the rebellion, on which Mackenzie's demand for responsible government had clearly meant that the Governor should choose ministers in whom the majority of the people's representatives had confidence, take their advice, whatever it might be, and change those advisors when they lost popular support. When Hincks resigned after losing majority support in Upper Canada, Elgin had betrayed the Reformers because he had not given them the opportunity to see if they could form a government. He had given the nod to Sir Allan MacNab on the advice, Mackenzie believed, of the corrupt Hincks. In an able speech on that occasion John Rolph had criticized Elgin's decision as not in accord with British constitutional practices.[56] Mackenzie could see no excuse for Elgin. He had accepted a Conservative government "not forced on him by an overwhelming majority." For that Reformers would not forgive him. The Montreal *Gazette* called Mackenzie's speech "decidedly one of the best of the session."

"Parliamentary control of the purse strings was by no means an automatic outgrowth of the winning of responsible government," J.E. Hodgetts has observed. "A long painstaking series of reforms had to be undertaken before that control was firmly established."[57] Mackenzie helped to bring about those reforms. He began by insisting that, in conformity with British usage, acts granting supply should show in detail for what services Parliament had voted the public's money. In 1851 he got Hincks to agree.[58] Prior to this time the acts had shown only the lump sum granted, not the items. Second, he objected that the members were not allowed sufficient time to consider the estimates before being called upon to vote on them. For example, in 1852 the estimates for that year were not presented in printed form until the very day the legislature was to adjourn. Third, Mackenzie was determined that the executive should show in detail how the money granted had been spent and should present the public with an intelligible set of accounts.[59] This was to be a long battle, not completely won in his day or by him alone.

Mackenzie asked for a complete statement of the public debt of Canada, the date and purpose of each loan, the rate at which the debentures had been sold, the state of the sinking fund, what the revenues and expenditures of the Post Office were, and which public officials were in default to the province of united Canada or its two predecessors.[60] As one newspaper put it, the Member for Haldimand was "a glutton for information."[61] Mackenzie also wanted "a real audit" of the public accounts. Hincks's finance committee, he complained, was appointed by himself to whitewash his office.[62] The MacNab-Morin ministry appointed Mackenzie to the Committee on Public Accounts. British tradition required a member of the opposition to be chairman[63] and Mackenzie was so named. He plunged into the work with alacrity.

The reports of this committee emphasized the great necessity of protecting the records from fire, pointed out that in the various departments the fiscal years ended at different times and noted that the Receiver-General's office had not balanced its books since 1849 until requested to do so by the Committee. Moreover, the accounts of the offices of the Receiver-General and the Inspector-

General were not being kept according to the same system and therefore did not "assimilate;" warrants did not always show to what account they were chargeable; and Hincks, as Inspector-General, had certified the public accounts for 1853 without examining them. The accounts of the Crown Land Department were not kept posted up to date; in fact, when inspected, were five months in arrears. Expenses incurred in collecting the various revenues were deducted before the receipts were paid over to the Receiver-General. In the process large sums had been "arrested" on their way to the public treasury and expended in various ways of which the people's representatives had no previous knowledge or opportunity to vote upon. The Committee recommended that these practices should cease since, while they continued, no efficient control of the revenue was possible. This reform had been instituted in Great Britain on the strong recommendation of the Parnell Commission on Financial Reform of 1831. Mackenzie had utilized the Parnell report in drawing up the famous Seventh Report on Grievances of 1835, and quoted its words in the second report of the Committee of which he was now chairman.

The Committee discovered also that money had been expended without the authority of Parliament or in excess of the authority given. The most scandalous incident was the expenditure on loading piers on the St. Lawrence below Quebec. £41,500 had been granted and appropriated by Parliament, £119,611 had been spent. The Inspector-General had not checked the accounts of the Crown Land Department nor those of the Post Office since the latter had come under provincial control. Incomes of officers in this department had been increased without the sanction of Parliament; no accounts had ever been rendered, no audit or examination had taken place. The Board of Works had not taken off a trial balance since 1852. The accounts of the land and timber agents were not audited by anyone. Several of them were in arrears and others had made no return at all. Mackenzie summed up this devastating indictment with the words, "It is scarcely possible to imagine a more imperfect financial system than we are describing...."[64] He promptly publicized large sections of the report in his *Message*.[65] As a result of the work of Mackenzie's committee the MacNab-Morin administration came "unanimously... to the conclusion on no account to spend a farthing without the previous sanction of Parliament."[66] But its supporters would not join in a resolution condemning its predecessors for different conduct.[67] Subsequently Mackenzie asserted that when he began to tell what he had discovered about books unbalanced for years and arrears of interest "forgiven by mere clerks," the books were shut against the Committee, he was "deposed" as chairman, and never again appointed to the Committee on Public Accounts.[68]

Mackenzie took care to include in the third report of the Committee one of his standing complaints: that estimates were not presented or appropriations granted until the year in which they were to apply was over or nearly over, and meanwhile the government had gone on taking the public money without authorization. That had been true for 1852 and 1853 and was again true for 1854. When the estimates for 1854 were finally presented, just before the recess, Mackenzie again complained that there was not time to give them adequate consideration. Once more he voted against various pensions and grants to sectarian institutions.[69] Parliament recessed on December 18 without accomplishing a long list of the reforms he was hoping for. He remained in Quebec for another three weeks, hard at work for his committee[70] and too busy to attend to some complaints that were reaching him about the Canada Company and agents of the Crown Land Department, although he did give them publicity in his *Message*.[71]

By 1855 Mackenzie's health had begun to suffer from the burden of activities he had laid upon himself as a member of Parliament, chairman of one of its most important committees and as a poverty-stricken publisher and correspondent for a struggling newspaper. He had been obliged to borrow from his colleagues, his subscribers were not paying up, he had to skip three issues of the *Message* and on February 17, 1855, he was to suspend it, later giving as an explanation the pressure of business at Quebec.[72] At this time he was in a despondent mood once more, hesitating to trust any longer in his own skill as an editor to do much good and perhaps disturbed by the loss of his committee chairmanship. The last issue of his *Message* contained a good deal of ranting criticism of Lord Elgin, accused the British government of sending out governors to thwart the popular will, accused the Assembly of slackness in the cause of human freedom and accused the voters of apathy and of apparently being content with such representatives. With this gloomy observation Mackenzie announced that he was suspending the *Message* at least until the session, which was to resume on February 23, should be over.[73] It ended on May 10 but the *Message* did not reappear until November 17.

Before the *Message* was suspended, James Lesslie and William McDougall, who for some time had been anxious to sell their publications, proposed that the *Message*, the *Examiner*, and the *North American* should be combined and that a company should be formed to get out a strong Reform weekly with Mackenzie as editor. They offered to give him a fixed salary and an interest in the paper proportionate to his subscription list. They also held out the inducement of a power press and the possibility that the new company might issue a daily.[74] Mackenzie declined to undertake the responsibility, just as he had when George Bruce made him a good offer in New York City. It was a wise decision, and probably a fortunate one for his would-be partners. Mackenzie could not have pulled in harness with anyone. James Lesslie, who seems to have been of a most forgiving spirit, then suggested that Mackenzie should write a weekly letter of several columns for the *Examiner* and enquired of him at what he valued his subscription list and the goodwill of the *Message*.[75] Lesslie's offer was accepted in part. After suspending the *Message*, Mackenzie supplied those of his subscribers still entitled to papers with *Examiners* instead and he accepted Lesslie's proposal that he should write a weekly column for his paper. These arrangements continued until the *Examiner* was absorbed by the *Globe* in September. As a correspondent Mackenzie proved to be not very dependable.[76] His continuing poor health during the spring of 1855 was probably the cause.[77]

By the time Parliament resumed Mackenzie was no longer chairman of the Committee on Public Accounts although he was still one of its members. In

October he had suggested to the Assembly that the Committee be instructed to report on the expediency of keeping the public accounts in a decimal currency. Permission had been given, but the Inspector-General, William Cayley, wanted it understood that the government was not committed to act on the report. This was the aspect of the Committee's work in which Mackenzie now engaged.

The question of adopting a decimal currency had been under consideration earlier. On Hincks's initiative an act had been passed requiring the public accounts to be kept in dollars and cents as soon as it should be found "convenient" and authorizing the government to introduce a coinage based on the decimal system.[78] This act, however, had shortly afterwards been repealed. Much information about the history of the decimal currencies of other nations was now compiled by Mackenzie and incorporated into the Committee's third report. In Canada accounts were already being kept in dollars and cents by many private businesses and the Reciprocity Treaty with the United States now made it even more desirable to adopt this system. The Committee recommended that after January 31, 1856, the public accounts should be kept in dollars and cents and that a decimal currency equal in value to that of the United States should be established.[79] No action was taken by the legislature until 1857, when a government bill passed requiring the provincial accounts to be kept in a decimal currency in future and recommending the general adoption of this practice throughout the country.[80]

Mackenzie's "opportune exposé" of the state of the public accounts led John A. Macdonald to suggest the formation of a Board of Audit and the appointment of John Langton as auditor.[81] Mackenzie tried to include in the Public Audit Act[82] several provisions that were not acceptable to his colleagues. He wanted the names of the banks used as public depositories to be published twice yearly. He would have required all educational and charitable institutions, not just those receiving all or part of their support from the government, to give an account of their receipts and expenditures and of the number of children freely maintained and educated by them. (No tax-dodging pseudo-charitable foundation would have escaped his scrutiny had he been a 20th-century legislator.) He proposed that every warrant issued bear the signature of the Inspector-General and the designation of the statute that authorized the expenditure. The rejection of all these proposals and the existence of two serious defects in the bill, one permitting payments to be made without Parliament's authorization but on warrants issued on order-in-council, the other requiring only their net receipts from the Post Office and the Customs Service,[83] may have been the reason Mackenzie voted against the bill in the end as he claims to have done.[84] Even without these provisions the Audit Act was a big step forward. Mackenzie could not have got it through by his own political influence, but the foundation for it had been laid by his persistent enquiries, propaganda and hard work, topped by the labour of colleagues on this "harmonious" Committee on Public Accounts, particularly John Young, a Liberal member from Montreal to whom Mackenzie paid public tribute.[85]

The Lower Canada section of the ministry had made it a condition of their forming the coalition with MacNab that they should obtain an act for separate schools in Upper Canada satisfactory to Roman Catholics. The Taché Act[86] of this session fulfilled this bargain by enabling Roman Catholic householders to elect trustees, set up a separate school and impose rates upon parents who sent their children to it. Those who chose to support separate schools were required to make a declaration to that effect to the clerk of the municipality in order to be exempt from paying local school rates. Their trustees were entitled to receive and dispense their share of the legislative grant for common schools without going through the municipal council of their township or reporting to the local school superintendent. This act did not enlarge the existing separate school privileges of Roman Catholics much, but it put them on a firm legal foundation by making it the *duty* of the municipal authorities to establish a separate school when 12 resident families asked for one. Apart from the principle at stake, the separate school bill angered Upper Canada because it came down from the Council at the tail end of the session when many Upper Canada members had already left Quebec and because it was imposed upon the predominantly Protestant upper province by French Canadian votes.[87] The demand for "rep. by pop." was strengthened by this bill. George Brown led the opposition to it. Mackenzie seems to have had only a small share in the debate. Instead of discussing the principle of the bill, he spent too much of his time showing up the inconsistent attitude of MacNab, who had formerly denounced Roman Catholics and Lower Canada in virulent language.

The Clear Grit platform of 1851 had demanded that the Legislative Council be made elective.[88] Mackenzie had not shown much concern about an elective council on his return to Canada. He had advised Reformers to let it alone "while it did no harm" and not to divert attention from more important topics.[89] By the time he had served one term in the legislature he had concluded that this change should be made. The Council had become an inefficient body whose unpaid members attended irregularly. It was hard to get a quorum; in consequence, the business of Parliament was impeded.[90] E.B. O'Callaghan, still keeping an eye on Canadian politics from Albany, prodded Mackenzie to inquire what the government's intentions were with respect to this reform, which had been one of the outstanding demands of Papineau and his supporters.[91] Morin brought the subject up during the session of 1852-53. In debate, his original proposals, which would have abolished property qualifications for both Council and Assembly, were much altered.[92] The Assembly adopted a series of resolutions as a basis for a bill. The Council was to be elected on the same franchise as the Assembly as Lord Elgin, disagreeing with the Colonial Secretary on this point, had wisely suggested. Previous members of the legislatures of Upper, Lower or united Canada were to be eligible for election and also persons who possessed £1,000 worth of real property, not £2,000 as the Colonial Secretary had proposed.[93] Initially Morin's scheme did not require members of the Legislative Council accepting office to go back to their constituents for re-election. Mackenzie moved an amendment to this effect and, despite the opposition of the two leaders of the government, it passed.[94] While the Assembly was debating reform of the Legislative Council, that body rejected, without debating its provisions, Drummond's Seigneurial Tenures Bill on which the Assembly had laboured.[95] The indignant Assembly then passed an address asking the imperial parliament for power to make the Council elective according to the scheme outlined in its resolutions. Its request was granted.[96]

The Legislative Council Bill introduced by the MacNab-Morin administration proved to be a more conservative measure than the scheme the Assembly had previously agreed on.[97] Mackenzie did succeed in securing the deletion of a provision that would have barred any person who had been found guilty of treason from being eligible for election to the Council.[98] He supported attempts to reduce the terms of both councillors and assemblymen, voted for Brown's amendment that the electoral districts should be arranged on the principle of "rep. by pop." and for his proposal that the Council should be subject to dissolution like the Assembly. Power to alter the property qualifications for members of the Assembly had been included in the enabling act. A.A. Dorion proposed to add to the government's bill a clause repealing the property qualification. He had Mackenzie's support. All these amendments failed. Mackenzie, who had no objection to an elective council, voted for the bill. Brown did not. He contended that a cabinet could not be responsible to two sets of elected representatives and he did not want to modify the constitution of Canada along American lines.[99] The bill would have required all 48 councillors to resign at once and would have set the qualification for the Council at £1,000 in real property, not £2,000.[100] The Council would not accept these provisions. At the next session a modified bill which met the Council's wishes was passed.[101] Mackenzie, who had voted for the Assembly's bill, opposed this one and subsequently he supported efforts to have the Council filled up at once with elected members instead of by degrees.[102]

The Sons of Temperance made a vigorous effort at this session to have a "Maine law" enacted for Canada: that is, a law to restrict the manufacture and sale of intoxicating liquors. In 1852 they had succeeded in putting through a bill merely to prohibit the sale of liquor on the line of public works. Mackenzie had given the Sons of Temperance his support ever since his return to public life. He had corresponded with Neil Dow and Horace Greeley as to the form a temperance law should take and had been advised that the law of Connecticut was the best model to follow.[103] He had brought in several petitions from the Sons of Temperance and at this session had been appointed to the Committee on Temperance. A deceptively large majority, 97 to 5, voted for the bill on its second reading, but there was a long struggle both in committee and after the bill was reported. The final debate began at three o'clock in the afternoon. Half a dozen supporters of the government, led by Hincks, carried on a determined night-long opposition to the bill, introducing vexatious amendments, repeatedly moving that the House adjourn and calling for divisions in the hope of wearying out the supporters of the temperance measure. "Though annoyed with the attack of my old enemy the ague... I stood it better than I thought I would have done." Mackenzie, writing his report for the *Examiner*, made this notation at five o'clock the next morning. The struggle continued. Messengers were sent to the various boarding houses to bring sleepy members to the House. There were more speeches, more motions. "Hope on. Hope ever. Try to do what is right and leave the issue with Him to whom the issues do belong," wrote the weary Member for Haldimand, trying to summon up the last vestiges of his strength. Finally at eight o'clock in the morning he could write triumphantly, "The day is ours. By a vote of 51 to 29 the House concurred in the Bill as it came from the Committee of the Whole."[104]

The triumph of the temperance advocates was short-lived. First they had to vote down a proposal that those who had invested capital in breweries and distilleries should be compensated. Then, when the bill came up for its third reading, it was killed when the Speaker ruled that since the bill related to trade it ought to have originated in a committee of the whole House.[105] No hint of this irregularity had been given during the long seven weeks' struggle. At the next session the advocates of temperance made another effort to get their bill through but nothing was accomplished except debate.[106]

At this session a bill was passed to amend the Civil List Act so as to increase the salaries of the judges and other officials, including those who held cabinet posts.[107] Mackenzie objected that cabinet officers should not vote themselves increases but should make that part of the bill apply only to their successors.[108] He objected also to the salaries of the Governor-General and his secretary being paid by Canada instead of by the imperial government which named them. In fact he objected to the entire permanent civil list because it withdrew about £75,000 a year "for many years to come from the wholesome control of the Legislature," and he proposed that it be repealed.[109] This would have been to renew the very question that had been at issue between Papineau and the government of Lower Canada. No one wanted that scene back on the boards. Mackenzie's opposition to the ministers' increasing their own salaries in this period of inflation did not add to his popularity. In response to a hint from MacNab, the members began drumming, singing and screeching in an effort to drown him out.[110]

Another bill that went against Mackenzie's fundamental convictions was the bill that allowed the government to issue £10,000 worth of debentures to assist the Law Society of Upper Canada to provide additional accommodation for the superior courts of Upper Canada in Osgoode Hall, Toronto. These debentures were to be financed by taxes on proceedings in the Courts of Queen's Bench and Common Pleas. Mackenzie was and always had been hostile to the Law Society, but in this case what he objected to was anything that made justice expensive for the poor man. He quoted John Stuart Mill's words that such taxes were "a tax on redress, a premium on injury."[111]

Then there was the proposal to grant additional aid to the Grand Trunk Railway, whose promoters were finding the costs of construction greatly in excess of their expectations. By 1855 the company's funds were exhausted and the railway was not finished. The government agreed to accelerate the rate at which its aid would be advanced but cut the total amount promised in accordance with the reduced mileage now agreed on. Before the session was over the Grand Trunk was back again, asking for more help. Several hostile motions were introduced either by Mackenzie or with his support. They asked for detailed information about the company's affairs, demanded delay and inquiry and proposed that the votes of those members who were stockholders in the railway be disallowed.[112] In the end £900,000 in additional aid was granted as a loan.[113]

On top of the new loan to the Grand Trunk, the expenses that the Seigneurial Tenures Act would entail, the increase in official salaries, and Mackenzie's discovery from his investigation of the public accounts that the Quebec and Montreal Turnpike Trusts and the borrowers under the Quebec Fire Loan Act had failed to pay either principal or interest on the sums lent them out of the Consolidated Revenue,[114] came the estimates for 1855. This was the last straw. "Of all the abominations in the form of 'supplies asked' which it had been my lot to peruse... nothing ever came up to the demands in the estimates for 1855," he declared.[115] He gave notice that if the Inspector-General moved to go into committee on supply, he would move for repeal of the union.[116] The Supply Bill included requests totalling some £46,200 for various charitable and educational institutions in Lower Canada, most of which were church controlled. These requests were almost twice as much as the £25,000 asked for Upper Canadian institutions, most of which were not under sectarian control.[117] A supply bill for 1854 with similar defects had been passed earlier in this parliament but not until that year was nearly over and until many expenditures for which authorization was then given had already been made without the previous consent of the legislature.[118]

Mackenzie made good his threat to move for repeal of the union.[119] As soon as he got up to speak, MacNab suggested that the House knew enough "to cough down useless debates." Some of the ministerial hacks then started to make such a noise by drumming on their desks that it was almost impossible for Mackenzie to be heard.[120] He argued that the repeal of the union would be in the best interests of both parts of the province, whose people were so different in life, language and habits. United Canada could not be easily governed from a capital placed at its eastern extremity. Above all, the existing arrangement was unfair to Upper Canada, whose population was under-represented in the legislature, contributed the major part of the revenue, received the minor part of the public appropriations and had legislation forced upon it contrary to the wishes of most of its inhabitants. Of the 20 members who voted for Mackenzie's motion 7 were Upper Canada Reformers of various shades; the rest were Lower Canada Rouges or Liberals.[121] Mackenzie was not discouraged by this vote. He believed he had set the ball rolling and that Upper Canada would never allow it to stop until the Act of Union was "blotted from England's statute book."[122] When the Supply Bill reached its final reading he voted no, supported by only two other members.[123]

At the end of May Mackenzie left Quebec, weary with the "rascally government" and depressed by his failure to accomplish anything during the session. His bill to abolish the property qualification for members of the Assembly had been defeated.[124] All his efforts to improve the electoral and parliamentary processes by having nominations and elections on the same day in all constituencies, elections held at fixed and convenient times of the year,[125] evidence in contested elections taken locally and promptly in the county courts,[126] roll calls on divisions taken in alphabetical order,[127] a majority of the elected members required for a quorum[128] — all had failed. His bill to exempt homesteads up to a certain value from seizure and sale for debt had been brushed off as a "U.S. Import,"[129] and he had been unable to secure more and badly needed justices of the peace for his county.[130] In addition he had been laughed at, sneered at and shouted down. But he was not yet ready to give up. He would fight again for the repeal of the union.[131]

# Chapter XVII

# "REP. BY POP." OR REPEAL OF THE UNION?

Shortly after his return home from Quebec, Mackenzie offered his entire printing establishment for sale. He had no need to resume publication of the *Message*. Since February, James Lesslie had reopened the columns of the *Examiner* to him and it was evidently through this medium that he planned to organize his campaign for repeal of the union. In the *Examiner* he published a summary of Upper Canada's complaints: the revenue of the united province, provided chiefly by Upper Canada, was being used to provide Lower Canada with railways, bridges, freehold tenure, roads, wharves, harbours, schools, convents, hospitals, jails, courthouses and payments to her sheriffs and jurors. He quoted the customs statistics for 1854. In the upper province £549,899 had been collected at the inland ports of entry; at Montreal £478,683 had been collected on goods destined chiefly for Upper Canada, and £196,699 at other Lower Canada ports, some of this also on Upper Canada trade. He pointed out that one small port in Upper Canada, Port Stanley, collected more in duties than 33 ports of entry in Lower Canada, and he reminded his readers that £180,000 had been spent on building landing piers below Quebec, where it was unlikely that the government would take in revenue equal to the annual interest on this expenditure. The true remedy for this unjust state of affairs in his opinion was dissolution of the union.

The ministerial papers promptly accused Mackenzie of disloyalty, "roundabout republicanism" and really aiming at annexation. Dissolution, they predicted, would mean that Upper Canada's trade, her railways and her canals would suffer; there would be a depression, discontent and a demand for annexation.[1] Mackenzie easily retorted the annexation charge upon his Tory critics. He characterized the Union as a device for ruling Canada not by representative government but by organized corruption. He reminded his constituents that he had said at the outset that the Union would not work well. He now announced bluntly:

> If there are any among you, be his creed and country what it may, who desire a continuance of French connexion as I have seen it in Quebec, I do not represent his sentiments and never can.[2]

This was a period during which ultramontane influences were on the increase in Lower Canada. The party which Lafontaine had once brought into co-operation with Upper Canada Reformers was becoming less concerned with the larger perspective than with the particular state-church problems of French Canada; it was becoming "decreasingly parliamentarian, increasingly authoritarian."[3]

To organize Upper Canada to demand repeal of the Union, Mackenzie planned to create a central repeal organization which would supply speakers to spark the formation of local associations.[4] Together, they would word a petition to the imperial parliament. Such political tactics had served Mackenzie well during the years 1835-37. One gets the impression that he looked back to those days — the days of his political influence — with nostalgia. He had not adapted himself to working through a more highly organized, centrally directed party structure. The weakness of his plan was that he did not name the members of the central committee to which he referred. The campaign seemed to be a one-man affair, dependent upon him alone for speeches and upon the *Examiner* for publicity.

Suddenly, on August 29, the *Examiner* ceased publication. It had been sold to George Brown, whose solution for Canada's problems was "rep. by pop." Mackenzie complained to his son that Lesslie had given him no hint of his intentions, and thus he was left without the means of putting his views before the public.[5] The *Globe's* policies, Mackenzie observed, were in the majority of instances "the very opposite of mine nor is time likely to bring us closer together."[6]

At this juncture a newspaper position of some kind was offered to Mackenzie through the agency of Daniel Morrison, then on the staff of the *Leader*. He was told he would have an opportunity "to say something editorially to the people" without having the burden of superintending the business affairs of the paper, and he was assured his political independence would not be compromised. Mackenzie's rejection of this offer probably may be explained by the closing sentence of Morrison's letter:

> Your scheme of dis-union — whatever you may think of it now
> — will be a woful [sic] failure. And God knows there's plenty
> of work for you to do without meddling with that. [7]

Mackenzie was not to be discouraged. During September and the first week of October he held a series of meetings in the counties of York, Wentworth, Haldimand and Lincoln, attempting to establish societies for the repeal of the Union and for democratic changes in the constitution. He wrote to James that he was "well received 'tho now and then those poor fools of Orangemen raised a riot."[8] This was a reference to the disturbances at Brampton and Dundas that broke up his meetings.[9] Brampton was an unfortunate choice for a meeting place. George Brown was also carrying on a campaign to plug his remedy for Upper Canada's grievances, "rep. by pop." He had preceded Mackenzie at Brampton. On July 22, addressing a gathering of Reformers and newspapermen, Brown had stressed the economic advantages of keeping Canada united and he expressed his own passionate conviction that she could obtain "rep. by pop." "if she would but elect representatives who would insist upon it." He won over his audience.[10] When Mackenzie arrived in September, he was pelted with rotten eggs.[11] At Dundas there was another fracas. At Galt he seems to have had a better reception. One who was present was amazed at the vigour and rapidity of his speech and gestures and at the torrent of statistics, invective and humour he poured forth.[12]

Mackenzie evidently hoped to have the support of the Rouges of Lower Canada. They had given him more votes on his motion for repeal than the members for Upper Canada, but Thomas Storrow Brown, whom he tried to interest in his plans, had become disillusioned with politics and replied that he did not care whether Canada was "separated into two divisions or chopped up into mincemeat."[13] On the whole, Lower Canada, where Papineau had once found supporters in his efforts to repeal the Union and establish republican institutions, had now accepted the Union. And why not? Under the union were not the French Canadians "the masters of Canada," as one of their own historians has acknowledged, and were they not also its financial beneficiaries, at Upper Canada's expense, as the wrathful Mackenzie realized?

Mackenzie also wrote about dissolution of the Union to Sir William Molesworth, who had become Colonial Secretary in the Aberdeen ministry. Horace Greeley promised to publish the letter in the *New York Tribune*,[14] although his hopes for Canada were not the same as Mackenzie's. Greeley wrote:

> You know that I am an annexationist. The time is coming when those states that persist in deifying slavery will secede from the Union and I am for letting them go peacefully…. Then I would like to form a union with Canada and have a Great Free Republic, the strongest and truest in the world. You and I will not live to see this, for the Reciprocity bill has postponed its advent but it is the right thing and so certain to come about. You see I too believe in Manifest Destiny. [15]

At length Mackenzie decided to resume publishing his *Message* even though it was, as he admitted to his son James, an unprofitable and wearisome burden on his shoulders. He felt that he must persevere, since the *Message* was now the only radical journal left, and with Parliament about to be held in Toronto once again, he could supervise it more easily. His first number told what progress had been made in the campaign for repeal. Some funds had been raised for the publication of propaganda. Nine members of the Assembly, whom he named, were said to be supporting the movement and there was evidently a central anti-union committee in existence in Toronto.[16]

Mackenzie reminded his readers that when first elected he had not "hastily agitated" for repeal but had always been opposed to the Union as, indeed, his *Gazette* and *Volunteer* show. He now urged repeal and the election of conventions in both parts of the province to draw up "home-made" written constitutions that should provide for an elective governor, and elective legislative council and assembly, elective officials at every level of local government, all for short terms, and the imposition of adequate checks on the legislature to prevent the ministers from abusing their powers. Obviously Mackenzie had been much influenced by the 1846 constitutional convention of the State of New York, which provided, theoretically at least, that power would return to the people at frequent intervals, and which prevented their being loaded with debt without their express consent. Other proposed solutions for Canada's political woes did not satisfy Mackenzie. He was not, of course, opposed to "rep. by pop." but he did not believe that the addition of four to six members from Upper Canada would prevent the log-rolling arrangements that had imposed upon Upper Canada laws that the majority of her people did not want and disproportionate financial burdens as well. Legislative union of all the British North American provinces would be no solution either; it would only make matters worse. As for a federal union, what, he inquired, would it do?[17] Mackenzie concluded his denunciation of the Union with these words: "We have only the shadow of a free constitution. We are in pecuniary bondage to the old world." His final complaint was that Canada had no control over her international affairs and might be plunged into war with the United States at any time by British policies.[18] All this came close to a demand not only for dissolution but also for outright independence and a republican constitution as well.

The second session of the fifth parliament did not commence until February 15, 1856. In this interval Mackenzie was able to get his *Message* well under way again and to build its cash subscriptions to the point at which he had good hopes of being able to maintain his paper. Prior to the meeting of Parliament, Morin retired and his place was taken by Etienne Taché. The MacNab-Taché coalition was supported in Upper Canada by Conservatives and by a remnant of the Hincksite Reformers, who were represented in this coalition cabinet by J.C. Spence, Postmaster-General, and by Robert Baldwin's son-in-law, John Ross, Speaker of the Legislative Council. The session was notable chiefly for a prolonged debate on the seat of government question and for the granting of additional aid to the Grand Trunk. Mackenzie was not appointed to the Committee on Accounts again, despite his valiant work during the previous session, but to the Committee on Contingencies, which he disliked and did not attend.[19] His chief concern through out the session was to win support for repeal of the Union.

The debate on the Speech produced criticism chiefly from the Rouges and from George Brown. The former regretted that no mention had been made of a general education measure for Lower Canada and criticized the working of the Seigneurial Tenures Act, which they disliked partly for its terms and partly because it placed so much patronage in the hands of the government;[20] the latter criticized the implementation of the commutation clause of the Clergy Reserves Act.[21] Mackenzie supported their strictures and, on his own part, deplored the government's failure to promise reduced taxation, temperance legislation and a legislative council bill based on the principle of representation according to

257

population.[22] His "rep. by pop." amendment was defeated,17 to 77, all the Lower Canada members present voting in the negative, a vote which, he pointed out, "must convince every candid Upper Canadian that Upper Canada has now no refuge left but to agitate for a repeal of the Union."[23] That, indeed, had been the purpose behind his motion. Mackenzie reminded the House that when the members of the present government were in opposition they had been in favour of "rep. by pop." but had now pledged themselves to the French to oppose it. In this connection he quoted from the Quebec *Gazette* a speech of MacNab's in which the latter had said the effect of the Union would be to make Upper Canadians "the serfs" of the French Canadians and that Upper Canada was coming to feel it would be more to her benefit to be ruled by "a neighbouring and kindred people." MacNab, unable to deny his own words — although he tried — treated Mackenzie to "opprobrious remarks."[24]

Early in the session the Corrigan murder trial shook the coalition and brought the MacNab-Taché government close to defeat. Robert Corrigan was a Protestant whom a group of Lower Canadian Catholics was charged with murdering. They were acquitted by a Catholic jury before a Catholic judge, in the teeth of the evidence, it was claimed. For Mackenzie the Corrigan trial was a clear illustration of his standing argument that the Hincks-Morin government and its successors, the MacNab-Morin and the MacNab-Taché administrations, had sold out the Reformers to priest-dominated Lower Canada and that the Union must be repealed. Mackenzie was tolerant of religious differences; it was ecclesiastical meddling in politics, whether Anglican or Roman Catholic, that he detested. Bishop Charbonnel warned him that the Irish Catholics in Haldimand, newly enfranchised under the Act of 1853, would take their revenge on him for his anti-Catholic sentiments. That did not silence him.[25]

The downfall of the ministry came over the seat of government question. At this session the Assembly decided by a vote of 67 to 56 that Quebec was the most eligible place for the permanent seat of government, all but 9 of the Upper Canada members voting in the negative. When the estimates for 1856 came up, including £50,000 for public buildings at Quebec, two of the government's Lower Canada opponents who preferred Montreal moved as an amendment a vote of no confidence in the ministry on the seat of government question.[26] Luther Holton, Member for Montreal, extended their amendment into a general vote of no confidence. Although the government was able to defeat Holton's amendment 47 to 70, it was left with a minority of six in Upper Canada.

The Upper Canada members of the ministry, except MacNab, used the vote on the seat of government question as an opportunity to assert the double majority principle and to claim they could not retain office as a government based on that principle unless they had the confidence of a majority of the members from Upper Canada. Their main object, however, was to strengthen the cabinet by getting rid of the nominal leadership of the aged and often absent Sir Allan MacNab. Their resignation obliged him to resign also. The Taché-Macdonald cabinet was then formed with the same Upper Canada members as before except that Philip VanKoughnet replaced MacNab. (John Ross had previously resigned over the Corrigan affair and had been replaced by J.C.

Morrison.) The new ministry survived a motion of no confidence debated for five successive days by a vote of 54 to 58 the latter figure including the votes of the eight ministers who had seats in the Assembly.[27] Mackenzie of course would not support them. "I cannot consent to be a prop to such rottenness," he wrote.[28]

Early in the session Mackenzie and Jacob DeWitt moved a resolution that the interests of both Upper and Lower Canada would be promoted by repeal of the Union. Despite a determined effort to shout him down by repeated cries of "Question, Question," Mackenzie delivered a speech setting forth the defects of the constitution under the Act of Union, the financial burdens which the Union had placed on Upper Canada and the futility of demanding "rep. by pop." That proposition, he pointed out, had already been voted down twice during the session, and 10 times since 1848. It was "a farce" to go on, as George Brown did, year after year introducing motions for "rep. by pop." which Lower Canada would never agree to and which would not solve the problems of the Union if she did. The remedy in Mackenzie's opinion was to petition Great Britain to allow Canada to make a constitution for herself which should be submitted to the imperial authorities so that they might see whether there was anything in it contrary to their interests. He failed to get a vote on his motion owing to the uproar created by the Attorney-General for Lower Canada, George Etienne Cartier, who moved adjournment and led the members in singing "Partant pour la Syrie."[29] When the debate was resumed the next day Mackenzie's motion was defeated, only 10 Upper Canada members supporting him.[30] A few days later a majority of the Upper Canada members gave their votes for "rep. by pop."[31] But this Assembly had been elected under the old franchise and in Mackenzie's opinion it no longer represented the country. J.S. Sanborn, an Independent member for Lower Canada, declared:

> No person can deny, no matter what can be said of Hon. Member for Haldimand, that that gentleman expresses the public sentiment of Upper Canada. [32]

After the reorganization of the government, when it was proposed to give a second reading to the resolutions of the Committee of Supply which included £50,000 for public buildings at Quebec, Mackenzie, as he had warned, moved the repeal of the Union. His motion was defeated, 21 to 65. On two subsequent occasions the persistent Mackenzie attempted to take advantage of the debates on supply to discuss the Union, only to be defeated.[33]

\* \* \*

The Speech from the Throne had promised legislation to reform the legal system. The purpose of the Upper Canada County Courts Amendment Act of the session was primarily to simplify and expedite the proceedings of those courts, but one of its clauses left it to the Governor-General-in-Council to determine the salaries of the judges within certain limits and according to the amount of work to be done.[34] The purpose of the Upper Canada Jurors Law

Amendment Act[35] was to increase the fees of the sheriffs and clerks of the peace. Mackenzie opposed these acts as he did all measures that added to court costs, increased the patronage at the disposal of the ministry or left to executive discretion matters which he thought should be regulated by the legislature. There was considerable support for Brown's motion that the salaries of the judges be fixed by law and some support for Mackenzie's proposal that the clerks of the peace be made elective,[36] but when he remarked that the counties should be allowed to elect their judges, on the ground that they would choose for themselves "far better than the centralized corrupt coalition could do it for them," and went on to say that the sheriffs ought also to be elected as in the United States "where the people are protected from such vicious or ignorant rulers as come here to mend their fortunes,"[37] he threw the House into an uproar. Nothing daunted, he added to these insults to the departed Elgin and to his successor the scholarly Sir Edmund Head by inquiring of the Speaker if, in connection with the subject before the House, it would be in order to move to dispense with "our feeble and ill advised executive and move to elect our governors." He declared that in his opinion there was "as good timber in Canada West as in any basswood ever imported." Amid "great uproar" the Speaker rejected his motion.[38]

Ill-advised language such as the above more than offset the good work Mackenzie did in exposing financial irregularities in the administration of the revenue or in pressing for democratic reforms or measures for the relief of the poor man. Nor did he help his campaign for the repeal of the Union. It was now quite clear that, however well-founded his criticisms of the Union might be, and however appealing the idea of dissolution might become to dissatisfied Upper Canadians, *he* was not the man to guide the province through so momentous a change with due regard for all the political, racial and economic interests that would be affected.

By the spring of 1856 the Grand Trunk, which was again in difficulties, appealed to the legislature for permission to issue £2,000,000 worth of bonds that should have preference over those guaranteed by the province. This privilege was granted. The Relief Act of 1856[39] specified how the new capital was to be spent and, by providing for a variety of local interests, garnered support. Mackenzie objected to aid to the subsidiary lines and to receiving the votes of those who were shareholders in the Grand Trunk.[40] The Relief Act finally passed, 52 to 33, with 20 Upper Canada members voting in the affirmative, 23 in the negative.[41] Mackenzie commented in his *Message*:

> It is idle to call it a measure of aid to the Grand Trunk; it is a
> measure of ruin... to give £2,000,000 and demand the construc-
> tion of unnecessary and unprofitable lines is an injury. [42]

Throughout the 1850s Canada financed the rising expenses of her government and her heavy borrowings to assist railways by increasing her tariff. Mackenzie continuously criticized the higher rates imposed on articles of common consumption or necessity. He argued that ultimately it was the farmer who paid for the government's railway policy. In 1856, when the tariff was increased again, by about 25% on the average,[43] Mackenzie backed John Young's efforts to substitute lower rates on items of general consumption[44] and also Brown and Galt's attempts to have consideration of the tariff postponed until the government should have submitted the estimates for the year and have made known what it planned to do for the Grand Trunk and for the North Shore Railway, which had also petitioned for assistance.[45]

Prior to the rebellion Mackenzie had criticized the chartered banks of Upper Canada because he regarded those corporations as privileged monopolies permitted to hold government and private deposits without paying interest upon them and to issue notes that were inadequately secured.[46] While he was in the United States the importance of a stable currency, the proper restrictions to be placed on banks of issue and the question whether public funds should be entrusted to the banks or safeguarded in an independent treasury were the main topics of the day[47] and frequently discussed in his own newspapers. In the legislature of United Canada Mackenzie returned to these subjects. He had long since come to accept banks and paper money as necessary evils but he was not satisfied that the public's interests were adequately safeguarded under Canada's existing laws. In every session he had made a determined effort to improve them and in this session he tried once more.

After 1841 the circulation of the chartered banks was limited to the amount of their paid-up capital and taxed 1%, and stockholders were subject to double liability.[48] In 1850 Hincks introduced a measure to satisfy the increasing demand for banking facilities in small localities and to widen the market for government securities. His Free Banking Act, like the New York act, was a general banking act that permitted non-chartered banks to be organized and to issue notes protected by the deposit of an equal amount of government securities with the Receiver-General.[49] It was also Hincks's policy to induce the chartered banks to increase their note issues. They were allowed to increase their capitalization and also empowered to issue additional notes if secured by gold, silver or any kind of debentures issued by the Receiver-General. On condition that they gradually reduce the circulation of their unsecured notes to three-fourths its average for the years 1849-50, they were to become exempt from the 1% tax.[50] Mackenzie was one of a small minority that opposed Hincks's measure because it left the chartered banks with a privilege, although a reduced privilege, that other banks did not enjoy. For this reason he voted against all the bank acts of the session of 1852-53.[51] He complained that the public was not protected against loss from unsecured notes. Nor was the government secured against loss, since bank notes were receivable for customs dues and for land, a practice which he mistakenly asserted had been terminated in the United States.[52]

Hincks's measures did not induce the chartered banks to increase their note issues as they had been expected to do. In debate during the session of 1854-55 Hincks acknowledged the failure of his policy. The country, whose economic life was being stimulated by the construction of railways and by the Reciprocity Treaty, needed increased banking capital; it was not to be had in Canada, and English capitalists would not supply it except through the large chartered banks which were not required to invest in low-paying government securities to protect all their notes, dollar for dollar. Therefore Hincks supported the bank legislation of the MacNab-Morin administration under which all new banks, and all existing ones permitted to increase their capitalization, could issue notes up to the amount of their paid-up capital, only one-tenth of which they were now required to keep in provincial or municipal debentures.[53]

Mackenzie had got himself insulted when he opposed the introduction of the bank bills in the session of 1854.[54] When bills for the incorporation of more new banks or for increasing the capitalization of old ones came up in 1856, he was the only member who opposed them.[55] The Quebec *Gazette and Chronicle* described his opposition as "groundless and factious." In a letter to the editors Mackenzie outlined his objections to the new system.[56] He distrusted the entire Consolidated Municipal Loan Fund scheme and therefore objected to banks being required to invest in its securities. The new acts did not oblige banks to redeem at their head offices notes issued by their branches, or to take their own notes at par in payment of debts due them. The new stock was not to be open to the general public but confined to the existing shareholders and directors. Unlike the free banks, the chartered banks were not required to make public the names of their shareholders, a proposal which had been called "impertinent" when Mackenzie first advanced it.[57] Nor were the banks required to show in their monthly statements the extent to which their own directors had been permitted to borrow from them. Mackenzie concluded that no additional security was provided for the public by these new bank acts and he drew attention to the fact that not all chartered banks were making the reports required by law.[58]

In a letter to the *New York Tribune* over the signature "Mercator," Mackenzie reiterated his strictures on the Canadian banking system, contrasting it with the New York system. The monthly returns of the Canadian banks were not made on oath. There were no bank commissioners or inspectors to check on them and the notes of chartered banks were not fully secured by government debentures. There was no independent treasury. The Bank of Upper Canada was the public treasury, yet it had become "so involved with politicians that its stock had fallen below par." Mackenzie pointed out that although the legal rate of interest was 6%, and the banks were consequently restricted to that figure, in practice the law was "nullified," since persons connected with the chartered banks did a great deal of business at 1% to 5% per month. "Our banks," he added, "are accused of lending their funds in large sums to their officers on speculation." He closed by publishing the latest statistics which showed that on the average the cash on hand of the banks was 5% of their liabilities and that 76% of their assets consisted of discounted paper.[59]

Mackenzie's constant criticism of the banks and the bank laws of Canada caused him to be mocked and ridiculed as one who just did not understand banking. He explained patiently what he had explained many times before, that he recognized the convenience of banks and bank notes. What he wanted was that these institutions should be made *safe* for depositors, that their paper be adequately secured and their capital and deposits lent to those who would "creatively and usefully use borrowed funds — not to mere speculators in land."[60] The chartered banks of Canada weathered the financial crisis of 1857 when it came, but two of those chartered banks were to fail in 1859 "under scandalous circumstances."[61]

Throughout his war on the banks Mackenzie was suspicious and inquisitive about the relations between the chartered banks and the government, and he was particularly hostile towards the Bank of Upper Canada. He believed that it was this bank that had brought about his initial expulsion from the Assembly of Upper Canada when he had opposed allowing it increased capitalization under its existing charter and had demanded that the bank supply the Assembly with a full statement of its affairs. In the session of 1852-53 he had asked for a detailed statement showing how much cash the government had to its credit, where it was deposited and at what rate of interest. He summarized the returns in the *Examiner*, pointing out that Canada had $2,000,000 on deposit in banks that were only paying her 3.5%, and $700,000 on which no interest was being paid.[62] Meanwhile those banks were lending to individuals at 6% and Canada herself was paying 6% on her debt of $6,250,000. Mackenzie was not the only one to regard this state of affairs as inadvisable. John Langton made a similar critical comment.[63]

Other banks that did more of the business of the country complained of the favouritism shown to the Bank of Upper Canada.[64] In the session of 1852-53, Mackenzie had advocated that the bank's monopoly of the government's deposits be ended.[65] At the next session a committee was appointed to inquire into the effects of the system upon the commercial interests of the province.[66] All it did was collect contradictory opinions from the rival banks and present them without conclusions or recommendations.[67] Mackenzie, however, bluntly raised the question whether the Bank of Upper Canada was safe.[68] It was his contention that the bank was using the government's deposits to make loans to "pets of the Executive and their partners" to enable them to speculate in land and railroad securities.[69] Since these assets would not be readily realizable, he feared that bank might find itself unable to meet the government's demands upon it and to take up its notes.

During the session of 1856 Mackenzie tried to get a legislative inquiry into the bank's affairs and he voted against a bill which in his opinion gave that institution "new and more dangerous powers".[70] Finally Mackenzie printed an open letter to Sir Edmund Head calling upon him to do his duty in protecting the people.[71] A similar open letter, this time to the Colonial Secretary, Henry LaBouchere, pointed out that nearly all the collectors of public revenue were ordered to deposit in the Bank of Upper Canada and that payments on government accounts were made in its notes. "If it were to fail with three or four million of its notes in the hands of our farmers... would you, Sir, have done your duty," he inquired.[72] The government's account was not to be withdrawn from the Bank of Upper Canada until 1 January 1864. The bank lived on sufferance for two years more. On September 1, 1866, it closed its doors. The government lost about a million, shareholders lost all their capital, $3,170,100, and depositors and note holders, whose claims stood at $1,117,826 when the bank closed its doors, lost heavily.[73]

The touchy question of education came before the Assembly at this session. George Brown led off with a proposal to abolish the separate school provision of the Upper Canada Common Schools Act. His motion did not come to a vote for some weeks and was then defeated. Meanwhile the debate had broadened out into a proposal to establish a uniform system of education for both sections of the province under which a common school education, not secular but non-sectarian, would be provided at provincial expense for every child. This was a reform long dear to Mackenzie's heart and he was one of the small group of members who supported it.[74] Mackenzie had always advocated placing the emphasis on common schools and had voted for a bill to increase the appropriation for common schools in Lower Canada.[75] But while he was ready enough to grant funds for education, he would aid only public schools.[76] Partly for this reason and partly because he thought it more essential to establish a good system of elementary education, he voted against what he called the government's "wicked measure"[77] appropriating the income from the Jesuits' estates and the so-called "unexpended balances" of the Lower Canada common school fund for the support of superior schools and for the establishment of normal schools in Lower Canada. John Langton, who had discovered that there were no unexpended balances for common schools in Lower Canada, wrote:

> The real object of the bill is to starve the common schools to build up the higher class of educational institutions which are under the control of the priests. Cartier, the Minister who introduced the bill... did not deny his knowledge of the truth to me and scarcely denied its object.... [78]

J.B.E. Dorion tried to have the Jesuit Estates appropriated for the support of common schools and Mackenzie, who regarded this property, which had long ago escheated to the Crown, as public property, supported him.[79]

When Mackenzie was first elected he was urged to secure the election of justices of the peace. A St. Catharine's correspondent observed:

> Executive patronage. This is a subject fraught with more evil and is more capable of destroying the liberties of the inhabitants than I think the people are generally aware of. [80]

Mackenzie heartily agreed. Haldimand had an inadequate number of magistrates — Cayuga, the county town, had none at all. The justices were usually named on the recommendation of the sitting member, but Hincks had ignored Mackenzie's recommendations, and when MacNab proposed to divide the patronage with him Mackenzie declined his offer.[81] He continued to complain and his county to suffer from the inconvenience.[82] At this session his recommendations for badly needed justices for Haldimand were, again, ignored.

All I could learn was that if I would not sell my independence,

Haldimand would have no new commissioners until they voted a more subservient person. [83]

All in all, the session of 1856 did not give him much satisfaction, whether on lands, railways, tariffs, schools or the union itself.

By the time Parliament adjourned on July 1 the Taché-Macdonald administration was weaker and there was a growing expectation that a general election would be called. Mackenzie, who had planned a visit to England and Scotland, concluded that he would have to remain at hand to canvass his constituency, where his opponents were already planning to run a resident "fully acquainted with the wants of the county."[84] Until Parliament met again in February 1857 he utilized his *Message* to continue his campaign for repeal of the union and to discuss the monetary theories of Isaac Buchanan.

\* \* \*

When Mackenzie revived his *Message* in December 1855 he had promised the publication of a *Repealers' Almanac* for 1856. It finally appeared in late April, probably delayed by the lack of advance orders to help finance it. The *Almanac* set forth Mackenzie's long-standing objections to the Union. It was not a true union but an inefficient and expensive arrangement under which the province had no fixed seat of government, maintained a double set of officials and records, had in effect a double executive, two separately organized judicial systems and two distinct educational systems. The increased wealth of Upper Canada was not due to the union, nor was it true that Lower Canada had paid Upper Canada's debts at the Union. The debts of both provinces had been charged to the Consolidated Revenue Fund, which meant that the old debts were being paid out of the customs revenue, three-fourths of which was provided by Upper Canada. On the contrary, it was the lower province that was a drain on the upper. To the argument that without the Union Upper Canada would be unable to export, that the French would hold the keys to the St. Lawrence, Mackenzie replied that Upper Canada had access to markets through her canals and lakes and American canals and railroads. She had no need to waste money on Lower Canada. Nor would dissolution of the Union deprive Upper Canada of revenue. The tremendous increase in customs revenue collected at her lake ports was proof enough of that. Finally Mackenzie asked "Who wants the Union?" Even George Brown's *Globe* had admitted:

> It is useless to deny that the proposal to dissolve the Union is very popular. We verily believe that if the point was submitted to the people of Upper Canada to-day, a majority would decide in favor of a dissolution. [85]

Mackenzie's pamphlet contained a mass of material, closely printed in 92 numbered columns, two to a page. It was forceful, but there was little in it that was fresh. The *Repealers' Almanac* sold for six cents a copy. It was a financial failure and one that its publisher acknowledged he could not afford to repeat.[86] The fact was that his almanacs and voters' guides had had their day. Canada West was now being served by many weekly newspapers and by some dailies. They received their news by telegraph, were being widely distributed by railways and were now free of postage. There was no need for the politically minded to wait for Mackenzie to make his painstaking compilations. Besides, public attention was being diverted from his gloomy jeremiads by George Brown, who was rapidly becoming the voice of western liberalism. Brown was predicting a rosy future for Canada West and particularly for Toronto when the Hudson's Bay territory should be turned over to Canada, when the virgin soil of the west should be opened up to enterprising farmers' sons, and when the new railway to Collingwood (the Ontario, Simcoe and Huron, later known as the Northern) and the North West Steamboat Company should pour the products of the west through Toronto.[87]

Mackenzie, on the other hand, was trying to warn the province of an impending financial crisis and depression. During the latter half of 1856 not only were the merchants coming under pressure, but the farmers, Mackenzie feared, would soon be also. They had been enjoying good prices during the Crimean War, but peace, which had been signed in March, was sure to cause a fall in the price of wheat. Then farmers would find it hard to pay 6% on their debts, let alone the 7% to which some persons wished to raise the legal rate of interest. "If we press the people too heavily, we imperil the whole fabric of society," Mackenzie observed.[88] On December 11 he noted that in a recent *Gazette* 22 columns of bankrupt notices had appeared for Upper Canada alone.[89]

Isaac Buchanan,[90] a wealthy merchant and a railroad promoter, was also predicting a commercial crisis and depression. What Buchanan wanted was to keep the country on an expansive course. He argued that, since the domestic commerce of the country was 20 times its foreign commerce, it should be the object of Canada's monetary policies to facilitate this domestic trade. Yet "the tie" between money and gold placed Canada's domestic economy at the mercy of fluctuations in its export trade. A decrease in exports relative to imports led to a withdrawal of specie from the banks, which then reduced their loans and discounts. The result of the shortage of specie was a shortage of "money" and consequently a fall in prices and restrictions on credit, which led to high interest rates. Together, they brought about unemployment and a depression.[91]

Buchanan's two remedies were a protective tariff for the budding industries of the province and the replacement of bank notes by government inconvertible paper — greenbacks. In short, expansion of the currency, not contraction. By some twist of logic he managed to believe that while the withdrawal of specie and bank credit would cause prices to fall, an issue of paper money would not cause inflation, since trade, "like a sponge," would only absorb money to the extent of its "limitations" and that any over-issue would "return" to the government.

Buchanan's favourite phrase was, "The Question of Money is the Question of Labor." He meant by this that the distress of the labouring classes could be remedied by substituting a paper currency with "a fixed value" for the bullion system. He urged the government to abolish the arbitrary and artificial standard of value which had been substituted for the only true one, the labour standard.[92] How this was to be determined — or maintained — he did not make clear. Buchanan seems also to have had some rather fuzzy and inchoate notions similar to those of the Douglas-Orage School of the 1920s.

> We cannot possibly overproduce [he wrote], if the law had not limited our money or instrument of exchanging commodities after we had produced them.

Monetary policy, he argued, should not be viewed merely as a question of the relationship between money and property already in existence but as

> machinery for the production of property and its distribution so as to give the greatest possible advantage to the industrious classes ... as opposed to the large rich annuitants and non-producers. [93]

Mackenzie had for years insisted that it was the government's duty to maintain a stable price level, that control of the currency was an attribute of sovereignty and should not be left to the banks. He had never accepted the idea of an irredeemable paper currency. Yet he agreed to publish Buchanan's notions as a monetary supplement to his *Message* and to see to it that the supplement was widely distributed. He took care, however, to make his own position perfectly clear in advance. He accepted Buchanan's business and money on condition he was to be free "to oppose politically tomorrow the men who may have essentially aided me today if I believe it just and right to do so." And should this prove to be the case, he was not to be accused of "ingratitude."[94]

Mackenzie found space for critical replies to Buchanan, purportedly written by a correspondent in New York City who signed himself "Ledger." The originals of these letters have not been found. Possibly they were written, if not by Mackenzie himself, then by John Windt or another of Mackenzie's old friends in the National Reform Movement. Ledger pointed out that:

> We cannot keep public functionaries honest under the present system ... what chance would we have under paper money.... If [Buchanan] is in earnest in his concern for labor it would be better for him to concern himself with a revision of the land laws.... As a general rule those who own the land will certainly own the people on it.

Ledger thought the most important reform was to limit the quantity of land a man could pass on to his heirs. The excess should be sold by government to the landless and the proceeds distributed among the heirs.

> Two or three generations under a righteous agrarian law of this

267

character... would make labor its own master essentially but while industrious classes can be duped with the bold cheat of paper money there is not much hope for them. A government sanctioning the use of paper money sanctions robbing the community — grinds the poor. [95]

Buchanan evidently took a leaf out of Ledger's book, drew up a land plan the nature of which is not known at this writing and suggested that Mackenzie print several hundred copies for distribution during his planned trip to Scotland. "Land—Land—Land—is the charm for the masses at home as it ought to be." [96] Continued and steady expansion of the economy was what Canada needed — and would be particularly good for men like Buchanan already at the top of the economic tree.

Buchanan's ideas met with a sympathetic response from Reformers in the counties of Huron and Bruce. They inquired whether he would contest the county at the next election in opposition to William Cayley, the Conservative incumbent. Buchanan declined "to attempt to work the present political system" and refused to stand for Huron and Bruce. He observed:

> A Council composed of any dozen gentlemen whom an utter stranger to Canada and its affairs, responsible in all things to London, may choose to invest with power and patronage, will not serve to cement British connexion [sic] with Canadian prosperity.

Buchanan advocated repeal of the Union, a written constitution, elective governors, separation of the executive and legislative power,

> and the People to keep the latter and the Power of the Purse in their own hands.... It seems [he remarked] that in a new country there is not a class of men to be trusted with the working of British Institutions.

He therefore advocated the American system "under which the duty of ministers is to carry out the law, not to make it." The only way to avoid annexation, he concluded, was for Canada to have a written constitution giving her "all the advantages of the state of things in the United States." [97] Later Buchanan was to take a much more conservative position, but his sentiments in 1856 were very similar to Mackenzie's, except that Mackenzie's democratic faith, even though by now somewhat battered, was stronger than Buchanan's and he was no longer convinced that "the state of things in the United States" was in all respects desirable. [98]

Buchanan seems to have regarded himself as Mackenzie's mentor at this time, as he had been the Browns' mentor in their earliest days in Canada. [99] Another detailed suggestion, almost a directive, was soon forthcoming from him. Relations between Great Britain and the United States were deteriorating rapidly. Great Britain had attempted during the Crimean War to recruit men in the United States. The plan was to send them to Nova Scotia, there to be sworn in and equipped. (Governor Head safely avoided involving Canada in these arrangements.)[100] When the activities of the British Minister to Washington, John Crampton, became known, he was required to leave the country and for a time it seemed that the United States might declare war. Buchanan feared that in these threatening circumstances the influence of the Reform Party might decline unless "some of its 1837 friends" set themselves right with the country.[101] He therefore advised Mackenzie to do so at once and enclosed an article which he thought would do the trick. Part of it survives. It was headed "Our Loyalty" and, referring to the Crampton crisis, said:

> Of course we cannot suppose that actual war will be precipitated but, if so, the Americans will find the British provinces united as one man. Such of us as made the mistake prior to 1837 of supposing Canada would be better off as part of the United States have seen the error of that opinion.

The rest of the article as it appeared in the *Message*[102] was Mackenzie's own. He told Buchanan that he could not write of his own loyalty in the way Buchanan had suggested and would have to make some changes.[103] He therefore said:

> Surely that man never breathed who loved his native land [Scotland, not England, be it remembered] with a warmer affection than the writer of these lines,— but does it follow that he should love ancient abuses? ... What good would it do them [the Imperial authorities] to see Canada crushed, embarrassed discontented, when such liberty as the Isaac Buchanan platform asks for might check what is evil and produce inconceivable benefits.... We ask only that British institutions shall not render a Canadian less free than an American republican. [104]

Buchanan was pleased with Mackenzie's course in "keeping off any suspicion of future loyalty" and sent him another letter for insertion in the *Message* signed, inaccurately, "Another Rebel."[105] It praised Mackenzie's sentiments, emphasized that the Reform Party had now cleared its skirts of disaffection and trotted out the well-worn argument of some of the ex-rebels that they had rebelled against the Family Compact, not against the mother country. "We now see that we were wrong in supposing that we could not get rid of them [their grievances] without violence...." To this Buchanan added Mackenzie's own admission that he had been wrong also in "supposing that the Know-Nothings in the United States would extend towards 'old Countrymen' any decent treatment." Mackenzie was reluctant to insert this contribution. He feared that its sentiments would be regarded as his own and that he would be accused of "wheeling round."

Why should I apologize for disaffection [he enquired] when every move that I have made has been for those healing measures which seemed most likely to remove all or many of the causes of disaffection? Why should I deny that I rebelled quite as much against Downing St. as against its pauper minions here? [106]

* * *

Despite a growing demand for a general election made known at a series of public meetings held during the fall and winter of 1856, the Taché-Macdonald ministry decided to meet Parliament again, convinced that the Reformers were too divided to be a serious threat to them. George Brown, meanwhile, was making a determined effort to get them to unite and to join with moderate Upper Canada Conservatives to form an effective Liberal-Progressive opposition party. The question was, would radical Reformers accept Brown who had once been their enemy? During the summer of 1855 some Clear Grits had been won over by his emphasis on the economic necessity of maintaining the Union; others still distrusted him, fearing he would never promote the constitutional changes they wanted — the extension of elective institutions, and the remodelling of the parliamentary system along American lines.[107] Moreover, they doubted his political consistency; one man called him "a Hincks in embryo... seeking to feather his own nest," and pointed out, with prophetic accuracy, that "he could not hold office a month without Lower Canada votes."[108] When Brown's opportunity came, he could not hold office 48 hours.

For Mackenzie the question was could he submit himself to a party led by George Brown. The *Globe*, he complained, had been "silent on principles", except the impractical one of "rep. by pop.," a proposal which Brown himself had opposed in 1850 and had characterized as "ungenerous," "unjust," "useless," and impossible of achievement.[109] Brown seemed to be ready to work not only with "sham Clear Grits" but also with arch-Conservatives opposed to the existing ministry. His attitude portended more coalitions but no radical measures to reform the existing system. "My fear of Brown is," Mackenzie confessed, "that he would want to play Hincks all over again."[110] Brown's legislative record, he felt, ought to deter Clear Grits from joining him. Brown had voted for supply bills that contained sectarian grants; he had voted against giving the people, or the county councils, power to choose their registrars, sheriffs and county judges; he had opposed abolition of the Court of Chancery, the creation of an elective legislative council and measures that would have restricted the government's patronage. He had favoured abolition of usury laws, supported legislation desired by the banks, and, Mackenzie hinted darkly, had had his reward in loans to acquire and develop his property in Zone township.

He wants his share of the patronage [Mackenzie concluded] and rep. by pop. will serve him until he can get his share of the plunder. [111]

On December 15, 1856, George Brown sent out a private circular to prominent Reformers proposing the formation of a united liberal party based on the following principles: "rep. by pop.," no sectarian grants of any description, a uniform system of state-supported secular education for the entire province, restriction on the power of the government to increase the public debt, the establishment of a voters' registry, free trade, incorporation of the Hudson's Bay territories with Canada, uniform legislation for the whole province and gradual assimilation of the legal system and local government institutions of Upper and Lower Canada. Members of the opposition and of the Reform press who found this platform acceptable for a Reform Alliance were invited to sign it. Eighteen members and thirty-five editors accepted it. Over their signatures invitations were then sent to every constituency in Upper Canada asking them to send delegates to a convention at Toronto on January 8, 1857, to discuss this platform.[112] The convention duly met and adopted Brown's proposals for a Reform Alliance with enthusiasm, although there was some dissatisfaction that vote by ballot had not been included and some uneasiness about the proposal to assimilate the institutions of the two parts of the province.

The Reform Alliance proposed to organize itself throughout the upper province by township and county committees and with a central committee at Toronto,[113] just as Mackenzie had hoped to organize his movement for repeal of the Union. But the members of *his* central committee, if indeed it existed, had never been named in the *Message*, nor was any platform yet agreed on for circulation to local organizations. Brown's central committee was composed of well-known Toronto businessmen, politicians and lawyers, eager, as he was, for the acquisition of the Hudson's Bay Company's territory, for the development of the agricultural and timber resources of the western part of Upper Canada, and for the expansion of the trade and commerce of Toronto.

Mackenzie, who had refused to attend any party caucus during the session of 1856,[114] was not invited to attend this one or to sign Brown's preliminary circular. He was invited to attend the conventions but did not go.[115] The fact was that Brown and Mackenzie were at opposite poles, the one advocating "rep. by pop.," a policy politically impossible of achievement, the other, dissolution of the union, a policy economically unattractive to many Upper Canada business interests. Both men regarded the Union as no real union at all. Brown proposed to make it a real union when "rep. by pop." should be achieved. He warned:

> The priest party have used their powers and most assuredly.
> Upper Canada Reformers will use theirs when they obtain the
> majority. These are united provinces and must be ruled on the
> same principles ... if we have one legislature we must have one
> law. [116]

Mackenzie, on the other hand, was disposed to dissolve the impossible Union and let French Canada retain her different institutions in a separate province. He wrote:

> I opposed the intended dismemberment of Lower Canada [by robbing her of Montreal] when the House of Assembly of Upper Canada asked for it; I am opposed now to coercion of a conquered race. [117]

Neither man was yet ready to advocate a third possible solution for Canada's political problems: a union of all the British North American provinces. They agreed in this, that a united French Canadian bloc would still hold the balance of power in such a confederation and that Upper Canada would continue to be "milked" for the benefit of all the poorer provinces.[118] A fourth possible solution —for Upper Canada—was annexation to the United States. But in Mackenzie's opinion exit from the Union by this door ought not to be attempted while entrance into the American federal republic was guarded by southern pro-slavery interests on the one hand and northern Nativists and Know-Nothings on the other. All that was left was an independent, land-locked Upper Canada. This was the solution he was to advocate in the end, with the possibility of annexation at some time in the misty future.

Mackenzie's reaction to the platform of the Reform Alliance was to poke fun at the idea of a country as deeply in debt as Canada adopting a policy of free trade, to characterize its proposals as neither new nor specific and to point out that several of them would readily be assented to by Conservatives.[119] This was superficial and exaggerated criticism. No complete reversal of the fiscal policy of the province was contemplated. The Reform Alliance planned to reduce customs dues as rapidly as was consistent with maintaining the public credit, *pari passu* with strict economy of public money and gradual liquidation of the public debt. It is true that certain proposals such as the introduction of "administrative reforms" and "constitutional restraints" upon the executive were vague, as Mackenzie complained, but if these remedies were not set forth in precise language they were accompanied by a bill of particulars as to the abuses they were intended to end. And many of these grievances to which the Alliance invited attention had been emphasized in Mackenzie's own *Message* for many months. Mackenzie was on firmer ground in criticizing the men who made or who now adhered to this platform. Some of them he regarded as staunch Reformers but the course of others — of Brown himself — had been inconsistent.[120] He was suspicious of Brown's sincerity as a Reformer and was ready to accuse him of being motivated primarily by a desire for office and of being ready to make another of the "calamitous coalitions" based on "evasions" and "degrading compromises" such as Hincks had made.[121]

> Our course is plain.... [he wrote] We repudiate [coalitions] and are ready to appeal to the Imperial Parliament for freedom to create other and better institutions.... Our present opinion is that an appeal there would be quietly successful. [122]

Alexander Mackenzie, George Brown's friend, tried to make Mackenzie see that his attitude would hurt him as well as the Reform Party.

Opposition from Tories is natural... but opposition from you is a very different matter and must result in either depriving you of all influence politically or in killing off a laudable attempt to unite all reformers under a close consistent organization. Are you prepared for either of these alternatives? [123]

A year earlier a similar warning had come from John White, who represented Halton.[124]

Towards the close of 1856 Mackenzie can hardly have been in a happy or confident mood. Like many another irascible, opinionated and harried parent, he had quarrelled with his two adolescent sons. In June 1855 William had been articled to Oliver Mowat for five years. This arrangement had lasted barely a year, if that long. In August 1856, after an argument with his father, the young man took himself off to New York where he obtained work with the Associated Press. He borrowed the money to travel with from Dr. Rolph.[125] George was sent away from home to work for a farmer, after some act of disobedience.[126]

Mackenzie had also reason to worry about his seat in Parliament. He had been receiving warnings that he could not count on re-election for Haldimand.[127] Old friends were becoming apathetic towards politics.[128] One of them observed that Mackenzie had been rowing upstream for 40 years and advised, "Better strike your colours."[129] Then George Brown's campaign for "rep. by pop." and for the formation of a Reform Alliance had been a great success and had won over several Clear Grits, while his own campaign for repeal of the union as a necessary preliminary to other reforms had barely got off the ground. To top it all, the Mackenzie Homestead Appeal, described below, was meeting with an indifferent response. It seemed that Upper Canada, dazzled by the glowing economic prospects to which George Brown was directing her attention with his emphasis on railways and acquisition of the Hudson's Bay territory, was no longer interested in creating the kind of society for which Mackenzie was still struggling manfully, a truly democratic society, of educated men, served by a frugal government and incorruptible representatives, enacting equal laws and developing the resources of the Canadas without adopting policies that promoted great inequalities of wealth or favoured special interests at the expense of the farmer and the labouring man. Was he coming to be regarded as a hopeless visionary — a has-been — to whom Upper Canada had no reason to be grateful, and was the indifferent success of the Mackenzie Homestead Appeal proof of this attitude on the part of the public? Discouraged and wounded in spirit, Mackenzie thought so.

When James Lesslie sold his newspaper to the *Globe* in August 1855, he had suggested in his valedictory editorial that a subscription be started to provide Mackenzie with a homestead in gratitude for his services to Canada.[130] Lesslie did not allow his idea to be forgotten. In March 1856 the project was presented to the general public. A central committee of five was chosen at a public meeting, Lesslie was made its secretary-treasurer and the publication of a pamphlet detailing Mackenzie's services to Canada as the justification for the financial appeal in his behalf was agreed on.

This pamphlet emphasized Mackenzie's constant concern for the poor man as shown by the legislation he had sponsored or tried to improve, reminded the public of his services in exposing governmental extravagances and mismanagement of the revenues and contrasted his incorruptibility with the venality and corruption existing in public life. With respect to the rebellion, the committee wrote that its members were convinced of Mackenzie's sincerity, "if not of his wisdom," in attempting to remove by force those evils which moral and constitutional means had failed to redress. Whatever people might think of the events of 1837 it had to be admitted that the political commotion of that period had produced beneficial results: the Durham Commission and all the constitutional changes which had followed. The pamphlet concluded as follows:

> What are the claims which he [Mackenzie] presents to the gratitude of the people of this province? If by long years of mental and physical labor, by the contribution of every shilling that the most frugal economy could spare, by the sacrifice of every domestic comfort, of every opportunity for wealth, of even the chance of competence, if by submitting to the sneers of the proud, the oppressions of the powerful, the insults and bludgeons of ignorant mobs, and often the peril of life itself, in the cause of freedom, a man can entitle himself to a People's Gratitude, then has Mr. Mackenzie, a claim upon the people of Canada, which it should be no less their duty than their pleasure to acknowledge and redeem. [131]

"I allowed the Homestead scheme to go on," Mackenzie explained, "not as desiring a shilling from the public without value — but because Upper Canada is greatly in my debt...." He was claiming from the government a portion of the expenses of his 1832 trip to England to present Upper Canada's grievances and saw no hope of being paid by united Canada, although Roebuck, the authorized agent of the Assembly of Lower Canada, had received $7,000 by a vote of the Assembly in 1851 for similar services.

Despite favourable notices of the Homestead Appeal in several news papers, six months later only £10 had actually been collected, a sum which Mackenzie chose to regard as the public estimate of his services as a public man. Some persons professed themselves willing to give if he would pledge himself to withdraw from public life and not to interfere "by voice or pen." To Mackenzie this was equivalent to offering him a bribe.[132] Unfortunately the Homestead Appeal had been launched at a bad time, before the farmers had received their returns from their harvest and when agricultural prices were falling. "At any other time in the past ten years, double the amount would have been raised," a friend explained.[133] James Lesslie, while deploring Mackenzie's caustic remarks upon the public's treatment of a devoted public servant and his interference in the matter, acknowledged that the limited response "was calculated to arouse the spirit of a less impulsive person" than Mackenzie. He looked for a better response after harvest.[134] And it came. In December Mackenzie was able to publish a handsome recantation of his charges against "old reform friends" and to name 14 members of Parliament who had contributed to the fund — including George Brown.[135] By February 1857 nearly $8,000 had been pledged, although not yet all collected. On February 26 Mackenzie resumed his parliamentary duties in a happier frame of mind.

## Chapter XVIII

# THE SESSION OF 1857: SQUATTERS' GRIEVANCES AND RAILWAY FINANCES

During the parliamentary session of 1857, February 26 to June 16, the support of the Macdonald-Taché government declined, the financial position of the province grew steadily worse, constitutional problems gave rise to extended but inconclusive debates and the difficult question of the seat of government remained unsettled. After a long debate it was to be decided to refer this last problem to the decision of the Queen,[1] a move which radical members, including Mackenzie, condemned as "at variance" with the principle of self-government. Her choice, Ottawa, was to be made known in January 1858.

At the beginning of the session the Assembly learned that Chief Justice Draper had been selected to go to England to watch over Canada's interests while a committee of the House of Commons considered what should be done about the chartered rights of the Hudson's Bay Company in Rupert's Land. Although Draper had been directed to make it plain that Canada was interested in settling the west and in preventing its falling to the Americans by default,[2] some Reformers objected to his appointment because they regarded his instructions as so vague as to indicate that the ministry had "little genuine interest in the annexation [to Canada] of all or part of Rupert's Land."[3] Others regarded the appointment of the Chief Justice as an impairment of the independence of the judiciary. Mackenzie objected because he detested the man and because he feared that the Hudson's Bay Company would be compensated for the surrender of its chartered rights in Rupert's Land at Canada's expense.[4]

There was not much in the governments program that proved acceptable to Mackenzie. He tried to give its bill for the more speedy trial of juvenile offenders not more than 16 years old the six months hoist. No one joined him in this effort. The bill was intended to avoid the evil of long imprisonment of such persons while they were awaiting trial by jury by giving them the option of a summary trial before two justices. Mackenzie's opposition to this bill, which one would certainly have expected him to support, arose from his fear that young offenders might be railroaded into prison. He wanted to amend it to provide that, where no parent or guardian was present to advise the child, he should have the right of appeal from the magistrates' sentence.[5] Mackenzie failed to vote on the bill for the provision of reformatories for young offenders and on one for the better management of prisons, jails and asylums, humane measures one would have expected him to support, except that they did not make mandatory government inspection of private institutions that should receive any public funds.[6] He voted alone against the government's bill for the gradual civilization of the Indian tribes not, however, because it permitted individuals to receive a 50-acre inalienable allotment and a cash payment in lieu of their share in the annuities and land reserved for their tribe — provisions of doubtful wisdom for the Indians — but because he believed the bill would injure settlers in the counties of Haldimand and Brant who were eager to have Indian land brought on the market,[7] many of them tenants on Indian land.[8] In Haldimand alone there were over 500 such persons. The government's civil service bill, which provided for deputy ministers as non-political heads for each department, salary increases at certain levels and a board of civil service examiners, did not receive his support, perhaps because of its weakness, although civil service reform was a topic on which he had sought information from James Stephens two years earlier when the Imperial Civil Service Reform Bill of 1855 was enacted.[9] In short, Mackenzie objected to every measure that increased the expenses of government or the patronage at the disposal of the ministry, no matter how desirable it might be in other respects.

Mackenzie frequently referred to the kind of responsible government Canada acquired after the Act of Union as a "sham," and quoted Papineau's remark that "servile and politically stupid Upper Canada had fallen into the trap of responsible government."[10] Until 1848 the practice was for the Governor-General to secure support for the ministers of his choice and for his policies by winning over members of the legislature with patronage appointments. After his return to Canada, Mackenzie came to the conclusion that Lord Elgin's ministers, although they yielded from time to time to his advice or pressure, used the patronage dispensed through him in the same way to maintain *their* majorities. A government so managed was not, in his opinion, a government responsible to the people. No political reform for which he agitated was therefore more important to him than one that would secure the independence of Parliament. He tried repeatedly to secure an act that would close all loopholes. The Independence of Parliament Bill passed in the session of 1853 was a more limited measure than two that private members had introduced.[11] It simply made ineligible for the Assembly in future all persons who held offices of emolument under the Crown, except ministers who held certain portfolios named, and it provided that a sitting member who accepted such an office thereby vacated his seat. Mackenzie approved of part of this bill, but voted against it because his proposal to exclude the solicitors-general from the legislature had been defeated. He objected to the law officers of the Crown having their time taken up by politics and having half their duties done for them by "members bribed with circuits."[12]

Although the Independence of Parliament Act was somewhat strengthened at the next session, its inadequacies soon became apparent. In 1855, 1856 and

1857 Mackenzie moved for returns of all appointments to offices of profit during the preceding 12 months and overcame the opposition of the printing committee to having them printed.[13] Rouge and Clear Grit critics of the government felt that members of the legislature who accepted contracts from the Crown or appointments on a per diem basis, such as commissionerships to revise the statutes or to carry out the Seigneurial Tenures Act, would not be Independent members. They were also opposed to the salaried posts of president and solicitor-general of the Grand Trunk being held by men who were members of the Executive Council, which framed the government's policy on aid to that railway.[14] In the session of 1857 two bills for securing the independence of the legislature were introduced, one by an Upper Canada Reformer, one by a Lower Canada Rouge.[15] Their bills were withdrawn when the government decided to introduce a bill of its own. This measure, evidently a much weaker one, was made stronger by amendments added during debate. Several attempts were made to exclude public contractors and directors of and shareholders in works receiving government assistance. These all failed. J.B.E. Dorion's milder proposal merely to deprive members of the Assembly who were shareholders in, contractors with or employees of such companies of the right to vote on questions in which they had a personal interest also failed.[16] These proposals went to the heart of the matter in this period of railway construction and were in line with Mackenzie's earlier attempts to deal with the problem of conflict of interests. As enacted, the government's measure made ineligible for either House those persons holding, directly or indirectly, any contract with the Crown or with any public officer or department.[17] This act also disqualified judges from sitting in the legislature and excluded a long list of office-holders from voting at elections.

Despite the failure of vital amendments Mackenzie voted for the government's bill which overcame some of the current practices to which he objected. But he was not satisfied and tried to obtain a second reading for a bill of his own, introduced earlier. This measure would have equated the employment of paid lobbyists with the offence of bribery and would have subjected any clerk, official or reporter of the House to dismissal if he accepted any gift for the purpose of influencing the legislature. His bill received the six months hoist by a vote of 33 to 12.[18]

For some time Mackenzie had been predicting an economic crisis and had been ridiculed for it.[19] He had called attention to the growing number of bankruptcies in the province, criticized the banking system, warned the government against increasing the provincial debt, cautioned the municipalities against borrowing to assist railways and protested against higher tariffs and heavier local taxation being imposed to carry the burden of public debt. During the early months of 1857 he could see the threatening clouds of a depression spreading over a province whose public and private debt owed abroad he estimated at $48,000,000.[20] The harvest of 1856 had been poor; the midge and rust had invaded the wheat fields; the price of wheat had fallen from $2.00 a bushels to $1.00, even to 50 cents in some areas;[21] and the *Canada Gazette* was full of notices of sheriff's sales. Two-thirds of the municipalities of Upper

Canada had already defaulted on their obligations to the Consolidated Municipal Loan Fund, and by 1858 practically all of them were to do so.[22] The banks had already begun to contract their circulation sharply — by $2,800,000 between October 31, 1856, and February 28, 1857.[23] Everywhere in the province money was tight.

As a means of attracting capital to Canada, the Legislative Council now proposed to allow any rate of interest to be charged, except by banks which would be limited to 7%. The penalties for usury had been abolished in 1853 but the legal rate had been maintained at 6% and that rate was still understood where no other rate was specified.[24] Mackenzie opposed the Council's "detestable bill" which in the end received the six months hoist from the Assembly. Four other bills to raise the rate of interest were also rejected.[25]

Various bills were advanced to charter additional banks, another method of easing tight credit. Mackenzie opposed them all, including one for the county of Haldimand,[26] and he again supported a bill to make banks take their own notes at par for debts due them.[27] He succeeded in getting a return printed showing the names and places of residence of the banks' stockholders. This document was criticized as a trashy, useless, 160-page volume printed at great public expense. Mackenzie, who had the example of Joseph Hume to guide him in this respect, pointed out that in case of failure a bank's creditors and noteholders would have to look to the shareholders for payment. It was therefore proper that the public should know who they were, how much stock they held (under double liability) and "whether they were 'men of straw' or wealthy."[28]

To assist the municipalities in their financial difficulties, the government brought in its Consolidated Municipal Loan Fund Amendment Bill. It modified the strict penalties imposed on defaulters by the existing act and gave the Governor-General power at his discretion to temper the wind to the shorn lambs.[29] Mackenzie opposed this act, particularly the discretionary power left to the Governor-in-Council. He tried to have the "villainous" Consolidated Municipal Loan Fund Act repealed, instead of amended. He called the amended bill an "electioneering bill" and predicted that the Governor's discretionary power would be used for political purposes.[30]

Although the province advanced the interest on the debentures of defaulting municipalities in 1857 and 1858, it did not take responsibility for the debts of the municipalities until 1859, by which time Mackenzie was out of Parliament. The fund was then closed, the 6% municipal loan fund debentures were replaced with 5% provincial debentures, defaulting municipalities were required to levy an assessment to provide for their share of these obligations and clergy reserve monies to which they were entitled were withheld and applied to their indebtedness.[31]

> Neither form of pressure brought the defaulters to time.... It may have been only a coincidence, but if so it is an interesting one, that in 1860 the chief defaulting municipalities in Upper Canada returned government supporters. [32]

From the start Mackenzie had not been far wrong in his prediction of the probable results of the Consolidated Municipal Loan Fund Act.

At this session Mackenzie's proposal that country coroners be elected by the freeholders as they were in England was negatived.[33] His motion that a special committee be named to draft a bill for voting by ballot also failed.[34] But two of his political reforms were at last accepted. His bill allowing cities to elect their mayors by a direct vote of the ratepayers passed its second reading, 55 to 4, but for some reason he believed he had little chance of getting it enacted and did not push it through the committee stage.[35] In the end he had the satisfaction of knowing that the ministry had accepted the principle of his bill and would make it part of the Upper Canada municipal bill they intended to introduce at the next session. This promise was kept and the privilege was extended, as one of his correspondents had suggested, to the election of mayors of towns also.[36]

Mackenzie was equally dubious about the fate of his controverted elections bill. He wanted the evidence in election cases to be taken before Parliament assembled by the judges of the county courts and then sent to the committees trying election petitions. Under the existing system, committees could appoint commissioners to go to the constituencies to do that work when it would be inconvenient or expensive for witnesses to come to them, but in such instances months often elapsed before commissioners began to gather evidence and sometimes cases dragged on into the next session. Mackenzie had introduced his bill twice before and seen it defeated.[37] This time J.A. Macdonald gave it his approval in principle. It was debated at length in committee and much amended but finally, to Mackenzie's surprise, it passed both houses. Baldwin's controverted Elections Act of 1851[38] had dealt primarily with the manner in which committees trying election petitions should be chosen and did not require the evidence to be taken promptly and locally. It was based on an imperial statute, 11 & 12 Vic., cap.98. Mackenzie's bill was based on an Act of Congress of February 19, 1851. The *Canada Law Journal* remarked that, taken together, the two acts conferred on Canada "a more complete machinery for the trial of controverted elections than exists in the United States or Great Britain."[39]

\* \* \*

One of the important concessions made by the government during the previous session had been the appointment of a Squatter Commission — something for which Mackenzie took to himself much credit.[40] For some time he had been receiving complaints about the government's land policies. Under pressure to make land available to settlers, the Hincks-Morin government had thrown open to sale and settlement the remaining Crown, school and clergy lands in Huron, Bruce, Wellington, Grey and Perth counties. The Land Act of 1853 left the terms of purchase to the Governor-in-Council. They were set at 10/- an acre, payable in 10 annual installments, and purchasers were limited to 200 acres. Settlement conditions were imposed: actual occupation, "immediate and continuous," the erection of a house and the clearing of two acres annually for five years.[41] Before these counties were officially opened to settlement several of them had been invaded by squatters. An order-in-council of August 9, 1853, had continued the pre-emption privilege which squatters had had under the Land Act of 1841, but the Crown land agents had been instructed not to allow pre-emption on "trivial pretences." The result was that after sales commenced squatters began to complain that the local agents were not allowing them their privilege, were selling their improved lots to newcomers and were also disregarding the 200 acre limitation. From other areas complaints came that the land agents were speculating in the land under their control and that honest men, despairing of getting a desirable location, were emigrating to the United States.

The agent for Huron County was was John Clark. Mackenzie received several letters of complaint about him and undertook to bring them to the attention of the Commissioner of Crown Lands.[42] He wrote:

> I find far more sympathy with the monopolists who grasp the
> public lands and never settle than for the squatter who sits
> down in the woods and makes Canada a country.[43]

He quoted the U.S. Commissioner of Lands on the value of pre-emption and contrasted American policy with the government's policy in the western peninsula:

> The value of the pre-emption policy [the American
> commissioner wrote] is no longer the subject of controversy. It
> is established by the history of every neighborhood and
> settlement throughout the West. This is said in full view of the
> fact that many fraudulent pre-emption claims are
> established.... But this class of cases when compared with the
> great body of honest claims made by men living upon the land
> is too inconsequential to weigh against our policy.... The title of
> the lands should pass immediately from the government to the
> men who are to cultivate the soil. So far as it may be avoided the
> speculator should not be allowed to intervene. [44]

Mackenzie presented Sir Edmund Head with a memorial offering to prove that the land regulations were being violated and he also brought the squatters' grievances up in the legislature. Petitions from the Lake Huron counties had poured in, and at length, on April 4, 1856, a commission of inquiry was appointed composed of Ogle R. Gowan, Grand Master of the Orange Order, and Dr. Morgan Hamilton of Goderich.[45] This action did not satisfy Mackenzie, who probably expected another whitewashing affair. He wanted the whole story laid bare, and therefore moved for a return of all lands of whatever classification sold or granted by the department between August 31, 1854, and June 31, 1855. His motion was opposed by the Commissioner of Crown Lands who saw "no need for such facts going to the public," and it was rejected, 15 to 60.[46] When the Squatter Commission got down to work, Mackenzie was informed that it was taking the evidence "very fairly."[47] The public soon learned that in eight townships in Huron County alone, especially in Turnberry, Howick and Grey, speculators had been allowed to acquire large quantities of land. One of the complainants sent Mackenzie a printed handbill in which one man offered for sale 10,000 acres of land, in blocks of 100 to 400 acres, all in one township, Howick. How could he legally have acquired it, Mackenzie asked, if the land agent had done his duty?[48] He concluded that a system of organized fraud had been set up and that the total of land so acquired would be found to exceed 100,000 acres.[49]

What mattered to the squatters was not that the details of the frauds should be publicized but what redress they would receive and how soon. About that Mackenzie had his doubts.[50] The longer the delay, the more the opportunity "for those who had grasped the land to sell out and gain fraudulently." What some speculators did in an attempt to regularize their position was to put a settler on a lot to comply with the settlement conditions, transfer some 50 acres to him and retain the balance for themselves.[51] Mackenzie kept needling the government for information about its intentions and continued publishing complaints from Huron and Bruce in his *Message*. He gave the names of well-known speculators, some of them occupying official positions, some of them sons of judges, who had managed to acquire large holdings in townships restricted by the regulations to 200 acres to a settler under settlement conditions.[52] "You are the only editor who takes part with the settlers in this part of the county," one of his admirers remarked.[53]

Shortly after the session of 1857 opened Mackenzie moved that the government produce the Squatter Commission's report, and the evidence, and state what action they had taken upon it, if any. His motion was agreed to but the document was not forthcoming promptly.[54] Meanwhile, all he could tell anxious inquirers was that the government claimed to be "hurrying" the report. When finally presented on April 17 it proved to be "a gigantic exposé of fraud, extortion and jobbing."[55] Some 63,000 acres had been dishonestly acquired by speculators, and in "this iniquity of encouraging poor men to settle and make improvements and then strip them of the fruits of their toil" a leading Reformer, editor McQueen of the *Huron Signal* was found to be involved. McQueen, who admitted guilt to the extent of 400 acres, was highly indignant that the commissioners made so much of his peccadillo but passed over in silence the much larger fraudulent purchases of some of those on the other side of politics.[56]

Joseph Cauchon, who had taken over the Crown Lands Department in January 1855, reported that he had found a disorganized, inefficient department in which there was a complete lack of discipline, in which incompetent idlers had been given appointments and where practices favouring speculators had been permitted.[57] Cauchon proved to be a more efficient commissioner than either of his predecessors, Rolph[58] or A.N. Morin.

Mackenzie acknowledged that both Governor Head and Cauchon had been very willing to have inquiry made when complaints were drawn to their attention but, impatient as usual, he demanded prompt action and nullification of the frauds. "If Head were really disposed to risk the wrath of the land jobbers," he remarked, "we would begin to believe in British governors."[59]

A tense situation was developing, particularly in Howick where, Mackenzie was told, squatters had organized themselves into companies to resist newcomers trying to take over their improved lots.[60] No action at all was taken on the complaints of the settlers in Huron and Bruce until March 1858, when an order-in-council issued directing that the disputes be settled immediately in accordance with the Land Act and the regulations.[61] Mackenzie concluded that the Gowan-Hamilton investigation had been a sheer waste of time and money. Everything had now to be done over again by the Crown Land Department. He wanted the commissioners' report to be published with the evidence, but since the Printing Committee and the government would not agree, he had to content himself with publishing a summary of the Bruce report in the *Message*, plus a strong condemnation of the government's conduct in suppressing the evidence.[62] No investigation was ordered for Wellington County until 1859, and as late as 1863 the complaints of settlers in the western peninsula had not been completely pacified.[63]

One explanation of the delay may be that Mackenzie, "the poor man's friend,"[64] the persistent champion of the settlers' cause, had resigned his seat at the close of the session of 1858 and was no longer present to needle the government. Another, that the efficient Cauchon had been eased out of the Crown Lands Department in April 1857. A more likely reason is that John A. Macdonald had never been sympathetic to the settlers in the western peninsula. "The peninsula must not get command of the ship," he warned. "It is occupied by Yankees and Covenanters."[65] For both political and economic reasons he had not approved the regulations that had implemented the Land Act of 1853. In his opinions actual settlement was "all humbug" and productive only of fraud and that, he told a friend, was the Governor-General's opinion too. Macdonald had not been anxious to see the Lake Huron lands opened to settlers, fearing that would interfere with "the long neglected country in the rear of Frontenac & with the Ottawa." "For political reasons the bal. of power should not go to[o] far West," he had warned. "If we want to preserve the Union Eastern Upper Canada must be pushed forward."[66] And he might have added that that was also the Governor-General's opinion.[67]

In 1854, as chairman of the Committee on Public Accounts, Mackenzie had succeeded after some difficulty in getting access to the accounts of the Crown Lands Department and had reported that some 50 agents were in arrears.[68] He could not get the government or the then-Commissioner to take action. Cauchon investigated, and found that in Canada West alone 31 agents were in default, one of them for almost £9,500, another for £6,280. He suspended them and ordered that in future all payments for land should be made through the Bank of Upper Canada.[69] The property of the Crown land agent for York, Ontario and Peel, and of his clerk, jointly the largest defaulters, was eventually seized and sold.[70] In another case the sureties of a Crown land agent were called upon to pay part of his debt. But no criminal prosecutions were undertaken and the defaulters were left at large. The same leniency had been shown to S.P. Jarvis, a defaulter to the extent of £6,000 of Indian Trust Funds.[71] Mackenzie observed that:

> The poor thief is sent to break stones. The rich land jobber, crown land agent or speculating judge though far more criminal, keep their coaches and are company for gentlemen. [72]

Mackenzie complained that although the Assembly "unanimously recommended" criminal prosecution of the defaulting Crown land agents, the Attorney-General had not undertaken it. All the Assembly did in 1857 was to inquire what course of action against the offenders was being recommended. In 1858 Mackenzie again pressed for action against the defaulters, one of whom by this time had been found to owe not £9,500 but £30,000, and in 1860 he was still reminding John A. Macdonald that he had not yet lived up to his promise to see justice done to the Indians. [73]

During July and August Mackenzie devoted a goodly amount of space in his *Message* to comments on the Gowan-Hamilton report and to denunciation of the evils of land speculation and land monopoly. He quoted from some 20 writers ranging from the learned Bishop Paley to Mike Walsh, the rough-and-tumble editor of the New York *Subterranean*, all of whom discoursed upon the theme of man's natural right to a share in the land. The government did not bring in a Crown lands bill designed to prevent the attempts at monopoly, the scandals or the disputes over squatters' "rights" until the session of 1858. This bill contained many detailed provisions to regulate the conduct of the employees of the Land Department. In future public land not subject to settlement duties was to be offered at auction twice a year at such upset prices and on such terms as the Governor-in-Council should establish. After that it was to be available for purchase at private sale. Free grants on some roads in new settlements were to be made on settlement conditions. Occupants of public land in actual possession (the bill avoided the word *squatters*) who had cultivated any portion in 1858 and had cleared five acres per hundred were to have a right of pre-emption in the purchase of 200 acres at the minimum price set for their district, provided they claimed it and paid the purchase price before the auction. Assignments of land being purchased would be recognized but assignments of mere rights to pre-emption would not in future be recognized. Thus the activities of men who were professional squatters would be halted, and the "right" of pre-emption was to be restricted to those already on the land. A land classification program was proposed to be instituted. In certain areas Reserve Forests of the Public Domain were to be set aside. The right of cutting in these areas was to be sold at auction. Occupants of public land not yet patented could have any timber dues they were called upon to pay applied to the purchase price of the land. They could also sell standing timber provided they paid in full for the land first. [74]

Mackenzie consulted several of his constituents about this bill, which was a Conservative government's answer to the complaints about the Land Department. He received a mixed bag of responses. [75] The chief criticism was that while there were some good points to the bill, too many matters were still left to executive discretion. Upper Canada radicals had little confidence in the executive's impartiality. They wanted detailed regulations in the law. They objected that no fixed minimum price had been established, as under the

American system. They wanted a land policy that would favour the landless man rather than the land speculator and from the Macdonald-Taché administration they were not likely to get it.

As it turned out, Mackenzie did not have to make up his mind on the bill, which was not proceeded in. Various clauses were not acceptable to lumbermen. They did not want settlers occupying small tracts in good timbered areas on credit, even though the proposed regulations were designed to prevent them from stripping the land of its merchantable timber without paying for it. Nor did they want timber berths laid off in blocks of stated size, with the right of cutting timber thereon sold at auction. They preferred the system under which they obtained licence to cut timber on Crown land, paid ground rent for the berth and timber dues on the quantity cut. "The Bytown lumbermen are furious... and are determined to resist," the *Message* announced.[76] Several firms petitioned against the bill.[77] No new land bill was enacted until 1860 and then no mention was made of Reserve Forests of the Public Domain nor of "rights" of pre-emption,[78] and the old system of managing the timber lands was continued.

Despite the provincial aid received in 1855 and 1856, the Grand Trunk had to come to Parliament for assistance again. In the past, six of its directors had been government appointees, some of them both salaried officials of the railway and members of the cabinet, which had to pass upon the company's pleas for assistance. This state of affairs had intensified criticism of both the government and the company. The Grand Trunk Bill presented at the session of 1857 contained a clause ending the practice of appointing government directors but this concession was not enough to sweeten the bill's other provisions for critics of the company. Nor was it enough to prevent the railway's securing public money without the consent of the people's representatives. It was subsequently discovered that between 1856 and 1861 the government made the Grand Trunk loans totalling $4,000,000 without securing the consent of Parliament. Some of these loans were interest-free and all but three of them had been made by an individual minister on his own responsibility without consulting the cabinet.[79] The Grand Trunk Bill of 1857 permitted the company to issue more preference bonds, and to ensure their sale (those previously authorized had not found buyers) the government gave up its first claim on the earnings of the road after operating expenses, on condition that the company complete the works mentioned in the Act of 1856. In addition the government agreed to pay out of the Consolidated Revenue Fund the interest on the bonds it had guaranteed until the railway should be able to pay interest on its other bonds *and* 6% on shares of common stock held by the public.[80]

Mackenzie called this bill a $16,000,000 "gift" to the Grand Trunk to bolster its securities in the English market.[81] He objected that as a condition of assisting the "bankrupt" railway, the company was being required to assist three shaky feeder lines in Upper Canada and to extend its main line in Lower Canada through unproductive territory to Rivière du Loup.[82] Again he tried to prevent the votes of those members who were shareholders in the Grand Trunk from being received.[83] As a clincher to his 45-minute speech, frequently interrupted by noises from the ministerial benches, Mackenzie moved that a general election be held under the new Franchise Act before any action was taken on the Grand Trunk's petition for aid. His motion was of course defeated.[84]

For Mackenzie one of the most awkward topics to come up during the session of 1857 was the proposed southern railway. It will be recalled that in 1836 the Niagara and Detroit had been chartered to build from some point on the Niagara River to Dunnville on the Grand, and through the Lake Shore townships to Sandwich on the Detroit, and that in 1851 the legislature had refused to renew the charter of this company which in the meantime had accomplished nothing.[85] Mackenzie had approved of this proposed railway. It would have given Haldimand connections with both Buffalo and Detroit by a shorter and cheaper route than either the Great Western or the Grand Trunk could provide, since by crossing the Grand at Dunnville it would avoid the Niagara escarpment.

Subsequently two rival capitalist speculators, Samuel Zimmerman and Isaac Buchanan, became interested in acquiring charters for a southern railway route across the peninsula.[86] Buchanan's primary interest had been the Great Western. This company had repeatedly tried to prevent the chartering of any road to the south of its line that would compete with it for the profitable American through traffic by what would undoubtedly be a shorter and cheaper route. Buchanan planned to secure control of two railways that had been chartered but not yet constructed, the Amherst and St. Thomas and the Woodstock and Lake Erie, to amalgamate them into one system, the Great Southwestern, and thus obtain control of a through route from Amherstburg to Suspension Bridge. Sooner or later the Great Western would need a second track. He planned to offer his Great Southwestern to the Great Western for this purpose. The latter company could then build it in its own good time and meanwhile could prevent a competitor from coming into existence.[87] The board of the Great Western, however, did not accept his scheme.

Samuel Zimmerman, together with Arthur Rankin, the Member for Essex, wanted to acquire a southern route across the peninsula in the interests of the Grand Trunk, which also did not want a southern route built unless it could control it. It is not worth while for our purposes to go into all the details of the fight between these interests. Suffice it to say that in 1857 a bill was brought in by the Zimmerman-Rankin interests to charter a southern line to be called the Great Southern.[88] It was opposed by Buchanan's friends, who asked that the amalgamation agreements he had made to create the Great Southwestern be confirmed by the legislature and that this road be permitted to cross the Grand River at Cayuga, instead of at Dunnville as originally specified.[89]

The point at which the crossing of the Grand would be made was a crucial matter for Mackenzie. Part of his constituency advocated Cayuga, part of it Dunnville. The latter group argued that the advocates of Cayuga were really working in the interests of the Great Western which wanted to defeat a competitive low-level route to the west. On the other hand, he was informed by the Warden of the County that in his opinion a majority of the people preferred a road through the centre of the county to one through its extremities, as the route through Dunnville would be.[90]

Mackenzie's comment on the struggle between the Buchanan and Zimmerman interests was that Buchanan professed the more liberal (political) principles but he thought the southern road should be made "on its own" and its route determined without reference to the interests of either the Great Western or the Grand Trunk. He acknowledged that Buchanan might think his failure to support him in railway matters smacked of ingratitude but that when he could not speak his mind on public questions he would retire from public life.[91] He also told Buchanan frankly that he had begun to suspect he was not "disinterested," that is, not sincerely anxious to see that the province got the best and cheapest route (in Mackenzie's opinion through Dunnville), but was concerned with promoters' benefits for himself.[92] George Brown, on the other hand, was strongly backing Buchanan and his Great Southwestern.[93]

No decision on the southern railroad was reached during 1857. When the Committee on Railroads investigated the conduct of both sets of promoters, it turned up much unsavoury information. Directors had been bribed, contracts and sub-contracts had been secured by the promoters for themselves and their friends at the expense of the stockholders, and the money of subscribing townships had been wasted.[94] "Buchanan, with all his professions about elective government and freedom is as rotten and as sordid as the others," Mackenzie wrote in disgust.[95] The question of the southern railway was not to be settled until the session of 1858. Buchanan's amalgamated companies were then rechartered as the Niagara and Detroit Rivers Railway.[96] It was to cross the Grand River at Cayuga. In the meantime a deal had been worked out between all the interests competing for the southern route. The charter of the Niagara and Detroit was loaded with the payment of certain claims to Ranking, Buchanan and the heirs of Zimmerman amounting to $500,000, or $4,000 a mile.[97] Mackenzie was importuned to support the charter with its change of route and financial burdens by politically important people in Haldimand, including the Sheriff of the county, who argued that if carried through Cayuga, the railway would be a feeder to the Grand Trunk.

> This would make it a provincial work... whereas if carried through Dunnville it will be a feeder to American lines and of little value as a Canadian work. [98]

William Harcourt, who succeeded Mackenzie in the legislature, wrote:

> For the credit of the county it was to be wished the road could be built independently of the disreputable associations with which the bill connects it. But the road will be built — jobs found — dishonesty cannot be helped. We want the road. [99]

Mackenzie could not overlook the dishonesty nor the change of route. He voted no.[100] The Niagara and Detroit Rivers Railway was never to be constructed, as he predicted. In the 1870s the Great Western, through its loop line, and the

Canada Southern, at length provided what Mackenzie had tried to secure since 1851, a through route that avoided the Niagara escarptment.[101]

* * *

At the close of the session of 1857, when the resolutions for the Supply Bill were being debated, Mackenzie had another opportunity to emphasize his standing objections to the government's policies and administrative practices and once more to use the occasion to demand repeal of the Union. By negative votes he called attention to the fact that the government had been making expenditures in advance of legislative sanction.[102] He pointed out that at a time when the United States was reducing its tariff for the second time in 10 years, Canada was raising hers, notably the rates on articles of common necessity, thereby making the country less attractive to immigrants.[103] He criticized all grants that enabled the government to increase its patronage by providing for additional customs house officers, fisheries commissioners, steamboat inspectors, river police, etc., and he opposed appointing and paying members of the Assembly to conduct criminal prosecutions for the government.[104] He voted against funds for the militia because he thought Great Britain should provide for Canada's defence while she remained a colony, exposed to the foreign policies of the mother country.[105] When the resolution on Indian annuities came up, he tried to add as a proviso that the Indian Department should be placed under provincial control.[106] And finally, he voted against the proposal of the Ways and Means Committee to grant a supply of £854,000 and to increase the public debt by £325,000 to enable the province to do so.[107]

On June 5, a few days before adjournment, when a motion to go into committee on supply was before the House, Mackenzie moved an excessively long amendment which he had previously published in the *Message*. It condemned the existing system of government in Canada under the Act of Union and the whole course of government since its passage, particularly the financial policies that had been adopted. He outlined a detailed list of reforms for which the province should strive, including repeal of the Union and acquisition by Canada of power to regulate her domestic affairs herself "without interference or check by the British Government or its agents." Although he firmly asserted the "undoubted constitutional right" of the people to hold a convention to discuss these constitutional changes or any other public questions without previously obtaining legislative sanction, he conceded that it would be expedient to have that sanction. He concluded by asking the Assembly to sanction and arrange for the calling of a constitutional convention, particularly for Upper Canada, and he outlined a scheme for the election of delegates from every city, town, village and township in that part of the province. Here was a contrast with 1837. This time he would go through the proper channels.[108] Through a convention he would demonstrate to the legislature what Upper Canada really wanted. He would request the legislature to inform the imperial parliament of Upper Canada's wishes and he expected the convention to endorse the reforms he and other radicals had been advocating. His proposals show the influence upon him of the method of summoning the New York State constitutional convention of 1846. Mackenzie's amendment was supported only by David Christie and Amos Wright from Upper Canada and by four Lower Canada Rouges. George Brown did not vote.[109]

On the third reading of the Supply Bill Mackenzie made one more effort — this time to add a clause for the appointment of commissioners to examine the whole system of public finance, including the practices of all the public departments, the management of the railway corporations that were in debt to the Crown, the affairs of defaulting municipalities and the system of letting public contracts. This comprehensive proposal was defeated 8 to 60, drawing support from five Lower Canada members and only three Clear Grits. The Supply Bill passed with only Mackenzie and three Lower Canada members in opposition.[110] In his *Message* Mackenzie put it bluntly and without shame:

> These votes will show that the views of the editor of this journal are entirely contrary to the opinions of men of all parties representing Upper Canada and his opposition is by them regarded as factious and a waste of time. [111]

# Chapter XIX

# RE-ELECTION AND RETIREMENT

After the parliamentary session was over Mackenzie indulged himself in a vacation. We know that he visited the township of Arthur and attended the Provincial Agricultural Exhibition at Brantford,[1] but we know little else about him. His correspondence for July and August is not extant and from September 18 to November 13 his *Message* was not published because his income from the papers's prompt-paying subscribers did not enable him to hire assistance during his absence. "Every number we publish with a loan," he told his readers, "but we mean to hold on and if necessary diminish the size of the weekly sheet." The *Message* was indeed in a bad way. By year's end it had not one-third as many paid-up subscribers as it had had the previous year.[2]

These losses can, no doubt, be attributed in part to the general economic distress, but the contents of the *Message* are also to be blamed. Mackenzie was criticizing imperial policies. In 1857 the Second Opium War occurred and received his condemnation.[3] On May 10, 1857, the Indian Mutiny had broken out. He sympathized with this revolt against British rule and said so in a series of articles in the *Message*, not omitting to criticize the East India Company, as he had the Canada Company, despite warnings that he would not increase the popularity of his paper by so doing.[4]

Before long Mackenzie turned his attention to Canadian politics again, particularly to the selection of candidates for the Legislative Council, soon to be elected. Then, on November 25, Taché resigned from the cabinet, the ministry was reorganized as the Macdonald-Cartier ministry, and Macdonald decided to bring on a general election immediately. Mackenzie did not compile a voters' guide this time. Instead, he provided his subscribers with free copies of a supplement issued by the *Globe* — a clear indication of his failing energy.[5]

Mackenzie, "the champion of reform," to quote the phrase applied to him by the Warden of Perth,[6] seems to have been really reluctant to run again. Cartier had sneered at him in the House as a person of no influence[7] and at the close of the session he himself had acknowledged his inability to obtain support for his policies from any political party. But when encouraging letters from his friends began to arrive, as well as requests for help for Reform candidates who evidently did not regard his influence as negligible,[8] he made up his mind to contest Haldimand again. He made the mistake, however, of not visiting his county at once. The result was that four other candidates, all local residents, came forward promptly, including his old opponent McKinnon who was vigorously supported by the *Sachem*. "If you will only come and spend a few days, matters will soon assume a different aspect," Mackenzie was assured. Finally he was persuaded, went down, worked hard, delivered speeches twice a day, each two hours long by his own estimate, and spent no more than £20 including his travelling expenses.[9]

In appealing to the voters Mackenzie reminded them of his record. He had always stood for equality of civil and religious rights, for support for education, for economy, for temperance, for improved municipal institutions and had "united in every effort to get the Great Northwest out of the grip of the Hudson's Bay Co." He had fought for an impartial marriage law, a wider franchise, an elective Legislative Council, elective county officers and elective township reeves with the powers of justices of the peace. He took credit for putting through an improved contested elections act, the Decimal Currency Act, and an act for the direct election of mayors. If again elected he promised to fight for the ballot and a measure for holding elections at stated times and on the same day in all constituencies.[10]

There were two topics of particular interest to Haldimand County on which Mackenzie had to take a stand: the Indian lands and the Grand River Navigation Company. Mackenzie, who had opposed the act providing for Indian allotments passed at the previous session, announced that he favoured bringing the Indian lands on the market. The Grand River Navigation Company had made the river navigable as far as Brantford and had greatly stimulated the agricultural development of the valley as well as its industrial enterprises, but the Company's revenues were becoming insufficient to carry its obligations. Its works were in disrepair, and it was near bankruptcy. Mackenzie was not in favour of assessments being imposed on the counties of Haldimand and Brant to assist the Company. He thought the government should take over the work as it had the Welland Canal Company,[11] an opinion shared by many of his constituents.

Although the election proved to be a victory for Mackenzie, it was not a triumph. He was hurt by his known opposition to chartering the Niagara and Detroit Rivers Railway, "with all its encumbrances upon it." He was also hurt by his slow start and by his opposition to a bank for Haldimand, an institution which he evidently mistrusted and which was soon to fall into disrepute.[12] He also had working against him the influence of a New Connexion Methodist minister, the Rev. N.C. Gowan, son of Ogle R. Gowan, Grand Master of the Orange Order, and perhaps also the influence of the Catholic hierarchy as Bishop Charbonnel had warned. Mackenzie received 978 votes, or 38% of the total cast in what dwindled down to a three-way contest on the second day. He carried five of the ten polling divisions and was the only candidate to receive some votes in all of them, although Samuel Amsden, his nearest competitor, who received 30% of the total votes, ran him a close second here.[13]

At the general election of 1851 Mackenzie had obtained 63% of the total vote in a two-way contest; 54% in 1854, in a two-way contest; 38% in this six-way contest. Between 1854 and 1858 the voting population of Haldimand, on the basis of votes cast, had increased by 255%, the actual number of Mackenzie's supporters by 153%.[14] But if we assume that there had been only two candidates, Mackenzie and Amsden, and that they would have shared the 1795 votes cast for the other four in the same proportion as they shared the total vote, Mackenzie would have received 54.6% of the votes. His hold on his county had certainly slipped — the presence of many candidates cannot be ignored — but it had not slipped as much as a straight percentage comparison with the general elections of 1851 and 1854 would indicate.

One of Mackenzie's workers explained that the new franchise had hurt him. Amsden was a merchant in Dunnville, and poor men in debt to him and unprotected by the ballot had been afraid to vote for Mackenzie.[15] Amsden's address to the voters had been very different from his. There was no political question, Amsden told them, that *he* cared very much about. He disposed of George Brown's chief interests, the opening up of the west and rep. by pop., as so much "claptrap." A southern railway that would serve their (Dunnville's) interests was the questions he was most interested in. That was what they wanted and they needed a representative "who could get it." The implication was that Mackenzie was not the man who could do that:

> You all know me as a business man. I have a large interest in this
> county and I believe my interests are identified with yours.
> Perhaps this principle may serve you in the present instance. [16]

These were doubtless the significant sentences in Amsden's address for any listeners who were in debt to him. Before the election Mackenzie had protested against Amsden's nomination on the ground that he was a customs house officer. Afterwards, Amsden protested that Mackenzie had not received a majority of good votes. Beyond filing, nothing more was heard of these protests.

The general election left the Macdonald-Cartier ministry in a minority in Upper Canada. The Liberals obtained 35 of Upper Canada's 65 seats,[17] defeating three members of Macdonald's cabinet in the process. George Brown had contested both North Oxford and Toronto and Mackenzie had supported him. Conservative newspapers used against Brown the same arguments that Mackenzie had used in their contest in Haldimand. The editor of the *Message* brushed off this awkward fact with the airy remark, "George Brown knows more of Canada's ruling politicians now than he did then."[18] His own suspicions that what Brown really sought was office and that in power he would be "another Hincks" were laid aside for the time being. In North Oxford Brown won 47% of the vote against two competitors. In Toronto there was a fairly even three-way contest for her two seats. Brown nudged out J. Luke Robinson, his nearest competitor for first place, by 51 votes.[19] When Brown chose to sit for Toronto, William McDougall became the Reform candidate for North Oxford, and both he and Brown appealed to Mackenzie for help in this by-election. He responded promptly with a *Message Extra* and by going in person to speak.[20] McDougall won. In Lower Canada, where there was much fraud at the elections, the ministry increased its strength and consequently was able to win the vote on the speakership for Henry Smith of Frontenac, 79 to 42.[21] Mackenzie was invited by Brown to a caucus of the opposition members prior to the opening of the session. While he did not approve of all Brown stood for he had no choice but to support him in opposition to Macdonald.[22] During the election he and Brown had on the whole been in agreement as to which candidates they would support or oppose.[23]

The government's program of legislation met with little criticism as such. Although the election had weakened the Macdonald-Cartier administration in Upper Canada, the opposition was able to muster at most only 40 negative votes on any paragraph of the reply to the Speech, and these included barely half-a-dozen Lower Canada votes from the far from homogeneous Rouges. Here was a clear indication that Brown would not get adequate support should the opportunity come for him to form a ministry.

At this session more time was spent discussing the contested elections than any of the pressing problems of the province. So numerous were the contested cases that Sir Edmund Head is said to have wanted public business delayed so that he could consult Lord Stanley as to whether he should go on with the present cabinet "or make such a compromise as would satisfy those hungriest for office and on other matters."[24] However this may have been, the government did seem to be dragging its feet. Four weeks of the session went by in which nothing was accomplished and then the ministry secured a recess of two weeks because the Speaker was "ill." Mackenzie regarded this excuse as a mere subterfuge. He was hissed when he suggested that the Speaker ought to appoint a deputy, as permitted by an act which Mackenzie himself had introduced at a previous session.[25]

The most flagrant election abuses had occurred in Quebec City, where the number of votes cast exceeded the adult male population. The investigation of the Quebec election, as well as that of others, dragged on for almost the entire life of this parliament. Meanwhile the ministry continued to govern, as Mackenzie said, through an illegal majority.[26]

To Mackenzie's disappointment his Controverted Elections Act did not expedite the settlement of these disputes as expected. Members whose elections were being contested hid themselves to prevent their being served with a notice of the petition against them within the time limit set by this law. Judges refused to hear petitions as commissioners under the act, with the excuse that the duties imposed were entirely different from those that belonged to their office. They doubted whether they could appoint deputies to carry on their ordinary judicial functions while they were hearing election petitions — although, as the *Globe* pointed out, the act specifically gave them that right.[27] Not only was Mackenzie's act rendered ineffective by obstuctiveness on the part of some judges, but clauses of Baldwin's act were also misused. Speaker Henry Smith, from whom Mackenzie had predicted impartiality need not be expected and whom he called a disgrace to Canada,[28] had seen to that.[29]

At the opening of the session the government had promised to amend the Controverted Elections Act, which had proved to have some weaknesses. They were well aware that they must make some move to counteract the public furore the fraudulent elections had created, not only among the opposition but among disgusted members of their own party as well.[30] Nothing was done at this session. At the next, Mackenzie's act was repealed but no new measure was put in its place.[31]

The government had also promised an amendment of the franchise acts and the compilation of voters' registers. Owing to the fact that the assessment franchise of 1853 and the old 40/- freehold franchise were both in use, the franchise was in a state of confusion. The municipal authorities had found it so difficult to compile voters' registers using the new system of assessments introduced in 1851[32] that the voters' register requirement of the law had been given up. As a result assessors and returning officers had in some instances let partisan political considerations influence their decision as to whether a man was entitled to vote.[33] The number of controverted elections in the recent contest made it imperative that the voters' registers be compiled. The new Franchise Act of this session wiped out the old 40/- freehold franchise and provided for the compilation of voters' registers based on the property qualifications of the Act of 1853, now expressed in decimal currency and slightly reduced, and on an assessment act no longer new and strange. By the time the Franchise Bill came up for its third reading Mackenzie had announced his intention to resign, and he did not vote. He had already criticized the bill in the *Message* because it did not provide for vote by ballot or prevent non-resident land-holders and lease-holders from voting.[34]

During this session, his last, Mackenzie continued to fight for his well-known principles and desired reforms, but not with his old vigour. He had come to realize that Upper Canada would not be guided by his light, that his day was past, and that it would be as well to entrust even minor reforms to more influential members.[35] He introduced only two proposals of his own: that all members of the Assembly be nominated and elected on the same day in all constituencies, and that a stated time be allowed to elapse between a dissolution and an election. John A. Macdonald, whose election tactics were thus inferentially criticized, blocked his efforts, just as Hincks had done with a similar motion in 1854. Mackenzie's other proposal was that a divorce court be created for Upper Canada that should take over from the legislature the task of hearing petitions for divorce. The idea was rejected.[36] In line with his previous efforts to reduce legal expenses, Mackenzie supported Brown's motion to abolish outright the separate surrogate courts of Upper Canada and to transfer their jurisdiction to the county courts,[37] a reform he had seen made in New York in 1846. Mackenzie joined in an attack on the separate school system of Upper Canada[38] and printed in the *Message* his own bill for repealing the separate school provisions of the Upper Canada education acts. He opposed the creation of one more ecclesiastical endowment by voting to deny the Sisters of Charity the right to reinvest funds, derived from the seigneuries they proposed to sell, in other lands, particularly Upper Canada lands,[39] and he again demonstrated his hostility to all organizations having a sectarian basis, whether Catholic or Protestant, by voting with the majority against the incorporation of the Orange Order.[40]

Although not active in proposing new legislation at this session Mackenzie was still hot on the trail of corruption, whether it involved theft of government debentures by an employee in the receiver-general's office, failure on the part of the ministry to see to it that those who had bought government toll roads paid for them, failure of government appointees to account for the interest on unexpended government funds in their care or irregularities in the accounts of collectors of customs. Several instances of the foregoing were publicized in the *Message*, but the Assembly refused to make the results of the audit of the customs houses part of its printed records.[41] Mackenzie tried once more to obtain the total abolition of imprisonment for debt and failed, 33 to 52.[42] He objected to increasing the tax on immigrants[43] and to raising the tariff again on articles of common consumption like tea, coffee and molasses, and he strongly denounced the increase in the tariff on woollens which, he felt, bore especially hard on the poor.[44]

The harvest of 1857 had been a poor one and that of 1858 was to be no better.[45] Mackenzie heard that in some areas the farmers were in great distress. Even their oxen were being seized and sold for debt. One Lobo Township farmer informed him that at the last division court between 400 and 500 suits had been instituted against debtors. He asked Mackenzie to procure "a stop law, otherwise all the little farmers in the back country must go to ruin."[46] Mackenzie succeeded in obtaining some relief for them. In 1857 an act had been passed amending the Upper Canada Common Law Procedures Act. The new act contained provisions which enabled the holder of a promissory note to get a judgement with costs against his delinquent debtor and to sell him out within 16 days unless, in answer to a writ of summons, he paid up within 8 days or appeared in court within 16 days to put in a defence. Previously it had been necessary for the creditor to sue for the note in court and get the verdict of a jury. Mackenzie had protested against these new summary procedures without effect.[47] They were supposed to go into operation on July 1, 1858. He succeeded in getting them suspended until January 1, 1860. This gave distressed farmers time to get another harvest which, it was to be hoped, would be more bountiful and sell at better prices than those of 1857 and 1858. Mackenzie's stop law was repealed at the next session, but the sections of the Procedures Act to which he had objected were repealed also.[48]

Another effort was made in 1858 to raise the legal rate of interest. The government's bill continued 6% as the rate to be understood where no rate was specified, but this was just window-dressing. Contracts voluntarily entered into at a higher rate of interest were now made valid, and the bill also provided that any rate of interest might be charged on bills of exchange and promissory notes that had less than a year to run. Mackenzie denounced this bill as one that would diminish the number of independent farmers and increase the number of tenants. In his *Message* he published the strong protest of Jacob DeWitt of La Banque du Peuple against the bill and against the act of 1853 which had repealed the penalties for usury. Reformers and Rouges stubbornly fought the new bill.[49] It was abandoned after a debate prolonged for four days.[50] After the "double shuffle" had increased the strength of the Conservatives, a different bill to consolidate the usury laws did pass. It restricted banks to 7% interest taken in advance but allowed individuals and all other associations to charge what rate they pleased.[51] Mackenzie, who in a few days was to announce his resignation, and who had given up futile opposition, did not vote.

Mackenzie also opposed the Jury Law Amendment Act for Upper Canada, which permitted a verdict in civil cases where the jury was not unanimous and altered the manner in which juries were to be selected. Under the previous act, the list of jurors had been compiled from the assessment rolls by elected officials. They listed the ratepayers according to the amount of their assessment and numbered the names of those on the top half of the list. The numbers of those who were to serve were then publicly drawn from a box by the Sheriff. Under the new act the jury lists were to be compiled as before but the names of those actually to serve were to be voted on by five "selectors." These persons were the Chairman of the Court of Quarter Sessions, the Clerk of the Peace, the Sheriff, and the Treasurer and Warden of the County.[52]

The passage of this act angered Mackenzie. He wrote to his son:

> I voted this morning [August 11, 1858], after one o'clock — one of 14 to preserve our popular jury laws which we struggled so hard to obtain. All are lost — five selectors of whom the government chooses four — select our juries — pack them... only 9 U.C. friends to free trial voted.... I'll get out of public life as fast as I can & leave the House, probably tomorrow.

On August 16th he did resign. He had been hooted at and insulted when he tried to stop this bill. It passed by the votes of Lower Canada members, "eager," as Mackenzie rather unfairly put it, "to destroy our institutions."[53]

Before the session ended three railway bills, the Southern Railway Bill, the Grand Trunk Bill and the Ontario Simcoe and Huron Bill, were disposed of. Not one of these measures pleased Mackenzie. The Southern, rechartered as the Niagara and Detroit Rivers Railway, has already been referred to. The Grand Trunk was empowered to increase its share capital and to build a bridge from Sarnia across the Detroit. Mackenzie attempted to have this bill postponed until the thorough investigation of the Grand Trunk's finances provided for by the Act of 1857 had been made. He also supported Brown's unsuccessful effort to deprive the company of the power to go on paying dividends out of borrowed money.[54] The Ontario, Simcoe and Huron had been in difficulties for some time. This railway, which J.C. Morrison and George Brown had helped to promote, had been chartered in 1849. It had been assisted on the same terms as the Grand Trunk with government debentures which were a first lien on the road. In 1856 the railway had defaulted on the interest payable on these securities. Mackenzie had succeeded in getting the Assembly to require a complete statement of the company's financial affairs before anything more was done for it. The report, when received, was not as detailed as he thought it should have been, particularly with respect to the company's large floating debt.[55] In 1857 the Ontario, Simcoe and Huron asked the legislature to allow it to raise more capital by issuing bonds that would have preference over those guaranteed by the government.[56] Mackenzie opposed this request. "A swarm of hungry locusts has settled upon this road, speculating, jobbing, contracting," he charged, an accusation which historians have since supported.[57] Like the two other railway companies assisted at this session, the "infamously conducted" Ontario, Simcoe and Huron got what it wanted as a result of what Mackenzie termed "log-rolling."[58] Mackenzie certainly realized that the Ontario, Simcoe and Huron had been a stimulus to the farms and the lumber industry north of Toronto, but, with an eye too attentive to scandals, his public comment was that this railway had been "nothing but a monstrous job from first to last."[59] It has been said of a later, politically more skillful Reformer that, although he wished for honesty and economy, he did not put economy before progress.[60] Mackenzie certainly put honesty before progress, especially as he believed Canada's tariff, which financed her corruptly managed railways, bore hardest on her farmers.

\* \* \*

Railway questions, however, were not the important ones in 1858, but the finances of the province and the future of the Union. Although no longer a member of the Committee on Public Accounts, Mackenzie followed its activities with keen interest. In 1857 the province had met its deficit by borrowing. In 1858, with another bad harvest and declining customs revenues in prospect, another deficit could be expected. Since this was not the year to put more provincial debentures on the market, Inspector-General Cayley proposed to raise the tariff again. The government's opponents prepared to scrutinize every penny of the accounts and to obstruct the Supply Bill until they could examine in detail the proposed tariff.[61] George Brown was a convinced free trader. Mackenzie, like his friend DeWitt, favoured a tariff policy that would foster home industries and create a home market for the farmer, but he did not favour a revenue tariff that would bear hard on the poor, particularly one that imposed specific duties, as this one did, instead of duties that would allow the cheaper grades of commodities used by the poor to come in at lower rates.[62]

After Cayley had introduced his proposals, Mackenzie delivered a speech that the *Globe* described as "a speech of great humour and power that kept the House in a ferment for some time."[63] He showed in detail the regressive nature of the government's tariff proposals and twitted Macdonald and his colleagues on their inconsistency in resigning from the MacNab-Morin ministry when it had lost the support of the majority of Upper Canada members, yet clinging to office now under the same circumstances. However tedious and discursive Mackenzie may have been on some occasions, he concluded this speech with a pithy and powerful peroration:

> Your government refuses to protect the poor man's lot of land in Huron and Bruce — it refuses to give him the ballot —it overwhelms him with taxation — it refuses to protect from seizure his furniture in hard times like these —it will not protect his homestead — it taxes his tea, sugar, coffee and

tobacco — it is never weary of impoverishing him — it sets up
Canada companies in Europe and drains Canada of the value
of lands made of great worth by our kindly neighbours — its
railway policy is a fraud — its financial schemes deceit.... I will
vote to remove the cabinet because it is corrupt, inefficient and
unfit to steer the ship of state into the haven of prosperity. [64]

The government attempted to have the resolutions on supply considered
before the evidence on fraud and corruption and the inaccuracies being brought
out by the Committee on Accounts had been examined. The opposition resisted
throughout an all-night session during which Mackenzie remained to support
them, never once leaving his seat.[65] Finally, when Brown's motion condemning
the government's financial policies was voted on, there was a majority of four
against the government in Upper Canada.[66] The fundamental question had now
to be faced: should a ministry in which the majority of Upper Canada members
had lost confidence remain in power supported by a majority of Lower Canada
votes?

Discussion of constitutional questions at this session had really begun with
the debate on the address. Brown had then moved that "rep. by pop." was "the
one question surpassing in importance all others."[67] His motion had been
defeated, 32 to 86, but the government had been left in a minority of six in Upper
Canada.[68] Subsequent debates on the federal nature of the union led to a
discussion of the double majority principle. Ministers, it was claimed, ought to
have a majority in both sections of the province. Laws ought not to be imposed
on one nation, contrary to its wishes, by the vote of the other nation. Only on the
double majority principle, therefore, could "rep. by pop." be refused. All three
propositions were defeated.[69] In the course of the debate on the nature of the
union, Malcolm Cameron had asked leave to introduce a "rep. by pop." bill. The
vote, when taken after many adjournments, was 42 to 64, with 41 of the
affirmative votes coming from Upper Canada, the largest number yet given.[70]

If George Brown felt like soaring in triumph, Mackenzie brought him back
to earth. He had had his motion for repeal of the Union ready for some time. The
moment had now come. He pointed out that both double majority and "rep. by
pop." had been voted down at this session as solutions for the political troubles
of the Union. In 10 years' time Lower Canada had given just one vote in favour
of "rep. by pop." At that rate the proposition might get a majority in 200 years!
He moved that it be resolved that the Union caused discontent, leaving the
inference unstated.[71] Mackenzie remarked in the *Message*:

Had Brown joined us long since for a repeal of the Union, and
had he not treated with contempt my proposition to petition
the real power of Canada, the House of Commons, reform
might by now have made real progress. [72]

As for double majority, Mackenzie regarded it as a temporary measure, "a jury
mast for a wrecked ship." The thing could not last and any governor who did

not tell the Colonial Office that would be faithless to his trust. "Hurrah for Repeal, even George Brown will have to come to it yet," Mackenzie predicted.[73] And George Brown did.

But George Brown had not yet lost hope of the union. Since the election he had been trying to work out a *modus vivendi* with the Liberals and Rouges of Lower Canada that would rest on "rep. by pop." for Upper Canada and also on some kind of constitutional guarantees for Lower Canada that her peculiar institutions would not be endangered. In response to Mackenzie, Skeffington Connor (Liberal, Oxford South), seconded by Brown, moved a moderate amendment to the effect that Upper Canada was not happy under the union with a ministry that did not have her confidence, and that she wanted constitutional changes, which were left unspecified. Ogle R. Gowan and J. Luke Robinson, two of the government's prominent Upper Canada supporters, moved in amendment "that this House does not desire steps to be taken to weaken the Union but to strengthen it." The debate lasted from three-thirty in the afternoon on July 28 until two o'clock the next morning, when this amendment was accepted, 68 to 34.[74] It seemed that the Macdonald-Cartier ministry had won its battle both with George Brown and with Mackenzie and would weather the session.

Somewhat later on the same day the ministry was defeated by a vote of 64 to 50 when E.V. Piché, one of the Rouge members, moved that Ottawa ought not to be the seat of government.[75] The Macdonald-Cartier government, which had asked for the Queen's decision, was at first divided over accepting it and was reluctant to let that fact become known. Now, forced to take a stand, it loyally accepted the Queen's choice.[76] The government's defeat on this occasion was the second of the session.[77] In addition, it had twice been left in a minority in Upper Canada, once during the debate on the Speech,[78] once on a direct vote of confidence introduced by J.S. Macdonald.[79] Now, defeated for the third time in Upper Canada, Macdonald and his colleagues chose to resign, seizing the chance to use the loyalty issue and to show George Brown and the opposition that while they had the power to obstruct, they did not have the power to govern.

Mackenzie had begun to speak of Brown in a more friendly tone by the time the elections were called. As the session wore on and it looked as if the Macdonald-Cartier government would be defeated, he had begun to hope that Brown would have a chance to form a ministry:

> His hold on the country is undeniable, but whether he would
> display in office ability enough to work such political
> machinery as Canada has will only be known by the results. [80]

The Brown-Dorion administration took office without sufficient support from Upper Canada Reformers, Lower Canada Liberals and Rouges. When it was promptly defeated on a vote of confidence, 71 to 31, Governor Head refused Brown a dissolution and the chance to appeal to the electorate, to which Brown believed himself entitled. The old ministry was then restored to power as the

Cartier-Macdonald ministry and its members performed what was called the "double shuffle." This meant that when they returned to power they took cabinet posts different from those they had previously held; then, almost immediately, they resigned their new offices and resumed their old ones. The purpose of this manoeuvre was to take advantage of a loophole in the Independence of Parliament Act of 1857 which required cabinet members on taking office to resign their seats and stand for re-election. However, if within a month they exchanged one portfolio for another, they were not required to go through this performance again. This provision had been designed to facilitate changes within a cabinet *in office*. It had not been intended to enable a defeated government to go out of office and come back in without facing the electorate again, even if this should occur within a month's time. The restored ministers were not anxious to face the public; the members of the short-lived Brown-Dorion administration were obliged to, since they had resigned their seats as required. Their supporters raged against the trick by which the Cartier-Macdonald ministry had escaped this obligation—and criticized the Governor-General, who had connived at it, but they had not the strength to have the legality of the double shuffle condemned by the legislature.[81] They therefore took their battle to the courts, where they were to be defeated.

After Brown's ministry was defeated Mackenzie made a speech stressing what he believed was "the real question," the differences between Upper and Lower Canada. No ministry could fairly represent their conflicting principles. In his *Message* he criticized the composition of Brown's cabinet, pointing out its incongruous nature and how the members had differed from one another in the past on such questions as separate schools, the Orange Order, Sabbath Day labour, aid for the grand Trunk and "rep. by pop." Brown's colleagues had been asking for time to formulate their principles as a cabinet, but in Mackenzie's opinion they could not have done it "had you given them until the resurrection."[82] To DeWitt he described Brown's cabinet as "a queer mixture of antagonisms," adding: "If this was the best he could do, his failure is proof of the folly of the Union altogether."[83]

Mackenzie had had no share in the negotiations preceding the formation of the Brown-Dorion government. When Brown had attempted to consult him he had refused "to be mixed up in their colonial cabinet making."[84] It is clear, however, that Mackenzie felt ignored.[85] The post that he coveted seems to have been that of Provincial Secretary. But this office was evidently regarded as a plum—there was "nothing to do"—and it had gone to Oliver Mowat "over the heads of every reformer of long standing in Canada." David Christie was another old Reformer who had been passed over. Mackenzie felt he should have been made Minister of Agriculture instead of J.E. Thibaudeau.[86] Nevertheless, Mackenzie supported the short-lived administration and joined in the effort to have the double shuffle declared unconstitutional by the Assembly.[87]

The ministerial rearrangements were completed by August 6. Ten days later the legislature was prorogued. Various important bills came up for final action during this time: a bill to refinance the provincial debentures, the Franchise Bill, the Usury Bill, the Supply Bill. Three important questions were debated: the future of the Hudson's Bay territories, the prospects of an Intercolonial Railway, the possibility of confederation. Mackenzie did not vote on any of these bills or topics. It was useless, and he knew it. On the last day of the session he stood up in his place and resigned his seat.[88]

Why, after winning a hard-fought campaign, did Mackenzie choose to resign at the close of a new parliament's first session and fail to vote on several important issues? His decision had been in the making for some time. He had been thinking of resigning since June 1857, when G.M. Prévost (Rouge, Terrebonne), had resigned his seat in disgust with political life.[89] Two months before the formation of Brown's cabinet Mackenzie had told Jacob DeWitt of his intentions.[90] What had discouraged him at that particular moment was John A. Macdonald's success in cutting down the time for private bills. Debate on this proposal had continued for 27 hours and without intermission and had ended in a victory for Macdonald.[91] "Our last safeguard was thrown down — the administration are everything — can do what they please," Mackenzie wrote in despair.[92] There would be little chance now to keep his proposed reforms before the members and the public! The government's new jury law and its success in winning all the controverted election disputes decided at that session, even in flagrant cases, were other causes of his disillusionment. The creation of the Brown-Dorion ministry may have created a flickering hope for a moment, perhaps even a personal hope. The double shuffle, the Governor-General's willingness to connive at this questionable device, his refusal to give Brown a chance to appeal to the voters, and the treatment he himself was receiving in the Assembly, all firmed his decision to give up his seat. These various matters, rather than differences from his constituents over the route of the proposed Niagara and Detroit Rivers Railway, were the important causes of his resignation.

The session had been the most unhappy one Mackenzie had yet endured. He was suffering from rheumatism and feeling the pressure of his parliamentary duties at his age. Never before had he been so irregular in his attendance at the Assembly.[93] In every session he had been subjected to discourtesy. This one appears to have been the worst. Wrote one reporter:

> No sooner is Mr. Mackenzie on his legs than the harmonious sounds begin: barking puppies and penny whistles are brought into requisition; the desk lids flap in cadence and Mr. Speaker... after smirking pleasantly, with vociferous cries of "Order"... serves to swell the jovial chorus. [94]

And not only discourtesy inside the House but mockery outside it. For example, the government organ, the *Colonist*, called him

> a toothless cur... suffered to bark and snap with impunity.... Nobody heeds what he does. He is treated as a nuisance. [95]

Mackenzie's reflections as he cleared his desk of its litter — printed copies of bills he detested, newspaper clippings by the dozens, scrawled copy for the

*Message*, jottings for speeches of protest that had been disregarded—must have been bitter. He was leaving political life at a time when the government was in the hands of a ministry in which Upper Canada had lost confidence, but which was being supported by a majority composed largely of Lower Canada members, many of whom had been corruptly elected. In the House, established rules and precedents were ignored by the Speaker and private members' time had been cut to a minimum. Corruption had been revealed in the Crown Lands Department, in the Department of Public Works and in the Customs Service. The accuracy of the government's own accounts was suspect. Public defaulters, although exposed, were not being criminally prosecuted. A depression prevailed. Farmers were being sold up and he had lost his long fight against the usurers. Canada would never be the democracy of his dreams. The Brown-Dorion government, the last faint hope that Clear Grits, Rouges, and Liberals together would solve Canada's constitutional problems within the union, had proved an ignominious failure.

DeWitt tried in vain to persuade Mackenzie not to abandon the field to the foe. Mackenzie replied:

> I am a very poor man, but to take $6 a day for three years' sessions and continue in this vile den of iniquity, I cannot, will not, do it. I can do no good, I know it. Why should I stay in the Assembly?[96]

DeWitt countered:

> Shall the ablest Sentinel of Freedom leave his post? [and he added:] Your delicacy ought not to outweigh the desires of your numerous friends that you keep your post.... Wait on the dealings of Providence for your remove.[97]

Friends in Upper Canada begged Mackenzie to reconsider. Men of integrity like him were needed, they reminded him, to prevent Canada "falling under the control of monied corporations,"[98] a fate which ultimately she was not to escape. He would not alter his decision not to sit in a parliament which he regarded as now illegal and he announced that he would not be a candidate "for any seat until after that dissolution which Head refuses to sanction."[99]

Some Reformers in Haldimand who conceded that "to sit with a government which maintains itself through any irregularity of organization would be revolting to an upright mind," were nevertheless disgruntled by Mackenzie's decision. He was putting the county to the expense of another election; he had deserted them in the hour of danger; and by his criticisms of Brown's cabinet he had weakened the cause of Reform in Haldimand. One such critic wrote:

> Many exceptions doubtless may be urged against Brown's cabinet, nevertheless they are the exponents of the present

302

opposition and any suggestion of an experienced Reformer against the said cabinet are eagerly caught up by the corrupt party and used as a weapon against Reform.... [100]

In a letter to the *Colonist* Mackenzie reiterated his criticisms of the "spotted and speckled politicians" who had been selected for Brown's cabinet, justifying in some detail his claim that "not once in ten divisions of late years have the members of the Brown-Dorion cabinet been in agreement." Worse still, he allowed his opinion that George Brown was a sham Reformer, who in office would be another Hincks, to surface, and he used the back files of the *North American* to show that William McDougall, now co-operating with Brown, had once shared this fear.

The *North American* had said:

> The real danger is that "Tories" will, with the aid of the *Globe* slip in under false pretences. That journal is not a Reform journal — the Editor is not, and never was, a Reformer. The only question on which he ever pretended to be with the Reform party, is that of Church and State and its adjuncts.... On all "radical", "democratic" reforms, George Brown *and his clique are with the Tories, and opposed to Reformers.* He opposed an elective senate, one of the most important constitutional reforms demanded by the Reform party.... He stoutly defended the Court of Chancery.... He never advocated Biennial Parliaments, or vote by Ballot... on every great question of principle that distinguishes the democratic reformer from the oligarchic Tory, Mr. Brown is against us. [101]

Mackenzie refused to give any advice on the choice of a Reformer to succeed him. He had stated that he would never again enter the existing House of Assembly, corruptly elected and unconstitutionally still in existence as it was, and therefore he felt precluded from advising anyone else to do so. Other Reformers might still have hopes of accomplishing something in the present House; he had not. [102] However, when the Reformers of Haldimand nominated William Harcourt to succeed him, Mackenzie gave this choice his approval. [103] Harcourt squeaked through at the by-election with a majority of only 16 votes in a two-way contest against Samuel Amsden, who contested the result. The trial of this election dragged on for three years until, just before the sixth parliament was dissolved, the committee decided in Harcourt's favour. [104]

Although criticism of the expediency of his resignation and of his weakening the Reform Party by criticizing Brown came from some, letters of appreciation and agreement came from others. In its issue of August 21, 1858, the Montreal *National* published an eloquent tribute to Mackenzie as one who had fought for the rights and liberties of the province. [105] It was several times suggested to him that he should run for the Legislative Council and obtain what one of his friends called "a calm retreat for your declining years." [106] He refused to be nominated. He had admitted earlier that he did not have the legal qualification, £2,000 worth of real estate,[107] and by 1858 he had come to detest the whole process of government in Canada. "The whole machinery of legislation is such a mockery," he told DeWitt,[108] and to James he wrote, "I could have gone in [he does not say how] but declined. I do hate humbug from my very soul."[109]

## Chapter XX

# FEDERATION, INDEPENDENCE
# OR ANNEXATION?

When informed by his father that he had resigned his seat in the legislature, James Mackenzie inquired how he planned to employ his time and proposed that he write his memoirs.[1] Somewhat earlier, Henry O'Rielly had suggested a "History of the Last Forty Years."[2] Mackenzie himself thought of bringing out promptly a brief duodecimo volume "exhibiting the condition of Canada's government and people," but the book, if begun, was never completed.

Paid subscriptions to the *Message* had been declining and in June 1858 Mackenzie decided to stop publishing it at the end of the year.[3] He explained:

> The *Message* is a loss to me, and I begin to see that something stronger than my newspaper will be needed to effect an improvement in Canada's affairs. [4]

The fact was the *Message* could not survive in competition with the big dailies which also published weekly editions. Moreover, the *Message* had become a different and decidedly less interesting paper than Mackenzie's subscribers had been accustomed to receive. Readers were not kept abreast of the daily doings of the Assembly. Although the voting record of the members was published in chart form from time to time, summaries of speeches were infrequent. Much use was made of quotes from the *Globe*, but material from a wide range of Upper Canada papers was not utilized. Mackenzie had notified his colleagues in the profession that he no longer wished to receive exchanges. He was "positively unable to read them whether good or bad." He was doing all the work of his newspaper himself and it now fatigued him to the point at which he had neither energy nor leisure left.[5] After the session closed, the *Message* appeared only infrequently, the issue of 24 December 1858 being the last for some months.

The record of Mackenzie's activities in the interval is incomplete. He tells us that he was "much engaged" but gives no details. In December 1858 Mackenzie publicly announced that he expected to leave Toronto about the middle of February 1859. We know that his relatives in Dundee and Alyth were definitely expecting him.[6] This journey, which had been planned twice before and postponed,[7] was not intended as a vacation. His earlier effort to convince the people of Upper Canada that they should sign a monster petition to the House of Commons for repeal of the Union had not succeeded. He was still hoping for petitions to carry with him, and he now had reason to think that the recent disgraceful election, the increased tariff and the conduct of the ministry had made Upper Canada more discontented with the Union. John Simpson, cashier of the bank of Montreal at Bowmanville, wrote that he feared hard times were not yet over:

> They can't be while we have a government that doubles our taxes every five years and then spends twice what they raise. The people are disheartened. Break up the Union for God's sake. Give it a helping hand at least. [8]

Mackenzie's intention, however, was to agitate not merely for repeal of the union but for independence for Canada as the only solution for her political problems.

In May 1859 Mackenzie wrote to Horace Greeley asking for letters of introduction to people who might help him with his project. Greeley had long favoured letting the southern states secede peacefully and effecting a union of the northern states with Canada when she should have secured her independence. He provided one letter of introduction[9] but replied that he knew scarcely anyone in England who would favour Mackenzie's project.

> Ships, Colonies, Commerce are so interwoven with all the traditions of British power that I should doubt your finding in all Great Britain one hearty supporter. [10]

Undeterred, Mackenzie went to New York about May 30,[11] but changed his mind about proceeding to England. By June 6 he was back in Toronto.

How Mackenzie, in his straitened circumstances, planned to finance his journey is a mystery. He had tried to get the committee in charge of the Homestead Fund, which had been raised to help his family in his old age, to let him have some of this money for his journey. When they refused, he is said to have abused them, and particularly the treasurer, James Lesslie, in unrestrained language.[12] Mackenzie's treatment of this old friend is inexcusable — but explicable. The project of visiting the Colonial Office with petitions from Upper Canada asking for redress of grievances suffered under the Union was dear to Mackenzie's heart. He was convinced that this method, which he had used successfully in 1832, was the only method that would produce results. Now these old friends of his would not permit him to try — and with what he regarded as his own money too! But they realized what he refused to realize, that this time he would not arrive at the Colonial Office carrying any weight. Determined to go, Mackenzie started from Toronto, perhaps hoping to obtain money in New York. We can only speculate that he may have tried, and failed. He covered up his failure by referring obliquely to political events in Europe which made his visit untimely.[13]

On his return to Toronto Mackenzie proposed to readers of his *Message*, revived on June 18, a 12 months' discussion of constitutional problems. On his part this meant agitation for dissolution of the union, "as our only remedy." What Upper Canada needed, in his opinion, was the power to make her own constitution and then to enter into "such alliances and confederations as may be for our permanent advantage." He outlined the sort of republican constitution he hoped she would make for herself by means of a "free Convention." Some of the provisions he suggested had been included in the draft constitution drawn up before the rebellion and also in the constitution issued from Navy Island. Mackenzie's attendance at the New York State Constitutional Convention of 1846 and his work for the National Reformers had a marked effect upon his proposals. He wanted an elective governor and elective officials at all levels, provincial and municipal, including judges, justices of the peace and officers of the militia. Despite the changes that Macdonald and Cartier had brought about in Canada's legal system, Mackenzie still criticized it and urged that the laws be simplified, costs reduced, a unified code of practice be established — and the Law Society of Upper Canada abolished. Still hostile to the Bank of Upper Canada and rightly suspicious of its financial soundness, Mackenzie called for "a divorce" between the banks and the state, but he did not specify what he would put in their place. Presumably he had the American Independent Treasury system in mind. Canada, like New York State more than a decade earlier, was burdened with a crushing debt as the result of creating her own transportation system. Mackenzie proposed that the same remedies be adopted: a constitutional check upon the legislature's power to borrow and a prohibition against loans by the state to incorporated companies unless — and here was a modification — assented to by the Governor and three-fourths of the Assembly. Many other provisions to bring about the various political, economic, humanitarian and educational reforms he had fought for throughout his legislative career were recommended. In particular, he wanted the land companies closed out, land sold to actual settlers only in future and the right of religious bodies to hold land in mortmain strictly limited.[14]

The pre-rebellion draft constitution and the Navy Island one had not been specific about the relation between the executive and the legislature, nor was Mackenzie specific now. Clear Grits and Rouges, dissatisfied with so-called responsible government under the Act of Union, and particularly with the executive's control of money bills, had resented the ability of Hincks and his successors in office to obtain majority support for their policies by the use of patronage. As a remedy, they had advocated the American system. Thomas Storrow Brown wrote:

> The only remedy is to remove the Cabinet from parliament. Put the ministers at their desks as heads of departments to carry out the laws and leave parliament free to legislate. In this way the ministers will be the servants & not the masters of the people.[15]

J.B.E. Dorion and Papineau held similar views.[16] No one had condemned the government's use of the patronage more vigorously than Mackenzie but, after his American experience, he could not be so naive as to suppose that merely to change from the British cabinet system to the American presidential system would leave the people's representatives free from the corrupting influences of the executive, although under the elective system they might be minimized. Once again, he did not fully commit himself on this question, unless his remark that he had "held by the cabinet system while it seemed possible to continue under it" be regarded as an admission that he had come to advocate the American system, or some modification of it — such as Smith O'Brien's plan for a colonial constitution under which members of the executive would be entitled to be present in the legislature to debate but not to vote.[17]

In September the *Message* contained a letter written by Mackenzie's eldest son, James, comparing Canada's government with that of Ohio and giving his thoughts on independence. By this time the younger Mackenzie had given up publishing the Kalida *Venture* and his seat in Ohio's legislature and had been elected to a judgeship. James made out a strong case for annexation — in the future. Canada was really an inland country with "a defective natural outlet to the sea." Much of her trade was already going via the New York State canals and railroads. The province was trying to expand her boundaries to include the fertile prairies. The natural outlet for their products would be the Missouri and Mississippi and their most profitable markets would be in the south. All geographic and commercial considerations, therefore, favoured annexation. As for Canada's constitution, the tendency of all constitutions on the American continent was towards giving the people "the largest possible control of their own affairs." In Canada, ministries went in and out of office as the legislative, and not the popular, majority demanded. The result was that Canada's provincial rulers bought their legislative majorities. James outlined Ohio's constitution, stressing its completely elective character, and he illustrated with figures the simplicity and economy of its legal system. He admitted that Ohio had gone through a period of extravagance and debt while her canals were being built. That era was over. The constitution now placed limits on the legislature's power to increase the public debt. Ohio's 3,000 miles of railways had been built entirely as corporate enterprises, without state aid. County and town subscriptions to such enterprises had been given in the past, but they were now forbidden by law. Ohio had also had its experiences with defaulters but they had had to flee the state to escape trial and had not been left at liberty like those in United Canada. James remarked, "That's the difference when a People manage their own affairs and when they are managed by a government 3,000 miles away."

Once independence had been achieved, American men of capital would "flock" into Canada, James predicted; not, apparently, to take up wild land but to purchase improved properties. "Improved land is cheaper in proportion to facilities for growth with you than with us." Canada's trade and industry would also be stimulated by access to capital and a continental market, and "the incoming American population would help determine the question of

308

annexation." (One may wonder whether Canadians of the 19th century found the prospect of hordes of Americans descending upon Canada to snap up bargains in improved properties a persuasive argument for their seeking independence as a prelude to annexation.) Could annexation take place? This brought James to the question of slavery, which we know he detested.[18] He was now brief — and legal — about it. The Dred Scott decision had been given in 1857. Congress could not interfere with slavery in the states where it existed nor prevent its extension to the territories. States would emancipate when it suited them to do so. But free northern territory could be added to the union without disturbing existing institutions. James concluded with the statement:

> It is better for all that the desire for change is not immediate. We have some preparatory questions to settle, and you have some experiences to endure of the folly of trying to import British rule and preserve popular responsibility. [19]

James's argument, not factually accurate about state aid to railways, did not reveal that under Ohio's free republican constitution, with elective officials, her people had had much the same kind of experience with her Loan Law — her Plunder Law as it came to be called — as United Canada had with her Guarantee Act and Consolidated Municipal Loan Fund.[20] Ohio's financial position was now sound, a public debt of $16 million for a population of 2,300,000. United Canada, with a population no larger, had a public debt of $48 million.[21] Ohio had not been one of those states that had defaulted on their obligations or repudiated them, but for some years it had been touch and go.[22]

Independence and a new constitution, with Ohio and New York as the models to go by: that was the future Mackenzie was advocating for Canada, with annexation in the offing. Meanwhile two other solutions for Canada's constitutional problems had been offered, one by Alexander Tilloch Galt, one by George Brown. In the recent session Galt, an Independent member from Sherbrooke, Lower Canada, had proposed that the Union should be changed to a dual federation, with a general legislature for topics of "national and common" interest. The Hudson's Bay Company's territories should remain under this government until they should be sufficiently developed and settled to be admitted as members of the confederation, and inclusion of the Maritime provinces should be promoted. Debate on Galt's proposals followed but no vote was taken.[23]

In the past George Brown had advocated "rep. by pop." as the remedy for Canada's political troubles and, anxious that Upper Canada should not become a land-locked province, crippled commercially, he had opposed repeal of the Union. Subsequently he had proposed constitutional changes within the Union to make it acceptable to both parts. During the parliamentary session of 1859 he discovered how difficult day by day co-operation with the Liberals and Rouges of Lower Canada could be. By the summer of 1859 he had moved one step further and was proposing the formation of a federal union limited to the two Canadas. This was a solution that could be implemented fairly quickly compared to federation of all the British provinces, and it could lead to a wider confederation some day. Brown had not lost interest in securing the prairie lands of western Canada from the Hudson's Bay Company for Upper Canada and the trade of the west for Toronto.

In September 1859 George Brown, whose spirits had been at a low ebb, decided to take a hand in Reform politics again. He convened a meeting of Reform members from the western and central constituencies of Upper Canada to discuss party policies. The 17 MPPs who accepted his invitation decided to invite all Upper Canada Reform constituencies to send delegates to a convention in Toronto on December 9. The convention circular stated that the delegates would have an opportunity to discuss written constitutions, dissolution of the union, a federal Union of all the British North American colonies or just one between the two Canadas, "or any other plan calculated... to meet the existing evils."

> Of the 520 delegates who attended... 273 were from the western counties and the Niagara peninsula... 178 from York and the central counties, and less than 70 from the eastern section of the province. [24]

Mackenzie approved of calling this convention. This was what Reformers had demanded in 1837 and what he had advocated on several occasions since his return to political life. He attended as an editor of an opposition paper, but as he was no longer a member of Parliament or a delegate from any constituency he limited himself to the role of an observer.[25] The convention, whose committees had been carefully selected in advance and tutored by Brown and his Toronto friends,[26] accepted the six propositions of the Resolutions Committee with one modification. It resolved that the Union had given rise to a heavy public debt, to burdensome taxes and to political abuses, and had created general dissatisfaction in Upper Canada. The delegates agreed that the double majority could be no permanent solution for the country's problems and that the prospect of a confederation of all the British North American provinces was too remote to be considered as a remedy. Restrictions on the borrowing and spending powers of both executive and legislature were declared to be necessary but insufficient reforms for existing evils. The fifth resolution stated that the most practicable remedy would be the formation of two or more local governments and the creation of a general government for matters of common interest; the sixth, that such a government should be based on "rep. by pop."

It was the fifth resolution that gave trouble. To maintain party unity and to conciliate those delegates who objected to a federal union with Lower Canada and who were almost ready to vote for dissolution, something Brown was anxious to prevent. William McDougall moved that the words "a general government" be changed to "some joint authority." These vague words, which dissolutionists and federalists could interpret to suit them, proved acceptable to the convention, particularly as the resolution provided that if Lower Canada refused to co-operate in setting up a joint authority, the party would "go... for a dissolution."[27] John A. Macdonald thought the convention had ended "in a fizzle" and in "an ignominious defeat for Brown." He asked, "Have they deposed Brown."[28] He had not been deposed, but his victory had yet to be consolidated. At the close, the convention decided to organize a Constitutional Reform Association with branches in every constituency. The central committee in Toronto was charged with the duty of formulating an address to report to the electors what had been agreed on.[29] The London *Free Press* called McDougall's compromise "an intangible illusion... a juggle... a mockery."[30] The committee's report was not published until February 22, 1860. In the meantime George Brown's *Globe* gave *his* interpretation of the work of the convention. Brown ignored McDougall's "joint authority." The delegates, he said, voted for a federal union.[31] George Sheppard was now preparing to leave the *Globe*. In the convention he had given a vigorous speech urging the delegates to pledge the party to constitutional reforms and to dissolution. He now complained:

> The constitutional struggle is now ignored by the *Globe*; at least
> I am not allowed to write about it. The one thing talked about
> is the prospect of getting office.... [32]

Mackenzie, who was far from content with the decisions of the convention, waited for a time to see what form the address of the Constitutional Reform Association would take. When it was not promptly forthcoming, he issued his own Appeal to the People of Upper Canada as an answer to the resolutions of the convention, and he made it the major part of his *Almanac for Independence and Freedom for 1860*. Mackenzie called Brown's federal union a "sham issue," only useful for election purposes.[33] He feared Upper Canada would have to wait as long for Lower Canada to assent to a federal government based on "rep. by pop." as it would for the assent of the Maritimes to a wider union. Brown proposed "to cure all our ills by a closer and costlier French connexion."[34] His scheme would require Upper Canada to support two governments and to pay the major part of the expenses for one of them. The constitutional changes the Clear Grits had long advocated — complete control by Canadians of their own civil list and their commerce,[35] and extension of elective institutions — had been ignored.

Both of the simple solutions for Canada's problems originally put forward by Brown and Mackenzie were clearly inadequate, and by 1860 both of them had come to recognize that fact. Brown had found it necessary to think beyond "rep. by pop." and was advocating federalism. Mackenzie was ready to admit that:

> Simple dissolution in 1860, a return to the system of 1791, with
> a very heavy debt, burdensome taxation and a line of tax
> gatherers all along the Ottawa would not mend matters much.

It would not give Upper Canada free trade with the United States nor power to establish a free constitution, although it would be infinitely better than the "new Union bill" with the French proposed at the Toronto convention.[36] Only

311

independence would give Upper Canada what she needed, and independence, Mackenzie argued, would be in the true interests of the mother country since it would relieve her of expense and causes of friction with the United States.

Independence was now Mackenzie's answer — independence, possibly followed by annexation to the United States. Annexation would unite "in one common bond the great interests of Agriculture, Manufacturing and Commerce throughout the northern continent." It was the true policy for Canada, Great Britain and the United States.[37] In his *Independence Almanac* Mackenzie did not openly advocate annexation as a step to be attempted before the slavery issue should have been settled, but the advantages of annexation were stressed throughout. The economic arguments for annexation used by the authors of the Annexation Manifesto in 1849 were reprinted and praised in language taken from the Prescott *Telegraph* of October 1849. "We never saw so many plain uncontroverted facts in so small a compass. They are naked truths told us in plain language."[38] Mackenzie concluded by renewing his suggestion that a petition asking for independence should be signed and sent to those members of the House of Commons who would be likely to favour it.[39]

All this was plainly inconsistent with the position Mackenzie had taken in 1849. He frankly admitted it. He had always believed independence to be the end towards which the colonial relationship was developing and in which it would terminate, and he had pointed out that for a landlocked Upper Canada annexation would be inevitable.[40] But in 1849, influenced by the Nativist movement and the existence of slavery in the United States, and probably to some extent by considerations of expediency, he had vigorously condemned annexation. He had said then that Upper Canada was not yet ready for independence and meanwhile he was willing to give the Union a fair trial. Well, the Union had been tried and, clearly, had failed.

No doubt anticipating that he would be criticized for his inconsistency, Mackenzie took the offensive. He accused George Brown of having "veered to every point of the compass that would pay," justifying his accusation by quotes from the *Globe*.[41] Brown was merely trying to unite an opposition party strong enough to topple the corrupt, railway-dominated group in power and to carry him into office. Throughout 1860 the columns of the *Message* contained one attack after another on Brown. They were regarded by some as wholly vindictive and motivated by jealousy.[42] Mackenzie can hardly have been free of some feelings of this kind. After all, Brown had apparently united the majority of Upper Canada Reformers behind him; Mackenzie had kept the allegiance only of the most radical. The *Globe* was flourishing, the *Message* dying. But there had been a brief period during 1859 when the *Globe* had come out for dissolution, a written constitution, and changes that would diminish the power of the executive, exclude the ministers from the legislature and extend elective institutions. These editorials had been permitted by Brown during a temporary period of frustration and anger caused by the irritations of the session and by the decision of the judges, handed down in December 1858, that the double shuffle had been legal. They had been written not by him but by one of his editorial writers, the radical George Sheppard, who was to leave the *Globe* before long.

For the ordinary reader, however, the pronouncements of the *Globe* and the opinions of George Brown were one;[43] yet when western radicals came to the convention they found the resolution on constitutional changes offered for their adoption worded so as to denigrate their importance. Also, there had been a moment in the life of the convention when it seemed that the radicals would get their way and that the convention would go for dissolution of the union, not for federation. This was the very thing Brown had planned to prevent by careful pre-convention strategy, since dissolution was not acceptable to the moderate and eastern wing of the Reform Party, nor in the economic interests of Upper Canada in the long run. It was George Brown's rousing speech that had brought the convention round to accepting McDougall's "joint authority" amendment. Brown had said:

> What true Canadian can witness the tide of Immigration now commencing to flow into the territories of the North West without hoping to have a share in the first settlement of that great and fertile country, and making our own country the highway of traffic to the Pacific? But is it not true wisdom to commence the federated system with our own country and leave it open to extension hereafter .... And how can there be the slightest question... between complete dissolution and the scheme of the committee? Is it not clear that the former would be the death blow to the hopes of future union, while the latter may at some future day readily furnish the machinery of a great confederation? [44]

As Mackenzie pointed out, Brown was advocating essentially what Galt had advocated in July 1858 and what Brown had then opposed.[45] He had put it to the Reform convention somewhat less boldly and less comprehensively than Galt, with more emphasis on the creation of a dual federation as a starter.

The semantic compromise, the "joint authority," skillfully offered at the right moment and dramatically supported by Brown's speech, was to be interpreted by the *Globe* essentially as federalism and all discussion of constitutional changes disappeared from its columns lest it should endanger party unity. No wonder that Mackenzie was critical of Brown. He had hoped that the convention would go on record as favouring the various reforms which he and the Clear Grits section of the party had been advocating. Brown had killed that hope. He had hoisted the flag of reform but he had staved off all real reform by urging a federal union with French Canada. Mackenzie believed that if the question of a simple dissolution of the union had been put before the convention it would have carried. By preventing such a motion Brown had prevented an appeal to England "for such remedies as only England can give." What was Brown now proposing to do? Nothing that was worth a brass farthing. He had taken none of the steps resolved on in the convention. He had destroyed his influence in Lower Canada and five of the Upper Canada Reformers had turned against him in the legislature. He had nullified the labours of the convention and accomplished nothing. He had wasted a year.[46] Mackenzie spent his last strength as an editor making it plain that in his opinion Brown had "paralyzed" the Reform Party. Brown did not succeed in bringing up his proposals for the dissolution of the Union and the creation of two local governments plus a joint authority in its place until April 16, 1860. After repeated exasperating postponements of the debate, they were defeated.[47]

These virulent criticisms of Brown brought down on Mackenzie once more accusations of being animated by personal pique. With more justice he was accused of inconsistency. During the general election of 1858 he had supported Brown, calling him "the man for the times." He had said he was for Brown because all the railroad jobbers, office seekers and Tory abettors of misrule opposed him. If the argument had been valid then, was it not still valid?[48] Mackenzie acknowledged that Brown had done good work on the Committee on Finance and he praised the manner in which abuses had been fearlessly exposed in the columns of the *Globe*.

> Where is the man who had worked like Brown to be the head of a party here," he asked. "Who could the opposition put in his place? ... He is the man for the times if Head's crew are ever to be got rid of. [49]

He was the man — but the trouble was he would not take what Mackenzie regarded as the right course. That was to forget the French, concentrate on the grievances of Upper Canada and ask the British government to allow Upper Canada to make her own constitution, to enjoy independence and to be free to enter some other confederation when — and if — she chose to do so.

\* \* \*

It will be remembered that in 1856 a subscription had been started to provide Mackenzie with a homestead in recognition of his services to Upper Canada. The fund accumulated slowly during the years of bad harvests and financial stringency. Of the $9,114.60 subscribed, $7,000 had been collected when the treasurer, James Lesslie, made his final report to the committee in charge on May 20, 1859.[50] A three-story brick house at what is now 117 Bond Street was purchased for the Mackenzie family and arrangements were made for a one-story brick addition. By October 1859 the family was occupying the new home. From time to time Mackenzie had acknowledged in the *Message* contributions to the Homestead Fund. They ranged in size from 50 cents to the $40.00 contributions of several members of Parliament. In his *Independence Almanac* Mackenzie thanked the people of Upper Canada for their gift to an "ancient public servant" and handsomely acknowledged the work of the committee, with particular mention of the labours of his much-tried friend James Lesslie. Mackenzie had at one time quarrelled with the members of the committee then in charge, and had even asked that no more contributions be made to the homestead.[51] He now made an apology:

314

I differed from the first committee on the manner in which the Homestead deed should be drawn but their views were quite conscientious and offered from the very kindest motives. [52]

Possibly they wished to restrict the deed in some way so that he could not burden the property to raise money for his planned trip to England or to continue publishing his *Message*. If so, it is not surprising that Mackenzie resented the committee's attitude. His pride would be touched. He regarded the Homestead Fund as a debt that the people of Upper Canada *owed him* for his services and his expenditures on their behalf, not as a charitable gift to be administered by a committee for the welfare of himself and his family in his old age.

When Mackenzie revived the *Message* in June 1859 he made such liberal use of cartoons that some of its issues look more like a comic paper than a serious political weekly. Without the long explanations attached, the cartoons would be pointless. During its final year the *Message* contained a *Life of Robert Bruce*, published in installments written, its editor claimed, especially for the *Message* by someone he did not name to illustrate "the curse of Papal and priestly interference in politics." Charles Kingsley's *Alton Locke*, "illustrating the slavery in which the workers are held" was also serialized. Letters from Jacob DeWitt criticizing the government's bank acts and its revenue policies and denouncing the repeated attempts to raise the rate of interest were utilized as articles, sometimes without the author's signature.[53] DeWitt was opposed to a revenue tariff on articles that had to be imported, but favoured a protective tariff for the benefit of Canada's budding industries. Mackenzie, who had long ago accepted the home market argument of Henry Carey, shared DeWitt's opinions. He was in favour of "incidental protection," but he also advocated free trade with the rapidly industrializing United States.[54] How he would reconcile these two policies, which were bound to conflict sooner or later, he did not explain. Another of Mackenzie's correspondents, John Windt, supplied him with useful material on interest rates and questions of land policy from the point of view of the National Reformers.[55] Windt's letters to the *New York Tribune* on Problems of Pauperism were also reprinted in the *Message*. Windt wrote:

> The solution of this problem involves not only the happiness but also the perpetuity of the Republic and perhaps the capacity of Mankind to maintain Free and rational government. [56]

Prescient words!

Not much time remained to the *Message* — or to Mackenzie. He continued to argue for independence and for land reform, kept the province in mind of its defaulters and urged his friends in the legislature to enlarge the list of exemptions for debtors and not to forget poor old John Montgomery who had repeatedly petitioned for compensation for the deliberate burning of his tavern in 1837 on the order of Sir Francis Bond Head.[57] Mackenzie criticized the

315

procedures of the division courts as ruinously expensive both to the small debtors who came before them and to their creditors, justifying his remarks with a reference to a recent sessional paper. By publishing an article from the *Upper Canada Law Journal* of April 1860 he drew attention to the fact that small debtors were being imprisoned for not having satisfied judgments against them, not for fraud or for obtaining credit under false pretences, which was all the Division Court Act, 13 & 14 Vic., cap.53, allowed.[58] Again he denounced the repeal of the laws against usury, pointing out that "New York and Ohio had gone back to 6%,"[59] and he drew attention to Edward Kellog's *Labour and Other Capital*. Kellog's argument was that if a rate of interest was permitted in excess of the rate at which the physical wealth of the country was increasing, then borrowers were called upon to repay more than they were able to supply and the result would be that property would tend to accumulate in the hands of capitalists.[60] Mackenzie was pleased to see a Homestead Exemption Bill and a measure for the abolition of property qualifications for election to the Assembly making progress in others' hands although they had not in his.[61] He took special satisfaction in pointing out to Upper Canada that in Great Britain the Lord Chancellor had introduced a Law and Equity Bill designed to extend the equity powers of the common law courts beyond those they had already been given by an act of 1854: "My ideas," he remarked, "are becoming fashionable."[62]

There was much denunciation of the Papacy and much ranting criticism of the government in the *Message* — an indication of Mackenzie's rapidly failing powers — but from time to time there was substance also. What there was not was what the *Globe* gave — detailed political news. "Tell us what Parliament is doing," one of Mackenzie's subscribers demanded. He replied that he would not waste time on their "useless speeches and moonshine schemes."[63] But contemporary Canadian news, the prospects of federation and of acquiring the Hudson's Bay territories, rather than theoretical discussions of economic policies or installments of novels, were what his readers preferred, and when they did not get it their subscriptions dropped off. By the close of 1859 Mackenzie had fewer subscribers than when he started in journalism in 1824, and he was reduced to pleading with old friends for support.[64] He admitted sadly to his son, "Nobody seems to care for my little *Message* now." It ceased publication abruptly on September 15, 1860.

Perhaps the old man got a little consolation in these unhappy days out of the visits of young John Ross Robertson, who used to drop in after school to learn about the hazards and problems of publishing a newspaper. Perhaps it was Mackenzie who drilled into him the wisdom of insisting on all subscriptions being paid in advance and of requiring all letters to the editor to be pre-paid. Of Editor Robertson it was to be said, "If there is anything wrong with the Eternal Councils not all the angels and arch-angels of Heaven will silence him." Truly, in this, another Mackenzie.[65]

Little occurred during the years 1859-1861 to lift Mackenzie's spirits. It is true that right up to the time of his final illness he was still being asked to make speeches at Reform or Temperance meetings, with the assurance that if he would consent to come, the money for his expenses could be found.[66] For

Mackenzie was hard pressed, even with the homestead, and his friends knew it. Then there had been a costly and unnecessary chancery suit with John Doel. It will be remembered that Doel had befriended Mackenzie. He had enabled him to qualify for the Assembly by selling back to him his land in Garafraxa and Dundas and taking a note, not a mortgage, for the large unpaid balance. When Mackenzie resigned his seat Doel wanted this unsecured obligation changed to a mortgage. Mackenzie's reluctance to give it offended Doel. Losing patience at last, Doel commenced a chancery suit against him which was dismissed when Mackenzie finally agreed to sign the mortgage.[67] His hesitation was probably due to a wish not to impair his qualifications for the Assembly. He had said he would not sit any longer in the "unconstitutional" Assembly of 1858, but he had not said he would not sit in another Assembly properly elected and legally sitting. A few weeks before his death in 1861 he was still dreaming of being a candidate again.[68] To Doel, and to James Lesslie, who had the task of remonstrating with Mackenzie and bringing him to reason, his conduct towards Doel must have seemed most ungrateful. The unnecessary chancery suit cost both sides money, and Mackenzie could ill spare it.

In late November 1859 Mackenzie had had the sad duty of helping to arrange for and being present at the exhumation of the bodies of Lount and Mathews from the potter's field, which was about to be sold, and their reburial in the Toronto Necropolis.[69] For what had these lives been sacrificed — these old friends of his? In retrospect, had it really been necessary? Mackenzie's own share of responsibility for attempting to hasten the slow tempo of reform may have tortured him as he stood by Mrs. Lount's side at the reopened grave. Perhaps as he walked sadly homewards he comforted himself with Macaulay's words that he had quoted in the first issue of his *Message*: "To trace the exact boundary between rightful and wrongful resistance is impossible.[70]

From Mackenzie's old friends in the legislature no cheering news came. Although there was still an Upper Canada majority against the government, the deeply divided Reform Party had accomplished nothing. It had become "a mere congeries of discordant opinions."[71] Brown was not holding the party together. The Lower Canada members of his short-lived administration had publicly differed from him as to what policies his cabinet intended towards Roman Catholics in Upper Canada and on the manner in which his government had planned to give additional assistance to the censitaires for the redemption of seigneurial rights.[72] In Upper Canada the Clear Grits' suspicions of Brown as no true Reformer, except on church-state issues, would not die.[73] David Christie wrote:

> The Convention resolutions, I fear, will not meet our case. Remedies which reach far beyond them are necessary. Brown has pursued a reckless and over-bearing course this session. Independent men do not like such treatment and they will not submit to them [*sic*]. At bottom, too, there is a want of confidence in him. The remembrance of his course at the election of 1854 inspires this state of feeling.[74]

And not only the election of 1854, but the manner in which the convention of 1859 had been manipulated and dominated, and the Reform caucus at first bullied and then ignored by Brown. Michael Foley in a speech of May 7, 1860, revealed their resentment to the Assembly and, as a consequence, the disorganization of the Reform Party.[75]

If Upper Canada's Reformers could not rely on Brown to fight for dissolution and the constitutional changes they wanted, what could be done? Mackenzie had planned to make the Colonial Secretary aware of Upper Canada's dissatisfaction with the Union himself. He had been unable to go to England, but there was still a chance of accomplishing his end. In the fall of 1860 Edward, Prince of Wales, accompanied by the Duke of Newcastle, Secretary of State for the Colonies, was to visit Canada. Here was a golden opportunity that should not be missed.[76] Toronto's fervidly loyal newspapers kept insisting that, despite the deep political discontent in Upper Canada, nothing must mar the Prince's visit. His Royal Highness should not be disturbed. Mackenzie agreed, but he could see no reason why the *Duke* should not be disturbed.[77] With the Colonial Office at their front door, so to speak, here was the chance for Upper Canada Reformers to make known their grievances under the Union and their desire for constitutional changes.[78] The royal visit — and the use Reformers could make of the Duke's presence — this was the chief theme of the *Message* in its last few issues. The articles were written in a moderate and pleasant tone, and the Queen, referred to contemptuously in 1838 as "that girl," had now become the Prince's "excellent mother."[79]

Although Mackenzie went to Montreal on the occasion of the Prince's arrival there, he had no intention of attempting to present such an address himself. He left that "to those whose positions authorize and allow it."[80] He was pleased to hear that George Brown intended to call the Duke's attention to the state of the country and he states that he was told that Brown had drawn up a document which, when signed by a majority of the Upper Canada opposition members, was to be presented to the Duke with a request for an interview.[81] A biography of the Duke of Newcastle in which an account of the royal visit is given, and several of Newcastle's reports to Palmerston are printed, makes no mention of such a document or of an interview with Brown.[82] Neither does Brown's biographer mention them, but he does refer to a Reform meeting held at Galt a few days after the Prince's visit to Toronto and before His Royal Highness and the Duke left the province.[83] In this indirect way Newcastle may have had his eyes opened to the discontent in Upper Canada.

Mackenzie's son William, who had been working for the Associated Press in New York since September 1856, became anxious to return to Canada and in March 1858 had asked his father to get him a position as clerk with some committee of the Assembly.[84] But Mackenzie was then about to resign his seat and would not have asked the administration then in office for any favours. It is not known exactly when his son returned to Toronto, but in February 1860 Charles Lindsey, who could approach a Conservative government, persuaded the Speaker, Henry Smith, to find a place for his brother-in-law. William seems to have been a rather unsteady young man. Within a month Smith was

318

complaining that William had come to him "in a very stupid state." He hoped he would "pull up."[85] In April 1861, when news of the outbreak of the American Civil War came, William, with other young men of Toronto, rushed off to Cincinnati and enlisted, at first for three months, later for three years.[86] The impetuous young man soon tired of military service but was persuaded by his elder brother to stick it out.[87] In April he was writing home from the field of Shiloh.[88] By December 1862 he was in hospital and on July 24, 1863, he was discharged, suffering from "hypertrophy and dilation of the heart."[89]

Mackenzie, too, was aroused to action by the war. He rejoiced in the triumph of the Republicans and the election of Lincoln.[90] At first he mistakenly believed that the cabinet in Washington would "gladly part friends" with the slave states and "shake hands permanently with the northern colonies."[91] A few months later he was "delighted" at the way the North had "stood up for the Union."[92] Was there at last a hope of bringing Canada into that union and could any efforts of his help along the good cause? The old man seems to have cherished that hope. On June 22, 1861, he informed James, "I leave for Washington in a day or two." He planned only a short absence. A general election had been called. He had to be back to vote and "perhaps" to be a candidate.

There was to be no journey to Washington and no candidacy. Mackenzie's strength was going. He was getting forgetful, mislaying his papers and neglecting to finish and post his letters to James. "I do fail fast," he confessed.[93] A letter that did get written and posted was one to George Brown making kind inquiries about him during his illness. He received a friendly and appreciative response from a man who could understand perhaps better than anyone else the arduous life Mackenzie had led.[94] "Life, James, is an uncertain boon," the father wrote in that last letter of June 22. There were just two months more of it, two months in which he became progressively weaker, unwilling to take stimulants or medicine, unable to write, anxious only to rest. On August 28, 1861, he died.[95]

> A gradual decay of his natural powers took place during the last few months and a few weeks ago he sank into a state of insensibility which yesterday evening ended in death.

So ran the *Globe's* report of August 29. The funeral took place on the following Saturday with the Mayor and Council, some 40 carriages, and many gentlemen on foot following the hearse to the Toronto Necropolis.[96]

Controversy surrounded Mackenzie even in death. Thurlow Weed, who had known Mackenzie for 40 years, wrote an obituary notice of him for the Albany *Evening Journal*. His characterization of Mackenzie although not uncritical was not unkind, but in the course of it he remarked that "undying hatred of the British Government" was Mackenzie's "ruling passion." "His last days and hours were given to a long labored letter bearing dates of 18th, 19th, 20th and 24th of August, 1861," that was "in his own hand," extended "over a dozen sheets," and was fortified with numerous documents — "all designed to prove that England intends and is preparing to take advantage of this Rebellion to avenge that of 1776." No such letter is now to be found in the Weed Papers in the library of the University of Rochester. Charles Lindsey denied that his father-in-law had the strength during the last month of his life to write any letter, much less one that, as Weed admitted, "would have taxed the strength of a well man." Lindsey accused Weed of "inventing the whole story for some base purpose of his own." One can only wonder whether Weed's article was a bit of war-time propaganda intended to stir up northern feeling against a country thought at the moment to be sympathetic to the South. For this purpose Weed may have made use of sentiment Mackenzie may have expressed, even in letters, at a much earlier time when he was suspicious of British policy in Texas.[97]

# Chapter XXI

# RETROSPECT

It is possible now to take a retrospective view of Mackenzie's post-rebellion career and to consider the sharply divergent estimates of him referred to in the first chapter of this study. A few days after his death both Liberal and Conservative newspapers printed judicial and temperate summaries of his career. Several of them can conveniently be read in Charles Lindsey's volume in the Makers of Canada series.[1] They all emphasized his personal integrity, his independence, his courage, his concern for efficient and honest administration of public affairs and his sincere if mistaken patriotism. They passed over his defects of character, touched on the rebellion lightly with cautious words of regret and stressed the constitutional changes it had hastened. A year later, Mackenzie's son-in-law, Charles Lindsey, published his *Life and Times of William Lyon Mackenzie*. This was a sympathetic but not uncritical biography written by one who had differed from Mackenzie in politics but who had had access to his private papers and the unique advantage of knowing him and his family intimately. In 1885 J.C. Dent's *Story of the Upper Canada Rebellion* appeared. Although Dent acknowledged Mackenzie's talents, he denigrated his character and his political achievements and elevated John Rolph at his expense. The *Story* called forth a long letter from James Mackenzie to Charles Lindsey flatly contradicting several of Dent's statements and also a hot response from John King, another of Mackenzie's sons-in-law, who entitled his rebuttal *The Other Side of the "Story"*.[2]

In 1908 Charles Lindsey, with the help of his son C.G.S. Lindsey, published a condensed version of his *Life of Mackenzie* in which a few errors in the original biography were corrected and some additional information was given. It had been intended by Messrs. Morang and Co., publishers of the Makers of Canada Series, in which Lindsey's revised biography was included, that W.D. LeSueur should provide the Mackenzie volume for their series, but the manuscript he produced was rejected by them and remained unpublished for many years. In 1979 A.B. McKillop edited and published LeSueur's manuscript with an informative introduction about the author, his place in Canadian historiography, his controversy with the Mackenzies and Morang, the influence of Mackenzie King in this affair and LeSueur's defence. LeSueur's *Mackenzie* was rejected because it did not fit in with what had been said in other volumes of the series about public men and the course of Canadian history. In addition, it was entirely out of sympathy with Mackenzie and did not present him as a "Maker" of Canada.[3] In Morang's opinion, scant justice had been done to his virtues and to his best qualities of head and heart and as much as possible had been made of his imperfections and weaknesses. LeSueur, on the other hand, considered he had made the real Mackenzie stand up and exhibit his feet of clay.

LeSueur's book was intended by him "to correct the extravagantly liberal view of the rebellion which has become a kind of tradition in Canada."[4] The author argued that Mackenzie had retarded rather than promoted the work of reform and the acquisition of responsible government. When Morang pointed out to him that Adam Short shared his views but had been more discreet in his *Sydenham*,[5] LeSueur vigorously defended the historian's right — and duty — to attack the sacred "myths" of history. However little one may agree with LeSueur's estimate of Mackenzie, it is impossible not to admire his sturdy independence and his refusal to make his work conform to the pattern set by other authors in the series who, he felt, had simply "hashed up" the opinions they regarded as prevailing without doing additional research of their own and who had emphasized the old theme of the acquisition of responsible government.[6] In addition to discussing this theme and Mackenzie's share in bringing about responsible government, or delaying its advent, LeSueur penned a damning estimate of Mackenzie himself: he frequently repeated statements that were "shockingly untrue," was guilty of "excesses of scurrility," misled the ignorant, ascribed the worst of motives to his opponents, and let his hatred of them dominate his interest in practical measures of reform. Nevertheless he had a soul above party politics and there was "a sound core of humanity in the man." These were the "essential ingredients in the rebel's character and actions."[7] This is harsh and not all of it specifically and adequately documented.

Writing in 1908, LeSueur considered that the problem of responsible government had not even then been solved. Government had

> only very partially been made responsible. What are the papers telling you every day about the corruption, the abuses, the waste of public money and the public domain that have sprung up under responsible government? [he inquired] People are becoming aware that they have placed altogether too much faith in the mathematical perfection of their political institutions and that it will take more to make a government responsible than to call it responsible.... My book forces attention upon the political situation of to-day.... It will make people see that for real responsible government they have to depend upon character — the mere machinery will never do it.[8]

It is amazing that a man who could see this — and write this — was not more appreciative of Mackenzie, who had stressed this very point for years. As early as 1832 he saw that responsible government would not be enough;[9] throughout his post-rebellion career in Canada he proclaimed that responsible government had proved to be "a sham" and kept bringing to light the same sort of abuses that LeSueur was complaining about in 1908. The explanation perhaps is that LeSueur was not well acquainted with Mackenzie's post-rebellion career. He could actually write:

> You cannot write the history of Canada for that period 1824-1838 and leave Mackenzie out but you could write the history from 1850 to 1861 and leave him out altogether. [10]

In a three-column article summarizing Mackenzie's career, published the day after his death, the Toronto *Globe* put it otherwise:

> No history of Canada can be complete in which his name does not occupy a conspicuous and we must add, not withstanding his errors, an honourable place ... he was the friend of purity and economy in the administration of public affairs. [11]

Surely this is not simply an instance of *nil nisi bonum*?

In recent years several other studies of Mackenzie have been made, some of which deal chiefly with the period up to the rebellion.[12] William Kilbourn's *The Firebrand* is a lively and imaginative account of the rebellion period and in many respects a perceptive and sympathetic although not uncritical account of Mackenzie himself. Kilbourn appreciates Mackenzie's power as a stump speaker and the hold he was able to get and long retain upon the affections of the rural population, but he takes the same view of Mackenzie's activities after his return from exile as LeSueur.

> In his old age he haunted the era of responsible government, an irrelevant nuisance, with his capering gestures of protest, amid the church parade of progress.[13]

It is hoped that the foregoing chapters provide a corrective for these estimates of Mackenzie's post-rebellion career. Mackenzie, one can be sure, would never have applied the phrase "church parade of progress" to Hincks's corrupt years in office, and if one wants to present Mackenzie himself in humorous terms, he might better be described as a dauntless little old man, persistently getting in the way of the big engines in a dirty railway shunting yard. J.B. Rea has given us an excellent chronological account of the development of Mackenzie's ideas during the pre-rebellion period and of the influence of the Jacksonians upon him.[14] Then there has been William Morrison's sympathetic but balanced appraisal of Mackenzie.[15] F.H. Armstrong's studies of his pre-rebellion career denigrate his character, his abilities as an administrator and the genuineness of his concern for the ordinary man.[16] More recently we have had from the pen of Paul Romney a careful study much less critical of Mackenzie as Mayor of

Toronto.[17] A.W. Raporich regards him as a man of inconsistent political ideas and "woolly" economic policies, fundamentally a romantic and an agrarian reactionary who, after his return from exile, "settled into a mood of cranky agrarian sectionalism."[18]

Several of Mackenzie's biographers agree with LeSueur that Mackenzie dragged Upper Canada "out of a course of steady constitutional development" and retarded the political development of the country. As Kilbourn has well put it, "There fled with Mackenzie ... a whole era of Canadian politics."[19] Others contend that it was the rebellion that hastened desirable constitutional changes in Canada.[20]

> It must be reiterated [said the Toronto *Globe*], that insurrection was the immediate cause of the introduction of a new system. It might have been gained without rebellion but the rebellion gained it. [21]

What is the fundamental significance of Mackenzie's career? An adequate discussion of this broad question and of these conflicting interpretations is beyond the scope of this study. It would take a chapter, if not a book to itself, plus careful consideration of the course of imperial history such as has been given in Oscar A. Kitchen's *Lord Russell's Canadian Policy* and recently in Phillip A. Buckner, *The Transition to Responsible Government*. But we can consider what are the facts of Mackenzie's post-rebellion life, how justified are the various estimates that have been made of his abilities, his character and his conduct, and how desirable were the reforms for which he fought.

In considering Mackenzie as a politician and reformer we need to ask first what his hopes for Canada were. In January 1837, Mackenzie summed up his position in these general terms:

> I wish to live long enough to see the people of this continent of the humblest classes educated and free, and held in respect according to their conduct and attainments without reference to country, color or worldly substance. [22]

The prime requisite to bring about a greater degree of social justice, he later came to realize, was peace, so that the work of reform could go forward. Unless it did, one need not expect that education alone, on which he always placed great emphasis, would prevent a rapidly rising crime rate such as was then occurring in England, despite the steady increase in her wealth.[23] Put in other terms, this meant that Mackenzie hoped Canada would yet become the ideal society of which he had dreamed in his early days when he was absorbing the ideas of British and American radicals.[24] He wanted her to be a land of equal opportunity for all, with no privileged clergy interfering in public affairs, with no grasping land speculators or money lenders, with no privileged corporations, with no extremes of wealth or poverty, but with education available to all, with the professions and trades open to all, with the natural resources of the country wisely and fairly administered by an honest, efficient, economical government elected by enlightened voters who *also* would have the general welfare at heart.

The question arises, in striving to establish his ideal egalitarian society, did Mackenzie ignore the important issues of his own day or did he contribute to their solution? But what were the important issues, and from whose point of view were they important? In the long run the important issues for Canada have proved to be the acquisition of the Hudson's Bay Company's territories, the creation of a federation of all the British North American provinces, and the construction of a transportation network to hold them together.

Mackenzie was hostile enough to the Hudson's Bay Company, but it was the same kind of hostility he had always shown towards monopolies and to the Canada Company. He wanted cheap fertile land for farmers' sons and he knew well enough that united Canada was running out of it. In one of his earliest political pronouncements made just prior to his return, he argued that the Company's territories should be opened to Canadian settlers, and subsequently he criticized the Macdonald-Taché government for failure to take vigorous enough action on the western question.[25] It is true that he later wrote that while Canada retained her colonial status he did not expect the territory to be well administered when she acquired it and, anyway, it had abundance of grasshoppers and no coal. But ought one to stretch this crotchety comment into "disenchantment" with the Canadian northwest as an area worth acquiring and settling?[26] While the shortage of cheap land continued Mackenzie was one of those demanding colonization roads and free grants for settlers in what proved to be an unsuitable area where "The Dark Druidical trees"[27] might better have been left untouched.

Mackenzie does not seem to have had A.T. Galt's great vision of a Canada stretching from sea to sea. Well acquainted as he was with the history of the United States, it is surprising that his imagination was not fired by the prospect of the gradual growth of a transcontinental federation of provinces, admitted one by one to the original nucleus in the way the American territories had been admitted to the union. At one time Mackenzie had favoured a federation of all the provinces. In 1834 he wrote to George Canning advocating a union of all the British North American colonies under a government:

> suitably poised and modelled, so as to have under its eye the resources of our whole territory, and having the means in its power to administer impartial justice in all its bounds, to no one part at the expense of another.... [28]

Upper Canada's experience under the Union had turned him away from the idea of federation. She had not been receiving impartial justice and he feared she would not under a confederation of all the provinces. Moreover, he could see only the difficulties and delays involved in such a scheme. The Maritimes were not ready for it and neither was Lower Canada. No relief for Upper Canada was in prospect and it was with Upper Canada he was primarily concerned. She would continue to be "milked" by her sister province and no doubt the poor

Maritimes would also plunder her should a federation ever be created. Mackenzie's vision was now myopic. He had become too busy scrutinizing the defects in Canada's existing political fabric to plan a new continent-wide garment for her.

From the point of view of Mackenzie's contemporaries, the important questions of the 1850s were secularization of the Clergy Reserves, abolition of the seigneurial tenures, reciprocity with the United States, the Grand Trunk, acquisition of more capital for development and the future of the Union. Mackenzie tried to make the first reform more beneficial to education and the second more helpful to the censitaires than to the seigneurs. He never advocated free trade either before or after his rebellion, but he consistently advocated freer trade relations with the United States.[29] His objection to the Grand Trunk was to its corruptive effect on public life, and to the manner in which government aid was provided through a tariff that bore hard on the poorer classes and increasingly threatened the life of the reciprocity arrangements with the United States. He raised the "rep. by pop." issue before George Brown did, and saw earlier than anyone else that it could not be obtained with Lower Canada's consent and that repeal of the Union must be effected. He appreciated as fully as Brown the difficulties Upper Canada might be exposed to if her export trade came to be at the mercy of Lower Canada and the United States, and he saw that the choice might have to be annexation. Its economic advantages were plain.

The issues of immediate importance from Mackenzie's point of view, once the Clergy Reserve question had been settled, and all religious denominations placed on a basis of equality before the law, were making responsible government more than an empty phrase, and providing laws and institutions to protect the interests of the poor man and his family. These objectives required that the legislature be made a really independent body of men, honestly elected on a wide franchise from constituencies of equal size. A high degree of local autonomy with elective officials at every level, an improved system of accounting for the public revenue, a land policy that would benefit settlers and immigrants and a sound banking policy — all were needed. The usury laws should be maintained, imprisonment for debt abolished and a simplified and less costly legal system instituted. Mackenzie fought the battles of the underdog — not always with discretion, not always fair to his opponents and not without a touch of personal vindictiveness towards some of them.

It should now be evident that, although Mackenzie had his own projects, his career in the legislature was not that of an unthinking obstructionist, an agrarian reactionary not alert to important issues of his day. He was well aware that in a railway age Canada would not remain an "untempted garden of an agricultural Eden," to borrow O.D. Skelton's phrase.[30] A struggle between the interests of commerce and agriculture was in progress — had been in progress, for that matter, since before the rebellion. Mackenzie had witnessed it again in New York State. His experience at the constitutional convention had shown him that the political weight of the commercial and financial interests had increased in the railway age and that of the agricultural interests had declined. He did not want that to happen in Canada. Of course the province must have railroads —

her farmers would be at a disadvantage without them — but he wanted them honestly and economically constructed on routes most in the *public* interest and not burdened with unjustifiable contracts to insiders. He was willing enough that vital internal improvements, such as roads and the canals on the Welland and St. Lawrence Rivers, and a trunk line railway, should be provincial enterprises undertaken with public funds. He was not willing that private enterprises, once undertaken, should be so assisted, unless as a result they became public, nor was he content to see provincial or municipal improvements like the toll roads later sold to private corporations. Aileen Dunham has charged that the Reformers

> failed to consider that debts incurred for public improvements are themselves assets, and if judiciously incurred ultimately carry their own remuneration. [31]

This criticism cannot be made of Mackenzie. He realized that "money borrowed for internal improvements fills the state with wealth,"[32] provided it is judiciously and honestly expended. He did not admit to himself that at the time there was no alternative to a revenue tariff as a means of financing the public debt incurred for sorely needed public improvements. Occasionally, as when reporting his trips on the railways, he admitted the great offsetting advantages the transportation revolution was bringing to the rural population, but more often his tone about the railways was one of complaint about their cost and the corrupt tactics of their promoters and of the politician who worked hand-in-glove with them.

Mackenzie gave up his earlier opposition to chartered banks. He only wanted them adequately regulated and their note issues made safe. And he certainly never advocated anything like a return to medieval barter! What he did not face up to was the fact that the province needed more capital for development and that under existing laws her banks and lending institutions were hampered in obtaining it. His object was to prevent the accelerating changes in commerce, industry and transportation from producing in Canada the extremes of wealth and poverty he had observed in the Old World and in the more mature economy across the lakes. He believed that high rates of interest, sharp contractions and expansions of the currency, high legal costs, a high tariff on necessities, a heavy burden of public debt, inadequately safeguarded issues of paper money and "privileged" corporations would produce those deplorable results. He wanted the benefits of banks and railways for the rural population without the social costs to them, without weighting down the balance of political power heavily in favour of the non-agricultural interests, and without destroying forever the hope of seeing his ideal egalitarian society created in Canada.

The debates at the New York State Constitutional Convention show that Mackenzie's "woolly" economic ideas, about banks, limited liability corporations and usury, were shared by many thoughtful men at this stage of the development of the North American continent. Mackenzie was not a

327

political Mrs. Partington senselessly trying to hold back the on-rushing tide of economic change. What he was really trying to do was to prevent that tide bringing in with it flotsam and jetsam and dirty oil slicks. Others refused to notice them; he still hoped to divert them from the shining sands of the New World. And he was, it is true, more concerned with the farmers than with anybody else. After all, they were still the major part of Upper Canada's population.

To the business men and politicians of the Union what was important was "growth," acquisition of capital to exploit the natural resources of the province, develop her budding industries, and provide a transportation network and financial services for her commerce and industry. The question was, who would pay and who would benefit? The policies adopted meant a heavy burden of public debt — sharp increases in the tariff and, for Upper Canada, heavier local taxation. Those who were responsible for her policies were convinced that rapid growth would eventually bring many benefits to all elements of society (including themselves) and that was more important than the theoretical assumptions of wild-eyed radicals about the potential evils. With Mackenzie, such men had no patience.

Mackenzie has been given full credit by his critics for his support of education. It was plain to him that if Canada was to become the self-governing society of educated freemen he envisioned, a system of publicly supported, locally controlled, non-sectarian schools was necessary, supplemented by public libraries and mechanics' institutes.[33] Mackenzie urged that such institutions should be supported out of Clergy Reserve funds and other provincial revenue. It has been said, however, that in his later years he developed a strain of "anti-intellectualism," and became critical of the academic colleges.[34] It is rather surprising to find the snobbish term "anti-intellectualism" applied, in this day and age, to Mackenzie because he proposed that in Canada the developing sciences of chemistry, botany and mineralogy should be stressed as well as the humanities (as was happening at that time at Yale) and because he supported David Christie's suggestion of university courses in scientific agriculture.[35] His *Message* of May 7, 1858, praised Justin Morrill's proposed Agricultural College Bill.

Mackenzie's attack on William Logan and the work of the Geological Survey is of course a disgrace to him, as much for its tone as its content. He refused to be satisfied with Logan's theoretical argument that there *could not* be coal at the *Bowmanville* site (where schemers had planted it). He demanded that that distinguished scholar and geologist waste his time by visiting Bowmanville himself, at once, to drill and find out. This would have been the impetuous Mackenzie's way of satisfying the public clamour on the question, and when Logan did not take it, Mackenzie criticized the entire operation — and cost — of the Geological Survey of Canada, whose creation he himself had originally advocated.[36]

What about women in Mackenzie's society of educated freemen? Is the claim that Mackenzie was "against the radical tide of feminism which had swept the eastern seaboard" and that "his sole concession to women would be to loosen their stays" completely justified? He was ready to admit women to university courses; he was prepared to make divorce easier to obtain, through the courts instead of by a Bill of Divorcement that had to make its awkward and dilatory way through the legislature.[37] He was anxious fully to protect their rights in their real property after marriage.[38] On the other hand, when Mackenzie was short of political news he printed many sickly-sentimental verses, stories and columns of advice on conduct, marriage and family life, meted out, on the whole, with even-handed justice to both sexes. But these little sermons of his, often lifted from some religious periodical or family-type journal, make a modern reader impatient with him. His fundamental duty was to provide for the large family he had fathered — and he did not do it. Mackenzie's image of himself was that of a fiercely independent, incorruptible journalist and devoted reformer. Only once — and briefly — could he bring himself to put his obligations to his family first.[39] Yet there is no doubt Mackenzie loved his children and desperately wanted to keep them all together under one roof. His distress and deep mental depression on their account is revealed from time to time in his letters.[40] Perhaps these black moods indicate the torment he experienced in choosing between his obligations to his family and his life's work.

In Mackenzie's newspapers there are many items that are simply fillers clipped by this hasty editor from his exchanges. It does not seem to me fair to say that "the diabolical and sensational was his stock in trade."[41] One of the items referred to in illustration of this charge is less than one-fifth of a column in a thirty-two column issue crammed with political news from England, the European continent, the United States and all the British North American colonies. But Mackenzie's journalism was uneven in character. When there was not enough political news, Mackenzie fell back on shipping news, financial news (prices current and bank note ratings), advice to farmers, household hints, some of the sickly stuff mentioned above — and the "sensational" items.

As a journalist, caution was not in him, nor much organization either. Mackenzie's *Colonial Advocate*, a commentator observed, "was a picture of his mind, exhibiting a piece of political patchwork without order, but all telling on public improvement."[42] The Draft Constitution for Upper Canada prepared on the eve of the rebellion is the most complete expression of Mackenzie's political ideas. On no occasion did this frantically busy and harried man sit down in academic calm to put together a fully integrated, theoretical scheme of things, political and economic. "I like to deal, and that thoroughly, with the age in which I live," he once wrote.[43] From time to time, as problems and personalities arose to trouble him, deal with them he did, striking his vigorous blows right and left. His language was "reckless" and unrestrained.[44] He showered abuse on opponents and critics, undeterred by their social rank or political authority. Governor Edmund Head, for example, was "an imbecile, useless and worthless,"[45] but this sort of thing was written by other editors of his day, even by the good George Brown who called Head "an embryo dictator" assisted by "a villainous pack of closet councillors," a man "unfit to breathe the free atmosphere of Canada in the middle of the nineteenth century."[46] Some of

Mackenzie's crudest and most violent expressions quoted by his critics are taken from his *Caroline Almanac* which was compiled, it should be remembered, when he was in jail and certainly in a tortured condition of mind and body.

It has been said that Mackenzie was "entirely unsuited to the life of politics,"[47] and with that judgement one must agree. As a representative he was indefatigable in serving his constituents, according to his lights, not theirs. For example, he refused to compromise with MacNab to get them more justices of the peace, and he refused to vote for a railway of whose incorporators and route he disapproved, even though influential constituents wanted it. He regarded it as his duty to serve a wider constituency than his own. As soon as he was elected, his correspondence was swollen by letters from those who had a grievance or an instance of corruption to bring to the attention of "the People's Friend." His *Message* was a sort of I.F. Stone's Weekly for his day. No member of the Assembly was quicker than he to draw attention to jobbing, or did so much to arouse the province to waste and dishonesty and unauthorized use of the public revenue. If one measures his legislative "weight" in this scale it was considerable.

When one comes to consider Mackenzie's relations with his colleagues in the Assembly, his weaknesses as a politician become evident. Horace Greeley's biographer tells us that Greeley tried to reform everything during his one lame duck session in Congress, martyrizing himself five or six times a day by voting against the whole House.[48] Similarly Mackenzie let his reforming zeal outrun his prudence. Greeley himself states, "I commenced resisting abuses and prodigal expenditures and soon had a whole nest of hornets about my ears."[49] In Canada Mackenzie followed his example. His colleagues found him a difficult member to work with. One of these complained that he was rash, headstrong and opinionated, and regarded no man's advice.[50] As T.S. Brown had earlier noted, he was too much wedded to his ideals, "to imagination of the brain, departure from which he considers as departure from principle."[51] Mackenzie sometimes voted for a bill that did not suit him down to the ground, but often he cast a negative vote against a desirable measure because it fell short of what he thought it ought to have been. A party man could not have indulged his egotism in this way, but Mackenzie was an Independent, not because all parties repudiated him but because he chose to be. Shortly before his return to Canada he gave his son some sound political advice when James, who had for several years been a member of the Ohio legislature, confessed his disillusionment with American party politics:

> Sail low and get along for a time ... perhaps you may do more
> good by remaining in the party and trying to get it to go as right
> as possible than you could in being an independent for in that
> case both parties would shut their ears to your message be it
> ever so sweet. [52]

After Mackenzie's return to Canada he was unable to follow his own sage advice for very long. He could not discipline himself to wear the collar of party and pull in harness with his Reform colleagues. At one time he had half admitted that one-man guerilla warfare could accomplish little, but in practice he resorted to it. In 1858 he expressed his attitude towards party government in words quoted from William Ellery Channing:

> Party spirit is singularly hostile to man's independence. In proportion as he ... judges by the service of his party, he surrenders his freedom as a man, the right of speaking his own mind. [53]

James evidently accommodated himself to party politics. He obtained a judgeship and later, in his turn, gave advice to his father: guerilla fights accomplish nothing. The few will think for the many. Faith in parties is necessary, and all of them will have corruption. "We must judge parties as we do individuals — by the balance of character they have."[54]

Of Mackenzie's political independence and integrity there can be no question. On his return to Canada he was offered the postmastership of Toronto, at the instance of Robert Baldwin it has been claimed. He replied, "No, they will think me an office-seeker, or bribed. I will work my way with my own brains and hands."[55] Hincks thought the proper course for Mackenzie at this point was to retire to private life with some honourable employment, but he would take nothing at the hands of the government.[56] He had not come back to Canada in the hope of obtaining an office from the Reform administration then in power. He had come back with the intention of pushing them along the road of reform faster — and further. Neither would he secretly consent, as some members did, to barter his independence during a session for some temporary patronage appointment to be subsequently bestowed. Nor was he connected with corporate enterprises seeking legislative favours. It was his absolute independence and political integrity that endeared Mackenzie to the ordinary man. "Little Mac" wanted nothing for himself, only what was in the public interest, and they knew it.

The Quebec *Gazette* recognized this quality in Mackenzie but it gave its comment an unpleasant twist.

> He wants men to be what they are not and never will be — disinterested actors on the stage of life. In a word, he measures everybody in his own bushel. The result has been that he has been left alone in his glory. Nobody believes in him. Those who pretended to be his friends have left him to sing his own praises. [57]

There was much unpleasant truth in this for Mackenzie. He did expect the electorate to vote for candidates who could see beyond their own economic interests or those of their particular constituents, and before he was through he was scolding "the People" as well as their parliament. He did sing his own praises. Over and over again he reiterated, "I have asked no favors, I seek no office...." He was as a legislator disinterested but he was not uninterested in collecting all he thought was his due. When the Homestead Fund was initiated he regarded it in that light. It was not uncommon in those days for such gifts to be made to political leaders: The Irish Patriots, Cobden, Henry Clay and others had been rewarded by their grateful countrymen. It would have added immeasurably to Mackenzie's stature as a public man if he could have returned to Canada and borne his losses with quiet dignity. But this would be to expect too much from a poor man, born to be an agitator, who believed he was being unjustly treated. One accusation that has been levelled at him is definitely untrue.[58] He did not petition the Baldwin-Lafontaine government or its successor for $12,000 in compensation for the pillaging of his newspaper establishment, bookshop, and bindery by the mob in Toronto during the rebellion, nor did he turn against them because they refused this "outrageous" demand. He *mentioned* the amount, but what he asked for was an accounting and whatever balance remained in Sheriff Jarvis's hands from the sale of his goods, and to this he was legally entitled.[59]

Isaac Buchanan's offer of money and Robert Hay's kind offer to furnish his home when he returned to Toronto were not accepted.[60] He borrowed from friends often, it is true. No man put his hand in his pocket for him more often than Henry O'Rielly. It is pleasant to record that O'Rielly could write to him:

> It rejoices me to say that in my whole life I never knew a gentleman more sensitive to all matters of personal independence and financial integrity. [61]

Not all Mackenzie's creditors would have endorsed these words. Mackenzie's correspondence reveals that there were some creditors in very humble circumstances who were indeed induced to give him credit when his star was in the ascendant and who were left waiting an unconscionably long time for their money. During Mackenzie's last days the knowledge that he had not succeeded in paying all his debts preyed upon his mind.[62]

Mackenzie has been accused of hopeless inconsistency,[63] of advocating representation of the colonies in the imperial parliament, of demanding responsible government at one time, although never really understanding it, and of stressing the need for a strong governor at another time, of expressing a preference for British parliamentary institutions, then for the elective institutions of the American republic, subsequently admitting he had become somewhat disillusioned with American democracy, next expressing regret for the rebellion, promising loyalty for the future, denouncing the annexationists and finally reverting to annexation at the end. On the face of it, all this appears to be the wildest inconsistency. One thing should be remembered: Mackenzie was primarily interested not in the form of a government but in the social effects it was producing. He began with a predilection for British institutions and the hope that Upper Canada would become predominantly a society of prosperous independent small freeholders. When he concluded that the government of the colony was not fostering but actually inhibiting the growth of such a society, he turned to whatever remedies were available and seemed to suit the time and circumstances.

In 1828, like Benjamin Franklin before him, he advocated colonial representation in the imperial parliament.[64] By this device, the wants and grievances of the people could be made known *directly* to the authority that could provide a remedy for them. His suggestion fell on stony ground. Mackenzie's next idea was to make the government of the colony itself responsive to the wishes of the people. It is clear from his letter to John Neilson of November 23, 1828, and his remark in the *Advocate* of May 16, 1833, that he fully understood what cabinet government meant in Great Britain at that time and what responsible government would mean in Canada, and he claimed that he was the first in Canada to agitate for it.[65]

Mackenzie soon recognized, as his letter of December 1836 to Joseph Howe shows, that responsible government might turn out to be a screen behind which dishonest men enriched themselves. All would depend on the character of the people's representatives and if they should be dishonest, self-seeking men, placemen, men corruptly elected, then a governor of "intelligence, popular character and great integrity might still be necessary to secure us the blessings of freedom."[66] (This was the situation that was to arise under Lord Elgin. In Mackenzie's opinion Elgin had the intelligence and the popularity but not the integrity. Instead of dismissing his ministers, as he thought Elgin could have done, the Governor stood aside and let the corrupt game go on.)

After Mackenzie returned from his visit to the Colonial Office in 1832, it seemed that Great Britain did not intend to allow Upper Canada to manage her internal affairs herself under a government responsible to her own legislature, and that obnoxious officials would continue to be appointed and sustained. He then attempted to obtain independence for the colony as a means of delivering her from "a lot of petty villains"[67] and procuring for her a constitution along American lines. He finally resorted to rebellion as a means to this end, accepted the offered help of some Americans, and urged upon the United States the desirability of annexation for the good of both that country and Canada. Before he made a trial of the republic, he believed that the American government, the choice of a "nation of freemen," was capable of demonstrating to less fortunate peoples the advantages of free, elective, republican institutions. When he became more informed about American political practices, about the nomination system, the caucus system, the spoils system, the Albany Regency, the Nativist movement, the corrupt elections, in which newly enfranchised immigrants permitted themselves to be used; when he saw, as he thought, that the nation of freemen was in reality controlled by a monied aristocracy of monopolists and slaveholders, he became disillusioned with republican institutions and said so more than once.[68]

In 1846 Mackenzie wrote:

> I have not a wish left to see Canada incorporated with the Union. If it obtain a direct representation in the British Parliament on the sagacious plan proposed by the far-seeing

Franklin, and renewed by Hume in the House of Commons, it may remain connected with Britain for years. Should that not take place, its annexation to these northern states is an event of no remote possibility. [69]

At that time Sir Charles Metcalfe was Governor and a Tory administration was in power. For the second time it seemed to Mackenzie that the only way for Reformers to get attention to their grievances was for the province to have direct representation in the imperial parliament.

Four years later, when he returned to Canada, the annexation movement was at its height. He opposed it, but he did not this time advocate Franklin's remedy. Originally he had condemned the Act of Union — and he continued to criticize some of its provisions — but the situation in Canada was no longer what it had been in 1841 or 1846. A Reform government was now in power and apparently responsible government was working under Lord Elgin. He was therefore willing to give the Union a trial in the hope that a Reform government, shepherded along the right path by Clear Grits and Rouges, would be able to prevent the economy and the government of Canada coming under the domination of monopolists and speculators. Consequently, on two occasions in 1851, when there was a motion for dissolution of the union, Mackenzie voted in the negative. In one of these instances, his vote was critical for the administration then in power, since there was a tie, broken by the Speaker's negative vote. [70]

Mackenzie had learned a lot in the United States, especially at Albany in 1846. Reforms were then made in the constitution of New York State that he was eager to introduce in Canada on his return, particularly an economical salary scale for government officials, the elective principle for the choice of officials at all levels, simplification of the legal system, tighter control of the public revenues and the public credit by the people's representatives, and a written constitution that would be a check upon both legislature and executive. In addition, every effort should be made to prevent the centralization of power at the capital. Gradually, however, Mackenzie came to realize that transferring "power" from the executive to the representatives of the people, or to local government officials, even when they were elected on a broader franchise, would not necessarily ensure honesty in the handling of public funds or prevent the kind of political "deals" which had disgusted him with the Democratic Party in the United States, in the days of the Albany Regency and Martin Van Buren. Towards the end of his career he sadly acknowledged that what had prevented — and would prevent — his ideal society from coming into existence was "the blackness of the human heart." [71]

Mackenzie had long believed, as did other persons of his day, that even without resort to the violent method of rebellion, the colonial relationship was bound to be terminated. On his return to Canada he did not conceal this opinion. He wrote:

Now we think there is no disloyalty in the opinion that a permanent or everlasting colony is an impossibility. The independence of this province may be distant half a century, but it is inevitable. It may be neither our interest or our duty to accelerate that event but wise statesmen will hardly ignore inevitable eventualities.[72]

At that moment Mackenzie was not disposed to accelerate independence. After a few years' experience with responsible government under the Union, he concluded that it was a revolting fraud, nullified in practice by the existence of a permanent civil list and by the patronage at the disposal of the executive. The whole scheme of popular rule had "resolved itself into a great gambling concern."[73] By 1855 it was clear to him that while the Union lasted Upper Canada would not get honest, economical government and the reforms he wanted for her. He began to agitate for dissolution of the Union and subsequently for independence as well.

The awkward question was, could an independent Canada, and particularly an independent land-locked Upper Canada, stand alone? Mackenzie had admitted that she could not; she must be either British or American. "Independent of both she neither can nor will be," he declared.[74] These were the facts of life as Mackenzie saw them in 1855. Yet he did not want annexation. As late as April 1856 he wrote to the Irish rebel, Smith O'Brien, that he was "truly anxious" to see Canada connected with Great Britain "by the mutual ties of affection and interest.... Republican rule is far less pure than I thought until I lived in the republic."[75] He still thought it possible for Canada to have elective institutions, even elective governors, under the British flag.[76]

There does not seem to be to be wild inconsistency in Mackenzie's course, *considering his ultimate aims and the changing circumstances under which he tried to achieve them,* until the end, when he was old, tired and bewildered. In April 1858 he acknowledged that he did not know what course Canada should take — he could not advise.[77] Yet not quite two years later he published his *Almanac for Independence and Freedom* in which he appeared to be advocating annexation, despite his earlier criticisms of the American republic. In the interval he had seen his own proposal for dissolution of the Union and independence voted down and Brown's proposal for "rep. by pop." and constitutional changes also voted down. Nothing had yet come of Galt's plan for a confederation of all the British North American provinces as far as he knew. Neither had anything come of the Reform convention of 1859.

What was the solution for Upper Canada, now insistently demanding "Rep. by Pop." and grown increasingly discontented with being ruled by a government whose majorities were furnished by Lower Canada? Would a federal union of all the British provinces under imperial authority ever be made? Would Upper Canada be impoverished by the federal tie? How free would she be to manage her internal affairs and her commerce? Annexation would have clear economic advantages for her — he pointed them out in the *Independence Almanac.*[78] Perhaps after all that would be the best solution. But who could tell what the outcome of the struggle over slavery would be? Would the union break apart? Would annexation just to the northern free states be possible? Who would foresee? All Mackenzie could advise was that Upper Canada achieve her independence and become free to take whatever course seemed the best when the mists cleared away. It did seem to him that annexation would offer overwhelming economic advantages. Yet he wavered.

Mackenzie had pinned his hopes on a society of independent freeholders governing themselves through completely elective institutions. In the United States he had discovered that the electorate and elective institutions could be manipulated by selfish men and that even a written constitution made by the people themselves was no adequate safeguard for liberty. Yet these were the political nostrums he had urged Canada to swallow. Even her own elective municipal officials were not behaving with the wisdom, justice and honesty that he had hoped for from the representatives of the people. The blackness of the human heart! He could not really justify annexation even to the free northern states as an ideal solution for Upper Canada. When asked to do so, he made an ineffective response, merely listing the evils in both countries in his *Message* of 25 February, 1860. In any event it was doubtful whether Canada was disposed to "look below the border" for relief from the political strains of an insupportable union. Had Mackenzie but known it, "No" was the answer Upper Canada was to give to this question when it was put to her by Conservative candidates during the elections of 1861.[79]

At the end, it was not so much inconsistency of which Mackenzie was guilty as indecision and confusion of thought. He who had once been so sure did not have the answer. Where was the path to the good society, the "true republic" he had hoped to live to see? The mists were closing in on him. He could not point it out except to emphasize the need for changes in the hearts and minds of men. To this extent he was, as Rasporich remarks, a moral crusader.[80]

Perhaps in the closing weeks of his life he comforted himself with the reflection that he had done something to improve the existing social order. The Court of Chancery had not been abolished, to be sure, but the whole system of jurisdiction and equity had been improved — and wasn't it his hammering away at that wretched court that had brought about — well, hastened — the changes? Then there was the new audit office. He had certainly shown them the need for *that*! The Squatter Commission? True, the settlers had not benefitted from it as much or as soon as he had hoped, but he had at least secured a hearing for them and exposed a couple of dishonest Crown land agents and got rid of them. He had preached the doctrines of the National Reformers, land for the landless. Canada had not adopted a homestead policy yet, but the idea had taken hold and maybe she would when she got those Hudson's Bay territories. He had done his best to reform election practices, institute the ballot and provide a better method of dealing with controverted elections. He hadn't succeeded but maybe the lessons he had tried to teach would not be forgotten. He had eased matters for unfortunate debtors and their families and he had saved enough of the working man's tools and equipment for him so that he could get started again. It was pleasant to think of those who had steadily aided him in this good work. Best of all, he had prevented distressed farmers being sold up during those bad years of poor harvests and low prices. He had warned the province about the Bank of Upper Canada, and the Municipal Loan Fund too, but his warnings had gone unheeded. There were some other good things he had worked for, and not alone — temperance, for example, and direct election of mayors, and a lower tariff upon goods the poor had to have. Revenue, now that was a problem. He had never really worked that out. Once he had thought of advocating an income tax — but it was too late now for him to concern himself about it.[81] Of course, if those rascally administrations had not been so extravagant, creating all sorts of new jobs, fisheries commissioners, and river police and what not, making grants to sectarian institutions, burdening the province with debts for those dishonestly managed railways, they would not need so much revenue. But he must not let himself get excited; he must rest; they were constantly telling him that. Was that the way of it, one wonders, in periods of lucidity during those distressing final weeks?

Mackenzie's contemporaries and students of his life are agreed in attributing to him certain qualities of mind and heart, certain characteristics of manner and defects of temperament. Those who knew him both before 1837 and in his days of exile and poverty frequently commented on his "indefatigable industry," regretting only that he did not apply it to his personal well being and that of his family. Housed in Mackenzie's slight and wiry frame was a dynamo of energy that enabled him simultaneously to carry on his legislative duties, burdensome committee work, a heavy correspondence and the conduct of his newspaper. Conscious of his abilities and full of restless energy, Mackenzie was determined to be noticed. He was confident and optimistic, impulsive and excitable, impatient of delay, intolerant of criticism and opposition. He *knew* he was justified in the steps he took during the rebellion years. As late as 1844 he could write to O'Rielly, "Neither do I or have I acknowledged even error, much less crime."[82] He was a suspicious man with a tendency to believe the worst before he had proof.[83] This, O'Callaghan told him, was his "corroding weakness."[84] LeSueur called it "the master passion and habit of his soul."[85] Moreover, he did not have the largeness of spirit that would have enabled him to rejoice in the successes of others — nor did he have a forgiving spirit towards those who opposed or criticized him. He was like a thistle. No one could touch him with impunity. At times he gave way to violent rages brought on by some totally unexpected frustration of a cherished plan, as, for example, when he was defeated for re-election in 1836, when he was arrested on leaving Navy Island, and when he turned on his friend Lesslie who blocked his plan to go to England in 1859. On more than one occasion Lesslie had deplored his "rashness," "impetuosity under defeat," and his "indomitable self-will." Even before the rebellion these characteristics had put a strain on Mackenzie's relations with the Lower Canadians and, as W.J. O'Grady admitted to Papineau and his friends, had tended to divide the Reformers of Upper Canada.[86]

Mackenzie had "talents of no ordinary kind."[87] He was an avid reader of history, of treatises on political economy and government, of journals of current comment, both British and American, of newspapers, both foreign and domestic. He was a first-rate accountant and he had a retentive memory. As a public speaker he came ready armed with facts, statistics, apposite historical parallels, quotations and uncomfortable references to the past political conduct of his critics. Burning with zeal and brimful of material for his topic, Mackenzie as a speaker was wont to be somewhat discursive and verbose, particularly in the opinion of those whose past conduct or opinions he could all too readily recall. *L'Avenir* commented on his "interminable verbiage."[88] On one occasion, when the Assembly was discussing the desirability of having the debates reported, George Brown poked fun at his habit of entertaining the members with reminiscences of the past commencing with "once upon a time" and of clinching every remark with "upon my sincerity." "It would be a matter for regret," said Brown, "if a single word that fell from him was lost." (Laughter)[89] Yet Mackenzie could be pithy and to the point. One who saw him in action during his last year in the legislature has described him thus:

> A small and rather decrepit looking old man with a great mass of grey hair tousled over his head. [The flaming red wig of earlier days had evidently been replaced.] His voice is full and clear — enunciation good — sentences pithy. He rose suddenly, leaped into the very heart of the question under discussion in a manner that was as eccentric as startling. [90]

As a stump speaker, "Little Mac" was unsurpassed. One who attended his meetings in Haldimand tells us:

> He was a host in an election. He depended almost entirely upon himself. Took no note of organization. He had a wonderful power of making friends and confounding opponents.[91]

He could entertain his audience, he could hold their interest by his reforming zeal, and he had that indefinable quality that enables a speaker to touch the minds and hearts of his audience and to know he has them with him.

Mackenzie was accused by Hincks of being an "unconscionable liar,"[92] in Sir Francis Head's narrative of "lying from every pore of his skin,"[93] by Dent of "concocting inconsistent and self-contradictory stories with the design of removing the obloquy of failure from his own shoulders to those of others,"[94] and by LeSueur of repeating shocking untruths.[95] There is no doubt that Mackenzie shaded the truth at times, and instances from his post-rebellion career have already been given. Like many a modern public relations man or official "spokesman," he tried to put a good face on untoward events so as to retain and intensify the support of the American public for the Canadian cause. It would, for example, have been utterly stupid of him to have revealed in his first speech at Buffalo any dissatisfaction with Rolph over the change of date, any division of opinion in reform ranks, or even in his letter to the *Watertown Jeffersonian* to have made some of the accusations that were later to come from his pen. Mackenzie has been accused of trying to shift the blame for the failure of the rebellion to other people's shoulders. Much of the evidence against him comes from persons anxious to clear their own skirts of complicity in the rebellion or of responsibility for its occurring at all or for its failure, and some of them were men ready enough to step forward publicly as leaders *after* all the risks had been taken. In this connection Dr. T.D. Morrison's letter is revealing[96] and Thomas Ridout's denunciation of Rolph and J.H. Price's estimate of him should be remembered.[97] It is clear, however, that complete accuracy has not been forthcoming from either side.

Mackenzie has been credited, even by LeSueur, with a sincere interest in the public welfare.[98] Rick Salutin points out that there were many changes in Mackenzie's stance, but stresses that he always remained committed "to one underlying goal, to serve the people of Canada" by the long list of reforms he struggled to obtain for them.[99] But was it *all* the people? Mackenzie has been accused of having no love for minorities, "especially blacks and Jews,"[100] and little concern for the Indians.

Two slighting references to Jews have been found, one to Head, who had a Jewish grandfather, and to his secretary John Joseph,[101] and one to "Jew usurers" in England.[102] Since Mackenzie would have been hostile to these persons in any event, are these items enough to base a general charge of anti-semitism upon?

Negroes who had escaped to Upper Canada were loyal to its government and a thousand of them had promptly offered their services in its defence against the rebels and their American supporters.[103] As has already been pointed out, when Mackenzie was asked what his stand was on slavery, he made it plain that he detested it with all his heart (his draft constitution for the "state" of Upper Canada forbade it and guaranteed the resident inhabitants of all colours all the rights of native Canadians), but as matters *then* were in the American *federal* union he could not support the abolitionists.[104]

There were 310 Indians in Haldimand when Mackenzie was first elected by that constituency. He was promptly asked to present to the legislature petitions for relief by some settlers who had been ejected from Indian land during the deep snows of March and deprived of their improvements. This was a tangled dispute about which Mackenzie moved cautiously until he knew more about it. Had these persons been encouraged to settle on Indian land by officials of the Indian Department, as they claimed; were they behind in payments for their land or rent for their leases or were some of them just squatters, as that department claimed; and had the petitioners, like others, been offered compensation for their improvements by the government before they were forcibly ejected from their homes?[105] Mackenzie presented the petitions of his constituents without effect[106] but subsequently he called for and obtained a return on the affairs of the Indian Department which showed that substantial sums had been paid out of the Indians' funds for the settlers' improvements.[107]

Another ongoing dispute in Haldimand related to the effect of an act passed in 1850 for the protection of the property of the Indians. Clause 3 of that act prevented creditors from obtaining a confession of judgement for debt from an Indian unless he was possessed of land in fee simple.[108] Creditors of the Indians, some of whom complained that they were owed from $100 to $600, and that the act had "secured the Indians in their dishonesty," petitioned Mackenzie to get this clause of the act abolished or at least made inapplicable to debts incurred before its enactment. Mackenzie introduced a bill for the relief of creditors of Indians but it was denied a second reading by a vote of 16 to 19.[109] Mackenzie's sympathies were clearly with the struggling settlers, who were his constituents, but he was at the same time critical of the conduct and the honesty of the Indian Department towards both the settlers and the Indians. When Chief Superintendent Samuel P. Jarvis was shown to be a defaulter originally to the extent of £600 of Indian Trust Funds, later for a much larger sum, Mackenzie publicized this fact in his *Message* of 18 July, 1857, and in his last year in the legislature reminded John A. Macdonald that he had so far failed to see justice done to the Indians as promised.[110]

Mackenzie has been accused of talking about the rights of labour until his profits as employer were threatened. In 1836 he resisted the efforts of the striking journeyman printers to get higher wages than their organization, the York Typographical Society, had previously agreed to accept. The journeymen's unexpected demand came at a time when Mackenzie was bound by his contract to do printing for the Assembly at a certain rate. There was also another element in the dispute: the efforts of the Society to restrict the number of apprentices an employer might have. Mackenzie was opposed to monopolies of every description, whether attempted to be created by workers, doctors or lawyers trying to restrict or control entrance into their craft or profession. He pointed out that the effect of such monopolies would be "to split the community into so many selfish and mischievous monopolies," like the guilds of past centuries. By the time Mackenzie returned to Canada he had become more sympathetic to organized labour. He supported the organized printers in their demands for higher wages during a period of rising prices and he paid these increased rates at a time when he was struggling to maintain his *Message* and his vigorous competitor George Brown was beating down the rate of wages.[111]

The sincerity of Mackenzie's concern for "the common man" has been called in question. He has been charged with not putting his hand into his own pocket for the relief of widows and orphans when an appeal was made in Toronto for their benefit in January 1833. Mackenzie had left for England in April, 1832, and did not return until August 1833. He has also been accused of failing to support the Toronto Mechanics Institute. This is surprising in one who had been an active member of such an institution in his native Dundee. The Toronto Mechanics Institute was created in January 1831 by a group of Toronto citizens led by James Lesslie. Mackenzie was not one of its officials either before the rebellion or after his return from exile,[112] but he certainly advocated legislative grants for mechanics' institutes and libraries.

It has also been observed that although Mackenzie wrote enthusiastic articles about elevating the poor, his accomplishments in this area do not equal those of Jesse Ketchum, the Baldwins or John Strachan.[113] No one should expect him to match the charitable activities of these wealthy men living comfortable lives with a degree of leisure that was never Mackenzie's. What Mackenzie spent for the public benefit was *himself* — about all he had after his return from exile.

On Mackenzie's emotional nature the poetry of Robert Burns and Thomas

Campbell had left a deep impression. In his childhood he had known poverty — he had felt it to his very marrow — and he understood the uneasy fears of the small tenant farmers and their longing for the independence that would come with land of their own. His sympathy with the poor and distressed was genuine. Often his publications contained quotations from his beloved Scottish poets. On the title page of his *Almanac of Independence & Freedom*, Mackenzie placed these moving lines from Campbell:

> The deep drawn wish, when children crown our hearth
> To hear the cherub-chorus of their mirth
> Undamp'd by dread that want may e'er unhouse
> Or servile misery knit those smiling brows;
> The pride to rear an independent shed
> And give the lips we love unborrow'd bread,
> To see a world from shadowy forests won.
> In youthful beauty wedded to the sun;
> To skirt our home with harvest widely sown,
> And call the blooming landscape all our own
> Our children's heritage in prospect long,
> These are the hopes, high minded hopes and strong,
> That beckon England's wanderers o'er the brine
> To realms where foreign constellations shine.
> The grey haired swain, his grandchild sporting round
> Shall walk at eve his little empire's bound
> Survey with pride, beyond a monarch's spoil
> His honest arms own subjugated soil.

Like many an emigrant of mature years, Mackenzie had found emigration to be a painful wrench that created an aching void not soon to be filled up, unless there seemed to be some prospect of hopes being realized. For those who put obstacles in the poor man's path, whether speculator, usurious money lender or corrupt Crown lands official, Mackenzie felt a deep and lasting scorn.

These were Mackenzie's qualities — and he had the defects of his qualities. That restless, uneasy temperament of his, that demonic temperament as it has recently been called, drove him to oppose the establishment of his day, blinded him to any good there might be in it, or in the men who supported it, led him to risk his domestic comfort and well being in political protest against it, and in the end to take gambler's chances in an effort to overthrow it. He had what Henry O'Rielly called a "starvation-like devotion to principle"[114] but this admirable quality also meant that he was not to be deterred by criticism, abuse or well-meant advice. He was determined and unyielding — self-willed, obstinate if one wants to use pejorative terms[115] — and he had the fortitude it takes to persevere, although at times he reveals something like a persecution complex. His energetic temperament was not an equable one. He went to extremes in words and actions. His mind's pendulum swung on a wide arc from moods of optimism and over-confidence to those of gloomy despair.

Finally, there is the question of Mackenzie's sanity, about which several critics in his own day and ours have had their doubts, somewhat justified by his conduct at *some* moments of his career.[116] But who has not seen stupid or irrational actions performed or threatened in moments of stress, excitement or anger by those usually capable of rational and intelligent conduct? To say of him that mind and nerves completely lost their balance after 1836 is surely an exaggeration. Throughout his life Mackenzie had firm friends, and not only among the unlettered; he enjoyed the respect of several very able men who were well aware that his was an excitable and impulsive nature, but who would have put his defects no stronger than that. Like another and more famous editor who fought for liberal causes all his life — Horace Greeley — Mackenzie died of "what the Victorians called softening of the brain." Greeley once protested, "But the world *does* move, and its motive power under God is the fearless thought and speech of those who dare be in advance of their time — who are sneered at and shunned through their days of struggle as lunatics, dreamers ... men of crotchets, vagaries and of isms."[117] But Greeley was more fortunate than Mackenzie in that the malady that closed his life was not seized upon by detractors to explain the whole of it.[118] Present-day students of mental health no doubt appreciate better than Bertrand Russell's contemporaries did his reference to "The ocean of insanity upon which the little bark of human reason floats." At times that ocean becomes tempest-tossed and the frail vessel rocks violently from side to side and seems about to founder. Some of us, more fortunate than Mackenzie, or more cautious in refusing to venture out upon an uncharted sea in search of the Happy Island of our dreams, go safely through life's calmer waters and *our* little boat makes no violent oscillations. Mackenzie called upon Reformers in Upper Canada to leave the safe shore, to push off and sail on until they arrived at the "newer world" of his dreams. They would go no farther than the safe harbour of responsible government. He found, too, that not all who called themselves Reformers were of "one equal temper of heroic hearts," determined to strive and not to yield. *He* had that unyielding temperament — and to the last.

# NOTES

## Abbreviations Used in Notes

| | |
|---|---|
| AHA | American Historical Association |
| *AHR* | *American Historical Association Review* |
| AO | Archives of Ontario |
| BHS | Buffalo Historical Society |
| *CHAR* | *Canadian Historical Association Reports* |
| *CHR* | *Canadian Historical Review* |
| DHS | Detroit Historical Society |
| *JCS* | *Journal of Canadian Studies* |
| *JLAC* | *Journal of the Legislative Assembly of [United] Canada* |
| *JLCC* | *Journal of the Legislative Council of [United] Canada* |
| *JLAUC* | *Journal of the Legislative Assembly of Upper Canada* |
| *JLCUC* | *Journal of the Legislative Council of Upper Canada* |
| LC | Library of Congress |
| MC | Mackenzie Collection (in PAC) |
| *MG* | *Mackenzie's Gazette* |
| MLP | Mackenzie-Lindsey Papers (in AO) |
| MTL | Metropolitan Toronto Library |
| NYHS | New York Historical Society |
| NYPL | New York Public Library |
| NYSL | New York State Library |
| OCP | O'Callaghan Papers |
| *OH* | *Ontario History* |
| OHSPR | Ontario Historical Society, Papers and Records |
| ORC | O'Rielly Collection (in NYHS) |
| ORP | O'Rielly Papers (in RPL) |
| PAC | Public Archives of Canada |
| PAQ | Public Archives of Quebec |
| PHS | Pennsylvania Historical Society |
| RPL | Rochester Public Library |
| UNCL | University of North Carolina Library |
| USNA | United States National Archives |
| WHS | Wisconsin Historical Society |

| | |
|---|---|
| *Debates* | *Legislative Assembly of Canada Debates* |
| *Documents* | *Select Documents of the Canadian Constitution* (Kennedy) |
| *Durham Report* | *Report on... British North America* (Lambton, Lord Durham) |
| *Events* | *A History of... the Navy Island Campaign* (E.G. Lindsey) |
| *Messages* | *A Compilation of the Messages of the Presidents* (Richardson) |
| *Legacy* | *A Legacy of Historical Gleanings* (Bonney) |
| *Life* | *The Life and Times of William Lyon Mackenzie* (Lindsey) |
| *Mackenzie* | *William Lyon Mackenzie* [Makers of Canada series] (Lindsey) |
| *Patriots* | *The Life and Times of the Patriots* (Guillet) |
| *Report &* | |
| *Despatches* | [of the Earl of Durham] (Lambton, Lord Durham) |
| *Story* | *The Story of the Upper Canada Rebellion* (Dent) |

# Chapter I Notes

1.  For Mackenzie's early life and the events of the rebellion, see Lindsey, The *Life and Times of Wm. Lyon Mackenzie* (1862); Dent, *The Story of the Upper Canada Rebellion* (1885); Kilbourn, *The Firebrand* (1956); King, *The Other Side of the Story* (1886); McKillop, ed., Le Sueur's *William Lyon Mackenzie* (1979); Read, *The Rising in Western Upper Canada* (1982).
2.  Finley, *The North Atlantic Triangle* (1975), p. 182 .
3.  This account of Mackenzie's early life is based chiefly on the essay of the Rev. H.J. Cockburn of Dundee, copy in the Catherine MacLean Papers in PAC.
4.  Mackenzie's interest in Upper Canada may have been aroused not only by the Lesslie family in Dundee but also by the British Government's program of encouraging, and in some instances assisting, the Scottish poor to emigrate there. Gates, *The Land Policies of Upper Canada* (1968), pp. 86, 91.
5.  Gates, "The Decided Policy of William Lyon Mackenzie," (1959); *Colonial Advocate*, 21 Feb. 1833; Rea, "William Lyon Mackenzie — Jacksonian?" (1968); Remini, *The Election of Andrew Jackson* (1963); MLP, D. Bruce to Mackenzie, 30 Aug. 1846.
6.  Lindsey, *Life* 1:213.
7.  Paul Romney, "William Lyon Mackenzie as Mayor of Toronto" (1975). For a critical view of Mackenzie as mayor see Armstrong, "William Lyon Mackenzie, First Mayor of Toronto" (1967).
8.  Lindsey, *Life* 1:319.
9.  Gates, *Land Policies of Upper Canada*, pp. 186-88.
10. Clark, *Movements of Political Protest in Canada* (1959), p. 371.
11. Brown, "A Brief Sketch of the Life and Times of the Late Louis Joseph Papineau" (1872); Schull, *Rebellion: The Rising in French Canada, 1837* (1977), pp. 53-72.
12. MLP, James Mackenzie to Charles Lindsey, 13 Jan. 1863.
13. Elinor Kyte Senior, *Redcoats and Patriotes: The Rebellions in Lower Canada, 1837-1838*, Canada War Museum No. 20 (Stittsville, Ontario, 1985), p. 52.
14. Dent set the date of this meeting at October 9 (Dent, *Story* 1:378), but surely it was held "Early in November" (Lindsey, *Life* 2:52). Colborne's request for troops to be sent to Kingston was made on October 24 and his request for them to be sent from Kingston to Lower Canada was made on November 6, leaving the upper province defenceless as Mackenzie said. (Lindsey, *Life* 2:54-56; Dent, *Story* 1:383.) On Rolph see Muggeridge, "John Rolph: A Reluctant Rebel" (1959); Dent, *Story*, passim; G.M. Craig, article on John Rolph in *Dictionary of Canadian Biography* 9:683-90.
15. This is the figure given by Nelson Gorham who claimed he "personally enrolled every one." (Rolph Papers, Gorham to Rolph, 18 Jan. 1885).
16. Cushing Papers, Mackenzie to Cushing, 14 Jan., 21 Nov. 1840; MLP, copy, Mackenzie to Levi Woodbury, Sec'y. of the Treasury, 9 Jan. 1841.
17. Buffalo *Commercial Advertiser*, 29 Nov., 6 Dec. 1837.
18. *MG*, 6 July 1839.
19. AO, Rebellion Papers, Voluntary statement of James Latimer, 21 Dec. 1837. John Cotton was proprietor of a coffee house in Buffalo. Lester H. Cotton, perhaps the person meant, was captain of the steamboat *Pennsylvania*.
20. Toronto *Examiner*, 30 Oct. 1850; Buffalo *Whig and Journal*, 6 Dec. 1837 quoted in Dent, *Story* 2:177.
21. Lindsey, *Life* 2:124. Dr. Cyrenius Chapin was an elderly physician who had served during the War of 1812. He is said to have visited Chippewa and the Short Hills early in December 1837. George Coventry believed that he had been informed of the planned uprising. Coventry, "A Concise History of the Late Rebellion in Upper Canada," (1919).
22. Bidwell had represented the counties of Lennox and Addington in the Assembly of Upper Canada and had been elected Speaker in 1828 and 1834. In the election of 1836 he had been defeated.
23. Burwell-Glenny Diaries, vol. 1, 12 Dec. 1837; B.F. Butler Papers, John A. Dix to Butler, 12 Feb. 1838.
24. Buffalo *Daily Commercial Advertiser*, 13 Dec. 1837.
25. Tiffany, "The Relations of the United States to the Canadian Rebellion of 1837-1838" (1905).

26.  Sutherland had been a printer and a newspaper publisher. At the time he was a lawyer of low standing in Buffalo. He was accused of being a deserter from the U.S. Marines. He himself claimed to have kept a military school and to have seen service in South America under Bolivar. (Bonney, *A Legacy of Historical Gleanings* [1875], 2:78; New York *Sun*, 31 March 1838; New York *Tribune*, 7 Sept. 1852); Lillian F. Gates, article on Sutherland *Dictionary of Canadian Biography* 8:851-54.

27.  Sutherland, *A Canvass of the Proceedings on the Trial of William Lyon Mackenzie* (1840), p. 10; *MG*, 6 July 1839.

28.  Bonney, *Legacy* 2:78-79.

29.  Waterbury, "Oswego County During the Patriot War" (1944), pp. 11-242.

30.  Bonney, *Legacy* 2:76.

31.  Rochester *Republican*, 12 Dec. 1837. (Italics added.)

32.  MLP, Lindsey section, Box 1, envelope 2.

33.  Bonney, *Legacy* 2:63-64. This statement like much of Bonney's *Legacy* is a hodge-podge and must be used with caution. It starts out as a letter to some unnamed person, probably the editor of the Albany *Advertiser*, has no signature, part of it is in quotes, and it also contains an extract from Head's despatches of December 19 which Van Rensselaer could not have seen by the date at the head of the letter, 11 Dec. 1837. There is also reference to Mackenzie's "precipitancy and rashness" having prevented Rolph and Bidwell from maturing plans for a more general rebellion. This seems to be an unacknowledged quote from the Montreal *Herald* of 28 April 1838, but it may, nevertheless, reflect Van Rensselaer's opinions or the information he got from Rolph, who was then in Lewiston.

34.  Bonney, *Legacy* 2:78.

35.  J.W. Taylor Letters, Sutherland to Taylor, 9 Feb., 19 April 1832.

36.  Bonney, *Legacy* 2:78-79; Sutherland, *A Canvass*, p. 12.

37.  MTL, The Affidavit of Samuel Wood in the unpublished Arthur Papers gives some support to this statement. Wood was taken prisoner at Pelee Island on 3 March 1838.

38.  *Niles Register,* 29 Aug., 18 Sept. 1846.

39.  Bonney, *Legacy* 2:78-80.

40.  Ibid., 80.

41.  Riddell, "A Patriot General" (1914-15); Sutherland, *The Trial of General Thomas J. Sutherland* (1838); PAC, Upper Canada, Civil Secretary's Letter Book, J.A. Macaulay to Colonel John Prince, 19 June 1838; OCP, Mackenzie to O'Callaghan, 15 March 1842.

42.  Lindsey, *Life* 2:129; Albany *Advertiser*, 29 March 1838; Bonney, *Legacy* 2:80.

43.  Bonney, *Legacy* 2:79. Names of the committee are given in "Illustrative Documents Relating to the Canadian Rebellion," BHS *Publications* VIII (1905): 119-47.

44.  Bonney, *Legacy* 2:81; Burwell-Glenny Diaries, vol. 1, 14 Dec. 1837; USNA, Misc. Letters, Dept. of State, Microfilm 179, Roll 85, Mayor Trowbridge to Sec. J. Forsyth, 14 Dec. 1837.

45.  Sutherland, *A Canvass*, p. 14.

46.  See *infra*, Ch. 4, p. 90.

47.  Marcy Papers, Marcy to Gen. P.M. Wetmore, 23 Dec. 1837; Porter Papers, Augustus Porter to Peter B. Porter, 9 Jan. 1838.

48.  Bonney, *Legacy* 2:81; *MG*, 6 July 1839; Unpublished Arthur Papers, Affidavit of Samuel Wood.

49.  Sutherland, *A Canvass*, pp. 17-53. Mackenzie had only unqualified contempt for Sutherland whom he described as "a poor pennyworth" (*MG*, 10 Nov. 1838).

50.  This reversal of sentiment was duly reported to Sir John Colborne. (Colborne Papers, Ogden Creighton to Colborne, 17 Dec. 1837.)

51.  Bonney, *Legacy* 2:81.

52.  Manning, *Diplomatic Correspondence of the United States, 1784-1860* (1942), 3:419-20; Spencer, "William L. Marcy Goes Conservative" (1944); New York *Tribune*, 28 Oct. 1845.

53.  Bonney, *Legacy* 2:80-82.

54.  Ibid., 65-66.

55.  Lindsey, *A History of the Events Which Transpired During the Navy Island Campaign...* (1838), p. 17.

56.  Toronto *Patriot,* 10 April 1838, quoting New York *Gazette*.

57.  Crosswell Papers, E. Crosswell to N.S. Benton, 13 Dec. 1827. Flagg was State Comptroller.

58.  Buffalo *Commercial Advertiser,* 13 Dec. 1837.

59.  Ibid., 6, 13, 14 Dec. 1837.

60.  Lindsey, *Events*, pp. 12, 15; for text of the proclamation, see Cruikshank, "The Invasion of Navy Island, 1837-8" (1936), pp. 7-84.

61.  Buffalo *Commercial Advertiser*, 18 Dec. 1837; Rochester *Democrat*, 23 Dec. 1837.

62.  New York *Albion*, 22 Dec. 1837; Buffalo *Commercial Advertiser*, 14 Dec. 1837, 13 Jan. 1838; Rochester *Republican*, 5 Jan. 1838; Rochester *Daily Democrat*, 23 Dec. 1837; Fred Landon, "The Democratic Uprising of 1837..." (1911).

63.  Woodbury Papers, E. Jewett to Sec'y. Woodbury, 12 Dec. 1837.

64.  Lindsey, *Life*, vol. 2, Appendix G; Bonney, *Legacy* 2: 81; Mackenzie Clippings, No.133, contain a note in Mackenzie's hand, "We agreed privately to put Rolph and Bidwell at the head of the provisional government."

65.  Rolph Papers, N. Gorham to T.D. Rolph, 3 May 1885.

66.  Lindsey, *Events*, p. 6; Lindsey, *Life* 2:142; On Chandler see Guillet, *The Lives and Times of the Patriots* (1938), pp. 32, 94, and Duff, "Samuel Chandler of St. John's" (1938), pp. 115-19.

67.  Lindsey, *Life* 2:131; A corrected proof sheet of the proclamation is in ORP, Box 4j.

68.  New York *Commercial Advertiser*, 6 Jan. 1838; Dent, *Story* 2:189.

69.  Woodbury Papers, E. Jewett to Sec'y Woodbury, 13 Dec. 1837.

70.  MLP, copy, Mackenzie to I. Buchanan, 21 Dec. 1845. Bidwell stated in a letter of 13 Dec. 1837 that he had had no communication with Mackenzie since arriving in the United States. C.B. Sissons, "Mr. Bidwell," *CHR* XXVII (1946): 376.

71.  Dent, *Story* 2:185-86; Bonney, *Legacy* 2:81.

72.  Graham Papers, I. Patterson to Dr. J. Graham, 15 Dec. 1837.

73.  Mackenzie Clippings, No.918 (from Buffalo *Journal*); Rochester *Republican*, 12 Jan. 1838.

74.  Bidwell Papers, M. Bidwell to H. Cassady, 31 Jan. 1838.

75.  MLP, Navy Island memoranda, 28 Dec. 1937.

76.  Butler Papers, J.A. Dix to B.F. Butler, 12 Feb. 1838.

77.  Bonney, *Legacy* 2:82-83, 92; MLP, Navy Island memoranda, 28 Dec.1837.

78.  Woodbury Papers, E. Jewett to Sec'y Woodbury, Fort Niagara, 4 Jan. 1838.

79.  Thurlow Weed Papers, Weed to Francis Granger, 31 Dec. 1837, 9 Jan. 1838.

80.  Bonney, *Legacy* 2:73-74; Albany *Argus*, 5 Jan. 1838.

81.  Porter Papers, Augustus Porter to Peter B. Porter, 9 Jan. 1838.

82.  MacNab Papers, Lt. Gov. Francis Head to Col. Allan MacNab, 21 Dec. 1837; Colborne Papers, J.B. Robinson to Colborne, 2 Jan. 1838, Head to Colborne, 26 Dec. 1837.

83.  Colborne Papers, Head to Colborne, 5 Jan. 1838.

84.  MacNab Papers, Head to MacNab, 31 Dec. 1837; Burwell-Glenny Diaries, vol. 2,10 Jan. 1838; Lindsey, *Events*, p. 9. A similar incident had taken place on December 27, according to an account in the Rochester *Telegraph*, 2 Jan. 1838.

85.  Colborne Papers, MacNab to Head, 11 Jan. 1838; Head to Colborne, 12 Jan. 1838.

86.  See Charles Grey's criticisms of MacNab in Ormsby, ed., *Crisis in the Canadas, 1838-1839: The Grey Letters and Journals* (1965), pp. 85-86.

87.  Curtis, *The Fox at Bay* (1970), p. 176.

88.  Albany *Argus*, 12 Jan. 1838; Lindsey, *Events*.

89.  Burwell-Glenny Diaries, vol. 1, 2 Jan. 1838; Welch, *Home History: Recollections of Buffalo ... Fifty Years Since* (1891), p. 277.

90.  MacNab Papers, — to Col. Kirby, 10 Jan. 1838.

91.  Poinsett Papers, vol. 9, p. 166, Joel R. Poinsett, Sec. at War, to Gen. Winfield Scott, 12 Jan. 1838, vol. 10, p. 18, Scott to Poinsett, 28 Jan. 1838; U.C. Stat., Vic. 1, caps. 1, 2, and 3. This legislation is discussed in Watt, "The Political Prisoners in Upper Canada" (1926).

92.  Bonney, *Legacy* 2:74.

93.  Ibid., 84.

94.  Ibid., 84, 87, 92; Cruikshank, "Invasion of Navy Island," describes this interview, pp. 69-70.

95.  "God grant them success. My heart is with the oppressed in both Canadas." Scott to Col. Worth, 12 Dec. 1837, quoted in Elliott, *Winfield Scott* (1937), 1:36.

96.  Bonney, *Legacy* 2:90.

97.  BHS, "Illustrative Documents," p. 123.

98.  Mackenzie's statement in Rochester *Daily Advertiser*, 20 March 1841; *Army and Navy Chronicle*, Jan. and Feb. 1838; Bonney, *Legacy* 2:90.

99.  USNA, RG 56, Collector of Customs, Cayuhoga, to Sec. Woodbury, 21 Jan. 1838.

100. Toronto *Patriot*, 2 Feb. 1838, quoting Buffalo *Commercial Advertiser*. A letter of similar tenor is printed in Mackenzie, *The Life of Van Buren*, p. 295.

101. Sanderson, ed., *The Arthur Papers* (1957-59), 1:196-98.
102. NYHS, Thomas C. Love to Henry Wise, 19 Jan. 1838.
103. OCP, L.J. Papineau to E.B. O'Callaghan, 16 Oct. 1842.
104. Marcy Papers, Marcy to P.W. Wetmore, 31 Dec. 1837.
105. Bonney, *Legacy* 2:84, 90.
106. St. Lawrence University Library, copy, T.V. Russell to G.H. Russell, Canton, N.Y., n.d.; Marcy Papers, Marcy to A.S. Greene, 1 Oct. 1838.
107. Rochester *Democrat*, 25 December 1837; Bonney, *Legacy* 2:88. Lindsey's statement (*Life* 2:163) that Mrs. Mackenzie arrived a few "hours" before the *Caroline* probably should read a few "days," since otherwise she could not have remained "nearly a fortnight." Head's safe conduct for Mrs. Mackenzie was dated Dec. 20.
108. Bonney, *Legacy* 2:89.
109. Rochester *Republican*, 28 Jan. 1838; Buffalo *Commercial Advertiser*, 5, 19 Jan. 1838; Albany *Argus*, 12 Jan. 1838.
110. Buffalo *Commercial Advertiser*, 5 Jan. 1838.
111. *MG*, 15 Dec. 1838.
112. ORP, D. M'Leod to O'Reilly, 15 Jan. 1838.
113. Colborne Papers, Arthur to Colborne, 25 April 1838, J.B. Robinson to Colborne, 15 Dec. 1838; Edgar, *Bishop Alexander Macdonnell and the Politics of Upper Canada* (1974), p. 186.
114. MLP, Mackenzie to Dr. E. Johnson, 13 Dec. 1837; BHS, "Illustrative Documents."
115. Affidavit of Samuel Wood in unpublished Arthur Papers in MTL.
116. Bonney, *Legacy* 2:90-91; Heustis, *A Narrative of the adventures and sufferings of Captain Daniel Heustis....* (1847), pp. 29-30.
117. MLP, R. Van Rensselaer to Mr. MacMahon, 24 Feb. 1840; New York *Commercial Advertiser*, 3, 5 April 1838, quoting Albany *Daily Advertiser*, 29 March 1838.
118. Bonney, *Legacy* 2:105; *MG*, 15 Dec. 1838.
119. Waterbury, "Bill Johnston, Patriot or Pirate?" (1949).
120. John Northman, "Pirate of the Thousand Islands" (typed ms. in Jefferson County Museum, Watertown, N.Y.). Northman is the pen name of a Canadian whose account was published about February 1838 in the *Watertown Times*.
121. MLP, D. Heustis to Mackenzie, 20 Nov. 1846. Heustis was an American from Watertown; Gibson was a surveyor who had been a member of the Upper Canada Assembly.
122. George Dawson to Mackenzie, 14 Dec. 1837, printed in Mackenzie, *Life of Van Buren*, p. 290.
123. MLP, C.H. Graham to Mackenzie, 2 Feb. 1838.
124. Graham Papers, Mackenzie to C.H. Graham, 30 Jan. 1838.
125. MLP, C.H. McCollum to Mackenzie, 22 Dec. 1837.
126. Brodeur's Transcripts, Robert Nelson to J.B. Ryan, 25 Feb. 1838. The transcriber may have mis-dated this letter, as it is dated after the affair was over.
127. ORC, Box 23, Mackenzie to O'Reilly, 4, 18 Feb. 1838.
128. Colborne Papers, James Buchanan to Colborne and to Madam Colborne, two letters of 13 Dec. 1837; Gates, "A Canadian Rebel's Appeal to George Bancroft" (1968); Brown, "Brief Sketch of ... Papineau" (1872).
129. Bonney, *Legacy* 2:96; ORC, Mackenzie to O'Reilly, 4 Feb. 1838; Mackenzie to Col. —, 17 Feb. 1838, printed in *MG*, 15 Dec. 1838.
130. Bonney, *Legacy* 2:97.
131. Colborne Papers, R.H. Bonnycastle (Lt.Col., Royal Engineers) to Captain George Phillpotts, 19 Feb. 1838. There is an excellent map in Haddock, *History of Jefferson County, New York* (1894), p. 153.
132. Graham Papers, Mackenzie to C.H. Graham, 30 Jan. 1838.
133. Colborne Papers, Phillpotts to Colborne, 9 Feb. 1838.
134. Ogdensburgh *Republican* quoted without date in *Niles Register*, 10 March 1838.
135. MLP, C.H. Graham to Mackenzie, 10 Feb. 1838. BHS, "Illustrative Documents," pp. 130, 132.
136. Graham Papers, David Gibson to C.H. Graham, 16 Feb. 1838.
137. ORC, Box 23, Mackenzie to O'Reilly, 4 Feb. 1838.
138. Bonney, *Legacy* 2:100; Albany *Argus*, 27 Feb. 1838; also n.31 above.

139. This act, which was not to be signed until March 10, 1838, permitted the seizure and detention of vessels, arms and ammunition about to pass the frontier when there was reason to believe they were intended to be used against any government with which the United States was at peace.

140. Heustis, *Narrative*, pp. 29-31; Wool Papers, Wool to Mrs. Wool, 22 Feb. 1838; Bonnycastle, *Canada As It Was* 2:79-99; PAC RG 5, A1, vol.165, Bonnycastle to Sec'y J. Joseph, 28 Feb. 1838.

141. Colborne Papers, Wool to Colborne, 21 Feb. 1838; USNA, letters received by the Adjutant-General's Office, 1822-60, Wool to Scott, 22 Feb. 1838.

142. Bonney, *Legacy* 2:98-101; Heustis, *Narrative*, p. 31-32.

143. Graham Papers, Mackenzie to C.H. Graham, 5 March 1838; Bonney, *Legacy* 2:104.

144. *Watertown Jeffersonian*, 5 March 1838, published a letter of Bill Johnston to C.A. Hagerman of Feb. 26, 1838.

145. Bonney, *Legacy* 2:99.

146. *Niles Register*, 10 March 1838, quoting Ogdensburgh *Republican*; St. Lawrence University Library, Judge Fine to Gov. Marcy, 21 Feb. 1838. (This letter is quoted only in part in a sales catalogue of J.S. Newman of Battle Creek, Mich.)

147. *MG*, 15 Dec. 1838.

148. Colborne Papers, copy, Colborne to Marcy, 31 Jan. 1838; Foster to Colborne, 18 Feb. 1838; Wool to Colborne, 21 Feb. 1838; USNA, Misc. Letters, microfilm roll 85, report of N.S. Benton 21 Feb. 1838.

149. Bonney, *Legacy* 2:102.

150. New York *Express*, 5 March 1838, quoting the Onondaga *Standard*.

151. MLP, Smyles to Mackenzie, 11 July 1843. This information came to light when the Baldwin-Lafontaine government was in power. J.H. Price, one of its members, revealed it, according to Smyles.

152. Bonney, Legacy 2:100.

153. Ouellet, *Lower Canada: 1791-1840* (1972), p. 312.

154. Graham Papers, D. Gibson to C.H. Graham, 16 Feb. 1838.

155. PAQ, copies of letters of Jan. 23, 29, 30, 31, 1838, unsigned and unaddressed, attributed by the archives to Papineau but clearly not written by him, whom they criticize, but by Chapman (alias for Robert Nelson) to whom replies are directed to be sent.

156. PAQ, copy, Papineau to Mackenzie, 12 Feb. 1838.

157. MLP, Chapman (Robert Nelson) to Mackenzie, 11 Feb. 1838; quoted more fully in Lindsey, *Life* 2:216-17; Wool Papers, Wool to Mrs. Wool, 28 March 1838, tells of his warning Chapman not to lose the sympathy of the United States.

158. MLP, the same to the same, 21 Feb. 1838.

159. ORP, Mackenzie to O'Reilly, Graham and Dawson, 22 Feb. 1838.

160. Kingston *Herald*, 20 Feb. 1838.

161. MLP, Chapman (Robert Nelson) to Mackenzie, two letters of 21 and 23 Feb. 1838.

162. Wool Papers, Wool to —, 26 Feb. 1838.

163. Wool Papers, Wool to Mrs. Wool, 7 March 1838.

164. Corning Papers, E.B. O'Callaghan to Erastus Corning, 6 March 1838.

165. New York *Evening Star*, 3, 6 March 1838; Gratz Collection, Wool to Marcy, 1 March 1838.

166. Fauteux, *Patriotes de 1837-8* (1950), p. 183.

167. VBP, M. Stirling to Van Buren, Watertown, 23 Feb. 1838.

168. Quoted without date in *Niles Register*, 10 March 1838.

169. MLP, M. Forward to Mackenzie, Watertown, 20 March 1840.

170. MLP, S.C. Frey to Mackenzie, Ogdensburgh, 14 March 1838.

## Chapter II Notes

1. Colborne Papers, Col. Foster to Colborne, 13 Feb. 1838.

2. Ibid., Capt. A. McLean to Colborne, 25 Jan. 1838, Maj. O. Creighton to Colborne, 6 Feb. 1838.

3. Guillet, The *Lives And Times of the Patriots* (1938), pp. 88-103.

4.      ORP, D. Gibson to O'Rielly, 5 March 1838; Graham Papers, D. Gibson to C.H. McCollum, 26 March 1838.
5.      Whelan Papers, Bill Johnston to Mackenzie, 8 March 1838.
6.      MC, Mrs. Mackenzie to John Mackintosh, 10 March 1838.
7.      Graham Papers, Mackenzie to C.H. Graham, 5 March 1838; New York *Commercial Advertiser*, 10 March 1838.
8.      MLP, C.H. Graham to Mackenzie, 8 March 1838; Whelan Papers, S.C. Frey to Mackenzie, 18 March 1838.
9.      MLP, Mackenzie to Dr. E. Johnson, 13 Jan. 1838.
10.     MLP, Samuel Hunt to Mackenzie, Hunt's Hollow, 26 May 1838; Graham Papers, C.H. Graham to Mackenzie, Rochester, 3 May 1838; MG, 16 June 1838.
11.     Graham Papers, Mackenzie to C.H. Graham, 21 Apr. 1838; on O'Rielly see Dexter Perkins, "Henry O'Rielly", RHS *Publications* VIII, pp. 1-24.
12.     ORP, copy, O'Rielly to Senator Silas Wright, 4 Apr. 1838.
13.     *MG*, 2 June 1838; Lindsey, *Life* 1:259-61.
14.     Graham Papers, Mackenzie to C.H. Graham, 21 Apr. 1838. Lount, a farmer and blacksmith, had been a member of the Upper Canada legislature representing Simcoe County. Mathews was a farmer.
15.     ORP, Mackenzie to O'Rielly, 5 July 1838.
16.     MLP, S. Hunt to Mackenzie, Hunt's Hollow, 28 May 1838, James Reid to Mackenzie, Rochester, 8 June 1838.
17.     MG, 2 June 1838.
18.     Larned Papers, M.S. Bidwell to J. Hunt, Ernestown, 22 May 1820.
19      Bonnycastle, *Canada As It Was* 1:271-72.
20.     New York *Commercial Advertiser*, 3 May 1838.
21.     *MG*, 12 May 1838; Mackenzie Clippings, No.232, note in Mackenzie's hand.
22.     *Arthur Papers* 1:71, 197. Arthur was authorized but not required to allow Bidwell to return to Canada. The Lieutenant-Governor objected on the ground that Bidwell had been trying to bring about "step by step that change in the institutions of the province which Mackenzie determined to effect by more violent means." (PAC, copy, C.O., 42, Vol. 450, Arthur to Glenelg, No.60, 8 Sept. 1838).
23.     Birge states that when he was in Toronto in the fall of 1837 he became acquainted with Mr. Bidwell and learned about the projected revolution from him. Birge and his brother-in-law, Judge Butler, then a member of the Michigan House of Representatives, promised their assistance if required. Birge also claimed that G.M. Dufort, who was sent to Toronto by Papineau about this time, was introduced to Bidwell, consulted with him about the proposed insurrection, and that Butler, Birge, and Dufort then left Toronto together for Detroit, where they organized a "war council" of influential citizens and officials. Birge's statement, which is in the MLP, is unsigned, but it is in the same handwriting as an unsigned letter of 22 Nov. 1840 which Mackenzie marked "From J.W. Birge." All in MLP.
24.     Dix, Memoirs of John Adams Dix (1883) 2:317; Marcy Papers, Marcy to P.W. Wetmore, 31 Dec. 1837; Bidwell Papers, Bidwell to H. Cassady, 4 Jan. 1838.
25.     Nevins, ed., *The Diary of George Templeton Strong* (1952), 1:88.
26.     Wright's letter to O'Rielly is not in the ORP but is quoted in part in O'Rielly's reply. (ORP, O'Rielly to Wright, copy, 4 April 1838.)
27.     Gratz Coll., a.l.s., Bidwell to J.A. Spencer, 6 March 1838.
28.     Mackenzie Clippings, No.233.
29.     C.B. Sissons, *Egerton Ryerson: His Life and Letters* (1937), 1:463; Victoria College Library, Ryerson Papers, S.S. Junkin to E. Ryerson, 13 May 1838.
30.     Gates, "The *Decided Policy of William Lyon Mackenzie*."
31.     MLP, Lindsey section, James Mackenzie to Charles Lindsey, 13 Jan. 1863; to C.G.S. Lindsey, 7 Dec. 1885.
32.     MLP, James Reid to Mackenzie, Rochester, 8 June 1838. For a discussion of this point see Lindsey, Life 2:52-56, and Dent, *Story* 2:15, 20-28, particularly Morrison's admission (p. 21) that Mackenzie was to be asked by Rolph to call a group of leaders together "to enter into two resolutions to effect the independence of the province...and to unite to do so by physical force. These were to be entered into without recording them."
33.     "History of the Recent Insurrection in the Canadas," *United States Magazine and Democratic Review* IV (Jan. 1838 - Dec. 1839): 73-104.

34.     ORP, Mackenzie to O'Rielly, 5 , 22 July 1838. Rolph explained his "tameness at Buffalo" with the excuse that his wife was a "hostage" at Toronto. (MLP, James Reid to Mackenzie, Rochester, 15 Aug. 1838.)

35.     ORP, Langtree and O'Sullivan to O'Rielly, 8 Sept. 1838; Rolph to O'Rielly, n.d.

36.     "History of the Recent Insurrection in the Canadas", loc. cit.

37.     Julius H. Pratt, "Origin of Manifest Destiny," AHR XXVII (1927-8): 797-98.

38.     "The Canadian Question," *U.S. Magazine and Democratic Review* I, pp. 1-15, 205-20.

39.     "The Banks and the Currency Question," *U.S. Magazine and Democratic Review* V (Jan.-June 1838): 3-17; Hershkowitz, "New York City, 1834-40: A Study in Local Politics" (Ph.D. diss., New York University, 1960), pp. 271-72.

40.     "Cotton and the Currency Question," *U.S. Magazine and Democratic Review* I (Oct. 1837 - Jan. 1838): 381-402.

41.     "British Colonization," *The British and Colonial Review* VI (1838): 472-503.

42.     *MG*, 21 July 1838.

43.     ORP, Mackenzie to O'Rielly, 5 July 1838.

44.     His Declaration of Intention was filed in the Marine Court of the New York on 5 Sept. 1838. On 11 April 1843, in the Court of Common Pleas of New York, he became an American citizen.

45.     Guillet, *Patriots*, pp. 104-13; Cruikshank, "The Insurrection in the Short Hills," OH*SPR* VII (1907): 5-23, and XXIII (1926): 180-222; Colin Read, *The Rising in Western Upper Canada, 1837-8: The Duncombe Revolt and After* (Toronto, 1982).

46.     MLP, James to Mackenzie, 6 June, 12 July 1838.

47.     Rumilly, *Papineau et son temps* (1977), 1:600, 601, 608; II, 27.

48.     *MG*, 10 Nov., 15 Dec. 1838.

49.     MLP, James Reid to Mackenzie, 1 July 1838.

50.     *MG*, 15 Sept. 1838.

51.     Gates, "Decided Policy"; *MG*, 6 Oct. 1838.

52.     Micah Ch. IV, verse 4.

53.     Reznick, "Social History of an American Depression," *AHR* XL (1934-5): 662-87.

54.     Gates, "Decided Policy."

55.     Hershkowitz, "New York City."

56.     For an illustration of the political power of the Bank of Upper Canada, see Baldwin Papers, John Ross to Baldwin, 28 July 1850.

57.     ORP, Mackenzie to O'Rielly, 5 July 1838.

58.     *Arthur Papers* 1:51.

59.     *MG*, 4 Aug. 1838.

60.     MLP, Thos. Hyatt, ed. Rochester *Daily Advertiser*, to Mackenzie, 2 July 1839.

61.     MG, 15 Sept, 27 Dec. 1838.

62.     *MG*, 28 Aug., 8 Sept., 27 Oct. 1838.

63.     MLP, S.C. Frey to Mackenzie, 8 Aug. 1838.

64.     MLP, E.B. O'Callaghan to Mackenzie, 14 Aug. 1838.

65.     MLP, James to Mackenzie, 6 Aug. 1838. At this time James was at Herkimer, working as a journeyman printer. See also Bray Hammond, *Banks and Politics*, pp. 652-55.

66.     Colborne Papers, draft, Colborne to C.A. Hagerman, 20 Sept. 1835; Lindsey, *Life* 1:243, 281-82.

67.     *MG*, 18 Aug. 1838.

68.     *MG*, 25 Aug., 8 Sept. 1838.

69.     PHS, Mackenzie to James Buchanan, 2 Dec. 1839.

70.     *MG*, 1 Sept. 1838.

71.     Mackenzie's criticism of American society and his fears for its failure are similar to those expressed by another unhappy observer, Francis J. Grund, in his *Aristocracy in America* (London, 1839).

72.     *MG*, 15 Sept. 1838.

73.     *MG*, 10 Nov. 1838.

## Chapter III Notes

1.  Lindsey, *Life* 2:199; Oscar A. Kinchen, *The Rise and Fall of the Patriot Hunters* (New York, 1956), Ch. 2; Edward P. Alexander, "The Hunters Lodges of 1839," NYHS *Proceedings* XXXVI (1938): 64-9.

2.  MLP, C.H. McCollum to Mackenzie, Nov. 1838; MC, James Mackenzie to Charles Lindsey, 23 Jan. 1863.

3.  MG, 22 Sept. 1838; Rumilly, *Papineau* II:27.

4.  MLP, R. Nelson, under alias of J. Pedlar, to Mackenzie, 2 Oct. 1838; DHS, Whelan Papers, S.C. Frey to Mackenzie, Massillon, Ohio, 9 Oct., 4 Dec. 1838.

5.  Colborne Papers, Arthur to Colborne, 22 Oct. 1838, General Clithero to Colborne, 30 Oct. 1838, pp. 5383-5, pp. 5249-50; PAC, Lieutenant-Governors' Internal Letter Books, R.G. 7, 16, Vol. 4, Arthur to Lt. Col. Brady, 26 Oct. 1838.

6   John Grant (a judge in Oswego County), Bernard Bagley, Samuel Moulson (Oswego Historical Society, 11th Report, p. 145).

7.  *MG*, 3 Nov. 1838, quoting *The Transcript*.

8   MLP, S.C. Frey to Mackenzie, Massillon, Ohio, 9 Oct. 1838. Frey was formerly a jeweller in Brockville, U.C.

9.  MLP, D. M'Leod to Mackenzie, Cleveland, 1 Nov. 1838.

10. MPL, James Reid to Mackenzie, Rochester, 7 Nov. 1838.

11. *Arthur Papers* 1:312-318, 346; Colborne Papers, Collector of Customs at Sandwich to J. Macaulay, 14 Aug. 1838, Arthur to Colborne, 29, 30 Sept., 22, 24 Oct. 1838, Collector at Gananoque to Col. Young, 8 Oct. 1838, Capt. de Rottenburg to Colborne, 11 Oct. 1838, H.S. Fox to Arthur, copy, 2 Oct. 1838.

12. On Van Schoultz see Ella Pipping, *This Creature of Fancy* (trans. from the Swedish by Naomi Wolford; London, 1971). Von Schoultz is shown to have been a not wholly stable, admirable, or truthful person and not accurately, although generally, referred to as Polish. M'Leod, *A Brief Review*, p. 254.

13. Richard A. Pierce, "Niels Von Schoultz," *Historic Kingston* XXXI (1970): 56-65.

14. Von Schoultz to Bierce, 20 Sept. 1838, printed in Talcott E.Wing, *History of Monroe County, Michigan* (New York, 1890), pp. 206-7.

15. See *supra*, Ch. 2, fn. 23. In Lindsey's account Bierce and Birge are confused. Birge has been variously identified as coming from Cazenovia, Rome and Syracuse. He has been described as a "travelling dentist" with "no fight in him."

16. Gen. L[ucius] V. Bierce, Histor*ical Reminiscences of Summit County, Ohio* (Akron, Ohio, 1852); Northman, "Pirate," p. 190; MC, James Mackenzie to Charles Lindsey, 23 Jan. 1863.

17. S.M. Myers' account in MG, 14 Nov. 1840.

18. MLP, J.W. Birge to Mackenzie, Cazenovia, 12 Dec. 1838.

19. Gardiner M. Chapin, *Tales of the St. Lawrence* (Rouse's Point, New York, 1873), pp. 358-382, contains E.W. Davis' "Narrative of the Prescott Expedition."

20. *Niles Register*, 24 Nov. 1838, quoting from the *Argus* of 14 November an unsigned article certainly written by Hiram Denio; St. Lawrence University Library, Canton, New York, letter, Hiram Denio to Mrs. Denio, 14 Nov. 1838. (Denio was a judge of the Fifth Circuit Court of New York and evidently part-owner of the *United States*, which he refers to in this letter as "my boat.") Letters from A.M. James, postmaster at Prescott in Mackenzie Clippings, No. 391; Syra*cuse Herald*, 11 June 1905, reprinting an account based on information from Col. John Sobrieski.

21. H.A. Mushum, "Early Great Lakes Steamboats. The Battle of the Windmill and After," *American Neptune* VIII (1945): 37-60. Mushum's account is based on Capt. James Von Cleve's "Reminiscences of Early Sailing Vessels and Steamboats on Lake Erie," the manuscript is in the Chicago Historical Society.

22. J.L. Churchill, *Landmarks of Oswego County* (Syracuse, 1895), pp. 161-2.

23. St. Lawrence University Library, letter, Hiram Denio to Mrs. Denio, 14 Nov. 1838.

24. Northman, "Pirate," p. 194. Woodruff was a colonel in the New York State Militia and sheriff of Onandaga County.

25. Guillet, *Patriots*, pp. 271-7.

26. St. Lawrence University Library, letter, Lt.-Col. N.S. Clark to Adj.-General John O'Connor, 12 Nov. 1838.

27. M'Leod, *Review*, pp. 256-7.

28.     *MG*, 22 Dec. 1838.

29.     MLP, J.W. Birge to Mackenzie, 12 Dec. 1838; *MG*, 22 Dec. 1838.

30.     MLP, James Mackenzie to Charles Lindsey, 23 Jan. 1863.

31.     *MG*, 7 Nov. 1840, contains Sebastian Meyer's account of Preston King's efforts to rescue the Patriots.

32.     USNA, Letters Rec'd, Adj.-General's Office, 1822-1860, Microfilm Roll 150, Col. Worth to Brig.-Gen. Eustis, 12 Nov. 1838.

33.     E. Waterbury, "Oswego County During the Patriot War," *Oswego Historical Quarterly* 8th publication (1944): 132, 140; Watertown *Jeffersonian*, 21 Dec. 1838.

34.     Guillet, *Patriots*, pp. 140-1.

35.     St. Lawrence University Library, copy, Thomas V. Russell to John R. Russell, Canton, N.Y., 14 Nov. 1838. The original of this letter is in the philatelic collection of Atwood Manley of Canton, N.Y.

36.     Franklin B. Hough, *History of St. Lawrence and Franklin Counties* (Albany, 1853), p. 661.

37.     W. Sherman to Mackenzie, 15 Sept. 1838. This letter, not now extant, was quoted by Charles Lindsey in a manuscript article, "Canada and Party Politics," ms. is in the Lindsey section of MLP.

38.     Wilson Porter Shortridge, "The Canadian-American Frontier during the Rebellion of 1837-1838," CHR VII (1926): 13-26,gives some support to this charge against the Whigs.

39.     VBP, Silas Wright to Van Buren, 6 March 1839.

40.     Waterbury, "Oswego County," pp. 182-6; NYPL, Flagg Papers, Silas Wright to A.C. Flagg, 25 July 1839; VBP, Silas Wright to Van Buren, 16, 17 March 1839, Judge Turrill to Wright, 25 Feb. 1839.

41.     On Theller see William Renwick Riddell, "Another Patriot General," *Canadian Magazine* XLVII (1916): 318-22; *MG*, 17 Nov. 1838; Edward A. Theller, *Canada in 1837-38* (Philadelphia, 1841; 2 vols).

42.     Philadelphia *Ledger*, 19-22, 24, 26, 28 Nov. 1838.

43.     Ibid., 1 Dec. 1838; OCP, Mackenzie to O'Callaghan, 22 Nov. 1838; Theller, *Canada* 2:258-65; *MG*, 24 Nov. 1838.

44.     WHS, Perrault Papers, O'Callaghan to Louis Perrault, 22 Jan.1839.

45.     James Daniel Richardson (ed.), *A Compilation of the Messages and Papers of the Presidents* (Bureau of National Literature, Washington, D.C., 1905-1917; 20 vols.), IV, 1699, 1703. Hereafter *Messages*.

46.     *MG*, 1 Dec. 1838, 26 Jan. 1839, 4 Jan. 1840.

47.     *Arthur Papers* 1:348; 2:27-31.

48.     VBP, A.C. Flagg to Martin Van Buren, 23 Dec. 1838; Flagg Collection, Martin Van Buren to Flagg, 28 Nov. 1838.

49.     VBP, Turrill to Van Buren, Oswego, 23 Dec. 1838.

50.     *Arthur Papers* 1:405; 2:28.

51.     *MG*, 22 Dec. 1838; *Volunteer*, 19 June 1841.

52.     MC, Mackenzie to James, Rochester, 9, 10 Jan. 1839 (misdated by Mackenzie 1838).

53.     MG, 13, 26 Jan. 1839.

54.     Whelan Papers, S.C. Frey to Mackenzie, 4 Dec. 1838; MLP, S.C. Frey to Mackenzie, 1 Nov. 1838; E.A. Theller to Mackenzie, 27 Nov., 10 Dec. 1838; D. M'Leod to Mackenzie, 1 Nov. 1838.

55.     Hough, *St. Lawrence and Franklin Counties*, p. 656.

56.     MLP, Batavia Committee to Mackenzie, 7 May 1839.

57.     *MG*, 4 May 1839.

58.     *Volunteer*, 29 May 1841.

59.     ORP, Mackenzie to O'Rielly, 18 Jan. 1839.

60.     MC, Vol. IX, circular, 12 March 1839. I have been unable to discover Moulson's Canadian background.

61.     MG, 14 Aug. 1838.

62.     MC, Mackenzie to James, 7 Dec. 1839.

63.     MLP, A.K. Butler to Mackenzie, Alexandria, N.Y., 18 April 1839; Charles Latimer to Mackenzie, Chicago, Ill., April and May 1839.

64.     A.K. Mackenzie's Canadian Refugee Association is said to have been responsible for the Short Hills affair. See Colin Read, "The Short Hills Raid of June 1838, and its Aftermath," OH LXVIII (1976): 93-109.

65.      PAC, Mss Group 24, circular of 9 March 1838; in A.K. McKenzie to W.L. Mackenzie, 29 March 1838; A.K. Mackenzie to C.H. Graham, 13 April 1838.
66.      PAC, U.C. Sundries, A.K. McKenzie to Sir George Arthur, 29 March 1838, quoted in Watt, "Political Prisoners," pp. 528-55.
67.      MG, 9 March, 27 April, 4 May 1839.
68.      MLP, W.H. Doyle to Mackenzie, 19 March 1839.
69.      MLP, Peter Watson to Mackenzie, Lockport, 1 April 1839; S.C. Frey to Mackenzie, Canton, N.Y., 16 May 1839; Charles Duncombe to Mackenzie, Hartford, Conn., 8 March 1839; Hugh Carmichael to Mackenzie, Cincinnati, 12 Dec. 1839; PAC, Mss Group 24 B18, C.H. McCollum to Mackenzie, 14 April 1839.
70.      MLP, James to Mackenzie, 13 May 1839.
71.      Colborne Papers, pp. 6539-45, Richard Airey to Capt. Halkett, 6 May 1839; Washington Globe, Feb. 25, 1839; Lindsey, *Life* 2:235-7. The material on which Lindsey based his statement is no longer to be found in MLP.
72.      MLP, James Mackenzie to Charles Lindsey, 13 Jan. 1862.
73.      MG, 9, 16, 23 March 1839.
74.      MLP, Caleb Cushing to Mackenzie, 31 March 1839.
75.      *MG*, 25 May 1839.
76.      *MG*, 11, 25 May 1839.
77.      *MG*, 30 March, 6, 27 April, 1 June 1839.
78.      *MG*, 14 March 1840.
79.      MLP, S.C. Frey to Mackenzie, 6 June 1839.
80.      *MG*, 23 Feb. 1839.
81.      MLP, David Bruce to Mackenzie, Burlington, N.J., 7 April 1839.
82.      *MG*, 16 March 1839.
83.      *MG*, 1 June 1839.

## Chapter IV Notes

1.       There is some evidence suggesting that Mackenzie unnecessarily risked a trial and, as it turned out, imprisonment. Because the trial had already been postponed twice, for what appeared to be flimsy reasons, he believed the government did not intend to try him at all. (*MG*, 20 Oct. 1838.)He wrote to H.S. Benton, District Attorney, about the futility of further proceedings. Benton replied that he must be prepared to stand trial in eight days' time at Canandaigua and that his case might come up on the first day of the session. When it did not, the impatient Mackenzie had petitioned the judges to have his trial stating that he had not and did not wish to avoid it. He was tried the next morning. (*MG*, 10 Aug. 1839; Cushing Papers, Mackenzie to Cushing, 4 Jan. 1840; Lindsey, *Life* 2:244.) William Larn, one-time editor of the Lewiston *Telegraph*, who had been arrested in connection with the Navy Island affair, informed S.C. Frey that "he was one of those Benton told to gohome on the pretence that he could not find witnesses against him." Larn claimed that Benton requested him to use his influence with Mackenzie to get his trial put off and when Larn reported that Mackenzie was determined to have his trial, Benton seemed enraged and said, "he shall be tried to his heart's content. He will find himself much mistaken if he thinks to be a great man at the expense of two governments." "Larn thinks," added Frey, "that if you had humoured the joke as he did, they never would have brought you to trial." (Whelan Papers, unsigned, but in Frey's handwriting, to Mackenzie, 18 Dec. 1839.)
2.       *MG*, 15 June 1839.
3.       William Lyon Mackenzie, *The Caroline Almanac* (Rochester, 1840), pp. 100-102.
4.       Sutherland, *Canvass*, pp. 14-15, 53.
5.       *MG*, 29 July 1839; ORP, a draft memorial for Mackenzie's release of 24 March 1840.
6.       See *supra*, Ch. I, pp. 17-18.
7.       *MG*, 6 July 1839; *Niles Register*, 21 Nov. 1835; *MG*, 29 June 1839; *Niles Register*, 9 June 1838.
8.       *Niles Register*, 6 July 1839; *MG*, 6 July 1839.

9. Rochester *Daily Democrat*, 21 June 1839.
10. *MG*, 6 July 1839.
11. *MG*, 20 June, 6 July 1839.
12. MLP, Nelson Gorham to Mackenzie, 7 July 1839.
13. *MG*, 13 July 1839; *Niles Register*, 6 July 1839.
14. *MG*, 13 July, 24 Aug. 1839.
15. Cushing Papers, Mackenzie to Caleb Cushing, 21 Nov. 1839.
16. *MG*, 9 Nov. 1839; Mackenzie, *Life of Van Buren*, p. 303.
17. MLP, various letters; *MG*, 13, 20 July, 24 Aug., 21 Sept., 25 Oct. 1839; *Volunteer*, 1 May 1841.
18. Lindsey, *Life* 2:253-68.
19. MLP, O'Callaghan to Mackenzie, 28 Nov. 1839; Dr. George Coombs to Mackenzie, 17 Dec. 1839.
20. *MG*, 3 Aug. 1839.
21. MLP, James to Mackenzie, 5 Aug. 1839.
22. PAC, R.G. 5, A1, vol. 185, W.T. Kennedy to Lt.-Gov. Head, 7 Feb. 1838.
23. Watertown *Jeffersonian*, 18 Jan. 1838.
24. *MG*, 22 June 1839.
25. *MG*, 25 May 1839.
26. *MG*, 17, 24 Aug. 1839.
27. Curtis, *The Fox at Bay*, Ch. 6 and 7.
28. *MG*, 14 Sept. 1839.
29. ORP, Mackenzie to O'Rielly, 6 July 1839.
30. *MG*, 14 Sept. 1839.
31. Thurlow Weed edited the Albany *Evening Journal* and was the political manager of the Whig Party in New York State.
32. MLP, W.J. Duane to Mackenzie, Philadelphia, 16 July 1839.
33. ORP, Mackenzie to O'Rielly, 26 July 1838. This was far from the truth as the early issues of the *Colonial Advocate* show. But Mackenzie was writing this for American readers.
34. *MG*, 17 Aug. 1839.
35. *MG*, 2 July, 3 Aug. 1839.
36. ORP, Mackenzie to O'Rielly, 11 Sept. 1839. The "papers" were memorials for his release and his affidavit of 13 Sept. 1839 that he had taken no part in Patriot enterprises since Hickory Island. Copy of the affidavit is in ORC, Box 22.
37. *MG*, 14, 28 Sept. 1839.
38. MLP, E.M. McGraw to Mackenzie, Detroit, 17 Sept. 1839.
39. PHS, Mackenzie to James Buchanan, 2 Dec. 1839.
40. ORP, Mackenzie to O'Rielly, 18 Oct., 11 Nov. 1839.
41. *MG*, 23 Nov. 1839.
42. MLP, draft petition of 23 Oct. 1839; Van Buren Papers, Mackenzie to Van Buren, 10 Jan. 1840.
43. MLP, S.D. Langtree to Mackenzie, Washington, 13 Oct. 1839.
44. ORP, Mackenzie to O'Rielly, 20 Oct. 1839.
45. *MG*, 2 Nov. 1839.
46. *MG*, 30 Nov. 1839.
47. *MG*, 29 Feb. 1840.
48. *MG*, 23 Aug. 1839.
49. Reznick, "An American Depression"; *MG*, 4 Jan. 1840; Richardson, *Messages* 4:1757-71.
50. *MG*, 4 Jan. 1840.
51. *MG*, 29 Feb. 1840.
52. MLP, S.D. Langtree to Mackenzie, 17 Nov. 1839; *MG*, 11 Jan. 1840; Mackenzie, *Life of Van Buren*, p. 290.
53. *MG*, 15 April 1840; Cushing Papers, Mackenzie to Cushing, 8 Jan. 1840.
54. VBP, Mackenzie to Van Buren, 10 Jan. 1840.
55. MLP, copies of Mackenzie to Gov. W.H. Seward, 14 Jan. 1840; Sec. John Forsyth to U.S. Marshall N. Garrow, n.d.; and Seward to Mackenzie, 27 Jan. 1840.
56. MLP, H.G. Sumner to Mackenzie, Stockbridge, N.Y., 11 Feb. 1840; VBP, Democratic Central Committee of Ohio to Van Buren, 13 Feb. 1840.

57.  MLP, T.S. Brown to Mackenzie, Tallahassee, Fla., 17 Mar. 1840. Brown was one of the prominent Lower Canada rebels.

58.  *MG*, 16 Nov. 1839; 15 April 1840.

59.  Lindsey, *Life* 2:260-2.

60.  MLP, O'Rielly to Mackenzie, Rochester, 30 Dec. 1839.

61.  ORP, Mackenzie to O'Rielly, 3 March 1840.

62.  Cushing Papers, Mackenzie to Cushing, 4 Jan. 1840.

63.  VBP, Mackenzie to Van Buren, 10 Jan., 10 Feb. 1840.

64.  Cushing Papers, Mackenzie to Cushing, 4, 18 Jan., 20 Feb., 26 March 1840.

65.  ORP, Circular of 1840; USNA, E 698, two boxes of petitions for Mackenzie's release.

66.  *MG*, 15 April 1840.

67.  *Niles Register*, vol. 58, pp. 75, 95, 107, 123, 169.

68.  Van Rensselaer had been sentenced to six months' imprisonment, a fine of $250, and to remain in prison until the fine was paid. (Bonney, *Legacy*, 2:126).

69.  *Congressional Globe*, vol. VIII, pp. 367-8; MLP, Cushing to Mackenzie, 26 Dec. 1840.

70.  *Congressional Globe*, vol. VIII, p. 368.

71.  *MG*, 16 May 1840. Evidently his release did not become known in Washington at once because petitions continued to be presented on his behalf. *Journals of the Senate*, 1840, pp. 365, 369. In his *Life of Van Buren* (p. 290), Mackenzie states that "the very day the Baltimore Convention met Van Buren was made to feel that my imprisonment had been a very great political blunder and I was instantly released." The convention, however, met on May 20.

## Chapter V Notes

1.   Cushing Papers, Mackenzie to Caleb Cushing, April 1839.

2.   *MG*, 13 April 1839.

3.   Norah Story, "Stewart Derbishire's Report to Lord Durham on Lower Canada, 1838," *CHR* XVIII (1937): 48-62.

4.   *MG*, 14 July, 28 Sept., 28 Nov. 1838; Oscar Kinchen, *Lord Russell's Canadian Policy* (Lubbock, Texas, 1945), Ch. 4.

5.   *MG*, 15, 29 Sept., 27 Oct., 13 Nov. 1838.

6.   *MG*, 27 Oct. 1838.

7.   Ordinances of the Special Council of Lower Canada, 1 sess., cap. 1, 2 sess., cap. 3; Aegidius Fauteaux, *Patriotes de 1837-8* (Montreal, 1950), pp. 396-7. On the government's difficulties in bringing Viger to trial, see Senior, *Redcoats and Patriotes*, p. 150.

8.   *MG*, 9 Dec. 1838.

9.   *MG*, 8 Sept. 1838.

10.  *Durham Report*, App. C, pp. 6-7.

11.  John George Lambton, first Earl of Durham, *Report and Despatches of the Earl of Durham* (Ridgways, London, 1839), pp. 307-17; *MG*, 20 Oct. 1838.

12.  *London True Sun*, 11 Nov. 1838, quoted in *MG*, 19 Jan. 1839. Cf. with S.D. Clark, *Movements of Political Protest in Canada, 1640-1840* (Toronto, 1959), pp. 320-22.

13.  *MG*, 13 July 1839; Lampton, *Report and Despatches of Durham*, p. 371.

14.  On the reception of the report, see Ronald Hyam and Ged Martin, *Reappraisals of British Imperial History* (London, 1975), pp. 79-80.

15.  *MG*, 17 Aug. 1839, 19 Oct., 9 Nov. 1840. Ellice was MP for Coventry and a member of the Committee of the Hudson's Bay Company, and seigneur of Beauharnois.

16.  *MG*, 20 April, 30 Aug. 1839; MLP, James to Mackenzie, 23 Aug. 1839; *Parliamentary Debates*, 26 July 1839, 3rd series, XLIX, 880; W.P.M. Kennedy, *Select Documents of the Canadian Constitution 1759-1915* (Toronto, 1918), pp. 443-7, 514-6.

17.  Gates, "Decided Policy."

18.  *MG*, 16 May 1840; OCP, Mackenzie to O'Callaghan, 25 Aug. 1844.

19.  *MG*, 17 Sept. 1840.

20.  *MG*, 8 June 1839.

21.  Colborne Papers, Mackenzie to Sir John Colborne, 8 March 1829.

22.  *MG*, 17 Aug. 1839.

23. John Beverly Robinson, *Canada and the Canada Bill* (London, 1839; reprint ed. New York, 1967), pp. 118, 168.

24. *Parliamentary Debates*, 19 March 1840, LII, p. 1344; 14 June 1840, LIV, p. 1143.

25. *Parliamentary Debates*, 13 April 1840, LIII, pp. 1055-57.

26. Helen Taft Manning, "Who Ran the British Empire, 1830-1850?", *Journal of British Studies* V (1965): 88-121; *JLAC*, 1841, p. 641 and App. B.B; William Ormsby, *The Emergence of the Federal Concept in Canada, 1835- 1845* (Toronto, 1969), pp. 55-56.

27. MLP, James to Mackenzie, 24 Nov. 1839; MC, Mackenzie to James, 12 Oct., 1 Dec. 1839; MLP, Ben Lett to Mackenzie, two letters of 10 March 1839. On Lett see Guillet, *Patriots*, Ch. 17, and Coventry, "A Concise History of the Rebellion." Lett was a farmer in Darlington Township. Lett took no part in the rebellion but was sympathetic to the Reformers. The brutal treatment of his mother and sister by soldiers turned him into a ruthless avenger.

28. MLP, E.A. Theller to Mackenzie, Detroit, 29 May 1840; D. M'Leod to Mackenzie, Cleveland, 12 June 1840.

29. MLP, W.A. Forward to Mackenzie, Watertown, 20 March 1840. (An M.W. Forward appears in the list of those who burned the *Sir Robert Peel* [Guillet, *Patriots*, p. 159]); MLP, C.H. McCollum to Mackenzie, 11 April 1840.

30. MLP, James Hunter to Mackenzie, Hartland, N.Y., 23 Feb., 30 May 1840; R. Alan Douglas, *John Prince: A Collection of Documents* (Toronto: The Champlain Society, Ontario Series IX, 1980), pp. 25, 28-31, 33-35. Prince had had prisoners taken at Windsor shot.

31. MC, G. Heron to Mackenzie, 27 Dec. 1839.

32. PAC, copy, C.O. 42, vol. 308, pp. 25-8; Arthur to Glenelg, 17 Jan. 1840.

33. *MG*, 16 May 1840.

34. MLP, D. M'Leod to Mackenzie, 12 June 1840.

35. The fire was not "accidental." (Buell Papers, Mackenzie to Andrew Buell, 17 June 1840; John W. Spurr, "The Night of the Fire," *Historic Kingston* XXXIV (1964): 57-65.

36. MLP, James to Mackenzie, Herkimer, 18 June 1840.

37. MC, Mackenzie to James, 6 July 1840.

38. MLP, D. M'Leod to Mackenzie, 31 Aug. 1840, quoting Mackenzie.

39. MLP, E.B. O'Callaghan to Mackenzie, Albany, n.d., 1840. O'Callaghan was an Irish physician who settled in Lower Canada, became editor of the Montreal *Vindicator*, a member of the Lower Canada House of Assembly, a supporter of Papineau, and fled with him to the United States. Eventually he settled in Albany and became the archivist of the State of New York.

40. MLP, T.S. Brown to Mackenzie, Tallahassee, Fla., 22 June 1840;Charles Durand to Mackenzie, Chicago, 24 July 1840. Durand, a lawyer of Hamilton, Upper Canada, had been banished for life.

41. MLP (signature torn off, to John Montgomery, 22 July 1840).

42. MLP, James to Mackenzie, Herkimer, 31 July 1840.

43. MC, James Mackenzie to Charles Lindsey, 23 Jan. 1863.

44. MC, Mackenzie to James, 27 Aug. 1840.

45. MLP, James to Mackenzie, 29 Aug. 1840.

46. MLP, 31 Aug. 1840, quoting Mackenzie's letter to him of 24 Aug. 1840.

47. MLP, M'Leod to Mackenzie, Cleveland, 24, 26 Sept. 1840.

48. MLP, W. Johnston to Mackenzie, 22 Sept. 1840. Johnston refers to Van Buren, Amos Kendall, his postmaster general, and Francis F. Blair, an influential Democrat.

49. *MG*, 23 Dec. 1840.

50. *National Gazette,* 28 Aug. 1840.

51. Garraty, *Silas Wright*, p. 163.

52. Cushing Papers, Mackenzie to Cushing, 11 Jan. 1841.

53. MC, Mackenzie to James, 27 Aug. 1840.

54. *MG*, 7 Sept. 1840, quoting House Exec. Doc. No. 10, 1st sess., 26 Cong.

55. *MG*, 17 Sept. 1840.

56. ORP, copy, O'Rielly to Mackenzie, 5 Oct. 1840.

57. Advertisements in *Rochester Daily Advertiser*, 5 Dec. to 14 Dec. 1840.

58. Cushing Papers, Mackenzie to Cushing, 11 June 1841.

59. *MG*, 23 Dec. 1840.

60. Theller's *Spirit of '76* at Detroit, James Mackenzie's *Freeman's Advocate* at Lockport, Dr. Cote's *North American* at Swanton, Vt., and Ludger Duvernay's *Patriote Canadien* at Burlington, Vt.

61. Whelan Papers, S. Moulson to Mackenzie, 18 May 1840; MLP, Rev. David Strang to Mackenzie, Peoria, N.Y., 23 July 1838.

62. *Congressional Globe*, 26 Feb. 1839, vol. VII, Appendix, p. 231.

63. *MG*, 27 April, 11 May 1839.

64. Duff Green Papers, copy, Green to —, Paris, 18 Jan. 1842; copy, Green to John Tyler, London, 31 May 1840; copy, Green to Nicholas Biddle, 24 Jan. 1842. Green was a southern Whig whom President Tyler sent on an unofficial mission to France and England.

65. Lindsey, *Life*, vol. 2, App. E; Stanley G. Ryerson, *Unequal Union* (Toronto, 1968), p. 327.

66. *MG*, 11 May, 3 Aug. 1839.

67. *MG*, 7 Sept. 1839.

68. Orestes Brownson, "Democracy and Reform," *Boston Quarterly Review* II (Oct. 1839): 478-517.

69. *MG*, 23 Nov. 1839.

70. MLP, James Hunter to Mackenzie, Hartland, N.Y., 2 Sept. 1839.

71. MLP, James to Mackenzie, 23 Aug. 1839.

72. *MG*, 1 June 1840.

73. MLP, James to Mackenzie, 27 Feb. 1840.

## Chapter VI Notes

1. ORP, Mackenzie to O'Rielly, 11 Feb. 1841.

2. ORP, Mackenzie to O'Rielly, 18 Dec. 1840.

3. MLP, W. Kitchener et al. to Mackenzie, Cincinnati, 30 March 1841; OCP, Mackenzie to E.B. O'Callaghan, 15 March 1841; ORP, Mackenzie to O'Rielly, 7 Jan. 1841.

4. Irving Abella, "The Sydenham Election of 1841," *CHR* XLVII (1966): 326-43.

5. MLP, Samuel McAfee to Mackenzie, Bertie Township, 24 Feb. 1841.

6. MLP, S. McAfee to Mackenzie, 24 Feb. 1841.

7. MLP, Joseph Wynn to Mackenzie, Queenston, 24 Feb. 1841.

8. *JLAC*, 1841, pp. 65-66; Jedediah Prendergast Merritt, *Biography of the Late William Hamilton Merritt, MP* (St. Catharines, 1875), p. 223.

9. *JLAUC*, 19 Dec. 1839, p. 40.

10. William G. Ormsby, "The Civil List Question in the Province of Canada," *CHR* XXXI (1950): 93-118.

11. MLP, J. Wynn to Mackenzie, Queenston, 24 Feb. 1841.

12. MLP, S. McAfee to Mackenzie, Bertie Township, 25 March 1841.

13. Toronto *Examiner*, 2 March 1841. Mackintosh had been vice-president of the Toronto (central) branch of the Canadian Alliance Society, organized by Reformers in 1834. Eric Jackson, "The Organization of the Upper Canada Reformers, 1818-1867," *OH* LIII (1961), 95-115.

14. MLP, copy, Mackenzie to George Lount, — April 1841. George was the brother of Samuel Lount.

15. *Advocate*, 13 March 1834.

16. Gerald M. Craig, *Upper Canada, The Formative Years 1784-1841* (New York, 1963), pp. 193-4, 240; George M. Wilson, *The Life of Robert Baldwin* (Toronto, 1933), pp. 25-6.

17. Toronto *Examiner*, 21 Aug. 1850; Baldwin Papers, John Carey to Baldwin, 28 July 1850.

18. PAC, R.G. 24, B24, Francis Hincks to Thomas Elliott, 16 April 1841.

19. MLP, copy, Mackenzie to G. Lount, — April 1841. The Bank of the People had been founded by Reformers. Hincks became its cashier. In Mackenzie Clippings 340A there is a brief account in Mackenzie's hand of Hincks' earlier support of the Tories.

20. OCP, Mackenzie to O'Callaghan, 5 April 1841; *Volunteer*, 17 April 1841.

21. Toronto *Examiner*, 1 June 1841.

22. OCP, Mackenzie to O'Callaghan, 5 April 1841.

23. Reserves equal to one-seventh of the land granted had been set aside for the benefit of a Protestant clergy.

24. Rochester *Volunteer*, 17 April, 3 July 1841; *JLAUC*, 1839, p. 309.
25. *Volunteer*, 15 May 1841; Kinchen, *Russell's Canadian Policy*, pp.119- 20; Knaplund, *Letters from Sydenham*, p. 121.
26. OCP, Mackenzie to O'Callaghan, 5 April 1841.
27. Lillian F. Gates, "A note on Dr. John Smyles," *OH* LVII (1965): 229-30. On Smyles, see also John S. Moir, "Mr. Mackenzie's Secret Reporter," *OH* LV (1963), 205-13; and Michael Brook, "Lawrence Pitkethly, Dr. Smyles and Canadian Revolutionaries in the United States," *OH* LVII (1965), 79-84.
28. MLP, Smyles to Mackenzie, 2 Aug. 1842. Smyles' reports are to be found in the New York *Herald* of 15, 22, 24 June, 7, 12, 14, 23 July, 2 11, 21 Aug., 2, 11, 18, 25 Sept. 1841.
29. MLP, Smyles to Mackenzie, Rochester, 12 Nov. 1838, 14, 29 Nov. 1839.
30. MLP, Neil Carmichael to Mackenzie, Cincinnati, 1 June 1841.
31. Edith Firth, ed., *Early Toronto Newspapers* (Toronto, 1961), p. 13. MLP, Charles Donlevy to Mackenzie, 11 Aug. 1841.
32. *Volunteer*, 8 May 1841.
33. MLP, Smyles to Mackenzie, 11 June 1841.
34. "Before the end of the session ten members of Parliament held major offices and nearly twenty others held minor offices under the Crown." Ronald Stewart Longley, *Sir Francis Hincks* (Toronto, 1943), p. 81.
35. *Volunteer*, 12 June 1841; MLP, Smyles to Mackenzie, 12 June 1841. For Parke's views see C.O. Ermatinger, *The Talbot Regime* (St. Thomas, 1904), pp. 240-1.
36. MLP, Smyles to Mackenzie, 24 June 1841.
37. MLP, Smyles to Mackenzie, 18 June 1841; *Volunteer*, 26 June 1841; *Debates* vol. 1, pp. 60-69. Draper was attorney-general for Canada West.
38. *JLAC*, 1841, pp. 64-6; *Kingston Chronicle*, 26 June 1841.
39. MLP, Smyles to Mackenzie, misdated letter of 21 July 1841, italics added.
40. Knaplund, *Letters from Sydenham*, p. 146.
41. *Kingston Chronicle*, 26 July 1841.
42. *Volunteer*, 3 July 1841. George M. Boswell represented Northumberland South.
43. MLP, Smyles to Mackenzie, 10 July 1841.
44. MLP, Smyles to Mackenzie, 23 July 1841.
45. MLP, Smyles to Mackenzie, 6, 23 July 1841. Smyles' reference was probably to Hermanus Smith of Wentworth.
46. *Volunteer*, 5 June, 24 July 1841.
47. PHS, Mackenzie to James Buchanan, 2 Dec. 1839; MLP, L. Bonnefaux to Mackenzie, 8 June 1841; *Volunteer*, 3 July 1841.
48. Elias Moore had been imprisoned for two months after the rebellion, indicted, bailed, but not tried. Read, *Rising*, p. 235.
49. *Volunteer*, 10 July 1841.
50. MLP, Smyles to Mackenzie, 15 July 1841.
51. MLP, Smyles to Mackenzie, 20 July 1841.
52. *Debates* (Montreal, 1970+), vol. 1 (1841), 608; *Kingston Chronicle*, 11, 14, 21 Aug. 1841.
53. Gates, *Land Policies*, pp. 236-38; MLP, Smyles to Mackenzie, 16 Aug. 1841; *Debates* vol. 1 (1841), 555, 620-1, 628-34.
54. Act of Union, clause 57.
55. MLP, Smyles to Mackenzie, 9 July 1841.
56. MLP, Smyles to Mackenzie, 14, 28 Aug. 1841.
57. *Kingston Chronicle*, 18 Aug. 1841, quoting the *Commercial Messenger*.
58. MLP, Smyles to Mackenzie, 23 July 1841.
59. New York *Weekly Herald*, 11 Sept. 1841; *Debates* vol. 1 (1841), pp. 745-59.
60. MLP, Smyles to Mackenzie, 16 Aug. 1841.
61. MLP, Smyles to Mackenzie, 16 Aug. 1841.
62. Such a bill was introduced in conformity to the resolution but not reported. (*JLAC*, 1841, pp. 488, 499, 612.)
63. New York *Weekly Herald*, 11 Sept. 1841.
64. Scrope, *Sydenham*, p. 224; MTL, unpublished Arthur Papers relating to the case of McLeod.

65.  Granger Papers, Thurlow Weed to Francis Granger, 9 March, 22 May 1841; R.C. Watt, "Case of Alexander McLeod,"EHR (1926):528-55; Frederick Merk, *The Fruits of Propaganda in the Tyler Administration* (Cambridge, Mass., 1971), p. 11; Albert Dennis Kirwan, *John J. Crittenden: The Struggle for the Union* (Lexington, Ky, 1962), pp. 144-6.

66.  Cushing Papers, Mackenzie to Cushing, 9, 13, 29 March 1841; Rochester *Daily Advertiser*, 6, 15, 20 March 1841.

67.  *Volunteer*, 24 July 1841; MLP, Cushing to Mackenzie, 18, 19 March 1841.

68.  Cushing Papers, Mackenzie to Cushing, 20 March 1841.

69.  Cushing Papers, Mackenzie to Cushing, 13 March 1841.

70.  MLP, E.B. O'Callaghan to Mackenzie, 21 March 1841; Donald M'Leod to Mackenzie, 25 March 1841.

71.  *Volunteer*, 24 July 1841.

72.  MLP, Nelson Gorham to Mackenzie, Fredonia, 21 Jan. 1841. This is a reference to an incident in which two Negroes were killed and several injured in an attempt to rescue from the hands of Sheriff McLeod an escaped slave accused of stealing who was being extradited. (*Constitution*, 4, 27 Oct. 1837.)

73.  *New York Herald*, 25 Sept. 1841; MLP, L.S. Woods to Mackenzie, 26 Aug. 1841; Henry Kalar to Mackenzie, Stamford, 14 Aug. 1841; Maria Wait to Mackenzie, 28 July 1841. Mrs. Wait was the wife of one of the Patriots who had been captured after the Short Hills affair and sentenced to transportation.

74.  Cushing Papers, Mackenzie to Caleb Cushing, 26 Oct. 1841; Robert Fairlie Wood, *Forgotten Canadians* (Toronto, 1963), pp. 9-10.

75.  MLP, D. M'Leod to Mackenzie, 28 March 1841.

76.  *Kingston Chronicle*, 13 Sept. 1841, quoting Buffalo *Commercial* of 6 Sept. 1841; Toronto *Patriot*, 17 Sept. 1841; MLP, Theller to Mackenzie, 10 Sept. 1841.

77.  MLP, Theller to Mackenzie, 13, 16 Sept. 1841; New York *Herald*, 27 Oct. 1841, quoting *Kingston Chronicle*; Onondaga *Standard*, 29 Sept. 1841, quoting the Niagara *Chronicle*.

78.  Onondaga *Standard*, 29 Sept. 1841.

79.  New York *Herald*, 27 Sept. 1841.

80.  MLP, S.C. Frey to Mackenzie, 1 Aug. 1841.

81.  MLP, D. M'Leod to Mackenzie, 26 April 1841.

82.  MLP, Papineau to Mackenzie, 27 Sept. 1841.

83.  New York *Herald*, 9-16 Oct. 1841.

84.  Ibid., 25 Sept. 1841.

85.  MLP, Papineau to Mackenzie, 1 Nov. 1841.

86.  MLP, James to Mackenzie, 5 Nov. 1841.

87.  MLP, same to same, 16 Dec. 1841.

88.  MLP, Ephraim Moulton to Mackenzie, 16 Nov. 1841.

89.  MLP, a memo of 20 Oct. 1841.

90.  *Volunteer*. An undated fragment of it survives in the Mackenzie Clippings. Its approximate date has been derived from an advertisement dated 29 Jan. 1842, announcing the opening of Mackenzie's law offices.

91.  MLP, Smyles to Mackenzie, 11 July 1843.

92.  MLP, Dr. A.K. McKenzie to Mackenzie, 15 Feb. 1842.

93.  PAC, C.O. 42, vol. 490, pp. 191-206, Bagot to Stanley, 14 March 1842.

94.  MLP, Mackenzie to Dr. A.K. McKenzie, 19 Feb. 1842, copied on verso of Dr. A.K. McKenzie's letter to him of 15 Feb. 1842.

95.  See note 93.

96.  OCP, Mackenzie to O'Callaghan, 1 April 1842.

97.  Rochester *Evening Post* Extra, 1 April 1842, quoted in New York *Evening Post*, 6 April 1842; Rochester *Evening Post*, 3 April 1842.

98.  New York *Herald*, 5 April 1842.

99.  OCP, Mackenzie to O'Callaghan, 1 April 1842.

100.  US Revised Statutes, CCLVII; *Congressional Globe*, 27 Cong., 2nd sess., XI, pp. 480, 730, 734, 891-2.

101.  MLP, Thomas Young to Mackenzie, 23 Feb. 1842; Adam Ramage to Mackenzie, 17 Jan. 1842.

102.  OCP, Mackenzie to O'Callaghan, 26 Feb., 5 March 1842; MLP, O'Callaghan to Mackenzie, 7, 15 March 1842.

| 103. | MLP, James to Mackenzie, 9 May 1842. |
| 104. | MC, Mackenzie to James, 3 June 1842. |
| 105. | MLP, James Allan to Mackenzie, 17 June 1842. |

## Chapter VII Notes

| 1. | PAC, R.G. 5, A1, vol. 185, Geo. Bruce & Co. to Lt.-Gov. Head, 24 Jan. 1838; MLP, Geo. Bruce & Co. to Mackenzie, 26 June 1838. |
| 2. | OCP, Mackenzie to E.B. O'Callaghan, 26 Feb. 1842; MLP, James to Mackenzie, 28 July 1842. |
| 3. | ORP, Mackenzie to Henry O'Rielly, 12 March 1842; MC, Mackenzie to James, 15 March 1842. |
| 4. | MC, Mackenzie to James, 15 Aug. 1842. |
| 5. | MLP, Dr. John Smyles to Mackenzie, 15 Sept. 1842. |
| 6. | *The Plebian Weekly*, 20, 28 July 1842. Gemmel was one of the prisoners taken at Short Hills and classified in the official lists as a labourer. (Lindsey, *Life* 2:390.) |
| 7. | MC, Mackenzie to James, 15 Aug. 1842. |
| 8. | ORP, Mackenzie to O'Reilly, 27 Aug. 1842, 18 Jan., 28 March 1843. |
| 9. | MLP, Adam Ramage to Mackenzie, Philadelphia, 23 Jan. 1843; O'Callaghan to Mackenzie, Albany, 29 Jan. 1843; J.T. Blain to Mackenzie, Columbus, Ohio, 14 Feb. 1843. |
| 10. | ORP, Mackenzie to O'Rielly, 12 March 1843. |
| 11. | ORP, Mackenzie to O'Rielly, 6 March 1843. |
| 12. | ORC, Mackenzie to O'Rielly, 7 Feb. 1843. The child was Isabel Mackenzie, born 6 Feb. 1843. |
| 13. | ORP, Mackenzie to O'Rielly, 26 April 1843; PHS, Mackenzie to John C. Spencer, 25 Nov. 1843; New York *Examiner*, 14 Oct. 1843. |
| 14. | ORP, Mackenzie to O'Rielly, 28 April 1844. |
| 15. | ORP, Mackenzie to O'Rielly, 28 March 1843. |
| 16. | MLP, Adam Ramage to Mackenzie, 2 Oct. 1843. |
| 17. | New York *Examiner*, 30 Sept. 1843. |
| 18. | ORP, Mackenzie to O'Rielly, 12 March 1843, 26 Sept. 1845. |
| 19. | MC, Mackenzie to James, 29 July 1843. |
| 20. | OCP, Mackenzie to O'Callaghan, 2 Jan. 1844. |
| 21. | Albany *Argus*, 8 Aug. 1836; New York *Examiner*, 30 Sept. 1843. |
| 22. | Bancroft Papers, copy, M. Van Buren to Nicholas Biddle, 17 July 1826. |
| 23. | New York State, Revised Statutes, Ch. 18, Title 2, Article 1, ss. 10, 14-18; Act of 1829, Ch. 94, s. 30. |
| 24. | The capital of the Safety Fund proved inadequate to the calls made upon it and the creditors of the insolvent banks were subjected to a long delay. Robert Chaddock, *The Safety Fund Banking System in New York, 1828-1866* (Washington: G.P.O., 1910), pp. 324-38; *Documents of the State of New York*, 66th Sess., 1843, No. 10, pp. 52-3. |
| 25. | New York *Examiner*, 7 Oct. 1843. |
| 26. | Curtis, *The Fox at Bay*, pp. 75-85; Flagg Papers, draft of letter of 30 Dec. 1839. Intended recipient not given. Possibly Van Buren. |
| 27. | *Report of the Proceedings and Debates of the Convention for the Revision of the Constitution of the State of New York* (Albany, 1821), p. 322. |
| 28. | New York *Examiner*, 30 Sept. 1843. |
| 29. | ORP, Lorenzo Sherwood to O'Rielly, 9 June 1844. |
| 30. | MLP, O'Rielly to Mackenzie, 17, 22 Oct. 1843. |
| 31. | O'Rielly Letter Books, Feb. to April 1843, O'Rielly to Silas Wright, 15 April 1843. |
| 32. | MLP, James to Mackenzie, Damascus, Ohio, 23 Oct. 1843. |
| 33. | MLP, James to Mackenzie, 23 Oct. 1843. |
| 34. | OCP, Mackenzie to O'Callaghan, 16 Oct. 1843. |
| 35. | MLP, O'Callaghan to Mackenzie, 20 Oct. 1843; OCP, Mackenzie to O'Callaghan, two letters of 24 Oct. 1843, 1 May 1844. |
| 36. | Lynn Gardiner Tyler, *The Letters and Times of the Tylers*, 3 vols. (Richmond, Va., 1884-96), 2:128. |

37. MLP, Thomas Fitnam to Mackenzie, Philadelphia, 24 Oct. 1843.
38. A copy of Mackenzie's letter of Oct. 27 1843 is appended to the above. I have been unable to find this reference to the *National Intelligencer*.
39. Robert Seager, *And Tyler Too* (New York, 1963), pp. 230-33.
40. MLP, Fitnam to Mackenzie, Washington, 29 Oct., 7 Nov. 1843.
41. MLP, J.R. Flanders to Mackenzie, Fort Covington, N.Y., Nov. 1843.
42. Tyler, *Letters and Times*, 2:129-132; *Niles Register* LXI (Sept. 1841- 1842): 257-261.
43. For Mackenzie's ideas about banks see my "Decided Policy," pp. 185-208; also MC, Mackenzie to James, 20 April 1840 and ORP, Mackenzie to O'Rielly, 1 Dec. 1843.
44. Charles Duncombe, *Free Banking. An Essay on Banking Currency, Finance, Exchange and Political Economy* (Cleveland, 1841); Cushing Papers, Charles Duncombe to Caleb Cushing, 10 Nov.1841.
45. Duff Green papers, copy, Duff Green to Tyler, London, 31 May1843; Merk, *Propaganda*, 19-22.
46. *MG*, 11 May, 7 Sept. 1839, 1 June 1840.
47. MLP, Fitnam to Mackenzie, 29 Oct. 1843.
48. MLP, James to Mackenzie, 11 Jan. 1844.
49. OCP, Mackenzie to O'Callaghan, 4 Dec. 1843; Lindsey, *Life* 2:284.
50. MLP, W.J. Duane to Mackenzie, 20 Nov. 1843; PHS, Mackenzie to J.C. Spencer, 25 Nov., 1 Dec. 1843.
51. MLP, Fitnam to Mackenzie, 20 Nov. 1843; USNA, Treasury Dept., Collectors Small Ports, Sec. G, No. 7, 9 Aug. 1843 to 6 Aug. 1844, J.C. Spencer to E. Curtis, 18 Nov. 1843.
52. PHS, Mackenzie to J.C. Spencer, 1 Dec. 1843, endorsed, "No Answer."
53. MLP, Fitnam to Mackenzie, 3 April, 4 May, 1844; Robert Tyler to Mackenzie, 28 April 1844.
54. ORP, Mackenzie to O'Rielly, 9 March 1844.
55. Duff Green Papers, E.J. Denio to Duff Green, 30 March 1844.
56. MLP, Fitnam to Mackenzie, 27 April 1844.
57. *Journals of the Executive Proceedings of the Senate*, Vol. VI, pp. 254, 338; Seager, *And Tyler Too*, p. 233.
58. MLP, Fitnam to Mackenzie, 4 May 1844.
59. MLP, O'Callaghan to Mackenzie, 31 May 1844.
60. ORP, Mackenzie to O'Rielly, 30 May 1844.
61. Seager, *And Tyler Too*, p. 232.
62. Ibid., p. 233.
63. OCP, Mackenzie to O'Callaghan, 25 July 1844; MLP, Dr. John Smyles to Mackenzie, 14 July 1844.
64. MLP, Fitnam to Mackenzie, 20 July 1844.
65. MLP, O'Callaghan to Mackenzie, 29 June 1844; Fitnam to Mackenzie, 20 July 1844; O'Rielly to Mackenzie, 21 July 1844.
66. New York *Express*, 25 July 1844.
67. MLP, Mackenzie to James, 5 Aug. 1844; OCP, Mackenzie to O'Callaghan, 24 Oct. 1844.
68. USNA, Treasury Dept., Sec. G, No. 8, Collectors Small Ports, Sec. Treasury to Van Ness, 14 Jan., 25 Feb., 6 May 1844, 29 Aug. 1846.
69. New York *Herald*, 26 Aug. 1844; New York *Democrat*, 27 Aug. 1844.
70. New York *Tribune*, 26 Sept. 1845.
71. Arthur G. Doughty and Norah Story, eds., *Documents Relating to the Constitutional History of Canada 1819-1828* (Ottawa, 1935), pp. 305-9, 351-5.
72. *Workingman's Advocate*, 24 Aug. 1844; New York *Democrat*, 18 Aug. 1844, quoting New York *Messenger* of 18 Aug. (Mackenzie Clippings No. 3856); ORP, Mackenzie to O'Rielly, 25 Aug. 1844; OCP, Mackenzie to O'Callaghan, 25 Aug. 1844.
73. On Nativism see Ray Allen Billington, *The Protestant Crusade* (New York, 1938), Ch. 8.
74. New York *Democrat*, 19 Aug. 1844, quoting New York*Messenger*, 18 Aug. 1844.
75. MLP, O'Callaghan to Mackenzie, 27 Aug. 1844.
76. Mackenzie Clippings, No. 3856.
77. New York *Democrat*, 27 Aug. 1844.
78. MC, Mackenzie to James, 5 Aug. 1844.
79. MLP, copy, Mackenzie to Thurlow Weed, 17 Oct. 1845.
80. OCP, Mackenzie to O'Callaghan, 25 June 1844.

81. MLP, copy of agreement with Burgess, Stringer and Co., 3 Feb. 1844; ORC, Mackenzie to O'Rielly, 9 March, 20 April 1844.
82. Helen Sarah Zahler, *Eastern Workingmen and National Land Policy, 1829- 1862* (New York, 1941), pp. 13-36.
83. *Workingman's Advocate*, 16, 30 March, 6 April, 8 June 1844.
84. Ibid., 25 May 1844.
85. Ibid., 8 June 1844.
86. Ibid., 15, 22 June 1844.
87. Ibid., 13 July 1844.

## Chapter VIII Notes

1. OCP, Mackenzie to O'Callaghan, 28 Dec. 1844.
2. MLP, Fitnam to Mackenzie, 11 Feb. 1845; OCP, Mackenzie to O'Callaghan, 19 April 1845.
3. OCP, Mackenzie to O'Callaghan, 16 Sept. 1844.
4. MLP, O'Callaghan to Mackenzie, 12 Nov. 1844.
5. ORP, Mackenzie to O'Rielly, 24 Dec. 1844.
6. OCP, Mackenzie to O'Callaghan, 1 June 1844.
7. ORP, Mackenzie to O'Rielly, 16 April 1844.
8. MLP, Burgess and Stringer to Mackenzie, 8 April 1845; ORP, Mackenzie to O'Rielly, 3 Nov. 1845.
9. New York *Tribune*, 24 Nov. 1845. So far, no complete copy of this second part has been found.
10. Theller, *Canada* 1:36, 56.
11. OCP, Mackenzie to O'Callaghan, 19 April 1845; MLP, O'Callaghan to Mackenzie, 25 April 1845.
12. William M. Holland, *The Life and Political Opinions of Martin Van Buren, Vice President of the United States* (Hartford, 1835), pp. 511-2.
13. Charles Grier Sellers, *James K. Polk, Continentalist* (Princeton, 1966), pp. 163-4.
14. Mackenzie's letter in *Tribune* of 6 Sept. 1845.
15. Duff Green Papers, Mackenzie to Green, 26 May 1845.
16. Polk Papers, Duff Green to President Polk, 22 May 1845; MLP, Duff Green to Mackenzie, 30 May 1845.
17. Chauncey S. Boucher and Robert P. Brooks, eds., "Correspondence addressed to John C. Calhoun, 1837-1849," Duff Green to Calhoun, June 1845, in AHA, *Annual Report*,1929, pp. 125-570.
18. Polk Papers, Van Ness to Polk, 4, 5 April 1845; General Council of Tammany to Polk, 9 May 1845; Van Ness to Polk, 10 June 1845.
19. MLP, Mackenzie to James, 7 June 1845; ORP, Mackenzie to O'Rielly, 2 Aug. 1845.
20. Years later Thurlow Weed gave an account of Mackenzie's visit to Albany to consult him about publishing the Hoyt papers. Weed states that Mackenzie came "unexpectedly" upon "this treasure" and "mined away silently until the gems were all collated [sic]." Mackenzie feared that if he attempted to publish this material in New York City, the news might leak out and he might be stopped by an injunction. Weed felt that he could not assist Mackenzie in publishing private letters of men to whom Weed was known to be personally and politically hostile. *Albany Evening Journal*, 2 Sept. 1861.
21. MLP, copy, Mackenzie to A.S. Doane, 1 Aug. 1845; Mackenzie to Thurlow Weed, 17 Oct. 1845. This letter is not marked a copy.
22. New York *Tribune*, 22 Sept. 1845.
23. Mackenzie, *Lives of Butler and Hoyt*, pp. 16-26, 31, 59-60, 69, 70, 75, 99, 104, 109-110, 121-2, 147-9.
24. New York *Tribune*, 26 Sept. 1845.
25. Mackenzie, *Lives of Butler and Hoyt*, p. 35.
26. Ibid., pp. 35, 149; New York *Tribune*, 2 Oct. 1845.
27. Wright-Butler Letters, Wright to Butler, 27 Feb. 1841.
28. *National Intelligencer*, 26 Sept. 1845, quoting *Commercial Advertiser*.
29. Wright-Butler Letters, Wright to Butler, 27 Jan. 1841; *National Intelligencer*, 27 Feb. 1841; New York *Times*, 26 Feb. 1841.

30. *National Intelligencer*, 20 March 1841; John C. Fitzpatrick, ed., "The Autobiography of Martin Van Buren," in AHA, *Annual Report*, 1918, vol. 2, p. 536.
31. New York *Tribune*, 22-26 Sept., 1 Oct. 1845.
32. *National Intelligencer*, 25 Sept. 1845.
33. New York *Express*, 23 Sept. 1845.
34. *The Subterranean*, 27 Sept. 1845.
35. Quoted in *National Intelligencer*, 25 Sept. 1845.
36. Quoted in *Tribune*, 14 Oct. 1845.
37. *National Intelligencer*, 27 Sept. 1845, quoting *Commercial Advertiser*, 23 Sept. 1845.
38. Washington *Union*, 25 Sept. 1845; *National Intelligencer*, 26 Sept. 1845.
39. New York *Tribune*, 25 Sept. 1845.
40. *New York Commercial*, 25 Sept. 1845.
41. Mackenzie, *Lives of Butler and Hoyt*, p. 98.
42. MLP, W.J. Duane to Mackenzie, 30 Sept. 1845, 21 May 1846.
43. OCP, Mackenzie to O'Callaghan, 13 Sept. 1845, with note appended by O'Callaghan; Mackenzie to O'Callaghan, 29 Oct. 1845.
44. OCP, O'Rielly to O'Callaghan, 28 Sept. 1845; MLP, O'Rielly to Mackenzie, 26 Sept. 1845.
45. MLP, James to Mackenzie, 9, 31 Oct. 1845.
46. New York *Tribune*, 26, 29 Sept., 14, 22 Oct. 1845; Gates, "Decided Policy."
47. Bogardus and Corryell's letters to the *Tribune* are quoted in Mackenzie's *Life of Van Buren*, p. 13, notes.
48. Mackenzie, *Lives of Butler and Hoyt*, p. 11.
49. New York *Evening Post*, 25 Sept. 1845; MLP, Mackenzie to Duff Green, 5 June 1845 (marked "not sent").
50. MLP, O'Rielly to Mackenzie, 26 Sept. 1845.
51. O'Rielly Letter Books, O'Rielly to Mackenzie, 3 Oct. 1845.
52. MLP, copy, Mackenzie to Weed, 17 Oct. 1845.
53. MLP, Mackenzie to James, 2 Oct. 1845.
54. MLP, Duff Green to Mackenzie, 30 May 1845; draft of letter Mackenzie to Duff Green, 5 June 1845; MC, Mackenzie to James,7 June 1845; Duff Green Papers, Mackenzie to Duff Green, 7 June 1845.
55. Duff Green Papers, draft, Green to editor of Charleston Mercury, 1 Oct. 1845.
56. MLP, Mackenzie to James, 12 July 1845.
57. ORC, Mackenzie to O'Rielly, 13 Jan. 1846.
58. MC, Mackenzie to James, 2 Oct. 1845.
59. OCP, O'Rielly to O'Callaghan, 28 Sept. 1845, punctuation supplied.
60. MC, Mackenzie to James, 2 Oct. 1845; MC, Rev. David Strang to Mackenzie, 16 Oct. 1845.
61. Duff Green Papers, draft, Green to editor of Charleston Mercury, 1 Oct. 1845.
62. Frederick Hudson, *Journalism in the United States from 1690 to 1862* (New York, 1873), p. 576.
63. New York *Daily Globe*, 23 Sept. 1845.
64. Polk Papers, F. Byrdsall to Polk, 24 Sept., 2 Oct. 1845.
65. New York *Herald*, 22 Sept. 1845.
66. Samuel Owen, ed., *The New York Legal Observer*, 12 vols. (New York, 1843-54), 6:343.
67. New York *Tribune*, 15 Oct. 1845; New York *Herald*, 14 Oct. 1845; *Western Law Journal*, 10 vols. (Cincinnati, 1846-1853), 3:101-9.
68. Washington *Union*, 25 Sept. 1845.
69. New York *Tribune*, 29 Sept. 1845.
70. MLP, Duff Green to Mackenzie, 2 Oct. 1845.
71. Duff Green Papers, Duff Green to Benjamin Green, 22 Oct. 1845.
72. New York *Tribune*, 22 April 1846.
73. Ibid., 22 Oct. 1845; New York *Herald*, 2 Oct. 1845.
74. MLP, copy, Mackenzie to Thurlow Weed, 17 Oct. 1845; A.S. Doane to Mackenzie, 23 Oct. 1845; copy of Agreement with Taylor.
75. MLP, Mackenzie to A.S. Doane, 14 Nov. 1845.
76. Mackenzie, *Life of Van Buren*, p. 281; MLP, Mackenzie to James, 20 Aug. 1848.
77. Mackenzie, *Life of Van Buren*, pp. 84-5. The New York constitution required the assent of two-thirds of the elected members of both houses of the legislature to laws granting or renewing charters of corporations.

78.  Mackenzie, *Life of Van Buren*, pp. 88-93.
79.  MLP, Mackenzie to James, 9 Jan. 1846.
80.  Curtis, *Fox at Bay*, p. 148.
81.  MLP, Mackenzie to James, 13 May 1846.
82.  New York *Tribune*, 22, 24 April 1846.
83.  "Political Corruption," *The American Review* III (1846): 455-64.
84.  John C. FitzPatrick, ed., "The Autobiography of Martin Van Buren" in AHA, *Annual Report*, 1918, vol. 2, p. 536.
85.  Mackenzie, *Life of Van Buren*, p. 17.
86.  Dennis Tilden Lynch, *An Epoch and a Man. Martin Van Buren and His Times* (New York, 1929), pp. 501-2.
87.  See fn. 84.
88.  ORP, Mackenzie to O'Rielly, 19 April 1846.
89.  MLP, D.W.[ebster?] to Thurlow Weed, 3 May 1846.
90.  Oliver L. Barb, ed., *Report of Cases Argued and Determined in the Court of Chancery of the State of New York* (New York, 1859), 3:320-2.
91.  New York *Tribune*, 27 June 1848.

## Chapter IX Notes

1.  MLP, Dr. John Smyles to Mackenzie, 6 May 1846.
2.  MLP, Mackenzie to James, 13 May 1846; Mackenzie to James Lesslie, 15 May 1846.
3.  Herbert A. Donovan, *The Barnburners* (New York, 1925), Ch. 1.
4.  MC, Mackenzie to James, 7 June 1845.
5.  New York *Tribune*, 14 Sept. 1846.
6.  Williamsburg is now part of Brooklyn.
7.  *Tribune*, 22 June, 14, 22, 25, 30 July 1846.
8.  *Convention Debates, Atlas*, p. 1059; *Tribune*, 10 Oct. 1946.
9.  *Tribune*, 11 July 1846.
10. *Convention Debates, Atlas*, p. 489.
11. Ibid., pp. 603-7; *Tribune*, 6 Aug. 1846. Mackenzie made a slip here in attributing this plan to Bascom instead of to Strong but put the matter correctly in *Tribune*, 2 Sept. 1846.
12. *Convention Debates, Atlas*, pp. 627, 630.
13. J.H. Aitchison, "The Court of Requests," *OH* XLI (1949): 125-32; Lindsey, *Life* 2:338, 356.
14. *Convention Debates, Atlas*, p. 640.
15. T.J. Randolph, ed., *Memoir, Correspondence and Miscellanies from the Papers of Thomas Jefferson*, 4 vols. (2nd ed., Boston, 1830), 4:288; *Tribune*, 17 Aug., 8 Sept. 1846.
16. *Tribune*, 28, 31 Aug., 3 Sept. 1846. *Convention Debates, Atlas*, p. 793.
17. *Convention Debates, Argus*, p. 585; ibid., *Atlas*, p. 793.
18. *Tribune*, 15 Sept. 1846.
19. See infra, Ch. 17.
20. William Dennis Driscoll, "Benjamin Franklin Butler: Lawyer and Regency Politician" (Ph.D. diss., Fordham, 1965), pp. 165-70, 260.
21. William Allen Butler, *The Revision of the Statutes of the State of New York and the Revisers* (New York, 1889), p. 22.
22. *Convention Debates, Atlas*, p. 196; *Tribune*, 4, 6 July 1946.
23. *Tribune*, 4 July 1846.
24. Ibid., 6 July 1846.
25. *Convention Debates, Atlas*, pp. 109, 117, 839-40; *Tribune*, 14 Sept. 1946.
26. *Convention Debates, Atlas*, pp. 1063-64; *Tribune*, 8 Oct. 1846.
27. J. Hampden Dougherty, *A Constitutional History of the State of New York* (2nd ed., New York, 1915), p. 170.
28. *Tribune*, 14, 15 Aug. 1846.
29. Mackenzie, *Life of Van Buren*, p. 303; *JLAC*, 1846, p. 267.
30. *Tribune*, 9 July, 24, 25 Aug. 1946; Mackenzie, *Life of Van Buren*, p. 303.

31.   *Tribune*, 14 Aug. 1846; *Manual for the Use of the Conventions to Revise the Constitution of the State of New York* (New York, 1846) includes a summary of the constitutions of the various states.

32.   *Tribune*, 19 Aug. 1846; *Reports of the Proceedings and Debates of the Convention of 1821 Assembled for the Purpose of Amending the Constitution of the State of New York* (Albany, 1821), pp. 517-19.

33.   *Convention Debates, Atlas*, p. 772; *Report of the Convention of 1821*, pp. 502, 514-15, 523-24.

34.   *Tribune*, 29 Sept. 1846.

35.   F.H. Armstrong, "Reformer as Capitalist: William Lyon Mackenzie and the Printers' Strike of 1836," *OH* LIX (1967): 186-96.

36.   *Tribune*, 26 Aug. 1846.

37.   See *supra*, p. 123.

38.   *Revised Statutes of the State of New York* (3rd ed., Albany, 1846-8), Part 1, Ch. 5, Title 4, sec. 26, 27; Griswold, *Law and Lawyers*, pp. 16-17.

39.   Alexis de Tocqueville, *Democracy in America*, ed. Philipps Bradley, 2 vols. (New York, 1945), 1:282-90; *Convention Debates, Atlas*, p. 799.

40.   *Convention Debates, Atlas*, p. 603.

41.   Ibid., pp. 779-80.

42.   Jabez D. Hammond, *A Political History of the State of New York* (Syracuse, 1852), p. 640.

43.   *Tribune*, 7, 9 Sept., 10 Oct. 1846.

44.   Ibid., 10 Oct. 1846.

45.   Ibid., 7, 9 Sept. 1846.

46.   *Convention Debates, Atlas*, pp. 588-89, 798-99, 801, 803, 813, 836-37. A bill to establish courts of conciliation was to be introduced in 1847 but was killed in committee. (*Journal of the Assembly of the State of New York* (1847): 935, 1053). In 1862 an act was passed creating a tribunal of conciliation in one district for three years, after which time the act was repealed (Lincoln, *Constitutional History* 2:164).

47.   *Tribune*, 13 June, 1846.

48.   Ibid., 13 July, 1946.

49.   *Convention Debates, Atlas*, p. 1059; *Tribune*, 10 Oct. 1946.

50.   *Tribune*, 2 Oct. 1846.

51.   *Convention Debates, Atlas*, p. 1078; *Tribune*, 12 Oct. 1846.

52.   *Tribune*, 30 July 1846.

53.   Ibid., 29 July, 5 Sept. 1846.

54.   David Maldwyn Ellis, *Landlords and Farmers in the Hudson Mohawk Region, 1790-1850* (Ithaca, N.Y., 1946) Ch. 7 and 8; *N.Y. Sess. Laws*, 1846, Ch. 274, 327.

55.   *Convention Debates, Atlas*, pp. 185, 265; *Tribune*, 1 July 1846.

56.   Henry Christman, *Tin Horns and Calico* (New York, 1945), pp. 156-57, 273; *Convention Debates, Atlas*, pp. 1051-52, 1062-63.

57.   *Tribune*, 13 July 1846; *Convention Debates, Atlas*, p. 265.

58.   *Tribune*, 2 Sept. 1846.

59.   Ibid.; *Convention Debates, Atlas*, p. 985; *Convention Debates, Argus*, p. 143; *Tribune*, 1 Oct. 1846.

60.   MLP, John Windt to Mackenzie, New York, 27 Aug. 1846.

61.   Christman, *Tin Horns*, p. 81.

62.   Constitution of 1846, Article 1, sec. 12; *Tribune*, 7 Oct. 1846.

63.   *Tribune*, 7 Oct. 1846.

64.   David Maldwyn Ellis, *A History of New York State* (rev. ed., Ithaca, N.Y., 1967), pp. 317-18.

65.   *Convention Debates, Atlas*, pp. 1022, 1026, 1076; *Tribune*, 10 Oct. 1846.

66.   MLP, Mackenzie to James, 12 Oct. 1846.

67.   *Convention Debates, Atlas*, pp. 461-63, 950.

68.   Ibid., pp. 182, 385, 985, 995.

69.   Lindsey, *Life* 2:346, 347, 354.

70.   *Tribune*, 1 July 1846.

71.   Ibid., 1 July 1846.

72.   *Convention Debates, Atlas*, pp. 999, 1004-05.

73.   Ibid., p. 1010.

74.   Ibid., p. 221.

75.     Ibid., pp. 775, 978-79, 1006, 1021.
76.     *Tribune*, 9 July, 30 Sept. 1846.
77.     *JLAC*, 1844, p. 1039; idem, 1847, p. 1083; Prov. Can. Stat., 13 and 14 Vic., cap. 28.
78.     *Tribune*, 5 Sept. 1846.
79.     ORC, Mackenzie to O'Rielly, 20 Aug. 1848.
80.     Ibid., 15 Sept. 1846.
81.     MLP, Mackenzie to James, 12 Oct. 1846.
82.     *Tribune*, 3 July, 8, 28 Aug., 5, 8, 23 Sept. 1846.
83.     Ibid., 14 Oct. 1846.


## Chapter X Notes

1.      MLP, George Bruce to Mackenzie, 9 Nov. 1846.
2.      MLP, Mackenzie to James, 29 Nov. 1846.
3.      MLP, Thos. Ewbank to Mackenzie, 18 Nov. 1846.
4.      MLP, H. Greeley to Mackenzie, 6 Oct. 1846.
5.      MLP, D. Bruce to Mackenzie, 22 Dec. 1846, and n.d., 1847; NYHS, H. Greeley to Thurlow Weed, 8 Jan. 1847.
6.      *Albany Patriot*, 6 Jan. 1847.
7.      MLP, G. Bruce to Mackenzie, 8 Mar. 1847, Nelson Gorham to Mackenzie, 3 Dec. 1846; OCP, Mackenzie to O'Callaghan, 6 Mar. 1847.
8.      MLP, O'Callaghan to Mackenzie, 8 Mar 1847.
9.      MLP, Mackenzie to James, 16 July 1848.
10.     ORC, Mackenzie to O'Rielly, 20 Aug. 1848.
11.     MC, Mackenzie to W. Nelson, 15 Nov. 1848.
12.     *Tribune*, 29 Sept. 1848.
13.     Lindsey, *Life*, Introduction.
14.     MTL has this item.
15.     MLP, O'Rielly to Mackenzie, Albany, 25 Nov. 1846, Pittsburgh, 14 July 1847.
16.     MLP, G. Bruce to Mackenzie, New York, 4 April 1847, T. Ewbank to Mackenzie, New York, 12 April 1847.
17.     ORC, Mackenzie to O'Rielly, 12 May 1847.
18.     ORC, same to same, 10, 14 Aug. 1847.
19.     *Tribune*, 26 Sept. 1846.
20.     MLP, O'Rielly to Mackenzie, 13 June 1847.
21.     Perkins, "O'Reilly," pp. 1-24.
22.     Robert Lutton Thompson, *Wiring a Continent* (Princeton, 1947), pp. 50, 51, 75, 88, 100.
23.     MLP, O'Rielly to Mackenzie, 14 July, Cincinnati, 12, 29 Sept., 16 Oct. 1847; ORC, Mackenzie to O'Rielly, 4, 14 Aug. 1847.
24.     LC, Manuscript Div., *Index to the James Monroe Papers*, p. viii.
25.     MLP, O'Rielly to Mackenzie, Washington, 5 Jan. 1849.
26.     ORC, Bound volume of manuscript material entitled "Material relating to the papers of James Monroe."
27.     ORC, Mackenzie to O'Rielly, 14 Aug. 1847.
28.     MLP, O'Rielly to Mackenzie, 8 Aug. 1847; ORC, Box 2, Mackenzie to O'Rielly, 26 Aug. 1847.
29.     It has been published in Stuart Gerry Brown, *The Autobiography of James Monroe* (Syracuse, 1959).
30.     Some of the letters had been included in Randolph's *Life of Jefferson* and a brief statement by Monroe of his claim on the government with supporting documents had appeared in the *National Intelligencer*, 14, 18 Nov. 1826.
31.     ORC, Box 2, Mackenzie to O'Rielly, 26 Aug. 1847.
32.     ORC, Mackenzie to O'Rielly, 28 Sept. 1847; MLP, O'Rielly to Mackenzie, Cincinnati, 28 Sept. 1847.
33.     ORC, vol. 5, Mackenzie to O'Rielly, 30 Nov. 1847, Box 14, 19 Jan. 1848.
34.     ORC, Box 2, Mackenzie to O'Rielly, 25 Oct. 1847, vol. 48, 3 Nov. 1848.
35.     ORC, Box 14, Mackenzie to O'Rielly, 19 Jan., Box 3, 20 March 1848.

36.    MLP, Mackenzie to James, 23 April 1848.
37.    ORC, Box 4, Mackenzie to O'Rielly, 12 April 1848.
38.    ORC, Box 4, Mackenzie to O'Rielly, 11 Oct. 1847, Box 14, 19 Jan, Box 4, 23 June 1848.
39.    "The Life and Death of a Great Newspaper," *American Heritage* (Oct. 1967).
40.    At 200 3rd Ave. (MC, George Mackenzie to Janet Mackenzie, New York, 24 Sept. 1848).
41.    MLP, Mackenzie to James, 16 July, 13 Oct., 25 Dec. 1848; ORC, Mackenzie to O'Rielly, Box 4, 16 Aug. 1848.
42.    ORC, Box 14, Mackenzie to O'Rielly, 19 Jan., Box 3, 7, 10, 11 Feb., 8 July 1848.
43.    MLP, O'Rielly to Mackenzie, Albany, 12 June 1848; ORC, "Monroe material."
44.    MLP, O'Rielly to Mackenzie, Washington, 25 June, O'Rielly to Sen. Westcott, Albany, 6 July 1848 (copy).
45.    MLP, copy, O'Rielly to Westcott, 9 July 1848, Mackenzie to James, 25 Dec. 1848; *National Intelligencer*, 5, 7 Dec. 1848; *Congressional Globe*, 1 Sess., 30 Cong., XVIII, pp. 998-99, XIX, App., pp. 1175-79.
46.    MLP, O'Rielly to Mackenzie, Albany, 12 June, 20 Aug. 1848.
47.    ORC, "Monroe material," Westcott to O'Rielly, 5 July 1848.
48.    ORC, draft, O'Rielly to S.L. Gouverneur, 8 Oct. 1848.
49.    ORC, S.L. Gouverneur to O'Rielly, Nov. 1848.
50.    ORC, Contract of 28 Dec. 1848 signed by Gouverneur and O'Rielly, copy of release signed by O'Rielly by his attorney, R.H. Gillet, 31st day of ___, 1849.
51.    MLP, O'Rielly to Mackenzie, Washington, 5, 12, 25 Jan. 1849; ORC, vol. 28, Mackenzie to O'Rielly, 17, 22 Jan. 1849, Box 14, 26 Jan. 1849.
52.    *Congressional Globe*, 30 Cong., 2nd Sess., XVIII, 163, 662, 638.
53.    ORC, "Monroe material," copy of release, 31 ___, 1849.
54.    ORC, Box 14, Mackenzie to O'Rielly, 26 Jan. 1849.
55.    Thompson, *Wiring*, pp. 152-54, 194, Chs. 5 and 6, App. 3, pp. 452-54; *Tribune*, 6 June 184
56.    Thompson, *Wiring*, Chs. 7 to 10, pp. 192, 343-44.
57.    ORC, Box 2, Mackenzie to O'Rielly, 4 Nov. 1847.
58.    *Tribune*, 13 Sept. 1847.
59.    Ibid., 12 Oct. 1847; ORC, Box 2, Mackenzie to O'Rielly, 11 Oct. 1847; MLP, O'Rielly to Mackenzie, Cincinnati, 16 Oct. 1847.
60.    *Tribune*, 29 Oct. 1847.
61.    Ibid.
62.    Ibid., 13 Nov. 1847; Weed Papers, Mackenzie to Thurlow Weed, 13 Nov. 1847; ORC, Mackenzie to O'Rielly, 15 Nov. 1847; MLP, William C. Hasbrouck to Mackenzie, Albany, 17 Nov. 1847.
63.    ORC, Mackenzie to O'Rielly, 18, 20, 23 Nov. 1847.
64.    *New York Commercial*, 26 Nov. 1847.
65.    *Journal of the Assembly of the State of New York*, 18 Jan. 1848; *Laws of the State of New York*, 71st Sess., Ch. 265; *New York Express*, 19 June 1848.
66.    ORC, Mackenzie to O'Rielly, 20 Aug. 1848.
67.    MLP, Mackenzie to James, 15 Nov. 1848.
68.    ORC, vol. 28, Mackenzie to O'Rielly, 7 Jan. 1849.
69.    There were several members of the *Tribune's* staff named Robinson. Possibly Mackenzie is referring not to the head proofreader, C.R. Robinson, but to W.E. Robinson, the writer of the articles signed "Richelieu." Don C. Seitz, *Horace Greeley* (Indianapolis, 1926), p.100.
70.    ORC, vol. 28, Mackenzie to O'Rielly, 22 Jan. 1849.
71.    ORC, Box 5, Mackenzie to O'Rielly, 25 Dec. 1848.
72.    MLP, O'Rielly to Mackenzie, Washington, 22 Jan. 1849.
73.    ORC, vol. 28, Mackenzie to O'Rielly, 22 Jan. 1849.

## Chapter XI Notes

1.    OCP, Mackenzie to O'Callaghan, 3 April 1846.
2.    *Western Herald*, 23 July 1841; *Debates*, vol. 1, pp. 240-1, 287.
3.    *Western Herald*, 18 Sept. 1841; New York *Weekly Herald*, 11 Sept. 1841; *Debates*, vol. 1, pp. 386-7, 729-34.

4.     *JLAC*, 1841, p. 488.
5.     PAC, C.O. 42, vol. 495, p. 345, Bagot to Stanley, 26 Sept. 1842.
6.     Guillet, *Patriots*, p. 131.
7.     MLP, J. Mackintosh to Mackenzie, Toronto, 29 Sept. 1843; Secretary Higginson to Mrs. Helen Mackintosh, 29 Sept. 1843.
8.     *The Statesman* (Kingston), 11 Oct. 1843; *Debates*, vol. 3, pp. 128-30; Jacques Monet, *The Last Cannon Shot*, p. 158.
9.     Rolph Papers, Hincks to Rolph, Kingston, 5 Nov. 1843. J.H. Dunn was Receiver-General in the Baldwin-Lafontaine administration. The *Welland Canal* was a newssheet published by Mackenzie in 1835. Its three issues criticized the management of the Canal's directors.
10.    ORP, Mackenzie to O'Rielly, 28 March 1843.
11.    *Debates*, 1844-5, vol. 1, pp. 395, 530; vol. 2, 1797.
12.    ORP, Mackenzie to O'Rielly, 21 Jan. 1845.
13.    Sir Charles Willis Kaye, *The Life and Correspondence of Charles, Lord Metcalfe*, 2 vols. (London, 1858), 2:345-6; Ormsby, *Emergence*, pp. 113-15.
14.    Quebec *Mercury*, 2 Oct. 1845; Thomas Storrow Brown, *1837, My Connection With It* (Quebec, 1898), pp. 37-8.
15.    MLP, Wolfred Nelson to Mackenzie, 6 March 1845.
16.    MC, Mackenzie to James, 7 June, 12 July 1845.
17.    MLP, I. Buchanan to Mackenzie, 13, 26 Nov. 1845.
18.    MLP, copies, Mackenzie to I. Buchanan, 18, 21 Dec. 1845.
19.    MLP, Mackenzie to James Lesslie, 15 May 1846; photostat, Mackenzie to John Neilson, 26 May 1846; Mackenzie to James, 6 July 1848.
20.    Duane's letter does not seem to have survived in the Papineau letters.
21.    MLP, John Ryan to Mackenzie, 13 March 1846.
22.    MLP, Mackenzie to James Lesslie, 15 May 1846.
23.    MLP, Mackenzie to James, 5 March 1847.
24.    PAC, Neilson Papers, Mackenzie to J. Neilson, 24 May 1847.
25.    Mackenzie's letters to Earl Grey, 23 Nov. 1845, in *Tribune*, 27 Nov. 1846 and 28 Nov. 1846, in *Elgin-Grey Papers* 3:1053-9.
26.    MLP, George Bruce to Mackenzie, New York, 4 April 1847.
27.    ORC, Mackenzie to O'Rielly, 28 Sept. 1847.
28.    Neilson Papers, Mackenzie to J. Neilson, 24 May 1847.
29.    MLP, copy of the petition, dated 6 Oct. 1847; James Lesslie to Mackenzie, 21 Jan. 1848; Mackenzie to James, 15 Jan. 1848.
30.    OCP, Mackenzie to O'Callaghan, 22 Dec. 1847.
31.    MLP, James Mackintosh to Mackenzie, Toronto, 22 Jan. 1848; James Lesslie to Mackenzie, Toronto, 21 Jan. 1848.
32.    MLP, copies, Mackenzie to I. Buchanan, 18, 21 Dec. 1845.
33.    MLP, Joseph Hume to Mackenzie, London, 20 Jan. 1848.
34.    Mackenzie to T.E. Campbell, 14 Feb. 1848, printed in *Elgin-Grey Papers* 1:228-34. Moodie had been shot by the rebels assembled at Montgomery's.
35.    MLP, Memo of Mackenzie to Robert Baldwin, 14 Feb. 1848.
36.    ORC, Box 14, Mackenzie to O'Rielly, 19 Jan. 1848.
37.    PAC, C.O. 42, vol. 495, No. 195, Bagot to Stanley, 26 Sept. 1842; No. 266, Stanley to Metcalfe, 3 Nov. 1843. Wilbur Devereaux Jones, *Lord Derby and Victorian Conservatism* (Oxford, 1956), p. 90.
38.    MLP, Hincks to Mackenzie, Montreal, 11 Feb. 1849; AO, Price Letter Book, H.H. Price to R. Baldwin, 6 Feb. 1843, gives some support to Hume's statement.
39.    MLP, Mackenzie to Wolfred Nelson, 2 April 1848, not sent. There is no record of the passage of an address asking for a general amnesty in the Assembly's *Journals* for 1848. Cf. John Charles Dent, *The Last Forty Years*, 2 vols. (Toronto, 1881), vol. 2, 135n.
40.    MLP, Dr. J.E. Barker to Mackenzie, Kingston, 26 Nov. 1848, 12 Jan. 1849.
41.    MLP, James Lesslie to Mackenzie, 8 Aug. 1848; Wolfred Nelson to Mackenzie, Montreal, 1 Sept. 1848.
42.    PAC, R.G. 7, Private Official Correspondence Miscellaneous, Mackenzie to Lord Elgin, 10 Sept. 1848.
43.    MLP, Mackenzie to James, 13 Oct. 1848; MC, Mackenzie to Wolfred Nelson, 15 Nov. 1848.
44.    MC, Wolfred Nelson to Mackenzie, 23 April 1848.

45.     Baldwin Papers, Opinions of the Attorney-General, 8 Aug. 1848, pp.218-30.
46.     *Elgin-Grey Papers* 1:226-7.
47.     Toronto *Examiner*, 24 Jan. 1849.
48.     Prov. Can. Stat., 9 Vic., cap. 107; 2 Vic., cap. 197.
49.     *JLAC*, 1849, pp. 37, 49, 60.
50.     *Elgin-Grey Papers* 1:227-8, 287-9. In a letter of 24 Aug. 1848, Elgin stated that Robert Nelson and Mackenzie were the principal rebels "now precluded" from returning. Yet in the *Tribune* of 15 July 1847 Mackenzie had announced that "within the last few weeks" Robert Nelson's disabilities had been removed, the Attorney-General for Lower Canada having entered a *nolle prosequi* for him. Nelson was displeased with Mackenzie for making public the fact that he was no longer an exile. He was so angered by the news, which came as a complete surprise to him, that he wrote Lord Elgin a brusque letter stating that he sought no pardon, had none to receive or to *give* (ORC, Mackenzie to O'Rielly, 4 Aug. 1847; OCP, Mackenzie to O'Callaghan, 23 July 1847; PAC, R.G. 7, A399, Nelson to Elgin, 7 July 1847.) In PAC there is no record of a pardon for Nelson being applied for or granted.
51.     *Tribune*, 30 Oct. 1849, 23 Oct. 1850, 17 Dec. 1851.
52.     PAC, R.G. 7, A399, Private Official Correspondence,Miscellaneous, Mackenzie to Hincks, 13 Feb. 1849. This letter, which was intended to be private, found its way into Elgin's files.
53.     MLP, Mackenzie to James, 7 Feb. 1849; ORC, vol. 26, Mackenzie to O'Rielly, 8, 19 Feb. 1849.
54.     MLP, Mackenzie to A.N. Morin, 1 March 1849, not sent. The reference is to the shooting of Col. Moodie and to the collapse of the spectators' gallery in the market hall at Toronto during a public meeting called to discuss taxes when Mackenzie was mayor. The boys were killed on this occasion. (Lindsey, *Life* 1: 315-6; *Tribune*, 20 April 1849.)
55.     MLP, A.N. Morin to F. Hincks, 2 March 1849; J. Prince to Dr. Barker, 7 March 1849.
56.     Toronto *Examiner*, 14, 21 March 1849, quoting Montreal *Herald* of 6 March 1849; Toronto *Examiner*, 27 March, 4 Sept. 1850; MLP, William Nelson to Mackenzie, E. Gwillimbury, 15 Dec.1849; A. to Mackenzie, 1 April 1849.
57.     Bonnycastle, *The Canadas* 2:45; *Canada* 1:191; *Canada As It Was*.
58.     Mackenzie to Grey, 14 Feb. 1848, in *Elgin Grey Paper*s 1:230.
59.     MLP, Mackenzie to James, 2 April 1849; J.M.S. Careless, *Brown of the Globe* , 2 vols. (Toronto, 1959), 1:89.
60.     Toronto *Examiner*, 28 March, 4 April 1849.
61.     MLP, Mackenzie to James, 2 April 1849.
62.     MLP, same to same, 2 April 1849.
63.     MLP, Anon to Mackenzie, 24 March 1849.
64.     Dent, *Last Forty Years* 2:144.
65.     MC, G. Baxter to Mackenzie, Kingston, 29 March 1849; MLP, James Lesslie to Mackenzie, 3 April 1849.
66.     MLP, Mackenzie to James, 2 April 1849.
67.     *Tribune*, 14, 17, 20, 24, 28 April, 19, 23 May, 4, 27 June 1849; Toronto *Examiner*, 25 April, 1, 9, 16, 23, 30 May, 6, 20, 27 June, 4, 11, 18, 23 July 1849.
68.     George Julian Duncombe Poulett Scrope, *Memoir of the Life of the Right Honourable Charles, Lord Sydenham* (London, 1844), pp. 149-5.
69.     PAC, R.G. 7, C, Private-Official Letters, Miscellaneous, Mackenzie to Lord Elgin, New York, 11 April, 16 Oct. 1849; Mackenzie to T.E. Campbell, New York, 28 May, 9 June 1849.
70.     *Elgin-Grey Papers* 1:103-115; Jean Paul Bernard, *Les Rouges* (Montreal, 1971), p. 51; Fernand Ouellet, *Papineau, Textes Choisis* (Quebec, 1958), p. 181; Monet, *The Last Cannon Shot*, pp. 328-30.
71.     Corning Papers, H. Dessaulles to Papineau, St. Hyacinthe, 26 Dec. 1839; L.J. Papineau to E. Corning, 13 July 1857.
72.     NYHS, H. Greeley to Thurlow Weed, 7 April 1849.
73.     MLP, H. Greeley to Mackenzie, New York, 11 May 1849.
74.     MLP, copy, Mackenzie to Hugh Maxwell, 30 June 1849.
75.     MLP, copy, Mackenzie to W.E. Benedict, 27 May 1849.
76.     Willard Grosvenor Bleyer, *Main Currents in American Journalism* (Cambridge, Mass., 1927), p. 164.
77.     MLP, Thos. Ewbank to Mackenzie, 30 May 1849.

78. MLP, Mackenzie to James, 14 Aug. 1849; ORC, vol. 30, Mackenzie to O'Rielly, 29 Oct. 1849.
79. *Tribune*, 14 Aug. 1849.
80. Careless, *Brown* 1:40.
81. MC, James Lesslie to Mackenzie, Toronto, 15 Nov. 1849.
82. Ernest Cockburn Kyte, ed., *Old Toronto* (Toronto, 1954), p. 136.
83. Toronto *Examiner*, 8, 22 Aug. 1849; *Colonial Advocate*, 2 Oct. 1834.
84. Toronto *Examiner*, 7 June, 8 Aug., 26 Sept., 17 Oct., 9, 21, 28 Nov. 1849.
85. Ibid., 22 Aug., 5, 13, 20, 26 Sept. 1849.
86. Ibid., 7 Nov. 1849.
87. Ibid., 13 Sept. 1849.
88. *Tribune*, 21 Jan. 1850.
89. Toronto *Globe*, 1 Jan. 1850.
90. Sandom Collection, Mackenzie to James Lesslie, 15 Feb. 1850.
91. Toronto *Examiner*, 10 Oct. 1849.
92. Cephas D. Allin and George M. Jones, *Annexation, Preferential Trade and Reciprocity* (Toronto, 1912), Ch. 1.
93. Ibid., pp. 106-14, 134, 141.
94. Ibid., pp. 154, 268, 325-7.
95. Toronto *Examiner*, 24 Oct., 26 Dec. 1849.
96. Ibid., 14 Nov. 1849.
97. Ibid., 15 Dec. 1849.
98. She would not necessarily have lost control of her lands. Texas did not.
99. Toronto *Examiner*, 27 June, 23 July 1849.
100. Ibid., 27 July 1849; Niagara *Mail*, 6 March 1850; *British Whig*, 17 April 1850.
101. Toronto *Examiner*, 27 June, 24 Oct., 7 Nov. 1849.
102. Patrick Shirreff, *A Tour Through North America* (Edinburgh, 1835), p.367.
103. MLP, P. Baxter to Mackenzie, Kingston, 5 Nov. 1849; Toronto *Examiner*, 14 Nov. 1849.
104. George M. Jones, "The Peter Perry Election and the Rise of the Clear Grit Party," *OHSPR* XII (1914): 164-75.
105. MC, J.E. Barker to Mackenzie, Kingston, Oct. 28 1849. Notation of refusal, 1 Nov. 1849, added in Mackenzie's hand.
106. MLP, Mackenzie to James Lesslie, New York, 23 Nov. 1849.
107. Allin and Jones, *Annexation*, p. 264, quoting the Toronto *Examiner* of 31 Jan. 1850. I have been unable to find this reference in the *Examiner*.
108. Toronto *Examiner*, 22 Oct. 1849.
109. MLP, Mackenzie to Lesslie, 23 Nov. 1849; Mackenzie to James, 9 Jan. 1850.
110. MLP, George Lount to Mackenzie, Barrie, 8 April 1850; Toronto *Examiner*, 19 Dec. 1849.
111. *JLAUC*, 1835, p. 396.
112. Toronto *Examiner*, 20 July 1849.
113. MLP, Mackenzie to James, 9 Jan. 1850.
114. MLP, James Lesslie to Mackenzie, Toronto, 23 Jan. 1850.
115. MLP, W.A. Stephens to Mackenzie, Erin, 12 Feb. 1850; Alex Davidson to Mackenzie, Niagara, 7 Feb. 1850; James Davidson to Mackenzie, Niagara, 24 Feb. 1850.
116. MLP, Mackenzie to James, 8 April 1850; Seward Papers, Mackenzie to Seward, 17 Jan., 5, 18 March 1850.
117. MLP, J. Lesslie to Mackenzie, Toronto, 30 Jan. 1850.
118. Sandom Collection, Mackenzie to J. Lesslie, 25 Feb. 1850.
119. Shenston Papers, Mackenzie to T.S Shenston, 26 June 1849.
120. MLP, J. Lesslie to Mackenzie, March 1850; Joseph Lesslie to Mackenzie, 19 March 1850.
121. MLP, J. Mackintosh to Mackenzie, Toronto, 25 March 1850.
122. MLP, Mackenzie to James, 8 April 1850.
123. Seward Papers, Mackenzie to W.H. Seward, 11 Sept. 1850.

## Chapter XII Notes

1. MLP, Mackenzie to his daughter Barbara, 9 June 1850.

2. Bonnycastle, *Canada* 2:108; Henry Scadding, *Toronto, Past and Present* (1884), p. 194; D.C. Masters, *The Rise of Toronto* (1947), p. 13; Elwood Jones and Douglas McCalla, "Toronto Waterworks, 1840-1877," *CHR* LX (1979): 300-323.

3. PAC, R.G. 7, A399, Private Official Correspondence, Miscellaneous, Mackenzie to Lord Elgin, New York, 11 April 1849; Mackenzie to T.E. Campbell, New York, 29 June 1849.

4. Charles Durand claimed that Baldwin authorized Stephen Richards to offer Mackenzie the postmastership of Toronto; Charles Durand, *Reminiscences of the Rebellion of 1837* (1898), p. 268.

5. MLP, Mackenzie to James Lesslie, 4 June 1850; J.S. MacDonald to Mackenzie, Toronto, 6 April 1850.

6. Toronto *Examiner*, 21 Aug., 30 Oct. 1850.

7. Toronto *Examiner*, 5 Dec. 1850; Robert Rumilly, *Papineau* (Montreal, 1977), I, p. 369.

8. Toronto *Examiner*, 28 Aug. 1850.

9. *JLAUC*, 1831-2, p. 12.

10. Toronto *Examiner*, 4 Sept. 1850.

11. Toronto *Examiner*, 25 Dec. 1850.

12. Toronto *Examiner*, 27 June 1850; MLP, Hincks to Mackenzie, 2 July 1850.

13. Toronto *Examiner*, 24 July 1850.

14. *JLAC*, 1851, p. 42.

15. MLP, Hincks to Mackenzie, 2 July 1850; *JLAC*, 1850, pp. 120, 127; MLP, copy, Mackenzie to Col. R. Bruce, 13 Aug. 1850.

16. Toronto *Examiner*, 31 July, 25 Dec. 1850; MLP, Merritt to Mackenzie, 11 July 1850.

17. MLP, Taché to Mackenzie, 20 Jan. 1851.

18. Lafontaine Papers, pp. 2163-6, Mackenzie to Lafontaine, 2 Aug. 1850; pp. 2355-2365, Mackenzie to Lafontaine, 17 Jan. 1851.

19. MLP, Lafontaine to Mackenzie, 20 Jan. 1851.

20. MLP, Baldwin to Mackenzie, 23 Aug. 1850.

21. MLP, Hincks to Mackenzie, 13 Feb. 1851; James Leslie, Prov. Sec., to Mackenzie, 6 March 1851.

22. MLP, Eastwood and Skinner to Mackenzie, Toronto, 24 March 1838.

23. Baldwin Papers, Mackenzie to Baldwin, 21 Sept. 1850. Draft of Baldwin's reply on verso.

24. MLP, Sheriff's account of 19 June 1852. Slightly different figures were given in A.N. Morin to Mackenzie, 3 July 1852.

25. MLP, W. Jarvis to J.H. Price, 27 Sept. 1853; W. Jarvis to Mackenzie, 27 Sept., 17 Oct. 1853; Mackenzie to W. Jarvis, copy, 5 Oct. 1853; notation on verso of copy of petition to obtain payment, 25 Oct. 1853; Secretary Chauveau to Mackenzie, 2 Dec. 1853.

26. *Globe*, 23 April 1851, quoting *Guelph Advertiser*.

27. Mackenzie Clippings, No. 2540; Sandom Collection, Mackenzie to James Lesslie, 25 Feb. 1850; MLP, Mackenzie to Lesslie, 15 May 1846; Hincks to Mackenzie, Toronto, 21 April 1850.

28. Sandom Collection, Mackenzie to Lesslie, 25 Feb. 1850; MLP, Memo by Mackenzie of settlement with Doel, 17 Sept. 1850. The qualification required was £500 in real property. Doel's daughter stated that her father had helped Mackenzie to qualify by making over to him a farm in Enniskillen township (OHS Scrapbook, 1924). At the general election of 1858 Mackenzie reported his qualifications to be the Garrafraxa and Dundasproperty, a lot in Bristol Village, township of Vespra (the gift of a friend), and one-tenth acre lot on Church Street, Toronto(PAC, R.G. 5, Election Records). How the last piece of property was acquired is not known at this writing.

29. MLP, W.H. Doel to Mackenzie, 25 May 1855.

30. Toronto *Examiner*, 30 Oct. 1850.

31. J.H. Price, who represented York South, had announced his intention of resigning. Later he changed his mind.

32. Toronto *Examiner*, 30 Oct, 12 Dec. 1850.

33. Toronto *Examiner*, 30 Oct., 13, 27 Nov. 1850, 2 April 1851.

34. Bernard, *Les Rouges*, p. 93; Careless, *Union*, p. 168; *Globe*, 21,23 March 1850; *North American*, 22 Nov. 1850; *Elgin-Grey Papers* 2:619-21.

35. *North American*, 14 Feb. 1851, quoted in Charles Clarke, *Sixty Years in Upper Canada* (Toronto, 1908), p. 65.

36. Toronto *Examiner*, 13, 15 Nov. 1850.

37. Toronto *Examiner*, 12 March 1851.
38. Hamilton *Spectator*, 13 Nov. 1850.
39. *North American*, 8 Nov., 6 Dec. 1850.
40. Toronto *Examiner*, 6 Aug. 1851. The letter is also printed in *Elgin-Grey Papers* 2:887-88.
41. MLP, Hume to Mackenzie, 21 April 1851.
42. Mabel Dunham, *The Grand River* (Toronto, 1945).
43. The figure 4,848, calculated from the Census of 1851, includes a small number of Indians of voting age. They were not distinguished from whites in the tables showing the voting age of the population.
44. William H. Smith, *Canada: Past, Present, and Future* (Toronto, 1851), 1:163-82; *Census of the Province of Canada*, 1851.
45. Rev Robert Bertram Nelles, *The County of Haldimand in the Days of Auld Lang Syne* (Port Hope, 1905), pp. 99-100.
46. Careless, *Brown* 1:123-9.
47. George Brown Papers, Hincks to Brown, 3 March 1851.
48. MLP, Hincks to Mackenzie, 29 March 1851 (incomplete).
49. Brown Papers, George Brown to Peter Brown, [13 April 1851].
50. Careless, *Brown* 1:130.
51. MLP, T.J. Wiggins to C. Lindsey, 16 Nov. 1862.
52. Brown Papers, G. Brown to P. Brown, [13 April 1851].
53. Toronto *Examiner*, 16 April 1851.
54. MLP, D. Ferguson to Mackenzie, 8 May 1851; a "Roger Sherman" letter by Mackenzie in *Tribune*, 8 March 1851.
55. *Census of the Province of Canada*, 1851.
56. Careless, *Brown* 1:131.
57. Toronto *Examiner*, 16 April 1851.
58. These journals were quoted in the Toronto *Examiner*, 30 April 1851.
59. MLP, Dr. James Grant to Mackenzie, Glengarry, 10 May 1851.
60. MLP, Charles Waters to Mackenzie, Van Kleek Hill, 5 May 1851.
61. MLP, H. Troy to Mackenzie, Newcastle, 17 May 1851.
62. MLP, John Bailey to Mackenzie, Missouri, 21 May 1851.
63. MLP, Duncan Ferguson to Mackenzie, 8 May 1851.

## Chapter XIII Notes

1. MLP, W. Nelson to Mackenzie, Montreal, 4 May 1851; MC, W. Nelson to Mackenzie, n.d.
2. MLP, D. Ferguson to Mackenzie, Caledonia, 29 May 1851.
3. Prov. Can. Stat., 13 and14 Vic., cap. 128.
4. Toronto *Examiner*, 23, 28 May 1851; *Debates*, 1851, pp. 81-83.
5. *Debates*, 1851, p. 83.
6. *Debates*, 1852-3, p. 243; *Debates*, 1850, p. 1511.
7. *Debates*, 1850, pp. 1492-3.
8. *JLAC*, 1851, pp. 13, 150, 169, 226.
9. *Debates*, 1852-3, pp. 1241, 1791-2.
10. MLP, Archibald Clark to Mackenzie, Chinguacousy, __ Nov. 1851.
11. MLP, James Reid to Mackenzie, Sharon, 30 May 1851.
12. MLP, Dr. James Grant to Mackenzie, Glengarry, 10 May 1851.
13. MC, Mackenzie to James, 4 May 1851.
14. *JLCUC*, 1830, p. 110.
15. Toronto *Globe*, 13 June 1851; *Niagara Chronicle*, 19 June 1851.
16. Toronto *Examiner*, 18 June 1851; *Debates*, 1851, pp. 363-73.
17. *JLAC*, 1851, pp. 20, 78.
18. *Message*, 16 June 1853. For Mackenzie's misstatement respecting New York, see Ch. 9, p. 217 and n. 46; *Debates*, 1852-3, pp. 339-43, 988-90.
19. U.C. Stat., 37 Geo. 3, cap. 13; U.C. Stat., 7 Will. 4, cap. 15.
20. *Debates*, 1851, pp. 1203-7; Toronto *Examiner*, 5 Aug. 1851.

21.  *JLAC*, 1852-3, p. 66, 1856, p. 666 and 1857, pp. 144-5; Prov. Can. Stat., 20 Vic., cap. 63.
22.  William Renwick Riddell. *Upper Canada Statutes* (Toronto, 1922), p. 147; *JLAUC*, App., pp. 57-61.
23.  Mackenzie, *Life of Van Buren*, p. 303.
24.  *JLAUC*,1836-7, pp. 77, 108, 380-389; U.C. Stat. 1 Vic., cap. 2.
25.  *JLAC*, 1845, p. 279.
26.  Prov. Can. Stat., 12 Vic., cap. 64; Toronto *Examiner*, 4 June 1851.
27.  The Act of 1837 required evidence to be taken in this way unless the court permitted an exception.
28.  Toronto *Examiner*, 2 July 1851; *Debates*, 1851, pp. 562-68.
29.  *JLAC*, 1851, p. 117.
30.  Baldwin Papers, Baldwin to John Ross, Toronto, 28 June 1851.
31.  Baldwin Papers, George Ridout to R. Baldwin, 28 March 1849; PAC, M.G. 24, B.30, Macdonald-Langlois Papers, vol. 1, W.H. Draper to J.S. Macdonald, 7 June 1849.
32.  Toronto *Examiner*, 2 July 1851; *Debates*, 1851, p. 570.
33.  *JLAC*, 1851, pp. 153-4; *Elgin Grey Papers* 2:891.
34.  PAC, M.G. 24, A16, Private letters from the Colonial Secretary, Earl Grey, to Elgin, 1 Aug., 15 Sept. 1851.
35.  Toronto *Examiner*, 2 July 1851; *Debates*, 1851, p. 570.
36.  MLP, James Kinnear to Mackenzie, Walpole, 21 July 1851.
37.  MLP, D. Ferguson to Mackenzie, Caledonia, 9 July 1851.
38.  Alan Wilson, *The Clergy Reserves of Upper Canada* (Toronto, 1968), p. 206.
39.  Francis Hincks, *Reminiscences* (Quebec, n.d.), p. 251.
40.  *JLAC*, 1849, p. 326.
41.  *JLAC*, 1850, pp. 5, 14, 46, 54, 70, 117.
42.  Prov. Can. Stat., 16 Vic., cap. 119; *Debates*, 1852-3, p. 919.
43.  J.K. Johnson, ed., *The Papers of the Prime Ministers*, vol. 1, 1836-1857, *The Letters of Sir John A. Macdonald* (Ottawa, 1968), Macdonald to Henry Smith, 20 Jan. 1856.
44.  Adam Shortt and Arthur G. Doughty, eds., *Canada and Its Provinces*, 23 vols. (Toronto, 1914), 18:532; Statutes of Ontario, 1881, cap. 5.
45.  Donald Swainson, ed., *Oliver Mowat's Ontario* (Toronto, 1972), p. 48.
46.  Toronto *Examiner*, 30 July 1851.
47.  MLP, M. O'Hare to Mackenzie, Belleville, 6 June 1851.
48.  *JLAC*, 1851, pp. 53, 95, 197.
49.  *JLAC*, 1851, pp. 108, 238; 1852-3, pp. 78-9, 212; 1857, p. 177.
50.  *JLAC*, 1851, pp. 117, 247; *Debates*, 1852-3, pp. 15, 114; Canada, *Bills*, 1852, No. 5; Toronto *Examiner*, 13 Aug. 1851.
51.  MLP, D. Ferguson to Mackenzie, 29 May, 2 June 1851; Prov. Can. Stat., 13 and14 Vic., cap. 74, sec. 3; *Debates*, 1851, p. 1643.
52.  *Debates*, 1851, p. 1133.
53.  Prov. Can. Stat., 14 and15 Vic., cap. 30; *JLAC*, 1851, pp. 92, 183.
54.  Toronto *Globe*, 16 June 1851; *Debates*, 1851, pp. 593-8.
55.  *JLAC*, 1851, p. 1870.
56.  *Niagara Chronicle*, 12 June 1851; Toronto *Examiner*, 18 June 1851; MLP, D. Ferguson to Mackenzie, Caledonia, 17 June 1851; A. Brownson to Mackenzie, Dunnville, 20 June 1851.
57.  Prov. Can. Stat., 8 Vic., cap. 48.
58.  *JLAC*, 1851, pp. 38, 47, App. LL.
59.  Hamnett P. Hill, *Robert Randall and the Le Breton Flats* (Ottawa, 1919), p. 61.
60.  *Macdonald Letters*, vol. 2, 3 Feb. 1858.
61.  Prov. Can. Stat., 22 Vic., cap. 96 (1858); *JLAC*, 1858, p. 923; Prov. Can. Stat., 22 Vic., cap. 33 (1859).
62.  MLP, William Howe to Mackenzie, Erin, 3 Feb. 1851; Gates, *Land Policy*, pp. 240-3; Alan Wilson, *The Clergy Reserves of Upper Canada*.
63.  Gates, *Land Policy*, pp. 244-250; *JLAC*, 1850, p. 74; Toronto *Examiner*, 2 July 1851.
64.  *Elgin-Grey Papers* 2:827; PAC, RG 7, vol. 131, Anon to Elgin, 15 Jan. 1853, no. 2.
65.  Careless, *Brown* 1:135.
66.  *JLAC*, 1850, pp. 73-88, 103-5; Careless, *Brown* 1:118; Longley, *Hincks*, p. 283.
67.  *JLAC*, 1851, pp. 6, 83; *Niagara Chronicle*, 19 June 1851; *Debates*, 1851, 406-10.
68.  *Globe*, 8 March 1851; Toronto *Examiner*, 12, 18 March 1851; *Elgin-Grey Papers*, 2:796, n. 2, 829, 832; Careless, *Brown* 1:133; Grey to Elgin, 11 July 1851, printed in *JLAC*, 1851, p. 231.

69.     MLP, John Reid to Mackenzie, 20 May 1851.
70.     MLP, Benjamin Davies to Mackenzie, 1 July 1851.
71.     Toronto *Examiner*, 12 March, 21 July 1851.
72.     *JLAC*, 1851, p. 38. A return asked for by Mackenzie showed that since 1835 25 appointments to existing rectories had been made, 10 of them by Lord Elgin, 5 of these in 1851 alone, but no new rectories had been created (App. O, App. M.M.).
73.     *JLAC*, 1851, pp. 56, 191, 204.
74.     *JLAC*, 1851, p. 199; *Debates*, 1851, p. 1049.
75.     *JLAC*, 1851, p. 355; Toronto *Examiner*, 19 Nov. 1851; Prov. Can. Stat., 14 and 15 Vic., cap. 175; *Debates*, 1851, pp. 1656-57.
76.     John S. Moir, *Church and State in Canada West* (Toronto, 1959), pp. 251-2.
77.     John George Hodgins, *Documentary History of Education in Upper Canada*, 28 vols. (Toronto, 1894-1910), 9:100, 226-7, 260, and 11:8-9.
78.     *JLAC*, 1851, pp. 157-8.
79.     Toronto *Examiner*, 16 July 1851; *Debates*, 1851, p. 785.
80.     Prov. Can. Stat., 14 and 15 Vic., cap. 32; *JLAC*, 1851, p. 32; Toronto, *British Colonist*, 4 July 1851.
81.     Sissons, *Ryerson* 2:245.
82.     MLP, S.T. Jones to Mackenzie, Hamilton, 23 June 1851; D. McCollum to Mackenzie, Montreal, 29 July 1851.
83.     *Debates*, 1851, pp. 1309.
84.     Toronto *Examiner*, 6 Aug. 1861.
85.     *JLAC*, 1851, p. 281; Prov. Can. Stat., 14 and 15 Vic., cap. 142.
86.     Toronto *Examiner*, 27 Nov. 1850; Careless, *Brown of the Globe* 1:165.
87.     Canada, *Bills*, 1851, No. 231.
88.     *Debates*, 1851, p. 1083.
89.     MLP, Dexter D. Everardo to Mackenzie, Font Hill, 5 Aug. 1851; *JLAC*, 1851, p. 205.
90.     Prov. Can. Stat. 14 and 15 Vic., cap. 5.
91.     Toronto *Examiner*, 25 June 1851; *Lord Durham's Report*, p. 107.
92.     *Debates*, 1851, p. 585; R. Alan Douglas, *John Prince* (The Champlain Society, 1980), p. 113.
93.     *Debates*, 1851, pp. 1510-11.
94.     *JLAC*, 1852-3; Toronto *Examiner*, 19 Nov. 1851.
95.     *JLAC*, 1851, pp. 220, 225, 236, 237; *Debates*, 1851, pp. 177-81.
96.     *JLAC*, 1851, p. 314.
97.     ORP, Mackenzie to O'Rielly, 4 Aug. 1851; *JLAC*, 1851, p. 715. The account of this incident in *Niagara Chronicle*, 26 July 1851, gave the credit not to Mackenzie but to Hincks; *Debates*, 1851, pp. 949-53.
98.     Toronto *Examiner*, 7 Aug. 1851.
99.     MLP, H. Davies to Mackenzie, 7 June 1851.
100.    *Debates*, 1847, pp. 854-5; Douglas, *Prince*, passim.
101.    Toronto *Examiner*, 7 Aug. 1850, 25 July 1851; George Roy Stevens, *Canadian National Railways*, 2 vols. (Toronto, 1960), 1:91-100.
102.    *Debates*, 1850, pp. 1409-11.
103.    Frank W. Walker, "Birth of the Buffalo and Brantford Railway," *OH* XLVI (1954): 81-90.
104.    *Mackenzie Message*, 23 Sept. 1853.
105.    Prov. Can. Stat., 12 Vic., cap. 84; 13 and 14 Vic., cap. 72.
106.    MLP, E.P. Wood to Mackenzie, Dunnville, 10 June 1851; A. Bronson to Mackenzie, 11 June 1851; L. Weatherly to Mackenzie, Dunnville, 14 June 1851.
107.    Toronto *Examiner*, 7 April 1852; Prov. Can. Stat., 14 and 15 Vic., cap. 51.
108.    *JLAC*, 11 Aug. 1851, p. 359.
109.    Toronto *Examiner*, 23 July 1851; Prov. Can. Stat., 14 and 15 Vic., cap. 121; *JLAC*, 1851, pp. 185, 343, 348.
110.    *Message*, 10 March 1854; 11 April 1854.
111.    Archibald William Currie, *The Grand Trunk Railway of Canada* (Toronto, 1957), pp. 247-53.
112.    Prov. Can. Stat., 12 Vic., cap. 29.
113.    George Ray Stevens, *Canadian National Railways*, 2 vols. (Toronto, 1960), pp. 61, 85.
114.    Prov. Can. Stat., 14 and 15 Vic., caps. 73, 75.
115.    H.V. Nelles, *Philosophy of Railroads* (Toronto, 1972), p. 140.
116.    Toronto *Examiner*, 20 Aug. 1851.

117. The St. Lawrence and Atlantic, which had been chartered in 1845, was to run from Montreal to the international boundary, there to connect with an American road, the Atlantic and St.Lawrence, whose terminus was Portland. (Currie, *Grand Trunk*, p. 6.)
118. *Elgin-Grey Papers* 2:889-90, reprint from the *Examiner*.
119. *Debates*, 1851, pp. 1575-82; Bernard, *Les Rouges*, p. 56.
120. *Debates*, 1851, pp. 1652, 1659.
121. MLP, D. Ferguson to Mackenzie, Caledonia, 5 July 1851.
122. *Debates*, 1852-3, p. 1601.
123. *Debates*, 1851, pp. 1223, 1245, 1343.
124. Toronto *Examiner*, 30 July 1851; *Debates*, 1851, pp. 460, 530, 1043.
125. MLP, John de Cew to Mackenzie, Cayuga, 16, 18 June 1851.
126. MLP, D. Ferguson to Mackenzie, Caledonia, 9 July 1851.
127. MLP, J.J. Wiggins to Mackenzie, Dunnville, 8 July 1851.

## Chapter XIV Notes

1. He had found himself at odds with the majority of French members over a bill relating to the seigneurial tenures of Lower Canada. (Bernard, *Les Rouges*, pp. 73-79.)
2. Shenston Papers, V. Hall to T. Shenston, 14 July 1851.
3. MLP, Lindsey section, W. McDougall to Charles Lindsey, 19 July 1851; Clarke papers, W. McDougall to C. Clarke, 25 July 1851.
4. Shenston Papers, G. Brown to T. Shenston, 23 Oct. 1851.
5. Toronto *Examiner*, 13 Aug. 1851; see note 8.
6. Careless, *Union*, pp. 172-3.
7. Shenston Papers, F. Hincks to T. Shenston, 14 July 1851.
8. MLP, J. Kinnear to Mackenzie, Woodstock, 15 Nov. 1851.
9. Toronto *Examiner*, 19 Nov. 1851.
10. Scatcherd had been the Reform candidate for London in 1836.
11. Mackenzie Clippings, No. 340B.
12. Toronto *Examiner*, 10, 17 Dec. 1851. H.J. Morgan, *Sketches of Celebrated Canadians* (Quebec and London, 1862) refers to this contest as Hincks' last election contest and gives him a majority of 64. Hincks contested South Oxford in 1854. See pp. 557-8.
13. Baldwin Papers, J. Ross to R. Baldwin, Belleville, 17 Sept. 1851; A. McMartin to Baldwin, Holland Landing, 14, 23 Oct. 1851.
14. Brown Papers, J.E. Price to G. Brown, 28 Dec. 1849.
15. Toronto *Examiner*, 10, 17 Dec. 1851.
16. Toronto *Examiner*, 26 Nov., 3 Dec. 1851; *Message*, 5 Jan. 1854.
17. Toronto *Examiner*, 17 Dec. 1851; *Globe*, 22 Dec. 1851.
18. Toronto *Examiner*, 5 Nov. 1851; MLP, D. Ferguson to Mackenzie, 22 Nov. 1851; MC, Mackenzie to James, 7 Dec. 1851.
19. Toronto *Examiner*, 10 Dec. 1851.
20. Paul G. Cornell, *The Alignment of Political Groups in Canada 1841-1867* (Toronto, 1962), pp. 102-3.
21. MLP, F. Hincks to Mackenzie, 30 Dec. 1851.
22. Shenston Papers, J. Ross to T. Shenston, Belleville, 9 Dec. 1851, 4 Feb. 1852.
23. Rolph Papers, Mackenzie to J. Rolph, 2 Jan. 1852.
24. Toronto *Examiner*, 10 Oct. 1849. See supra, Ch. 13, p. 295.
25. Toronto *Examiner*, 17 Dec. 1851.
26. Baldwin Papers, M.S. Bidwell to R. Baldwin, New York, 31 Oct. 1852.
27. MLP, Lesslie to Mackenzie, 7 March 1850.
28. MLP, Note of 10 Oct. 1850 for £47/8/4.
29. MLP, F. Hincks to Mackenzie, 21 April 1850.
30. Baldwin Papers, J.A Price to Baldwin, 21 Dec. 1842, 12 April 1843.
31. Rolph Papers, Mackenzie to J. Rolph, 11 Feb. 1852; MLP, S. Richards to Mackenzie, 3 April 1852.
32. ORP, Mackenzie to H. O'Rielly, 1 March 1852.

33. MLP, Mackenzie to James, 7 Dec. 1851.
34. Rolph Papers, Mackenzie to J. Rolph, 8 March 1852.
35. MLP, D. M'Leod to Mackenzie, 5 Jan. 1852.
36. MLP, J. Rolph to Mackenzie, 2, 12 Jan. 1852.
37. Rolph Papers, Mackenzie to J. Rolph, 11 Feb. 1852.
38. Rolph Papers, Mackenzie to J. Rolph, 11, 14 Feb. 1852.
39. MLP, J. Rolph to Mackenzie, 7 June 1852 (partly illegible).
40. MLP, Mackenzie to J. Rolph, 14 June 1852 (copy on verso of the letter of June 12 to Rolph, which was not sent).
41. Prov. Can., State Book M, p. 22.
42. MLP, J. Rolph to Mackenzie, 19, 21 June 1852.
43. See notation on verso of letter of June 12.
44. MLP, Mackenzie to Rolph, 28 June 1852 (marked "not sent").
45. See verso of letter of June 12.
46. MLP, J. Rolph to Mackenzie, 20 July 1852.
47. *Message*, 17 March 1853.
48. MC, Mackenzie to James, 4 Aug. 1852; MLP, J. Lesslie to Mackenzie, 2 Oct. 1852.
49. Toronto *Examiner*, 18 Aug., 15 Sept. 1853; MLP, W.K. Graham to Mackenzie, 21 Aug. 1852.
50. *JLAC*, 1852-3, p. 9.
51. *JLAC*, 1852-3, pp. 9, 85; Toronto *Examiner*, 14 April 1852.
52. *JLAC*, 1852-3, pp. 828-9. On the abuses of this office and the difficulties of independent editors such as Mackenzie see Robert A. Hill, "A note on Newspaper Patronage in Canada during the late 1850s and early 1860s," *CHR* XLIX (1968): 44-50.
53. E. Russell Hopkins, *Confederation at the Cross Roads* (Toronto, 1968), p. 102.
54. Prov. Can. Stat., 16 Vic., caps. 38, 39, 73.
55. Stevens, *Railways*, pp. 85, 283. The eastern terminal was later changed to Rivière du Loup.
56. *Message*, 19 Feb. 1853.
57. *Message*, 25 Dec. 1852.
58. *Message*, 17 Feb. 1853.
59. *Message*, 3 March 1854.
60. Currie, *Grand Trunk*, pp. 35-6; Longley, *Hincks*, pp. 234-41; Nelles, *Philosophy of Railroads*, p. xliv.
61. Prov. Can. Stat., 16 Vic., cap. 22; E.P. Neufeld, *The Financial System of Canada* (Toronto, 1973), pp. 463-4.
62. *Message*, 24 Oct. 1856.
63. Prov. Can. Stat., 12 Vic., cap. 81, sec. 117; 14 and 15 Vic., cap. 109, sec. 36; *Globe*, 7 Oct. 1852.
64. *Message*, 25 Dec. 1852; *Debates*, 1852-3, pp. 732-4.
65. Toronto *Examiner*, 25 June 1851.
66. Donald Grant Creighton, *British North America at Confederation: A Study Prepared for the Royal Commission on Domestic-Provincial Relations* (Ottawa, 1963), p. 69.
67. *Message*, 25 Dec. 1852.
68. *Debates*, 1852-3, pp. 1890-1903.
69. Toronto *Examiner*, 15 Sept. 1852; *JLAC*, 1852-3, pp. 251-2, 554-8; Prov. Can. Stat., 16 Vic., cap. 80.
70. *JLAC*, 1852-3, pp. 1054-5; *Message*, 10 March 1853.
71. MLP, W. Spink (Clerk of the Legislative Assembly) to Mackenzie, 6 Feb. 1852.
72. MLP, J. Rolph to Mackenzie, 2, 22 Jan. 1852.
73. Hincks, *Reminiscences*, pp. 288-96; Wilson, *Clergy Reserves*, pp. 209-10.
74. *JLAC*, 1852-3, p. 569.
75. Alexander MacKenzie, *The Life and Speeches of George Brown* (Toronto, 1882), pp. 45-50; *JLAC*, pp. 155-64; *Debates*, 1852-3, pp. 449-65.
76. *Debates*, 1852-3, p. 519.
77. Hincks, *Reminiscences*, pp. 291-2; Wilson, *Clergy Reserves*, p. 210; *JLAC*, 1852-3, pp. 143-4.
78. Toronto *Examiner*, 1 Sept. 1852; *Globe*, 2 Oct. 1852.
79. *Globe*, 31 May 1853.
80. *Message*, 4 Aug. 1853.
81. Prov. Can. Stat., 16 Vic., cap. 152; *JLAC*, 1852-3, pp. 539-40, 643.

82.     *JLAC*, 1852-3, p. 609; *Globe*, 25 Oct. 1852, gives the population of the new constituencies; *Message*, 19 Jan. 1854.

83.     *Message*, 31 March 1853.

84.     John Garner, *The Franchise and Politics in British North America* (Toronto. 1969). p. 87.

85.     *JLAC*, 1852-3, pp. 375-6; *Message*, 3 Feb. 1853.

86.     *JLAC*, 1852-3, pp. 898-9.

87.     *JLAC*, 1851, p. 95. In Lower Canada tenant-purchasers of the British-American Land Co. had been granted the franchise in 1849.

88.     Toronto *Examiner*, 25 June 1851.

89.     Jones, "Peter Perry Election"; *The Witness*, quoted without dates in *Globe*, 8 Nov. 1849; Toronto *Examiner*, 20 March 1850; MLP, John Kirk to Mackenzie, Canboro, 19 April 1851; James Grant to Mackenzie, Martinstown, 7 June 1851.

90.     Prov. Can. Stat., 16 Vic., cap. 153.

91.     For Canada East the 40/- freehold was retained, or its equivalent in another tenure. In municipalities that should compile an assessment roll, the other classes named above were to be entitled to vote.

92.     *Message*, 25 Aug. 1853; *JLAC*, 1852-3, p. 864.

93.     Mackenzie Clippings, *Leader*, dates missing; Edward Thompson, *The Life of Charles, Lord Metcalfe* (London, 1937), p. 356.

94.     *JLAC*, 1854-5, p. 240; *Message*, 24 Nov. 1854.

95.     Clarke, *Sixty Years*, p. 108; Prov. Can. Stat., 37 Vic., cap. 9.

96.     Prov. Can. Stat., 16 Vic., cap. 182; *JLAC*, 1852-3, pp. 948-9; *Message*, 14 April 1854.

97.     MLP, T. Wiggins to Mackenzie, Dunnville, 24 May 1851; Dr. James Grant to Mackenzie, Glengarry, 10 May, 7 June 1851.

98.     MLP, W. Gibbons to Mackenzie, St. Catharines, 27 April 1851; D. D'Everardo to Mackenzie, Fonthill, 6 March, 5 April 1851; H.J. Williams to Mackenzie, 1 Sept. 1852.

99.     *JLAC*, 1852-3, pp. 65, 399, 755-6, 897; *Message*, 2 June 1853; Prov. Can. Stat., 16 Vic., cap. 177.

100.     Canada, *Bills*, 1851, No. 276; *JLAC*, 1851, p. 227.

101.     Prov. Can. Stat., 13 and14 Vic., cap. 53, sec. 89.

102.     *JLAC*, 1852-3, pp. 1065-7; *Debates*, 1852-3, p. 368.

103.     Canada, *Debates*, 22 Sept. 1854; *JLAC*, 1854-5, pp. 140, 1109.

104.     *Message*, 16 June 1853.

105.     *Message*, 3 April 1857.

106.     Prov. Can. Stat., 20 Vic., cap. 57, sec. 23.

107.     *JLAC*, 1857, p. 418; *Message*, 22 May 1857; Canada, *Bills*, 1857, No. 16.

108.     Prov. Can. Stat., 22 Vic., cap. 19, sec. 151; 23 Vic., cap. 25

109.     Gates, *Land Policies*, pp. 247-8.

110.     Toronto *Examiner*, 13 Oct., 17 Nov. 1852.

111.     Gates, *Land Policies*, p. 282.

112.     Ibid., pp. 256-62, 281, 284-7.

113.     *North American*, 14 Feb. 1851, quoted in Clarke, *Sixty Years*, p. 65; Toronto *Examiner*, 15 Sept. 1852.

114.     Toronto *Examiner*, 26 May 1852.

115.     Toronto *Examiner*, 26 May, 19 June 1852; Rolph Papers, Mackenzie to Rolph, 31 May 1852.

116.     *Debates*, 1852-3, p. 1492.

117.     Toronto *Examiner*, 25 May 1852. A similar criticism of the government's railway policy was made a year later by T.C. Keefer (Nelles, *Philosophy of Railroads*, p. xxxvi).

118.     MLP, R. Chisholm to Mackenzie, Alexandria, 25 March 1853.

119.     MLP, Canada Co. to William de Cew, 30 Nov. 1852; William H. Smith, *Canada* 2:168, 170, 198.

120.     The Company was allowed to retain one-third of the agreed-on purchase price for expenditures on internal improvements (this applied only to the Huron Tract). Some persons argued that the Company's land really cost it about 1/- an acre since it paid by installments, took title proportionately, and its land became taxable by degrees.

121.     *Message*, 21 April 1854.

122.     *Message*, 17 Feb., 10 April 1853.

123. MLP, John Young to Mackenzie, Fullerton, 14 Dec. 1853.
124. *JLAC*, 1852-3, pp. 421-2, 540-51.
125. *Message*, 18 Aug. 1853.
126. *JLAC*, 1856, pp. 252-3; *Message*, 11 April 1856.
127. MLP, D. Fox to Mackenzie, Toronto, 12 June 1851; J. Burley to Mackenzie, Kingston, 6 June 1851; J. Jackson to Mackenzie, Madoc, 3 June 1851.
128. MLP, J. Stevens to Mackenzie, 7 Oct. 1850; J. Jackson to Mackenzie, Madoc, 3 June 1851.
129. Prov. Can. Stat., 12 Vic., cap. 30.
130. Ontario, Dept. of Lands and Forests, Report, 1907, p. 210.
131. MLP, J. Andrews to Mackenzie, 2 Aug. 1852.
132. *JLAC*, 1852-3, p. 208, App. QQQQ.
133. *Message*, 15 Sept. 1853.
134. *Message*, 24 Nov. 1853.
135. *Globe*, 8 Nov. 1849, 29 March 1850; Toronto *Examiner*, 20 March 1850; MLP, Platform, 4th riding of York, 30 Oct. 1851, and Platform, West Oxford, 6 Nov. 1851.
136. *JLAC*, 1852-3, p. 140.
137. Toronto *Examiner*, 22 Sept. 1852.
138. *JLAC*, 1852-3, p. 69; Canada, *Bills*, 1852-3, No. 28.
139. George Macaulay Trevelyn, *History of England* (New York, 1928), p. 556.
140. *Debates*, 1852-3, p. 401.
141. Toronto *Examiner*, 22 Sept. 1852; *Debates*, 1852-3, pp. 390-401.
142. *Globe*, 21 Sept. 1852.
143. Ibid.
144. *Debates*, 1852-3, pp. 690-7; *British Colonist*, 5 Oct. 1852; *Message*, 19 Jan. 1854.
145. *Debates*, 1852-3, p. 401.
146. *JLAC*, 1852, p. 221.
147. *JLAC*, 1856, p. 494. 148. Toronto *Mirror*, 15 Oct. 1852, printed Mackenzie's letter to Lesslie of 5 Oct. 1852 [Toronto *Examiner*, 6 Oct. 1852].
149. MLP, J. Lesslie to Mackenzie, 29 Sept. 1852.
150. MLP, J. Lesslie to Mackenzie, 8 Oct. 1852.
151. Rolph Papers, W. McDougall to J. Rolph, Toronto, 12 Dec. 1852.
152. Clarke Papers, W. McDougall to C. Clarke, 2 Feb. 1853.
153. *North American*, 3 Feb. 1853.
154. Clarke Papers, W. McDougall to C. Clarke, 2 Feb. 1853.
155. MLP, W. Spink to Mackenzie, 7 Jan. 1852; *JLAC*, 1852, pp. 347-61.
156. MC, Mackenzie to Jacob Keefer, 1 Oct. 1853.
157. *Globe*, 21 June 1853.
158. *Haldimand Independent*, 22 Aug. 1851.
159. *JLAC*, 1851, p. 351; Toronto *Examiner*, 13 Aug. 1851.
160. *JLAC*, 1852-3, p. 958.
161. *JLAC*, 1852-3, p. 1015; Prov. Can. Stat., 16 Vic., cap. 185; *Message*, 16 June 1853, 3 March 1856.
162. MC, Mackenzie to his daughter Janet Lindsey, 9 June 1853; *Message* 19 May 1853.
163. *Message*, 25 Dec. 1852, 10 March 1853.
164. *JLAC*, 1852-3, p. 182; *Globe*, 22 March 1853.
165. *Globe*, 12 Dec. 1853.
166. Alexander Mackenzie Papers, G. Brown to A. Mackenzie, 26 March 1853.
167. *JLAC*, 1852-3, p. 575; *Globe*, 11 March 1853.
168. *Globe*, 24 March 1853.
169. *Message*, 4 Aug. 1853.
170. *JLAC*, 1852-3, p. 801.
171. *JLAC*, 1852-3, p. 752.
172. *Message*, 23 June 1853.
173. *Globe*, 30 June 1853; *Message*, 23 June 1853; *North American*, 23 June 1853 quoting the *Patriot*; *JLAC*, 1852-3, pp. 1122-5.
174. *JLAC*, 1852-3, pp. 120, 695; *JLAC*, 1852-3, pp. 113, 705.
175. *JLAC*, 1852-3, p. 1037.

1. MLP, George Bruce to Mackenzie, New York, 8, 10, 14 Feb., 3 March 1854; MC, J. Windt to Mackenzie, New York, 4 Dec. 1853.
2. *Message*, 14 July 1853.
3. MLP, J.S. Macdonald to Mackenzie, 7 July 1853.
4. MLP, David Christie to Mackenzie, 31 Dec. 1852.
5. *Message*, 12 Jan. 1854.
6. MC, Mackenzie to James, 6 March 1854; A.H. Young, ed., *The Roll of Pupils of Upper Canada College, Toronto, January 1830 to June 1916* (Kingston, 1917), pp. 388-9.
7. *Message*, 8 Sept. 1853.
8. *Message*, 15 Dec. 1853, quoting *Leader* of 10 Dec. 1853.
9. Prov. Can. Stat., 16 Vic., cap. 153.
10. MLP, D.H. Loucks to Mackenzie, 3 Dec. 1853; *Message*, 1 Dec. 1853, quoting the *Globe*.
11. Clarke Papers, W. McDougall to C. Clarke, 2 Feb. 1854.
12. *Message*, 7 April 1854.
13. *Message*, 5 Jan. 1854, quoting the *Examiner*.
14. *Message*, 9 June 1854.
15. Careless, *Brown of the Globe* 1: 01.
16. *Message*, 4 Aug., 15 Dec. 1853, 5 Jan. 1854.
17. Theodore Walrond, ed., *Letters and Journals of James, Eighth Earl of Elgin* (London, 1872), p. 143; John Lyle Morrison, *The Eighth Earl of Elgin* (London, 1928), p. 137.
18. *Leader*, 10 Dec. 1853.
19. J. Rolph to W. McDougall, 20 Dec. 1853, printed in *Message*, 5 Jan. 1854.
20. *Globe*, 16 Feb. 1854.
21. *Message*, 17 Feb. 1854.
22. MLP, D. M'Leod to Mackenzie, Quebec, 21 Feb. 1854.
23. *Message*, 3 March 1853.
24. *Message*, 13 Aug. 1853.
25. *Message*, 14 July 1853; William Menzies Whitelaw, "Responsible Government and the Responsible Governor," *CHR* XIII (1932): 364-86.
26. *Message*, 25 Aug. 1853.
27. *Message*, 21, 28 July 1853. For the changes see Dent, *Last Forty Years* 2: 278.
28. MLP, John Schofield to Mackenzie, South Pelham, 12 Jan. 1854; A. Clark to Mackenzie, Chingacousy, 19 Jan. 1854; G. Bolton to Mackenzie, Albion, 19 Jan. 1854.
29. *Message*, 24 March 1854.
30. Longley, *Hincks*, pp. 238-9; Hincks, *Reminiscences*, pp. 355-8; Careless, *Union*, p. 185.
31. Clarke Papers, W. McDougall to C. Clarke, 17 Sept. 1853.
32. Longley, *Hincks*, pp. 234-41; *Message*, 4, 18 Aug., 15, 29 Sept., 17 Nov., 8 Dec. 1853, 5 May 1854.
33. *Message*, 29 Sept., 10, 24 Nov. 1853, 5 Jan. 1854.
34. *Message*, 10, 31 March, 1 Sept. 1853.
35. *Message*, 27 Jan., 27 July, 4 Aug., 17 Nov. 1853, 19 Jan., 31 March 1854.
36. *Message*, 26 May 1854.
37. *Message*, 12 Jan. 1854.
38. *Globe*, 22 Dec. 1853.
39. Careless, *Brown* 1:205; *Globe*, 10 May 1853; Bernard, *Les Rouges*, p. 172.
40. *Message*, 14 July 1853.
41. *Message*, 19 May, 4 June 1853.
42. *Message*, 6 March 1854, 21 July 1854.
43. *Message*, 21 July, 4 Aug., 8, 15 Dec. 1853.
44. *Globe*, 12 Dec. 1853.
45. *Message*, 15 Dec. 1853.
46. Clarke Papers, G.B. Thomson to C. Clarke, 16 Feb. 1853.
47. MLP, J. Holmes to Mackenzie, 31 Dec. 1853.

48.     *Message*, 2 June, 1 Sept. 1853; Lindsey, *Life* 1:287. After the McNab-Morin administration came into office, J.A. Macdonald, Attorney-General, reported on these claims. He dismissed the claim for interest briefly and pointed out that the other claim had not been fully substantiated both as to Mackenzie's responsibility for money borrowed by the Committee of the Home District for his journey and as to the extent of the financial assistance he had received from them. Following Macdonald's report, the Executive Council took no action on Mackenzie's petition but after Confederation the Legislature of Ontario granted his widow $4,000. *Macdonald Letters* 1:265-8; Charles Lindsey, *William Lyon Mackenzie*, Makers of Canada Series, vol. 6 (Toronto, 1912).
49.     *Message*, 10 Nov. 1853.
50.     *Globe*, 2 Nov. 1852.
51.     Gates, *Land Policies*, p. 281.
52.     *Globe*, 2, 9 Nov. 1852; William Lyon Mackenzie, *Head's Flag of Truce* (Toronto, 1854), pp. 1-3.
53.     *JLAUC*, 1837-8, Appendix, p. 406.
54.     *Globe*, 9 Nov. 1852; *Debates*, 1852-3, pp. 1184-5.
55.     Mackenzie, *Flag of Truce*, p. 2; *Globe*, 9 Nov. 1852; Rolph Papers, G. Thompson to Rolph, 14 April 1854.
56.     *Globe*, 9 Nov. 1852; Mackenzie Clippings, No. 227.
57.     Document is in the Rolph papers.
58.     J. Morgan Dix, *Memoirs of John Adams Dix* 2:314-5; italics added.
59.     MLP, Lindsey section, James Mackenzie to Charles Lindsey, 28 May 1886.
60.     *JLAC*, 1852-3, App. SSSS.
61.     Carl Wittke, ed., *History of the State of Ohio*, 6 vols. (Columbus, Ohio, 1941-44), 4:127, 281, 283-4; *Message*, 19 Jan. 1854.
62.     *Message*, 5 May 1854.
63.     *JLAC*, 1854, pp. 2-3, 24-31; *Message*, 7 July 1854.
64.     *Globe*, s.w., 29 June 1854; *Message*, 7 July 1854; Cayuga *Sachem*, 23 June 1854.
65.     *Quebec Gazette*, 23 June 1854.
66.     *Message*, 7 July 1854.
67.     MLP, Dr. W. Alwin to Mackenzie, Brooklin, 23 Jan. 1854.
68.     MLP, A. Clark to Mackenzie, 18 Jan. 1854.
69.     *North American*, 4 April 1854.
70.     Clarke Papers, Draft, C. Clarke to W. McDougall, 24 April 1854.
71.     *Message*, Extra, 10 July 1854.
72.     *Message*, 21 July 1854.
73.     MLP, B. Foley to Mackenzie, Cayuga, 18 March 1854; J. White to Mackenzie, 8 April 1854.
74.     Cayuga *Sachem*, 10 May, 14, 21 July 1854.
75.     *Message*, 21 April 1854, quoting Cayuga *Sachem* and *The Independent*.
76.     *Message*, 9 June 1854; MLP, John Kent to Mackenzie, Caistor, 21 Sept. 1854.
77.     MLP, W. Holmes to Mackenzie, 31 March 1854. Other warnings came from J. Fergus, June 1854; H. Kennedy, 29 Aug. 1854; T. Tipton, 27 Dec. 1854.
78.     *Message*, 28 July 1854.
79.     *Message*, 21 July 1854.
80.     *Message*, 4 Aug. 1854.
81.     MLP, Mackenzie to W. Carroll, 3 July 1854.
82.     *Message*, 21 April 1854, quoting Montreal *Gazette*.
83.     *Message*, 21 July 1854.
84.     *Message*, 14 July 1854.
85.     MLP, D. D'Everardo to Mackenzie, Pelham, 28 July 1854.
86.     MLP, W. McDougall to Mackenzie, 13, 18, 19, 20 July 1854; *Globe*, 3 Aug. 1854.
87.     Shenston Papers, F. Hincks to T. Shenston, 6 Aug. 1853.
88.     Shenston Papers, F. Hincks to T. Shenston, 31 Aug. 1854; Hincks, *Reminiscences*, p. 317.
89.     *Message*, 7 July 1854.
90.     *Message*, 21 July 1854, quoting Oxford *Sentinel* of 13 July 1854.
91.     *Message*, 1 Sept. 1854.
92.     Cayuga *Sachem*, 21 July 1854.
93.     MLP, W. Carroll to Mackenzie, 14 April 1859.

94.  *Message*, 1 Sept. 1854.
95.  Computed from partial returns in *Globe* of 3 Aug. 1854 and Mackenzie's overall figures in *Message* of 1 Sept. 1854.
96.  *Message*, 4 Aug. 1854.


## Chapter XVI Notes

1.   *JLAC*, 1854-5, pp. 5-6, italics added.
2.   Hincks, *Reminiscences*, p. 333; *Documents relating to the Resignation of the Canadian Ministry in September, 1854*, pamphlet (Quebec, n.d.), p. 12.
3.   *Globe*, 19 April 1855.
4.   *JLAC*, 1854-5, p. 13. On the scandals, see Longley, *Hincks*, pp. 236-41.
5.   *Message*, 15 Sept. 1854.
6.   Sissons, *Ryerson* 2:284; Baldwin Papers, [J. Ross] to William Young, Attorney-General of Nova Scotia, 27 Oct. 1854.
7.   MLP, David Christie to Mackenzie, 19 Feb. 1855.
8.   *Message*, 22 Sept. 1854.
9.   MLP, David Christie to Mackenzie, Brantford, 2 Oct. 1854.
10.  *Message*, 20 Oct. 1854.
11.  *Debates*, 1854-55, pp. 150-7.
12.  *Message*, 22 Sept. 1854; *JLAC*, 1854-5, p. 146.
13.  *Macdonald Letters* 1:235.
14.  *JLAC*, 1854-5, p. 173, App. AAAA.
15.  *JLAC*, 1854-5, pp. 177-8; *Message*, 20 Oct. 1854.
16.  *JLAC*, 1854-5, p. 297.
17.  *Mirror of Parliament*, 9 Nov. 1854.
18.  *Message*, 17 July 1854; Cayuga *Sachem*, 7 July 1854.
19.  Toronto *Examiner*, 2 Aug. 1854.
20.  *JLAC*, 1854-5, pp. 261, 320; *Message*, 27 Oct. 1854.
21.  *Message*, 17 Nov., 1 Dec. 1854.
22.  MLP, J. Lesslie to Mackenzie, 17 Nov. 1854.
23.  MLP, W. McDougall to Mackenzie, Toronto, 23 Oct. 1854.
24.  *Globe*, 5, 12 March 1855; *Debates*, 1854-5, vol. 13, p. 373.
25.  JLAC, 1854-5, pp. 649, 901-3; Wilson, *Clergy Reserves*, p. 216.
26.  Rumilly, *Papineau* 1:608.
27.  Baillargeon, "La tenure seigneuriale a-t-elle étée abolie par suite du plaintes des censitaires?", *Revue d'Histoire de l'Amérique Française{aise* XXI, pp. 64-80; S.D. Clark, *Movements of Political Protest*, pp. 320-1.
28.  MLP, D. Armstrong to Mackenzie, Montreal, 30 March, 8 April 1853.
29.  *Message*, 4 Aug. 1853, 14 July 1854.
30.  Canada, *Bills*, 1851, No. 285; Hincks, *Reminiscences*, pp. 304-5; *Debates*, 1851, pp. 1550, 1672-4. A bill to promote commutation was later introduced but its terms were unsatisfactory to Lafontaine (*Debates*, 1851, pp. 1602-7, 1612-13).
31.  *JLAC*, 1852-3, p. 56; Hincks, *Reminiscences*, p. 305.
32.  Canada, *Bills*, 1852-3, No. 142.
33.  *Message*, 5, 12 May 1852.
34.  Munro, *Seigneurial System*, p. 233; William Smith, *History of Canada From Its First Discovery to the Peace of 1763*, 2 vols. (Quebec, 1815), 1:202, App. 46, vol. 2, p. 189; Richard Colebrook Harris, *The Seigneurial System in Early Canada* (Madison, 1966), pp. 64-5.
35.  *JLAC*, 1852-3, p. 839, 1852-3, pp. 52-3, 483, 519-20.
36.  *Message*, 10 Nov. 1854.
37.  Hincks, *Reminiscences*, p. 306.
38.  *Message*, 10 Nov. 1854.
39.  *Message*, 24 Nov. 1854.

40. *Message*, 4 Dec. 1854.
41. *JLAC*, 1854-5, pp. 332-6.
42. *Message*, 18 Dec. 1854.
43. *JLAC*, 1854-5, p. 390.
44. *JLAC*, 1854-5, pp. 543-66, 570-4.
45. Louis P. Turcotte, *Le Canada sous l' Union*, 2 vols. (Quebec, 1882), 2:236-7; Prov. Can. Stat., 22 Vic., cap. 48 (1859).
46. Marcel Trudel, *The Seigneurial Regime* , Canadian Historical Booklet No. 6 (Ottawa, 1971), p. 21; Louis Hartz, *The Founding of New Societies* (New York, 1964), p. 225.
47. *Message*, 9 Feb. 1855.
48. *JLAC*, 1854-5, pp. 565-6.
49. *Globe*, 25 Dec. 1854.
50. PAC, M.G. 24 A34, Newcastle to Elgin, 1 May 1853; Microfilm C.O. 42, Roll A, 396, Elgin to Newcastle, 30 May 1853.
51. Hincks, *Reminiscences*, pp. 303-10.
52. The Hon. Amelia Murray, *Letters from the United States, Cuba and New York* (New York, 1856), p. 89.
53. *Debates*, 1854-5, pp. 1853-60; *Message*, 5 Jan. 1855, quoting the *Colonist*.
54. William Menzies Whitelaw, "Responsible Government and the Responsible Governor," *CHR* XIII (1932): 364-86.
55. *Message*, 5 Jan. 1854.
56. *Debates*, 1854-5, pp. 119-24.
57. J.E. Hodgetts, *Pioneer Public Service: An Administrative History of the United Canadas, 1841-1867* (Toronto, 1955), p.97.
58. *Message*, 9 June 1853.
59. *Debates*, 1852-3, vol. 11, pt. 2, p. 682.
60. *Message*, 26 May 1853; *JLAC*, 1852-3, pp. 226-7, App. T.T.
61. Montreal *Herald*, 2 Oct. 1854.
62. *Message*, 21 April 1853.
63. Herbert R. Balls, "John Langton and the Canadian Audit Office," *CHR* XXI (1940): 150-76.
64. *JLAC*, 1854, App. J.J. (2nd report).
65. *Message*, 29 Dec. 1854.
66. *Macdonald Letters* 1:235.
67. *JLAC*, 1854-5, p. 210.
68. *Message*, 28 June 1858.
69. *JLAC*, 1854-5, pp. 510-21, 537.
70. MLP, Mackenzie to William Carroll, __ Jan. 1855, copy.
71. George Bolton Papers, Mackenzie to Bolton, 26 Oct., 17 Nov. 1854; G. Lightwell to Mackenzie, Goderich, 2 Dec. 1854; *Message*, 5 Jan. 1855.
72. MLP, J. Frazer to Mackenzie, Fonthill, 29 Jan. 1855; D. Christie to Mackenzie, Brantford, 12 Jan., 2 Feb. 1855; *Message*, Extra, 17 Nov. 1855.
73. *Message*, 9 Feb. 1855.
74. MLP, J. Lesslie to Mackenzie, 15 Nov. 1854.
75. MLP, J. Lesslie to Mackenzie, 26 Jan. 1855.
76. MLP, J. Lesslie to Mackenzie, 2 May 1855.
77. MLP, B. Wait to Mackenzie, 18 April 1855. Wait referred to "overwork and exposure."
78. Prov. Can. Stat., 14&15 Vic., cap. 47.
79. *JLAC*, 1854-5, App. J.J.
80. Prov. Can. Stat., 20 Vic., cap. 18.
81. *Macdonald Letters* 1:235.
82. Prov. Can. Stat., 18 Vic., cap 78.
83. Balls, "John Langton and the Audit Office."
84. The final vote on the bill was not recorded.
85. *Globe*, 21 March 1855; *Examiner*, 18 April 1855.
86. Hodgins, *Documentary History* 12:36; Taché Act, 18 Vic., cap. 131.
87. *JLAC*, 1854-5, pp. 1286-7; *Globe*, 6 June 1855.
88. Clarke, *Sixty Years*, p. 65.
89. Toronto *Examiner*, 18 May 1852; *Message*, 25 Dec. 1852, 7 Jan. 1853; MLP, Mackenzie to J. Lesslie, 23 Nov. 1849.

90. *Message*, 23 Jan. 1853.
91. MLP, E.B. O'Callaghan to Mackenzie, 24 Aug., 23 Sept. 1852.
92. *Leader*, 28 Sept. 1852; *Globe*, 4 June 1853.
93. *JLAC*, 1852-3, pp. 944-5.
94. *Message*, 19 June, 4 Aug. 1853.
95. See *supra*, pp. 357-388.
96. Hincks, *Reminiscences*, p. 306; Turcotte, *Le Canada sous l'Union* 2:201; *JLCC*, 1852-3, pp. 483, 519, 527.
97. *JLAC*, 1854-5, p. 761; Toronto *Examiner*, 16, 28 March 1855; *Globe*, 26 March 1855.
98. Toronto *Examiner*, 23 May 1855.
99. *JLAC*, 1854-5, pp. 1083-7, 1095; Careless, *Brown of the Globe* 1:181.
100. Canada, *Bills*, 1854-5, No. 66.
101. *JLAC*, 1856, pp. 147-8, 174-5, 193-4; 19-20 Vic., cap. 140; *Message*, 21 March, 4 April 1856.
102. *JLAC*, 1857, pp. 67-8.
103. MLP, A. Greeley to Mackenzie, New York, 14 Nov. 1854; N. Dow to Mackenzie, Portland, 20 Nov. 1854.
104. Toronto *Examiner*, 9 May 1855; *JLAC*, 1854-5, pp. 198, 929-38.
105. *JLAC*, 1854-5, pp. 952, 957-8; Toronto *Examiner*, 18 April 1855.
106. *JLAC*, 1856, pp. 67-9, 237-8.
107. Prov. Can. Stat., 18 Vic., cap. 89.
108. Toronto *Examiner*, 6 June 1855.
109. *JLAC*, 1854-5, pp. 1170-3. Mackenzie was referring not to the civil list clauses of the Act of Union but to the Canada Act of 1846 which had replaced them and which also provided for a permanent civil list, but not for annual legislative grants.
110. Toronto *Examiner*, 6 June 1855.
111. 18 Vic., cap. 122; *JLAC*, 1854-5, pp. 911-2, 959; Toronto *Examiner*, 2 May 1855.
112. Toronto *Examiner*, 8 Aug. 1855; *JLAC*, 1854-5, pp. 329-3; Oscar Douglas Skelton, *The Life and Times of Sir Alexander Tilloch Galt* (Toronto, 1966), pp. 34-6.
113. Prov. Can. Stat., 18 Vic., cap. 174.
114. Toronto *Examiner*, 13 June, 29 Aug. 1855; *JLAC*, 1854-5, pp. 944-5.
115. Toronto *Examiner*, 16 May 1855.
116. Toronto *Examiner*, 30 May 1855.
117. *JLAC*, 1854-5, pp. 1181-1203.
118. *JLAC*, 1854-5, pp. 485-506.
119. *JLAC*, 1854-5, p. 1145.
120. Toronto *Examiner*, 30 May 1855; *Message*, 18 Jan. 1856.
121. *JLAC*, 1854-5, p. 136.
122. Toronto *Examiner*, 7 July 1855.
123. *JLAC*, 1854-5, p. 1146.
124. *JLAC*, 1854-5, pp. 148, 1102; *Message*, 13 Oct. 1854.
125. *JLAC*, 1854-5, p. 140.
126. *JLAC*, 1854-5, pp. 119, 247; *Message*, 24 Nov. 1854.
127. *JLAC*, 1854-5, p. 3; *Message*, 6 Oct. 1854.
128. *Message*, 13 Oct. 1854.
129. *JLAC*, 1854-5, pp. 45, 1028; *Message*, 13 Oct. 1854; *Mirror of Parliament*, 7 May, p. 207.
130. *JLAC*, 1854-5, pp. 204-5.
131. MLP, Mackenzie to James, 25 May 1855.

## Chapter XVII Notes

1. *Leader*, 2 Aug. 1855; Toronto *Examiner*, 15 Aug. 1855.
2. Toronto *Examiner*, 29 Aug. 1855.
3. Jacques Monet, "French-Canadian Nationalism and the Challenge of Ultramontanism," *CHAR* (1966): 41-55.
4. Toronto *Examiner*, 1 Aug. 1855.
5. MC, Mackenzie to James, 24 Sept. 1855.
6. Toronto *Examiner*, 29 Aug. 1855.

7.     MC, D. Morrison to Mackenzie, 7 Sept. 1855.
8.     MC, Mackenzie to James, 24 Sept. 1855. A handbill displayed in Mackenzie House, Toronto, advertises the place and date of some of these lectures.
9.     *Message*, 11 April, 13 June 1856.
10.    Careless, *Brown* 1:206; *Globe*, 23 July, 6, 14, 24 Aug. 1855.
11.    MLP, Peter McNaughton to Mackenzie, Brampton, 14 Dec. 1855.
12.    James Young, *Public Men and Public Affairs in Canada* (Toronto, 1912), p. 87.
13.    MLP, T.S. Brown to Mackenzie, 27 Aug. 1855.
14.    I have been unable to find this letter in the *Tribune*.
15.    MLP, H. Greeley to Mackenzie, 14 Aug. 1855.
16.    *Message*, 17 Nov. 1855.
17.    *Message*, 7, 14 Dec. 1855.
18.    *Message*, 7 Dec. 1855.
19.    *Message*, 25 April 1856.
20.    MLP, F.B. (Bourassa?) to Mackenzie, 23 Feb. 1856.
21.    *JLAC*, 1856, p. 46.
22.    *JLAC*, 1856, pp. 38-55.
23.    *Repealer's Almanac*, 1856, column 50.
24.    *Message*, 29 Feb., 7 March 1856.
25.    *Message*, 21 March 1856.
26.    *JLAC*, 1856, pp. 514, 532.
27.    *JLAC*, 1856, pp. 543-4.
28.    *Message*, 30 May 1856.
29.    *JLAC*, 1856, p. 364; *Globe*, 23 April 1856; *Message*, 25 April 1856.
30.    *JLAC*, 1856, pp. 364-5, 375, 604.
31.    *JLAC*, 1857, p. 328.
32.    *Message*, 2 May 1856.
33.    *JLAC*, 1856, pp. 566, 724-5, 738.
34.    Prov. Can. Stat., 19 and 20 Vic., cap. 22.
35.    Prov. Can. Stat., 19 and 20 Vic., cap. 92.
36.    *JLAC*, 1856, p. 484.
37.    Mackenzie apparently accepted as accurate the *London Morning Chronicle's* statement that Elgin had "bagged £100,000 out of his governship" and had cleared part if not the whole of the mortgage on his estate (*Message*, 11 Feb. 1856).
38.    *Message*, 9, 16 May 1856.
39.    Prov. Can. Stat., 19 and 20 Vic., cap. 111.
40.    *Message*, 9 May 1856.
41.    *JLAC*, 1856, p. 702.
42.    *Message*, 16 June 1856.
43.    Prov. Can. Stat., 19 and 20 Vic., cap. 10.
44.    *JLAC*, 1856, pp. 196-8; *Message*, 18, 25 April 1856.
45.    *JLAC*, 1856, pp. 422-3.
46.    Gates, "Decided Policy."
47.    Reznick, "Social History of an America Depression."
48.    Neufeld, F*inancial System of Canada*, p. 84; Roeliff Morton Breckenridge, *The Canadian Banking System* (Toronto, 1894), pp. 88, 91; Prov. Can. Stat., 4 and 5 Vic., cap. 29.
49.    Prov. Can. Stat., 13 and 14 Vic., cap. 21.
50.    Prov. Can. Stat., 14 and 15 Vic., cap. 70; 16 Vic., cap. 162; *JLAC*, 1851, pp. 209, 216, 304.
51.    *JLAC*, 1852-3, pp. 371, 797; *Message*, 24 Nov. 1853.
52.    *Message*, 12 May, 20 June, 21 July 1853. The specie circular had been quietly repealed in 1838 (Curtis, *Fox at Bay*, pp. 129-30).
53.    Prov. Can. Stat., 19 and 20 Vic., cap. 3.
54.    *JLAC*, 1854, pp. 391-2, 395-7.
55.    *JLAC*, 1856, pp. 493, 668.
56.    *Message*, 8 Dec. 1854, quoting Quebec *Gazette* and *Chronicle*, 20 Nov. 1854.
57.    *Leader*, 28 Sept. 1854.
58.    *Message*, 2 Oct. 1856.
59.    *Tribune*, 8 Dec. 1856; Neufeld, *Financial System*, Ch. 15.

60.     *Message*, 31 Oct. 1856.
61.     Skelton, *Sir Alexander Tilloch Galt*, p. 125; *Message*, 21 April 1860.
62.     Toronto *Examiner*, 29 Sept. 1852; *JLAC*, 1852-3, pp. 15, 340, 753, and App.
63.     W.A. Langton, *Early Days in Upper Canada: Letters of John Langton from the Backwoods of Upper Canada and the Audit Office of the Province of Canada* (Toronto, 1926), pp. 243-4.
64.     MLP, J. Simpson (Bank of Montreal) to Mackenzie, 31 Aug. 1852.
65.     *Message*, 2 Nov. 1854.
66.     *JLAC*, 1854, pp. 207, 240.
67.     *JLAC*, 1854-5, App. E.E.
68.     *Message*, 1 Dec. 1854.
69.     Toronto *Examiner*, 29 Sept. 1854.
70.     *JLAC*, 1856, p. 668; *Message*, 20 June, 12 Sept. 1856; Prov. Can. Stat., 19 and 20 Vic., cap. 121.
71.     *Message*, 17 Oct. 1856.
72.     *Message*, 12 Sept. 1856.
73.     Neufeld, *Money and Banking in Canada*, p. 146; A.B. Jamieson, *Chartered Banking in Canada* (Toronto, 1953), p. 14; Breckinridge, *Canadian Banking System*, p. 174.
74.     *JLAC*, 1856, p. 436.
75.     *JLAC*, 1856, p. 419; Prov. Can. Stat., 19 and 20 Vic., cap. 14.
76.     *Message*, 7 March 1856.
77.     *Message*, 28 March 1856; Prov. Can. Stat., 19 and 20 Vic., cap. 54.
78.     Langton, *Letters*, pp. 250-1.
79.     *JLAC*, 1856, pp. 246, 310-4. See also Monet, "French-Canadian Nationalism," pp. 48-49.
80.     MLP, W. Gibbons to Mackenzie, 23 Dec. 1851.
81.     *Message*, 9 April 1858.
82.     On the important role of the justices see J.A. Aitchison, "The Municipal Corporation Act of 1849," *CHR* XXX (1949): 107-22.
83.     *Message*, 29 Feb. 1856.
84.     *Message*, 30 June 1856.
85.     *Repealer's Almanac*, col. 12, quoting *Globe*, 10 July 1855.
86.     *Message*, 17 Oct. 1856.
87.     Careless, *Brown* 1:211-2, 221-3.
88.     MLP, Mackenzie to Isaac Buchanan, 25 March 1856.
89.     *Message*, 11 Dec. 1856.
90.     See *supra*, Ch. 11, p. 246.
91.     Crawford D.W. Goodwin, *Canadian Economic Thought* (Durham, N.C., 1961), pp. 82-3.
92.     *Message*, 28 March, 4 April 1856.
93.     *Message*, 18 April 1856.
94.     Buchanan Papers, Mackenzie to I. Buchanan, 3 March 1856.
95.     *Message*, 4 April, 2 May 1856.
96.     MLP, I. Buchanan to Mackenzie, 4, 10 April 1856. A copy of The Land Plan may be in the extensive Buchanan Papers in PAC; unhappily, the author was unable to read the tissue copies.
97.     *Message*, 27 June 1856, quoting *Huron Signal*!
98.     Buchanan Papers, Mackenzie to I. Buchanan, 17 June 1856.
99.     Careless, *Brown of the Globe* 1:36-9.
100.    D.G.G. Kerr, *Sir Edmund Head: A Scholarly Governor* (Toronto, 1954), p. 197.
101.    MLP, I. Buchanan to Mackenzie, 17 June 1856.
102.    *Message*, 27 June 1856.
103.    Buchanan Papers, Mackenzie to I. Buchanan, 17 June 1856.
104.    *Message*, 27 June 1856.
105.    MLP, Buchanan to Mackenzie, 28 June, 1 July 1856.
106.    Buchanan Papers, Mackenzie to I. Buchanan, 12 July 1856.
107.    MLP, J. Malcolm to Mackenzie, 13 Sept. 1856; D. Christie to Mackenzie, Brantford, 18 Sept. 1856.
108.    MLP, James Jones to Mackenzie, Stamford, 25 Nov. 1856.
109.    *Message*, 5 Sept. 1856, quoting *Globe* of 26 July 1850.

110. *Message*, 15 Aug. 1856.
111. *Message*, 5, 26 Sept. 1856.
112. Brown Papers, vol. 2, circular of 15 Dec. 1856.
113. Careless, *Brown* 1:234-7.
114. *Message*, 16 Nov. 1856.
115. *Message*, 20 Feb. 1857.
116. *Repealers' Almanac*, quoting *Globe*, 10 July 1855.
117. Ibid., col. 6.
118. Ibid., col. 16.
119. *Message*, 9 Jan. 1857.
120. *Message*, 30 Jan. 1857.
121. *Message*, 16 Jan. 1857.
122. *Message*, 23 Jan. 1857.
123. MLP, A. Mackenzie to W.L. Mackenzie, Port Sarnia, 22 Jan. 1857.
124. MLP, John White to Mackenzie, 8 Dec. 1855.
125. MC, W.L. Mackenzie Jr. to his father, 5 Dec. 1857; Rolph Papers, W.L. Mackenzie Jr. to John Rolph, 2 Aug. 1856. Dent mentions this incident *(Story of the Rebellion* 2:322). He puts the documents referred to in the plural. One such letter and one note signed by William remain in the Rolph Papers.
126. MLP, John White to Mackenzie, 8 Aug. 1856.
127. MLP, J.W. Smith to Mackenzie, Balmoral, 20 June, 17 Nov. 1856; 30 Jan. 1857.
128. MLP, D. Ferguson to Mackenzie, Caledonia, 14 Aug. 1856; Thos. Brothers to Mackenzie, E. Gwillimbury, 14 Aug. 1856.
129. MLP, James Jones to Mackenzie, Stamford, 14 Oct. 1856.
130. *Message*, 3 Oct. 1856. I have not been able to find Lesslie's valedictory in the *Globe*.
131. Donald M'Leod, *The Mackenzie Homestead. Minutes of Proceedings at Two Meetings held in Toronto preparatory to an Appeal being made to the people of Canada on behalf of an old faithful and talented public servant, William Lyon Mackenzie, Esq., M.P.P., with the address of the Central Committee* (Toronto, 1856).
132. *Message*, 3 Oct. 1856.
133. MLP, J.M. Campbell to Mackenzie, Durham, 26 March 1857.
134. *Message*, 17 Oct. 1856.
135. *Message*, 5 Dec. 1856.

## Chapter XVIII Notes

1. *JLAC*, 1857, pp. 92-134.
2. *JLAC*, 1857, App. 17.
3. John S. Galbraith, *The Hudson's Bay Company* (Los Angeles, 1957), pp. 343-4; Hopkins, *Confederation*, p. 105.
4. *Message*, 13, 27 Feb., 6 March 1857.
5. Prov. Can. Stat., 20 Vic., cap. 29; *JLAC*, 1857, p. 437.
6. Prov. Can. Stat., 20 Vic., cap. 28; *JLAC*, 1857, p. 454.
7. Prov. Can. Stat., 20 Vic., cap. 26; *JLAC*, 1857, pp. 473-4; *Message*, 5 June 1857.
8. *JLAC*, 1854, p. 342.
9. Prov. Can. Stat., 20 Vic., cap. 24; *JLAC*, 1857, p. 604; MLP, James Stephens to Mackenzie, 13 April 1855; Hodgetts, *Pioneer Public Service*, pp. 42-3.
10. Toronto *Examiner*, 8 Aug. 1849.
11. Canada, *Bills*, 1852-3, Nos. 2 and 7; *JLAC*, 1852-3, pp. 14, 22.
12. Prov. Can. Stat., 16 Vic., cap. 154; *JLAC*, 1852-3, pp. 1014-5; *Message*, 12 March, 4 Aug. 1853.
13. *JLAC*, 1854-5, pp. 762, 1099-1100, App. SSS; *JLAC*, 1856, pp. 215, 482, App. 45; *JLAC*, 1857, pp. 32, 423, 448, App. 49.
14. *Message*, 11, 25 April 1856.
15. Canada, *Bills*, 1857, No. 8; *JLAC*, 1857, pp. 31, 168; Canada, *Bills*, 1857, No. 50; JLAC, 1857, pp. 45, 69.

16. *JLAC*, 1857, pp. 155-7.
17. *JLAC*, 1857, pp. 176-7; Prov. Can. Stat., 20 Vic., cap. 22.
18. *JLAC*, 1857, pp. 124, 675; Canada, *Bills*, 1857, No. 142.
19. *Message*, 27 March, 25 July, 9, 15, 22, 29 Aug. 1857.
20. *Message*, 12 June 1857.
21. MLP, Dr. J.M. Jarron to Mackenzie, Dunnville, 20 March 1857; Robert Leslie Jones, *History of Agriculture in Ontario, 1613-1880* (Toronto, 1946), pp. 198, 203, 204; Hanson Orlo Miller, *A Century of Western Ontario* (Toronto, 1949).
22. *JLAC*, 1857, App. 34; 1858, App. 40.
23. *Message*, 27 March 1857.
24. See Ch. 14, p. 329.
25. *JLAC*, 1857, pp. 185, 304, 451, 553, 555; *Message*, 12 March 1857.
26. *JLAC*, 1857, p. 637; *Message*, 12 June 1857.
27. *JLAC*, 1857, p. 150.
28. *JLAC*, 1857, App. 11; *Message*, 4 Sept. 1857.
29. Prov. Can. Stat., 20 Vic., cap. 20.
30. *Message*, 5 June 1857; *JLAC*, 1857, pp. 609-10, 616.
31. Prov. Can. Stat., 1858, 22 Vic., cap. 84; 1859, 22 Vic., caps. 14 and 15.
32. Skelton, *Galt* (reprint, Toronto, 1966), pp. 111-2.
33. *JLAC*, 1857, pp. 124-5.
34. *JLAC*, 1857, pp. 232-3; *Message*, 24 April 1857.
35. *JLAC*, 1857, p. 173; *Message*, 29 April 1857.
36. Prov. Can. Stat., 22 Vic., cap. 79; *Message*, 12 June 1857; MLP, W.T. Bronson to Mackenzie, Guelph, 28 March 1857.
37. *Message*, 3 April 1857.
38. Prov. Can. Stat., 14 and15 Vic., cap. 1.
39. Prov. Can. Stat., 20 Vic., cap. 23; *Message*, 12 March 1858, quoting *Canada Law Journal*.
40. Bolton Papers, Mackenzie to George Bolton, 16 Dec. 1856.
41. Gates, *Land Policies*, pp. 291-4.
42. MLP, Robert Johnston to Mackenzie, Howick, 14 March 1856; Bolton Papers, Mackenzie to George Bolton, 17, 26 Nov. 1855; Bolton to J. Clark, 2 Nov. 1855.
43. *Message*, 21 March 1856.
44. *Message*, 18 Dec. 1857.
45. *Repealers' Almanac*, col. 69; *Message*, 9 May 1856.
46. *JLAC*, 1856, p. 495.
47. *Message*, 20 June 1856.
48. *Message*, 24 Oct. 1856.
49. *Message*, 11 Dec. 1856.
50. Bolton Papers, Mackenzie to Bolton, 16 Dec. 1856.
51. *Message*, 11 Dec. 1856.
52. *Message*, 6 Feb., 20, 27 March, 15 May 1856.
53. MLP, John Irwin to Mackenzie, 20 July 1857.
54. *JLAC*, 1857, p. 32; PAC, M.S. Group 24, B18, vol. 9, Mackenzie to G. Bolton, 17 March 1857.
55. *JLAC*, 1857, App. 32; *Message*, 24 April 1857.
56. MLP, Alex. Campbell to Mackenzie, 20 July 1857; *Message*, 6 Feb., 7 Aug. 1857.
57. *Message*, 10 April 1857; *JLAC*, 1856, App. 25.
58. Murray, *Letters*, p. 74.
59. *Message*, 10, 24 April 1857.
60. *Message*, 13 Feb. 1857.
61. *JLAC*, 1858, App. 22.
62. *Message*, 23 April 1858.
63. Gates, *Land Policies*, p. 293.
64. MLP, John Grant to Mackenzie, 9 June 1857.
65. *Macdonald Letters* 1:340, J.A. Macdonald to Brown Chamberlain, 20 Jan. 1856.
66. Ibid., pp. 333-6, Macdonald to Henry Smith Jr., 20 Jan. 1856.
67. Kerr, *Head*, pp. 171-2.

68.     *Message*, 27 Feb., 17 April 1857.
69.     *Message*, 27 Feb. 1857.
70.     *Message*, 7 Aug. 1857, 16 April 1858.
71.     Douglas Leighton, "The Compact Tory as Bureaucrat: Samuel Peter Jarvis and the Indian Department," *OH* LXII (1981): 40-53.
72.     Message, 8 May, 10 July 1857.
73.     *JLAC*, 1857, p. 32; 1858, p. 140, App. 22; *Message*, 12 May 1860. (Jarvis had died in 1860 and his estate was in chancery.)
74.     Canada, *Bills*, 1858, No. 115; *JLAC*, 1858, p. 355.
75.     MLP, E. Malcolm to Mackenzie, Brant County, 28 June 1858; T. Tipton to Mackenzie, Oneida, 22 June 1858; John Kirk to Mackenzie, Caistor, 24 June 1858; Anon. to Mackenzie, Norwich, 24 June 1858.
76.     *Message*, 2 July 1858.
77.     *JLAC*, 1858, pp. 800, 816, 825.
78.     Prov. Can. Stat., 22 Vic., cap. 2.
79.     Currie, *Grand Trunk*, p. 91.
80.     Prov. Can. Stat., 20 Vic., cap. 111.
81.     *Message*, 1 May 1857.
82.     *Message*, 1 May 1857.
83.     *JLAC*, 1857, pp. 311-4.
84.     *Message*, 15 May 1857; *JLAC*, 1857, pp. 304-5, 404.
85.     See *supra*, Ch. 13, pp. 303-05.
86.     *JLAC*, 1853, p. 716; *JLAC*, 1857, p. 117; J. Davis Barnett, "An Election without Politics," *OHSPR* XIV (1916), 152-62.
87.     Currie, *Grand Trunk*, pp. 256-9.
88.     *JLAC*, 1857, p. 244.
89.     *Message*, 1 May 1857.
90.     MLP, J.A. Brown to Mackenzie, Dunnville, 20 April 1857; Richard Martin to Mackenzie, Cayuga, 20 April 1857.
91.     Buchanan Papers, Mackenzie to I. Buchanan, 16 Sept. 1857.
92.     Buchanan Papers, Mackenzie to I. Buchanan, 14 Nov. 1857.
93.     *Message*, 15 June 1858; Careless, *Brown* 1:210-1, 227-8.
94.     *JLAC*, 1857, App. 6.
95.     *Message*, 4 May 1857.
96.     Prov. Can. Stat., 22 Vic., cap. 118.
97.     *Message*, 12 June 1858.
98.     MLP, J.A. Martin to Mackenzie, 23 March, 20 June 1858.
99.     MLP, William Harcourt to Mackenzie, 24 April 1858.
100.    *JLAC*, 1858, pp. 954-7; *Message*, 24 Dec. 1858.
101.    Currie, *Grand Trunk*, pp. 200-1; *Message*, 6 Aug. 1858; J.J. Talman, "Development of the Railroad Network of South Western Ontario," *CHAR* (1953): 53-60.
102.    *JLAC*, 1857, p. 521.
103.    *JLAC*, 1857, pp. 84, 701; *Message*, 20 March, 20 Nov. 1857.
104.    *JLAC*, 1857, pp. 486-92.
105.    *JLAC*, 1857, p. 525.
106.    *JLAC*, 1857, pp. 518-9.
107.    *JLAC*, 1857, p. 670; Message, 12 June 1857.
108.    MC, Mackenzie to E.B. O'Callaghan, 8 April 1857.
109.    *Message*, 22 May 1857; *JLAC*, 1857, pp. 640-5.
110.    *JLAC*, 1857, p. 700.
111.    *Message*, 17 June 1857.

## Chapter XIX Notes

1.     *Message*, 21 May 1860; Bert Good Latzer, *Myrtleville, A Canadian Farm and Family* (Southern Illinois University Press, 1976), p. 65; MLP, J.W. Campbell to Mackenzie, 29 Aug. 1857.

2.      *Message*, 18 Sept., 27 Nov. 1857, 22 Jan. 1858.

3.      *Message*, 19 June 1857.

4.      *Message*, 17 July, 14 Aug. 1857; MLP, W.J. Reese to Mackenzie, 17 Sept. 1857; Rev. J. Strang to Mackenzie, Galt, 21 Sept. 1857.

5.      *Message*, 20, 27 Nov. 1857.

6.      MLP, W. Hamilton (Warden of Perth) to Mackenzie, 1857.

7.      MLP, G. Williams to Mackenzie, Dalhousie, 10 June 1856.

8.      J.W. Small to Mackenzie, Oneida, 29 Oct. 1857; Dr. J. Frazer to Mackenzie, Welland, 16 June, 26 Nov. 1857; S. Davidson to Mackenzie, 17 Dec. 1857.

9.      MLP, Samuel Darling to Mackenzie, 10 Dec. 1857; MC, Mackenzie to Jacob DeWitt, 2 Jan. 1858; *Message*, 5 Jan. 1858, quoting *Globe*.

10.    *Message*, 1 Jan. 1858.

11.    Grand River *Sachem*, 29 Dec. 1857.

12.    This bank was the International Bank at Cayuga. In 1863 the Legislature repealed its charter. MLP, Dr. J.J. Jarron to Mackenzie, 5 Dec. 1859; *JLAC*, 1863, pp. 109, 291.

13.    *Message*, 8, 15 Jan. 1858; *Macdonald Letters* 2:8; PAC, R.G. 5, B28, Election returns for Haldimand.

14.    *JLAC*, 1858, App. 28.

15.    MLP, T.J. Wiggins to Mackenzie, 9 Jan. 1858.

16.    *Message*, 18 Dec. 1857.

17.    Cornell, *Alignment*, p. 108. The two Upper Canada seats shown by Cornell as vacant had been won by Liberals. One of the members died. The election of the other was contested. New writs were issued and both seats went to Liberals.

18.    *Message*, 4 Dec. 1857.

19.    *JLAC*, 1858, App. 28.

20.    MLP, W. McDougall to Mackenzie, 7, 13 April 1858; G. Brown to Mackenzie, Telegram, 7 May 1858; John McWhimsie to Mackenzie, 27 April 1858.

21.    *JLAC*, 1858, p. 21.

22.    MLP, Mackenzie to Aemelius Irving, 16 Feb. 1858.

23.    *Message*, 27 Nov. 1857.

24.    *Message*, 26 March 1858.

25.    *Message*, 25 March 1858; Prov. Can. Stat., 19 and 20 Vic., cap. 41. This act had been designed for just such an emergency, but it had been carelessly worded in a way that permitted the Speaker to name a deputy for a temporary absence only when he was about to leave the chair. *JLAC*, 1856, p. 187.

26.    Garner, *Franchise*, p. 209; *Message*, 5 Feb. 1858.

27.    *Message*, 5 Feb., quoting the *Globe*.

28.    MC, Mackenzie to Jacob DeWitt, 21 Jan. 1856; Canadian Library Association microfilm, *Debates*, Feb. 25 1858.

29.    Garner, *Franchise*, p. 209; *Message*, 19 March 1858; *JLAC*, 1858, pp. 86-9.

30.    Garner, *Franchise*, p. 212.

31.    Prov. Can. Stat., 22 Vic., cap. 11.

32.    The new assessment act of 1851 had abolished the long-standing arbitrary valuation of £1 an acre for cultivated land, 4/- for wild land and had required that all land be assessed at its true value.

33.    Garner, *Franchise*, pp. 109-10; MLP, H. Bleeker to John Ross, Sidney, 30 April 1854.

34.    Prov. Can. Stat., 22 Vic., cap. 82; *Message*, 8, 29 Jan. 1858.

35.    *Message*, 13 Feb. 1857, 28 May 1858.

36.    *JLAC*, 1858, pp. 253-4, 766.

37.    *JLAC*, 1858, p. 167.

38.    *JLAC*, 1858, pp. 739-41; *Message*, 25 April 1858.

39.    *JLAC*, 1858, pp. 368-9, 471-2; Prov. Can. Stat., 22 Vic., cap. 18.

40.    *JLAC*, 1858, pp. 412-3.

41.    *Message*, 12 Feb., 14, 21 May, 6 Aug. 1858; *JLAC*, 1858, p. 916.

42.    *JLAC*, 1858, p. 923.

43.    *JLAC*, 1858, p. 501; Prov. Can. Stat., 22 Vic., cap. 3.

44.    *JLAC*, 1858, pp. 857, 897; *Message*, 12 March, 2, 16 July 1858.

45.    At least in Haldimand County. MLP, J.W. Small to Mackenzie, Selkirk, 16 Aug. 1858.

46.    MLP, Charles de Long to Mackenzie, Lobo, 7 Feb. 1858.

47.    Prov. Can. Stat., 20 Vic., cap. 57; *JLAC*, 1857, p. 369.

48.    Prov. Can. Stat., 22 Vic., caps. 10, 32; *Message*, 23 April 1858.

49.    *Message*, 19 March, 16 April 1858.

50.    *JLAC*, 1858, pp. 216, 255, 389, 392, 409, 499, 607.

51.    Prov. Can. Stat., 22 Vic., cap. 85.

52.    Prov. Can. Stat., 13 and 14 Vic., cap. 65; 22 Vic., cap. 52; 22 Vic., cap. 100.

53.    MLP, Lindsey section, James Mackenzie to Charles Lindsey, 11 Dec. 1885, quoting Mackenzie's letter; *Message*, 27 Aug. 1858; *JLAC*, 1858, pp. 124-5, 980-1.

54.    *JLAC*, 1858, pp. 865-75; Prov. Can. Stat., 22 Vic., caps. 52, 53.

55.    *JLAC*, 1857, App. 6.

56.    Currie, *Grand Trunk*, pp. 261-2; *JLAC*, 1857, p. 964.

57.    *Message*, 6 March 1857; H.Y. Hind et al., *Eighty Years Progress in British America* (Toronto, 1863), pp. 218-20; Stevens, *Railways*, pp. 261-2; Currie, *Grand Trunk*, pp. 389-96.

58.    Prov. Can. Stat., 22 Vic., cap. 117; *Message*, 2 Jan., 16 July 1858.

59.    *Repealers' Almanac*, col. 66.

60.    Donald Swainson, ed., *Mowat's Ontario* (Toronto, 1972), p. 46.

61.    *JLAC*, 1858, pp. 720-1, 748, 764, 810.

62.    *Message*, 19 March, 6 Aug. 1858; MLP, J. DeWitt to Mackenzie, 2 July 1858.

63.    *Globe*, 9 March 1858.

64.    *Message*, 12 March 1858.

65.    *Message*, 28 June, 2 July 1858; *JLAC*, 1858, pp. 742-50, 855-9, 898-900.

66.    *JLAC*, 1858, p. 898.

67.    JLAC, 1858, p. 121.

68.    *JLAC*, 1858, p. 122.

69.    *JLAC*, 1858, pp. 145, 486-7, 877-82.

70.    *JLAC*, 1858, pp. 641, 834-5; *Message*, 6 July 1858.

71.    *JLAC*, 1858, pp. 886-7.

72.    *Message*, 16 July 1858.

73.    *Message*, 2 April 1858.

74.    *JLAC*, 1858, pp. 886-7, 929-30; *Message*, 6 Aug. 1858.

75.    *JLAC*, 1858, p. 931.

76.    David B. Knight, *A Capital for Canada* (Chicago, 1977), pp. 241-53.

77.    *JLAC*, 1858, p. 893. In divisions which followed, the government had been sustained.

78.    *JLAC*, 1858, p. 841.

79.    *JLAC*, 1858, pp. 841-3.

80.    *Message*, 14 May 1858.

81.    *JLAC*, 1858, pp. 974-6.

82.    Mackenzie's comment in Montreal *Gazette*, 6 Aug. 1858.

83.    MC, Mackenzie to DeWitt, 27 Oct. 1858.

84.    *Message*, 26 Nov. 1858.

85.    MC, Mackenzie to DeWitt, 27 Oct. 1858.

86.    *Message*, 6 Aug. 1858.

87.    *JLAC*, 1858, pp. 935-7, 973-6.

88.    *JLAC*, 1858, p. 1038.

89.    *Message*, 5 June 1857.

90.    MC, Mackenzie to J. DeWitt, 28 May 1858.

91.    *JLAC*, 1858, pp. 506-16.

92.    MC, Mackenzie to DeWitt, 27 May 1858.

93.    MC, Mackenzie to DeWitt, 10 April 1858.

94.    *Message*, 21 May 1858.

95.    *Message*, 21 May 1858.

96.    MC, Mackenzie to J. DeWitt, 10 Aug. 1858.

97.    MLP, J. DeWitt to Mackenzie, 12 Aug. 1858.

98.    MLP, John Kirk to Mackenzie, Caistor, 14 Aug. 1858.

99.    *Message*, 27 Aug. 1858.

100.   MLP, M.L. Holmes to Mackenzie, 4 Oct. 1858.

101.   Toronto *Daily Colonist*, 1 Oct. 1858.

102.   Haldimand Historical Society, Mackenzie to James McIndoe, 26 Aug. 1858.

103.   *Message*, 26 Nov. 1858.

104. *Macdonald Letters* 2:180; *JLAC*, 1861, p. 137.
105. MLP, Joseph Papin to Mackenzie, Montreal, 23 Aug. 1858.
106. MLP, John Murray to Mackenzie, Oneida, 9 May 1858; Thos. Cowan to Mackenzie, 27 Sept. 1858; John Kirk to Mackenzie, Caistor, 28 May 1858.
107. *Message*, 25 July 1856.
108. MC, Mackenzie to DeWitt, 27 Oct. 1858.
109. MLP, Mackenzie to James, 23 Sept. 1858.

## Chapter XX Notes

1. MLP, James to Mackenzie, 15 Sept. 1858.
2. ORC, Mackenzie to O'Rielly, 14 July 1858.
3. MLP, M. Gould to Mackenzie, Caledon, 5 June 1858.
4. MC, Mackenzie to J. DeWitt, 10 Aug. 1858.
5. Young, *Public Men* 1:815; MLP, J.A. Gemmell to Mackenzie, Sarnia, 22 May 1858.
6. *Message*, 24 Dec. 1858; MC, George Robertson to Mackenzie, Alyth, Scotland, 1 April 1859; George Mackenzie to Mackenzie, Dundee, 1 April 1859.
7. See *supra*, p. 421; MLP, Mackenzie to James, 4 June 1858.
8. MLP, John Simpson to Mackenzie, Bowmanville, 14 June 1859.
9. MC, H. Greeley to G.J. Holyoak, 9 May 1859.
10. MLP, H. Greeley to Mackenzie, 14 May 1859.
11. MLP, John Mc. A. Cameron to Mackenzie, 30 May 1859.
12. Dent, *Story of the Rebellion* 2:325.
13. W.L. Mackenzie, *An Almanac for Independence and Freedom for the Year 1860* (Toronto, 1860), cols. 43-4; *Message*, 29 June 1859; Ford Collection, Mackenzie to David Bruce Jr., Toronto, 6 June 1859. (The Derby government had been defeated. The period of ministerial instability which followed was not one in which Mackenzie could expect to get any attention paid to his ideas about Upper Canada, more especially as there was war on the continent.)
14. *Message*, 2, 23 July 1859.
15. MLP, T.S. Brown to Mackenzie, Montreal, 27 April 1858.
16. MLP, J.B.E. Dorion to Mackenzie, 4 April 1859; Brown, "Sketch of Papineau."
17. *Message*, 23 July 1859.
18. See *supra*, pp. 128-29, 355.
19. *Message*, 13 Sept. 1859.
20. Harry N. Scheiber, *The Ohio Canal Era: A Study of Government and the Economy, 1820-61* (Athens, Ohio, 1969), pp. 110, 131, 192-3, 285-7.
21. Based on U.S. Census of 1860 and Census of Province of Canada, 1861; *JLAC*, 1863, Sess. Paper 10.
22. Ernest L. Bryant, "The Financial History of Ohio," *University of Illinois Studies in the Social Sciences* (Champaign-Urbana, 1912), 1:80-1.
23. *JLAC*, 1858, pp. 815-6.
24. Fred Landon, *Western Ontario and the American Frontier* (Toronto, 1941), pp. 245-6; Careless, *Brown* 1:295-9.
25. *Independence Almanac*, col. 26.
26. Craig Brown, comp., "Upper Canada Politics in 1850's," *Canadian Historical Readings* (Toronto, 1967), p. 24.
27. *Independence Almanac*, col. 52; Careless, *Brown* 1:317-23.
28. MLP, Lindsey section, J.A. Macdonald to Charles Lindsey, 12 Nov. 1858.
29. *Independence Almanac*, cols. 23-27.
30. Elwood H. Jones, "Ephemeral Compromise: The Great Reform Convention Revisited," *Journal of Canadian Studies*, III (1969): 21-8.
31. Brown, "Upper Canada Politics in the 1850's," p. 35.
32. Ibid., p. 36.
33. *Independence Almanac*, cols. 28-9.
34. Ibid., col. 35.
35. Hodgetts, *Pioneer Public Service*, p. 273.

36.     *Independence Almanac*, cols. 26-7, 32.

37.     *Independence Almanac*, col. 42.

38.     *Independence Almanac*, cols. 17-19.

39.     *Independence Almanac*, col. 42.

40.     See *supra*, pp. 266-67.

41.     *Independence Almanac*, cols. 1, 2, 44.

42.     MLP, Andrew Irving to Mackenzie, Pembroke, 2 Feb. 1860.

43.     Careless, *Brown* 1:302-3; M.H. Lewis, "A Reappraisal of George Sheppard's Contribution to the Press of North America," *OH* LXII (Sept. 1970): 179-88.

44.     Careless, *Brown* 1:321.

45.     *Independence Almanac*, cols. 27, 53.

46.     *Message*, 11 Feb. 1860, quoting Hamilton *Times*; *Message*, 14, 21 April 1860.

47.     *JLAC*, 1860, pp. 376-7.

48.     MLP, Andrew Irving to Mackenzie, 19 March 1860.

49.     *Message*, 19 March 1860.

50.     *Message*, 19 Nov. 1859; *Independence Almanac*, col. 46.

51.     Lindsey, *Life* 2:298; *Message*, 28 Jan. 1860.

52.     *Independence Almanac*, col. 46.

53.     MC, Mackenzie to J. DeWitt, 11 April, 26 May 1858; MLP, DeWitt to Mackenzie, 14 April, 21 July 1858.

54.     *Message*, 28 July, 6 Aug. 1859.

55.     *Message*, 11 Nov. 1859.

56.     *Message*, 11 Feb. 1860, 26 April 1858.

57.     On Montgomery see E.A. Lacey, "The Trials of John Montgomery," *OH* LII (1960): 141-58.

58.     *Message*, 21 April, 13 July 1860; *JLAC*, 1860, sess. paper 31.

59.     *Message*, 24 March, 16 June 1860; Franklin W. Ryan, *Usury and Usury Laws* (Boston, 1921), pp. 212-3.

60.     *Message*, 18 Feb. 1860; Edward Kellog, *Labour and Other Capital* (New York, 1849).

61.     *Message*, 14 April, 16 June 1860.

62.     *Message*, 30 June 1860.

63.     *Message*, 3 March 1860.

64.     *Message*, 10 Dec. 1859.

65.     Ronald Poulton, *The Paper Tyrant* (Toronto, 1971), pp. 17, 21, 32.

66.     MLP, Wm. McDougall to Mackenzie, 19 Jan. 1861; M.L. Ferguson to Mackenzie, 9 May 1861; G. Gibson to Mackenzie, 27 June 1861; M. Smith, S. Oxford, to Mackenzie, 24 June 1861.

67.     MC, J. Lesslie to Mackenzie, 12 March 1859; MC, Box 11, Receipt from E.H. Blake for cost of chancery suit; injunction obtained by Doel, 27 Jan. 1859; P. McGregor to Mackenzie, 12 March 1859.

68.     MC, Mackenzie to James, 22 June 1861.

69.     *Message*, 3 Dec. 1859.

70.     *Message*, 25 Dec. 1852.

71.     MLP, Hon. Alan Wilson to Mackenzie, 24 April 1860; John Rose to Edward Ellice, 20 April 1860, quoted in Creighton, *John A. Macdonald, The Young Politician*, p. 297.

72.     Creighton, *Macdonald*, p. 288.

73.     MLP, Letters to Mackenzie from D. Christie, 11 Sept. 1856; J. Malcolm, 13 Sept. 1856; James Jones, 25 Nov. 1856.

74.     MLP, D. Christie to Mackenzie, 11 Sept. 1856.

75.     Creighton, *Macdonald*, pp. 297-8; Canadian Library Association, microfilm, Parliamentary Debates, 7 May 1860.

76.     *Message*, 28 July 1860.

77.     *Message* 8 Aug. 1860.

78.     *Message*, 1 Sept. 1860.

79.     *Message*, 1 Sept. 1860.

80.     *Message*, 21 July, 1 Sept. 1860.

81.     *Message*, 28 July 1860.

82.     John Mardineau, *The Life of Henry Pelham, Fifth Duke of Newcastle* (London, 1908).

83.     Careless, *Brown* 2:105.
84.     MLP, William Mackenzie to his father, — March 1858.
85.     MLP, Lindsey Section, Henry Smith to Charles Lindsey, 20 Feb., 21 March 1860.
86.     MC, Mackenzie to James, 22 June 1861.
87.     MC, James Mackenzie to Charles Lindsey, 2 Nov. 1862.
88.     MC, W.L. Mackenzie Jr. to Master Charles Lindsey, 21 April, misdated 1861 instead of 1862.
89.     MLP, Lindsey Section, James Mackenzie to Charles Lindsey, Lima, Ohio, 13 June 1863; USNA, copy of discharge papers of William L. Mackenzie Jr.
90.     MC, Mackenzie to Dr. John Kirk, 10 Jan. 1861.
91.     MLP, Lindsey Section, Mackenzie to Amos Wright, 28 March 1861.
92.     MLP, Mackenzie to James, 22 June 1861.
93.     Ibid.
94.     MC, George Brown to Mackenzie, 29 May 1861.
95.     Lindsey, *Life* 2:299.
96.     Toronto *Globe*, 3 Sept. 1861.
97.     Albany *Evening Journal*, 2 Sept. 1861; Lindsey, *Life* 2:299.

## Chapter XXI Notes

1.      Lindsey, *Mackenzie*, Ch. 16.
2.      King, *Other Side* (Toronto, 1886); MLP, Lindsey Section, James Mackenzie to C.G.S. Lindsey, 7 Dec. 1885.
3.      LeSueur Papers, Morang to D. LeSueur, 6 May 1908.
4.      LeSueur Papers, W.D. LeSueur to Morang, 14 July 1907.
5.      LeSueur Papers, Morang to LeSueur, 5 Sept. 1907; LeSueur to Morang, 11 May 1908.
6.      LeSueur Papers, LeSueur to Morang, 11 May 1908.
7.      McKillop, LeSueur's *Mackenzie*, p. xxiv.
8.      LeSueur Papers, LeSueur to Morang, 23 March 1908.
9.      Gates, "Decided Policy of Mackenzie."
10.     LeSueur Papers, LeSueur to Morang, 10 June 1907.
11.     Toronto *Globe*, 29 Aug. 1861.
12.     David Flint, *William Lyon Mackenzie: A Rebel Against Authority* (Toronto, 1971); Rick Salutin, *1837: William Lyon Mackenzie and the Canadian Revolution* (Toronto, 1976); Colin Read and R.J. Stagg, *The Rebellion of 1837 in Upper Canada* (The Champlain Society, Toronto, 1985).
13.     Kilbourn, *Firebrand*, p. 125.
14.     Rea, "Mackenzie — Jacksonian?", pp. 223-35.
15.     William Morrison, "William Lyon Mackenzie: His Contribution to the Canadian Political Tradition," *Wentworth Bygones*, No. 6, 1965.
16.     Armstrong, "Reformer as Capitalist," 187-96; "William Lyon Mackenzie: The Persistent Hero," *JCS* (Aug. 1971): 21-36; "Critic in Power," 309- 31.
17.     Romney, "Mackenzie as Mayor of Toronto," 416-36.
18.     Anthony W. Rasporitch, *William Lyon Mackenzie*, Canadian History Through the Press series (Toronto, 1972).
19.     LeSueur, *Mackenzie*, p. 389; Armstrong and Stagg, article in *Dictionary of Canadian Biography*, pp. 496-510 vol. 9, on Mackenzie; Kilbourn, *Firebrand*, p. 216; Read, *Rising*, p. 211.
20.     McKillop, LeSueur's *Mackenzie*, Introduction, pp. xvi-xviii.
21.     Toronto *Globe*, 29 Aug. 1861.
22.     *Quarterly Anti-Slavery Magazine* II (1836-7): 350-1. A similar but more detailed statement of his views was made in a letter to the *Examiner* shortly before his return to Canada (Rasporich, *Mackenzie*, p. 13).
23.     MLP, Mackenzie to James, 12 July 1845.
24.     Gates, "Decided Policy."
25.     See *supra*, Ch. 18, p. 469.
26.     Rasporich, *Mackenzie*, p. 14, n. 32.
27.     Michael Cross, "The Dark Druidical Groves," Ph.D. thesis, University of Toronto, 1968.

28.      Lindsey, *Life* 1:56.
29.      Gates, "Decided Policy of Mackenzie"; *Constitution*, 1 Feb. 1837; *Message*, 2 July 1859. See *supra*, Ch. 19, p. 492.
30.      Skelton, *Galt*, p. 47.
31.      Aileen Dunham, *Political Unrest in Upper Canada, 1815-36* (Published for the Royal Colonial Institute, Imperial Studies No. 1, London, 1927), p. 137.
32.      See *supra*, Ch. 10, p. 232.
33.      MLP, D. D'Everardo to Mackenzie, July 2 1851.
34.      Rasporich, *Mackenzie*, p. 12.
35.      *Message*, Feb. 22 1856, 24 Dec. 1858 quoted in Rasporich, *Mackenzie*, pp. 144-6.
36.      Rasporich, *Mackenzie*, p. 12; Bernard J. Harrington, *Life of Sir William Logan, Kt.* (London, 1883), pp. 124, 263-5; *Message*, 4 June 1858.
37.      Rasporich, *Mackenzie*, p. 11; *Message*, 24 Dec. 1858, cited by Rasporich, *Mackenzie*, p. 145. See *supra*, Ch. 20, pp. 503-04.
38.      *JLAC*, 1852-3, p. 1037; see *supra*, Ch. 14, p. 354.
39      See *supra*, Ch. 8, p. 189.
40.      See *supra*, CH. 8, p. 189, Ch. 14, p. 334.
41.      Rasporich, *Mackenzie*, p. 12.
42.      Gates, "Decided Policy."
43.      OCP, Mackenzie to O'Callaghan, 6 March 1847.
44.      McKillop, LeSueur's *Mackenzie*, p. 41.
45.      *Message*, 5 June 1857.
46.      *Message*, 28 Dec. 1858, quoting *Globe*.
47.      Craig, *Upper Canada*, p. 210.
48.      Glyndon G. Van Duesen, *Horace Greeley* (Philadelphia, 1958), p. 128.
49.      Henry Luther Stoddart, *Horace Greeley* (New York, 1946), p. 289.
50.      See *supra*, Ch. 13, pp. 287-8.
51.      OCP, T.S. Brown to E. O'Callaghan, 7 March 1844.
52.      MLP, Mackenzie to James, 27 Jan. 1848.
53.      *Message*, 24 Dec. 1858.
54.      MLP, James to Mackenzie, 29 July 1857.
55.      Charles Israel, *Reminiscences of the Rebellion of 1837* (Toronto, 1898), p. 265.
56.      MLP, Lindsey Section, Francis Hincks to Charles Lindsey, 27 April 1875.
57.      Quebec *Gazette*, 16 Oct. 1856.
58.      Dent, *Story* 2:308-9; David Flint, *William Lyon Mackenzie: Rebel Against Authority* (Toronto, 1971), p. 181.
59.      See *supra*, Ch. 12, p. 270.
60.      Lindsey, *Mackenzie*, pp. 505-6.
61.      MLP, Henry O'Rielly to Mackenzie, 20 Dec. 1849.
62.      Lindsey, *Life* 2:299.
63.      McKillop, LeSueur's *Mackenzie*, p. 114.
64.      *Colonial Advocate*, 8 June 1828.
65.      Neilson Papers, Mackenzie to John Neilson, 27 Nov. 1825; *Message*, 5 March 1858.
66.      William Smith, *Political Leaders of Upper Canada* (Toronto, 1931), p. 114.
67.      *Message*, 30 April 1858.
68.      MLP, Mackenzie to James Lesslie, 15 May 1846; Mackenzie to James, 5 March 1847; MC, Mackenzie to John Neilson, 25 Feb. 1847.
69.      Mackenzie, *Life of Van Buren*, p. 288.
70.      *JLAC*, 1851, pp. 140, 202.
71.      *Message*, 18 May 1858.
72.      Toronto *Examiner*, 12 Dec. 1858.
73.      *Message*, 26 Sept. 1856.
74.      *Message*, 13 March 1855, 7 March 1857; New York *Tribune*, 9 Oct. 1855; *Message*, 7 May 1855.
75.      MC, Mackenzie to W. Smith O'Brien, 20 April 1858.
76.      *Message*, 27 June 1855.
77.      *Message*, 30 April 1858.
78.      *Independence Almanac*, col. 30.

79.     Careless, *Brown* 2:47.
80.     Rasporich, *Mackenzie*, p. 11.
81.     MLP, Lindsey Section, an unidentified newspaper clipping, n.d. I have found no reference to an income tax in the Journals.
82.     ORP, Mackenzie to O'Rielly, 27 March 1844.
83.     OCP, L.J. Papineau to E.B. O'Callaghan, 22 Nov. 1844.
84.     MLP, E.B. O'Callaghan to Mackenzie, 12 Nov. 1844.
85.     McKillop, LeSueur's *Mackenzie*, p. 190.
86.     MLP, Lesslie to Mackenzie, 20 Oct. 1852; Rumilly, *Papineau* 1:369.
87.     Toronto *Leader*, 4 Oct. 1856.
88.     *L'Avenir*, 18 Dec. 1853.
89.     Can. Parl. Debates, 7 May 1855.
90.     P.B. Waite, "A Nova-Scotian in Toronto," *OH* LV (1963): 155-9.
91.     R.B. Nelles, *Haldimand*, p. 57.
92.     LeSueur Papers, LeSueur to Morang, 30 April 1908.
93.     Head, *Narrative*, p. 3.
94.     Dent, *Story* 2:14.
95.     McKillop, LeSueur's *Mackenzie*, p. xxiv.
96.     Dent, *Story* 2:21-2.
97.     See *supra*, Ch. 15, p. 369; Ch. 14, p. 315.
98.     McKillop, LeSueur's *Mackenzie*, p. xxvi.
99.     Rick Salutin, *1837*, p. 88.
100.    Armstrong and Stabb article on Mackenzie in *Dictionary of Canadian Biography* 9:508.
101.    Referring to Lt.-Gov. Head and his civil secretary John Joseph, Mackenzie ended an article, "O but what we lose in Christians (from Cholera) we gain in Jews." *Constitution*, 26 July 1837, cited by Armstrong in *Journal of Canadian Studies* (1971), 21-36; Ged Martin, "Sir Francis Head: The Private Side of a Lieutenant-Governor," *OH* LXXIII (1981), 145-70.
102.    Salutin, *1837*, p. 179.
103.    Robin W. Winks, *The Blacks in Canada: A History* (Montreal, 1971), p. 151; Ged Martin, "British Officials and their Attitude to the Negro Community," *OH* LXVI (1974), 79-88.
104.    See *supra*, Ch. 5, pp. 122-23.
105.    MLP, numerous letters to Mackenzie, July 7-30 1851.
106.    Prov. Can.,*Debates*, 1851, pp. 196, 226.
107.    *Message*, 15 May 1853.
108.    Prov. Can., 13 and 14 Vic., cap. 74, sec. 3.
109.    Prov. Can., *Debates*, 1851, pp. 1184, 1643.
110.    See *supra*, Ch. 18, p. 462.
111.    Armstrong, "Reformer as Capitalist"; Sally Zerker, "George Brown and the Printers Union," *JCS* X (1975): 42-48.
112.    Masters, *Toronto*, pp. 45-46; OA, Mechanics Institute of Toronto, Annual Reports; F.H. Armstrong, "The Persistent Hero," *JCS* VI, pp. 21-36.
113.    Armstrong and Stabb article on Mackenzie in *Dictionary of Canadian Biography* 9:508.
114.    MLP, H. O'Rielly to Mackenzie, 1 March 1848.
115.    OCP, H. O'Rielly to E.B. O'Callaghan, 28 Sept. 1845.
116.    Kilbourn, *Firebrand*, p. 126; Dent, *Story* 2:326-27.
117.    Stoddart, *Greeley*, p. 83.
118.    "'It was not lunacy,' said Choate [Greeley's physician]. 'It was an exhausted brain that could return to normalcy ... it did not.'" (Stoddart, *Greeley*, p. 220) Dr. James Richardson, Mackenzie's physician, also declared, "No doubt of W.L. Mackenzie's sanity can be entertained for one moment..." (MLP, Dr. Richardson to Charles Lindsey, 7 Nov. 1877).

# SOURCES

There are two groups of Mackenzie papers. The one in the Archives of Ontario, owned by the late Col. C.B. Lindsey, has been referred to as the Mackenzie-Lindsey Papers; the one in the Public Archives of Canada has been referred to as the Mackenzie Collection.

There are also two groups of O'Rielly papers. The one in the Rochester Public Library has been referred to as the O'Rielly Papers; the one in the New York Historical Society has been referred to as the O'Rielly Collection. O'Rielly's name has been spelled as he preferred it to be.

When letters between W.L. Mackenzie and his son James are cited, the son's surname has been omitted.

## ABBREVIATIONS

| | |
|---|---|
| AHA | American Historical Association |
| *AHR* | *American Historical Association Review* |
| AO | Archives of Ontario |
| BHS | Buffalo Historical Society |
| *CHAR* | *Canadian Historical Association Reports* |
| *CHR* | *Canadian Historical Review* |
| DHS | Detroit Historical Society |
| *JCS* | *Journal of Canadian Studies* |
| *JLAC* | *Journal of the Legislative Assembly of [United] Canada* |
| *JLCC* | *Journal of the Legislative Council of [United] Canada* |
| *JLAUC* | *Journal of the Legislative Assembly of Upper Canada* |
| *JLCUC* | *Journal of the Legislative Council of Upper Canada* |
| LC | Library of Congress |
| MC | Mackenzie Collection (in PAC) |
| *MG* | *Mackenzie's Gazette* |
| MLP | Mackenzie-Lindsey Papers (in AO) |
| MTL | Metropolitan Toronto Library |
| NYHS | New York Historical Society |
| NYPL | New York Public Library |
| NYSL | New York State Library |
| OCP | O'Callaghan Papers |
| *OH* | *Ontario History* |
| OHSPR | Ontario Historical Society, Papers and Records |
| ORC | O'Rielly Collection (in NYHS) |
| ORP | O'Rielly Papers (in RPL) |
| PAC | Public Archives of Canada |
| PAQ | Public Archives of Quebec |
| PHS | Pennsylvania Historical Society |
| RPL | Rochester Public Library |
| UNCL | University of North Carolina Library |
| USNA | United States National Archives |
| WHS | Wisconsin Historical Society |

# PRIMARY MATERIALS

Arthur Papers (a small collection in MTL, not included in those published).
Baldwin Papers, in MTL.
Bancroft Papers, in NYHS.
Barker, J.A., Papers, in BHS.
Bidwell Papers, in AO.
Bolton, George, Papers, in MTL.
Bourke, Edward, Papers, in LC.
Brodeur's Transcripts, in PAC.
Brown Papers, in PAC.
Buchanan Papers, in PAC.
Buell Papers, in PAC.
Burton, C.M., Papers, in DHS.
Burwell-Glenny Diaries, in BHS.
Butler, B.F., Papers, in Princeton University Library.
Clarke Papers, in AO.
Colborne Papers, photocopies in PAC.
Corning, E., Papers, in Albany Institute.
Crittenden Papers, in LC.
Croswell, E., Papers, in NYHS.
Cushing Papers, in LC.
Flagg, A.C., Papers, in NYPL and Columbia University Library.
Ford Collection, in NYPL.
Granger, F., Papers, in NYHS.
Graham, C.H., Papers, in PAC.
Gratz Collection, in PHS.
Green, D., Papers, in UNCL.
Hincks Papers, in PAC.
Lafontaine Papers, in PAC.
Larned Papers, in DHS.
LeSueur Papers, in AO.
Lindsey, Charles, Papers, in AO (these contain letters and also drafts of articles, some of which contain
    citations from letters not now extant, so far as is known).
Macdonald, J.S. Langlois, Papers, in PAC.
Mackenzie, W.L., Clippings (numbered envelopes of newspaper clippings, name and date not always
    preserved on clippings, in AO, which has a topical index to them).
Mackenzie-Lindsey Papers, in AO. Cited as MLP.
Mackenzie, W.L., Collection of Papers, in PAC. Cited as MC.
Mackenzie, Alexander, Papers, in PAC.
MacNab, A.N., Papers, in AO.
Marcy, W.L., Papers, in LC, and also in NYHS.
Merritt, W.H., Papers, in PAC.
Neilson, J., Papers, in PAC.
Nelson, R., letters in Brodeur's transcripts and in PAQ.
O'Callaghan, E.B., Papers, in LC and PAC. Cited as OCP.
O'Rielly, H., Papers: in RPL cited as O'Rielly Papers (ORP); in NYHS cited as O'Rielly Collection
    (ORC).
O'Rielly Letter Books, in NYHS.
Papineau, L.J., Letters in PAQ (but see comment Ch.1, n.155).
Patchin Family Papers, in DHS.
Perrault, L., Papers, in WHS.
Poinsett, J., Papers, in PHS.
Polk Papers in LC.
Porter, P.A., Papers, in BHS.
Rolph, J., Papers, in PAC.
Sandom Collection, in MTL.
Seward, W., Papers, in University of Rochester Library.
Shenston, T., Papers, in AO.
Taylor, J.W., Papers, in NYHS.
Weed, T., Papers, in NYHS and Rochester University Library.
Van Buren, M., Papers, in LC. Cited as VBP.

Whelan Papers, in DHS.
Woodbury, L., Papers, in LC.
Wool, J.E., Papers, in NYSL.
Wright, S., Papers, in St. Lawrence University Library.
Wright-Butler Papers, in NYPL.
Various official letters in AO, PAC and USNA.

## SECONDARY MATERIAL

### Articles

ABELLA, IRVING MARTIN. "The Sydenham Election of 1841." *CHR* XLVII (1966): 326-43.
AITCHISON, J.A. "The Municipal Corporation Act of 1849." *CHR* XXX (1949): 107-22.
————. "The Court of Requests." *OH* XLI (1949): 125-32.
*AMERICAN HERITAGE*. "The Life and Death of a Great Newspaper," Oct. 1967.
ALEXANDER, EDWARD P. "The Hunters' Lodges of 1839." *Proceedings of the New York Historical Association* XXXVI (1938): 64-69.
ARMSTRONG, F.H. "Reformer as Capitalist: William Lyon Mackenzie and the Printers' Strike of 1836."*OH* LIX (1967): 186-96.
————. "William Lyon Mackenzie, First Mayor of Toronto: A Study of a Critic in Power." *CHR* XLVIII (1967): 309-31.
————. "William Lyon Mackenzie: The Persistent Hero." *JCS* (Peterboro, Ont.) VI, 1971 21-36.
BAILLARGEON, GEORGES. "La tenure seigneuriale a-t-elle été abolie par suite des plaintes des censitaires?" *Revue d'histoire de l'Amérique française {aise* XXI, 64-80.
BARNETT, J. DAVIS. "An Election Without Politics." *OHSPR* XIV(1916): 152-62.
BOUCHER, C.S. and R.B. BROOKE, eds. "Correspondence Addressed to John C. Calhoun, 1837-1849." AHA *Annual Report* 1929, 125-533.
BROOK, MICHAEL. "Lawrence Pitkethly, Dr. Smyles and Canadian Revolutionaries in the United States, 1842." *OH* LVII (1965): 79-84.
BROWN, THOMAS STORROW. "A Brief Sketch of the Life and Times of the Late Louis Joseph Papineau." *Dominion Monthly*, Jan. 1872,3-20. ["Papineau"].
BROWNSON, ORESTES. "Democracy and Reform." *Boston Quarterly Review* 11 (Oct. 1839): 478-517.
COVENTRY, GEORGE. "A Concise History of the Late Rebellion in Upper Canada to the Evacuation of Navy Island." *OHSPR* XVII (1919): 116-74. ["Concise History"].
CRUIKSHANK, E.A. "The Invasion of Navy Island, 1837-1838." *OHSPR* XXXI (1936): 7-34.
————. "The Insurrection in the Short Hills." *OHSPR* VII (1907): 5-23, and *OHSPR* XXIII (1926): 180-222.
DUFF, LOUISE BLAKE. "Samuel Chandler of St. John's." Welland County Historical Society *Papers and Records* V (1938): 115-119.
FITZPATRICK, JOHN C., ed. "The Autobiography of Martin Van Buren." AHA *Annual Report* 1918, vol. 2.
GATES, LILLIAN F. "The Decided Policy of William Lyon Mackenzie." *CHR* XL (1959): 165-208. ["Decided Policy"].
————. "A Note on Dr. John Smyles." *OH* LVII (1965): 229-30.
————. "A Canadian Rebel's Appeal to George Bancroft." *New England Quarterly* XLI (1968): 96-104.
HILL, ROBERT A. "A Note on Newspaper Patronage in Canada During the Late 1850s and Early 1860." *CHR* XLIX (1968): 44-50.
JACKSON, ERIC. "The Organization of the Upper Canada Reformers, 1818-1867." *OH* LIII (1961): 95-115.
JONES, EDWARD and DOUGLAS McCALLA. "Toronto Waterworks, 1840-1877." *CHR* LX (1979): 300-23.
JONES, ELWOOD H. "Ephemeral Compromise: The Great Reform Convention Revisited." *JCS* III (1969): 21-28.
JONES, GEORGE M. "The Peter Perry Election and the Rise of the Clear Grit Party." *OHSPR* XII (1914): 164-75.
LACEY, E.A. "The Trials of John Montgomery." *OH* LII (1960): 141-58.
LANDON, FRED. "The Democratic Uprising of 1837, and Some of Its Consequences." Royal Society of Canada *Transactions*, 3rd series, XXV (1911), section 2, 89-98.
LEIGHTON, DOUGLAS. "The Compact Tory and Bureaucrat: Samuel Peter Jarvis and the Indian Department." *OH* LXII (1981): 40-53.

LEWIS, M.H. "A Reappraisal of George Sheppard's Contribution to the Press of North America." *OH* LXII (1970): 179-88.

MANNING, HELEN TAFT. "Who Ran the British Empire, 1830-1850?" *Journal of British Studies* V (1965): 88-121.

MARTIN, GED. "British Officials and Their Attitude to the Negro Community." *OH* LXVI (1974): 79-88.

———. "Sir Francis Bond Head: The Private Life of a Lieutenant Governor." OH LXIII (1981): 145-70.

MOIR, JOHN S. "Mr. Mackenzie's Secret Reporter." *OH* LV (1963): 205-13.

MONET, JACQUES. "French Canadian Nationalism and the Challenge of Ultramontanism." *CHAR* 1966, 41-55.

MORRISON, WILLIAM. "William Lyon Mackenzie: His Contribution to the Canadian Political Tradition." *Wentworth Bygones*, Nov. 1965.

MUGGERIDGE, JOHN. "John Rolph, A Reluctant Rebel." *OH* LI (1959): 217-29.

MUSHUM, H.A. "Early Great Lakes Steamboats: The Battle of the Windmill and After." *American Neptune* VIII (1945): 37-60.

NORTHMAN, JOHN [pseud.]. "Pirate of the Thousand Islands." Typed MS in Jefferson County Museum, Watertown, N.Y. ca. Feb. 1838.["Pirate"]

ORMSBY, W.C. "The Civil List Question in the Province of Canada." *CHR* XXXI (1950): 93-118.

———. "Sir Charles Metcalfe and the Canadian Union," CHAR (1961): 35-41.

PERKINS, DEXTER. "Henry O'Reilly." Rochester Historical Society *Publications* VIII, 1-24.

PIERCE, RICHARD A. "Niels Von Schoultz." *Historic Kingston* XXXI (1970): 56-65.

———. "Political Corruption." *The American Review* III (1946): 45-54.

REA, J.E. "William Lyon Mackenzie — Jacksonian?" *Mid-America* L (1968): 223-35.

READ, COLIN. "The Short Hills Raid of June, 1838, and Its Aftermath." *OH* LXVIII (1967): 93-109. ["Short Hills"]

REZNICK, SAMUEL. "The Social History of an American Depression." *AHR* XL (1934-5): 662-87.

RIDDELL, WILLIAM RENWICK. "A Patriot General." *Canadian Magazine* XLIV (1914-15): 32-36.

———. "Another Patriot General." *Canadian Magazine* XLVII (1916): 218-22.

ROMNEY, PAUL. "William Lyon Mackenzie as Mayor of Toronto." *CHR* LVI (1975): 416-36.

SHORTRIDGE, W. SHERMAN. "The Canadian-American Frontier During the Rebellion of 1837-1838." *CHR* VII (1926): 13-26.

SPENCER, J.V. "William M. Marcy Goes Conservative." *Mississippi Valley Historical Review* XXXI, no.2 (1944): 205-24.

SPURR, JOHN W. "The Night of the Fire." *Historic Kingston* XXXIV (1969): 57-65.

STORY, NORAH. "Stewart Derbyshire's Report to Lord Durham on Lower Canada, 1838." *CHR* XVIII (1937): 48-62.

TALMAN, J.J. "Development of the Railroad Network of South Western Ontario." *CHAR* 1953, 53-60.

TIFFANY, ORIN EDWARD. "The Relations of the United States to the Canadian Rebellion of 1837-1838." Buffalo Historical Society *Publications* VIII (1905): 3-114.

UNDERHILL, F.A. "Some Reflections on the Liberal Tradition in Canada." *CHAR* 1946, 5-17.

WAITE, P.R. "A Nova Scotian in Toronto." *OH* LV (1963): 155-59.

WALKER, FRANK W. "Birth of the Buffalo and Brantford Railway." *OH* XVII (1954): 81-90.

WATERBURY, EDWIN M. "Bill Johnson, Patriot or Pirate?" *Oswego Historical Quarterly* Eleventh Publication (1949): 108-68. ["Bill Johnson"]

———. "Oswego County During the Patriot War." O*swego Historical Quarterly* Eighth Publication (1944): 11-241.

WATT, R.C. "The Case of Alexander McLeod." *English Historical Review* (1926): 528-55.

WHITELAW, WILLIAM MENZIES. "Responsible Government and the Responsible Governor." *CHR* XIII (1932): 364-86.

ZERKER, SALLY. "George Brown and the Printers Union." *JCS* X (1975): 42-48.

## SELECTED BOOKS AND MEMOIRS

ALEXANDER, Dr. ALVA STANWOOD. *A Political History of the State of New York.* 2 vols. New York, 1906.

ALLIN, CEPHAS DANIEL, and GEORGE M. JONES. *Annexation, Preferential Trade and Reciprocity.* Toronto, 1912.

BARB, OLIVER E., ed. *Report of Causes Argued and Determinied in the Court of Chancery of the State of New York.* Vol. 3. New York, 1859.

BELLASIS, MARGARET. *"Rise, Canadians!"* London, 1955.

BERNARD, JEAN-PAUL. *Les Rouges.* Montreal, 1971.

BIERCE, LUCIUS VERUS. *Historical Reminiscences of Summit County, Ohio*. Akron, Ohio, 1852.
BILLINGTON, RAY ALLEN. *The Protestant Crusade*. New York, 1938.
BLEYER, WILLIAM GARRISON. *Main Currents in American Journalism*. Cambridge, Mass., 1927.
BONNEY, CATHARINE V[an] R[ensselaer]. *A Legacy of Historical Gleanings*. 2 vols. 2nd ed. Albany, 1875.
BONNYCASTLE, Sir RICHARD HENRY. *The Canadas in 1841*. London, 1841.
———. *Canada and the Canadians in 1846*. London, 1846.
———. *Canada As It Was, Is and May Be. With Considerable Additions, and an Account of Recent Transactions by Sir James Edward Alexander*. 2 vols. London, 1852.
BOYCE, GERALD E. *Historic Hastings*. Belleville, Ont., 1967.
BRECKENRIDGE, ROELIFF MORTON. *The Canadian Banking System, 1817-1840*. Toronto, 1894.
BROWN, Craig, comp. "Upper Canada Politics in the 1850's." In *Canadian Historical Readings*. University of Toronto Press, 1967.
BROWN, STEWART GERRY, ed. *The Autobiography of James Monroe*. Syracuse, 1959.
BROWN, THOMAS STORROW. *1837: My Connection With It*. Quebec, 1898. [*1837*]
BUTLER, WILLIAM ALLEN. *The Revision of the Statutes of the State of New York and the Revisers*. New York, 1889.
CARELESS, J.M.S. *Brown of the Globe*. 2 vols. Toronto, 1959.
———. The *Union of the Canadas*. Toronto, 1967.
CHADDOCK, ROBERT E. *The Safety Fund Banking System in New York, 1828-1866*. Government Printing Office: Washington, 1910.
CHANCELLOR, WILLIAM ESTERBROOK. *A Life of Silas Wright, 1795-1847*. New York, 1913.
CHAPIN, GARDINER M. *Tales of the St. Lawrence*. Rouse's Point, N.Y., 1873.
CHITWOOD, OLIVER PERRY. *John Tyler, Champion of the South*. New York, 1939.
CHRISTIE, ROBERT. *A History of the Late Province of Lower Canada*. 6 vols. Montreal, 1866.
CHRISTMAN, HENRY. *Tin Horns and Calico:A Decisive History in the Emergence of Democracy*. New York, 1945.
CHURCHILL, J.L. *Landmarks of Oswego County*. Syracuse, 1895.
CLARK, SAMUEL DELBERT. *Movements of Political Protest in Canada, 1640-1840*. Toronto, 1959.
CLARKE, CHARLES. *Sixty Years in Upper Canada*. Toronto, 1908.
COREY, ALBERT B. *The Crisis of 1830-42 in Canadian American Relations*. New Haven, 1941.
CORNELL, PAUL G. *The Alignment of Political Groups in Canada,1841-1867*. Toronto, 1962.
CRAIG, GERALD M. *Upper Canada: The Formative Years, 1784-1841*. New York, 1963.
CREIGHTON, DONALD GRANT. *John A. Macdonald, The Young Politician*. Boston, 1952.
———. *British North America at Confederation: A Study Prepared for the Royal Commission on Dominion Provincial Relations*. Ottawa, 1963.
CROSS, MICHAEL. "The Dark Druidical Groves: The Lumber Community and the Commercial Frontier of British North America." Ph.D. diss., University of Toronto, 1968.
CURRIE, ARCHIBALD WILLIAM. *The Grand Trunk Railway of Canada*. Toronto, 1957.
CURTIS, JAMES C. *The Fox at Bay: Martin Van Buren and the Presidency, 1837- 41*. Lexington, Ky., 1970.
DENT, JOHN CHARLES. *The Last Forty Years*. 2 vols. Toronto, 1881.
———. The *Story of the Upper Canada Rebellion*. 2 vols. Toronto, 1885.
DIX, MORGAN. *Memoirs of John Adams Dix*. 2 vols. New York, 1883.
DONOVAN, HERBERT D.A. *The Barn Burners*. New York, 1925.
DOUGHERTY, J. HAMPDEN. *A Constitutional History of the State of New York*. 2nd. ed. New York, 1915.
DOUGHTY, Sir ARTHUR G. *The Elgin-Grey Papers*. 4 vols. Ottawa, 1937.
———, and NORAH STORY, eds. *Documents Relating to the Constitutional History of Canada 1819-1828*. Ottawa, 1935.
DOUGLAS, ALAN. *John Prince: A Collection of Documents*. The Champlain Society, Ontario Series XI. Toronto, 1980.
DRISCOLL, WILLIAM DENNIS. "Benjamin Franklin Butler, Lawyer and Regency Politician." Ph.D. diss., Fordham, 1965.
DUANE, WILLIAM J. *Narrative and Correspondence Concerning the Record of the Deposits*. Philadelphia, 1938.
DUNCOMBE, CHARLES. *Free Banking: An Essay on Banking, Currency, Finance, Exchange and Political Economy*. Cleveland, 1841.
DUNHAM, AILEEN. *Political Unrest in Upper Canada, 1815-36*. Published for the Royal Colonial Institute, Imperial Studies No. 1. London, 1927.
DUNHAM, MABEL. *The Grand River*. Toronto, 1945.
DURAND, CHARLES. *Reminiscences of the Rebellion of 1837*. Toronto, 1898.

EDGAR, R.J. *Bishop Alexander Macdonnell and the Politics of Upper Canada.* Toronto, 1974. [*Macdonnell*]

ELLIOTT, CHARLES WINSTON. *Winfield Scott, The Soldier and the Man.* 2 vols. New York, 1937.

ELLIS, DAVID MALDWYN. *A History of New York State.* Rev. ed. Ithaca, N.Y., 1967.

———. *Landlords and Farmers in the Hudson Mohawk Region, 1790-1850.* Ithaca, N.Y., 1946.

ERMATINGER, C.O. *The Talbot Regime.* St. Thomas, 1904.

FAUTEUX, AEGIDIUS. *Patriotes de 1837-8.* Montréal, 1950.

FINLEY, JOHN L. *The North Atlantic Triangle.* Toronto, 1975.

FIRTH, EDITH, ed. *Early Toronto Newspapers.* Toronto, 1961.

FLINT, DAVID. *William Lyon Mackenzie: A Rebel Against Authority.* Toronto, 1971.

FUESS, CLAUDE. *The Life of Caleb Cushing.* 2 vols. New York, 1923.

GALBRAITH, JOHN S. *The Hudson's Bay Company.* Los Angeles, 1957.

GARNEAU, FRANÇOIS XAVIER. *A History of Canada from the Time of Its Discovery Till the Union Years, 1840-41.* Trans. Andrew Bell. Montreal, vol.1 1862, vol.2 1866.

GARNER, JOHN. *The Franchise and Politics in British North America.* Toronto, 1969.

GARRATY, JOHN ARTHUR. *Silas Wright.* New York, 1949.

GATES, LILLIAN FRANCIS. *The Land Policies of Upper Canada.* Toronto, 1968.

GILLET, RANSOM H. *The Life and Times of Silas Wright.* 2 vols. Albany, N.Y., 1874.

GLAZEBROOK, G. de T. *Sir Charles Bagot in Canada.* Oxford, 1929.

GOODWIN, CRAWFORD D.W. *Canadian Economic Thought.* Durham, N.C., 1961.

GRISWOLD, EDWIN M. *Law and Lawyers in the United States.* Cambridge, Mass., 1965.

GRUND, FRANCIS I. *Aristocracy in America.* London, 1839.

GUILLET, EDWIN C. *The Life and Times of the Patriots.* Toronto, 1938. [*Patriots*]

HADDOCK, J.A. *History of Jefferson County, New York.* Philadelphia, 1894.

HAMMOND, BRAY. *Banks and Politics.* Princeton, 1957.

HAMMOND, JABEZ D. *A Political History of the State of New York.* Syracuse, 1852.

HARRINGTON, BERNARD J. *Life of Sir William Logan.* London, 1883.

HARRIS, RICHARD COLEBROOK. *The Seigneurial System of Early Canada: A Geographical Study.* Madison, Wis., 1966.

HARTZ, LOUIS. *The Foundation of New Societies.* New York, 1964.

HEAD, Sir FRANCIS BOND. *A Narrative.* London, 1839.

HENDERSON, JOHN L.H. *John Strachan, 1778-1867.* Toronto, 1969.

HERSHKOWITZ, LEO. "New York City, 1834-1840: A Study in Local Politics." Ph.D. diss., New York University, 1960. (Microfilm, Ann Arbor, Mich., University Microfilms.)

HEUSTIS, DANIEL. *A Narrative of the Adventures and Sufferings of Captain Daniel D. Heustis and His Companions in Canada and Van Dieman's Lands During a Long Captivity, with Travels in California and Voyages at Sea.* Boston, 1847.

HILL, HAMNETT P. *Robert Randall and the Le Breton Flats.* Ottawa, 1919.

HINCKS, FRANCIS. *Reminiscences: Documents Relating to the Resignation of the Canadian Ministry in September, 1854.* Pamphlet. Quebec, n.d.

HIND, H.J., et al. *Eighty Years Progress in British America.* Toronto, 1863.

HODGETTS, J.E. *Pioneer Public Service: An Administrative History of the United Canadas, 1841-1867.* Toronto, 1955.

HODGINS, JOHN GEORGE. *Documentary History of Education in Upper Canada.* 28 vols. Toronto, 1894-1910.

HOLLAND, WILLIAM M. *The Life and Political Opinions of Martin Van Buren, Vice President of the United States.* Hartford, 1835. [*Van Buren*]

HOPKINS, E. RUSSELL. *Confederation at the Cross Roads: The Canadian Constitution.* Toronto, 1968.

HOUGH, FRANKLIN B. *History of St. Lawrence and Franklin Counties.* Albany, 1853. [*St. Lawrence & Franklin Counties*]

HUDSON, FREDERICK. *Journalism in the United States from 1690-1862.* New York, 1873.

HYAM, RONALD, and GED MARTIN. *Reappraisals in British Imperial History.* London, 1975.

ISRAEL, CHARLES. *Reminiscences of the Rebellion of 1837.* Toronto, 1898.

JACKMAN, SIDNEY. *Galloping Head.* London, 1958.

JAMIESON, A.B. *Chartered Banking in Canada.* Toronto, 1953.

JENKINS, JOHN STILLWELL. *History of Political Parties in the State of New York.* Auburn, 1846.

JOHNSON, CRISFIELD. *History of Oswego County.* Philadelphia, 1877.

JOHNSON, J.K., ed. *The Papers of the Prime Ministers.* Vol. 1, *Letters of Sir John A. Macdonald, 1836-1857.* Ottawa, 1968. [*Prime Ministers*]

JONES, ROBERT LESLIE. *History of Agriculture in Ontario, 1613-1880.* Toronto, 1946.

JONES, WILLIAM DEVEREAUX. *Lord Derby and Victorian Conservatism.* Oxford, 1956. [*Derby*]

KAYE, JOHN WILLIAM. *The Life and Correspondence of Charles, Lord Metcalfe.* 2 vols. London, 1858. [*Metcalfe*]

KEILTY, GREG. *1837: Revolution in the Canadas As Told by William Lyon Mackenzie.* Toronto, 1974.

KELLOG, EDWARD. *Labour and Other Capital and the Rights of Each Secured and the Wrongs of Both Eradicated.* New York, 1849.

KERR, DONALD G.G. *Sir Edmund Head: A Scholarly Governor.* Toronto, 1954. [*Head*]

KENNEDY, W.P.M. *Select Documents of the Canadian Constitution 1759-1915.* Toronto, 1918. [*Documents*]

KILBOURN, WILLIAM. *The Firebrand.* Toronto, 1956.

KINCHEN, OSCAR S. *Lord Russell's Canadian Policy.* Lubbock, Texas, 1945.

KINCHEN, OTTO ARVLE. *The Rise and Fall of the Patriot Hunters.* New York, 1956. [*Hunters*]

KING, JOHN. *The Other Side of the "Story".* Toronto, 1886.

KIRWAN, ALBERT DENNIS. *John J. Crittenden: The Struggle for Union.* Lexington, Ky., 1962.

KNAPLUND, PAUL. *Letters from Lord Sydenham to Lord John Russell.* London, 1931.

KNAPPER, GEORGE, ed. *Travels in the Southland: Journal of Lucius V. Bierce with a Bibliographical Essay.* Columbus, Ohio, 1854.

KNIGHT, DAVID B. *A Capital for Canada: Conflict and Compromise in the Nineteenth Century.* University of Chicago Department of Geography Research Paper 182, 1977.

KYTE, ERNEST COCKBURN, ed. *Old Toronto.* Toronto, 1954.

LAMBTON, JOHN GEORGE, first Earl of Durham. *Report and Dispatches of the Earl of Durham.* Ridgways, London, 1839. [*Report & Despatches*]

———. *Report on the Affairs of British North America from the Earl of Durham.* London, 1839. [*Durham Report*]

LANDON, FRED. *Western Ontario and the American Frontier.* Toronto, 1941.

LANGTON, W.A., ed. *Early Days in Upper Canada: Letters of John Langton from the Backwoods of Upper Canada and the Audit Office of the Province of Canada.* Toronto, 1926. [*Letters*]

LATZER, BERT GOOD. *Myrtleville. A Canadian Farm and Family.* Southern Illinois University Press, 1976.

*Legislative Assembly of Canada Debates.* Edited series reprinted from *JLAC* with extracts from newspaper comment on the day's debates. Montreal, 1970 —. [*Debates*]

LINCOLN, CHARLES. *Constitutional History of New York.* Rochester, 1906.

LINDSEY, CHARLES. *The Life and Times of William Lyon Mackenzie.* 2 vols. Toronto, 1862. [*Life*]

———. *William Lyon Mackenzie.* Makers of Canada Series, vol. 6. Toronto, 1912. [*Mackenzie*]

LINDSEY, E.G. *A History of the Events Which Transpired During the Navy Island Campaign to Which is Added the Correspondence of Different Public Officers with the Affidavit of Individuals in the United States and Canada.* Lewiston, 1838.

LIPSCOMB, ANDREW A., ed. *The Writings of Thomas Jefferson.* 20 vols. Monticello edition. Washington, 1903-04.

LONGLEY, RONALD STEWART. *Sir Francis Hincks.* Toronto, 1943. [*Hincks*]

LYNCH, DENNIS TILDEN. *An Epoch and a Man: Martin Van Buren and His Times.* New York, 1929.

LYON, CALEB. *Narrative and Recollections of Van Dieman's Lands During a Three Years Captivity of Stephen S. Wright Together with and Account of the Battle of Prescott.* New York, 1844.

MACKENZIE, ALEXANDER. *The Life and Speeches of George Brown.* Toronto, 1882.

MACKENZIE, WILLIAM LYON. *Mackenzie's Own Narrative of the Late Rebellion with Illustrations and Notes, Critical and Explanatory, Exhibiting the Only True Account of What Took Place at the Memorable Seige of Toronto in the Month of December, 1837.* Palladium Office, Toronto, 1838. A reprint of this item was published in Rochester, 1839.

———. The *Carolina Almanac and American Freeman's Chronicle for 1840.* Rochester, N.Y., 1840.

———. The *Sons of the Emerald Isle or Lives of One Thousand Remarkable Irishmen.* New York, 1844.

———. The *Lives and Opinions of Benjamin Francis Butler and Jesse Hoyt.* Boston, 1845.

———. The *Life and Times of Martin Van Buren.* Boston, 1846.

———. The *Repealer's Almanac.* Toronto, 1856.

———. An *Almanac for Independence and Freedom for the Year 1860.* Toronto, 1860.

MACKIRDY, KENNETH ALEXANDER, comp. *Changing Perspectives in Canadian History.* Notre Dame, 1967.

M'LEOD, DONALD. *A Brief Review of the Settlement of Upper Canada... and of the Grievances Which Compelled the Canadas to have Recourse in Defence of Their Rights and Liberties, in the Years 1837 and 1838.* Cleveland, 1841. [*Review*]

———. The *Mackenzie Homestead: Minutes of Proceedings at Two Meetings held in Toronto preparatory to an Appeal being made to the people of Canada on behalf of an old faithful and talented public servant, William Lyon Mackenze, Esq., M.P.P., with the address of the Central Committee.* Toronto, 1856. [*Homestead*]

MANNING, WILLIAM R. *Diplomatic Correspondence of the United States. Canadian Relations 1784-1860.* 3 vols. Carnegie Endowment for International peace, Washington, 1942.

MANSFIELD, EDWARD D. *Life and Services of General Winfield Scott.* New York, 1852.

*Manual for the Use of the Convention to Revise the Constitution of the State of New York.* New York, 1846.

MARSH, ROBERT. *Seven Years of My Life or A Narrative of a Patriot Exile.* Buffalo, 1847.

MARTIN, CHESTER. *Foundations of Canadian Nationhood.* Toronto, 1955.

MARRYAT, Capt. FREDERICK. *A Diary in America with Remarks on Its Institutions.* Ed. Sidney Jackman. New York, 1962.

MARTINEAU, JOHN. *The Life of Henry Pelham, Fifth Duke of Newcastle.* London, 1908.

MASTERS, D.C. *The Rise of Toronto.* Toronto, 1947.

McKILLOP, A.B., ed. W.D. LeSueur's *William Lyon Mackenzie.* Toronto, 1979.

MERK, FREDERICK, and LOIS MASTERSON MERK. *Fruits of Propaganda in the Tyler Administration.* Cambridge, 1971. [Progaganda]

MERRITT, JEDEDIAH PRENDERGAST. *Biography of the Late William Hamilton Merritt, M.P.* St. Catharine's, Ont., 1875.

MILLER, NATHAN. *The Enterprise of a Free People.* Ithaca, N.Y., 1962.

MILLER, HANSON ORLO. *A Century of Western Ontario.* Toronto, 1949.

MOIR, JOHN S. *Church and State in Canada West.* Toronto, 1959.

MONET, JACQUES. *The Last Cannon Shot.* Toronto, 1969.

MONROE, JAMES. *A View of the Conduct of the Executive in the Foreign Affairs of the United States.* Philadelphia, 1797.

MORGAN, HENRY J. *Sketches of Celebrated Canadians, and Persons Connected with Canada, from the Earliest Period in the History of the Province Down to the Present Time.* Quebec and London, 1862.

MORGAN, ROBERT J. *An Embattled Whig.* Lincoln, Neb., 1954.

MORRISON, JOHN LYLE. *The Eighth Earl of Elgin.* London, 1928. [*Elgin*].

MORTON, W.L. *The Critical Years.* Toronto, 1964.

MUNRO, WILLIAM BENNETT. *The Seigneurial System in Canada.* New York, 1907.

MURRAY, the Hon. AMELIA. *Letters from the United States, Cuba, and Canada.* New York, 1856.

NELLES, H.V., ed. *Philosophy of Railroads and Other Essays by T.C. Keefer.* Toronto, 1972.

NELLES, Rev. ROBERT BERTRAM. *The County of Haldimand in the Days of Old Lang Syne.* Port Hope, 1905. [*Haldimand*]

NEW, CHESTER WILLIAM. *Lord Durham: A Biography of John George Lambton, First Earl of Durham.* Oxford, 1929. [*Durham*]

NEUFELD, E.P. *The Financial System of Canada.* Toronto, 1973.

————. *Money and Banking in Canada.* Toronto, 1964.

NEVINS, ALLAN, ed. *The Diary of George Templeton Strong.* 4 vols. New York, 1952.

*Ontario Historical Society Scrapbooks.* 1924.

O'RIELLY, HENRY. *Settlement of the West: Sketches of Rochester.* Rochester, 1838.

————. *Notices of Sullivan's Campaign.* Rochester, 1842.

ORMSBY, WILLIAM, ed. *Crisis in the Canadas 1838-39: The Grey Letters and Journals.* London, 1965.

————. *The Emergence of the Federal Concept in Canada, 1835-1845.* Toronto, 1969.

OUELLET, FERNAND. *Papineau, Textes choisis.* Québec, 1958.

————. *Lower Canada 1791-1840.* Montreal, 1972.

OWEN, SAMUEL, ed. *The New York Legal Observer.* 12 vols. New York, 1843-1854.

PAPINEAU, LOUIS JOSEPH. *Histoire de l'insurrection au Canada.* Edition Lemeac. Montréal, 1968.

PEARSON, W.H. *Recollections and Records of Toronto of Old.* Toronto, 1914.

PIPPING, ELLA. *This Creature of Fancy.* Translated from the Swedish by Naomi Wolford. London, 1971.

POULTON, RONALD. *The Paper Tyrant.* Toronto, 1971.

RANDOLPH, THOMAS JEFFERSON, ed. *Memoir, Correspondence, and Miscellanies from the Papers of Thomas Jefferson.* 4 vols. 2nd ed. Boston, 1830.

RASPORICH, ANTHONY W. *William Lyon Mackenzie.* Canadian History Through the Press series. Toronto, 1972.

READ, COLIN. *The Rising in Western Upper Canada 1837-8: The Duncombe Revolt and After.* Toronto, 1982. [*Rising*]

————, and RONALD J. STAGG. *The Rebellion of 1837 in Upper Canada: A Collection of Documents Edited with an Introduction by Colin Read and Ronald J. Stagg.* The Champlain Society incorporated with the Ontario Heritage Foundation. Toronto, 1985.

REMINI, ROBERT V. *The Election of Andrew Jackson.* New York, 1963.

RICHARDSON, JAMES D., ed. *A Compilation of the Messages and Papers of the Presidents.* 20 vols. Bureau of National Literature, Washington, D.C., 1905-1917. *[Messages]*

RIDDELL, WILLIAM RENWICK. *Upper Canada Statutes.* Toronto, 1922.

RIPPY, J. FRED. *Joel R. Poinsett: Versatile American.* New York, 1968.

ROBINSON, JOHN BEVERLY. *Canada and the Canada Bill.* London, 1839. Reprinted New York, 1967.

RUMILLY, ROBERT. *Papineau et son temps.* 2 vols. Montréal, 1977.

RYAN, FRANKLIN W. *Usury and Usury Laws.* Boston, 1921.

RYERSON, ADOLPHUS EGERTON. *The Causes and Circumstances of Mr. Bidwell's Banishment by Sir F.B. Head, Correctly Stated and Proved by a United Empire Loyalist.* Kingston, 1838.

RYERSON, STANLEY G. *Unequal Union.* Toronto, 1968.

SALUTIN, RICK. *1837: William Lyon Mackenzie and the Canadian Revolution.* Toronto, 1976.

SANDERSON, CHARLES R., ed. *The Arthur Papers.* 3 vols. Toronto, 1957-59.

SCADDING, the Rev. HENRY. *Toronto, Past and Present.* Toronto, 1884.

SCHEIBER, HARRY N. *The Ohio Canal Era: A Study of Government and the Economy, 1820-1861.* Athens, Ohio, 1969.

SCHULL, JOSEPH. *Rebellion: The Rising in French Canada 1837.* Toronto, 1977.

SCOTT, Lt.-Gen. WINFIELD. *Memoirs of Lieut.-General Scott LL.D. Written by Himself.* 2 vols. New York, 1864.

SCROPE, GEORGE JULIAN DUNCOMBE POULETT. *Memoir of the Life of the Right Honourable Charles, Lord Sydenham.* London, 1844.

SEAGER, ROBERT. *And Tyler Too.* New York, 1963.

SELLERS, CHARLES GRIER. *James J. Polk, Continentalist.* Princeton, 1966. *[Polk]*

SENIOR, ELINOR KYTE. *Redcoats and Patriotes: The Rebellions in Lower Canada, 1937-1838.* Canada War Museum No. 20. Stittsville, Ont., 1985.

SHAW, RONALD E. *Erie Water West: A History of the Erie Canal, 1792-1854.* Lexington, Ky., 1966.

SHEPPARD, GEORGE. *Martin Van Buren.* New York, 1899.

SHIRREFF, PATRICK. *A Tour Through North America.* Edinburgh, 1835.

SHORTT, ADAM, and ARTHUR G. DOUGHTY, eds. *Canada and Its Provinces.* 23 vols. Toronto, 1914.

SIETZ, DON C. *Horace Greeley.* Indianapolis, 1926. *[Greeley]*

SISSONS, C.B. *Egerton Ryerson: His Life and Letters.* 2 vols. New York, 1937. *[Ryerson]*

SKELTON, OSCAR DOUGLAS. *Life and Times of Sir Alexander Tilloch Galt.* Toronto, 1966. *[Galt]*

SMITH, N. PERRY. *A History of Buffalo and Erie County.* 2 vols. Syracuse, 1884.

SMITH, WILLIAM. *History of Canada Fromm Its First Discovery to the Peace of 1763.* 2 vols. Quebec, 1815.

SMITH, WILLIAM. *History of the Post Office in British North America.* Cambridge, England, 1920.

SMITH, WILLIAM. *Political Leaders of Upper Canada.* Toronto, 1931.

SMITH, WILLIAM H. *Canada: Past, Present, and Future.* 2 vols. Toronto, 1851.

SOMERS, HUGH JOSEPH. *The Life and Times of the Hon. and Rt. Rev. Alexander Macdonnell.* Washington, 1911.

STANLEY, JOHN LANGLEY. "Majority Tyranny in Tocqueville's America: The Failure of Negro Suffrage in New York State in 1846." Ph.D. diss., Cornell University, 1966.

STEVENS, GEORGE ROY. *Canadian National Railways.* 2 vols. Toronto, 1960. *[Railways]*

STODDART, HENRY LUTHER. *Horace Greeley.* New York, 1946.

SUTHERLAND, THOMAS JEFFERSON. *Three Political Letters Addressed to Dr. Wolfred Nelson, Late of Lower Canada, Now of Plattsburgh, New York.* New York, 1840.

———. *A Canvass of the Proceedings on the Trial of William Lyon Mackenzie....* New York, 1840.

———. *The Trial of Gen. Thomas J. Sutherland.* Buffalo, 1838.

SWAINSON, DONALD, ed. *Oliver Mowat's Ontario.* Toronto, 1972. *[Mowat's Ontario]*

THELLER, EDWARD A. *Canada in 1837-38.* 2 vols. Philadelphia, 1841.

THOMPSON, EDWARD. *The Life of Charles, Lord Metcalfe.* London, 1937.

THOMPSON, ROBERT LUTTON. *Wiring a Continent.* Princeton, 1947.

de TOCQUEVILLE, ALEXIS CHARLES HENRI MAURICE CHEREL. *Democracy in America.* Henry Reeve text. ed. Phillips Bradley. New York, 1954.

TREVELYAN, GEORGE MACAULAY. *History of England.* New York, 1928.

TRUDEL, MARCEL. *The Seigneurial Regime.* Canadian Historical Booklet No.6, Ottawa, 1971.

TURCOTTE, LOUIS P. *Le Canada sous l' Union 1841-67.* 2 vols. Québec, 1882.

TYLER, LYNN GARDINER. *The Letters and Times of the Tylers.* 3 vols. Richmond, Va., 1884-96.

VAN DEUSEN, GLYNDON G. *Horace Greeley.* Philadelphia, 1958. *[Greeley]*

WADE, MASON. *The French Canadians.* New York, 1955.

WALROND, THEODORE. *Letters and Journals of James, Eighth Earl of Elgin.* London, 1872. *[Elgin]*

WELCH, SAMUEL MANNING. *Home History: Recollections of Buffalo During the Decade from 1830 to 1840 or Fifty Years Since.* Buffalo, 1891.

WHITFORD, NOBLE EARL. *History of the Canal System of the State of New York.* 2 vols. Albany, 1906.

WILSON, ALAN. *The Clergy Reserves of Upper Canada: A Canadian Mortmain.* Toronto, 1968.

WILSON, GEORGE E. *The Life of Robert Baldwin.* Toronto, 1933. [*Baldwin*]

WING, TALCOTT E. *History of Monroe County, Michigan.* New York, 1890.

WINKS, ROBIN. *The Blacks in Canada.* Montreal, 1971.

WITTKE, CARL, ed. *History of the State of Ohio.* 6 vols. Columbus, Ohio, 1941-44.

WOOD, HERBERT FAIRLIE. *Forgotten Canadians.* Toronto, 1963.

YOUNG, A.H. *The Roll of Pupils of Upper Canada College, Toronto, January 1830 to June 1916.* Kingston, 1917.

YOUNG, JAMES. *Public Men and Public Affairs in Canada.* Toronto, 1912.

ZAHLER, HELEN SARA. *Eastern Working Men and National Land Policy 1829-1862.* New York, 1941.

# INDEX

reforms, 163; becomes candidate for Assembly from Haldimand, 173-76; results of election and importance of his victory, 178; legislative initiatives, 1851, 185-94; hostility of members to Mackenzie, 194-5; role in election of 1854, 197-88; reelected in Haldimand, 199; rejects Rolph's offer of a job, 202-204; opposes Consolidated Municipal Loan Fund, 205-206; loses support of Lesslie and chance to publish in *Examiner*, 216; establishes *Mackenzie's Weekly Message*, 216-17; issues of the 1852-53 legislative session, 205-221; debates George Brown on the Union, 226-27; reprints story of his escape in the *Message*, 227; discusses Head's Flag of Truce, 228-29; visits his son James and comments on political advantages of Ohio, 230; denounces abrupt dissolution of parliament, 231; issues Voters Guide, 232; receives less support in Haldimand in election of 1854, 232-33; his help sought by other reformers, 233; loses influence in the Reform party, 235; rages against new MacNab-Morin coalition, 236-37; criticizes Elgin on occasion of farewell address, 244-45; discovers irregularities and scandalous practices as chairman of Committee on Public Accounts, 245-47; advocates records management, 245, Board of Audit created as result of his exposé, 248; legislature accepts his recommendations of change to decimal currency, 248; moves for repeal of the Union, 252; summarizes Upper Canada's complaints in *Examiner*, 254; plans campaign for repeal of the Union, 252, 254-56; resumes publication of *Message* urging repeal of the Union and creation of constitutional conventions, 256; opposes measures of Taché-Macdonald ministry, 260-64; insults the Governor-General and diminishes his own influence, 260-61; publishes *Repealers' Almanac*, 265-66; opposes formation of Reform Alliance by George Brown, 270-71; opposes measures that increase expenses of government, 277; his controverted elections bill passes, 280; complains of land regulations being violated, 280; publishes squatter's complaints, 283; opposes charter for proposed southern railway, 285-88; calls for a constitutional convention, 288; runs in general election of 1858, 290-93; publishes instances of corruption in *Message*, 295; gets a Stop Law passed for benefit of debtors, 295; opposes jury law amendment act, 296, supports Brown-Dorion cabinet, 299; criticizes double shuffle, 299-300; resigns his seat, 301-302; revives *Message* to agitate for dissolution of Union and power to make new constitution, 306-307; comments on Reform Convention of 1859, 311; regards Civil War as opportunity for Canada to be brought into the Union, 319; attacks George Brown's plan of federation, 313-14; death occurs, 319; controversy over obituary by Thurlow Weed, 319-20; newspaper

estimates of 321; biographies of, 322-24; retrospective analysis of his life and policies including attempts to prevent economic changes that would produce extremes of wealth and poverty, 325-30; attitudes on land policy, railways, banks, education, , 325-29; weaknesses as a politician, 330; attitude towards minorities, 339-40; his character and talents, 337-42

Printed in Canada